PAUL SCOTT

a life

Paul photographed by Helen Craig for 39 Writers of Hampstead *in 1962.*

PAUL SCOTT

a life

HILARY SPURLING

The novelist destroys the house of his life and
uses its stones to build the house of his novel.
Milan Kundera, *Art of the Novel*

HUTCHINSON

LONDON   SYDNEY   AUCKLAND   JOHANNESBURG

Also by Hilary Spurling

Ivy When Young. The Early Life of I. Compton-Burnett 1884–1919 (1974)
Secrets of a Womans Heart. The Later Life of I. Compton-Burnett 1920–1969 (1984)

Handbook to Anthony Powell's 'Music of Time' (1977)
Elinor Fettiplace's Receipt Book (1986)

This edition first published in 1990 by
Hutchinson

Random Century Group Ltd
20 Vauxhall Bridge Road, London SW1V 2SA

Random Century Australia (Pty) Ltd
20 Alfred Street, Milsons Point, Sydney NSW 2061,
Australia

Random Century (NZ) Ltd
9–11 Rothwell Avenue, Albany, Auckland 10, New
Zealand

Random Century South Africa (Pty) Ltd
PO Box 337, Bergvlei 2012, South Africa

British Library Cataloguing in Publication Data
Spurling, Hilary
    Paul Scott: a life
    1. Fiction in English. Scott, Paul, 1920–1978
    I. Title
    823.914

ISBN 0–09–173984–5

Set in Sabon by Deltatype Ltd, Ellesmere Port

Printed and bound in Great Britain by Butler and Tanner Ltd,
Frome, Somerset.

Contents

For Bryan, who wanted me to write this book,
and whose encouragement has made so many
do their best, as I did, to oblige.

Preface and Acknowledgements

Fame and fortune on a scale inconceivable in his lifetime came to Paul Scott when Granada's television series, *The Jewel in the Crown*, was shown in 1983, five years after he died. It coincided with, and helped to release, a wave of nostalgic enthusiasm for the British Raj which would have astonished its author. It is easy to forget the stubborn reluctance to contemplate the end of Britain's affair with India that remained widespread in this country at all levels throughout Paul's career as a novelist. He was already dying when he received the Booker Prize for *Staying On* in 1977, and with it his first ironic inkling that his books had at last broken through the resistance against which he had struggled so doggedly and for so long.

He himself had no Indian background or connections, apart from a relatively brief wartime experience. His lifelong commitment to the subcontinent was the first but by no means the last, and certainly not the hardest, of the puzzles he set for a biographer. In 1988 I travelled across India in Paul's footsteps and, when the journey was completed, I flew on halfway round the world on a hunch to Tasmania to visit an old friend of his, who had known him as a very young writer at the start of the Second World War in London. Conversations with Ruth Sansom clarified much that had seemed inexplicable before, and confirmed my growing sense that a crucial part of the answer to how and why Paul wrote the Raj Quartet lay in something that had happened before he ever set foot in India.

Paul's letters to the Sansoms, which I read in Tasmania, are now deposited with the bulk of his private papers in the McFarlin Library at the University of Tulsa in Oklahoma. To people who find their contents as disconcerting as I did at first, I can only give the answer Paul gave himself, when he vigorously defended the authors of *The Secret Lives of Lawrence of Arabia* against charges of malice or muck-raking. He insisted that concealment or half truths in a biography do no service to its subject. When Nirad Chaudhuri's life of Clive raised the question of whether a biographer can hope to show any human being in a strictly historical light 'without feeling called upon to pronounce judgement for or against', Paul decided that it was probably impossible: 'The catch lies in the phrase "called upon". No one calls upon a writer but himself. His own choice of subject suggests an empathy (or an antipathy). Either way, judgement has been entered before he begins . . .'

In this sense, my judgement was entered before I began, and my greatest debt is to Penny Scott and her daughters who agreed at that preliminary stage that the only point in their authorising or my undertaking a life would be to paint as full, truthful and accurate a portrait as possible. None of us foresaw then that this biography would explore sides of Paul of which his immediate family knew nothing, and I should like to emphasise that this is my view of his story, not theirs, and that my reconstruction of his early life relies almost entirely on other sources. No one but me is to blame for gaps, imbalances and shortcomings.

* * *

I should like to thank Penny Scott for her steady and unconditional support, and for her patience in answering my questions. Carol and Sally Scott were unreservedly generous from the start with practical help, information and insights in many long and searching conversations about their father. I owe more than I can say to all three for the courage and confidence with which, in practice as well as theory, they stuck to Paul's principle that a writer should pursue his or her chosen subject with no strings attached.

My next debt is to Ruth Sansom for sharing so much of the past as well as for making me so welcome in the present. My best thanks go to Peter Scott (especially for his photographs) and his wife Eileen, and to Paul's cousins Sheila Wright, Edna Donagh, and Pauline Hildesheim. After his family, I owe most to Paul's many friends, especially those who presided in India over the writing of the Raj Quartet, chief among them Dorothy Ganapathy in Bombay and Dipali Nag in Calcutta. Without their kindness to a stranger for the second time, my book would have been much the poorer. I should like to thank also most particularly Neil Ghosh's sister, Nilima Dutta, in Calcutta, Goodie Singh in Delhi, Coocoo and Manohar Malgonkar in Jagalbet, whose hospitality made my travels as pleasant as they were instructive.

My special thanks go to Mollie Hamilton (M. M. Kaye) and Peter Green for guidance and encouragement at all stages, including some of the trickiest junctures of my imaginary journey. I owe much to Paul's writing friends, especially James Leasor, Kay Dick and the late Mary Patchett; to his publishers, Roland Gant and Charles Pick of Heinemann, and John Willey of William Morrow Inc. (who wrote me a memoir but could not read my manuscript, because it was still unfinished when he died); to his literary agent, Dorothy Olding, in New York; and most of all to Bruce Hunter of David Higham Associates in London, who first asked me to write this book, and whose calmness, sympathy and resourcefulness have been an unfailing support ever since.

I am grateful to all the people who went out of their way to help me in India, especially to Sue and Partap Sharma and to Foy Nissan in Bombay; to P.C. Chatterji in New Delhi; to Dr V.R.N. Prasad in Aurangabad; to Robert Sykes of the British Council, to his wife Laura, and to Pearson Surita in Calcutta. I owe a particular debt to Caroline Warton (née Davies), as also to Geoffrey Ridehalgh, Olive Corben, Barbara Whelan (née Phillips) and Peter Lumley. In Southgate and Palmers Green I learned much from Graham Dalling, a prince (if I may paraphrase Paul's friend, the late E.M. Almedingen) among Local History Officers; also from Mrs Arnold, Malka Baker, Mrs Ethel Collins, Mr Michael Collins, Betty Jukes, Mr and Mrs Munns and, among Winchmore Hill Collegiate School's old boys, from F.G. Rudling, Ralph and Douglas Watkinson, Norman Read and Rex Vicks. On the war years, I had invaluable help from Lt Col P.J. Emerson, Hon. Sec. to the Indian Army Association, and from Narice Arlen, David Atkins, Geoffrey Bide, Brigadier Shelford Bidwell, Lt Col Kenneth Capel Cure, R.H. Elliott, Alan K. Hill, Major P.G. Malins, E.J. Scilloe (who wrote a memoir describing the formation and adventures of D Coy., 8th Bn, The Buffs), and Capt. R.P. Williams (who sent me a detailed account of his training and Paul's in 12 Platoon, B Coy. Belgaum). I am also grateful to Gen. A.S. Chopra in Belgaum, Major-Gen. P.K. Palit, Brig. V.J. Moharir and Brig. A.K. Sahukar in Delhi.

Apart from word-of-mouth, my chief sources have been the complementary collections of Scott papers at the Universities of Tulsa, Oklahoma, and Texas at Austin. Tulsa's McFarlin Library contains a very nearly complete record of Paul's voluminous correspondence (the letters he received and carbon copies of his answers) between 1960 and his death together with typescripts of lectures, articles, reviews, obituaries, his reader's reports for publishers, the manuscript of *Staying On*, his play scripts and sketches, press cuttings and other miscellaneous papers. The Harry Ransom Humanities Research Centre at Austin holds all the other surviving manuscripts, notebooks and working drafts of the novels, some correspondence, Paul's library of books on India, and his working files as an agent in the archive of Pearn, Pollinger and Higham (afterwards David Higham Associates). My warmest gratitude goes to Sidney F. Huttner and his knowledgeable staff at McFarlin – Caroline S. Swinson, Jennifer Carlson and Milissa Burkart – and, at HRC, to Cathy Henderson and Ken Craven.

My best thanks go to Paul's friends, supporters and students in

Tulsa: Warren Brown (who played me the Chekhovian Farewell), Sally Dennison, Patti Floyd, Harriet and Jim Leake, Maureen Modlish, Brian Murray (who wrote a memoir), Kay Scully, William Wheeler and Steve Wood. I owe a special debt to Dr Thomas F. Staley in both Tulsa and Texas; to Professor R. W. Louis, who welcomed both Scott and his biographer to the British Studies group at Austin; to Francine Weinbaum whose thesis was first in this field; to Professor R. J. Moore for sharing the historian's perspective in *Paul Scott's Raj*; and to Sir Denis Forman of Granada, who put *The Jewel in the Crown* on television, and whose enthusiasm proved infectious.

I should also like to thank all those who gave me information, assistance or advice: Dr Roger Atwood, Brian Baker of Doncaster Libraries, David Bell, Elizabeth Berridge, Toni Block, Ronald Blythe, David Bolt, June and Neville Braybrooke, John Bright-Holmes, Kenneth Brown, AGRA, Professor D. M. Burjorjee, Michael Bywater, Librarian to the Institute of Chartered Accountants, Simon Callow, Paul Cashmore, Dr Nag Chaudhuri, Colin Chambers, Gerda Charles, Krishan Churumani, John Clay, Olive Corben, Adèle Dogan, Judi Dooling, Christopher Dowling at the Imperial War Museum, D. J. Enright, Barbara Everett for a moral tutorial, Penelope Farmer, Alison Fincham at Wellington College, Philip French, Armita Ghosh, Martyn Goff, Giles Gordon, Gerald Hanley, Marjorie Harris of the Swanwick Writers School, Carl Harrison of Lewisham Libraries, Donald Hayden, Mrs A. Heap of Leeds Local History Department, Helen and Ben Higham, Christopher Hibbert, Jacqueline Korn, Audrey Lambert, Inder Malhotra, P. C. Manaktala, Isha Mellor, Reginald Moore, Christina and Donald Morley, Joan Power of Turramurra, N. S. W., for a remarkable piece of detective work, Martin Pick for a memoir, Frances M. Pilkington, Erin Pizzey, Gerald Pollinger, Alice Lindsay Price, Anthony Rota, Philip Rushworth, Tim Scott, Alan Smith, Maurice Temple Smith, Ian Spring, Julian Symons, Judge Robert Taylor for a Scott-Wright tour, Nigel Viney, Sheila Watson, Dame Veronica Wedgwood, Elisabeth Wigin for an essential clue, Lord Willis, Barbara Woodgates and Ian Wright.

Lastly, my thanks go to my editor, Richard Cohen, for starting me off and seeing me through, and to my designer, Margaret Fraser, for a handsome finish. I am also truly grateful to the Authors' Foundation for timely help with travelling expenses, and to the Hawthornden International Retreat for Writers, Drue Heinz and her committee, Dr McAleer and the staff for six weeks' privacy and peace last autumn at Hawthornden Castle, where I wrote the middle section of this book and set up enough momentum to write the rest.

HILARY SPURLING, *Holloway, June 1990*

OPPOSITE *Bourne Hill, Palmers Green, between the wars: the Scotts' house, where Paul 'really began to write', is on the left.*

PART ONE

1920–1943
The Poet in Him

'I imagined the poet in him as an unborn twin,
one that could be cruel to him as well as kind.'

CHAPTER ONE

Half close your eyes here – and you're in Mayapore

The last story Paul Scott ever finished was his version of *Cinderella*. He wrote it just over a year before he died, and reworked it at intervals during the next nine months. 'The tale is like a looking-glass in which you see yourself if you gaze into it long enough,' he wrote in the final draft.[1] The happiness of his Cinderella does not depend on magic, or the intervention of a handsome prince. When her sisters go to the ball, she is left behind, alone in her shabby working clothes, imagining pictures and patterns in the flames of the kitchen fire. Her ball takes place in her head. Much the same might be said of a great many writers who feel themselves shut out or cold-shouldered by the rest of the world. But Paul Scott drank in with his mother's milk a sense of being on the outside looking in, and it is scarcely an exaggeration to say that he could not have written the books by which he will be remembered – the Raj Quartet and its pendant, *Staying On* – if he hadn't remained essentially an outsider, like his Cinderella, to the day he died.

He was born on 25 March 1920, at 130 Fox Lane in the north London suburb of Southgate. He said long afterwards that he had been twice born – first in London in the ordinary way, and a second time twenty-three years later when he was shipped out as a soldier to India in the Second World War.[2] He hadn't wanted to go, and he didn't instantly take to the subcontinent, but there was something about it that he recognised in his bones. By the time he sailed for home three years later, he was obsessed by the place. India had entered his bloodstream. In the end it would be British India that enabled him to look back, to see a pattern in his past, to make sense without rancour of the world in which he grew up. 'When I lived [in Southgate], I knew nothing of India,' he said: 'Returning, I see images of India everywhere

... the maidan, the club, the cantonment, the governor's residence. Only the names were different.'[3]

The Scotts' house was at the top or newer end of Fox Lane, roughly equidistant from the more select residential quarters of old Southgate and Palmers Green, but still well within what Paul called cantonment limits. It was a small, semi-detached redbrick villa, decorated like countless others with white-painted bow windows, a fancy porch, minute front garden and crazy-paving path. Theirs was the house the builder had put up for himself, which gave it a touch of distinction. Parts of the district were still in the hands of developers throughout Paul's childhood, with bricks, tiles and drainpipes stacked along patches of muddy, unmade road. Fox Lane kept its grass verges until well after the second war, and it still has its wooden pen for impounding stray cows.

Paul was born in his parents' upstairs front bedroom. He was the second of their two sons, and they named him Paul Mark: 'You've got a Peter. Now you'd better have a Paul,' said his father's cousin Ada, who was visiting at the time.[4] Mark was his mother's maiden name. It was also the name of his great uncle, Mark Scott, the family's wealthiest and most illustrious relation, a Yorkshire mill-owner whose promised state visit to Southgate was keenly anticipated by Paul's mother. Tom Scott, Paul's father, had come down from Headingley in Leeds to settle in London round about the turn of the century, and remained a good Yorkshireman, following the county cricket scores to the end of his life and declaring, if Yorkshire lost, that the team had not so much been beaten as *robbed of victory*.[5] He was a freelance commercial artist in partnership with his three unmarried sisters, producing illustrations and advertising display work for the fashion trade. Paul described the atmosphere of his early years as 'polite, suburban bohemianism'.[6]

His father was the only artist – indeed the family took considerable pride in his being the only professional man of any description – at their end of Fox Lane. It meant they had standards and a certain state to keep up, which was no joke in Southgate in those days, when elaborate, unwritten rules governed every move you made: which church you attended, which clubs you joined, which schools you chose for your children, what you wore, who you spoke to and where you shopped, even which seats you sat in at the cinema. Much depended on where you lived. People with Rolls-Royces who took foreign holidays lived on the Broad Walk overlooking Grovelands Park, within a stone's throw of Fox Lane but separated by an impassable gulf. Solidly prosperous tradesmen lined Alderman's Hill ('Call it Government House Road', said Paul),[7] on the other side of Fox Lane going south. If you carried on beyond Alderman's Hill past the shopping parade (or bazaar) or turned right at the bottom, heading for Haringey or Edmonton, you passed out of cantonment limits into working-class territory, where costers were said to keep coal in the bath and walk their donkeys in at the front door. This was a no-go area for anyone brought up in Palmers Green or Southgate. From the point of view of the respectable citizenry on higher ground in Fox Lane, it might – as Paul said – just as well have been Black Town. 'In Palmers Green when I lived there we were as aware of social distinctions as they were in Mudpore,' he explained long afterwards: 'to that extent, India was *never* a surprise to me.'[8]

Paul's father had a studio, ten minutes' walk from the house, on the old village High Street near the maidan, otherwise Southgate Green. The Scotts had initially set up their fashion studio at Streatham in south London, where premises and labour were cheap. Southgate, still very much a village when Tom Scott and his sisters moved up there just before the first war, must have reminded them of their native Headingley, also built on high ground to the north of the city with hills and fields beyond. Both suburbs offered clean air, green spaces, easy access to town and country. Communications were good and rents comparatively low. Tom Scott's house and studio were rented because 'his sort of person' didn't own property: 'It was almost vulgar to own a house. You rented whatever was available wherever you found yourself on station, as the raj used to say.'[9]

It was the Scott family, with their polite codes of behaviour and their nice social distinctions, that set the tone for Paul's childhood. His mother, who came from south London, enthusiastically endorsed the outlook and values that went with her husband's sort of person. Frances Scott was a woman of powerful poetic imagination and driving will. All her life she consoled herself for reality's shortcomings with rich and extravagant dreams. She had written unpublished novels herself as a girl, working in a cupboard by candlelight: the night before her wedding in 1916[10] she said she read them all through and burned them. Her elder son Peter, who was two years older than Paul, took after no one in particular. But Paul had her own strong, distinctive Mark family nose, and with it she passed on her creative energy and a burning sense of what he might do in the future. He had been a ten months' baby: she said she had carried him an extra month in the womb to allow time for his remarkable brain to develop. She had resented her pregnancy, wanted nothing more to do with the messy and distasteful business of sex, and had in any case hoped for a girl.[11] But Paul was a prodigy in her eyes from birth. He walked and talked before he was one and, according to his mother, who could never have enough of his achievements, he came pretty close to writing his first poem too.[12] She had unheard-of ambitions for him; he grew up under the spell of his mother's imagination, and the spur of her great expectations. He was to fulfil her promise, redeem the hopes of her girlhood, make good the disappointments of a life that had never quite come up to scratch.

Paul always insisted that he had a perfectly ordinary childhood, comfortable, happy and protected. He and his brother were the only children in a family heavily weighted towards the other end of the age scale. Their father had himself been the only boy in a household of women, petted and made much of by six sisters none of whom ever married. Peter and Paul grew up in a circle of elderly maiden aunts, and Paul in particular energetically returned their interest. He was an enchanting infant, comical, astute and precocious. His sayings were treasured, his doings marvelled over, his jokes passed round the whole family. He seems to have been, even as a very small child, sharply aware of other people and unusually receptive. The earliest symptom he diagnosed in himself as a writer was an intense curiosity:[13] he said it could prove dangerous later, but in childhood it meant that he gave as much as he got from the fond, admiring female relations bending over his cot.

All his life he remained an exceptional listener. People to whom he gave his full attention agree that there was nothing to match it. He listened with a sympathetic concentration that was irresistible, and the first voice he listened to was his mother's. He must have heard her building dream castles for him to inhabit almost before he could understand what she was saying; and as soon as he could stagger to his feet, he brought her offerings in return – a toy boat with a bead in the bottom which he said was a 'little abayling', or a ring case with a coin lodged in its slot, which he called a 'doe-gift'.[14] Already he knew how to please her, and perhaps already he could hear, beneath her challenging, confident voice, another message, equally insistent but harsher and more plaintive. Paul's mother seldom talked about her past, except sometimes to recolour and recast it in a more satisfactory form. How much she told Paul, and how much he guessed, is impossible to say. But there can be no doubt that, for all the bold front she put on in public, Frances Scott was the forerunner of a line of lonely, vulnerable, insecure wives in his books, women whose energies have found no outlet and whose talents run slowly to waste.

Marriage had been the high point of Frances Scott's career. She was thirty in 1916, when she married a man sixteen years older than herself and shook the dust of south London off her feet for good. It was a drastic step for a working girl, even one who had already landed a highly superior job in the counting house of one of London's brand-new West End department stores. The Mark family, like the Scotts, originally came from the north, and Frances met her future husband on the strength of the Yorkshire connection. One of his employees had taken her along to a dance in the Scotts' studio at 28 Criffel Avenue, Streatham. She was lively, artistic, resourceful, full of enterprise and sympathy, with a neat figure and an eye for a stylish turnout: she could be captivating when she cared to be, and family tradition ever afterwards maintained that she set her cap at Tom Scott.

Frances's brothers and sisters all agreed she had done exceptionally well for herself. As the eldest daughter, she had learned early to hold her own, if not set the pace at home for five brothers. All the Marks were nicely spoken, immaculately dressed, very particular about points like table manners and turnout. The girls had been brought up to keep a good table, the boys knew how to treat a lady, and, in a family that believed in putting on a show, no one put up a better show than Frances. She was her father's favourite, in some ways the one who most nearly took after him. 'All the drive and go came from my grandfather,' said a niece who had been brought up in considerable awe of her dashing Auntie Frances: 'She and her father were very close.'[15] William Mark had always believed his eldest daughter would go far and, considering the odds stacked against them, Frances's marriage was a triumph for her own and her father's combined drive and go.

William Mark had been one of three brothers, sons of the village schoolmaster at Wildboarclough, near Macclesfield in Cheshire, all of whom went to sea. He was a sailor on Deptford docks when he courted Eliza Hannah Mawson Elliott, the illegitimate child of a farm labourer's illiterate daughter from the Yorkshire village of Fenwick, just outside Doncaster.[16] He gave up the sea to marry her in 1878 at the Wesleyan Chapel on Brixton Hill. She was twenty-four, he was three years younger, and prospects could hardly have been worse for a young couple running away to seek their fortunes at a time of severe unemployment, rioting and chronic distress all over south London. The Marks had three sons in three years before Frances was born on 1 May 1886, in a labourer's cottage in Deptford. Her father described himself on her birth certificate as a paperhanger (papering the walls was generally the only means of keeping the bugs down in the tiny crowded lodgings of the London poor). In 1886, the worst in a series of bad years for the building trade, which remained slack throughout the decade, a builder's or decorator's labourer could expect to earn something under £1 a week – supposing he were lucky enough to find work. Even the most expert manager could not make those wages stretch to feed a family of six on much more than bread, margarine and tea.[17] The Marks rented rooms at 83 Dennetts Road in a terrace of ten mean little houses – two up and two down – between the Rising Sun public house on one corner and the Earl of Derby on the next. Drink was the only available palliative in what was inevitably, for people at the bottom of the social heap like William Mark, a life of grinding hardship, insecurity and malnutrition.

Frances, who prided herself in later life on her delicate constitution, once said she had been so small at the age of four 'that they were afraid to allow me to walk by myself without someone holding my hand, in case the wind lifted me off my feet.'[18] There were two more little brothers, and a baby sister who died, before Frances was six. Round about this time their father moved the whole family back up to Yorkshire in search of work as a painter and decorator, settling in Potternewton, one of the poorest inner city districts of Leeds. Here a rapidly expanding ring of outer suburbs like Headingley provided plentiful opportunities, and, by the time a second daughter, Alice, was born in 1893 (Ruth completed the family in 1896), their father was describing himself as 'housepainter (master)'. If this meant he could afford to employ someone under him, his relative prosperity does not seem to have lasted, for he was soon back in London, trying his hand at various trades, including caretaking and catering. In Paul's novel *The Bender*, Vi Spruce – who was the nearest her son ever came to a direct portrait of Frances Scott – insisted that her father had been a master builder, and bitterly resented her sister's matter-of-fact correction: 'Master drinker, Vi.'[19]

Frances Scott, like Vi Spruce, found it hard to face or forgive the conditions into which she had been born. Want of space, want of privacy, want of peace and quiet were the rule among the working people of south London and, if Frances hid in a cupboard to write, it signalled a mental as much as physical retreat into a world of romance. There were not many other escape routes from a life that offered for the most part only drudgery, ill-health, insecurity, overcrowding and constant childbearing on starvation wages. Frances's mother bore nine children in fifteen years and dinned into them the hard philosophy it taught her. 'My mother's words come back to me,' Frances's youngest sister Ruth wrote at the end of her life to her nephew Paul: 'Never buy friendship . . . Take a tip, my dear, look after your own – hang other people. It doesn't pay to be decent. . . . Life certainly is not a bed of roses.'[20] All her sayings suggest the pessimism and disillusionment that bred a corresponding cynical, humorous stoicism among women whose experience commonly defeated hope. 'My mother would have said – well, you haven't got her to thank for it,' Ruth

wrote, when a niece failed to deliver a favour, ' – and called me a fool
to believe in people.'[21]

If Paul inherited a measure of Yorkshire grit from his father, from
his mother he got a double share of self-reliance, self-containment and
stubborn northern pride. All the Marks set store by 'getting on',
'making something of yourself', not letting life get the better of you or,
if it did, never letting anybody know. Frances's five brothers – George,
William, Wilfred, Harry and Bert – had each been set to learn a trade,
but they were overtaken by the First World War after which, although
they all survived physically, they seem to have lost the courage or
stamina to get on. For the girls, leaving school at twelve to go out to
work meant a choice between domestic service and piecework in a
sweatshop or factory, working twelve hours or more a day for roughly
half a man's wages. Frances's post as cashier in a drapery or
department store represented already an enormous advance on the
hand she had been dealt at birth. Her youngest sister Ruth remained a
domestic servant living in a single room on Brixton Hill to the end of
her working life: throughout the 1920s and 1930s she was earning ten
shillings (50p) a week, with her lunch thrown in, as cook-general to a
family in Croydon.[22] She died in her seventies, as she had lived, in
comfortless poverty, with no savings and no possessions to speak of,
nothing but a few sticks of furniture in a council flat ('just a Rabbit
Hutch,' she wrote to Paul, 'not even an easy chair')[23] on Brixton Hill,
where her parents had been married almost a century earlier.

This was the fate Frances Mark married to escape. Crossing the
river and moving the dozen or so miles north to Southgate meant, so
far at least as her family was concerned, that she had passed beyond an
invisible barrier. It was almost more of a mental, even spiritual passage
than a physical journey. Tom Scott had installed his sisters on
Southgate High Street in a gabled, three-storeyed house called
Wyphurst, with leaded casement windows and a steep-pitched roof in
the picturesque, post-Voysey Edwardian style. It was set back behind a
high brick wall with pillars at the corners and a gateway beneath an
arch in the middle, opening on to the broad, leafy street where Leigh
Hunt had once lived, not far from Charles Lamb's country retreat and
Tom Hood's Rose Cottage on Winchmore Hill. Even after the First
World War, this part of Southgate retained traces of the rural charm –
the thatched cottages, the country lanes, the shady glades and groves –
that had attracted romantic poets and essayists in the previous
century. Wyphurst itself had a pretty, sheltered garden with roses and
a flowering creeper round the door. Inside it was furnished with family
portraits, watercolours, books and albums, old Mrs Scott's piano and
other Victorian pieces originally salvaged from Headingley. From

their studio window at the top of the house, Tom and his sisters looked out over the cricket pitch to the tall spire of Christ Church. This was the heart of old Southgate. 'Half close your eyes here', said Paul, ' – and you're in Mayapore.'[24]

To anyone born and brought up in the grimy, teeming, tightly-packed back streets of Deptford and Brixton, it must have seemed another world. But it was one from which Frances was still in some sense excluded. 'My father's family looked down on my mother's, who all lived in south London', said Paul: 'Really Black Town, that.'[25] Tom's sisters had never warmed to his much younger wife, who must have seemed to them pushy, intrusive, a presence altogether too alien for them to accommodate. Tom was fifty the year Paul was born, the eldest of his three sisters getting on for sixty. A gulf remained fixed between the generations. 'My father . . . had two homes,' Paul wrote. 'Or rather one and a half. He rented the houses which from time to time my mother, my brother and I lived in – and he slept in – and paid half the rent of another house where he had his studio.'[26] Paul's accounts of his childhood often make his father sound like a lodger in his mother's house. Tom spent all day at the studio, and the evenings as well if there was a rush of work, disappearing after breakfast and not returning until after dark. 'My father kept his married life separate from his real life,'[27] said Paul, who seems to have learned very early to identify work as a central saving activity for human beings, and one that removed them from the perplexity and conflict of living with other people.

If work gave Tom a retreat, Frances had none. She had made it clear to her own family that visitors would not be welcome in her new home; but it can't have taken her long to discover that physical proximity had brought her no nearer to the world of carriage folk, bespoke tailors and gentlemen's clubs which her husband continued to inhabit in her imagination. Instead, she found herself cooped up alone all day with no support system, no outlet for her formidable gifts, no one to turn to for consolation or company but her two small sons. Too common for her in-laws, too proud to admit where she came from or that she had a sister in service, Frances used her indomitable imagination to close the gap between dream and reality. Paul must have sensed her isolation and loneliness very soon: for him one side of his mother always remained a Cinderella looking on at a ball to which she had no hope of being invited.

The world Frances actually occupied proved an unfriendly and sharply critical environment. It would have been inconceivable in Southgate in those days to admit to having relatives south of the river. People suspected of far less serious failings – eating in the kitchen, for instance, or doing the washing at a weekend – found themselves forced by the pressure of their neighbours' disapproval to pack up and leave the district. The inhabitants of Fox Lane and the suburban streets round about were a rootless people whose insecurity made them hostile to anyone but their own kind. None of them had been there for long. The whole area had been farmland until the first decade of the century. For the raw new society that replaced the old rural framework the most urgent need was cohesion, and the prime virtue conformity. Stiff penalties were imposed on anyone who didn't know what was done, and what wasn't. Frances Scott had deliberately cut herself off from her own background when she married, as so many wives were to do later in her son's books. If she felt, like Lucy Smalley sailing out to India as a bride in *Staying On*, that her husband had rescued her from a future too dismal to contemplate, she must have realised – like Lucy as soon as she reached her destination – that the marriage which was to have solved her problems had in fact made them more complicated.

Southgate had its own hierarchy, graded by seniority and status as strictly as anything in British India. Ranks automatically closed against intruders who might weaken the neighbourhood's fabric, or lower its social tone. People in Fox Lane, and on Bourne Hill where the Scotts lived later, were regularly snubbed or cut for speaking with the wrong accent, shopping in the wrong clothes, sometimes even for living (as the Scotts did in both cases) on the wrong side of the street. Conformity could be tricky in a world where even your virtues might count against you. The drive, the efficiency, the good head for figures that had secured Frances Mark of Brixton a coveted job in a counting house were now as likely to give her away, much as Lucy Smalley's shorthand marked her in India 'as a girl who had once had to work for a living'.[28] It was part of the unwritten code of Southgate and Palmers Green that no gentleman permitted his wife to go out to work any more than he ate in the kitchen, pushed his children's pram or let them play in the street. The shame of it would have been hard to live down in a respectable street like Fox Lane, especially for someone whose own credentials would not bear inspection and whose husband's could at best be described as bohemian.

Things might have been easier if Tom Scott had brought in a steady income, or taken the train every morning like other people's husbands to a recognised job in the city. Even a war record would have helped. Frances's own brothers, although hopelessly unpresentable on other counts, had at least served in the trenches: Tom, who had been too old to fight but looked younger, was once accosted on the corner of Oakfield Road, as he turned out of Fox Lane on his way to the studio, by two women who hissed him for being a civilian in wartime. Fox Laners were known for their nosiness, and for thinking too much of themselves for their own good. The whole street had a reputation for living, socially speaking, beyond its means. Suburban Southgate was full of people moving up from one class to another who found an ultra-modern semi-detached house with all the latest labour-saving devices (gas brackets, running hot water, porcelain bathroom fittings) more expensive than they had bargained for, and not just in money terms. Social anxieties made for defensiveness and mutual suspicion rather than solidarity among neighbours whose collective reach often exceeded their individual grasp.

In a sense all Fox Laners shared the same fantasy of gracious living, with their pocket-sized shrubberies at the front, their bow windows with decorative stained-glass strips opening on to long, narrow gardens at the back, and their tradesmen's doors at the side. The Scotts had a screen in their tiny hall to divide the front from the back quarters (which consisted of a kitchen and scullery so dark and pokey the light had to be left on all day) and, although the house was so small you could have heard a raised voice anywhere in it, there was a set of bells on the kitchen wall to summon the maid. Anyone with any self-respect in Fox Lane kept a servant, usually a very young girl from the surrounding countryside – or later in the hungry 1930s from Wales – whose family were glad enough to have one less mouth to feed. She wore overalls in the morning, black with white cap and apron for best, and she slept in the minute spare bedroom, or at a pinch under the stairs. The Scotts had one girl who could never understand why they needed clean plates for the second course at dinner: at home, anyone as fussy as that would simply have turned the plate over and finished eating off the back.[29]

Frances had all the Marks' innate respect for etiquette, their sense of style, their love of finery and pretty things. To the end of her life she took pleasure in a talent for exquisitely delicate laundering and the daintiest imaginable needlework, making the pointed lace trim for her sheets and pillow cases, crocheting all her own mats, doilies, runners and matching table linen. Her house was immaculate, and so was her family. Like Lucy Smalley in *Staying On*, she observed the proprieties and, like Lucy, she firmly suppressed any urge to protest against the system that kept her in her place, 'bottled up and bottled in, and brainwashed . . . into believing that nothing was more important than to do everything my place required.'[30] Frances's rebelliousness had been fully expended on her obstinate refusal to accept the common fate of her kind. Her own and her parents' experience of poverty and insecurity had been too calamitous in the past, her hold on the present remained too precarious, to permit the luxury of opposition. Her instinct was to comply and, when the pressure became unbearable, to take refuge in what Lucy apologetically called 'this tendency to imagine, to fantasize, to *project*'.[31]

It is only in her old age, in an interior monologue running right through *Staying On*, that Lucy takes a long, clear, critical look at her past, reviewing her own attitudes and other people's, her inability to flower or flourish within the system that had given her such meagre and grudging nourishment. Paul wrote *Staying On* at the very end of his life. His mother had been dead six years when he started it, and it proved to be the last novel he published. But one of the things that had interested him, almost from the start of his career as a novelist, was recording the confessions of ordinary, apparently insignificant, indeed publicly almost invisible, married women accustomed, like Lucy, to live out their lives in the background of other people's. Lucy rehearses her monologue in her head. Others – Dorothy Gower in *The Alien Sky*, Mrs Hurst in *A Male Child* – pour out their troubles to a listener who turns up by chance, a boy or young man who has played no part in the past, and who can be relied on neither to judge nor intervene in the present.

In each case, he is an extraordinarily understanding, sympathetic, all but anonymous stand-in for the narrator or novelist. In *Staying On*, Lucy's confidant is an imaginary young man. Dorothy Gower's, in *The Alien Sky*, is real but remains passive. What absorbs him is not so much Dorothy's actual words as the desolation behind them: 'He was listening to her voice, hearing it as a voice crying over a deserted landscape, not filling it with sound, but echoing its emptiness.'[32] Paul grew up as a small boy in Fox Lane listening to the cry of his mother's voice in spoken or unspoken monologue; and what it said was put into words by Lucy Smalley trying to make sense in her seventies of her lifelong feelings of inferiority and deprivation, the humiliations she had endured, her self-suppression, her hope of achieving stability and self-esteem through marriage, and the slow seeping away of that hope in frustration and disappointment.

There were, of course, many other elements incorporated in Paul's portrait of Lucy Smalley. But the women in these three novels each took something in the first place from his mother: Lucy, her courage and optimism in youth and the protective bulwarks she built against encroaching age; Mrs Hurst, the bitterness of a life lived almost entirely by proxy through her husband and sons; Dorothy Gower, the corrosive effect of self-repudiation. Dorothy, heroine of *The Alien Sky*, is the first of these partial portraits, the furthest from Frances Scott in outward circumstances, and the one whose story is most dramatic. She is unhappily married to a British journalist in India on the eve of Independence in 1947: Tom Gower, like Tom Scott, comes of a strongly liberal background which gives him a political generosity and a social confidence denied to his wife. Dorothy is a Eurasian, child of an English father and a 'native' or Indian mother which meant, in British Imperial India, someone brought up from birth to deny and reject her origins.

She sees herself as an outcast, child of a father who felt that marriage had dragged him down to his wife's level, and a mother who could never forgive her husband for failing to 'pull her up to what he'd once been'.[33] Her own marriage was based on a lie born of desperation. Her whole life has been poisoned by what she sees as a dual rejection: she bitterly resents the subterfuges forced on her by the need to claim kinship with the British, to whom she can never belong, while loathing the land that simultaneously gave her birth and taught her to be ashamed of it. This was the common predicament of Eurasians in India. It was one of the things Paul recognised in his bones in the 1940s, as the subcontinent gradually brought home to him social and emotional patterns he had known, perhaps without understanding, from infancy. Hence the special tenderness, running through almost everything he wrote, for children of mixed marriages, half castes, Eurasians, anyone born into one culture and brought up to aspire to another.

It was this aspiration that by turns brightened and darkened Paul's childhood. He was his mother's golden boy: if she saw herself in some lights as Cinderella, Paul was cast from birth or even before as the Prince Charming who would make her world come right. He was everything she could have desired: gifted, artistic, engaging, sensitive, and sufficiently determined to break through the stifling petty restrictions that had proved too much for her in the end. But there was another side to Paul, the side that could never live up to her hopes, however hard he tried. She pictured him as, on the one hand, a wayward poetic genius with the world at his feet, and, on the other, a safe, dependable breadwinner who would redeem the family fortunes. For him, the two sides were irreconcilable. Re-visiting Fox Lane after his mother's death, Paul diagnosed the split in himself from birth: 'I was born in that room. March 25 1920. An Aries. Impulsive, impatient, but a hard worker. Head in the clouds. Feet on the ground. Sometimes. A practical dreamer.'[34]

He might have been describing the pair of brothers who crop up again and again in his books – one of them brilliant, impulsive, charming but unreliable, a dreamer with his head in the clouds; the other a dull, dogged hard worker with his feet on the ground. The second is generally though not invariably defeated or rejected in favour of the first, who is their mother's favourite. A thread of fraternal rivalry between two young men, usually but not always blood brothers, runs through all but the last of Paul's novels. It is the central theme of the first four, and it recurs thereafter in various forms, sometimes relegated to the periphery but always present, until it is finally resolved in the strange relationship between Hari Kumar and Ronald Merrick which is at the core of the Raj Quartet.

Paul's own brother seems to have played relatively little part in shaping this theme in fact. Peter, two and a half years old when Paul was born, promptly joined the admiring ring round the new baby, by his own account abandoning the role of rival easily and early. From the start he fell in with Paul's habit, established in infancy and unquestioned throughout their childhood, of commandeering whatever was going with a determination which by and large suited them both. Separated by a huge age gap from everyone else in the family, regularly thrown together and left to their own devices, they formed a close, jokey, mutually supportive and protective alliance against elders in general, relatives in particular; and by common consent they presented a united front when it came to placating and appeasing the presiding deity at home. Their mother was energetic, amusing, inquisitive, something of a card, adept at turning anything that happened into a drama. But she was also exacting and what the boys called 'quick to temper', full of vexations, liable to erupt at any moment in outbursts which could be volcanic. If Paul monopolised his mother's admiration – 'There was *nothing* he couldn't do,' said Peter – he also bore the brunt of assuaging her dissatisfactions. A precocious awareness of the burdens she bore, together with his own childish attempts to lighten them, made him in some ways responsible beyond his years. When the two boys spent holidays with their cousin Sheila, her nanny said it was always Paul who 'mothered' Peter and packed his things. It was Paul, too, who once flooded the whole house when his mother was out, trying to wash down the passage for her, and swab the coloured tiles in the hall.

Paul was the adventurous, resourceful one of the brothers, always the one to chance his arm and, in case of trouble, the one who got it in the neck. Peter, like his father, preferred to keep his head down. So long as Paul was prepared to take the lead, Peter seemed content to cede both the privileges and the pains of seniority. Peter went to school first, but Paul made it his business to catch up and pass his brother as soon as he got the chance. Once roles were reversed. Peter at seven was invited to spend the summer at an hotel in Scarborough as companion to a child of the proprietors who were family friends: Paul's indignation and incredulity at being the one left behind were still fresh in his memory half a century later.[35] Perhaps this was one of the rankling infant injustices he had in mind when he defined the role of literature from its earliest beginnings in fairy tale and fable down to modern times as essentially one of dissent:

Poor Cinderella. Is it fair that she should scour the pots and pans while her sisters, all the big wide world, go to the ball? Poor Desdemona. Poor Jane Eyre. Poor Oliver Twist. Poor Uncle Tom. Even, poor Becky Sharp. The lessons of injustice and inhumanity are learned very early, and we respond to them even as children who are surrounded by love and happiness and comfort. It is as though we were born with some racial memory of pain and misfortune.[36]

1924 was the year of Peter's trip to Scarborough. It was also the year he started school, which meant that the four-year-old Paul, left behind once again, began spending more and more time at the studio. 'Throughout my childhood, from the age of four or five, I walked from Fox Lane every Saturday morning, with my brother, to visit the Studio. My mother was jealous of it,' said Paul. 'I don't blame her.'[37] The visits provided his first regular excursions away from home and his first outside influence, one that profoundly affected him. Both boys were made welcome by their aunts, Florence and Laura (two older Scott sisters, Jessie and Kate, had died young before the family left Leeds, and a third sister, Maude, died of cancer when Paul was a very small child). Florrie, who was fifty-six in 1924, worked in the studio with Tom. Laura the youngest, who was fifty-one, kept house, and painted flowers in her spare time. The studio itself occupied the top floor at Wyphurst, running the length of the house with a dormer window at the front, and another window at the back from which you could see the garden and the trees on the green. A table in front of each window held drawing boards propped up for Tom and Florrie. The rest of the space was a jumble of bits and pieces, spare pens, paints, brushes, chalks, pencils, supplies of paper and card: the usual artist's organised disorder of materials, props, clients' specifications, half-finished or discarded work, together with dummies, dress stands and batches of the new season's hats, coats, wraps, jackets and frocks.

Tom copied fabrics with minute exactitude, the more highly patterned the better: Florrie contributed faces, limbs and general outlines, showing where the garments were to fall. They worked in Indian ink with mapping pens, and coloured inks for colour work, or lamp black with Chinese white for highlights. Speed and accuracy were essential in a workroom ruled by seasonal pressures where deadlines had to be met, jobs rushed through for the press, mail order

catalogues and display cards for spring and autumn fashions somehow completed on time. Tom and Florrie formed a production line:
she sketched features of her own invention in freehand to start him off
on the far more laborious, methodical business of accurately repro-
ducing a particular client's design. There was something forthright
and free about Florrie, who had a contented and generous disposition,
strong features and an incisive set to her jaw. No matter how busy
their father might be, Florrie had time for her nephews, and both boys
found her great fun. In 1924, it was Florrie who took Paul in hand and
taught him to draw: for him the studio remained ever afterwards 'a
sort of basic childhood country',[38] as it seems to have been for whole
generations of Scotts. Thirty years later, Paul's younger child, Tom's
granddaughter, found his last studio a magical place with its coloured
pastels, pens and sharpened pencils, its jars of newspaper spills, its
comfortable promise of peace and order.

Tom's own father, a wine merchant by profession, had been a gifted
amateur artist who married into a family where everyone painted and
drew. As a boy, Tom himself lived round the corner in Leeds from his
older cousin, George Wright, a highly successful painter of horses and
hunting scenes, who regularly exhibited at the Royal Academy. Tom
and his sisters, together with George's own younger siblings – Louise
(known as Louie), Philip and Gilbert Wright all became professional
artists – were trained at home, and all in varying degrees shared the
family gift for graceful fluidity of line, bright jewelled colouring, crisp
composition, vivacious and delicate detail. In later life, Tom excelled
at copying the folds and fall of a dress, the curves of underwear and
corsets, the most intricate floral designs on printed silks and cottons. If
a visitor in a flower-patterned frock called on his wife, he would sit
contemplating her in silence, working out how best to paint what she
wore. He specialised above all in the furs whose arrival marked off the
summers of Paul's childhood:

Because the autumn catalogues were always published in August or
September, the wholesale and retail furriers used to send their stuff to him in
the spring and early summer. Cascades of mink – and astrakhan, silver fox,
musquash and the despised rabbit – tumbled out of the immense brown paper
parcels which came by Carter Paterson and the LNER [London & North
Eastern Railway], and covered his summer studio ankle deep in winter
opulence.

My mother, who sometimes posed for him, one hand on hip, the other
indicating a vista, always complained that the only time she wore sable was in
June when it was too hot to enjoy it.[39]

The studio gave Paul his first contact with the world of work which became a source of professional fascination, and a private refuge, all his life. It taught him habits of contemplation and concentration he never lost. He learned how to observe accurately, how to analyse and record, how to pick out the salient detail, how to use colour and highlights, how to block out an overall composition before attempting to fill in the outline. He and Peter had both inherited something of the family facility with pen and pencil, and Paul always remained a cartoonist, and an intermittent painter of landscape.

Wyphurst was not the only studio to which he had access. Tom, Florrie and Laura Scott had been brought up to think of themselves as brother and sisters, rather than cousins, of the four Wright girls and three boys (the Scotts' mother had been a Wright, and the Wrights' mother a Scott, which made, as Paul liked to point out, for a thoroughly incestuous relationship between the offspring). The Wrights ran their own thriving fashion studio between the wars on the top of Richmond Hill in Surrey, where five or six of the seven lived and worked together with their families in an enormous, ugly but imposing mansion called Kingsbury.

The house had been snapped up just after the first war by Gilbert Wright, who split it into flats and threw out two wings, occupying the left-hand extension himself with his wife and only surviving child, a daughter called Sheila who was mid-way in age between Peter and Paul. The right-hand wing housed a studio with ample working space for Gilbert himself, his brothers, sisters, employees and apprentices, or 'students', who were learning the trade. Fashion work supplied their bread and butter, but they still painted coaching and hunting scenes, catering to the upper end of the calendar and card market, turning out glossy, seductive, essentially reassuring images of a rural past polluted or lost by industrial expansion. The business provided a comfortable living for a thriving artistic community at Kingsbury, which was divided into separate quarters for Gilbert's two spinster sisters, Louie and Ethel (as the only Wright woman who didn't paint, Ethel took charge of the housekeeping, like Laura at Wyphurst); a married sister, Connie Best, with her husband and son; and the eldest brother, George, who hunted with the Old Surrey and Burstow, and was often away on his travels, painting horses up and down the country for favoured clients. The third brother Philip, who specialised in sporting life, 'lived out' with his wife and son at Barnes, while the fourth sister, Mabel, moved in as a widow on her return from Canada, having buried three husbands (which entitled her, as she said, to call herself the Female Bluebeard). Kingsbury and its occupants supplied models for the rambling family house called Aylward, in Paul's third novel *A Male Child*, with its odd-shaped landings, makeshift partitions and cargo of imperious, elderly sisters alternately bullying and indulging their brother-in-law, Rex Coles, who is in part at least a direct portrait of Gilbert Wright.

Gilbert was the moving spirit at Kingsbury, the youngest and most audacious of the whole family, the one who most tried his sisters' patience and the one for whom Paul afterwards retained a soft spot: 'Of course, my favourite uncle was always Uncle Gilbert. He was a bit of a lad. Always running off with unlikely women and having to be brought back. He went in for Port, as well as barmaids. He also wore spats. And a little brown bowler. Quite an Edwardian nut. It was he who decided they all ought to cut a dash in Richmond.'[40] Gilbert had a chauffeur who drank, and a series of limousines, including a Buick ('a beautiful, buff-coloured thing,' said Peter, who never forgot being driven in it with Paul as a treat all the way to the coast and back, escorting Sheila on her way to a seaside holiday), which was replaced by a Rolls-Royce with a crest on the door. There was a butler ('who liked Port and barmaids too, but Port most,' Paul wrote, 'and was unsteady with the plates')[41], a gardener, and a nanny for Sheila. In the Wright household, as in the Scotts', age had the upper hand over youth. George's two daughters were so old they might as well have belonged to another generation so far as Peter and Paul were concerned; Philip's son David and Connie's only child, Tony Best, were respectively seven and six years older than Paul, and Tony in any case was mostly away at boarding school.

Peter and Paul came over at weekends, travelling by open-topped 29 bus, which had a canvas cover for the knees in wet weather, and which carried them from Southgate to Finsbury Park, where they changed to the underground, catching another bus at Hammersmith for Richmond.[42] They were regularly invited to stay in the summer, to be company for Sheila who was much alone, seeing little of her parents and forbidden to make friends with the neighbourhood children. She liked and looked up to Paul, who pitied her loneliness and was especially fond of her in return. The three of them played in Richmond Park, along the river bank, in the large garden with its trees and shrubberies or, when it rained, in the house. The Wrights, critical and cantankerous, became star turns in the private cabaret carried on by Peter and Paul over the next half century or so. Both boys were champion mimics, both liable at the drop of a hat to hold long, hilarious, impromptu conversations in the fruity tones of Gilbert, who lisped, and Louie, the oldest and fiercest of the Wright sisters, who was deaf and made expert, offensive use of her ear trumpet.

No outsider could hope to be considered good enough for a Wright. Sheila's mother suffered bitterly from a sense of inferiority and rejection; Philip's wife chose to live out; George's was considered 'K.O.M.', or common, by the family. 'None of them ever got on,' said Peter: 'Paul always said the Wrights quarrelled all winter over cards and all summer over croquet.' They played croquet in long, concentrated serial battles lasting for weeks on end with matches 'as hard-contested as Wimbledon',[43] and as furiously disputed afterwards. Often at dinner, which the families took together in a communal dining room, the separate tables weren't speaking. If it wasn't croquet or bridge scores they complained about the heating arrangements, or the inadequate performance of individual members. Sheila was brought up by the powerful, proprietorial Wright women to count herself second best from birth on account of inferior blood. So were her cousins David Wright and Peter and Paul Scott. 'You must remember that they were their fathers' sons,' she said, 'but an outsider bore them: the woman who had married into the family.'

Paul and Sheila grew up with something of the ambivalent closeness of siblings just as their fathers, who were double cousins, had done before them. 'It was as close to incest as you could get,' Sheila said: 'Paul used those words to me.' Tom Scott, who came between Philip and Gilbert in age (the three were known as The Three Mustgetbeers), had always treated their sisters as his own. The Wrights might patronise him, contrasting their prosperity with his lack of it, and generally disparaging his relatively low-grade commercial practice as what they called artistic potboiling, but Tom remained part of the family concern. When the Wrights won the prestigious contract for the Harrods catalogue between the wars, Tom was called in to help out with the furs; and when, round about 1931, one of Gilbert's hunting scenes was chosen for the front of the Prince of Wales's Christmas card – which, as Paul said, 'put poor George's nose further out of joint'[44] – the Scotts were as proud as if Tom had done it himself.

But it was not for nothing that the Scotts had moved up to Southgate before the First World War, putting as much distance as possible between themselves and the Wrights. Family disapproval of George's wife, and Gilbert's, was mild compared to the family's feelings when Tom brought home a working girl young enough to be George's daughter. Frances Scott was never made welcome at Kingsbury. At one point, the Wrights broke with her altogether, relenting only in favour of her two sons.[45] Perhaps in some sense the ban came as a relief to Paul's mother, who had even less defence than Sheila against the intolerance of the Wright women. Paul, growing up with a foot in both camps, watched and noted their behaviour. As a child there was little he could do to smooth his mother's path. But the Wrights' plummy tones lived on long after their deaths in Paul's and Peter's comic imitations; and a more sombre sense of their mother's humiliation at the hands of her social superiors informed passages like this one, in *Staying On*, where Lucy Smalley remembers what it felt like to be treated like dirt by

those awful women who had condescended and taken every nasty little advantage of her as a junior wife who was not in a position – no, not in a position – to tell them where they got off but instead, oh yes instead, under an obligation to bear their treatment meekly not just for [her husband's] sake but because a hierarchy was a hierarchy and a society without a clear stratification of duties and responsibilities and privileges was no society at all.[46]

Frances Scott could not afford, any more than Lucy Smalley, to defy the social hierarchy that despised her. The Wrights were her best allies in the battle to disown her own past and the fate to which it had condemned her. Their very existence gave point to her ceaseless struggle to make ends meet without letting standards slip on hopelessly inadequate funding. 'One side of my family was quite well-off,' Paul wrote, 'the other side (mine) quite poor. Weekends in Richmond (a Rolls, a chauffeur, menservants and a nanny) were set off against years in Southgate (Shanks pony, the bus and making do). My father was ... usually in trouble with the bank manager.'[47] The Wrights offered practical help: they might poach orders but they also put work Tom's way and, in an emergency, they could be touched for a loan. But, perhaps more important, they represented a family access card to the spacious world of Frances's imagination. From their large house in Richmond, they looked back to memories of another, much more splendid establishment, a house called Kirklees in the country with a stream running through the grounds, which Gilbert and Tom remembered from their Yorkshire boyhood. Sheila and her cousins grew up on stories of Kirklees, emblem of solidity and success, symbol of all the family aspired to and all that threatened forever to slip through their grasp, origin perhaps of the lost land of prosperity and content that figures in so many of Paul's early novels. Kirklees became a family legend. Throughout their childhood, in time of hardship or discouragement at home, Peter and Paul were familiar with their mother's rallying cry: 'We can hold up our heads because of the Wrights.'

Kirklees seems to have been, in fact, the property rented by the Wrights' father in the 1890s at 10 Hollins Lane, Leeds. This was the site of some of the highest and grandest houses in Headingley, newly built in styles ranging from Renaissance villa to medieval crenellated, perched on a ridge so that prosperous manufacturers with their backs to the city might gaze out at the front, over the valley falling steeply away to a beck in the bottom, to a magnificent view of green fields and hills stretching as far as the eye could reach. George Wright the elder, father of the three horse painters, had been manager of a carpet factory, which might explain why he named the place that crowned his career after the ruined priory called Kirklees, then in the heart of heavy woollen carpet country between Leeds and Huddersfield. The Wrights had originally made their money (like the Brights in Paul's novel *The Bender*) from coal. Old David Wright (Gilbert's grandfather and Tom's) had prospered as a coal merchant in Hunslet, part of Leeds' expanding smoky sprawl of pottery and brickfields, railway yards, gas works and acres of tiny workmen's cottages. It was his son George, the carpet man, who moved up to the much more salubrious suburb of Headingley, when he married Elizabeth Scott in 1859, the year before her brother, George Bewick Scott, married George Wright's sister Ruth.[48]

The Wrights always claimed that the family's artistic streak came from their side (and certainly there had been Wright families of potters producing Leeds creamware, plain and painted, at the Hunslet pottery throughout the nineteenth century). The Scotts counterclaimed with an illustrious ancestor of their own, the wood engraver Thomas Bewick. Paul's brother was christened Peter Bewick Scott, and Paul himself enjoyed a connection which seems to have arisen, naturally enough in an outstandingly competitive family, without any basis in fact. Paul's grandfather, George Bewick Scott, had taken the name in the first place from his mother Elizabeth Bewick (no relation to the engraver, although she came from Stamfordham, part of the same little clutch of Northumbrian villages as his birthplace at Ovingham).[49] Her descendants believed she had been 'travelling companion to a lady of rank',[50] or lady's maid, before her marriage in 1830 to a railway engineer from Jarrow called Thomas Scott. The couple moved down by stages to Leeds, following his trade, and placing their sons, when they left school at twelve, in good jobs as clerks with the Midlands Railway on five shillings a week. The middle son, Mark, found an opening at Selby with an oil-seed- and grain-crushing mill, which brought him prosperity, and eventually power as the town's leading Liberal reformer. George, the eldest, set up in the 1860s soon after his marriage as a wine and spirit merchant and wholesale ale bottler at 7 Bond Street in the centre of Leeds.

George Scott's only son, Tom, was born in 1871: a date which his own son Paul often cited as giving him his stake in the mid-Victorian scene. Paul felt himself formed in childhood more by his parents' and grandparents' outlook than by what he called 'post-war twentyism':

'we're not just of our time,' he said. 'We inherit our own memory, and the memories and attitudes of our parents.'[51] The Scotts were passionately committed to the Liberal cause. Paul's father would have been ten in 1881, when the ageing Gladstone made a triumphal, four-day progress through Leeds with speeches, a banquet, scores of loyal addresses, a tumultuous reception from the chamber of commerce and a mass meeting at which half a million supporters assembled to celebrate their booming, trade-based economy, secured by Imperial expansion abroad and the onset of democracy at home. Coal and railways were key factors in this prosperity. Paul inherited his father's pride in a family founded, on the one side, by the successful railwayman Thomas Scott and, on the other, by the even wealthier David Wright, who was agent for Middleton colliery. He also inherited the Scotts' Liberal tradition, and he was one of the first to insist, almost a century after his father's birth, that England's gain was India's loss: that the derelict cotton mills which dotted the Yorkshire and Lancashire landscape in the 1970s were as much a monument to the British raj as any statue of Queen Victoria.[52]

The Scotts' decline and fall came long before the empire's. Paul's grandfather, always more interested in radical reform than in minding the shop, was said to have been ruined (like the Spruces in *The Bender*) by standing bail for a friend who absconded without paying. Young Tom, making his way by this time in the hotel trade, would have been hard put to support his parents and his five unmarried older sisters. His Wright cousins, meanwhile, had turned out to be on to a good thing. George built up a fashionable horse portrait practice in the first decade of the century based on Rugby and Oxford, while Gilbert – never one to pass up a lucrative opening – detected rich pickings to be found on the side in London's infant fashion trade. By 1900, the Wrights were renting premises in Forest Hill in south London and, in 1906, the whole family moved into a capacious, semi-detached villa at 99 Honor Oak Park, which they named nostalgically 'Kirklees'. Here, between Catford and Dulwich, they founded what became between the wars the 'Gilbert and Louise Wright Art Studio'; and here, at a rather more modest establishment a few miles westwards in Streatham, they were joined by Tom Scott, arriving with his father, mother and sisters to set up a Scott fashion studio.

It was a drastic uprooting, and no doubt the two sides of the family were drawn together afterwards by their common exile from Yorkshire. But the Wrights had always been restless, energetic, surefooted, the kind of people who readily adapt to a society in flux. The flourishing new suburbs both families lived in – Headingley, Forest Hill, Honor Oak Park, Southgate and Palmers Green – were part of a convulsive social upheaval taking place all over England as the great industrial centres, which had sucked in whole populations from the fields round about, now spewed them back out to the countryside. 'Here come the clerks, the respectable middle class and the respectable artisans of England,' said Paul in Palmers Green, '. . . encouraged to come here by the building of railways and houses by speculators . . . Outer London, north and south, is a vast complex of action and reaction, cause and effect.'[53]

As he grew older, this complexity increasingly fascinated Paul. He was himself the product of genteel suburbia, like George Spruce in *The Bender*, 'of middle-class origin on his father's side, lower middle amounting to working class on his mother's, a poor relation'.[54] Like George, he was taught early to think of himself as a gentleman and never to admit to working-class origins. It took him a long time to make terms with this inbred self-contempt, and longer still to see what a boon his sense of alienation had been to him as a writer. 'One of the earliest signs of the so-called creative instinct in childhood is self-absorption,' he wrote, 'the feeling that you are somehow separate from your environment and can't identify with it really satisfactorily – plus the feeling that this inability, far from being *wrong*, ought to be cultivated.'[55] As a small child, Paul was friendly, outgoing, alert, fondly remembered by his girl cousins as full of mischief and fun. But he also had a withdrawn, brooding side which he cultivated in long hours spent alone at home, or drawing quietly in the studio:

This self-absorption is a form of curiosity, and after a while when it's worked itself out, a different kind of curiosity takes its place and is just as sharp – a curiosity in *other* people. There is something common to both forms. That is the curiosity in the environment – in the physical surroundings. That doesn't change, and I suppose the child who is going to be a writer is more curious about his surroundings than the child who wants to be – and is – part of them. . . . I think it's true to say that in the absence of a real one, the creative child will invent his own unhappy childhood. He is a natural rearranger. A natural rejector.[56]

There would be many stages to go through before Paul could look back without anger on the childhood that made him an outsider in his own country. He wrote about it at first hand in *The Bender*, in some ways his favourite among his own books, and the only one that has no connection whatsoever with India or the Near East. He said India provided the metaphor he needed as a writer: 'I don't think a writer chooses his metaphors. They choose him.'[57] He himself had no obvious connection with India (except a great aunt, George Scott's sister Anne Lindsey, whose husband built bridges for the raj), or with the kind of old India hands who recognised themselves in his books, and to whom places like semi-detached, suburban Southgate remained 'totally foreign – as India is not foreign to the more privileged upper middle classes'.[58] Paul himself never belonged to the ruling élite of district commissioners, police superintendents and government aides he wrote about in the Raj Quartet. But he maintained that England's wealth, the period of Imperial strength and prosperity ushered in by the industrial revolution, was largely founded on India's, and that it was a debt owed by the whole nation, not just by the privileged few who had sailed out from Britain to serve the Imperial power. By the time he finished the Quartet, he had come to feel that the link with India ran through his mother's people as well as his father's, and, to show what he meant, he quoted a passage from the fourth and last volume, describing a room full of sleeping British soldiers in Bombay in August, 1945:

The faces were those of urban Londoners and belonged to streets of terraced houses that ended in one-man shops: newsagent-tobacconist, fish and chip shop, family grocer, and a pub at the corner where the high road was. What could such a face know of India? And yet India was there, in the skull, and the bones of the body. Its possession had helped nourish the flesh, warm the blood of every man in the room, sleeping and waking.[59]

Wright hunting scene from Paul's grandmother's album.

CHAPTER TWO

Slow dreamy boats of recollection and swift thrusting boats of ambition

Paul was six when he started as a general reader and, in his own phrase, 'went critical' as a writer, sitting on the floor beside the bookcase at Fox Lane reading his first adult book, which was *Three Weeks* by Elinor Glyn.[1] Only an exceptionally liberal and easygoing family would have allowed a child of six access to this notorious shocker, generally held to be one of the most scandalous stories of sexual misconduct in the language before *Lady Chatterley's Lover*. Paul not only read it without anyone apparently minding, but used it as a convenient cover behind which to take down and deface his father's Melrose edition of Walter Scott's Waverley novels scribbling methodically on the title page of each volume with a soft 3B pencil. It was a protest against everything he found repressive and forbidding, impossible to live up to, in his mother's view of the Scott heritage:

The author of *Waverley* was not claimed as a connection; indeed, he had been explicitly disowned; but I judged otherwise. Only a grown-up and therefore tiresome Scott of my own ilk could have been responsible for such a mournful-looking set of books: the letter-press niggardly, tight-worked on the page, the paper harsh and grainy to the touch, the cloth binding a dark unsympathetic green, fussily embossed with a design of horrid thistles, the illustrations in gloomy monotone, mostly of insipid ladies looking frightened out of their wits on inhospitable battlements or at the tops of stone stairways on which – it could not be soon enough for me – they seemed about to come croppers. So: *that* with the pencil to Sir Walter, and *that* across a frontispiece portrait in Lockhart, the likeness by Raeburn which, although clean-shaven, was conclusive evidence of an implacable relationship with the stern, bearded patriarchs whose portraits hung like ill-omens in dark corners of the hall and landing of the house I lived in.[2]

Paul had confused Sir Walter Scott with 'an uncle whom I detested', presumably his namesake and great uncle Mark Scott, chief of the dismal Yorkshire patriarchs whose achievements seemed as threatening to a small boy as their bushy beards. He was caught redhanded by his mother – 'Wait until your Father sees this' – but his vandalism fell flat that night at the seat of authority: 'Well, Father Saw it. Fortunately it turned out that he was himself a Dickens and Thackeray man, and was mainly concerned at the waste of his 3B pencil which (he gently pointed out), although encased in wood, did not grow on trees.'[3] Paul wondered afterwards whether his interest in Scott had perhaps been taken as an early declaration of literary intent. At all events, no more was said, no rubber was produced, and the defiled Melrose edition went back to its shelf until Paul himself devoured Scott in his teens.

As a precocious six-year-old, he preferred the seductive vista of adult life glimpsed in *Three Weeks*, whose Edwardian hero – 'he was just a splendid English young animal of the best class' – offered a more appealing namesake: 'Paul was young . . . and fair and strong. He had been in the eleven at Eton and left Oxford with a record for all that should turn a beautiful Englishman into a perfect athlete. . . . As for his mother – Lady Henrietta Verdayne – she thought him a god among men!'[4] This was heady stuff. Paul Verdayne's sentimental education at the hands of a nameless Balkan beauty of mature years and untold sophistication centres on the mysteries of upmarket adulterous passion, with what was then probably the most popular erotic encounter in fiction staged on a tiger skin uncomfortably strewn with rare books. But *Three Weeks* also covers table manners ('Then they played with the tea, and she showed him how he was to drink it with lemon'),[5] turnout ('No Roman Empress with her bath of asses' milk could have had a more wonderful toilet than she'), and the finer points of how to treat a lady. Paul Verdayne's *soignée* seductress turns out to be an indulgent and surprisingly maternal creature, teasing him ('You must tell me why you were upset, baby – Paul!'), teaching and caressing him with a 'strange tenderness which might have been a mother's watching the gambols of her babe'. His nationality is one of the things that excites her most (' "I love the English" she whispered. "I have known the men of all nations – but I love the English best. They are straight and just – the fine ones at least. They are brave and fair – and fearless" '). She makes three weeks' courtship and seduction pass 'at boiling-point of excitement and bliss'. The real Paul said he didn't understand a word of it, but he must have grasped the thrilling message that there was nothing in the world to beat the prospects of a young gentleman born in time of Imperial confidence into the noblest nation on earth. Moreover, Edwardian literary discretion meant that, although Paul Verdayne is in fact being taught how to make love, the lesson is described in language that would apply just as well to his having at last learned to read:

What was this marvellous thing which had happened to him? . . . now he was a man and knew what life meant in its greatest and best. That was part of the wonder. . . . Nothing small would ever again appeal to Paul. His whole outlook was vaster and more full of wide thoughts.[6]

Much of the Lady's teaching would have been perfectly acceptable in any respectable home, especially her romantic views on manliness and motherhood ('You must always reverence your mother, Paul, and accept her worship with love').[7] The chivalric code would have been strongly reinforced when Paul Scott finally joined Peter at school in the autumn of 1928: 'I went to one of those private schools that used to be described as for the sons of gentlemen. My father was a gentle man, by which I mean he seldom raised his voice in anger,'[8] Paul wrote in one of several essentially deprecating accounts of his education. Winchmore Hill Collegiate School had been opened in 1906 in purpose-built premises on the highly desirable, tree-lined northern heights of Southgate by an energetic and ambitious schoolmaster named John Temblett-Wood.[9] Peter and Paul, or Scotts 1 and 2, attended the College, a preparatory branch run for mixed juniors by the headmaster's wife in a small hall a few doors down from their house in Fox Lane. The school believed in King and Empire, church and country, loyalty, patriotism, the ethics of service and sacrifice, and the moral imperative of games-playing. It aimed at 'Sound Teaching based on Common-sense Principles'[10] rather than academic distinction. Boys were prepared for the university of life, or for London public day schools like Merchant Taylors and the City of London, from which they might matriculate to other, more selective universities.

Relatively inexpensive private schools, like Winchmore Hill Collegiate, springing up all over the Home Counties before and after the First World War, got a bad name because they gave unscrupulous, ill-qualified proprietors unlimited opportunities to trade on the snobbery and prejudice of gullible parents who had no means of telling if they were being taken for a ride. The Collegiate was admittedly founded (as George Spruce said of his school in *The Bender*) 'for the education of the sons of gentlemen who had gone down, but kept afloat mainly by local tradesmen who had come up.'[11] In other words, it helped supply the binding element essential to a society in transition. Its prime aim was to endorse the aspirations, strengthen the confidence and refine the manners of new recruits to the middle class. John and

Jessie Temblett-Wood were enthusiasts of genuine conviction and principle, who made no bones about the fact that what they offered – and what their customers wanted – was social more than intellectual training. The headmaster, renowned as 'a proper old stickler'[12] or disciplinarian, was widely respected for the significance he attached to social credentials, and the inculcation of correct speech and grammar. Pupils imbibed a version of what Paul later diagnosed as Kiplingesque double talk,[13] but in the years immediately after the first war it was impossible for a small boy to remain impervious to the sense of a heroic, national and Imperial destiny actively instilled on all sides, at home and at school, where it was impressed on even the youngest pupil that he put on a whole apparatus of duty and privilege with his uniform of grey shorts, red blazer and grey cap with red banding.

Peter and Paul in their cherry-coloured blazers were a source of pride and satisfaction to the whole family. Their schooling was a luxury – 'the only luxury he afforded himself,' Paul said of his father[14] – but one that all agreed was essential. Collegiate parents and pupils alike respected the red-and-grey cap as a badge of honour, to be looked after, lived up to, and if necessary defended in case of attack by boys from the local board school: fast runners and good fighters in cut-down clothes with boots too big for them, who used filthy snotrags instead of clean handkerchiefs, and whose heads as often as not were shaved for ringworm. In the frontier spirit of pioneering Southgate in those days, schools like Winchmore Hill saw themselves in some lights as the bulwarks of a beleaguered community prepared at any moment to protect itself against rebuff and threat. On one side were the cockney Edmontonians, suspected of harbouring disaffection as well as ringworm and fleas, marked out by the way they spoke as 'little better than foreigners'.[15] On the other were the carriage or chauffeur-driven car folk, set apart by their almost equally impenetrable manners, their public-school accents and educations, although in Southgate in the 1920s these were more likely to be international financiers and anglicised Greek bankers than the original county families, whose seats had been demolished along with the rest of the recent rural past.

Names of pubs like the Cattermole Arms, the Dog and Duck, the Stag and Hounds, the Woodman at the top of Fox Lane and the Fox at the bottom, commemorated its passing. One of the first cinemas in the district (the Queens Hall, where Paul first saw *Grand Hotel*)[16] remained a converted, lath-and-plasterwork farmhouse on Green Lanes. Hedge Lane, leading off Green Lanes (the two are now the A111 and A105 respectively: fume-ridden, traffic-choked main routes into central London), was still partly bordered in Paul's boyhood by its towering white hawthorn hedge, festooned with dogroses, briony, wild hops and honeysuckle. There were cool, tiled dairies where trippers from the city could buy fresh eggs and glasses of milk from the odd farm that had not yet capitulated to the developers. A friend of Paul's who grew up in Hedge Lane remembered Farmer Watson of Huxley Farm striding along in his thick country tweeds and leather leggings, followed by a train of derisive boys from the newly-built terraced houses round about.[17] To the farmer, these strange urban boys, and their white-collared fathers who disappeared each morning with rolled umbrellas down the underground, represented the horde of invading barbarians who had laid waste to his world. For the boys, 'Potty Watson' with his red face, truculent manner, and a defiant red rose in his buttonhole, was a crackpot senselessly trying to stem the tide of progress and civilisation which would inevitably root out his hawthorn hedge and pave over his cornfields, just as it had already chopped down the orchards, filled in the ponds and reduced Winchmore Hill woods to a manageable, decorative remnant of the great forest belt that once stretched from Barnet and Enfield Chase to Lea marshes in the Thames Valley.

This was the cohesive vision of the future towards which institutions like Winchmore Hill Collegiate were enthusiastically working. The school motto was *Conjunctis viribus*, or All Pull Together. Those who couldn't or wouldn't fit in had to pay a price. Any child who had ever earned money running errands, or attended a ragged school, would be found out at once by his fellows. Boys were adept at the sort of cross-examination that makes other boys squirm: questions about what their fathers did, whether they could afford a car and where they went for the holidays. One boy in Paul's year remembered being narrowly interrogated as to how much his mother got to spend each week on the housekeeping.[18] Tom Scott retained all his life the Yorkshire accent which, Paul said, was ridiculed out of him before he was ten:[19] 'In this middle to lower-middle-class residential area, I was very early aware of social distinctions. Most of the children who went to the College lived in grander houses. I and my brother, living at 130 Fox Lane, went there because my father was the only Professional Man in that part of the road. He couldn't afford it. But we went.'[20]

It was in what he called middle childhood that Paul began to understand his mother's mixed feelings about her relations, and the difficulty of reconciling the two worlds to which he belonged. His Mark grandmother died of a stroke in her seventies in the summer of 1926. He was too young to remember her, or only as part of that shadowy company who figured in his mother's stories of family births and deaths, cradles, coffins and bridal wreaths, the saga of a people whose funerals were always far more splendid than their lives. Paul's grandmother had had a hard life but she made a good end: the beautiful broderie anglaise night-dress she had worn on her deathbed was carefully put away, along with Paul's own first knitted boots, to be brought out and admired on special occasions. Frances Scott treasured her relics and stories of the past. She told her daughter-in-law long afterwards that she had peopled her house in Fox Lane with family ghosts, thronging so thickly that she had to stand aside to let them pass on the stairs; and she had a battered silver ring set with a green stone, said to have been damaged when it was hacked from the finger of an ancestor who had been hanged on a gibbet in the fifteenth century.[21] This sounds like a possible plot for *The Keepsake*, Frances's favourite of the novelettes she had burned on the eve of her wedding, and the only one whose title she could remember. Paul wondered afterwards whether they had existed at all: 'Perhaps they were never really written. She had a powerful imagination.'[22]

Paul grew up as a child hearing more or less gruesome stories like this one at family gatherings. Before his grandmother's death, his Mark grandparents held regular musical evenings on Saturdays at their house in Upper Norwood, when an old-fashioned sing-song round the piano was followed by a hospitable spread of beef aitch-bone, mashed potato and salad, with a fine lemon jelly to follow. Paul's mother, in some ways still part of a tougher, more robust, roistering tradition than anything admissible in genteel Southgate, was proud of her ability to sink half a pint of gin as if it were water; and she insisted on her sons learning early to hold their liquor. 'I was taught to drink from the age of six,' Paul said: ' – whisky, port, gin, wine – the lot, anything the adults drank, I drank too – diluted, I grant you, but who knows? – perhaps my mother laced my bottle with gin when I was an infant. I wouldn't put it past her.'[23] This was the world that produced characters like Vi Spruce from south London in *The Bender*, and Barbie Batchelor from Camberwell in the Raj Quartet, a drab, pinched world of hardship relieved by occasional sprees and drinking bouts, dances at the local Temperance Assembly Hall or the annual church charity social, a world of funny uncles and disreputable fathers always short of what they call the ready, perpetually struggling to support champagne tastes on beer incomes, liable at the slightest encouragement to break out in disorderly music-hall turns or snatches of 'Champagne Charlie'.

Peter and Paul did not see a great deal of the Marks. Their Aunt Alice sent handsome presents, and both boys remembered an outing with her to the 1924 Wembley exhibition to see the Flying Scotsman and the Giant Soap Bubble. Ruth would sometimes come over to

Southgate on her day off bringing their cousin, Wilfred Mark's daughter Edna, who was suitably impressed by the glamour and vitality of her Auntie Frances, the space and comfort in which the Scotts lived, the games Paul invented for them to play. 'He was really a ball of fun. Up to every trick that was going. Paul got culture from the Scotts,' she said, 'but he was a true Mark.' She meant that he had inherited his mother's and grandfather's imaginative drive, their generous instincts, their sense of occasion, love of finery and ability to make things hum. He had the true Mark's assertive temperament, but he was also a true Scott; and, if it was the Mark in him that concocted schemes and built wildly ambitious dream castles, it was the dogged, practical, foot-on-the-ground Scott that carried them through. It took a long time for Paul to acknowledge how much he had in common with his father, 'a kind, gentle, humorous man'[24] whose mildness masked an unyielding stubborn detachment. Tom Scott was tall, broad-shouldered, generally silent, cut off by a courtliness that seemed already antiquated to his younger son. Paul as a child saw his father as a 'strong, sometimes stern, always heroic figure',[25] remote and unapproachable, belonging to a different generation from his lively, dramatic, dissatisfied mother. It suited Frances in some moods to build her husband up to heroic proportions, just as she might cut him down to size when confronted with the sort of passive resistance that exasperates Vi Spruce in *The Bender* ('Sitting there, she said, on his backside in his good north light painting little pictures when Mr Proctor next door goes off every morning in his car earning good money like a proper husband should').[26]

Tom responded with resignation and a muffled, unobtrusive humour. His sons called him 'the old Josser', which suited him so well that he was soon known to the whole family as 'Josser'. He played little part in the everyday round of the household at Fox Lane. Physical absence at the studio all day was compounded at home by absent-mindedness. 'He was always losing things,' said Peter, remembering one Christmas eve which Josser celebrated so enthusiastically over drinks with his friend George Proctor that he came home without the briefcase containing toys for the children's stockings. 'Father Christmas brought me odds and ends this year,' Paul said, in the matter-of-fact way that made everyone laugh. As Tom advanced into his sixties, deafness added to his isolation. He had an ear trumpet, improvised by Frances from a length of metal shower hose and two tin funnels in imitation of one that belonged to his even more ancient cousin, Louie Wright: Josser and Louie once had a row down these ear trumpets, each getting more flushed and rednecked as they bawled at one another through their funnels, to the delight of Peter and Paul who

mentally stored scenes like this for replaying later with a flourish of
imaginary trumpets. But even before deafness forced him back in on
himself, Tom retreated increasingly into the memories he shared with
his sisters. The past was bright, warm, peopled, hospitable, a time of
hope and companionship when both Scotts and Wrights prospered,
before Tom and his sisters left Leeds in a slow spiral of financial and
social descent. 'He lived in his past,' said Paul: 'I learned to live in it
too.'[27]

'I regret knowing so little about my own father, and having almost
nothing to remember him by,' Paul wrote to his own children at the
end of his life.[28] One of the few relics that survived both Paul's death
and his father's was a cigar box containing a lock of brown hair in a
folded paper, several pressed roses, a single tiny white kid glove with
pearl buttons, and a poem 'To Nell' in Tom's writing, dated New
Year's Day 1894; there was also a Christmas card to 'my darling' from
'your loving little Nell', a second of Tom's poems lamenting her
illness, and a black-edged mourning card announcing the death of
Ellen Oldroyd, aged 22, in May 1896. The Oldroyds of Providence
Avenue, Headingley, figured prominently in family reminiscences of
Leeds, and in group photos which show Tom himself in his twenties,
looking sturdy, handsome and confident in a natty suit and straw
boater. Whatever lay behind this box of mementoes, and however it
came into Paul's possession, it was a sharp reminder of how easily the
past may be romanticised. Paul grew up with a father who turned his
back on the present. He himself came to understand this attitude too
well to be able to share it, settling instead for the vigorous sense of
history he assigned to Mildred Layton in the Raj Quartet, 'vigorous
because it pruned ruthlessly that other weakening sense so often found
with the first, the sense of nostalgia, the desire to *live* in the past.'[29]

The Wrights of Richmond tried literally to put this dangerous desire
into practice. 'I was brought up by elderly maiden aunts,' said Paul's
cousin, Sheila Wright: 'So was Paul – and we had a very Victorian
attitude.' Sheila believed in the end that her father's optimistic refrain
– '*You*'ll never have to earn your living' – only reinforced the
conventional constraints designed to control and weaken her sex. For
Paul, watching what happened to Sheila, the lesson was salutary. His
own Wyphurst aunts were very far from the prim, protected stereotypes of Victorian spinsterhood. Florrie played the piano, Laura
painted in water-colours, but they were both strong, resourceful, self-
reliant women whose liberal and independent outlook was a part of
the old-world charm that struck everyone who met them. In some
ways they could be surprisingly modern: Peter and Paul called them by
their Christian names, Florrie and Laura, which was by no means the

custom for small boys addressing even closely related old ladies in the 1920s.

Paul loved and respected them both, especially Florrie, who figures occasionally in his writings as his 'anti-Shavian aunt',[30] the one with a weakness for Walter Scott and a positive passion for Mark Twain. Florrie entertained her small nephews, sitting between them in the arbour at the far end of the long, thin Fox Lane garden, telling them stories, sometimes of her own invention, sometimes drawn from the past or the Bible. 'How are you going to get your piano up there?' Paul once asked sceptically, giving her a straight look, when she talked about going to heaven. The boys attended Christ Church with their parents, and would both in due course be confirmed into the Church of England, but their churchgoing was more a social than a religious observance. Florrie, who had no time for hypocrisy, seems to have talked to them as frankly as if they were adults. 'Florrie told Peter and me (when she was about 60) that she hated the age she was born in,' Paul wrote: ' "All so nice on the surface", she said, "and extraordinary things going on behind the scenes." '[31] Florrie was sixty in 1928, when Paul was eight years old. Nearly half a century later he found out one of the things she had meant from George Wright's daughter, Enid, a courtesy aunt and another of his favourite relations. Enid, who lived at Seaford on the south coast, is the 'seaside aunt' who turns up sometimes in his essays and letters, the conventional, romantic, conservative aunt who claimed to have read Daphne du Maurier's *Rebecca* nine times.[32]

She was in her seventies when she told Paul the sad story of his Aunt Kate, Florrie's and Laura's older sister, said to have been the most beautiful of the five Scott girls, who died, aged eighteen, in 1884. She had been pregnant at the time: her seducer was a cousin, one of Mark Scott's sons from Selby, who came to stay with Kate's parents and alarmed her so much that she begged never to be left alone with him. Afterwards, not daring to tell her parents, she concealed her condition, perhaps even tried to abort the baby.[33] Florrie Scott would have been fifteen, Tom and Laura respectively thirteen and twelve, the year their sister died and, although the cause of her trouble could not have been mentioned in front of them, Florrie at least was old enough to recognise something extraordinary going on behind the scenes. Another of their cousins, George Wright – the future horse painter – had hoped to marry Kate, and opening shots fired over her grave marked the start of what proved a long-lasting feud between the Wrights and Mark Scott. Paul's father possessed altogether nearly three dozen Yorkshire first cousins (including the seven Wrights, who were double cousins), all of whom endlessly married, quarrelled,

worked with or wronged one another, and whose affairs still
mysteriously hung in the air of Paul's childhood. He could never sort
them out, but they gave him an abiding sense of the past, its importance,
and the dangers of either denying or over-simplifying it. Young as he was
to receive it, Florrie's warning about the Victorian age bit deep.

Paul's aunts when he knew them earned their own livings,
something rarely possible for women of their class and generation. It
gave them a measure of control over their lives, a courage and lack of
self-pity which remained ever afterwards qualities that touched Paul's
heart in the women he liked. He grasped very early what it meant to be
without professional occupation: the contempt it invited, and the
helpless dependence to which it condemned girls like his contemporary, Sheila Wright, who bitterly regretted having been treated like a
toy or a trophy by her charming and chivalrous father. 'The Wright
men – and my father in particular – had a very high opinion of women.
When he took you out, his manners were wonderful. I was never
allowed to put a piece of coal on the fire for fear of hurting myself,'
Sheila said: 'I wasn't allowed to clean my own shoes. *I wasn't trained
for anything.*' She felt that Paul, unlike her father or her other boy
cousins, sensed something wrong in her predicament. Certainly in
later life he responded, both as a man and a novelist, with particular
warmth, respect and attention to the plight of spare, unmarried or
unsatisfactorily married women traditionally expected to live out their
lives on the sidelines as passive observers. Paul once said that he wrote
novels in order to give a voice to people who would otherwise remain
inarticulate,[34] and one of the unexpected strengths of the Raj Quartet
is the way in which from time to time it looks at a male-dominated
society sidelong, so to speak, through the eyes of people like Barbie
Batchelor and Edwina Crane: modest, impoverished, elderly spinsters
so insignificant as to be virtually invisible to the more powerful and
articulate members of the British community in India.

This sort of woman is frequently obliged, as Mrs Hurst explains in *A
Male Child*, to depend for survival itself on her powers of observation.
Society had no real use for her once she failed to negotiate the marriage
market, and, even if she succeeded, her future was by no means
assured: 'nature demands that she keeps alert for any slightest sign of
failure in the man, because she depends on him for life and
livelihood. . . . And so . . . your so-called intuitive woman takes to
watching and interpreting every shadow of expression on her man's
face. If he's losing confidence, her training in observation detects it as
surely as the wart on the end of his nose, and so she bolsters him up,
praises him, *pushes* him, you see, into regaining confidence.'[35] Paul's
mother was this sort of woman. She encouraged in her sons a practical

helplessness which was her own guarantee of survival, and she paid the price of unremitting vigilance required, in a man's world, by what Mrs Hurst calls female intuition ('Sometimes I've grown dizzy in the exercise of my talent, and I can't claim to have exercised it with success. If anything, it has only been a source of anxiety to me, but then . . . the talent itself has its roots in anxiety, hasn't it?').[36] Paul had been a witness to the anxieties and painful distances within his parents' marriage, and to the different compensations each evolved in self-defence. As a very small boy, he had access to his mother's fantasies, and also to the world of work in which his father found refuge. 'I tend to write about people in relation to their work,' he wrote, looking back later on these formative years, 'which strikes me as . . . no less important than their private lives, because this work is so often affected by their sense of personal deprivation.'[37]

Like many of his generation, Paul found his own escape in the cinema. The Palmers Green Palmadium opened on Green Lanes in the year of his birth, a vast, marble-fronted, resplendent, red, white and green palace with a pipe organ for the first house (a live orchestra came in at three o'clock), private boxes and a tea-room. Paul paid his first visit when he was six. 'The film was silent, of course, and was called *The Keeper of the Bees*, and it turned me into a cinema addict – rather a precocious one, because I remember complaining when the talkies came that standards had gone down, with all that singing, dancing and colour.'[38] For nearly a decade Paul remained a fanatical, increasingly knowledgeable and active film fan. He became expert on makes of planes and the comparative performance of air aces in films like *Wings* or *Dawn Patrol*. He was strong on horror, provided the films were in costume, but violence in a contemporary context, among people 'wearing the kind of clothes my parents and relations wore', upset him so much that he was once physically sick, and had to be stopped from watching any more.[39] Romance was a speciality: blasé, debonair, already something of a ladykiller at seven, Paul could make everyone laugh in Woolworths just by asking for a copy of *Gentlemen Prefer Blondes*.[40] Picture-going set the pattern of the whole week. The boys either went straight from school on Friday afternoons, or stopped on the way home to inspect the stills outside the cinema. Florrie and Laura doled out tuppence per nephew on Saturday mornings: 'We blew it on film magazines, since we both had ambitions to produce and direct epics. The *Film Weekly* and *Picturegoer* were in those days (Thirties) 2d a week. I remember the smell of the new editions, as one bought them on Friday evening, on the way home from school.'[41]

Paul had by this time co-opted Peter in a bid to pre-empt the threat of the talkies by founding their own silent studio:

By 1929, my brother and I had set up in the film business as producers, directors, designers and photographers . . . The films we produced were drawn in Indian ink, with mapping pens, on long narrow strips of greaseproof paper, which we gummed together and passed through a projector made out of a cigar box, a 60-watt bulb, and the lens from an old pair of binoculars. The images we drew were free-hand. Frames of dialogue were interspersed to help the stories along. When it came to close-ups of the leading characters we traced these from photographs of popular stars. The whole was projected on to a screen painted silver and authentically edged in black.

The business of making films absorbed me for about four years. When my elder brother grew out of this exacting occupation, he contributed technical assistance. The projector became infinitely more sophisticated. The screen was only revealed to the audience after a velvet curtain had been raised by invisible wires and had disappeared mysteriously behind an immense gilded proscenium arch made of painted plywood. By this time too my films were running for sixty minutes and had become more sophisticated with some sequences in colour. Romance, drama, comedy, costume and modern – one film would take me an entire autumn to complete, to be ready for its Christmas Gala release. I suppose we never gave more than two shows a year. The *creation* of the film was the main thing. The stories were all more or less original, but the stars were real, sub-contracted from Paramount, Fox, RKO and Metro-Goldwyn-Mayer. My last epic was a sophisticated comedy called *The Girl in the Porch*, and starred Miriam Hopkins, Alice White (making a comeback) and Fredric March. Coming across it years later and riffling it through my fingers, I noted that scenically it was distinctly avant-garde. And script-wise, just a little naughty. Unconsciously so, I think. But at last I understood a remark by my headmaster that while this boy's English essays showed promise, he lacked discrimination.[42]

Film shows were for years the highlight of Christmas at Wyphurst, drawing a gala audience of parents, aunts and visitors, sometimes including Sheila ('they were cranked by hand: very Heath Robinson') and her mother. Peter remained all his life an expert cameraman. Paul had hankerings to direct, or even act, on the grounds that script-writing was altogether too easy: 'The business of creating a plot and characters seemed to come perfectly naturally. Unconsciously I had absorbed the lessons of the cinema and also of the many books I had now read.'[43] His taste developed much earlier in films than in books. His favourite reading remained Jack London, Zane Grey and Lew Cody's stories in *Wild West* ('or was it *Western Magazine*?')[44] long after he had graduated in the cinema to the psychological subtleties of Joan Crawford playing Sadie Thompson in *Rain* ('I can't be sure that at the age of thirteen I got all the sexual nuances, but I got the other

The family's most illustrious relative, Tom's Uncle Mark Scott of Selby.

TOP   Tom Scott in his palmy days as a young bachelor, before the family was ruined and left Yorkshire.

BOTTOM   Tom's sisters, Jessie, Maude, Kate, Florrie and Laura Scott, at home in Headingley.

RIGHT   Frances Scott with her elder son, Peter.

Album drawing by Paul's grandfather, the wine merchant turned artist, George Bewick Scott.

Water-colour from her own album, by Paul's grandmother Ruth Scott, born a Wright.

Coaching Scene by George Wright.

TOP 'Huntsman and Hounds in Full Cry' by
Tom Scott's cousin, George Wright.

ABOVE Tom Scott, at 18, already showed
the keen interest in the female form he would
exploit professionally in partnership with his
sister, Florrie: 'She did faces, hands, legs and
feet, and sometimes toned down the shadows
of his over-exuberant bosoms,' wrote Paul.

RIGHT Fashion drawing by Tom Scott. 'My
mother, who sometimes posed for him . . . ,
always complained that the only time she
wore sable was in June when it was too hot to
enjoy it.'

Arch opening on to the garden at Wyphurst, the Scotts' Fashion Studio on Southgate High Street: Paul's 'basic childhood country'.

Mr and Mrs Scott with Peter and Paul, wearing the school caps and blazers that gave satisfaction to the whole family.

The Collegiate School.

Charles Drakes, the English Master ('Scott 2 could be an author if he wanted to be'), and the Headmaster, John Temblett-Wood, in 1929.

The boys with their father and their Aunt Alice Mark on a trip to the seaside at Eastbourne.

Peter and Paul.

The old Queen's Cinema, Palmers Green, where Paul first saw Grand Hotel.

Fredric March in Dr Jekyll and Mr Hyde *(1932), an image that haunted Paul for the rest of his life.*

Joan Crawford as Sadie Thompson in Rain: *'at the age of 13 . . . I got the major points about bigotry, inhumanity, lust and the power principle.'*

major points about bigotry, inhumanity, lust and the power principle').[45] He was fascinated by the sinister ambiguity of Fredric March's performance in *Dr Jekyll and Mr Hyde*, becoming adept at imitating March's transformation from one self to the other. 'It fascinated him, that did,' said a schoolfriend, who more than fifty years later still vividly remembered Paul's features writhing ('he had a very rubbery face'), constricting and dissolving as Jekyll's identity was inexorably lost in Hyde's.[46]

This ghastliest and most gruesome of all Paul's boyhood setpieces supplied an image that possessed him for the rest of his life and, even on a strictly mechanical level, his imagination always functioned most fluidly in film terms. He said his novels came to him in the first place as moving images – 'a vision that is mobile, audible, alive' – materialising on a blank screen. It might be a white wall, a sheet of white paper in the typewriter, or the blank white screen of the mind upon which, if he stared long and patiently enough, the initial image would appear. With *The Birds of Paradise*, the birds themselves surfaced apparently out of nowhere like the picture behind the credits in a title sequence ('I can't remember just what began it. It was probably the name itself, swinging up in the dark of a sleepless night and hovering there like the bar of a trapeze, pausing fractionally for the grasp of my comprehension before sweeping down and away, taking me into the fabulous world where the birds called and mated').[47] *The Jewel in the Crown* came to him as a girl running, although at the time he had no idea where to or what from.[48] (She is still there in the first sentence of the published text, if not in the opening shots of the film eventually based on it.)

The central image, once given, had to be subjected to rigorous, sustained interrogation by the conscious intelligence standing in as director, technician and designer ('If it is a good hard image it will stand. Nothing will erode it. But it is extremely difficult to co-ordinate it with all the sequences of images it gives birth to').[49] Novel-writing for Paul always remained a process that went back to the home-made films of his childhood: a sequence of images flickering in and out of focus, speeded up, slowing down, juxtaposed on one another, starting to leap and jump as the whole thing gathered momentum, unfolding a story only partly under the writer's conscious control. He never entirely threw off the powerful spell of that early film-going. When what he called the cameras of the imagination[50] began to turn, he became oblivious to everything else. Like his father, he developed a phenomenal ability to blank out time and space. He said that anyone wanting to write had to surrender so completely to the images on his inner screen that he could walk through a rainstorm without noticing he carried a folded umbrella.[51]

The year the boys set up in the film business, 1929, was also the year they moved up to the Collegiate School on Winchmore Hill. 'When I was ready to go,' Peter said, 'Paul came too.' Paul was remembered as something of an outsider, a quiet boy (he had by their standards much to keep quiet about) who kept himself to himself. He and Peter remained inseparable. 'Tweedledum and Tweedledee, I called them,' said their friend Geoffrey Ridehalgh, who was fascinated by the Scotts' aloofness and by the defensive, derogatory, irresistibly funny running commentary they kept up in private: 'They were always together. They didn't bother with *anyone* else.' Geoffrey was the only boy admitted to their company, partly perhaps because he was another solitary figure isolated at school by trouble at home, and partly because of a mutual loathing of games.

The bond between the brothers had been reinforced by the licensed ragging of new boys, which went on 'every day, every break, on the stairs, in the playground'[52] for at least half a term without interference from staff or prefects, and further strengthened on the playing field. 'Peter and Paul were hopeless at sport,' said Geoffrey. 'When it came to football, they really only stood about in heaps.' Geoffrey was older than either of the Scotts and made friends with them only in his last year, 1930–31, when the pair moved up as a unit into the top form. In a fiercely competitive, sporting school, disaffection united the three as nothing else could have done. They would lurk on the sidelines of hockey on Tuesdays, football on Wednesday afternoons and Saturday mornings, making off as soon as they decently could to walk home together, collating and comparing the latest films. The two older boys relied on Paul's endless flow of stories and impersonations: 'He was quite a romantic,' said Geoffrey, 'even Peter would listen with open mouth.' On their walks, Paul provided amusement; and on Sports Day, when the other two skulked in the background, it was Paul who kept his end up as an athlete, avoiding team games – 'I liked to win on my own'[53] – but regularly finishing first or second in the high jump, the 100 and 220 yard sprints. He took prizes in his first three years until 'a rival turned up and beat me so consistently at the things I shone at that, youthlike, I lost interest and wrote poems instead.'[54]

His parents must have felt their financial sacrifice amply justified by Paul's performance. The few school stories he himself volunteered in later life were nearly all memories of being encouraged, giving satisfaction and achieving modest success. He shot up the school, 'always a shining light in class',[55] famous for being able to memorise any passage after a single reading. He read Shakespeare's *Henry VIII* when he was ten, stirred by a history lesson on Katherine of Aragon whose story troubled him even at that tender age. He said that her lines

I am a most poore Woman, and a stranger
Born out of your Dominions

picrced his heart, and that it was 'thc revclation of *Henry VIII*' that
first showed him the classics could speak to contemporaries.[56] As for
his own compositions, his chief problem was to keep them within
manageable limits. By the time he was fourteen and beginning to
transfer interest from film-making to the written word, his essays
regularly ran to twelve pages apiece. He could always make the class
laugh when he read them aloud, and he never forgot a comment by the
handsome and popular English master, Charles Drakes, overheard
handing one particularly ambitious, eighteen-page effort to another
master: 'Scott 2 could be an author if he wanted to be'.[57]

Natural perversity made him instantly decide to be an artist instead,
or perhaps go into films but, however wide the possibilities seemed to
him at fourteen, his future prospects were beginning to narrow for his
parents. Paul was the sort of boy warmly approved by the headmaster,
who kept a Merit Book for high achievers and never judged his pupils
solely by their parents' ability to pay. But John Temblett-Wood died,
aged 57 in January 1930, soon after Paul transferred to the senior
school. The new headmaster was his only son Kenneth, who had
rowed for Cambridge and taken a degree, which was more than could
be said for his father, or for Charlie Drakes, on whom the actual
running of the school increasingly devolved. Kenneth Temblett-
Wood, feeling that the Collegiate could no longer afford the luxury of
being too particular as business started to slump, increased numbers
by widening the intake and advertising special terms. The Sports Day
programme for 14 July 1934 offered 'One Guinea EACH TERM' off
for new entrants, which was a bargain reduction on fees of four
guineas per term. The Scotts, like the Spruces in *The Bender*, probably
got cut rates for the second boy (especially such a creditable boy as
Paul was turning out to be), but it was never easy to pay the fees
regularly. Like George Spruce, Paul grasped as a very small boy the
need to placate the two great powers, landlord and bank manager,
who grew steadily sterner and more difficult to appease as the 1920s
drew to a close.

These were hard times for the fashion trade, made worse by the
menace of photography which was expected to drive men like Paul's
father out of business before long. There was talk of mushroom
studios, cut-throat competition, the undercutting of reputable concerns with professional standards, commissions falling off and rates
being forced down. The self-employed, always vulnerable, were
peculiarly so in the depression when unemployment raged through the
land like a plague. The writer Ted Willis, growing up over the same

years as Paul in a respectable working-class street in north London, remembered an atmosphere that chilled even a child whose father earned a steady wage in a safe job: 'it was impossible not to sense and to share the atmosphere of fear and foreboding which lay on the district like a frost'.[58] In Southgate, thin, shabby men could be seen hanging round the station, collecting in crowds at building sites on the off chance of a job, hawking matches and shoelaces from door to door. Sudden moves and midnight flits became commonplace; people who could no longer manage the rent would pack up and leave without a word to the neighbours. Children at school got used to finding each term that one or two had been removed without warning during the holidays. Whole families vanished leaving no address. 'It wasn't talked about,' said a Southgate contemporary of Paul's. '*Nothing* was ever said. People had their pride. The price of failure in Fox Lane was pretty high. There was no safety net: if things went wrong, you couldn't afford to hang around for long.'[59]

The Scotts left Fox Lane in 1933. The business had been so badly hit that the only solution was for the whole family to cram in with the aunts at Wyphurst. Paul's account makes no bones about the extent of the calamity:

I was thirteen then. But of course you can't have two women running a kitchen. The first six months were terrible. The rows were terrible. It was a house divided. The studio was up there, behind the attic window. Even that was divided, by a partition, to give my brother and me a bedroom. For weeks at a time half the household wasn't speaking to the other half. I suppose this taught me something. Taught me to see both sides of a question. I loved my parents. I loved my aunts. By nature I'm a very emotional person. I think the first six months in this house affected my ability to express it – except in writing.[60]

Paul's mother and his aunts would scream at one another from the head and foot of the stairs. The memory of these shouting matches left him with a lifelong horror of scenes, raised voices, any kind of domestic drama. His remedy was to retreat into himself, as his father did more than ever in this turbulent period when old dissatisfactions resurfaced, and suppressed feelings boiled over in furious recrimination. Paul seldom talked afterwards about what had happened, save to reiterate his determination never again to lose control of his life, or let emotion get out of hand if he could help it. His mother's loss and bitter humiliation must have been dreadful to see. The move brought back the uncertainties of her childhood, spent flitting from one tiny, overcrowded lodging to the next with the constant anxiety of inadequate wages failing to meet unpaid rent. Cut off from all familiar supports, determined not to admit distress, unable any longer to hold up her head in front of the neighbours, Frances could hardly expect much comfort from her own family, perhaps not even from her sister Ruth, the cook general, whose warmth and admiration had sustained her in the past.

Frances had always played the dauntless elder sister, sharing her triumphs with Ruth as well as domineering over her shamelessly. Ruth, generous and self-deprecating, visited Fox Lane on sufferance, and thankfully accepted a place in the background of Frances's life. 'My sister so always impressed on me – I must not this, and that,' Ruth wrote to Paul long afterwards,[61] explaining her reluctance ever to put herself forward or propose a visit to relations who might be ashamed to receive her: 'My sister gave me such a frightening description of everything, I felt unable to make the effort.'[62] Ruth had provided not only a loyal audience but a physical bolthole, when loneliness and frustration at home became too great for Frances to bear. 'I remember how often she left home and came to me for 2 or 3 weeks running with never a penny piece,' Ruth wrote towards the end of her life in a long, reflective letter to Paul about his tyrannical mother: 'that was when you were schoolboys, and I earned ten shillings per week and my lunch.'[63] When tempers ran high, Frances's instinct all her life was to storm out. She could never reconcile herself to spending time in the doghouse: a lesson Ruth, as the youngest in a large family, said she had learned very young. Frances had made her own bed, but being obliged to lie on it at Wyphurst turned her finally from the husband who had failed her to her younger son, who from now on bore the full brunt of her dreams, ambitions and plans.

Losing her own home was not the last of the disasters pending in those first months spent sharing a roof with her sisters-in-law. Peter left school at seventeen in the summer of 1934, and found a job selling cars, which must have been a relief. The family decision to pool resources at Wyphurst had temporarily staved off the need to remove Paul from school too. He was fourteen in March 1934. Whatever he himself thought of his prospects – school after all provided a peaceful orderly refuge, and hope for the future, when he needed them most – there was never any real question of further education. A university scholarship might have been available if his parents could have faced the stigma of putting him through the state education system (Southgate County School in Fox Lane was known locally as 'the matriculation shop', because of its impressive examination record), but such things were beyond the Collegiate's compass. The staff did their best – able, receptive, hard-working, Paul must have been a pleasure to educate compared to some – but there was nothing more they could teach him, as his mother said, using a comforting formula from her own childhood (Frances' brothers had had to go out to work younger even than Paul). Paul's own explanation was that he had reached matriculation level but that his parents had been too unworldly or too badly advised to grasp that attaining the standard meant nothing without actually studying the syllabus and sitting the exam.[64] For a long time the subject remained too painful to dwell on, but he explored it cautiously forty years later in a long, autobiographical letter to his own grown-up children:

The thing is that because I was bright, academically, & the school was fairly progressive & not absolutely tradition-bound, I was in the top form at the age of 13, or 14, I can't remember which. It doesn't matter & I was a fairly tall boy anyway & if I was good at the academics, I was no slouch on the race-track, or on the field events, & given the mood I could knock up a run or two at cricket (tho' I preferred catching the other chaps out). I ought really to have stayed longer at school, I suppose, to learn about unselfishness & working with others, & not always thinking just of myself & of trying to make it, alone – but just before I was 15 the family money ran out.[65]

Paul left school probably at the end of the 1934 autumn term. No help was forthcoming from the Wrights in Richmond (in at least two of Paul's novels, *A Male Child* and *The Bender*, deaf ears are turned to an urgent appeal for funds to prevent the younger of two brothers from having to leave school prematurely, and go out to work for an accountant), although Paul later maintained that Gilbert had offered him a place in his studio. He himself still assumed he would become some sort of artist or writer and, when he told the story afterwards, he often used the same curiously formal wording to describe how he discovered his mistake: 'It was with some surprise that eventually I heard that my father had decided that I should become an accountant.'[66]

It was a crushing blow. His father's decision demolished all the imaginary futures he had, however vaguely, constructed for himself. Like a similar decree announced in the same formal way by Bill Conway's father in *The Birds of Paradise*, it cracked Paul's world straight up the middle. Up till now, he had taken it for granted that his future lay in the same sort of sphere as the rest of the family: like young Bill Conway he had been happy to dawdle beside the stream, launching 'slow dreamy boats of recollection and swift, thrusting boats of ambition and expectation'.[67] *The Birds of Paradise*, which explores as one of its central themes a son's rejection in adolescence by his father, was the first novel Paul embarked on after his own father's death. Bill Conway's father is a District Commissioner in India whose son had seen his whole boyhood and schooling as a preparation for following him into the high tradition of the Indian Civil Service. Bill looks back on a life shaped and soured by the arbitrary decision that he should go into the City instead, which he takes to be his father's way of turning 'thumbs down on me'. Almost harder to bear than the change of plan itself is the brutal lack of preparation or explanation. The stern, admired, omnipotent father of childhood seems to have turned without warning into a curt, contemptuous stranger.

Bill Conway's portrait of his younger self – as a smug, conceited, condescending prig, stuffed with self-deluding, white supremacist fantasies about the British Raj – corresponds to Paul's gloomiest visions of himself when young. The two share the same vulnerability, which invites the same disillusionment. But, at the end of his life, Paul came to see more and more of himself in the father who had apparently repulsed him so cruelly. He told a disturbing story about how he had tentatively admitted he would like to write, whereupon his father asked what he would most dislike to do, announcing, when Paul said accountancy, that he was to be an accountant. The punchline sounded to at least one listener like 'a kick in the stomach',[68] although Paul insisted that he bore no grudge. His attitude was as ironic and as profoundly ambivalent as young Conway's in *The Birds of Paradise*: 'He *thanks* his father for organising his life in such a way that he grew up to have money and leisure. He *thanks* his father for saving him from the discomfort of life in the East. . . . But deep in his heart he regrets never having had the splendid things which he believed would have compensated him for the discomforts. He is not blaming his father. He is genuinely paying tribute to his father's common-sense. But his heart does not quite agree with his head.'[69]

Paul blamed his real father long and steadfastly for what he saw as a betrayal. This was the first of many points at which the roads forked in his life, forcing him to choose between the gay, gifted, irresponsible, dreamy side of his nature and the dull, dependable breadwinner. This time the choice was made for him but, although Paul cited his father, the responsibility seems to have lain in fact with his mother. It had been Frances in consultation with Charlie Drakes who agreed that Paul should leave school, and it was Frances who accompanied him to Wheatley's employment agency near Piccadilly Circus, which had already fixed up Peter, and now produced a vacancy in an accountant's office for Paul. 'It was *chance*,' said Peter, pointing out that, at a time when there were commonly fifty boys after a single job, anyone might count himself lucky to take whatever was going. Frances was the family manager. 'She was the dominating one,' said Peter, who strongly disputed Paul's subsequent accounts of being browbeaten by their father: 'It would have been something that went on under my nose, *if* it ever happened.'

The truth was probably that Frances urged her younger son towards mutually exclusive goals: 'She had a vivid imagination,' Paul said. 'This I inherited. She imagined me as an accountant.'[70] On the one hand, Paul was to make his mother's wildest dreams come true ('She's determined he'll be Poet Laureate one day,' said Tom Scott).[71] On the other, he was to hold down a steady job (bank manager represented the summit of earthly aspiration for much of respectable, middle-class Southgate) with a regular income for the rest of his working life and a pension at the end of it, so that, in a phrase Paul quoted that bears the authentic ring of passionate urgency, '*someone in the family not be poor*'.[72] Paul acknowledged in the end, and perhaps he had an inkling at the time, that what happened was not his father's fault. 'I much miss knowing things about my own father,' he wrote on the last page of his letter to his own children, 'another silent, stubborn, morose man, who at times I hated because he seemed to give me nothing, but obviously gave me all he had to give.'

Paul could never bring himself, then or later, to blame his mother, and perhaps at bottom he blamed his father not for asserting his will but for the opposite: for failing to assert it, for absenting himself, not so much for turning thumbs down as for washing his hands of responsibility. Tom Scott was the model for the painter of calendars and Christmas cards, Harry Spruce in *The Bender*, 'whose face had every so often been composed into lines of sympathy for people whose problems he had somehow avoided getting mixed up in before going back to his spare-room studio to paint snow.'[73] All that can be said for sure is that Paul as a boy felt desperately let down by a father who bowed to pressure from the bank manager, who couldn't even keep their own roof over the family's head, and who seemed indifferent to his son's shock and bewilderment. Sheila Wright said that Paul's father, her Uncle Tom, reminded her of Dickens' Mr Micawber: he had that gentleman's old-world gallantry, and his sweet disposition, as well as his iron determination never to confront the consequences for other people of his own everlasting need for pecuniary accommodation.

If there was a touch of Micawber in Tom Scott, there was undoubtedly something of David Copperfield in Paul himself. Both suffered exquisitely from what Paul called 'that delicate nerve of superiority which vibrates in children'.[74] David Copperfield, like his creator, found the shame of being removed too soon from school, and sent out to work, swallowed up in a despairing sense of being discarded, of talents turned down and thrown away. Paul remained sensitive all his life to the hurt inflicted in childhood on people like Malcolm Muggeridge's father, employed at thirteen as a shirtmaker's clerk: 'The effect on him of having to become a wage earner at such a tender age may be compared with the effect on Dickens of finding himself at the blacking factory. He became an ardent champion of the underdog.'[75] So at a similar age did Paul himself. He also perfected Copperfield's defence mechanism, the ability to deny and conceal his dismay from even those closest to him. 'At the time you wouldn't have known there was anything wrong,' said Peter Scott. 'I think at the time Paul wouldn't have minded much. It was only later that it rankled.' At the deepest level, imagination works slowly. For Paul, this episode lit a smouldering, long-burning fuse of misery and resentment that worked itself out only long afterwards in his life and work. If he explored aspects of his relationship with his father in *The Birds of Paradise* (1962), and with his mother in *The Bender* (1963), it was *The Jewel in the Crown* three years later that unlocked and drew on his own devastating early memories of expulsion and helplessness.

Boys prematurely removed from school, or otherwise cheated of a future they had taken for granted, form a common pattern in Paul's early fiction: Tim Spruce in *The Bender*, Alan Hurst in *A Male Child*, and Bill Conway in *The Birds of Paradise* correspond most closely to his own experience. But the one whose loss is most poignant, grave and irreversible is Harry Coomer, or Hari Kumar, in *The Jewel in the Crown*. Kumar is a young Indian dispatched by his father to an English public school in order to prepare him to take his place among the Imperial rulers of his own country. When his flourishing school career is cut short without warning by his father's financial collapse and death, Kumar is shipped back to India to survive as best he may on charitable handouts from reluctant relatives with whom he has nothing in common. An English public school background has left him hopelessly ill-fitted for life as a native on the wrong side of cantonment lines in British India. He earns a pittance in a dead-end job with nothing to look forward to save loneliness and insecurity. He is appalled by the physical circumstances, the sights and smells of deprivation, overcrowding, disease, the lack of hygiene and privacy in his new home, but it takes time for him to realise fully how much he has lost. Far worse than any physical hardship is the discovery that he has become literally invisible to the only people with whom he feels at home. His education had been designed to put him on an equal footing with the British: nothing in it had prepared him for the shock of being plunged without hope of rescue or recovery into the world of the poor and powerless.

Some inkling of Kumar's sensations would have been familiar, at any rate in apprehension, to anyone growing up in lower middle-class Southgate between the wars. Paul's friend, Clive Sansom, described how stubbornly people like his parents and Paul's struggled to preserve their position on a slippery social scale. 'One false move and they might slip down; but if they kept their foothold, there was a chance that they, or at least their children, might climb a few inches higher.'[76] Sansom, whose family lived ten minutes' walk away from Fox Lane, had been carefully taught as a small boy never to set foot over the boundary with Edmonton ('Beyond that, in our childhood mythology, lay poverty, disease and nameless depravity'). This was where Paul, only half joking, would later locate the dividing line between the cantonment and the native quarter, or Black Town. Tom Scott's missed foothold, followed by the experience of being knocked off the ladder himself, had given his son an unforgettable glimpse of how easily the social pits might yawn for him too. When people in India asked him long afterwards how an Englishman had been able to get under the skin of the Indian characters in his books, Paul replied that he had imagined what he would have felt himself in their place. Hari Kumar is in some sense a self-portrait, a projection of all that was eager, confident, hopeful in the young Paul, the promise that had burgeoned at school and been nipped in the bud when he left. Paul once said, looking back, that his experience in adolescence had made him a displaced person,[77] and that displacement is nowhere more vividly expressed than through Hari Kumar in the Raj Quartet.

CHAPTER THREE

Muse on the warpath

It was made painfully clear to young Scott, as soon as he asked for a job, that his superior schooling entitled him to no special treatment in the marketplace where his talents were now for sale. If anything, it put people's backs up ('We spoke too proper for the people we had to live amongst,' as George Spruce says in *The Bender*, 'but not proper enough for the people who lived the way our old Ma made us think we lived. Sons of a gentleman. Well.')[1]. A boy without even School Certificate, never mind Matriculation, cut no ice at interviews. Under-age, over-educated and without the lowliest qualification, Paul was turned down out of hand by C. T. Payne, the elderly accountant running his own old-fashioned, one-man firm to whom he presented himself at Regent's Arcade House in Regent Street.

Payne, nearing retirement age with no son to succeed him and inadequate funds to support a partner, had evidently hoped for something weightier, more experienced, altogether less naïve and ingenuous by way of an assistant, but Paul, looking absurdly young in his business suit and trilby hat, persuaded him to change his mind. Paul's sympathetic enthusiasm and shining determination were always, even at that age, hard to resist. Events proved Payne a shrewd judge. As for Paul, in those lean years of hunger marches and lock-outs, it was a feather in anybody's cap to have landed a job at all, let alone one in the heart of the West End. For the next twenty-five years, the seedy area around Regent Street and Piccadilly Circus would remain Paul's familiar London beat, first marked out in Payne's lunch breaks when any spare time was spent dreamily exploring the back lanes of Soho and Bloomsbury's second-hand bookshops. 'I shall not pass unheard . . .' he wrote in the most ambitious of the poems produced at this period: 'They shall say of me/ "That stone the corner one/ he touched it as he passed along this way".'[2]

Regent's Arcade House was a rabbit warren of small businesses, erected at the beginning of the 1920s and let off cheaply in the depression to some fifty or sixty tenants, sixteen of them crammed in on the floor where Paul worked. Payne's office came between a boot and shoe manufacturer and Olga Jackson, Chiropodist. Paul never forgot the text on the office calendar: 'You cannot see Beauty with miserable eyes' (untrue, according to Paul, who said trees and sky never seemed lovelier to him than in his deskbound youth), or the office typewriter on which he learned to type, banging out poems with two fingers in the lunch hour when its official handler was absent.[3] The chief duty of an accountant's boy – or junior audit clerk, the title to which Paul was swiftly promoted – was to add up accurately, and as fast as a finger could travel down columns of pounds, shillings and pence. Paul acquired this skill with characteristic speed and took equally characteristic satisfaction in it, between bouts of the grief and resentment natural to all clerks employed to function as human computers: 'here are the hours/ of toiling the pain and the horror/ of hours relentless and hours without/ Hope – ' he wrote in a spurt of genuine feeling at the close of the long, imitative, rhetorical poem about Christ's suffering which he composed after four years with Payne.[4]

Paul worked five days plus Saturday mornings for fifteen shillings a week,[5] which was half as much again as his Aunt Ruth earned as a cook-general. His wages eventually doubled, bringing the total to £75 a year, or roughly what an unqualified junior teacher might expect to bring in at a private school (Malcolm Muggeridge was earning £260 a year by 1930 as leader writer on the *Manchester Guardian*, 'adequate then for two adults, one child and a car!').[6] Payne might be a notorious skinflint but even his meagre rate seemed enviable to Geoffrey Ridehalgh, who had left school before either Peter or Paul, and was still unemployed at nineteen when they ran into him in the street. They recommended 'old Wheatley' who fixed Geoffrey up as office boy to the Trade Protection Society in Oxford Street on thirty shillings a week, and the three boys promptly resumed their old habit of walks and talks. 'Everything was always Paul's idea,' said Geoffrey: 'Peter tagged along, occasionally making a remark, critical or cryptic. I suppose I tagged along too.' They quartered London, exploring the galleries, making photographic expeditions to places like Brompton Oratory or the Albert Memorial. Peter spent almost a whole month's salary on a Voigtlander camera and Paul, who acted as darkroom assistant, would spend hours going through the prints with Geoffrey, criticising angles, exposure, texture and composition.[7] Peter and Paul, who were musical, attended Sir Henry Wood's promenade concerts in the old Queen's Hall. All three became regulars at the Old Vic theatre, the National Gallery, and the Sadler's Wells ballet (where seats cost eighteenpence, or you could stand for a shilling). 'We were poor as church mice,' said Geoffrey, 'but we made it stretch.'

They would meet on Saturdays, as soon as they were released from their offices, for lunch at Lyons Corner House. Paul said that ninepence, intelligently laid out at Lyons, could provide sausage-and-mash with coffee, or (his favourite) patty and chips for 5½d with a Swiss bun and coffee for 2½d. 'Plus 2d tip, I think, or maybe a penny. Anyway, less than a bob. If one spent 1/1d one felt positively daring.'[8] He enjoyed distributing largesse and cutting a dash with the waitresses, who gave and got special sympathy. 'As for Nippies — one remembers many of them with a sort of rushed affection. They always looked so hot, poor things, from standing near those infernal tea machines that used to gush steam . . .': nearly thirty years later, in one of only two novels set in London, he included a 'casual party help who had once been Nippy of the Year and had a certificate to prove it . . .'.[9] Some of the nippies, like the clerks they served, were little more than children, working long hot hours on a minimal wage for penny tips, and it was typical of Paul to register their condition, both at the time and in a book later. 'I didn't want you to lose the important years, the emotional ones of full puberty,' he wrote to his own elder daughter, who had begged to be allowed to leave school at sixteen, 'by having also to cope with the idea of survival by going out to work'.[10]

For Paul, the idea of survival meant driving himself unmercifully. He gave up film-making to listen instead to the other side of his nature, 'the one that says you have to work that much harder than the next person just to keep level'.[11] After putting in a full day at the office, he studied book-keeping at night, going to classes three evenings a week, working at English and maths in an attempt to matriculate on his own, and, when he felt a despairing suspicion that standards were slipping, adding a correspondence course as well. 'I grew early into the habit of having no leisure,'[12] he said of these years, when under the crushing pressure of his father's failure and his mother's anxiety he acquired a mistrust of leisure that never left him. Peter, who took life more stoically, was startled at the depths of his brother's dissatisfaction one day when Paul, looking up from his books, announced that he had no intention of staying stuck in an office for ever: he meant to be a writer. He was beginning to admit it again, tentatively at first, to himself and others, however absurd it might seem for a suburban clerk with no knowledge of the literary world and little access to books. There was

no serious bookshop, not even a public library in Palmers Green. Paul
joined a book club, sent away for books, or bought them on hire
purchase from an elderly itinerant bookseller called Mr Fullbrook,
'who used to call at the office with a fascinating square leather bag full
of riches. I bought Zola, Anatole France, Hardy, Remarque,
Chesterton and Maurois. . . . It was the beginning of my own library,
and I remember Mr Fullbrook with affection. He was the first member
of the book trade I knew personally. He once read my poems and
handled the situation with charm and tact.'[13]

Paul said that the encouragement he got from Mr Fullbrook marked
the start of a literary apprenticeship that ended nearly twenty-five
years later when he finally became a full-time writer. 'Mr Fullbrook
was a good beginning. He tramped the streets with a heavy bag,
knocked at doors, and smiled, and handled books as if he cared about
them, and wanted you to care.' For the next four or five years Paul read
voraciously. He ran through Walter Scott, Arnold Bennett, the whole
of Trollope's Barsetshire Chronicles, 'buying them one by one in the
Everyman edition',[14] and launching out in all directions at once on the
Abbey Classics: '*Daphnis and Chloe*, Petronius Arbiter & *Vathek*. . . I
used to read them on the tube when I ought to have been reading
Mercantile Law or the Law of Contract and the Principles of
Auditing.'[15] He was beginning to get back his breath and his balance
after a knockout blow to his confidence. Payne was gratified by his
application at the office and Fullbrook gave him a foot in the door – at
least a toe in the crack – of the book world.

The pressure at home had eased as soon as outgoings on Peter and
Paul were converted into income, and the financial situation improved
sufficiently for the family to leave Wyphurst. 'In 1936, having
recouped some of his losses, my father moved us out of High Street –
leaving his studio there like some sort of Holy Grail,' Paul wrote
drily,[16] describing the Scotts' return to a roof of their own at 15
Cannon Road, a cul-de-sac off Cannon Hill, not far from Southgate
High Street, the Mall and the old village green in the respectable heart
of the cantonment ('Over there's Northmet House. Call it the
Governor's residence. Call Cannon Hill Artillery Road'). They took
over the house from a family called Bruce (Brenda Bruce grew up to
become a distinguished actress). It was a thoroughly satisfactory
move, celebrated by father and son at the Cherry Tree Inn on the
green, where Tom Scott bought Paul, at sixteen, his first pint of beer.

Peter and Paul, who had scarcely if ever invited anyone home, now
began asking Geoffrey round as a regular thing on Saturday nights.
Paul called the trio 'The Three Mustgetbeers',[17] reviving the name
used half a century earlier in their hopeful youth by Tom Scott and the

Wright brothers. Mrs Scott, always at her most expansive in company, celebrated Saturdays with an elaborate meal (once it was a brace of pheasant), served under brisk sniping fire from her sons, whose witticisms she took in the derisive Yorkshire way as no more than her due. Geoffrey never got used to the boys teasing their mother, or to the fact that neither of them ever lifted a finger to help her. If anything needed doing in the garden, it was Geoffrey who came round to lend a hand with the digging while Paul looked on sardonically and cracked jokes from the sidelines: 'Paul was not practical. He could hardly even cut the grass. The only thing he could do was write.' But Paul's impracticality was in a sense his mother's triumph. Male helplessness on the domestic front is the traditional guarantee of female power, and Mrs Scott throve on a system which reduced her household in general, and Paul in particular, to almost total dependence at home. These evenings with her sons and their friend at Cannon Road re-created on a smaller, more sedate scale something of the Marks' old sociable, musical Saturday nights in south London. The boys would improvise on the piano, or sit up talking for hours in sessions which invariably included both parents. 'They were always there,' said Geoffrey. 'All the time. We never had the room to ourselves. Very close it all was. Everything had to stop while it was shouted out to Mr Scott.'

Deafness had finally closed on Tom Scott, who seems to have completed his retreat placidly and without reluctance into passivity, a state of withdrawal known in the family as 'The Silence of Dean Maitland' after a novel by Maxwell Gray published in the same year as R. L. Stevenson's *Strange Case of Dr Jekyll and Mr Hyde,* and offering another sensational variation on the theme of a divided self that appealed so strongly to Paul. Cyril Maitland is an ethereally fair and pure young curate who develops into an outstandingly popular preacher, renowned for his saintly disposition and tipped for high office in the church, but so tormented by a secret history of fornication, bloodshed, perjury and betrayal that he finally confesses his crimes from the pulpit to a packed congregation and drops dead in his own cathedral stall. This kind of fiction catered to much the same emergent, newly affluent, socially ambitious and inquisitive middle class in the 1880s as the Wrights' hunting prints. Like the James Bond books nearly a century later, *The Silence of Dean Maitland* combines a gripping plot with tips on social refinement, and a morality based at bottom on a highly developed sense of class. Dean Maitland's illegitimate son, brought up in dangerously democratic America, returns home to demand his rights but is brought to his senses by his father's death, abandons his impudent claim to an Oxford education ('I don't want to be a gentleman now . . . that is all knocked out of me'),[18] and settles with tears of repentance for the more suitable position of office boy. The book gives an interesting glimpse of what Paul meant when he said that a child belongs as much to the period in which its parents grew up as to its own.

The Scotts spent three years in Cannon Road. 'I was happy in that house,' Paul said. 'Mostly, I think, because I was beginning to write seriously. Poems mostly. And reading, reading. Youth, what energy! Marvellous, really. A social life too. Nights at the pub. Learning to dance. Taking a girl out.'[19] Paul's first piece of what he called deliberate writing was a three-act play, based on John van Druten's sensational West End success *Young Woodley*, 'about a family very different from my own . . . set . . . in their drawing-room which was considerably more luxurious than any I had ever entered.'[20] The lure of the theatre was reinforced for Paul by a vague but illustrious connection with Charles Laughton, whose meteoric rise to fame in Hollywood and the West End in the 1930s outstripped even Frances Scott's wildest dreams. Laughton was the eldest son of a family of northern hoteliers: he himself had triumphantly remodelled the stuffy, respectable Pavilion Hotel, Scarborough, as a fashionable watering place before thankfully making off to the Royal Academy of Dramatic Art in London in 1924. This was the summer made memorable for Paul by Peter's trip to Scarborough as the guest of Charles's uncle and aunt, Tommy and Flo Laughton. Flo's sister, Emmie Land, was an honorary aunt in the Scott household: a friend from Tom's hotelkeeping youth, something of a trial to Frances, she was apt to come down to London in the summer, when the hotels filled up, and park herself on the Scotts, where her celebrated nephew supplied a promising theme whenever conversation became competitive. Stories of the Scarborough hotel trade, and especially of the doings of Charles' autocratic mother, loomed large in Paul's childhood and resurfaced more than forty years later in his last novel *Staying On*, where Smith's Hotel in the Indian hill station of Pankot still sounds an echo of the Laughtons' Pavilion Hotel with its formidable proprietress terrorising her compliant husband, cowed staff and meekly submissive guests.[21]

Paul never actually met Charles Laughton but he was always an encouraging presence in the background, someone who had just left or hoped to drop in whenever the boys took tea with Miss Land at the Langham Hotel in Portland Place. Laughton's career, as bitter as his own in its early disappointments, was an omen for Paul as he wandered round Bloomsbury – 'largely unaware that this was one of the hearts of the publishing world, but sniffing the remote, misty yet somehow earthy air of the business of words' – or grew so absorbed in Walter Scott's *The Antiquary* that he overshot his stop on the tube, and had to get out at 'a curious place called South Kensington'.[22] Paul himself started writing a novel at eighteen in the bedroom he shared with Peter at 15 Cannon Road in time stolen from his textbooks on mercantile law, economics, the theory of bankruptcy and receivership, the casting up of trial balances. The book was called *Rachel*, set in Bloomsbury, with a hero down from the north (about which Paul said he knew as little as he did about Bloomsbury), who stepped bravely off the train at King's Cross but lost impetus before he had carried his suitcase as far as Fitzroy Square. 'I saw myself as a poet and playwright,' said Paul. 'As yet the world of the novel seemed too vast and laborious.'[23]

All his powers of endurance and concentration were swallowed up in the drudgery of evening classes. He had had his first taste of success at seventeen when he won a silver medal from the Royal Society of Accountants (Tim Spruce – whose career with the accountants Bartle, Wallingford in *The Bender* closely follows the early stages of his creator's – wept when he won the gold medal in his own accountancy finals). He had a second taste the year after, when he came fifth overall in the preliminary accountancy examinations (an alternative to matriculation in general subjects like English, history and maths),[24] a triumph that went far to repair earlier disappointments. His employer had no formal qualifications: 'old Payne', like 'old Bartle' in *The Bender*, had worked his way up from the bottom, picking up the job like Paul as he went along. The London Stock Exchange, enormous in those days by contemporary standards, included quantities of small businesses, often one-man firms which, considering the modest fees charged by accountants like Payne, could hardly expect to have their books kept by anyone but an unqualified junior clerk.

Payne's clients ranged from a Spanish importer of Canary Island tomatoes in Bloomsbury to estate agents in Streatham. What Paul liked best was being sent out on his own for a day's auditing, jaunts on which he proved, like Tim Spruce in *The Bender*, 'unexpectedly good at handling old clients, getting a name with them, in fact'.[25] He possessed already a novelist's talent for drawing people out, unravelling their affairs, listening patiently to their rambling stories, sifting out and memorising salient points: 'I . . . grew early into the habit of meeting people against the background of their work. There were solicitors in Norfolk Street, dentists in Harley Street, linen importers in the City, wholesale "robe" merchants in Islington, and a poor chap who had been swindling the income tax for years and used to cry in the office because the commissioners had caught up with him.'[26] Clients' affairs supplied the basis for a wildly inventive, fantastically embroidered running serial delivered after hours to an audience consisting of Peter and Geoffrey. 'We would meet up, perhaps at the pub in the evenings, to listen to Paul yarning away about the different people he met with the audits,' said Geoffrey. 'It was wonderful entertainment – what he'd seen, what he'd heard, the people he'd met and their crummy lives. He'd keep us amazed. More and more scandal would come out – all the little shady bits.'

Paul was developing skills more suited in the long run to fiction than to accountancy but, for the moment, his examination results did much to repair his confidence, improve his standing in the office and make his family feel they could hold up their heads once again on their own account. News of his successes reverberated round the relations: cousins on both sides were told, even the Wrights were impressed. Gilbert had little enough to boast about himself by this time. His financial house of cards was on the point of collapse with debts, always pressing, now beginning to crush him. His business and his marriage were both on the rocks. He had divorced Sheila's mother in 1936 (a stigma almost impossible to exaggerate for a woman defined by her marital status, even though she was the innocent party), disbanding the Richmond studio and putting Kingsbury up for sale. His brother George had retired to the seaside, still painting horses. Gilbert had installed his ex-wife with his daughter in one flat, his sisters in another on slender means. 'Oh, no, Sheila. *His own* come before wife and child,' was the aggrieved reaction of the Wright women when Sheila suggested that her mother's alimony might have first call on her father's resources. 'I was supposed to be part of the family, and yet I wasn't their own,' said Sheila, who remembered with gratitude all her life the Scotts' kindness at this point, and Paul's sympathy in particular. She had always had a soft spot for him, a fondness he returned with the delicacy that disarmed and delighted women all his life. Sheila never forgot their feelings for one another in their late teens, her tenderness for him, his protective affection, a romantic intimacy if anything intensified by his holding her physically at arm's length.

Paul, who loved dressing up, was something of a dandy at this stage. After years of pinching self-denial, cutting back and making do, success always produced in him an upsurge of generosity, the desire for promiscuous spending, a liberal impulse to treat himself and others to luxuries he could not afford: 'between 17 & 20 I was a bit of a peacock,' he wrote twenty years later to the novelist Muriel Spark,[27] in one of those moments of unconditional well-being which always brought out the dandy in him. He went to his first dance at seventeen, reacting with the scornful impatience of that age when his father asked why he wasn't wearing white gloves.[28] By the time he started *Rachel*, he was becoming more sure of himself with girls. 'I was also taking out a waitress with yellow hair. She wore net gloves which made me feel a bit of a lad.'[29] This was Edith Payne (no relation to the firm), who worked just behind Paul's office in Argyll Street, in one of the cafés where he had felt so warmly towards the nippies. Edith spent Christmas 1938 with the Scotts at Cannon Road, and Paul was invited back to supper to meet her family at home on Millbank where, 'hoping thereby to gain some sort of favour', he rashly presented her little brother with his Hornby train set ('I had a marvellous LNER train – black tank engine plus a set of Pullman coaches', he wrote long afterwards, mourning that long-lost bribe).[30]

In this optimistic and expansive mood, Paul was experimenting on all fronts with an energy heightened for people of his generation by the sense that time was running short. They had grown up in the shadow of war, hearing news of Hitler's activities filtered through stories absorbed in infancy of friends, fathers, uncles, cousins swallowed up by the trenches. 'As each year went by, it got worse,' said Geoffrey Ridehalgh. 'We had been brought up on the 1914–18 war. We knew it would come.' For Paul, the prospect of war with Germany acted more as a stimulus than a dampener. Energies that might have been expended at university were poured out in a study programme that made up in flexibility and freedom from prejudice anything it lacked in intellectual rigour. 'One goes to university to exercise the mind, not cripple it,' Paul wrote thirty years later,[31] by which time he had well-founded misgivings about the academic approach to literature. 'What on earth is a "self-taught" writer?' he asked tartly, reviewing what seemed to him a condescending, cold-hearted, superficial and typically academic biography of H. G. Wells, 'or conversely a "taught" writer?'[32]

Paul made a practical start by sending off ten poems to a firm called the Cambridge Literary Agency, which undertook to offer three of them to suitable editors at a fee for 'expenses' of half-a-crown each. He borrowed the money – seven shillings and sixpence, a sizeable sum or half his original wage packet – from his mother who took to calling him, only half teasing, 'the Future Poet Laureate' ('This did not actually irritate me. I merely felt that she was a little premature').[33] While confidently awaiting developments, anticipating a summons from Faber & Faber, and – 'the first of the writer's disciplines' – learning to watch for the post, Paul turned out more poems ('to ensure that I had a major body of mature work to show them when they got round to sending for me'), and prepared designs for his first slim volume of verse:

This would be published in boards. I would have a pale green cloth, quarter bound in slightly darker green leather. I designed the colophon in the shape of a tasteful sprig of lime-blossom whose smell then reminded me of nothing so much as the hopes and ambitions of youth but which I have since learned to connect with the smell of funerals.[34]

The double avenue of lime trees running up Bourne Hill, Palmers Green, would have been coming into flower when the Scotts moved there in June 1939, to a house big enough to provide Peter and Paul for the first time with separate bedrooms. Lime-blossoms, in poems written over the next few years, always spell happiness and hope: their funereal aspect came twenty years later, when Tom Scott lay dying in the Bourne Hill house at the season of lime-blossom. The Scotts settled at number 63, near the top of the hill, next but one to the waterworks, round the corner from their old house in Fox Lane, and closer still to the Broad Walk which borders Grovelands Park. Paul's was the room to the right at the front over the garage: 'the room where I really began to write – I mean in the sense of writing things that were published.'[35]

His poems had come back without ever having reached Faber, rejected even by magazines like *Great Thoughts* and *The Lady*, but one thing Paul's upbringing had taught him was to accommodate failure with equanimity. He changed his tactics and was rewarded in quick succession by two letters to the editor published in *Picturegoer* (paid for at a princely half-a-crown each), followed by two more in the *Palmers Green and Southgate Gazette*. The last, which made fun of the social aspirations of local shop assistants trying to pass themselves off as gentlemen, caused quite a stir in W. H. Smith's when Paul dropped in on the day of publication[36] and casually disclosed his identity. He enjoyed his brief notoriety and, more important, that strange sense of a separate existence conferred on, or confirmed in, a writer by first seeing his name in print.

The last year or two before the war was, for Paul, a springtime when anything seemed possible. At the office there was the doubling of wages, talk of promotion, dreams of a junior partnership, even perhaps of one day taking over the practice. He was enjoying himself and the responsibility Payne gave him. He was also working seriously for his intermediate accountancy examinations, and doing so well that the decision whether or not to enter the profession struck him, looking back afterwards, as a close-run thing. In retrospect something seemed to have been holding him back. 'Sallying forth for a day's auditing in Streatham, with my sandwiches in my brief-case, and in the evenings immersed in the mysteries of double-entry, depreciation and wear and tear I never once, never once convinced myself of my impersonation. I did not feel like an accountant. . . . I was now quite clear in my mind that I felt like a writer.'[37]

Payne's client in Streatham was Gerald Armstrong, an estate agent who lived in Forest Hill, a man considerably older than Paul with some knowledge of the world and artistic interests, a lover of ballet and – most attractive of all to a budding dramatist – a playgoer who kept up with the trends. Armstrong for his part was charmed, as many of Payne's clients must have been, by this unusually bright, deferential, helpful and handsome young auditor with his remarkable yellow-brown eyes. Like young George Spruce in *The Bender*, Paul looked well and knew it in a pair of black bathing trunks. If, as George's aunt insisted, the world can be divided into rulers and ruled, with a separate section for charmers – who reach the top by virtue of a pressing desire to rise rather than any innate advantage of wealth or position[38] – then Paul put himself as a boy and young man firmly into the third category. He said in coldly self-critical moments that the knack of pleasing people, or rather the time and energy he gave to it, had been a mistake.[39] But, at eighteen, it was the only outlet for a generous nature cramped and restricted by circumstances.

Paul was ripe for guidance, starved not only of companionship but of criticism and advice. He urgently needed someone like Armstrong, a more sophisticated older man with whom he could talk about books, theatre, the arts, and to whom above all he could submit his own plays and poems. 'One needs a mentor,' Paul insisted later to other young writers, 'otherwise it's very lonely. You need someone to tell you to go on.'[40] Armstrong as a confidant had the advantage of knowing Paul in his official capacity, understanding the constraints it put on him, and being only too anxious to help him throw them off. 'So for a year or two before the war I led this double life,' Paul wrote; 'I always seem to have done that.'[41] He meant working by day in the office, putting up a highly successful impersonation of an accountant, while simultaneously leading an unsuspected separate existence in his own time as a free spirit, poet and visionary. He expressed what this felt like long afterwards in a neat metaphor, when Barbie Batchelor in *The Towers of Silence* remembers from childhood her mother's saying that her father had a lot of the poet in him: 'After that I used to watch him hard. I imagined the poet in him as an unborn twin, one that could be cruel to him as well as kind.'[42]

There can be no doubt that, at an age when Paul craved encouragement, Gerald Armstrong brought out the poet in him. Armstrong was the first genuine aesthete he had ever met, and it was presumably under his influence that, about this time, Paul read Oscar Wilde's *The Picture of Dorian Gray*. A faint glow of Wilde's own scandalous aura still shone even from the Everyman edition of what remained in those days a useful manual for undercover poets, artistic misfits, anyone who felt himself misunderstood or turned down by society. For homosexuals it served as code-book, talisman and guide at a time when precious little else in print offered support or comfort, let alone basic information. It held Paul spellbound. *Dorian Gray* describes, in even lusher and more potent prose than Elynor Glyn's *Three Weeks*, the sentimental and worldly education of yet another romantic, ingenuous youth of obliging plasticity and startling good looks ('Grace was his, and the white purity of boyhood, and beauty such as old Greek marbles kept for us').[43] But the story takes on subtler and more sinister overtones through Dorian's portrait, which coarsens and ages, growing 'bestial, sodden and unclean', leaving its subject free to pursue his evil debauches while remaining apparently untouched. A similar duality had already fascinated Paul in *Dr Jekyll and Mr Hyde* (and for that matter *The Silence of Dean Maitland*). There was something about this central conundrum that he understood, or absorbed, at the deepest level of consciousness. The split self, the double life, the strange relationship between the real face and the face in the portrait or mirror: these are all images that worked down in the end to the core of his life and art.

Dorian Gray freed a part of Paul that had been, in his own phrase, groping for an identity. Attitudes, images, words, whole phrases from it are sprinkled thick on the letters and poems of the next few years. 'Philistine' and 'aesthetic' or 'decadent' became for a time his highest terms of abuse and approval; themes of youth, beauty and betrayal preoccupied his imagination. Wilde's aesthetics always come as an immense relief to anyone struggling alone to assert him or herself as an artist in unpropitious circumstances. Paul was already in revolt against Palmers Green, rejecting its narrow standards and aspirations, making fun of its morals, 'affecting to despise all this as terribly suburban'.[44] He had long written poems, but now he started to dress the part. He experimented with a curved pipe and a poet's black polo-necked jumper worn with matching black handkerchief in his breast pocket; or, for playwriting, a Paisley dressing-gown and slicked-back hair. He learned to make the most of a cigarette-holder, positioned between thumb and forefinger, palm uppermost, arm extended, the whole pose set off by a look of languid disdain on the face.[45] If he got his aesthetics from Wilde, his attitudes came from Noël Coward. The poet in him responded extravagantly to the narcissism of both, and to their theatricality.

'I used to act in front of mirrors & give stupendous performances,' Paul wrote, looking back on these years. 'Rupert Cadell in *Rope* – Othello & a little character I made up, a young Belgian who dies with the name of a little woman in Brussels on his lips.'[46] Fantasies sprouted. The punishing self-discipline of working by day and studying by night had made forbidden pleasures out of the simplest things, like idleness, or 'walking through the running leaves in Grovelands Park – with my long hair flying in the wind – & living for the wind.'[47] Paul's tastes still inclined to the *fin de siècle* and the Georgian. Rupert Brooke was his model. He said he lived in beauty,[48] his 'words slipped from a poet's silvered tongue', he prided himself on outstanding decadence. He described his new friend Gerald Armstrong as 'the eternal poseur',[49] and boasted that Gerald's personal history exceeded Dorian Gray's ('Oscar would have loved him for "copy" ').[50] Gerald, who was homosexual, seems to have been responsible for initiating Paul into the jokey camp world of code words, private signals, mocking insinuations and that delight in artificiality which is a defensive as much as offensive reaction to society's disapproval. 'All my synthetic passions are real to me – / I who have shut my heart from reality' was Paul's 'Epigram' for this period.[51]

Gerald had a scathing tongue when he wanted to tease, but he was a staunch ally against the philistines of Palmers Green. His gallantry charmed Mrs Scott, whose welcome contained perhaps a touch of relief. Always chary of Paul's success with girls, she seems to have cultivated Gerald almost as assiduously as he cultivated Paul, inviting the Armstrongs over, encouraging them to stay, accepting drives in their car, even spending weekends with the couple in Forest Hill. Gerald had a wife called Doris, friendly, attentive and so acquiescent that Paul characteristically felt sorry for her.[52] But his compunction was swallowed up in what he called 'naughtiness', the clandestine delights of provocation and defiance, thrills to which Wilde must have introduced generations of young men for whom his appeal lies as much in society's outraged reaction as in any particular acts he advocates. In between poems Paul dashed off a series of one-act plays – 'my outrageous morality plays' – of which his favourite was a kind of rake's progress in rhyming couplets called *The Atonement*. 'Well, anyway, no other play can touch *The Atonement* for downright lewdness,' Paul wrote complacently, clinching his point with a synopsis which suggests the lighthearted tone of his relations with Gerald: 'The chief figure is the *Bad Boy* who reads naughty books, e.g. Byron – & who then rushes all over the continent seeking fulfilment of his reading – only to find he's something quite different. Someone gets 2 years in prison & the Bad Boy is shamed – thus producing the Epilogue – with a chorus of artists, poets & Ballet dancers. EXEUNT.'[53] The man who ended up in prison was a magistrate, the Bad Boy's lover. 'Embrace me, & pray do not be shy' runs the only surviving couplet from this outrageous affair: 'Desist! a Philistine draws nigh!'[54]

Paul was enchanted to find that he, too, could be 'something quite different'. His early poem, 'It Never Happened' (the title comes from *Dorian Gray*), looks back to a spring, summer, autumn and winter when the poet and his lover picked bluebells, held hands 'And rushed, laughing, down a springy slope/ In Sussex', stood together flushed and panting to catch their breath, or ventured out 'bareheaded into a summer shower,/ And kissed the standing drops/ Upon each other's brow.'[55] Paul told a friend that the love poems of these years were all written to 'persons of my own sex', and that Gerald was the man with whom he was having an affair.[56] Gerald was presumably the companion with whom the poet lay:

> half-waking
> In the twilight, beneath a lime-tree,
> In July, understanding nothing
> But the tender presence of each other . . .

This was July 1939, when the pleasures of peace – making love, writing poetry, even wandering the countryside – seemed snatched from the shadow of war. People had been operating on borrowed time ever since the Munich conference the year before had brought temporary respite from German aggression. Like other young intellectuals in the 1930s, Paul had subscribed to the *New Statesman*, becoming a radical and a pacifist under the influence of C.E.M. Joad but, when it came to the point, he wavered between the Peace Pledge Union and the Territorial Army, in the end joining neither.[57] Peter and Paul were taking their annual seaside holiday in lodgings at Felixstowe when Hitler's demands on Poland forced a crisis in August 1939. People were glued to the wireless, parliament was recalled, plans for evacuation were set in train. On 1 September, German troops crossed the Polish border and their aeroplanes attacked the capital. Saturday, 2 September was the day Paul afterwards recalled as 'the last but one day of peace, when Warsaw had been bombed, & Peter & I sat on the deserted beach at Felixstowe, throwing interminable pebbles into the sea.'[58] The British ultimatum was delivered next day, and the prime minister Neville Chamberlain declared war with Germany. 'On 3 September I put away the Laws Relating to Bankruptcy and Receiverships – my parents quite understood – so that I could spend my last months of freedom letting loose the three muses of poetry, prose and drama.'[59]

The autumn of 1939 was for Paul the prelude to a period of intense imaginative activity. The mobilisation of Britain and France, the

Paul and his parents, photographed by Peter.

Clive and Ruth Sansom, and Paul in 'those heavenly days before the war': 'did we eat? or only live, and talk, and listen?'

German conquest of Poland, the Russian advance into Finland produced a strange state of suspension for boys waiting to be called up by the services, while the civilian population prepared for attack from the air. Paul, with the past closed off behind him and the future still unimaginable, seized the present to turn out a stream of works by which at a pinch he might be remembered. 'I wonder what happened to him?' Paul asked afterwards:

I wonder what happened to the impatient and carefree youth who wrote a whole chapter of a novel between dinner and bedtime, a three-act play between Monday and Friday, and composed a sonnet in the short time it took one morning to shave the hopeful fluff from chin and cheeks, and did not care who admired or scoffed at these brilliant sparks that seemed to fly so casually from the crater of his apparently volcanic talent?[60]

By the time he wrote this the exuberant youth had turned into a middle-aged man, and the volcanic talent had dwindled, or concentrated itself, to 'a single rather cold blue flame – not unlike the pilot light of a gas appliance – thin and steady, waiting for a supply of fuel from which it can create the likeness of an explosion.'[61] But Paul said afterwards that the first half of 1940 was one of the most fruitful periods of his life: an explosion of creative energy which he put down to his encounter with a second mentor,[62] a poet and teacher who promised intellectual and imaginative delights headier than anything Gerald Armstrong had to offer. This was Clive Sansom, who lived with his wife next door to the Scotts in the top flat at 61 Bourne Hill. Meeting his first real, live man of letters, always a momentous step for any young writer, was one of those times when luck behaved like a lady to Paul. New Year 1940 was so bitterly cold that rivers iced over, people skated on the boating pond in Broomfield Park, and the Sansoms' pipes froze, forcing Clive to go next door for advice and buckets of water. Paul never forgot the excitement of coming home one evening in early February to be told by his mother that they had a poet as their upstairs neighbour: 'I asked his name. She told me. I said I had never heard of him. She said, "That's what he said about you when I said you were a poet, too, so I gave him some of your things to prove it."'[63]

Sansom, who was ten years older than Paul and had grown up less than a mile away in Hedge Lane, had abandoned his own office job five years before to concentrate on writing, and encourage people to read and speak poetry. He was making his way on the freelance's precarious path, working part-time at the London Speech Institute in Fitzroy Square, editing *Speech News*, lecturing at training colleges, teaching evening classes, examining for the London Academy of

Music and Dramatic Art. Every spare moment was given to poetry: his poems had been appearing spasmodically for years in poetry magazines or the national newspapers and, at the beginning of 1940, he was already putting together his first slim volume of verse. His flat was full of the irresistible litter of literary life – typescripts, galley proofs, correspondence with publishers, a letter from Richard Church, a token postcard from Bernard Shaw, books above all. 'Books came before everything else in our home,' wrote Sansom's wife, Ruth. 'Book cases multiplied year by year until every room in the house was a library first and a bedroom or hall second.'[64]

The Sansoms were sized up over tea by Paul and his mother (who remained frankly baffled). Clive himself was more impressed by Paul than his poems: 'They are easy and fluent to read, but still somewhat Brookeish,' he wrote in his diary. 'He does not seem to have read any of the recent moderns.'[65] Clive promptly took Paul's education in hand, picking up where Mr Fullbrook's classics had left off, introducing him to Auden, Isherwood, Cecil Day Lewis and – peculiarly congenial to an excitable temperament – Stephen Spender. Spender's *Poems, 33* supplied Paul with tags and titles for at least another decade, but the revelation that knocked him sideways was T. S. Eliot. If Gerald Armstrong presided over the lush pastures of Wildean flirtation, friendship with Clive meant breathing a keener, cooler, more bracing atmosphere that, poetically speaking, sent Paul reeling. He seems to have gone from Brooke to Eliot at a single bound, which was more than could be said for the literary establishment at a time when C. S. Lewis, then a distinguished don teaching English literature at Oxford, could still dismiss each fresh effort of Eliot's as another stop on 'the short road from *The Waste Land* to the wastepaper basket'.[66]

Clive's class at the Speech Institute that January was comparatively advanced, but his bold claim that Eliot's poetry would be generally accepted by the year 1980 was more than even his students could stomach: 'He will be regarded as a pathological specimen,' one said indignantly.[67] Admiration for Eliot was commonly held even, perhaps especially, by poetry lovers to be little short of subversive. Clive and Ruth, already regarded as queer fish on Bourne Hill, would have seemed queerer still if their neighbours had suspected them of spending a great part of the winter rehearsing a pioneering, part-sung, part-spoken recital of *The Waste Land*, which they performed together at the Ethical Church. 'We were both out of time and place and living only in *The Waste Land*,' wrote Ruth.[68] So, very soon, was Paul. He said at the end of his life that Eliot had been the strongest and most enduring influence on him as a writer; and the staggering impact of *The Waste Land* may be seen in the long poem, saturated in Eliot's rhythms and religious imagery, which he began writing at once under Clive's tutelage.[69]

Clive's energetic conviction was always infectious. 'He was slight in build with a wide forehead, large expressive grey-green eyes, a strong nose and generous mouth,' wrote Ruth. 'The face was animated by a fire within, and a directive mind. From the tips of his fingers and toes he was tremblingly alive. He felt passionately about everything. . . . His profile resembled Hardy's and Keats' and Browning's . . .'[70] (Clive was proud of the fact that the Hardys, Brownings and Sansoms all came originally from the same part of Dorset.) Ruth, working at the Speech Institute on a scholarship from Tasmania, had met him as a fellow student and fallen in love with his vitality, his ability to catch fire, his determination to live and breathe poetry. They were married in June 1937, at the Quaker meeting house on Winchmore Hill (both afterwards became Quakers) for the sake of its connection with Charles Lamb, whose grave Ruth had discovered by chance in the overgrown churchyard at Edmonton. From their first meeting in 'those heavenly days before the war',[71] the Sansoms pooled poems and plans with Paul. Clive, who had grown up on music hall turns at the Wood Green Empire, was an excellent mimic, and he and Paul would change identities, put on foreign accents and generally send themselves up, reducing Ruth and each other to helpless laughter.

They played the same records over and over again. Tchaikovsky's 'Symphonie Pathétique' became their theme music, along with Ravel, Debussy, a sort of Russian 'Jingle Bells' called 'Troika', and the mournful lilt of Coward's 'Matelot, matelot/ Where you go/ My heart goes with you . . .' Paul afterwards improvised a saucy French sailor with intellectual leanings called Jacques de Matelot:[72] he could call all his life on a capacious repertoire of character parts, or *alter egos*, plucked out of the air to express or relieve his feelings, and it was the whimsical, amorous, frisky and frivolous Jacques – along with an even more boisterous character called Ivan Kapinski – who encapsulated the sillier side of that lime-scented summer with the Sansoms.

The sense of isolation and oddity imposed on all three in Bourne Hill underlies Ruth's account of the gratitude, relief and excitement each felt at finding a kindred spirit:

There was an immediate affinity between us and Paul as though we had known each other in some former life. . . . Our minds interlaced. It was Paul who invented the 'Jetty Pail', a chain of office, to be presented to each one who achieved this distinction by mutual agreement when a new poem was written by one of the three. There was almost daily coming and going, we to Paul to listen in delight to records of Tchaikovsky, & Paul to us for poetry and conversation. . . . I hear Paul's voice forty-five years later as we walked down Bourne Hill under the hedge of flowering May. It was the first year of the war, and people were fearful of spies. As a couple approached us Paul said in a loud undertone: 'De bomb – under de *gas works*.'

We walked at times to Grovelands Park, up the hill, beneath the soft perfumed lime trees, heightened by the soft English rains.

Did we eat? or only live, & talk, & listen? I remember only the great yellow gooseberries, & cod roe and celery on Sunday afternoons.[73]

Paul was swept up in a triangular relationship which absorbed him to the increasing exclusion of Peter and Geoffrey (both of whom were conscripted into the army by early summer). Clive introduced the Russian playwrights to Paul who, on the strength of a sketchy acquaintance with Chekhov and innumerable repeats of 'Troika', dashed off a new playlet called *The Blue Waltz*,[74] which catches the mood of this three-sided friendship much as *The Atonement* reflected relations with Gerald. The piece, which has no plot to speak of, revolves round three central characters, drifting or dancing to the melancholy strains of the Blue Waltz. Paul himself is the exuberant extrovert, Ivan Kapinski, getting steadily tipsier on music, ice-cream and vodka, playing the fool to an audience consisting of his older and wiser friend, Stepan Ilyaitch, and the tough, independent, unsentimental Anna Gavrialich. Clive was Stepan and Ruth Anna (the two would turn up again as Steven and Annie, together with the snowbound landscape of 'Troika', in Paul's only published play, *Pillars of Salt*). Neither Stepan's appreciation nor Anna's deflationary comments can restrain Ivan, whose tearing spirits, boundless self-confidence and faith in the future mirror at least one side of Paul that summer when he, too, could get drunk on nothing stronger than gooseberries and lime juice[75] (Clive had a horror of alcohol, which the three never touched).

No less intoxicating were the delights of sprung rhythm, another of the mysteries into which Clive initiated Paul in bouts of improvised incantation which left the three limp, giddy and mutually elated. The Sansoms both belonged to the London Verse Speaking Choir, part of a movement which would lead after the war to a widespread resurgence of verse drama and spoken poetry. Anything written by one of the three was immediately chanted aloud to the others before being criticised, analysed and competitively assessed. Paul's poetic output changed gear and shot forward like an engine kept too long ticking over: 'Under the encouragement I got from next door I began imperceptibly to suppress impulses which produced the kind of work which they tenderly put to death with a few well-chosen but not hurtful words, and – greedy for praise – give fuller rein to impulses which produced work they took more seriously, because in it they heard – not echoes – but the faint sound of my own voice.'[76] That sound is almost too faint to hear in the three loosely connected long poems Paul wrote in the opening months of 1940: 'The Creation', 'The Dream' and 'The Cross', eventually published as one under the name *I, Gerontius* (after the protagonist of 'The Dream'). 'It records the thoughts and emotions experienced by the author before entering the Army,' Clive wrote in his introduction. 'War and human suffering are its background, the desire for religious belief its implication.'

This was a generous, if not strictly inaccurate description of a work crammed with impressions Paul had picked up at the Sansoms', and shaped according to the incantatory techniques they used to tip themselves over into what Clive called 'the hinterland of consciousness'. Paul himself claimed that 'The Cross' had been dictated to him in the course of a single night during which he surrendered joyfully, and without a struggle, to 'my Muse . . . on the Warpath again'.[77] Clive complained with some justice that parts of the poem had been lifted piecemeal from his own writings. The whole is a ragbag of Sansomian themes, ranging from Confucius to the Pharaoh Akhnaten (who ranked high in Clive's pantheon as the founding father of pacifists), from Sodom and Gomorrah to more edifying biblical borrowings (Paul had politely declined Clive's invitation to attend Quaker meetings on Winchmore Hill on the grounds that communal faith in an unseen being went against his grain as an individual),[78] including the dreams of Naboth and Gerontius, the betrayals at Gethsemane and Calvary. Above all *I, Gerontius* reflects its author's bewitchment by Wilde and Eliot, the one overtaken by the other, both at their most incantatory:

> If we consider the ends
> the ends leading to the greatest end
> and the greatest end ending forever
> If we consider Life
>
> Let it be said we consider
> all things all things considered
> by us and all things to us
> inspirations to the great end
>
> Then we consider nothing
> or considering nothing can
> be nothing to us forever
> then Nothing attained

Nothing attained Nothing
Desolate is the cry and great the shoutings
accompanying this void
this empty masquerade of living

I saw many masks in the moonlight
striving to attain the moon.

The masks and the moonlight come from Wilde's *De Profundis*, which Paul read with the Sansoms. The rest confirms C. S. Lewis's worst fears about Eliot's influence on the young. Paul insisted that it was essential to try out other people's styles: 'You have to be able to do them properly before you are free as a writer,' he explained a generation later to his own younger daughter,[79] who was experimenting at eighteen with a set of strikingly similar writing exercises, including a long poem about Christ in the garden at Gethsemane (*Gethsemane* was one of the titles Paul eventually discarded in favour of *I, Gerontius*).[80] Paul passed on to her much of what Clive had said to him at this tentative stage in his own development. The long, detailed letter to his daughter in which Paul analyses the same faults that had made him impatient with his younger self – banal conception, second-hand mannerisms, synthetic emotion, technical immaturity – clearly reflects something of those devastatingly accurate group criticism sessions at the Sansoms':

The imagery is all borrowed, isn't it? . . . Why don't you write the poem again in free verse. . . . Alternatively . . . study every line with a view to substituting an original phrase for a cliché phrase.

There is a tendency to wrap your meaning up in archaic words and phrases, which is a way of attempting to make poetry consciously, I should say self-consciously. . . . 'But' is a favourite word of yours which you should get rid of promptly! It is a sort of poetic 'yet' or 'only' and, like certain sickly phrases of music, immediately conveys a stock, ready-made emotion: in this case, an emotion about poor suffering humanity. But. We are but little children weak. If you strip the first stanza of 'buts' and archaic juxtapositions . . . you'll see that you are stating something that doesn't quite make sense . . . what does it *mean*? A good exercise for rewriting this poem would be to write it in words of one syllable in prose.

Paul disowned *I, Gerontius* in later life, and destroyed his own copy. But, at the time, it was a declaration of intent, one that established his credentials as a poet in the eyes of his friends and himself. The first two parts were finished by May 1940, although 'The Cross' still needed alteration ('The Eliot part was struck right out,' Paul wrote cheerfully, posting the manuscript off with Clive's approval to Faber & Faber, who returned it immediately).[81] Each part was typed out in turn by Clive before being neatly bound by the author in thick white art paper, secured with brass fasteners, signed and dedicated to the two Sansoms. On 24 May Clive received the supreme Order of the Jetty Pail, 'conferred . . . for distinguished services in the field of Blasphemy and Wit', and signed in council by Paul and Ivan Kapinski, who were respectively President and Vice-president.[82] Kapinski, whose favourite word was 'Exhilarating!', flourished and grew that summer as Paul drew the others in after him to a kind of serial Russian fantasy. So, in a more languid vein, did another of his imaginary *alter egos*, the decadent poseur J. W. Cynara, who was roped in as the Jetty Pail's secretary. The Jetty Pail pendant itself changed hands regularly, its progress recorded by Paul who kept meticulous accounts for the Order, called meetings, and issued elaborately lettered certificates, citations, membership cards, presentation scrolls and a Royal Grand Star of the Supremeship. The President's office bore Payne's address, 232–60 Regent Street, at any rate for typed communications. Clive was elected Chief Meany. 'Well, you old Meany,' wrote the President, resting from his labours on 'The Cross', 'I have written nothing of importance for quite a while – but when it does come! Wham!'[83]

Considering that Paul was already nineteen when they met, and Clive (by this time wholly committed to pacifism) a married man of twenty-nine, all this was no doubt an absurdly juvenile way of letting off steam in face of impending doom. But Clive, too, had grown up too fast, missing what Paul called the important years, 'the emotional ones of full puberty',[84] by going out to work as an office boy at the London office of the Sheffield ironworks which employed his father as a commercial traveller. Like Paul, he ruthlessly hoarded spare time for writing. He was nineteen when his first poem was published in the *Observer*. 'I have always led a double life,' he wrote: 'From the age of fourteen I wanted to write. From sixteen I wanted above everything to write poetry.'[85] He knew only too well what it meant to be regarded as a freak in the world in which he lived while struggling alone to get out of it, without guidance, without any but the most basic schooling, and with severely limited access to books. Clive had found no one to give him the practical encouragement he gave Paul (who would in turn go out of his way all his life to help other writers), or to sustain him in an emotional predicament that corresponded in some ways closely to Paul's own.

Clive understood a good deal about Paul's problems at home. He, too, had been his mother's favourite, the younger of two brothers, in a closely knit, domestic unit of three which largely excluded his father. William Sansom drank heavily, and his terrifying violence when drunk

was a disgrace which cut the family off from their neighbours even
more effectively than the Scotts' financial troubles. Her husband's
retreat into alcoholism and aggression turned Mrs Sansom to her
younger son with a generous, passionate, unconditional love, which
he returned with an ardour beyond his years. But the force that had
given him courage and confidence as a boy threatened to smother him
as a man, and, although his mother came in the end to accept his
marriage, the process had been protracted and painful. Clive described
it in a bitter poem about trust and betrayal, 'Loyalties',[86] which
begins:

> For nine months' lodging in the womb
>   I must pay rent for ever.
> To match my Mother's will
>   Shall be my will's endeavour;
> And if my instincts tell
>   What I, not she, would do,
> I must deny their promptings
>   . . . *and a far cock crew* . . .

Clive's solutions were ascetic and spiritual. The isolation, iron sense
of purpose and relentless self-discipline of a writer's life provided his
escape from the human emotional chain ('The extramural world/
Interprets state as mother/To pay for being warped/ We each must
warp each other . . .'). He must have foreseen what would inevitably
happen to Paul, who remained still wrapped up in his mother. Frances
Scott was her son's staunchest ally and defender. She entered into his
plans, applauded his successes, delighted in his unique abilities,
mighty brain and formidable powers of concentration ('He never
hears when I call him for dinner, and I have to go up to his room where
he is composing his poems, and touch him gently, to bring him back to
reality').[87] She believed without reservation in his genius and, in
moments of discouragement, she could make Paul believe in it too.
Something of her persists behind each of the women in his works who
possess this talent. He explored its implications from inside through
Mrs Hurst in *A Male Child*, and showed it in action from outside in a
television play, *Sahibs and Memsahibs*, in the person of Nan Forrest, a
divorcée who infuriates the Colonel's Lady by flirting with all the
young cadets: 'She is what? 38? She is blonde, strikingly handsome,
young enough to make a cadet feel a bit of a dog. . . . She is liked
because she seems so easy to like, laughed with because it's so easy to
laugh with her, confided in because you know you can trust her . . .
adored because she proves one capable of adoration.'[88] Mrs Forrest is

lonely, socially ostracised, rejected by the world to which she would have liked to belong, dependent on her wits and charm to improvise an alternative existence. She has the courage and gallantry Paul admired in his mother, who found men always more malleable than women, and who to the end of her days had a knack of getting to know people, winning their confidence and drawing them out.

But there was another side to Paul's mother. She was a martyr to nerves and indigestion. Even her strongest supporters agreed that she had no staying power in relationships. She took people up with enthusiasm but she was apt to drop them just as capriciously. If she was Paul's keenest admirer, she was also his most exacting critic. She and Paul would indulge in bouts of competitive repartee, each capping the other in a kind of crescendo of sarcastic vituperation. At the end of his life, Paul insisted to his students that a writer's eventual achievement depended partly on the strength and egotism of his or her writing personality, partly on how strictly that personality had been controlled: 'however egotistical and strong your writing personality is, the *alter ego* – the reflection of you that looks at what you are writing and have written – must be a critic that is almost impossible to please, or get a good mark from.'[89] Both these attributes in Paul – the strength of his self-assertion as a writer, and the ruthlessness with which he learned to control it – went back to his relationship with his mother in these formative years at home when nothing had as yet come between them.

'He is your life – the same as he is mine,' she said a year later when Paul eventually brought home a serious rival for his affections.[90] But for the moment she rightly diagnosed no real threat in either of the Sansoms, or for that matter Gerald Armstrong, who wooed her with flattery and flowers, and indulged her propensity to talk for hours about Paul. She was discreet, if not positively encouraging, about the state of affairs between Paul and Gerald. 'I think Mrs Scott knew about Paul's escapade,' said Ruth Sansom. 'She once asked me in an agitated state, "*Is* Paul a homosexual?" I wasn't sure: we hadn't talked about it. I was very ignorant. *She* obviously didn't know anything about it.'[91] Like Mrs Scott (and indeed most respectable women from Queen Victoria downwards until well into the second half of the twentieth century), Ruth knew nothing about homosexuality, had never so far as she knew met any homosexuals, and couldn't have identified them if she had. With no means of recognising, let alone deciphering the various protective codes evolved for fear of blackmail or prosecution, Ruth was as perplexed as Paul's mother. Clive found a paperback with a chapter on homosexuality, which Mrs Scott apparently read, and no more was said on the matter.

Gerald's charms were in any case waning as Paul became more and more engrossed in the Sansoms. 'I hope you will not disappear until I am in the service of the Country,' Paul wrote in June to Clive, who had applied to the tribunal for conscientious objectors, 'as now Geoffrey is gone – and Peter not getting back at weekends I shall be a very lonely little poet! My friend Gerald Armstrong is also going to be a Conscientious Objector & is very worried & keeps himself to himself, & there is no comfort from that quarter as he is angry with me for changing my mind about objecting too. I think he is looking for someone to take my place!!!'[92] Paul loathed the thought of war as deeply as Clive.[93] He seriously considered applying for exemption as a pacifist but he knew well enough what it meant to be deprived of privilege, and it had given him a lifelong mistrust of claims for special treatment, or of being set apart from ordinary people. This dread of inverted élitism, of being singled out, even in some sense mysteriously privileged, was one of the things that turned him in the end against homosexuality. He had introduced his two mentors in February, very soon after he first met the Sansoms, but the meeting had not been a success: Ruth instinctively mistrusted Gerald, and Clive, realising more clearly what was involved, remained understandably cagey.

But Clive was neither shocked nor surprised when Paul ventured tentatively two months later to show him *The Atonement*. 'I did not reply to the naughty answer to the naughty play,' Paul wrote on 24 May, 'because I do not quite know whether your naughtiness hid genuine disapproval of the content.' 'Naughty' became something of a catchphrase between Paul and Clive, who exchanged naughty poems, played naughty tricks and told one another naughty stories. It signified much the same as 'decadent' in the campaign against philistinism articulated for both of them that summer by Wilde, at his most moving and magisterial in *De Profundis* ('In their heavy inaccessibility to ideas, their tedious orthodoxy, their worship of vulgar success, their entire preoccupation with the gross material side of life, and their ridiculous estimate of themselves and their importance, the Jews of Jerusalem in Christ's day were the exact counterpart of the British philistine of our own').[94] It was Clive, always anxious that people should be brought as far as possible to understand themselves, who suggested Paul read the long letter – part dignified public statement, part agonised private recrimination – Wilde wrote to his lover from prison.[95] Ruth, who read the book at the same time as the two men, astonished Paul by her sympathy with Wilde, something he had not conceived possible in a woman. He himself was still more dazzled by Wilde's romantic rise than impressed by the sombre realities of his downfall.

With the Sansoms preparing to move to the country near Oxford, and Peter and Geoffrey already gone, the lonely little poet received his own call-up papers at last with something like relief. He was to join his regiment on Wednesday 17 July. He packed Palgrave's *Golden Treasury* with Everyman's *Golden Book* of modern poetry[96] and took tearful leave of his aunts, shedding tears once again on his last afternoon at the thought of all he owed Clive and Ruth, who crept up the front path late that night to drop two final farewells through the letterbox of number 63. Ruth came back next morning, after Paul had left for the station, with a word of consolation for Mrs Scott, who replied:

My dear Friend,

I have read your kind note in my darling's room. I am overwhelmed. I must do some cooking this morning but if you would walk with me in the park this afternoon & will you both have a cup of afternoon tea with Tom and I when we return.

Much love & many grateful thanks for your understanding & sympathy. His dear heart was full as he left

Frances[97]

Frances Scott's ambivalence puzzled Ruth on this walk. She asked if Ruth loved Paul and, when Ruth said yes ('I was very innocent then: now I don't know *what* she meant'), gave her a pair of gold and amethyst earrings as a keepsake, a token of her affection, possibly some sort of safeguard against Paul's return. Ruth herself felt it was precisely because she was safely married that Frances entrusted Paul to her: it was a way of holding on to him as much as of letting him go. His mother must have suspected that, even if Paul survived the war, he would never now be an accountant, and perhaps she guessed, when he cut off his long flowing hair on the army's instructions, that sooner or later it would mean the end of the poet in him.

CHAPTER FOUR

A twin who could be cruel as well as kind

Paul joined the army as a private soldier on ten shillings a week in the first batch of civilians called up to form the 8th Battalion, the Buffs, in improvised billets at Dropmore Hall, near the village of Burnham, a few miles outside Slough. Most were boys of twenty like himself, from London or Kent, clerks, labourers, shop assistants, tough customers from Bermondsey with no knowledge of the army and little enough of the outside world. Many had never spent a night away from home before in their lives. They were met at Taplow station and marched back to Dropmore by their platoon sergeants, the battalion's only experienced soldiers, nearly all survivors from the catastrophe at Dunkirk the month before, remnants of other regiments hastily assembled and made up to sergeants to train the new intake.[1] Not a man in the battalion was there by choice: Paul, who saw himself as a pilot, always said the RAF had turned him down because he wrote poems. His first day was spent standing about in the hot sun with other raw recruits, brooding on the darkness of fate, but by nightfall he felt better, having got the first lines of a lugubrious new poem: 'If this should be/ The last time I beauty see/ With eyes the loveliest of me . . .'[2]

Mealtimes were disgusting, sanitary arrangements primitive and, at a time when whole regiments were being raised from scratch all over the country to repel invasion, there was no kit or equipment to speak of. Each man was given a straw palliasse, a metal bowl, mess tin, knife, fork and spoon. Otherwise there were Lee Enfield rifles (some had to make do with antiquated First World War survivals, or even drill-purpose dummies), and spades with which to set about fortifying the camp and the surrounding countryside by digging trenches. Paul's

hair, already cropped before he left London, was savagely shorn by the
regimental barber. He lived for the post, reading letters from home in
snatched moments of privacy on the latrine. He said he felt like a
prisoner in Sing Sing.[3]

But he also found himself unexpectedly pleased with the place, his
companions and the restfulness of routine. By his own account, he
liked living under canvas in glorious sunshine beneath the Buckinghamshire beechwoods, smelling the bracken and the familiar scent of
lime trees. He liked excursions into Maidenhead to sample the
teashops and cinemas, as well as boating on the river at weekends. He
liked even the unending drill, signing himself exuberantly 'Paul Mark
Time', and remembering to the end of his life 19 Platoon, D Company,
marching out resplendent after three months with 'bags of swank'.[4]
Army life removed the burden of choice:

I enjoyed the cessation of intellectual exercise, I enjoyed the monotony, the
sleeping on bare earth sometimes, the rising at impossible hours and shaving
in cold water; the gradual achievement of proficiency, the utter pettiness of
administrative detail, the outward gloss, the inner corruption; the preoccupation with rights and privileges, the mass emotionalism, the private malice. I
had found in myself an unexpectedly broad streak of the banal.[5]

This is the narrator of *A Male Child*, who has much in common with
his creator. The austerity of army routine appealed to the puritan in
Paul. The other side of his nature luxuriated alternately in thoughts of
death and dreams of fame, picturing himself after the war as a
successful poet, more in Coward's style than Sansom's ('cool nights in
old flannels on a river reading Shelley by moonlight'), entertaining his
friends on his own yacht and buying a house in the country for his
mother.[6] He finished his poem about beauty and posted it off on 28
July, making it quite clear to the Sansoms that his vision required
shoring up not shooting down ('I can't be practical in the army, so
please don't make me do too much criticism'). After nearly six months'
unremitting imaginative exertion, he welcomed and probably needed
a period of mental stagnation and physical effort, with its corollaries
of fatigue and sensual pleasure. He said he felt cramped, and would
like to 'rush across the fields with Tchaikovsky in front, improvising
on a violin'.[7] Five years later, towards the end of his stint in the army,
he looked back indulgently on those innocent 'days as a khaki-clad
civilian at Dropmore', when time hung suspended between Slough and
Maidenhead, 'which is another way of saying Despond, and a mental
preoccupation with sex'.[8]

A golden glow pervaded those first heady months in an all-male
environment. One of Paul's first moves at Burnham had been to size up

the local talent. By the first week of August, he was already dating 'a young lady' (she is never mentioned again in letters to the Sansoms), but even before that he had found a friend. 'Have met a DECADENT person (in the way I mean) who likes Tchaikovsky – Keats & Shelley. He also looks well.'[9] Frances and Tom Scott came down for the day at the end of July, followed by the Sansoms for a picnic on the river the weekend after. 'Let us always be frank,' Paul wrote a few months later to Ruth: 'Just as we were that time in Maidenhead when we sat & discussed sex for so long over tea.'[10] Paul's frankness that afternoon was enough to alarm both Sansoms. Ruth, in whom Paul was beginning to confide his private affairs more freely than he could to Clive, wrote anxiously from London, and received in reply a ringing, if not altogether reassuring affirmation of Paul's sexual creed:

It is true that women fail to interest me generally. You will have already gathered that from the various conversations we have had concerning sex. Also you will have gathered with what man I have an affair – & also that all my love poems are written to persons of my own sex. This may seem unnatural to you – it does to most people – but I think you will understand & appreciate that it is a popular failing with people of my type!

For me sex is an all-important – I should say *the* most important part of life. All emotions & creative instincts are (to me) based on the sexual impulse in man. For me proof of this is shown in the fact that artistic people – who experience more complicated emotions than others – are on the whole very highly sexed in either one way or another. And yet an artistic person can live his sex life in his art – so that for long periods – sometimes indefinitely – the sexual act is unnecessary for him. At other times – mostly in periods of artistic inactivity – his actions will become of a highly emotional & physical character . . .

Life is certainly very complicated – but sex itself should not be the cause of complication but the simplifier. A perfect sex life is a perfect life.

Sex is the great Simplifier. It sets aside all loyalties – ties & bonds & restrictions. Accept the need for sex & the mental troubles of the moment will pass away.[11]

By this time Clive, who had always known or guessed more than Ruth, was understandably worried on Paul's account. Behaviour that had been harmless enough on Bourne Hill carried serious risks in the army, and Clive was sufficiently disturbed by the Maidenhead picnic to arrange a meeting with Gerald Armstrong to whom he delivered some sort of warning. He never told Ruth what was said at this lunch, but she guessed he would have emphasised Paul's youth, inexperience, vulnerability, and the stiff penalties exacted in his new life for indiscretion. Gerald responded frostily: 'Dear Clive . . . May I express to you my gratitude for the lesson that one is never too old to learn and for your explanation that confidences, sometimes given in all sincerity, may be misplaced.'[12] Paul was delighted to picture Gerald tying himself in knots: 'I expect he smoked endless cigarettes explaining his relations with me!' he wrote that August to Clive. 'Its funny – but I see nothing wrong in it, you know – except certain pricks of conscience as regards Doris. It is always the way & makes life very hard. I don't know whether he told you his life history – but it is most interesting – & exceeds "Dorian Gray" – Oscar would have loved him for "copy". We have spent some wildly happy – lush – luxurious times together – & always I shall remember them as the greatest achievement in my life.'[13]

Paul in this mood clearly felt no regrets for the life he had left behind him. The only two fellow privates mentioned by name in letters to the Sansoms from Dropmore were Peter Lumley, who lived in Chelsea round the corner from Augustus John's local drinking club, and whose uncle was the couturier Edward Molyneux; and the actor Stephen Badham who, under his stage name of Stephen Arlen, had worked on several of Paul's favourite West End hits, including *Rope*, *George and Margaret*, and *Ghosts*. Badham, who would go on to become successively manager of Sadler's Wells, the English National Opera, and the newly-founded National Theatre, was married to a Scottish dancer from Pavlova's company.[14] He and Lumley were both unequivocally heterosexual, but they brought a whiff of a worldly, cosmopolitan, faintly raffish bohemianism incomparably more sophisticated, both socially and sexually speaking, than anything Paul had yet known, and it made him feel already a long way from the suburban mores of Palmers Green. It also made him less inclined to take seriously either Clive's qualms about his predicament, or his attempts at consolation: 'After all, there's nothing very unusual in it – except in degree. It happens in teachers' training colleges, for instance, to the extent of about 40% of the population, I believe. And it is even more frequent among artistic people.'[15] Clive explained that everyone contains some element of the opposite sex and that any sexual partnership works better when the balance is even, as between himself and Ruth, so that there could be no possessiveness ('One doesn't need the other in order to gratify their sense of *power*').

It was a shrewd warning but it came too soon for Paul, who was in any case too absorbed in his new life to pay attention. He found it impossible to drop back into the familiar pattern, even with the Sansoms, when he got his first Sunday pass and spent a few hours in London on 25 August.[16] Two weeks later he got his stripe as Lance-Corporal and, working under Corporal Badham ('we get on like a house on fire'),[17] discovered a talent for organisation which made their platoon one of the best-run in D Company. Badham, seven years older than Paul, would be celebrated all his life for his sympathetic knack of getting the best from his staff. The natural flair for solving problems, handling emergencies and cutting through red tape, which made him a brilliant, if unconventional administrator, had already been developed by the discipline of stage management, compared to which the army was child's play. Paul blossomed under his tuition, throwing himself into the business of building up the platoon, and planning to get Badham to read the script of Clive's play, *Akhnaten*. He was also thinking of showing his own poems to Lumley. They were the first contemporaries Paul had come across who belonged automatically to the world of casual public school privilege and power he had read about in books (both had in some sense turned it down, preferring a measure of independence and firmly resisting all invitations to apply for officer training). Both had mixed freely with poets, painters, actors, artists of all sorts. Paul was enchanted by Lumley's flamboyance – 'dear old Lumley is a darling – always broke (he comes from Chelsea)'[18] – by Badham's unorthodox methods, by their combined gaiety, warmth and self-confidence. 'There are a number of people really worth knowing,' he wrote happily to the Sansoms at the end of September. 'Life is really worth living at the moment.'[19]

If Badham and Lumley stood out as freaks in that company, they were freaks who were tolerated with good humour and even respect. Lumley's scarlet pyjamas became something of a byword in the battalion:[20] he said that, of the seven fellow soldiers who shared his tent in July 1940, none had ever seen a man wear pyjamas before but, by the time he left, all seven had bought pyjamas themselves. Most people slept in their clothes, considered bathing dangerously detrimental to health, and took it for granted that only madmen read books. Paul kept his head down as he had done at school, extracting what satisfaction he could from ferocious company drill, and dreading the scarcely less ferocious kit inspections which cost him endless anxiety over boots insufficiently polished, trousers inadequately pressed, rifle improperly cleaned, kit incorrectly laid out or minus so much as a buttonstick (Paul was hopelessly at sea when it came to scrounging missing items, which was the normal method of kit replacement with no questions asked in that shrewd and resourceful company). The commanding officer of D Company was Captain H. E. Smith, also a former civilian and a figure infinitely remote at that stage in the war, although Paul had reason to feel grateful to him later. Lumley's CO in B Company was the novelist R. C. Hutchinson, who had had a phenomenal success two years earlier with his Russian revolutionary epic, *Testament*: Paul longed to confess that he, too, meant to be a writer one day, but never got further than an encouraging feeling that 'such close proximity to the author of *Testament* was an augury for the future'.[21]

For all his efforts at roughing it and mucking in with the others, he struck several of his companions in that first year of the war as seriously out of his depth. Clive was not the only one who felt nervous on Paul's behalf. The company clerk was another twenty-year-old called Edward Scilloe, a north London cockney, shorthand typist to a silk importer in civil life, and a veteran of the Boys' Brigade which made him far more at home than most with the mysteries of military turnout, discipline and drill. One of nature's fixers, like Badham, with an equal love of the army, of setting things to rights and seeing them run smoothly, Scilloe earmarked Paul as his assistant ('Having to lay out his kit was hard on him. There was a lot of taking the mickey. He was very quiet, very shy – he really tried to be a soldier. But army life must have been agony for him'). By mid-September it was generally agreed, in view of Paul's book-keeping experience and his painfully evident impracticality, that the company office was the best place for him.

The Battle of Britain raging in the air that September put a sudden stop to training activities for the Buffs' new 'adolescent battalions',[22] which had been specifically raised to guard the south coast. D Company, in the 8th Battalion, was hastily posted to Slough to put up a smoke screen round makeshift munition factories, then down to Marazion in Cornwall in the middle of October to spend ten days running-up improvised coastal defences. Paul's platoon was quartered in the Godolphin Hotel at St Hilary, a mile or so inland on the high spine of the Cornish peninsula. Eddie Scilloe remembered Paul's misery and his bleeding hands as they set about entangling guard post and clifftop in loops of barbed wire. Paul himself remembered only romantic, Arthurian dawns breaking over St Michael's Mount as he took down the blackout at first light, and the magical march back to the coast to entrain for an unknown destination: 'As we marched . . . I looked at the sea, & it was the colour of opals – pink, blue, grey,' he wrote long afterwards to his eldest daughter. 'And I have never forgotten that, although it was 36 years ago. Next morning we woke up to find ourselves in Torquay!!'[23]

Torquay, which welcomed its first troops with effusive relief, proved an unexpectedly safe place to be in the autumn of 1940 as waves of German bombers concentrated night after night on London. D Company headquarters were established in the Maycliffe Hotel, St Luke's Road, and the unparalleled luxuries enjoyed by the boys at the Maycliffe – soft beds, cushy jobs and a bar on the premises – became a

running grievance to the rest of the battalion, who slept on bare boards
with no privacy and nowhere to put anything between punishing
forty-eight-hour stints of guard duty. Paul settled down efficiently
under Scilloe's wing to sorting out Captain Smith's hopelessly
muddled imprest account, submitting returns, keeping records and
organising the weekly pay parade. He wrote to Clive from the
Maycliffe on 29 October, jubilantly anticipating home leave and
catching up with old friends. 'Geoffrey is cutting his leave short to
spend a bit of time with a queer boy in Cardiff – who is a medical
orderly in the RAF. He seems very bucked about it. Evidently a very
aesthetic boy who adored my poem "If I must die before my heart
grows old" – who gives Geoffrey sentimental monologues – terribly
us. He was madly jealous of Gerald – as we have known each other
since we were 12 – & went everywhere together. When I think – I am so
blessed with friends of this order – that I am at times a little humble for
it – but perhaps that is a pose like the rest of my life!!!!!'

Paul's days as a poseur were about to be brought to an abrupt end.
The battalion was growing increasingly unsettled at news of death and
destruction in London, where nearly everyone had family or friends at
risk. The distant glare of fires in the capital had been visible from
Dropmore on the night sky, and the first bomb fell on Southgate on 26
August, the night after Paul's visit home on his first Sunday pass.
Regular air raids throughout September intensified the month after,
with bombs dropping for as many as five nights in succession. One
hundred and eighteen bombs and two mines fell on Southgate in just
under three weeks that October.[24] Winchmore Hill sports ground was
destroyed, and water was cut off on Bourne Hill when the mains were
hit. 'We have indeed been in the thick of it,' Frances Scott wrote to
Ruth on 23 October. 'There is hardly a window left in Compton,
Orpington, Hazelmore, Arlow, Fernleigh or Highfield Roads. It is
terrible to behold. On Sunday night a bomb exploded in Fox Lane &
demolished two houses also one behind the reservoir it made us jump.'

After a month of sleepless nights in the air raid shelter followed by
devastation next morning, the Sansoms had taken refuge with a friend
at Charlbury, near Oxford. The three Wright sisters, who had come
over from Richmond to stay with their cousins Florrie and Laura at
Wyphurst, were so appalled by conditions in Southgate that, when
they left on Thursday 7 November, they fled London altogether,
planning to hole up in Cornwall for the duration. A stick of bombs fell
that night on Southgate High Street, blowing out all the windows at
Wyphurst. 'The Broadwalk is very badly damaged it was a terrible
night I quite thought it was the end for us,' Frances wrote afterwards
to the Sansoms.[25] At 10.30 next morning a time bomb, which had lain

unsuspected all night under the kitchen floor at Wyphurst, exploded and destroyed the house. Florrie was killed instantly, along with a neighbour, who had gone in to ask how she was. Laura, dreadfully injured, died four days later in hospital.[26] Tom, who had left late for the studio that morning, arrived to find one sister dying, the other dead, and his life's work in ruins.

'Father does not yet realise, I think, the greatness of the loss which we all suffered,' wrote Paul,[27] who reached home the following Thursday, after travelling all night, on seven days' compassionate leave. Geoffrey, who had arrived back from Wales just in time to hear the Wyphurst explosion, was dispatched by Mrs Scott to tell Peter, stationed with his regiment in Kent. The double funeral at Christ Church on Friday 15 November was the first Paul had ever attended and, although he had long since abandoned any faith in conventional religion, the beautiful, sombre words of the burial service were almost more than he could bear. 'I dared not look on anyone, but watched always the trees and the sky and the long bare horizon, which my Dear Aunts loved so well.'[28] The rest of the week was taken up with arrangements, condolences, business affairs, and a visit to Gerald Armstrong at Forest Hill. Paul went up to town to consult another old friend and client of Payne's, a solicitor called Henry Wilfred Howard Smith, and to visit the accountants who had taken over Payne's firm. The nights brought fresh raids: 'I don't know how London stands it,' Paul wrote,[29] hearing for the first time the drone of German planes overhead and the answering crash and thud of the guns. It rained endlessly all week. Frances dried out what little could be salvaged from the debris of Wyphurst. Every stick of furniture had been smashed along with the paintings, books, Florrie's piano and all the ornaments except for a single Japanese vase, one of a pair, which survived intact. Paul's 'basic childhood country', the studio and everything in it, lay buried under a surprisingly small heap of rubble.

Paul returned to Torquay after the funeral with a sharp sense of unreality ('Coming back was a strange experience. I felt as if somehow this was my home, and the week I had spent at Southgate merely an interlude').[30] His surface calmness hid an inner confusion which he poured out to Clive in a letter full of arrogance, uncertainty and the despairing knowledge that he had not yet begun to find his own voice as a writer:

Auden, Eliot and Isherwood. Emulation was once the height of my ambition . . . but there is only one person now to whom I hold acknowledgement . . . Paul Scott . . . great or bad . . . I cannot let him linger any more in echoes . . . he has wandered about his own shore of wisdom and humanity . . . and has seen his own horizon blessed by a rising sun of recognition of his spirit . . .

ambition had led him upon many shores already claimed by the Great Ones, and his glory was reflected, but on coming into a New shadow of sorrow he did not recognise, and was not recognised, until he saw that the glory was his own reflected face. Lend me all aids to my triumph. Let there be Loud Voices and Singing when the veil arises and lets the full inspiration in him up to the skies and beyond the reach of others. I pray you think kindly of him.[31]

Genuine grief and shock underlay these disjointed visions of death and glory and celestial choirs. Paul's heroic destiny as an endangered, possibly doomed young poet had been confirmed by his mother's unconditional faith in him, by Peter's and Geoffrey's belief in his future, no doubt also by the neighbours' admiration and pity for the dashing figures the two bereaved brothers cut in khaki at this early stage of the war. Young Mrs Arnold, in the flat below the Sansoms next door on Bourne Hill, never forgot the solemn sight of Peter and Paul in uniform, kneeling in church with their parents for what everyone knew might be the last time. Clive's book of poems, *In the Midst of Death*, had been privately published that autumn. Paul himself wrote from Bourne Hill, at Clive's suggestion, to Peter Baker, who had advertised a new wartime publishing venture under the rousing title *Resurgam!* The first Resurgam broadsheet, which contained twenty-one recent poems by the editor himself, was issued from Catterick Camp where Second Lieutenant Baker was training with the Royal Artillery, and published by the Favil Press in South Kensington. Paul's fantasy of being hailed by Loud Voices and Singing was inspired by Baker's call to arms: 'It is my conviction that culture must be preserved in war-time even more securely than in peace. . . . there must be a platform for those of our younger poets who have something new, something significant to say. . . . God willing – and you, the reader, willing – here is that platform.'

Daydreaming in a letter to Clive did not prevent Paul being businesslike with Baker ('this is the thing I have been waiting for . . . a platform'),[32] and arranging for Clive to back him up with a professional reference in the next post. The lonely little poet with his head in the clouds might have surfaced again on this visit home, but he could still keep his feet on the ground. Paul regained Torquay covered with spots, confused, tired, excitable, in a highly susceptible state of suppressed emotion. A boy from the RAF playing Max Bruch's violin concerto, as an amateur soloist with the town band at a Pavilion concert, brought tears to his eyes:

I was in love for a brief period. I was in love with the dim shadow in my eyes which reflected my dear, dear brother – I thought he was Peter for a moment or two – playing as I would give my life to see him play on a platform with the applause of the crowd ringing into his soul like eternal salvation from his deep sorrow. When it was all over I said to myself: 'That is a great experience you have passed through. . . . Clap louder and you might regain the affection you have just felt, though he is rather a plain boy.'

Dear Clive. Why am I loved by so many? There are a number you know who have loved me for my spirit, and the eternal conceit is ours, ours the waiting and the sad hours of watching and the suffering ours . . . I have tried so hard to be good to my friends, yet at times have been most disloyal. Clive, I have the strangest temperament . . . I love life so passionately that I should be glad to die and know that others were at peace at last with the wind.[33]

There was a good deal of wind in Paul's letters from Torquay that December. He could never entirely suppress a glint of self-mockery when writing to Clive ('the eternal conceit is ours, ours the waiting and the sad hours of watching' was a parody of 'The Cross', itself an Eliot-esque pastiche on a theme which might fairly have been described as the importance of being earnest). But weariness and dissatisfaction were the keynotes. Office staff were not exempt from the company's regular cross-country runs up and down the steep little hills at the back of the town, and Paul encapsulated the experience in a gloomy poem about wind, bare hills, dull rain, the desolation of fields and dry leaves:

> . . . memory seems but wind
> coming and going and sweeping hills
> and I remember in grey silence
> the love of Wind and rain and tall trees which stir
> my great passion like old wounds . . .[34]

The winds of memory, 'coming and going and sweeping hills', were to become in future an essential activating agent, sowing and fertilising imaginative seed in periods like this one of blank brooding withdrawal. All his life, Paul filled his creative bucket at the well of depression. Office routine alternately distracted and maddened him. He said in a letter to Ruth that the army was driving him crazy. He pictured himself weeping in darkness and the rain falling like tears from spent lime blossom. He felt drained and dismal, and he wished this world might pass unheeded by him ('I would have given *my life* for Life – its comedies – tragedies – & beauties. I held my pen ready – & my head full of courage. I gave to everyone I loved – & now only memories assail me. That each precious memory is too precious to be recorded is my personal tragedy').[35] At the end of this letter, written on night shift in the Duty Room at the Maycliffe while waiting for an invasion that never materialised, Paul took up the Sergeant Major's scratchy borrowed pen to write yet another wan poem about rain, tears, and wind bearing the petals of youth through the orchards of youth, stirring the scented lime blossom of beauty and memories. The sentiments, the imagery, even the phrases and rhythms come from Wilde at his washiest. Dorian Gray had given his life for Life with a capital L, driven by terror of letting his youth be contaminated by age, habit and the hopeless monotony of ordinary existence.

But this kind of affectation was for Paul, as for Dorian, strategic and experimental, 'merely a method by which we can multiply our personalities'.[36] The lonely, listless little poet who wrote regularly to the Sansoms had a vigorous companion in the person of Ivan Kapinski of Torquayovitch, who burst out ten days after the funeral at Southgate and commandeered Paul's correspondence with Ruth. There is more than a touch of Dorian Gray about this decadent Muscovite with his well-appointed bachelor establishment, his butler and household staff, his daily round of parties, receptions and *conversaziones*, his gossip and scandal, his endless flirtations with society ladies and his cynical indifference to their broken hearts. But irrepressible energy remained Kapinski's chief characteristic; and his creator's taste for the seedier end of the social scale swiftly declared itself in the running saga of Little Anna, Kapinski's scullery maid, who was married off pregnant (her employer indignantly denying responsibility) in Torquay cathedral, and subsequently gave birth to such a rapid fire of babies that she was a mother of six before she was twenty. Her story in letter after letter became so convoluted and pathetic that Ruth (or Big Anna) could never be sure, even at the time, whether this second Anna really existed or not.

Kapinski wrote more freely to Anna than Paul could to Ruth, dwelling on fond memories of elderly aunts, and hoping for a favourable response from the editor of *The Russian Era* to his 'treatise on Misery' (it ran to sixty instalments in pamphlet form, priced complete with carrier 'at the welcome sum of £100').[37] Kapinski took over as president of the Jetty Pail from Paul, who promptly founded a brand new club, the Ancient Order of the Stooges, which Ruth and Clive were invited to join by completing typed application forms ('Not only am I a fully qualified stooge myself, but my father and grandfather were regular stooges, & my wife shows signs of developing along the same lines'). Kapinski's thoughts, in his blacker moods, ran much on wasted youth, death, life, art and sex. He could switch at will from urban roué to army veteran, brooding so intently for hours on end – 'He sits and watches the far-off hills when he goes at dawn to the outside lavatory'[38] – that, like Paul, he sometimes lost touch altogether with his surroundings. Often the two identities were indistinguishable. 'My life is always disjointed in these times of taxes and headaches,' Kapinski wrote from Torquayovitch. 'My 20 years weigh heavily on me. I wake at night and think I have lived twenty years. Two more lifetimes such as this, & I may be dead or ill with some disease.'[39]

Kapinski's escapades provided useful relief from a reality too wretched and uncertain to contemplate for long in the winter of 1940–41. Hitler, who had already occupied Czechoslovakia, Belgium, Holland, Austria and France, stood poised to take England. People on the south coast had got used to the bombers heading inland each night, and to hearing news of destruction next morning. Paul, doubling as Orderly Sergeant, scanned the airwaves for signs of enemy landings. He and Eddie Scilloe (whose family home in north London was bombed flat soon after Wyphurst) took it in turns to telephone battalion headquarters each morning to report on the state of the sea. Rumoured sightings of German paratroopers had caused an alert even before the company left Buckinghamshire; and it was Corporal Scilloe who had to ring round the local pubs, cinemas and billets when all troops were ordered to stand by to repel attack one Sunday night in Torquay.

As Christmas approached – for Paul, as for most of his companions, this would be the first he had ever spent away from his family – the company grew collectively jumpier. Frayed nerves reached snapping point. There was a heavy snowfall on New Year's Day 1941. Badham told his wife afterwards that some of the younger soldiers on coastal guard duty for up to forty-eight hours at a time had been driven to the verge of suicide by cold, exhaustion and exposure.[40] One of the married men in D company blew his brains out that Christmas on account of an unfaithful wife. Four months later another NCO, whose whole family had just been wiped out by a bomb, would avenge himself by shooting down a German escaping from a crashed plane in Brixham harbour. According to Eddie Scilloe, Paul was one of the quiet ones who were always the most worrying, the men who tried to bottle things up and confided their troubles to no one. Scilloe did his best, patiently checking Paul's rifle for him, rehearsing the ritual laying out of kit, even listening to the poems ('I had to grin and bear it') otherwise best kept dark in the army. He sensed the nervous tension underlying Paul's carefully controlled exterior, his apprehensiveness, the intensity of his longing for a commission. In his first months in the army, Paul had taken it for granted that the arrival of a commission was only a matter of time. Later he felt less sanguine. He hoped for an Intelligence posting (like Peter Lumley), having failed to pass the officers' selection board (Badham passed and left that February for OCTU). Again, Paul said he had been turned down because he wrote poetry and blamed his company commander, Captain Smith, for not having warned him to keep his mouth shut.[41] Smith was plump, gingery, unsoldierly, almost painfully keen to do the right military thing. Paul would later pass on some of his attributes to Teddie Bingham, Susan Layton's fiancé in the Raj Quartet, who was 'partly based on a fellow I knew in the army, when I was only a private and he was an officer . . . He was such an awful fool on the surface that he made me miserable because underneath you could see how good he was. But nobody noticed it (except, I suppose, his mother, if he still had one).'[42]

In January, 1941, Paul was overtaken by some sort of crisis, hinted at perhaps beforehand in asides to Ruth about the love and treachery of friends. 'How strange it is that people are so double-faced,' he had written to her on 22 December: 'We go through Life & trust many of them – but soon we discover their defects.' Six days later a letter from Kapinski – the last he was to write for many weeks – reported a purge, involving the imprisonment or deportation of friends to Siberia, and cheerfully contemplated the same fate for himself ('I am going to bed now as I am due at the Ministry for transportation to Siberia tomorrow. I cannot think what for. As always, Ivan Kapinski'). Paul's correspondence with the Sansoms breaks off at this point. On 18 January, he lost his stripe as lance-corporal and reverted to private.[43] Corporal Scilloe said his kit had failed to come up to scratch at a surprise inspection; Paul himself told his brother that he had been caught writing something he shouldn't have in a letter to his friend, the solicitor Howard Smith, one of several of Payne's former clients who had been charmed by Paul's eagerness, and by the infinite trouble he took to please. Peter assumed that Paul had accidentally given away dates or troop dispositions, but it seems likely that he had committed some more personal indiscretion, especially if he wrote to Smith in the same terms he used to other older men who had taken him under a protective wing ('Dear Clive, why am I loved by so many . . .'). Ruth came eventually to suspect some kind of sexual stumble, and Paul himself confirmed as much in muffled and fragmentary reports of the affair in later life.

At the time, the Sansoms corresponded anxiously with Peter, who put Paul's perturbation that January down to loneliness ('It must drive him nearly mad, not being able to see any of his friends for weeks on end'),[44] and his mercurial artist's temperament. Paul's next communication from Torquay was a chastened and characteristically enigmatic account of Siberian exile: 'My dear Ruth and Clive. I have not written for years. It seemed years. I have not wanted to write to anybody – & know you will understand! . . . Things are no different here. . . . The days follow upon each other in the same monotonous ritual. One day

Siberia will not seem so bad. It is just a matter of changing one's habits & of accustoming oneself to the climate.'[45] He supposed his bitterness would eventually pass, begged the Sansoms to visit him, asked forgiveness for his apparent lack of feeling ('I am so very sorry if this letter seems cruel in parts'), and ended with an appeal quite unlike his usual style of pretence in its simplicity and heartfelt directness: 'PS – Don't ever stop loving me.'

Clive and Ruth felt Paul was in such distress that one or other must go to him. His trouble could hardly have come at a worse time for the Sansoms, who had just begun three months' basic agricultural training in a Quaker camp run for conscientious objectors at Spicelands in Kent. They were too involved in learning how to work the land from dawn each day to freezing dusk to take time off lightly for travelling, always slow and uncertain in unheated, blacked-out wartime trains, especially along the south coast. After much deliberation Ruth made the journey in the first week of February, taking with her a poem from Clive, 'For Paul. January 1941, Torquay':

For One in Darkness

Is it a comfort to the mind to know
That other minds have been enclosed in night,
And that all nights, however dark they grow,
End in eventual and increasing light?

Each man is individual and alone,
Tramping the desert at his spirit's core,
Where all advice is dead, all friends unknown,
And faith and reason wage unceasing war –

But others walked that desert and that night,
Crossed the uncharted lands where you must go,
And found the green oases and the light . . .
Is it a comfort to the mind to know?

Ruth found Paul in a state of extreme agitation. Time was short. She booked a bed at a boarding house, and he managed to get the evening off at the last minute so that they could eat together. Paul, unable to rest at night because of tormenting dreams, broke down and wept ('It made me feel so much better just to be able to sit & tell someone all I had in my heart – I can see that I was suddenly physically overcome & unable to understand why you were with me so unexpectedly').[46] He had always talked easily to Ruth but he couldn't explain what was wrong. She understood only that he was distraught and deeply divided: 'It was a tug-of-war between destruction and creativeness.'

Nearly fifty years later, re-reading Paul's wartime letters and remembering his desperation that February, she saw his predicament more clearly: 'He joined the army and was caught out in homosexual practices. He was threatened with exposure and imprisonment by one of the senior officers. The fear of this remained with him all his life. He read Oscar Wilde and decided to control his impulses.'[47]

Exact details of the threat Paul faced, or thought he faced, are hard to establish. Some sort of showdown seems to have produced a period of turmoil, followed by the long, slow, drastic readjustment charted in his letters that spring and summer. The setback of January 1941 embittered the whole of his army career. It gave him a lasting grudge against authority: once returned to the ranks, he took the better part of a year to regain his coveted stripe, and another eighteen months to be permitted to apply again for the commission he had anticipated as a matter of course at the end of his basic training. He seldom talked in later life about his first months in the army. But twenty or thirty years later he did confide partially and obliquely in another woman friend, who reached independently much the same conclusion as Ruth. This was Mollie Hamilton, the novelist M. M. Kaye, one of the people who remained closest to Paul throughout the second half of his life. With her, as with Ruth, his confidences were enigmatic but she gathered from odd remarks that, at a particularly vulnerable stage in his development as a very young man, someone had dealt a shattering blow to his confidence. Paul never specified the sex of the person who had betrayed him – 'He never said "he" or "she". It was someone he trusted & loved & admired, who let him down badly'[48] – nor precisely what it was that had been done to him. But he said enough to suggest that the threat came from a man with some kind of sexual hold over him, that what he feared was disclosure, and that there had been an element of blackmail.

This was as far as he was ever prepared to go on the subject, and probably a good deal further than he went with anyone else. Dorian Gray had urged silence and suppression as the best method of dealing with an experience too painful to face: 'If one doesn't talk about a thing, it has never happened.'[49] The longest and most personal of the love poems written at the time of Paul's affair with Gerald was called 'It Never Happened'.[50] Dorian's strategy became habitual with Paul in later life, but what seem to be echoes of the shock he sustained in January 1941 sound constantly in his books. Something like the experience glimpsed by Ruth and others in fact clearly lies behind a relationship which fascinated Paul in fiction: the punitive connection between an obsessive authoritarian officer and the youth he selects as his victim. The older man is generally a more or less sadistic and deeply repressed homosexual, whose plight is treated warily in the early novels but with increasing explicitness in later books ('the truth was he was punishing himself for sins only his subconscious mind had knowledge of . . .').[51] Subsequent experiences supplied new settings and supporting characters, fresh twists, an alternative model for the older man, until the original incident, coming and going on the winds of memory, probably no longer bears any close resemblance to the relationship between, say, Major Craig and Cadet Ramsay in *The Mark of the Warrior*, or Major Reid and Lieutenant Sutton in *The Chinese Love Pavilion*. But it reappeared for the last time, in its simplest and atmospherically most autobiographical form, in the story of Major Merrick and Lance-Corporal Pinker (called Pinky) in *A Division of the Spoils*, the fourth and final novel in the Raj Quartet.

Pinker is twenty, 'a reserved, studious and hard-working young man',[52] drafted into the army and shipped out to India in wartime, sheltered, unworldly, young for his age, only just beginning to realise and accept the nature of his homosexuality: 'He knew he couldn't help being what he was and he didn't hate himself, but he couldn't have borne to be found out.'[53] He makes tentative advances to an Indian boy, which to his joy are accepted, only to find himself caught out by Merrick, blackmailed into complicity, reported to his superiors and left to await arrest, exposure and imprisonment. The physical symptoms of panic are described with extraordinary vividness: Pinker suffers giddiness, nausea, vomiting, diarrhoea, all the involuntary emissions said to afflict convicted men approaching the gallows. Shock gives way to despair, lethargy, numbness, a period of semi-consciousness as tormented days merge indistinguishably into sleepless nights. Worse even than the unbearable present is the prospect of future disgrace for his family. Pinker's commanding officer affords what protection he can: 'Richardson's was the last friendly face he was likely to see until he came out of prison. But he did not think he would ever come out. He would die of terror and humiliation. He hoped so. How could he ever face his parents again if he survived to be sent home?'[54] After several days of excruciating suspense, hope begins to rekindle as the expected charge fails to materialise. The affair peters out with a new posting for Pinker, who weeps from relief as he packs his possessions, including the new wrist watch he had meant to give away as a love token:

Pinky stopped, sat down, and looked at the watch: the gift of his parents when he joined up. Then he threw it on the floor and stamped on it with the heel of his boot until it was in pieces. This was what he had done with his life so far . . .[55]

Paul's parents gave him a gold watch as an early twenty-first birthday present when he went home on leave in the second week of March 1941.[56] That month marked a decisive turning point. Like Pinker, Paul set his boot, metaphorically speaking, on the life lived by his previous self and ground it underfoot. Ruth's visit to Torquay had come at the height of his despair, when he couldn't sleep or talk coherently or control his tears. The letter he wrote her and Clive immediately afterwards showed the first signs of recovery: 'Quite suddenly I understand why it is that I have been tortured so – and that is that it has been necessary – & that I should unburden my heart at an unbearable stage was also intended for my "Brush with the Spirit" as you say, Ruth – & now the first milestone is reached – & I know that as the way continues & at times I shall be tortured again – I shall know that I shall live to see happiness again. O, my heart goes out to you. Paul.'[57]

By the time he wrote this the worst was behind him. His equilibrium was further restored by the prospect of going home for a week on 6 March for the 'glorious Bean-feast'[58] laid on by his mother, who had hoarded ration coupons, supplies, precious tins of dried milk and coffee for months to celebrate Paul's coming of age. Geoffrey also managed to get leave, and Peter turned up at the last minute on a twenty-four-hour pass. The Blitz on London continued that spring: a bomb in Fox Lane in February demolished a house opposite the Woodman pub, killing a passer-by, while another fell in the roadway further up Bourne Hill, tearing up drains, destroying gas pipes and smashing the neighbours' windows. Mrs Scott was roped in as a fire-fighter by the Women's Voluntary Service, provoking much ribaldry from Paul at the thought of his father left in command of the kitchen ('also he remarked considering the way he & Peter were pushed around when at home, he feels sure it will be nothing for me to tackle a bomb,' his mother reported drily).[59] This was the first time the family had been together since the aunts' deaths, and it did them all good. Paul feasted, paid visits, inspected bomb craters, received tributes and donations (including, from Charles Laughton's aunt's bottom drawer, an attaché case, a set of mauve stationery and an elderly bar of chocolate – 'or was it soap? The parcel was wrapped in a way which would have made the Ministry of Supply weep & tear its hair. I did').[60]

He returned to Torquay on 13 March in an altogether calmer mood, although muffled echoes of former distress still sound occasionally in his letters. 'Have you heard that I am crazy, and am going to be locked up in a dungeon for the rest of the war?' he wrote to Ruth on 14 March. 'Will you come and give me biscuit and cake through the bars of the cage or dungeon so that I can remember my former life. It is all

CIVILIANS BRAVELY ENDURE WHILE BRITAIN GIRDS HER LOINS

Brute force hits civilians.

WOMEN KILLED
Memorial Homes Damaged

head. I've got it as a memento!"

Mr. Bester added that it was well for him that the tile came down flat. "Had it come down edgeways," he added with a wry smile, "it might have been a different story and someone else would have told it to you!"

A neighbour, who enjoyed the distinction of being, at one time, the oldest postman in London, had a very narrow escape from injury. He was walking along a public footpath near the end house which was demolished, when a friend in the main road called to him.

The retired postman, Mr. "Johnnie" Brooks, responded to the call and walked away from the doomed houses. They crashed behind him! The passageway in which he had been standing was choked by falling brickwork.

There were some forty to fifty people within a twenty yards radius of the scene, and a few complained of shock.

was treated for shock, but soon recovered. The child was unhurt.

Mr. George Bester told a newspaper reporter that he was attending to his damaged windows,

Wyphurst in ruins after the explosion of the bomb which killed Paul's aunts in November 1940.

Private Scott, sketched by himself, returning home on leave in March 1941 to be greeted by his mother in her new role as WVS recruit.

very difficult, and one cannot think what is going to happen from one day to another. I have often tried to read my thoughts, but I am such an awful speller in my subconscious.' In imagination, if not in fact, Paul had clearly anticipated the same sort of consequences as Pinker, whose fears of guardroom and glasshouse were scarcely exaggerated. A charge of homosexuality, or gross immorality, carried if anything even graver penalties in the army than in civilian life. Soldiers had no choice but to accept conformity as, in Paul's words, 'the safest and most comfortable thing'.[61] More than a quarter of a century later, he explained why this policy suited him in a long, reflective letter to his nineteen-year-old younger daughter, newly installed at university and experiencing her own first taste of institutional rough treatment:

Day by day you can't, in any organisational life, fight the system. You can think your thoughts . . . sometimes to get the *best* out of people . . . it is sensible to drift in their direction, to see where they take you, still thinking your thoughts. But sometimes you find your thoughts adjusting, getting nearer to their right level. Meanwhile you haven't alienated the person whose level is so different from your own. It sounds a bit creepy, and perhaps erosive of integrity, but in the end it is other people you have to live with, and integrity is never a hard and fast thing that you're born with. It is malleable, to the extent that year by year you become a different person. . . . Not sure what I'm trying to say at this juncture; except don't despair . . . you are probably a bit like me, a very slow maturer . . .

Certainly no one is standing over you, like a sort of shadow of Nemesis – at least not from this end! It may look as if they are, from your end . . . but perhaps they look like Nemesis mainly because you resist them inwardly.[62]

For Paul himself this was the heart of the matter. Whatever pressures the army may have brought to bear at the beginning of 1941, he had come up against something he dreaded and distrusted in himself. More than any external threat he feared, like Dorian Gray, 'the still more poisonous influences that came from his own temperament'.[63] Looking back six months later, he said his old self had died that spring and been replaced by another.[64] He fell back increasingly on Wildean imagery of masks and mirrors to describe his predicament. His letters are full of the divisions that fascinated Dorian: the split between body and spirit, the frightening gap between the real face and its beautiful, unreal, eternally perfect reflection in the portrait or mirror. Dorian Gray had opted for an image uncontaminated by experience. Wilde himself, immersed in the horror and humiliation of prison seven years later, resolved on the opposite course in one of the most sombre and haunting passages of *De Profundis*:

The important thing, the thing that lies before me, the thing that I have to do if the brief remainder of my days is not to be marred, maimed and incomplete, is to absorb into my nature all that has been done to me, to make it part of me, to accept it without complaint, fear or reluctance.[65]

This Wildean consolation came to mean much to Paul. It supplied a kind of text or key to his career as a novelist; it enabled him to contemplate his younger self at the end of his life without recrimination or pity; it lay behind the practical advice he always gave to other writers, and to those who wanted to write. It reappears in its pithiest form, midway through *A Division of the Spoils*, in Captain Richardson's parting words of comfort to Lance-Corporal Pinker: 'No experience, however disagreeable, is ever wasted.'[66]

Paul said that the conflict between his mother and aunts in a divided house when he was thirteen had affected his ability to express emotion; and the shock he sustained in the army seven years later seems to have put the lid on it. He told Ruth his thoughts were unreadable because he was such an awful speller in his subconscious, but his letters to her that spring and summer spell out clearly enough his intention of burying one side of himself: the sentimental narcissist, the effusive and effeminate little poet with the flowing golden hair and silver tongue, the dandy he told Muriel Spark long afterwards had surfaced in him between the ages of eighteen and twenty. He pictured himself approaching a junction: '& Paul – what of him – shall he go on – or backward. Shall he know reality or dreams,' he wrote to Ruth on 3 April. Over the next few months, in spite of hesitation and waverings, he turned his back on the daydreamer with his head in the clouds, settling instead for the soldier and realist with both feet on the ground. By 26 August, he had effectively split in two – 'myself is glancing over my shoulder as I write this letter' – and he said the self behind his shoulder was the one who had been suppressed in the spring: 'In what way have I changed? In no way. In what way have I looked at myself of late? I have gazed in the same mirror but seen a different reflection – that is the only way I can explain the change in myself.'

This was Paul's answer to Ruth's continued perplexity about his sexual preferences. The affair with Gerald Armstrong, long since over in practice, had come to a full stop with what turned out to be Paul's last visit to Forest Hill on his leave in March.[67] There was no clean or immediate break with the old Paul, who would still on occasion wistfully size up his chances with the more civilised and better-looking of his army companions (he was attracted, like Pinker, not to younger boys but to sensitive, vigorous and athletic contemporaries), and who still intermittently lamented his state in stanzas about lost youth and lime blossom. He had been plucked from his original slough of despond, immediately after Ruth's visit in February, by a letter from Peter Baker, promising to include something of Paul's in a projected anthology, *Poets of This War*, and holding out hopes of devoting a whole *Resurgam!* Broadsheet to his religious trilogy.[68] Baker's encouragement could hardly have been better timed. It was not much more than a year since Paul had made designs in his head for an imaginary first published collection: even without a lime-blossom colophon, the Broadsheet was a dream come true, and perhaps its author remembered Wilde's warning in *De Profundis*: 'The first volume of Poems that in the very springtide of his manhood a young man sends forth to the world should be like a blossom or flower . . . It should not be burdened by the weight of a terrible and revolting tragedy; a terrible revolting scandal.'[69]

It was Clive, apprehensive as always for Paul and nothing if not practical, who had persuaded Baker to publish the trilogy by privately offering to subsidise costs on condition that his contribution should not be disclosed, then or later, to Paul.[70] The scheme worked admirably. Paul threw himself into preparations, urging Clive to supply an introduction,[71] begging both Sansoms to help find a title, and settling eventually for *I, Gerontius* by way of Robert Graves' novel, *I, Claudius*. Paul spent his twenty-first birthday book token from Geoffrey on the second of the *Claudius* novels, together with Eliot's two new poems, 'Burnt Norton' and 'East Coker', the latter published the previous autumn as a highly successful pamphlet by Faber.[72] He was contemplating a second assault on Fabers himself, once the trilogy had come out, as well as planning publicity (he had furtively rearranged W. H. Smith's book display at Palmers Green in favour of Clive's *In the Midst of Death*, and looked forward to a prominent place himself on Smith's Torquay bookstall), and discussing interpretations with Ruth, who was to read the entire work at the Poetry Society in Portman Square in July. Paul was jubilant. His debt to Clive, greater even than he knew, was promptly acknowledged in a poem ('I am writing my masterpiece!') called 'Out of the Darkness'.[73]

This turned out to be yet another rambling bulletin from the hinterland of consciousness ('a man carrying a cross/ walking the Hill/ despairing hoping/ searching beyond despair/ and beyond hope . . .').[74] It was taken down according to Paul as if from dictation the week he got back from leave, and completed one night the week after, between 2 a.m. and 4.30 a.m., in the room he shared at the Maycliffe with three other soldiers who snored throughout. He said it was the work of a soul in torment, but the Sansoms, celebrating the end of their Spicelands training with a weekend in mid April at

Torquay, remained sceptical. 'I remember crouching upon the floor of the Clydesdale Hotel,' Paul wrote nostalgically four years later to Clive, '& reading the rather absurd verse to you & Ruth, perfectly aware of the blank looks of amazement on both your faces ... I realised that the whole thing was not an overwhelming literary masterpiece.'[75] Paul commemorated this visit at the end of April in a playlet, 'Farewell' by Ivan Kapinski,[76] depicting Ivan saying goodbye to Anna and Stepan under a clouded sky on Torquay railway station: although he always remained attached to the Sansoms, fond of Ruth and profoundly grateful to Clive, 'Farewell' marked the beginning of the end of the most intense phase of their triangular friendship.

CHAPTER FIVE

The same mirror but a different reflection

Paul was by this time moving towards a different allegiance, first signalled a month earlier with a letter signed in three persons: 'Ivan Kapinski. Paul Scott. Jacques de Matelot (new one)'. 'Jacques is whimsical and nearly twentyone,' Paul explained in a postscript. 'He is very amorous and fond of ladies.'[1] The whole company was making a determined effort that spring to overcome its collective inexperience and gaucherie with girls. Eddie Scilloe said that of the thirty men who had joined up in his platoon in July 1940, only two possessed girlfriends until they sorted themselves out at regular company dances in Torquay's Co-op Hall or the Marine Spa Hotel, clumping round the floor in army boots with WAAFs from Babbacombe and local hospital nurses. One sign of the change in Paul was attendance at these weekly hops. Another was the jokey, anonymous running commentary on D Company he started writing that March in the regimental paper, *The Dragon*: 'It does not interest me – it won't interest you,' he wrote, enclosing a cutting for Clive, 'I just wanted you to see how "normally" I could write!'[2]

Paul launched himself on what he called 'the normal road'[3] with a spectacular ten-day bender, starting on 25 March, his twenty-first birthday, and throwing a party two days later with crates of beer at the end of the Marine Spa dance, after which he had to be delivered back to the Maycliffe in a taxi by a waitress from the Epicure, and put to bed by his room-mates. Opportunities for debauchery in the blackout in Torquay's respectable pubs, dives and dens like the Epicure, the Burlington, the Gibbons Hotel and Paul's favourite, Addison's Café, were strictly limited, if only by chronic shortage of funds among both nurses and soldiers, but Paul made the most of them. 'I have now an awful reputation in Torquay,' he wrote complacently to Ruth at the end of his bender, ' – & cannot go into my favourite haunts without meeting females of a notorious character. "Mary of the Epicure", "José of the Gibbons", "Dot" etc. etc. . . .'[4] His mood veered wildly between elation and despondency. The barmaids he teased, flirted and joked with, and who generally finished up telling him their life stories, tended to regard him admiringly as something of a card ('Right, ducks. You are a one – always knows what he wants, does Paul').[5]

With men he was less assured. Peter Lumley, whose twenty-first birthday fell on Sunday 30 March, five days after Paul's, ran into him drinking alone that night in a pub. Lumley, depressed on his own account by the collapse of his date with a girl, pooled his dejection with Paul, who responded by making a tentative pass, and couldn't help shedding tears when it was politely rejected. Both were initially taken aback, then drawn together by their common sorrow. 'Peter & I were discussing my being queer,' Paul reported to Ruth. 'He's not – but understands – coming from Chelsea.' Coming from Chelsea also made Lumley more tactful than most about the plight of an unpublished poet: 'Peter is fond of poetry & he read my new one & thought it was marvellous – he told me quite honestly – he is always very frank.'[6] The pair moved on from the Epicure to the Gibbons, growing steadily merrier, with Lumley urging Paul to ask up to ten guineas for *I, Gerontius*, and insisting wildly that there was a living to be made as a poet. But the lasting impression Paul made that Sunday night was of unhappiness and confusion. 'He was very mixed-up in more ways than one,' Peter Lumley said long afterwards: 'nice looking. Gentle and quiet, rather unsophisticated, and *very sad*.'

Paul produced the opposite effect at the Marine Spa two days later, when he strode across the floor to a group of nurses from Rosehill Children's Hospital, singled out the most attractive and asked her to dance. She was twenty-one, enchantingly pretty and popular, putting in time as a junior nurse while waiting to join the WAAF. Paul said she had poetry in her eyes: to her he seemed tall, slim and as handsome as he was charming. She told him she liked reading, played the piano, and had taken elocution lessons at boarding school.[7] He called her the Girl with the Golden Voice. Her real name was Barbara Phillips ('Barbara gets excused all over the place when she is on the floor,' Paul reported with satisfaction to the surprised Sansoms).[8] They danced together for the rest of the evening, and Paul had fixed a date for Barbara's day off the following Saturday by the time he rolled home at half past one in the morning. Next day Paul wrote to Ruth, itemising the almost unbroken whirl of celebration in ten hectic days since his birthday, and describing the scene when he turned up that evening with his brother

Peter (on a twenty-four-hour pass) and Lumley back at the Gibbons:

There they all were lined up at the Bar – Mary – Dot – José behind it – thousands & thousands of faces all saying 'Ducks'.

Then there is Pauline who looks like Margaret Sullavan – and Mary Bennett – there *was* Joyce Bachelor (only 17 – & never been kissed) – Gladys of the Co-op who sat in the most expensive seats at the cinema – a new one is Kay of the Burlington who gives one a free entrance ticket to the cinema for a free one at the dance . . . You may think I'm doing wrong – but I'm not – here is the truth as I see it. The woman at Addison's has a son in the navy – & is still having to work for a living – Dot is a kind-hearted woman who was so pleased that two young soldiers took out her landlady for a bit of fun [Paul and a friend called Reg Baker had insisted on treating the pianist from Addison's Café]. Mary is a girl who 'loves us all' & spends her money on us all to give us a good time. She has a squint eye & glasses – probably has some secret sorrow she is hiding. José of the Gibbons is a prostitute who doesn't mind shouting it from the roof tops – she has a defiant look in her eyes, has once had a classical beauty which has been ruined by vice & hardship.

Pauline has her husband in the army. 'I don't like leading this sort of life but its better than sitting at home & remembering – ' Mary Bennett is the same. Kay of the Burlington is out for a good time. 'Why bother to save up when one day you will be dead' – But Barbara – whom I have known for an hour or less has a calm clear vision – & music & poetry in her eyes. She is a nurse – need more be said. She speaks beautifully – & Paul – what of him – shall he go on or backward. Shall he know reality or dreams. He is 21 – & is afraid he will never be 22 . . . Yet if these things all come again – & he is not there – he would be happy & every time a limetree blossoms he will sing . . . for he has walked in Beauty & has seen the Despair in beauty – & the kindliness in ugly things.[9]

The writer of this letter stands poised between his two selves: the familiar dreamer – with his artificial tears and his everlasting lime blossom and his earnest attachment to Beauty and Despair – is briefly elbowed aside by an altogether tougher customer, an unsentimental observer sympathetically alert to the individual anxieties and loneliness behind the painted façades and professional bonhomie of barmaids, waitresses, receptionists, the hard-working good-time girls of wartime Torquay. It is a curious aside from an immature twenty-one-year-old with troubles enough of his own. It sounds, however faintly, Paul's authentic note as a writer, the voice of his own which both Clive and Lumley had urged him to cultivate, the voice of the small boy who read Shakespeare's *Henry VIII* for the sake of Katherine of Aragon, and the voice of the novelist who would one day give unexpected dignity and power to lonely, defeated, stoical, unwanted women like Marion Hurst, Edwina Crane and Barbie Batchelor.

Paul kept his date with Barbara on Saturday, 5 April, walking her back afterwards under a bright moon through the steep woods at the back of the children's hospital. Two days later he wrote her a poem, 'Strange Meeting', 'To B—'.[10] She was struck almost equally by the poem (apart from a token lime, she made him think of apple blossom, old cathedrals and green meadows under cool summer skies), and by the fact that Paul asked for it back (he sent it to the editor of *Poetry Quarterly*, who turned it down). For the rest of the month they spent every spare moment together, dancing, walking and talking. 19 and 20 April was the weekend of the Sansoms' visit when Paul first realised he was not a natural disciple of Eliot. There was a route march the Friday afterwards, twenty-two miles in full pack to Teignmouth with no exemption even for HQ clerks. Paul got back just in time to meet Barbara at Addison's, only to find she had promised to produce him at the Spa dance to please her superior, Sister Avery, whom Paul dimly remembered having met. He capitulated reluctantly, lightheaded with exhaustion, beginning also to feel oppressed by Barbara's boarding-school background, construing her diffidence as disapproval and claiming she refused to dance with him, which was hardly surprising once she found herself playing Rosaline to Penny Avery's Juliet. 'As things went on, Penny and I danced together and . . . I suddenly found myself madly in love with her, and we were talking as if we had known each other for ages; I told her all about my poetry . . .' Paul wrote next day to Clive. 'She has a warmth, an emotional outlook just like mine; she likes the same little things as myself . . . She is engaged, but then I can't worry about that. I suppose this sounds rather like a Dorothy Dickson Open Letter in the *Daily Mirror*, What Shall I do Now?'[11]

What Paul did next was to concentrate his considerable powers of will, imaginative sympathy and emotional magnetism on Penny Avery. The speed of their courtship was a legend ever afterwards among their family and friends. She had been struck the moment she saw him by his crispness, his dignity, his compelling yellow-brown eyes, above all by an intrinsic authority she couldn't understand in a private soldier. The tune was 'In the Mood' the first time he asked her to dance: 'My heart skipped a beat. His arm round my waist was loose, impersonal, as was the long cool hand that held my own as we moved onto the floor. This may may be a poet but he was no dancer. Stiffly, he held me at arm's length.'[12] Paul's aloofness, his air of distance and untouchability, his exotic reputation in that company as a poet, only intensified his attraction. He told her at once that they were made for one another, and that he intended to marry her. The two felt themselves enclosed at the centre of a magic circle in which neither could focus on anyone else. Penny was dazzled. In the next few heady

weeks Paul overwhelmed her, just as he took command of their group
in the bar, insisting that everyone drink along the shelves from right to
left, sampling the bottles at random in whatever order they came – gin,
whisky, rum, lemonade, liqueurs – with each person paying in turn for
his or her round. It was a trick he had learned at his mother's knee,
when the two boys would finish up whatever the grown-ups were
drinking. It mesmerised Penny, who from that first day had eyes for no
one but Paul.

She was lively and strikingly handsome with a natural poise
enhanced by rich auburn hair and elegant long legs. The rumour ran
that she had totted up at least seven proposals by the time she met Paul,
and had been engaged three times already. She had been ceremonially
piped aboard the ship of her current fiancé, a naval commander named
Pawle ('from whom she receives unwanted Bridge lessons by post,'
wrote Paul,[13] enjoying his conquest over an unseen but not inconspicuous rival stationed that summer in Alexandria). She was a highly
successful nurse, advancing rapidly up the ladder of promotion, older
than Paul although still absurdly young for a Ward Sister, senior to
him in rank, and in some ways far more experienced. At that
highwater point in her career, she struck everyone who met her as
formidably capable in her own right. Self-reliant, energetic, resourceful, she was everything that appealed most to Paul in a woman. But she
had also a gentleness and deep-seated humility which he found
irresistible. Her mother had died when she was a baby, leaving her and
an older sister to a father ill equipped to take responsibility for two
small daughters. Penny, brought up by a series of unenthusiastic
relations, had had independence thrust upon her at an early age. If
Paul's problem at home had been the overriding urge to escape from
his mother's domination, Penny as a child had found no figure in
authority who could return her love, no one she might turn to, lean on
or trust. In this sense she was, as Paul said, made for him. Penny's self-
abnegation matched Paul's longstanding and increasingly urgent need
to assert himself. 'Paul Scott didn't court nor woo me,' she wrote long
afterwards:

He was there. He took charge of everything, and made decisions. He
corrected me when my opinions of people, events, and situations did not
coincide with his own. . . . He could discuss singers, ballet, plays, opera, in
depth, and I was bewildered, and yet I listened to him, learning from him,
being kept on my mental toes, and I found quite soon that I agreed with him,
and fell in with his wishes. . . . Paul was sound, reliable. He was the anchor I
searched for.[14]

One of Penny's charms for Paul was precisely her eager receptivity:

unlike his mother – or the Sansoms when it came to poetry – she could be counted on never to criticise or answer back. After the past few turbulent months her soothing attentions proved infinitely restful. Paul's growing happiness that summer preoccupied him to the partial exclusion even of *I, Gerontius*, which came out at the end of May and was immediately noticed (in a paragraph prudently submitted beforehand by the author) only by the *Palmers Green and Southgate Gazette*.[15] By this time he was in any case immersed in army manoeuvres. The battalion moved in mid-May to Stover camp at Newton Abbot for a month's intensive training. 'We shall be out most of the week playing Cowboys and Indians,' wrote Paul (who was shortly afterwards shot to pieces by one of his own section with a mock bomb – coal dust, flour and water wrapped in the *Daily Mirror* – in a surprise attack on company HQ).[16] He said he loathed almost everybody and that they were all, himself included, wearing masks.

Newton Abbot was at least within reach of Penny and Torquay, which was more than could be said for the company's next posting in June to Falmouth in Cornwall: 'personally, I think it is one of the most loathsome provincial towns I have ever set eyes upon,' wrote Paul dismally, reverting to Jacques de Matelot's expressive tongue to convey his feelings: '*Et après avoir vu les femmes terribles de Newton Abbot – et les femmes de la ville de Falmouth, je me dis "Tout mes jours je m'appellerai – Bachelor"* '.[17] Paul took time off between stints of anti-aircraft duty to visit his father's ancient Wright cousins, Louie, Mabel and Ethel, in refuge from the Blitz at Flushing, only to find the three sisters whose grim disapproval had darkened his childhood transformed into a trio of charming little old ladies, set out on a sofa and simply delighted to see him ('*not a bit like the Wrights*', he reported disbelievingly to Peter). In an autobiographical fragment long afterwards he said they made him feel 'big-booted and ham-fisted', insolently masculine with his army boots and his big hands blunted and dirtied by manipulating a Lee Enfield rifle. 'What did they make of the change in me, I wondered. But perhaps in a world so full of change I was something stable from the past.'[18]

Change was much on Paul's mind throughout that long, hot summer. At the end of June his platoon spent a week in the remote and beautiful Cornish hamlet of Mylor Creek, bathing, sunbathing and boating in their spare time. Paul and an equally unskilful friend rowed themselves 'across, and occasionally up, the creek'[19] in a dinghy belonging to the best-selling novelist Howard Spring (a favourable notice from Spring was said after the war to be worth up to a thousand copies sold: Paul, alternating with him as a book reviewer in the 1960s on *Country Life*, was not well received when he rashly confessed to having been one of the private soldiers who helped themselves to the great man's boat in wartime).[20] Spring had retired to the banks of the creek in 1939 to write *Fame is the Spur*. By June 1941 he was working on his memoirs – 'High up in the air the barrage balloons that float over Falmouth have been suspended like huge silver sharks nosing into a grey sea'[21] – while Paul, a true Londoner, basking in his borrowed boat, gazed stonily 'at the deep sincerity of the Cornish landscape' and dreamed 'of Piccadilly at 2 p.m. on a Saturday in May or June'. He missed Penny badly: 'I long for Torquay, and all that Torquay meant to me.'[22]

But seven days of tranquillity and torpor at Mylor were what he needed for a kind of mental and emotional stocktaking, 'completely up-ending myself and having a brain spring-clean'.[23] He had been reading Charles Morgan's *The Voyage*, which is on one level a schematic, sub-Balzacian debate about marriage, artistic bohemianism versus bourgeois respectability, the conventional lives people lead and the possibility of their changing course. 'I feel . . . as if I were reading – not my history – but an appreciation of my life', Paul wrote. 'It has been a great help.'[24] He couldn't quite see himself as the hero, Barbet Hazard, an unworldly innocent who lives with his mother in provincial nineteenth-century France, writing lyrics and minding the family wine business, eventually throwing it up to realise his dream by becoming a simple peasant craftsman making barrels. Paul had in some ways more in common with the book's other protagonist, the Parisian diseuse Thérèse Despreux, who builds a career by ruthlessly sacrificing all human ties for the sake of her art. The book ends with the pair of them sailing into the sunset, united in spirit, separated in the flesh, each following his or her own individual star. Metaphorical voyages, journeys and travelling occupied Paul's thoughts a good deal over the next few weeks. He envied Clive's voyage to a new way of life as a market gardener at Worth in Surrey, and longed to embark on his own. In the poem he wrote that summer, 'Mylor Creek', the poet is a traveller at journey's end, resting by the seashore, like Paul, who spent his last Sunday at Mylor alone, looking out to sea and remembering the deserted beach at Felixstowe where he had sat with Peter the day before war was declared. 'Mylor Creek',[25] which celebrates escape from past danger and looks forward to renewal and rebirth in the future, becomes in the second of its three sections a love poem to Penny:

> Yes, I could sit here and watch
> those tiny sails
> feeling almost happy again.
> I could compare this shore

with one I knew before my pain
had stretched my limbs
enabling me to reach from shore to shore
but see no beauty anywhere.
But here – Yes. I could be happy.
If I should hear your voice
like a dim echo, vibrating those steep walls
now green with sea-hands, and sea-care,
this place would be my choice . . .
Yes, here – this journey's end –
forgetting-place, full with a dozen memories
might be a fitting place
to meet, and plan what will come later in the year.

The event being planned for later in the year was Paul's marriage to Penny, and it was no accident that he put it at the centre of the poem which, in his view, marked yet another complete change in him as a writer. The passing of his old writing self was commemorated on 4 July at the Poetry Society's 'Resurgence Reading', organised by Peter Baker, with Ruth reading *I, Gerontius* and another young poet, Patricia Ledward, reading from Clive's poems ('I should give my life to be there, I think,' Paul had written, holed up in the West country).[26] The programme was disrupted in the end by Frances Scott who fell into a fit of nervous coughing midway through Paul's poem, got up to go, and could be heard descending every step of the uncarpeted stone stairs leading from the first floor at Portman Square to the flagged hall below, then explaining what had happened in ringing tones to the doorman.

She had cause to feel agitated, both by the event itself which was a culmination she had planned for and dreamed of almost since Paul was a baby, and by the ordeal to come, for Paul proposed bringing Penny home to meet his parents at the end of July. It was a confrontation dreaded by both sides. Paul announced his intention to Penny so curtly that she wondered if she had done something wrong: an impression confirmed when she met Paul's mother, who looked her over on the doorstep at 63, Bourne Hill with an expression so fierce and a ramrod bearing so stiff with disapproval that Penny felt sure she must have offended. Mrs Scott, who showed no emotion in public, had even stronger reason in private to find her visitor intimidating. No one had ever seriously encroached before on her monopoly of Paul. She alternated between shutting Penny out altogether, enveloping Paul in reminiscences of the past or plans for the future, and overwhelming her with detailed instructions as to how to look after him. It was made plain from the start that no matter what Penny might do she could never hope to come up to Mrs Scott's standard as housekeeper, companion or muse.

Paul, whose part cannot have been easy, arranged excursions to get him and Penny out of the house. They took tea with Pat Ledward at her flat in Earls Court, going on to a prom concert and coming back afterwards for coffee. There were outings with Peter to see Hermione Gingold in cabaret, and *Coppélia* at Sadler's Wells, as well as a visit to the Armstrongs, who had moved to Stanmore.[27] It was altogether a tense and uneasy visit; disturbing for Penny, who felt she was picking her way unaided over a minefield for which she had not been prepared, and perhaps more unsettling still for her hostess, who must have felt as if a mine thought to be safely under control had blown up in her face. Paul's relief, when at last they set off with their bags for the station, was so violent that Penny was mystified. He had first proposed to her in a crowded dance hall, and he put a ring on her engagement finger in the railway carriage packed with people on the journey back to Torquay. It was a family heirloom, the green stone in a battered silver setting which Mrs Scott claimed had been hacked from the finger of an ancestor hanged as a highwayman.[28] Whatever the truth of its origins, all parties understood well enough that it was an ominous ring.

But Paul's mind was made up in that week of demolition, upheaval and partings. Shortly afterwards he sent Peter a poem written in the ironic modern manner, clearly a relief after the solemn quasi-religious incantations and the gushing Brooke phase: 'Charing Cross Station'[29] is an account of seeing Peter off on the train back to billets over congealing cups of coffee in the station buffet. It describes the strains of the past week on leave, the tensions and cross-currents at home, the brothers' mutual reluctance either to look forward to an uncertain future or to evoke the past by playing Tchaikovsky's Sixth Symphony ('on the whole we do it rather well – the careless concern of being unconcerned;/ the "Do you remember?" and/ "After the war", so and so . . .').

Peter was posted to Gibraltar in September, and Paul's own coveted Intelligence posting arrived in August, which meant a week's trial before being made up to corporal and installed at Brigade HQ in Totnes. The job had been originally offered to Eddie Scilloe who, reluctant to leave D company himself and knowing how desperately Paul longed to move, had managed to pass on the posting. Paul told Clive in a letter which simultaneously hinted at marriage and gave news of Private Kapinski, said to have both feet in the grave as far back as the spring, last heard of serving with the Russian army near Smolensk (the German invasion of Russia was sweeping down on

Penny Avery.

Penny and Paul at Bourne Hill.

Wedding group, Torquay, 23 October 1941: bride and groom flanked by best man and bridesmaid, Percy Avery on right, Tom and Frances Scott on left.

Leningrad, then Moscow, meeting ferocious resistance all through the summer and autumn of 1941), now reported missing altogether. Paul could hardly have declared more emphatically his sense that he had done with one side of himself. He spelt out his position even more clearly to Ruth on 26 August.

Winter is approaching again . . . I *must* find my new way of Life soon or I shall rapidly grow stale again as I did last winter. And it was not *I* who was recalled to Life in the Spring. Myself is glancing over my shoulder even as I write this letter . . . In what way have I changed? In no way. In what way have I looked at myself of late. I have gazed in the same mirror but seen a different reflection – that is the only way I can explain the change in myself. You know to what I refer. It was a passing phase essential to my necessarily wide understanding of Life. . . .

I lay my new self – or my own self newly expressed – before you for your consideration. In the meantime, please write . . . In my detachment I seem to grow even more dependent upon others. Loneliness has a great deal to do with it. Even though now I have someone who returns the affection I have thrown out to the winds, even though we are wildly happy, & sensibly considerate in that mutual affection – we are still both lonely, because we must walk unmasked among masks, which is far worse than wearing yourself a mask.

On 30 August Paul travelled up to town to say goodbye to his brother on embarkation leave for Gibraltar, where Peter received a telegram announcing Paul's official engagement on 23 September. 'He couldn't believe it,' said Geoffrey Ridehalgh, who vividly remembered the enormity of that announcement, and the foreboding it caused: '*We couldn't believe it.*' The marriage took place exactly one month later on 23 October 1941, in Christ Church, Torquay. Like many wartime weddings, it was hasty, impromptu, ill attended, fraught with misgiving, resentment, and hurt feeling on the part of family and friends. The bride, radiant in chalk blue with a posy of violets, was given away by her father, Percy Avery, who arrived alone because Penny's stepmother said she had better things to do than attend weddings in wartime.[30] Mrs Scott had threatened not to come either ('*She* couldn't believe it,' said Geoffrey. 'The war was bad enough. *But now this* . . .'), relenting only at the last possible moment just in time to catch the train with Josser in tow. Paul said afterwards that all he could ever remember about his own wedding was the sound of himself and his best man, Reg Baker, clumping up the echoing aisle of the empty church in their army boots (which was odd, because wedding photos show he was married in his own civilian clothes). If Paul's friends had been incredulous, Penny's were apprehensive: the bridesmaid and the best man had each privately warned her to be careful. Even her father, charmed by Paul's deference and his habit of addressing the older man as 'sir', urged her not to become a slave to her husband's whim. The only two people absolutely certain they had done the right thing were the bride and groom. 'I married a poet and I was terrified,' said Penny, whose qualms were strictly literary: 'I didn't know anything about poetry, and I didn't know what it might mean. But I wanted that man.'[31]

They spent the afternoon at the cinema watching Laurence Olivier and Vivien Leigh in *Lady Hamilton*,[32] retired that night to the Clydesdale Hotel, and made the most of the remaining five days of Paul's leave in the spot he had dreamed of at Mylor, the Regent Palace Hotel at Piccadilly Circus. The time passed in a whirl of London pubs, cinemas and theatres, window-shopping in the Regent's Arcade, and a literary lunch with Pat Ledward at which Penny was presented at last to the Sansoms. The introduction was not a success: they tried but failed to be nice about nursing, while she felt hurt and excluded by the private Jetty Pail jargon – 'crazy talk' – they shared with Paul. Corporal and Mrs Paul Scott returned to Devon to start married life in a rented room of their own – 11, Denby Road, Paignton – where they met whenever they could make Paul's days off from Brigade HQ coincide with Penny's from the Rosehill Hospital. Their den (or denski to Ivan Kapinski, who still put in the odd appearance that autumn) was a large ground-floor room with a big bay window, space for Paul's books from Bourne Hill, and his most precious possession – a treasure beyond rubies in wartime – a remodelled Remington typewriter, which had been part of Penny's trousseau as a wedding present. It was one of Paul's jokes that he had married her for it.[33]

He told Penny herself he had married her because she never made scenes: he loved her for the gentleness which contrasted so strongly with his mother's assertive and demanding personality. He puzzled Mollie Hamilton long afterwards by saying that he had married Penny for protection and safety: 'Protection. He used that word to me.' Marriage was admittedly a wise precaution for anyone who had feared persecution in the army on homosexual grounds, but Penny protected him against unstable elements in his own temperament rather than any risk from outside. Her own home background had been deeply disturbed. Her father had provided neither physical nor emotional security: son of a Skegness newspaper proprietor, he had dabbled in journalism, risen to captain in the first war, and tried his hand afterwards at various occupations including agent for the Tory party in three different northern constituencies. When his second wife made it clear that there was no room at home for a pretty and talented teenage stepdaughter, he had put up no opposition. He was a man of parts, pragmatic and versatile, a prime figure skater, rifle shot and tenor singer, skilled stenographer, collector of precious stones, expert on astronomy and church architecture. It was said of Percy Avery that he wielded a facile pen[34] and Penny, who had his facility with words, had inherited also his buoyancy: a gift for staying on the surface in even the most dangerous seas, and an almost limitless capacity for negotiating hidden reefs and submerged emotional rocks. Early unhappiness had taught her endurance, and an instinctive generosity towards those in trouble. Helping others was already a highly developed speciality, and Paul throve on it.

Marriage produced in him a spurt of sustained creativity, marked by yet another complete about turn as a writer. He immediately started a 'modern play' called *Brilliant City* ('positively the best thing I've ever written, & definitely the best thing I've ever read').[35] Poetry was largely abandoned, although a sentimental 'Young Man's Prayer' made the usual return journey up to town and back, being rejected by *John O'Londons Weekly* in March 1942.[36] 'Mylor Creek', posted off months before to Wrey Gardiner's *Poetry Quarterly*, one of the choosiest of wartime literary reviews, returned unexpectedly at the end of the month in the shape of proofs for correction (Paul's first contact with a real, live professional editor was by telephone from the Duty Room at Brigade HQ).[37] Pat Ledward included a couple of his pieces in *Poets of This War* (a Resurgam anthology, co-edited by Baker under the name of Colin Strang), which also came out that spring. *Brilliant City* was finished by early July, faithfully typed out by Penny, and forwarded for comment to Clive and Gerald Armstrong, by which time Paul was already enthusiastically at work on a new play called *Pillars of Salt*.

His friends not unnaturally had reservations. Clive privately blamed marriage for destroying Paul's interest in poetry. Gerald, bitterly aggrieved and resentful, sent a long, cruel letter saying that Paul should stick to writing about what he knew, avoid bogus emotion and concentrate on acquiring some sort of structural technique. The criticism, all the more wounding because it was perfectly true, arrived out of the blue when Paul was alone (Penny was away nursing her father), and crushed him utterly: 'It has shaken the very base of my belief in myself, something that my wife has fostered most beautifully for me during the past year.' He wondered if he would ever write again. A dreadful fog clouded his brain. Every time he tried to put pen to paper he heard a sarcastic voice jeering at him: 'I would think of something and then somebody would say SENSELESS, CAN'T BE DONE, ABSURD, WHERE'S THE POINT, WHERE'S THE PLOT,

WHERE IN HELL IS THE PLOT . . . what am I to do, Clive? What on earth am I to do?'[38] Clive and Penny between them picked up the pieces over the next few weeks. Penny, whose unconditional loyalty to Paul was matched all their lives only by her burning indignation against his detractors, entered into his desperation with a vehemence that instantly made him feel better. Clive wrote sensibly about *Pillars* and consolingly about *City*.

Meanwhile war news, in the autumn of 1942 and the following winter, grew steadily bleaker. The Germans had not yet lost the upper hand in the battle for Stalingrad, or in the Western Desert, while in the Far East, after the fall of Singapore, the Japanese were driving the British ignominiously back up through Burma to a far from secure refuge in India. Urgent demand for troops, coupled with the lifting of the threat of invasion in Britain, meant that the Buffs 8th Battalion faced disbandment at the end of the year. Paul had achieved his third stripe, having been promoted to sergeant in August, but married life in Paignton looked more than ever precarious. He caught measles on his leave in November, and spent an extra three weeks at home in Bourne Hill being nursed by Penny and fussed over by his mother. He had a batch of poems back from the Favil Press (Baker's publishers) with a critical letter from the director, E. A. Lowy, congratulating him on having got over the insincerities of *Gerontius* ('such a waste of energy and talent'), and urging him to write instead from his own experience – 'which after the first staggering effect . . . I read to be an encouragement!!!!!!!!!!!!!' The poem Paul sent Lowy was his final answer to the lines Clive had written for him in despair at Torquay almost exactly two years earlier: the response he couldn't give at the time to Ruth's anxious entreaties, when she had found it impossible to make contact with a Paul almost unrecognisably changed, white-faced, crop-haired, hysterical, woefully disguised by his army uniform.

Soldier, Tell Us the Tricks

Say, soldier! Tell us the tricks,
    the tackle of your trade;
The passage of your hours;
    the plans that you have made –
Of what you think – what consider?
Tell us of the slow process,
That gradual change
    from man to soldier – ?

And what can I say, what reply?
    There is no answer.

> The tale is hidden in the eye.
> The soldier's here – the man is not:
> man's voice was lost;
> The sex decayed
> By the bitter bayonet – the chattering shot
> The growth delayed.
> The brief days of youth,
> And its forgotten past,
> Cannot be commanded to appear,
> We hope they may at last
>   – some other time – some different year.[40]

Lowy took Paul out to lunch at the beginning of February 1943, offering to publish this poem and any more like it[41] in the Favil Press series, *Poets Now*. But by this time Paul had more pressing matters in hand. He had been given permission at last to apply again for a commission before a two-day selection board at Derby (part of a new drive to make up the officer shortfall by widening recruitment). Penny, who realised what this was likely to mean, remembered ever afterwards the streamers and paper hats at a Forces' New Year party blotted out by repressed tears as the dancers advanced and retreated, clasping hands, in the ritual observance of Auld Lang Syne: 'As the dance ended Paul swung me round into his arms and we stood silent, with that magical oneness that excluded the others.'[42] They had four more weeks together before Paul was passed by the board at the end of the month, and ordered to report on 17 February for training as an officer cadet at Wrotham in Kent.

But he had been there barely a week before it seemed as though, after nearly three years' waiting and hoping, his chances of becoming an officer had slipped through his fingers for a second time. All cadets were ordered to form up for inspection by a group of officers accompanied by a sergeant major, who inserted his pace stick beyond the man next in line to Paul, dismissed those drawn up on one side, and informed the crestfallen remainder that they had been drafted overseas.[43] They were to report after seven days' embarkation leave to No. 1 District Transit Camp, in the Great Central Hotel at King's Cross in London. On 25 February the Sansoms got a telephone call, and this time it was Clive who couldn't believe his ears when he heard Paul's destination: 'He has been told it is to India, but I suspect that is a "blind" ', he wrote in his diary. But there had been no mistake. Paul sailed for India from Liverpool in March, 1943, in draft RZGXG aboard the troopship RMS *Britannic*.

PART TWO

1943–1964
The Young Executive

CHAPTER SIX

Falling in love with India

'When I write about the India of the raj, as I do, I'm using it, always have used it, as a metaphor,' Paul said at the end of his life, thinking of his favourite definition of the novel as an extended metaphor for its author's view of life: 'India is my extended metaphor.'[1] British India, when Paul landed there in the summer of 1943, had reached the beginning of the end. The Japanese, having beaten the British back up through Burma the year before, stood poised for invasion. The people of India, seeing their rulers humiliated and apparently powerless to protect them, reacted with mixed feelings: to many Indians the Japanese army seemed less like a threat than a rescue force, which would enable the subcontinent to rise against its British oppressors. For the British themselves, struggling to cope simultaneously with Japanese aggressors hammering at the door and civil disruption within the gates, this disastrous year marked the lowest point in their fortunes. The Raj itself, barely beginning to suspect what the future might hold, had only another four years to run.

It seemed still solidly in place, its systems, beliefs and customs functioning as smoothly as ever, in the glimpses of station and cantonment life available to a young subaltern in wartime. It was only looking back, over the next two decades and more, that Paul realised he had arrived at a moment of drastic transition in a society about to succumb to overwhelming pressure from both within and without. The four novels of the Raj Quartet represent his final attempt to map what he found in June 1943, to explore Britain's relationship with India, and to see its ultimately disastrous conclusion as part of a chain of post-war upheaval and dissolution with causes reaching far back into the past. 'I don't think a writer chooses his metaphors,' he said. 'They choose him.'[2]

Like most of his fellows on the *Britannic*, Paul knew virtually nothing about India, hadn't wanted to go there, and was not initially impressed by what he found. Among the precursors, if not agents of impending change at this stage in the war were the shiploads of young cadets, like himself, bearing down on the subcontinent ready to be turned into ECOs: Emergency Commissioned Officers, the kind of men who would never under normal conditions have considered (or been considered by) the Indian Army, men without preconceptions who had little understanding of the imperial tradition and no particular interest in prolonging it. People like Paul (who did not care for Kipling, and had not yet read *Passage to India*) could never understand why they should not treat Indians as equals, nor why it was axiomatic that Indians could not be allowed to govern their own country. Paul would later describe the sea change, beginning round about the Suez canal, that came over even the least prejudiced English people on the voyage out as they slowly absorbed a system of values they would not have countenanced at home.[3]

But troops in the self-contained world of a ship like the *Britannic*, making the long journey by the Cape round Africa, were largely insulated from outside influences. Few had been abroad before, or at most on a day trip across the Channel. The convoy travelled slowly, and the *Britannic* slower still, being delayed by engine trouble off Sierra Leone, putting in for repairs at Lagos, and breaking down altogether at Cape Town, where she was forced to stay behind while the rest steamed ahead. After weeks at sea the sight of a Union Jack as big as a house flying over Cape Town, the enthusiastic reception on shore, and the fact that everyone spoke English, brought home forcefully – and for the first time to most of the cadets – the meaning of red on the map. 'You suddenly realised what an empire was,' said another prospective novelist, James Leasor, who had been the man next in line to Paul at Wrotham on the morning the draft was made up for India (the two got to know one another on board the *Britannic*, where they were detailed to bring out the ship's newspaper). This first taste of Imperial hospitality contrasted sharply with recent experiences in England. Cars lined the dock to greet the ship, appreciative hosts hungry for news of home came every day with invitations to explore their land of plenty, prosperity and astonishing natural beauty. The cadets were billeted at Pollsmoor race course underneath Table Mountain with nothing to do but enjoy being fêted (parts of the city – what Paul called Black Town – were strictly out of bounds). There was unlimited sunshine, subtropical seabathing, lights on at night, ham-and-eggs three times a day for all who pleased, ample supplies of fresh fruit with pineapples for sale by the roadside:[4]

luxuries unheard of at home where people had almost forgotten what life was like without blackout regulations, petrol coupons and rigorous food rationing. Paul remembered ever afterwards the sense of physical and moral well-being conferred by the place and its appreciative inhabitants.

After six luxurious weeks left behind in Cape Town, passengers from the *Britannic* finished their voyage in the *Athlone Castle*. Paul by this time had discovered a circle of congenial like-minded friends, including Jimmy Leasor, a boy called Paddy Love and an aspiring artist called Bob Mason. They discussed plays and paintings, circulated manuscripts, formed a ballet club to scandalise more conventional elements. Paul's particular friend was James Corben, a cricketer and army PT instructor, former head boy of Kings School, Canterbury, veteran of the international touring Public Schools Eleven, tall, sociable, 'a man . . . with no intellectual gifts, happy, extrovert, ideal "officer-material" '.[5] The phrase describes Alan Hurst (in Paul's third novel *A Male Child*), a character who owes much to Jim Corben, and who is also first encountered as an officer cadet bound for India in wartime abroad the *Athlone Castle*. Alan belonged, like Jim, by temperament and upbringing to 'what I call the Kingston-bypass era, with its weekend cricket, open sports cars and road-house crawls . . . He had no politics other than those which prodded the patriot in him, no gift for words or analytical thought, no apparent liking for the world of books and the men who wrote them (or, more pertinently in that once-present company, intended to write them) and he thought us collectively an odd bunch.' If Paul was charmed by Jim's energy and openness, Jim was intrigued in return by Paul's easy familiarity with contemporary literature, theatre and politics: 'I have got a FRIEND, a real friend. I mean a friend for life,' he wrote back to London from Cape Town.[6] One of the things that drew them together was Jim's falling passionately in love with a girl in South Africa (Paul would put this affair in his first novel), or rather his despair at parting and Paul's attempts to console him as the ship left Cape Town.

India, when they eventually reached it in the second week of June, came as a shock. They had encountered the monsoon a few days out from land in the Arabian Sea ('I had never seen anything like it: sea and sky merged, and it was difficult to say whether the sea was being sucked upwards or the sky downwards in vertical rods of water').[7] For miles outside Bombay the water was churned yellow with mud. As they came in to land, scavenging kitehawks swooped out of the sky to snatch biscuits from the hands of soldiers lining the deck. Nothing had prepared them for the stupendous press of numbers described by Rupert Croft-Cooke, another writer bound that summer for the same cadet course as Paul: 'the ceaseless murmurous stream of people in tens of thousands down every vista of Bombay, something unceasing which in Europe has only momentary parallels, as if the road were filled for ever with the crowd struggling out of a football stadium after a cup-tie.'[8] Half the *Athlone Castle* cadets were destined for the officer training school at Bangalore, the rest – including Paul, Jim Corben, Jimmy Leasor, Paddy Love and Bob Mason – for OTS, Belgaum. They took the Deccan Express, travelling south through the legendary land of the Mahrattas, fought over by heroes from Akbar and Aurangzeb to the future Duke of Wellington. Paul was reminded prosaically at Poona of Clapham Junction with palms.[9]

His destination on the whole depressed him. 'I hated Belgaum,' he said at the end of his life. 'I've been back there several times in recent years. I don't hate it now – how could I? – but when I'm there I remember how much I hated it.'[10] Built on a plateau high in the Western ghats ('a little bit of Salisbury plain in the Indian hills'), Belgaum was the traditional home of the Mahratta Regiment, hugely swollen in wartime. The place is generally graceless in Paul's recollections, or in scenes inspired by it in his books ('I had never hated the army so much as I did in this . . . drearily familiar and horribly anonymous area of roads and pathways, directional signs, inhospitable huts and characterless rooms – the makeshift, impermanent jerry-built structures that seem to rest for sole support on the implacable and rigid authority of military hierarchy').[11] Cadets, forbidden to set foot in the city itself, were confined to cantonment and camp. They lived in high, airy barracks, partitioned off like loose boxes, with primitive sanitary arrangements (thunderbox and canvas bath) and wooden verandahs. Birds flew freely in and out. Red dust from the Deccan sandstone got into everything in the monsoon – clothes, skin, even the white of an egg. Cadets wore antiquated, Boer-War topees, and learned to cool off in the sweltering heat by drinking hot tea which emerged almost at once as sweat through their pores. Part of Paul's depression was no doubt physical, for he fell ill almost at once with dysentery, and a mild but debilitating and persistent jaundice, which turned his bathwater yellow, and meant that for weeks he could eat nothing except cauliflower cheese[12] (army catering made no concessions to climate: dishes like curry and kedgeree were simply added to the standard repertoire of stew, chops and heavy steamed or baked puddings).

Illness cannot have been easy to bear on top of the punishing routine of basic training in torrid monsoon weather. Cadets were issued with bicycles, and became adept at cycling by numbers, mounting and dismounting to order, riding to attention on sight of an officer. The school was staffed in wartime mostly by rejects and casualties, men who would have been at the front if not disabled by wounds, pulled down by malaria, disqualified by stupidity, incompetence or some more specific failure to make the grade. Day-to-day training was in the hands of NCOs, leathery, experienced old quartermasters and sergeant instructors who subjected their charges to the usual brutal infantry regime of PT before breakfast, drilling, marching, battle courses and petty harassment over discipline. There were lectures on map-reading, weapons, ammunition, and a course in 'Roman Urdu' (a purely phonetic approximation, which paid no attention to the written language, let alone literature) taught by a lively and likeable Eurasian Lieutenant Joseph.

Paul enjoyed Urdu but was dismally defeated by motor maintenance, always heavy going for impractical intellectuals. Rupert Croft-Cooke managed to pass the crucial, end-of-term Motor Transport test by bribing a mechanic the night before: Paul, who had mastered morse code, swapped places with Jimmy Leasor for whom the internal combustion engine held no secrets, sitting Leasor's morse test for him in exchange, so that each passed with honours in the other's name. The pair, both accredited writers by this time, collaborated again on a camp newspaper: they discussed work in hand (Paul was tinkering with *Brilliant City*, Jimmy had already embarked on his first novel), and swapped daydreams about their respective professional futures. Paul, who still saw writing as a lofty spiritual calling, was scathing about Jimmy's notion of being a Hollywood scriptwriter. But neither found much opportunity to write in a timetable taken up with tough route marches, complicated TEWTS (tactical exercises without troops), lessons in survival carried out in the dense, primeval jungle stretching south towards Goa. Cadets, who would soon be fighting the Japanese in Burma, learned how to move silently and fast, improvise rafts, and kill a cobra by spitting it with the tip of a kukri before chopping its head off.

Much of the detail of camp and landscape, the physical setting, the mock manoeuvrings of war games and tactical exercises showed up again in Paul's novel, *The Mark of the Warrior*, fifteen years later. But subtler and more complex impressions took longer to digest. Cadets at Belgaum were under surveillance: for six months every move they made, social as well as military, was discreetly noted. The Indian Army had traditionally been a military élite, taking its pick each year from the Sandhurst cadet crop, turning over its leavings to the British Army, and severely restricting its intake of Indian officers to whom it offered little chance of promotion and no social equality. If defeat in 1942 had been a rude shock, so was the immediate need to absorb large numbers of new recruits from home with barely time to lick them into military, let alone moral shape. Cadets were automatically made members of the Belgaum Club, which admitted no Indians, just as they were expected to frequent Green Hotel – a smart little outfit standing in a grove of flamboyant trees, shaded by banyan and mango and surrounded by trim beds of canna lilies, beside the bandstand on the regimental parade ground – which was restricted to Europeans only. They were encouraged to visit the large, shady bungalows of British residents in the cantonment, to play tennis and attend play readings at the rectory. Their behaviour and bearing were assessed according to a venerable and highly developed intelligence system, strained to its utmost in wartime by the huge influx of ECOs ('The old standards go by the board. . . ,' as someone says bitterly in Paul's TV play, *The Colonel's Lady*: 'So many thousands of officers wanted over so many months. Quantity's what counts with them, not quality').[13] The selection process worked on the tacit understanding that each cadet should be given enough rope to hang himself, and watched to see what he did with it.

The wartime cadets in *The Mark of the Warrior* undergo comparatively crude, straightforward tests of manhood, involving courage, powers of leadership and ruthless determination to kill. Paul's uneasiness at the far more insidious testing going on behind the scenes at Belgaum was voiced in retrospect by a character in *The Jewel in the Crown*, another liberal-minded young Englishman whose first reactions to the subcontinent had been bewilderment and dismay: 'I hated India – the real India behind the . . . myth. I hated the loneliness, and the dirt, the smell, the conscious air of superiority that one couldn't get through the day without putting on like a sort of protective purdah.'[14] A crash course in putting on this kind of protection was as essential a part of the cadets' training as jungle survival or Urdu. They were paired off at the start (Paul shared with Bob Mason), each couple sharing a sitting room, bedroom, bath house and bearer. Boys who had never had a personal servant before were naturally charmed by half shares in a bearer whose job was to polish his masters' boots, press uniforms, make beds, run baths, or sit cross-legged on the verandah cleaning kit with great pots of blanco and brasso. 'The word went round: We're sahibs now.'[15]

But initial enthusiasm was qualified on Paul's part by reservations. It became clear that according to the army's elaborate social hierarchy the 1943 intake of cadets represented for the most part scrapings from the bottom of the officer barrel, and that Belgaum etiquette could be as inflexible as Southgate's when it came to what was done and what not. Paul had been familiar from earliest childhood with this kind of subtle, invidious discrimination from which there was no appeal. Even before he reached India, the old divisions had been brought home again on the troopship by an encounter with a boy called Clayton, also from Palmer's Green – 'within a stone's throw of where I was born'[16] – also bound for Belgaum. The two could not conceivably have met at home: Clayton, whose parents lived in a house overlooking the park opposite the Broad Walk, belonged by Paul's own account to another world. But the gulf between Scott and Clayton was as nothing compared to the gulf dividing both from someone like their Urdu instructor Lieutenant Joseph, whose claim to be a Yorkshireman was belied by his distinctive lilting intonation, the 'chi-chi' Eurasian accent universally despised even – perhaps especially – by those born to it. There were no white women in Belgaum except for a handful of official wives, and the local half-caste girls, often exquisitely beautiful with their alabaster skins and delicate dolls' features: Jimmy Leasor remembered a girl at a dance, who claimed to come from Sheffield, saying desperately when pressed to specify which part of Sheffield, 'the cantonment'. Similar experiences lie behind characters like the Eurasian Lieutenant Johns in *Johnny Sahib*, and the girl in *Alien Sky* who is cruelly exposed for describing herself as a native of Brighton. Paul, in these first months in India, had already begun cultivating the sensitivity which would make him, as a novelist, so attentive to half-castes and hybrids, people refused entry to one world and forced to court rejection by another.

But, if tensions within British India made him feel at home, Paul was as perplexed as his companions by the reception they got from the Indians themselves. Far from welcoming the new arrivals, who had crossed half the world to come to their aid, the townspeople of Belgaum seemed hostile and resentful. 'When we got to India in the middle of 1943, the Quit India riots were still very fresh in people's memories. We weren't allowed to stray far from the school – in case the locals chucked stones at us. You felt the strength of feeling against us right from the beginning . . .'[17] The Quit India campaign, unleashed against the British after the imprisonment of Congress leaders in August 1942, was where Paul eventually chose to begin his reckoning in the Raj Quartet. *The Jewel in the Crown* starts with civil unrest, outbreaks of violence, crowds gathering, the British community in India feeling itself alarmingly vulnerable to attack. Later, in the two middle volumes of the sequence, the British sense of isolation and danger, of a tide inexorably rising to swamp them, is symbolised by a stone thrown at a wedding in the late summer of 1943, and by a mutilated bicycle dumped ominously on the verandah of a particular officer's quarters: incidents reminiscent of stones thrown and bicycles abandoned on the streets of Belgaum (Jimmy Leasor remembered a wretched incident that summer, when one of the OTS's regimental staff sergeants blew his brains out on account of a scandal over missing bicycle parts turning up for sale in the bazaar).

Paul himself, with only the haziest grasp of the political situation, let alone the historical complexities behind it, was in no position at this stage to do more than register an atmosphere of gathering threat. He seemed unusually grave to his fellow students, speculative and self-contained, as he began for the first time to feel obscurely troubled by the ignorance and indifference about India in ordinary English people, like himself, whose government ruled the subcontinent in their name. Information about what was happening to the Congress politicians gaoled without trial, or to their sympathisers swallowed up by prisons and detention camps, was even harder to come by on the spot at the time than it proved to be when Paul came to write about it twenty years later at home. Cadets were rigidly segregated by the single, spinal road that divided the cantonment from Belgaum itself, where some fifty thousand people crammed into narrow streets to scrape a living from the local cotton mill, soap factory, tannery, and the produce of vegetable growers in the villages round about. The cantonment seemed spacious by comparison with its bougainvillea and lemon groves, its well-kept Anglican church of St Mary's (red sandstone with cloistered portico, flying buttresses and gothic arches), its Rex and Globe cinemas, its cafés, its Chinese diner (where jaundiced cadets feasted rashly on too much fatty food), its tongas and traps, its gaily-painted shops, stalls, fish market, fruit sellers and Swami's bakery: 'like every road in India, the Belgaum streets were busy with pedestrians, turban, fez, congress cap, mingling and passing by in talkative processions. The lean country women in their harsh-coloured saris, never without a burden and rarely without children, passed in groups. A herd of goats, a few lazy water buffaloes, a *pai* dog or two, scurrying chickens, noisy children. . . ,' wrote Rupert Croft-Cooke: 'I never grew tired of it.'[18]

Paul remained critical and aloof, ill at ease with imperial attitudes, uncomfortably aware of strains he could not identify, instinctively sympathetic to the grievances of the disaffected young Indian intellec-tuals from whom he and his kind were so carefully protected. He struck Jimmy Leasor in those days as morose and mocking: 'He was always an outsider. Solitary, beak-nosed, saturnine. He had a waspish tongue: Scott was always sneering at the officer class.' Jim Corben, who called Paul affectionately by his middle name of Mark, knew a far less defensive, more humorous, hard-drinking soldierly character with a sardonic relish for army efficiency never entirely extinguished by exasperation with army red tape. Scott and Corben both enjoyed their reputation as potential subversives, unreliable, independent-minded, too inquisitive by half, the kind of tricky customers liable to let down King and Empire when it came to the crunch. At the end of the course in early December, both were commissioned into the Service Corps, disobligingly known as the Rice Corps, Flying Grocers or Jam Stealers and generally considered to be about as low as it was possible to get in the Indian Army. Even the most obstreperous cadet in *The Colonel's Lady* is tamed by the threat of ending up in the Service Corps ('I'll have him posted to a unit he'll be ashamed to wear the badges of . . .') as opposed to a crack posting like the Rifle Brigade or the Gurkhas. Clayton from Palmer's Green joined the Gurkhas, going on to become a paratrooper and, after the war, a planter of tea in Assam: 'The East had called him in a way it never quite called me,' Paul said ironically.[19]

Things improved as soon as he left Belgaum. The Service Corps contingent was drafted for three months to the RIASC Training School at Kakul in Kashmir (now the national Military Academy, the Sandhurst of Pakistan), where they found themselves on top of the world, four thousand feet above sea level on the slopes of the Hindu Kush, in a great saucer-shaped valley surrounded by snow-capped mountains. It was brilliantly sunny by day, bitterly cold at night: 'battledress weather. But I'm *very* comfortable,' wrote Paul,[20] who had a room of his own with pictures on the walls, books (including Clive's newly published *The Unfailing Spring* on his bedside table), and a fire burning all day in his grate. Kakul remained a pleasant memory to the end of his life. He enjoyed as much as his companions the thrill of putting up a pip and being admitted at last to the dubious, desirable officer class, sampling at first hand the romantic wildness of the North West Frontier together with the creature comforts devised to cheer those who served on it. Paul and his friends never quite got over their sense of make-believe. 'Do you remember . . . that dear old ginger-haired bearer who "cleaned" Bob Mason's paintbox and sewed a button on the buttocks of my trousers,' Paddy Love wrote fondly long afterwards to Paul – 'the man who startled us by inquiring if we had any invisible mending in what seemed to be the desolate area between Russia, Tibet and Afghanistan?'[21]

They celebrated the Christmas of 1943 in excellent spirits with a round of festivities, including a mounted Musical Chairs at the race course on New Year's Day, when the staff acted as bookies, and the Belgaum contingent all bet on Jim Corben, the only serious rider among them, who gave his friends a run for their money by reaching the last two rounds on a mule.[22] Jim – six feet tall, muscular, grey-eyed, already balding at twenty-one – was always one for making things hum. He loved dressing up, improvising on the piano, violin or harpsichord, getting up a play or an impromptu singsong. 'He was a giggler, Jim was,' said his future wife: 'Always in the thick of things. Paul was quiet and reserved, but he came alive in Jim's company.' They developed a double act just as Paul had done with his brother, building up a repertoire of running jokes, film gags, take-offs of senior officers, and wildly inventive mimicry. They mounted a highly successful Christmas production of Ian Hay's *The Housemaster*: Jim, who could get round anyone from the Colonel downwards, was the director and moving spirit: Paul played the juvenile lead, Philip de Pourville,[23] the assistant science master or Junior Stinks Beak who, after an unprepossessing start, ends up winning the hearts of both the heroine and the boys.

It was an agreeable introduction to the orderly, undisturbed, immemorially trivial Anglo-Indian social round of amateur dramatics, garden parties, tennis or bridge at the club, gin fizz and *nimbupanis* on the verandah at sunset. It must have seemed an almost weirdly insulated world in the opening months of 1944, which saw whole cities devastated in Germany, ferocious fighting on the Russian front, and dramatic developments in Burma, where the long-awaited Japanese invasion of India, beaten back against all odds in the Arakan in February, switched north to an advance on Imphal in March. Paul completed his three months' training at Kakul that month and, after a week's leave in the pretty little hill station of Abbottabad, moved on for a month to the Motor Transport School at Lahore, then back up to the Air Supply training depot at Chaklala near Rawalpindi. 'One felt one was never going to get a real job,' he said, looking back. 'But of course these were among the best known cantonments. In the midst of a war one was living the old pre-war Indian military and civilian life.'[24] However much it exasperated him at the time, Paul would make good use later of this brief but intense immersion in a way of life that seemed impervious to change. He was as appalled as many of his fellow cadets by a society so hidebound and ingrown that it treated the imminent collapse of Western civilisation as an unwarranted intrusion on its own comfort ('Lahore; Ambala; high, cool messes with silent bearers grouped round a morose Colonel for whom the war could only mean the remorseless shelf of neglect; a dying-on-the-feet, out of date and limited by tradition and experience').[25] Sometimes it seemed as though he would be condemned to waste time for ever. 'I am terrified of stagnating in an Indian station – be it in the plains or in the hills,' Paul wrote to Clive after a month in the sticky, pre-monsoon heat of Lahore: 'I've seen the results a year or two in a place has on people, and I must avoid it at all costs.'[26]

Paul and Jim Corben relieved frustration and boredom with the regular benders that had cemented their friendship from the start. Jim, who had been taught like Paul to hold his liquor at an early age in a hard-drinking family, dated his adult initiation to attempts to drown his sorrows in Cape Town ('Jim always said that's where he learned to drink,' said his wife: 'I think they had hollow legs, those two'). Paul's habit of nerving himself with a bottle went back to his own time of trouble in Torquay, when drink had given him courage for escapades like the spree which started just before he met Barbara and ended with his proposal to Penny. He had scarcely touched alcohol, according to Ruth, in innocent, abstemious Bourne Hill days when all any of them needed for intoxication was a mixture of lime juice and sprung rhythm. Later Paul drank to release the masterful, bold and incisive side of himself he found hard of access when sober. It was the aspect caught by Bob Mason in an oil sketch, done at lightning speed while he and Paul waited for the bar to open in the Abbott Hotel at Abbottabad at the end of March, 1944. 'The sketch showed me with my "one pip", pretending to be a Second Lieutenant & wearing my "Sam Browne" of which I was proud, but also amused by, & no doubt thirsty by the look of concentration & dedication!' Paul wrote on the back of the painting. 'The crimson background represents what in India they called an almirah, which means a wardrobe. In this hung my smart new uniforms!'[27]

Th portrait went everywhere with him for the rest of the war, hanging in huts and tents, and afterwards on the wall of his study at home in London. Like the picture of Dorian Gray, it recorded its youthful subject at a high point, confident and composed against a crimson background of hope. Paul had Dorian's dilemma much in mind that summer as he took stock of his position, looking back over the past four eventful years, and assessing how far they had changed him. If his determination to write remained as firm as ever, writing itself became less and less practicable. He had used the interlude of relative privacy and peace at Kakul and Lahore to scrape together a handful of pieces ('Songs from India')[28] which he tentatively posted to Clive, but essentially he had made no advance, nor was likely to, on the point reached with *Brilliant City* and *Pillars of Salt* at the end of 1942. Clive and Penny laboured tirelessly on his behalf as agent and secretary, Clive circulating manuscripts, Penny typing and retyping drafts written or corrected in India. Clive discussed strategy with another Quaker conscientious objector, the man with whom he worked the market garden at Tinker's Orchard, a character actor with little-theatre connections called Jonathan Field.

It was probably on his advice that Clive sent *Pillars of Salt* to the

Unity Theatre, which had built up a considerable reputation in the 1930s as a left-wing theatrical launchpad, and mounted an energetic programme of plays at its St Pancras headquarters in wartime. Clive called there on 8 September 1943, to discuss possible performance with the head of the play clinic, Mary Wren, who arranged a Sunday reading for *Pillars* that autumn.[29] Plans for a production by the company's Outside Show group were eventually shelved but news of the reading, reaching Paul in Belgaum, inspired him to spend his eight days' leave in Bombay at the end of the course working on a third play, *After Our Labours*, already begun on the troopship. Jimmy Leasor, who was himself by this time sending his novel home to his mother by instalments on airgraph forms, remembered *Brilliant City* as Paul's work in progress at Belgaum. *After Our Labours* was rushed through by Christmas ('It was consigned to the post rather as I imagine an appeal to the Home Secretary for leniency'),[30] and by May Paul had got as far as designing the sets for a fourth play to be called *The Pilgrim Michael*.

All these plays were more or less allegorical and, judging by readers' reports at the time and by the script of the only one that survives, more or less callow. All four attempt universality by examining contemporary situations in settings which acknowledge no specific date or location. Paul himself was dismissive in retrospect about them, especially *Brilliant City* ('It was about people rebuilding things after a disaster, a city, no less. It sounds and was frightful'),[31] but at the time they represented the closest he had yet come to exploring the world he lived in. *Pillars of Salt* takes place on the mountainous frontier of an aggressive fascist state preparing to annexe the neighbouring country: its two heroes are brothers, a pair of patriotic young prospective blackshirts speaking in vaguely transatlantic monosyllables ('GARTH: I guess you sort of feel things pretty much, don't you? STEVE: Guess I do'),[32] who find themselves slowly turned to stone, or salt, by governmental atrocities perpetrated on their Jewish countrymen, and who finally join the resistance. Paul had his doubts as soon as Penny sent him the revised script in India, and he was even more dubious about *After Our Labours*, preferring to forget it almost at once in favour of the as yet unwritten *Pilgrim Michael*. 'The rough theme is that a country owes its soldiers nothing,' he wrote on 17 May 1944 to Clive, adding ominously: 'I am trying to analyse the meaning . . . of abstractions like devotion – patriotism – faith – reality – wisdom – & happiness.'

Clive, who had a shrewd grasp of his pupil's strengths and limitations as a writer, diagnosed a split between intellect and feeling, pointing out tactfully that Paul possessed the kind of Shakespearian imagination that worked best from the concrete and particular, rather than from abstractions. He had predicted Paul's future course pretty accurately in an encouraging little poem about him, 'Soldier in Exile', dated January 1944 ('Across wild hill and arid plain/ I carry England in my brain ... in my mind, whose secret eye/ Projects the films of memory,/ The Wilderness where nothing grows/ Shall blossom as the English rose').[33] Although his prescription offered no immediate comfort, Clive was right in the long run: Paul's chief task as a writer in wartime was absorption, recording on the reels of memory experiences that would resurface twenty or thirty years later in the Raj Quartet.

His attempts to explore the war and its consequences, alternately bombastic and stilted in *Brilliant City* and *Pillars of Salt*, seemed absurdly flimsy by comparison with what was happening that spring to the Sansoms 'far away in Inglistan'.[34] 1944, when Ruth found a teaching job and Clive worked long hours for a commercial market gardener in Reigate, proved their worst year of the war. In February, a 250lb bomb demolished their lodgings, leaving Ruth miraculously unhurt in bed: Clive, coming home from fire-watching duty at the cinema in Reigate, found remnants of their blue-and-green painted furniture dangling at a crazy angle in space, two walls of their room missing, half the floor gone and no sign of his wife. Anxiety and homelessness compounded damage done by heavy physical labour to an already frail constitution weakened by ill health, inadequate diet, and chronic shortage of sleep after more than three years in the Blitz. Clive nearly died that summer from a perforated ulcer: 'Did I make a fool of myself? Did I scream loudly before the doctor arrived?' he asked anxiously as soon as he came round from the emergency operation, explaining with relief when Ruth assured him that he had uttered no sound: 'I was screaming inside.'[35]

But even physical collapse scarcely interrupted the steady stream of reassurance he sent in answer to Paul's evasive but increasingly urgent appeals for help. 'There is only one possible way of living in India, unless you are to become hopelessly homesick – anyway one takes steps, hopes for events to materialise,' Paul wrote from the Air Supply School at Chaklala on 7 May: 'Afraid I must talk about it to someone, Clive – and certainly I don't wish to worry anyone at home.' The key to Paul's otherwise unexplained difficulty seems to be the letter he had written to Ruth, nearly four years earlier, identifying sex as the root of artistic energy: 'All emotions and creative instincts are (to me) based on the sexual impulse in man.' The correspondence with Clive ostensibly discussed Paul's future as a writer but both parties tacitly acknowledged that what was at issue was an emotional and sexual as much as an artistic dilemma. By Paul's own account, the strictly sexual impulse burned low in time of artistic activity, but inability to write meant that there could be no relief for mounting inner tension. By the summer of 1944, he had produced nothing but scraps and jottings for almost two years and, although he still talked of schemes like *The Pilgrim Michael*, the prospect of setting pen to paper looked increasingly remote: 'poor Michael is sick & his pilgrimage interrupted,' Paul wrote when the monsoon broke in May, watching huge blobs of rain spatter like liquid gas spray on the dusty ground outside. Present circumstances, and the likelihood of an imminent posting to the battle front on the Burmese border, gave an ironic twist to passages like this one, but Michael, however sickly, embodied a genuine problem for his creator:

He stands at a T junction – (a cross roads is much too ordinary for Michael). There are two clearly defined courses for him. One is to follow the road of his desire, which is free & undisciplined – with strange new twists & turns. The other is a normal road – but if he walks it he will stand a better chance of meeting mankind on mankind's *self-imposed* level. I think & hope he will walk this road & work out his drama in a straight & simple way – so that any message can have the chance of being understood by all.

How important this – (especially in writing for the stage) to write in conjunction with *acceptable* trends. How exciting to prune one's emotional tree down to its bare significance . . . It would be far easier to write freely – damn the public & turn the stage inside out & roundabout – filled with strange movements – faces & lights & complexities. But the best way is the hard way. The result seems simple & unassuming – yet how much more severe discipline is required . . .[36]

The normal road was always the harder and more challenging for Paul. Discipline stimulated him. He made it sound far more tempting than the free and easy road of desire: 'How important . . . to write in conjunction with *acceptable* trends. How exciting to prune one's emotional tree . . . how much more severe discipline is required . . .' This is the voice of the puritan conscience, the harsh, exacting, unappeasable side of Paul's nature, his critical sense: what he would call later, when he read Lorca, his *duende*. But it is clear from his letters to Clive that, for the moment, Paul still saw his situation in Wildean terms. He faced the same choice as Dorian Gray between self-discipline and the 'wrong, fascinating, poisonous, delightful' path of dissipation. For Paul, as for Dorian, marriage had been a purifying and protective measure, a love that might 'shield him from those sins that seemed to be already stirring in spirit and in flesh'.[37] Paul had turned his back on these in the opening months of 1941, and, when they stirred again in India, he vowed himself for a second time to 'the normal road', the puritan's stony sacrificial path which, in Dorian's view, could lead only to disaster: 'mad, wilful rejections, monstrous forms of self-torture and self-denial, whose origin was fear . . . '.[38]

It would be another twenty years and more before Paul could begin to explore the monstrous consequences of fear and self-denial through the character of Ronald Merrick in the Raj Quartet. What he feared at this stage was not repression but its opposite. In later life, when he came to look back on himself as a young man, he talked much of the renunciations required from a writer: 'Perhaps only those who sacrifice themselves completely are truly memorable,' he wrote when he finished the Raj Quartet.[39] His letters to the Sansoms between 1940 and 1945, and more specifically this exchange with Clive in 1944, show him deliberately rejecting Dorian Gray's road of undisciplined desire. At some fundamental level, his nature craved repression: it was self-indulgence that threatened Paul both as a man and a writer, and the fight against it pushed him steadily towards what he called 'the morose side' in the summer of 1944. He had long cultivated the habit of blanking out or switching off attention, a knack both envied and resented in the army. 'We'd be having a hilarious evening, we'd be nearly drunk, and Paul would go quiet,' said Jim Corben,[40] who learned to bear patiently with his friend's abstractions which could last for hours, sometimes for whole days at a time.

Some found Paul's withdrawals unnerving. Others put his aloofness down to drink ('Moody devil. Drinks like a fish and never shows it,' one of Paul's friends had warned Penny).[41] To Jimmy Leasor it looked more like inverted snobbery, the chip on the shoulder of a Rice Corps subaltern who came from the wrong social drawer and would have been made to feel it by experienced hands in clubs and regimental messes ('people who are probably Artillery on their mother's side,' Paul wrote cheerfully to Clive).[42] 'He brooded and drank on this,' said Leasor, who sensed in Paul from the start a sharp sense of exclusion: 'he always wanted to be accepted.' Paul in those days was already fascinated by places like the Imperial Hotel, the Turf Club at Poona, the Gymkhana Club and the Willingdon in Bombay. They appealed to him as an observer, and also perhaps to the self that longed to be accepted, what he called the sahib in him, the authoritarian who believed in control, repression, pruning the emotional tree. Long after Paul's death, when *The Jewel in the Crown* was shown on television, James Leasor recognised at once the Scott he had known in the army: '*Merrick*. That's him, that's him. When I saw him on the box, I recognised so much.'[43]

Paul said once that he looked in the mirror in order to see himself in the third person:[44] mirrors supplied him all his life with a convenient metaphor for the mysterious process by which a writer multiplies and manipulates reflections of himself. Drink became for Paul a means of both releasing and subduing the unruly warring selves whose conflict would in the end deepen and enrich his most ambitious work. A great part of the next twenty years would be spent struggling to record clearly and honestly what he saw in his inner mirror. He detested and longed to destroy much that he found reflected there: he told his wife that he could not bear to see the sneering face that looked back at him from the mirror.[45] 'The only time Paul's two halves found unity was when he was writing . . .', Ruth Sansom wrote long after Paul's death and Clive's. 'I see now that when Clive was unable to write during the war & at various times before and after the war, he also destroyed his body, not by drink, but by ulcers and migraines rather than let his body take possession of him . . . In a sense, writing was the child of the union, and it was a very demanding child.'[46] Clive had always been as carefully contained, as deeply divided, as enigmatic and allusive as Paul. Each knew that, in time of trouble, he could rely for understanding on the other. Paul acknowledged news of Clive's illness (its gravity seems to have been kept from him) for the first time in a letter of 5 July, reporting his own frustrations ('God alone knows how long I shall be out here & writing seems impossible'), and the sensation, so familiar to both, of reaching screaming point inside:

Do you remember Torquay? It is full circle again. . . . Sometimes I wish my nerves weren't so strong – because my inside has suffered so often from a breakdown – but the old nerves keep on going. I suppose on the whole I magnify every time I feel ready to scream until that is all I can remember. But I seem to have that strange capacity for remaining cheerful in the eyes of casual observers with whom I come in contact – though I am becoming on the morose side gradually – & can do nothing about it.

The trouble is I can offer no reasonable grounds for complaint & would be as happy as a sandboy if I were completely normal. But it's the old question of living two lives at once – & *it is* becoming rather a strain.

Dear Clive, write to me . . . I wish I could believe wholly in God for I have often found temporary relief inside a church – but that is always spoiled by the place resembling too much the known places of childhood. I cannot, either, let myself be unfaithful to my wife, for there can be only one woman in the world for me – I strongly believe this – tho' I could I suppose draw a curtain over impatience & patience & forget myself. 'Last night, ah! yesternight – '

Write, Clive,

As always   Paul.

PS Kapinski is dead.

Clive responded by sending two poems written with Paul in mind. One was the cheerful 'Soldier in Exile', which urged him to look on the bright side; the other was 'The Enemy',[47] a grim, terse little parable written the autumn before – a year almost to the day after the Scotts' wedding – which confronted the treacherous Trojan horse Paul and Clive both knew so well. 'Paul stamped out the tendency towards homosexuality,' wrote Ruth. 'And I see this as his great fear – that it might, without Penny's help, grip him, as it did Oscar Wilde . . . Clive's short poem "The Enemy" grew out of this situation.'[48]

The Enemy

No cause to fear by sea
That mortal Enemy.
Man's adversary waits
Always within the gates,
Lurking till he can find
Division in the mind.
Lest the heart's fortress fall
Turn inward from the wall
To where that Horse still stands
We built with our own hands.

This was effectively the end of Paul's apprenticeship to Clive. There was no break: they continued to correspond, Clive sending measured advice, Paul vehemently affirming his credo of constraint, reiterating the need for a writer to curb spontaneity and self-expression in the interests of clearing a way for his characters ('I write with, of and *for* emotions . . . DISCIPLINE. I *mean* that one must discipline oneself to present emotions . . . if I am to write successfully – I hate every word I write – because it is other people talking *through* me & they say what they like & I disagree heartily').[49] But there was nothing more Paul could learn from Clive. When he started writing again, after the war, his efforts to contain and express himself would be part of a protracted, internal battle in which there could be neither help nor reinforcement from outside.

By July 1944, Paul had also at last reached the end of his military apprenticeship. The letter reporting Kapinski's death was written nearly a month after he had finally joined his air supply unit in Bengal on 13 June. He was second in command of one of three platoons or sections in No 1 Indian Air Supply Company, RIASC, behind the lines at Comilla, where General Slim had established his 14th Army headquarters during the battles for Imphal and Kohima, fought out over the past three months with relentless ferocity on both sides. The fighting was by no means over and the only road to Imphal still remained blocked, but by June the Japanese had sustained appalling losses, their onslaught had weakened and they were beginning for the first time to contemplate the possibility of retreat. Air supply was a key factor in Slim's plan to avenge the disaster of 1942. His initial victories over the Japanese in the Arakan and at Imphal were both inflicted by troops supplied entirely from the air, and they smashed for good the legend of Japanese invincibility in the jungle. The recapture of the Imphal road on 22 July meant much to the men of the 14th Army, whose retreat from Burma two years earlier had ended with their straggling into Imphal – exhausted, starving, sick, looking more like scarecrows than soldiers – to spread demoralisation and panic throughout British India.

No 1 Air Supply Company was the first of its kind.[50] It had been founded to support Wingate's legendary Chindit expedition behind enemy lines in 1943, and with others had since proved its worth by maintaining guerrilla groups in the Chin Hills as well as supplying more conventional fighting forces beleaguered in the Arakan and under siege in Imphal. By the time Paul joined the company (nearly two hundred Indian soldiers commanded initially by three British officers), it was exhausted but triumphant. Officers and sepoys had been working flat out seven days a week, sometimes twenty-four hours a day, ever since the 'Arakan Flap' in February had been followed almost immediately by the 'Imphal Flap'. Desperately needed new recruits inevitably came in for a mixed reception. Proprietary feelings ran high and tempers short. Paul, who had flown in from Calcutta and cadged a lift by jeep from the airfield to the camp in Comilla, never forgot the greeting he got from his commanding officer, Major Kimber: 'Where the hell have *you* been?'[51]

Kimber was short, fiery, indefatigably energetic, an enthusiastic disciplinarian, inordinately proud of his company and its achievements. He suffered from prickly heat, an excruciating rash all over his body which he relieved by stripping off in monsoon rain, and which he immediately insisted on displaying to Paul. He ran a tight, effective, self-sufficient operation, and he made Paul in his brand-new bush hat and dapper uniform painfully conscious of having arrived too late to see action (at least two future novels would deal with the initiation of a raw, inexperienced, as yet unblooded young subaltern at the hands of a battle-scarred major running a unit based on Kimber and his company). Paul's immediate superior in 10/10 Section was Tony Colegate, an immensely popular captain of conspicuous dash and devil-may-care reputation: Colegate, like Johnnie Sahib, the eponymous hero of Paul's first novel, was cocky, piratical, blue-eyed with a challenging stare and a battered hat with the brim jammed down. 'He was a bit of a busker. He had a lot of heart but no sense. Difficult, being his 2 i/c . . .' Paul wrote to a mutual friend after the publication of *Johnnie Sahib*: 'I sent him the script because, so clearly, it was really about him and me . . . Working for Tony meant keeping what nowadays is called a low profile, and sometimes covering up for him.'[52] Colegate had celebrated the first lull in the fighting for months by taking leave in anticipation of being relieved by Paul, whose first move was to select a new havildar, or sergeant. He chose at random a naik called Narayan Dass, 'a sturdy, rather silent little Madrassi',[53] industrious, efficient, unswervingly loyal ever afterwards to Lieutenant Scott, who enjoyed both his devotion and his rare, dry wit.

Paul's arrival coincided with a major administrative overhaul, the outbreak of what General Slim called an orgy of planning,[54] unleashed by the decision to chase the Japanese back down through Burma without waiting for a road to be built. The unconditional vindication of air supply proved to be in some sense its practitioners' undoing: what had been an independent operation, run on thoroughly unorthodox lines by freebooters like Kimber and Colegate, was now to be placed on an established footing and handed over to planners, desk johnnies with no firsthand experience, RAMOs and FAMOs (Rear and Forward Air Maintenance Organisations), regarded by the companies on the ground with universal mistrust, resentment and ill will. The 14th Army, already nicknamed the Forgotten Army, was well aware that neither the British public nor the War Office had any great confidence in its ability to fight, let alone win a murderous campaign against a peculiarly vicious and hitherto unbeaten foe on inadequate resources over impossible terrain in an outstandingly unhelpful climate. 19 Division, which No. 1 Company was earmarked to supply, lacked the mystique of more glamorous fighting forces in the Pacific, or the liberating D Day armies in Europe. Even association with romantic desperadoes like Wingate (lost in a plane missing over Burma that spring) and his legendary Chindits could not disguise the fact that air supply companies were essentially industrial units with a uniformed management and labour force. Slim himself compared them to the mail order department of a great department store, supplying plain and fancy goods with promptitude and exactness.[55]

The work required diligence, steadiness, detailed concentration and organising ability. 'Fascinating. Inglorious. But memorable,' wrote Paul, who enjoyed sorting out accounts, drawing up schedules, juggling limited resources against urgent demands, setting himself to deliver the trickiest orders: 'working out how many parachutes you needed to drop a jeep successfully – or a canoe, feather-weight, plus two or three chaps who were going to reassemble it on the ground and paddle up a creek to disaster or its opposite.'[56] At the height of the battle, the supply system had reckoned to process four hundred aircraft a day, and to 'turn round' (unload, reload and refuel) each plane in ten minutes flat. Drops covered everything from fuel, weapons, ammunition, engine and Bailey bridge parts to rations, including live sheep, goats and chickens with legs tightly bound. Demand rose from the original estimated 150 tons per day to a drop of 2,000 tons daily in the last stages of the race for Rangoon in May 1945. All hands worked night and day to service the circling bombers, huge lumbering RAF Dakotas, small fierce US Mitchell B 25s, each plane touching down at one end of the airstrip almost before the last had taken off at the other. Paul described the airfield in one of its regular flaps crowded with jostling aircraft, convoys of lorries, men hurrying between them, pilots waiting impatiently, and the Major barking orders, shouting for transport, darting tirelessly among his Indian loaders: 'the end of the runway was thick with jockeying Mitchells swinging their tails, shaking their flaps, hunching themselves to hustle forwards and throw themselves into the air; one; two; three; four. Two craft taking the strip at once. It wove itself into an earsplitting, audible pattern.'[57]

The heroic pioneering phase of air supply was already over by the time Paul reported for duty in 1944. Emergencies, accidents, crises of every description were from now on to be anticipated by consolidation, careful preparation and planning. Paul's methodical approach went down well at CAATO (Comilla Army/Air Transport Operation), the organisation designed by Kimber's predecessor as company commander, Tom Newman, to rationalise the old hit-or-miss system of cadging, scrounging and triumphs of chaotic improvisation. Paul got on readily with Major Newman, but the new bureaucratic control did not please Tony Colegate, who frankly despised unnecessary tidiness, form-filling and people who set store by office routine. When the company was ordered to move up from Comilla to Imphal itself, it was Paul who led 10/10 Section's convoy of lorries,[58] set up its headquarters at Tulihal airstrip, and instituted an orderly office with a flexible system of stock control. The section lived, slept, worked and messed within sight and sound of the airfield. Dass kept the ledger book, writing up what was available each morning on a blackboard, 'so that a glance at the board, and a glance at the demands, showed what the transport and collection problems might be at the end of the day'.[59]

Jim Corben had by this time joined the company as Motor Transport Officer, and he and Paul resumed their old double act, ribbing one another, swapping stories, working so smoothly together that the sepoys could not believe they weren't brothers ('It must be the likeness in our hawklike beaks,' wrote Jim).[60] Paul described in *Johnnie Sahib* the difficulty of winning cooperation from men whose allegiance was already wholeheartedly pledged to Colegate, but letters and recollections from this period make it clear that he rapidly established his own base at the table under the blackboard, where he and Corben sat side by side, coordinating the flow of lorries and material, dovetailing the packing, loading and drops with their havildar clerks: Dass, Nimu Purkayastha, Hari Rahman (known as Sunshine), and C. R. Nag of the MT platoon.

The great fertile plain of Imphal was remote and self-sufficient, an idyllically beautiful valley watered by the Manipur River, ringed with jungle and cut off by precipitous mountains from the rest of India. There were plentiful wild geese and duck on the lake, every pond teemed with fish, palm trees, bamboo and malacca cane thickets flourished alongside fruit orchards and vegetable gardens. Raspberries grew on the hillsides with purple iris, white jasmine and dog roses. The little town of Imphal itself had its miniature British cantonment with large sprawling bungalows for government officials, an engineer's house, a school and an English cemetery. It had been an isolated, paradisal place, reminding nostalgic visitors of the Sussex Downs, until 1942, when the first Japanese bombers arrived. 'In 1944 it was an advanced suburb of Armageddon. Beyond the Logtak Lake – it was still there, reed-rimmed, silent, pale blue – lay the border ridges, and beyond them, Burma,' wrote another prospective novelist, John Masters,[61] who as a regular Gurkha officer had served with Wingate's Chindits, and would shortly be appointed second in command of 19 Division under General Pete Rees.

It was characteristic of both men that, where Masters eventually produced the gripping, fast-paced, highly-coloured *Road Past Mandalay*, Paul chose to concentrate in his book on the Burma campaign (which also ends with the taking of Mandalay) on an inconclusive minor power struggle in an anti-romantic setting behind the lines during a lull in the fighting: 'in *Johnnie* not a shot gets fired in anger,' he wrote, defending himself hotly against the charge of writing jungle adventure stories. 'The fire is all temperament, male temperament. These men are running a business. True, the dividend for the shareholders is survival, but as in any other business that was ever run that consideration isn't necessarily the one uppermost in the minds of the management.'[62] Paul came in the end to dislike *Johnnie Sahib* ('you are right, that first frightful little novel ... was autobiographical')[63] as much as the rest of his early work, partly perhaps because he had transferred plot, setting and personnel wholesale from fact to fiction. Place names are imaginary but people remain intact: Dass and Nimu appear under their own names (Paul had written to ask their permission first),[64] and there is even a dim but dependable Scottie (Paul's inevitable army nickname) under the Major's command. But Paul put most of himself into Jim Taylor, the over-imaginative, apprehensive, untried new subaltern destined to take over from Captain Johnnie Brown, whose flamboyant individualism and flagrant disregard of regulations eventually force the Major to sack him just as Kimber reluctantly replaced Tony Colegate in the autumn of 1944: 'it took 3 or 4 weeks, after Tony's sacking, for Kimber to agree I should put up three pips,' wrote Paul, who was promoted captain in command of 10/10 Section on 4 November. 'I remember the night very well (Imphal) when he suddenly looked across and said "You'd better put up that other pip, Scottie." '[65]

A platoon is one of the four best commands in the army, according to Slim, 'because it is your first command, because you are young, and because, if you are any good, you know the men in it better than their mothers do and love them as much.'[66] Paul certainly tended his men like a mother, and ruled them as strictly as his own mother had controlled him. The Section (later renamed 10/10 Platoon) numbered by this time roughly one hundred and thirty men, mixed Hindus, Muslims, Sikhs, Christians and Nepalese. Paul supervised their different diets, inspected their drinking water, sorted out family problems, inquired after their children and sent his respects to their wives. He flew with them when he could, making a point of going on the next sortie after a crash to encourage the ejection crews, and enjoying the occasional landing in a clearing 'somewhere in Burma', so long as he could pop back by nightfall in time for a drink in the mess.[67] Paul always insisted that he was an urban Londoner, happiest in Piccadilly Circus, ill at ease in the backwoods whether of Mylor or Manipur. He seldom if ever regaled his family after the war with the kind of stories Jim Corben liked to tell about clearing the tortuous single-track Imphal road by shoving broken-down lorries down the sheer mountainside, or finding himself dying of thirst in the jungle with the siren voices of invisible Japanese soldiers luring him from the trees (after the war Jim would never sleep without a full jug of water on his bedside table in case this nightmare came back). One of Jim's most hair-raising Scott-and-Corben adventures described how the pair of them, lost on a mission without a pilot, somehow negotiated the flight back to base with Jim handling the controls and Paul navigating.[68]

Paul's own recollections were more matter-of-fact. He instigated practical innovations, like the section blackboard and a separate

TOP LEFT *Jim Corben, who recognised Paul on the troopship bound for India in 1943 as* 'a FRIEND, *a real friend, I mean a friend for life'.* TOP RIGHT *Flight Sergeant Peter Green, another lifelong friend picked up in India, eventually the model for Sergeant Guy Perron in the Raj Quartet.* LEFT *Cadet Scott being licked into shape in 1943 at OTS, Belgaum: 'The word went round: We're sahibs now.'* ABOVE *Jimmy Leasor, already working on his first novel at Belgaum, and Bob Mason who would paint the portrait that went everywhere with Paul for the rest of his life.*

INES OF COMMUNICATION'

A new play by Paul Scott
based on his novel 'Johnnie Sahib'

★

CAST IN ORDER OF APPEARANCE

tenant Taylor, R.I.A.S.C. (Jim)	David Oxley
ildar-clerk Nimu	Roger Snowdon
adar Moti Ram Sahib	Abraham Sofaer
by Jan Mohammed	Charles Thomson
Major	Edward Evans
tenant-Colonel Baxter	Patrick Waddington
tain Scott (Scottie)	John Boyd Brent
tain Parrish (Bill)	Michael Rathborne
tenant Ghosh (Ghoshey)	Hugh Munro
ildar Dass	Peter Elliott
tain Brown (Johnnie)	Patrick Troughton
tenant Johns	Neil Gibson
by Kaisa Ram	Y. Yanai
or Shelley	Michael Kelly
tenant Smith (Geoff)	Brian Kent

OTHERS TAKING PART

J. Deromos, A. Gaffor, V. Giondo, G. Martin
M. Rahaman, B. Weeraperuna

*The action takes place in India and Burma
between July 1944 and March 1945*

SETTINGS BY CLIFFORD HUET
in association with Frederick A. Knapman

★

DUCED   BY   IAN   ATKINS   AT   8.15

*Paul's professional
debut as a writer: the
play based on his
experience of supplying
the 14th Army in
Burma, and broadcast
by BBC Radio on 12
February 1950.* ABOVE
RIGHT *The 14th Army
on the move in the
winter of 1944/45,
marching south to
Mandalay at the end of
a supply line manned by
Captain Scott's No. 1
Coy.* RIGHT *Paul,
standing second from
left, with Bob Mason
and Jim Corben,
garlanded, in centre.*

NCOs' mess ('The idea was . . . to give the NCOs a sense of self-importance . . . & it kept the NCOs from being too familiar with the men under them').[69] He had protested when Jim called him a peppery little captain – 'I don't mind the peppery,' he told Penny indignantly, 'it's the little I can't stand' – but, from below, he seemed peremptory and masterful enough. Dass cherished all his life the memory of a punishment dished out by his officer to a group of troublemakers made to drill at the double, with heavy parachute bales on their backs, running up and down and saluting each time they passed Captain Scott's open office door.[70] Paul himself said that trying to do business in India, given the Indians' fatalistic sense of time and disconcerting habit of telling people what they wanted to hear, drove him wild with irritation. He contained it by developing what became a lifelong instinct for soothing ruffled feelings, forestalling scenes and averting crises: his fictional *alter egos*, from Jim Taylor onwards, are pacific and placatory, adept at preventing people like Colegate and Kimber from reaching boiling point ('The whole damned patrol was like a row of kettles under which you had to keep turning down the gas . . .').[71]

The 14th Army offensive was timed to go off at the beginning of December, with 19 Division making at top speed for Mandalay as a diversionary measure, while the main advance was secretly concentrated seventy miles south on Meiktila. Supplies and equipment were, in Slim's view, deplorably inadequate, his fleet of available aircraft lamentably depleted, his lack of outside support made up only by the unlimited ingenuity, skill and determination of officers and men both in and behind the lines. His scheme for crushing the Japanese army between the hammer of Mandalay and the anvil of Meiktila proved brilliantly successful. 19 Division covered two hundred miles in the first twenty days, hacking their own road out of the mountains with picks and shovels as they went, crossing the Irrawaddy in early January, and racing down at top speed on Mandalay at the beginning of March. John Masters vividly describes the night of 10 March, which he spent in hand-to-hand combat, battling his way with the 4th Gurkhas up through the tunnels, fortified temples and covered stairways inside Mandalay Hill, until at dawn next day he stood on the summit with his CO, General Rees, looking out over the ancient palace of the kings of Burma. Paul had less glamorous memories of the same night: 'I was probably one of the first junior officers to know that we'd got Mandalay back, because I'd spent hours loading about 20 Dakotas with 88 shells which they were battering the city with, crashed into bed about midnight, & then was called out ½ hour later & ordered to offload the planes & get them reloaded by dawn with 44 gallon drums of petrol for tanks – which of course meant 19 Div had got Mandalay & was going forward. We made it.'[72]

Slim's army was by this time collectively high on exhilaration from one end to the other of its lengthening and increasingly precarious supply line ('There was a limit to human endurance,' he wrote of his air supply companies and crews in *Defeat Into Victory*, 'and they must be near it').[73] Paul found time in the week of his twenty-fifth birthday in March 1945 to draw up a progress report on his first quarter of a century for Clive, but it was a stilted and self-conscious exercise. The present had engulfed the past. If the race for Mandalay had been punishing, the 370 mile sprint south to Rangoon was a breakneck gamble against not only the Japanese but the monsoon, expected to start in mid May. In the event it broke two weeks early on 1 May, the day before a stray pilot reconnoitring the city reported the famous slogan written on the roof of Rangoon gaol: 'JAPS GONE PULL FUCKING FINGER OUT' (the last part was modestly garbled in Slim's published account to *exdigitate*). News of victory in Europe that month seemed hardly more than a satisfactory footnote to this triumphant capitulation. The fall of Rangoon was the signal for yet another orgy of planning, re-equipping and regrouping in preparation for the invasion of Malaya that would avenge the loss of Singapore, with which the whole campaign had begun. No 1 Air Supply Company was promptly posted from Imphal north to the base camp at Agartala (Comitarla, with its general hospital and nearby river in *Johnnie Sahib*, is a cross between Comilla and Agartala). Almost exactly a year had passed since Paul had joined his section. Kimber was once again suffering the torments of prickly heat – 'On the day the rain came I went out of my basha into the compound and saw him standing in the downpour wearing nothing at all and shouting for joy'[74] – and this time it was Paul's turn to celebrate a lull in the fighting with a month's leave.

He spent the month of June sampling the night life of Calcutta, followed by the delights of a houseboat on the Dal Lake in Kashmir with Jim Corben, who made an excellent travelling companion, amusing, convivial and tirelessly inquisitive. Both were in a state to take satisfaction in everything from the journey itself – Paul never tired of the pleasures of Indian trains with their mahogany-lined carriages, well-appointed private compartments and leisurely meals in the dining car – to the rituals of arrival. 'Two cases, gramophone records, bedding rolls,' wrote Jim: 'Then Calcutta, a hurried lunch in the Grand, and then a raid on the gramophone shop. Next the pictures.'[75] They indulged in an orgy of listening after months without music (entertainment for the troops seldom went beyond film shows and the odd ENSA touring group: Paul had been amazed to find Noël Coward – 'my rival!' – turning up with a pianist in Comilla the week after he got there himself).[76] Calcutta remained ever afterwards his favourite among Indian cities, and in it his favourite haunt was the Grand Hotel on Chowringhee, with its courtyard and balconies, its spacious view over the tree-lined maidan, its elegant shops and stalls that made him think fondly of the Burlington Arcade in Piccadilly. The place was crammed with officers on leave, sleeping six to a room, drinking or dancing under coloured lights in the great central court with the beautiful Eurasian girls whose plight always stirred pangs of fellow feeling in Paul. Nina Mackenzie in *Johnnie Sahib* is the first of a procession of girls in his books 'dancing at the Grand Hotel in skirts absurdly short',[77] coupling in hotel rooms, in soldiers' billets, in the backs of taxis and trucks, girls who have learnt from experience to take any risk, endure any humiliation, bite on any bullet in pursuit of the elusive British or American passport that would guarantee not only a living but an identity and a homeland.

Paul held that anyone who sat long enough in the Grand Hotel must eventually meet someone he knew, or pick someone up if he didn't. It was in Firpo's bar, next door to the Grand on Chowringhee, that he first met Flight Sergeant Peter Green, a jaunty character in a battered bush hat, also newly back from Burma and still smarting from what the RAF considered the frightful fiasco of not having been needed at the last minute to take Rangoon. Four years younger than Paul, Peter was a classicist with a scholarship to Cambridge from Charterhouse, and a horror of being type cast. He explained that he had refused a commission on the characteristically rational grounds that no one below Squadron Leader enjoyed as much power and freedom as a warrant officer in the RAF. He was working at the time for Intelligence which provided an admirable excuse for getting about, sniffing the air, asking questions and generally covering a good deal of ground in India. He and Paul took to one another at once: they shared the same sharp slanting humour, and the same iron determination to write. Each appreciated the other's dry wit, and also his own luck in finding another optimist who still believed in a life to come after the war when people would once again read and write books.

Peter was everything Paul liked best: civilised, inquiring, unorthodox, hard-drinking with an imperturbable gaiety that masked uncommon intellectual openness and generosity. For his part, Peter recognised immediately that Paul would succeed as a writer: 'I never doubted it for a moment. Rod of tungsten.'[78] They plunged straight into one of those wide-ranging serial conversations covering pretty well everything, but especially gossip and books, which they would continue on and off in one continent or another over the next twenty years and more. In a sense, this meeting at Firpo's was a replay of that other chance encounter four years earlier with Peter Lumley (himself now also an Intelligence Sergeant in Field Security) at the Gibbons Hotel in Torquay. 'At the time I thought he was trying to pick me up,' Peter Green wrote, 'and looking back I'm not sure that in a weird kind of way he may not in fact have been doing just that.'[79] Peter, who served in one of the RAF's most blatantly homosexual units, had become expert at recognising and gracefully fending off this kind of advance: like Lumley before him, he thought none the worse of his new friend, and, when the war summoned them separate ways, each retained a vivid, vigorous and thoroughly congenial impression of the other.

Plans were well in hand in the summer of 1945 for Operation Zipper to retake Malaya. By early August Paul was in Bombay, preparing with his section to sail for Port Swettenham in the Malacca Strait some two hundred miles up the coast from Singapore, when the first reports arrived of atom bombs dropped on Hiroshima and Nagasaki. The war was virtually over before 10/10 Section embarked on SS *Samaflora*, and the Japanese had surrendered unconditionally by the time they landed on Penang Island in September. They camped the first night in a coconut grove, where Paul took pains to supplement the men's dry rations with fresh pineapples, although he could not prevent their being rained out at midnight by an auspicious but drenching downpour.[80] He had caused a first-class row on the troopship by insisting, as the commander of the only Indians aboard, that the British soldiers be prevented from spitting in his men's drinking water.[81] On land, the chief problem was homesickness: Dass remembered Paul consoling a lovesick young sepoy, who wept aloud from grief and loneliness.[82] He himself found leaving India as much of a shock as arriving had been, only this time in reverse. What shocked him about Malaya was its lush greenness, its civilised orderliness, the broad tarmac roads with traffic lights stretching into the jungle. '*Beautiful* country, Malaya, *marvellous*, clean, prosperous country — no signs of poverty or misery at all,' he said, 'it was irresistible: at any moment you expected Dorothy Lamour and Bob Hope to emerge from the bushes, it's that sort of place.'[83] After two and a half years away from home, Paul felt unbearably homesick not for England but for India. He missed its sticky heat, its dusty hills, its vast spaces and teeming population: 'It was at that moment I realised that I had fallen in love with India . . . all I wanted to do was get back and gaze at those barren, arid plains.'[84]

He and his section were detailed for mopping-up operations, sorting out logistics, administering civilian programmes, organising the transport of supplies and weapons. They spent a month on Penang, followed by six weeks on the mainland – 'in a village called Sungei Patani (or was it Bukit Mertagam?)'[85] – before moving to Singapore at the beginning of December. Stories of Japanese atrocities were commonplace: Havildar Dass encountered a group of weeping women whose husbands had been marched away as labourers on the Siam railway, and who had themselves been forced to flee with their children, leaving their homes to scratch a subsistence living from the jungle.[86] Allied troops were treated as liberators, entertained by girls from establishments with names like The Happy World, and welcomed by Chinese merchants who brought out stocks of silk stockings, scent and fountain pens. 'A lot of stuff had been hoarded in back rooms and under counters in Penang and Singapore from pre-Jap invasion days,' said Paul,[87] who treated himself to the Malayan kris which afterwards hung in his study in London, and would become a sinister central motif fifteen years later in *The Chinese Love Pavilion*. But he had invested too much imaginative energy and feeling in India to pay more than perfunctory attention to this new environment. Perhaps his most salutary experiences in Malaya were two encounters with elderly ladies, both British memsahibs who had returned to Singapore after the occupation, and who left him with an impression of toughness, dispossession and disorientation which he never forgot. He gave one a lift in his jeep: 'She didn't speak all the way from one end of the island to another but when she got off she said, "It is hard for people like me to thank people, but I do, even though I am bitterly ashamed to be seen *walking*, and so obviously in need of a lift." '[88] He met the other at Kalland airport while waiting for a plane to Rangoon: she told him she had spent the war in a Javanese prison camp and was going home to Kuala Lumpur to look for traces of her house or her husband:

Her plane and mine were announced at the same time. When we stood up I reached for her bag to carry it for her. She pushed it out of my hand quite viciously (before then she had seemed perfectly normal and gentle), and shouted, 'No, no. It's because people like me always had our bags carried for us that what happened to us happened.' And off she strode, lugging her heavy suitcase.[89]

The company's old commander, Tom Newman, had turned up again as a colonel at Allied Land Forces headquarters in Singapore, with Paddy Love as his assistant and plans to rope Paul in with a RAMO staff posting. But Paul took energetic precautions to evade his clutches, wangling paperwork, cadging lifts, flying out to Rangoon without official permission, and turning up thankfully in Calcutta on 31 December 1945, with only ten rupees in his pocket: 'The Field

Cashier was shut for three days for the New Year holiday. But I knew that if I sat in the lounge of the Grand Hotel, Calcutta, for an hour or two another friend would turn up who would lend me fifty chips or so.'[90] He finally tracked down and joined the remainder of No. 1 company far away to the north, 'left behind by the war, in a beautiful, beautiful place near Bihar, completely bare and empty, all living on pecans.'[91] This was the vast anonymous sprawling expanse of Chas Transit Camp: 'that bloody desert place,' Havildar Purkayastha wrote gloomily,[92] but to Paul it was a dream come true ('After just three years, the country was in my bones'). He loved 'the great open rolling land of Bihar' with its hilly, streamy contours, its emptiness and isolation, the austerity and luxuriance of its flame of the forest trees: 'the trees were completely bare, and then suddenly all this red, flaming flower comes out of them. And I just sat there for five months absorbing it all . . . I was in love with it all.'[93] There was nothing to do but wait for repatriation, and nowhere to go but Ranchi (a seventy-five-minute fast jeep ride), where the club barman mixed a powerful cocktail, and the local Carew's gin flowed freely at a smaller and tattier but friendly version of the Grand Hotel (Calcutta itself could be reached on a 48-hour pass by express train from Dhanbad).[94] Many British soldiers were exasperated beyond bearing by what seemed a pointless, enforced marking time on top of the six years of war that had already swallowed their youth, but Paul was not impatient to be gone: 'in Bihar for the next six months I sat, doing little, but absorbing India.'[95]

This time of contemplation and contentment expanded in memory (it lasted in fact four months, from early January to the end of April 1946, when he left for Bombay to join a troopship sailing for home in May). Thinking is the cheapest and one of the most effective of all long-range weapons, according to General Slim, who had also sat for months at an earlier stage in the war absorbing India, reviewing the past, pondering the future, revolving plans for turning defeat into victory; and there can be no doubt that, whether consciously or not, in a literary sense Paul at this point was doing the same. A delayed critical report on *After Our Labours* from Clive's friend, the actor Jonathan Field, had finally caught up with him in Singapore ('he says a great deal too much in its favour. It is best forgotten, I think,' was Paul's laconic comment),[96] and a further bulletin was forwarded in December reporting Clive's own latest triumph with *Pillars of Salt*. He had put it in for an international Jewish play competition organised by the parliamentary Anglo-Palestinian society, with a committee of judges headed by Harold Rubinstein who placed *Pillars* fourth out of 155 entries. Paul's jubilation was tempered by his sense that the time had come to turn his back on past disappointments and invest in a fresh plan of campaign.

Virtually everything he wrote from now on would draw more or less deeply on Indian themes. His counterparts in book after book – from Jim Taylor in *Johnnie Sahib* to Tom Brent in *The Chinese Love Pavilion*, Bill Conway in *The Birds of Paradise* and Guy Perron in the Raj Quartet – would reproduce the state of brooding abstraction Jim Corben encountered so often in Paul himself during their last weeks together in Bihar. Five years in the army had taught Paul the habit, which remained an unvarying ritual for the rest of his life, of clearing his mind last thing at night, sorting and storing the day's impressions, or simply blanking them out. Jim Taylor does it sitting on the edge of his camp bed surrounded by sleeping soldiers, and so does Guy Perron who, in the last but one of Paul's novels, has perfected the ability to switch off the sound made by obstructive or opinionated superiors: 'Perron listened attentively for . . . ten seconds . . . and then tried to tune in to what he called his other ear: the one that caught the nuances of time and history flowing softly through the room.'[97]

Sergeant Perron, who turns up in the final book of the Raj Quartet with an undercover job in Intelligence in the summer of 1945, owes much in attitudes, background and looks to Peter Green. But he also serves as a stand-in or spokesman for the author himself, who had tried to tune in an inner historical ear while waiting, like Perron, for the abortive Operation Zipper to sail from Bombay in August. Paul's initial arrival on the subcontinent had coincided, like Perron's, with a wave of anti-British feeling, and his departure would be followed by a far more savage and destructive tide of violence at the time of partition in 1947. He hadn't wanted to come and, before he sailed, he had shared the unthinking, insular view that India generally speaking represented bad news: 'bad news in my case because I knew we ought not to have it and should jolly well give it back.'[98] Devolution became the standard official policy of the post-war Labour government elected in Britain in 1945. Its advantages would be eloquently expounded in the Raj Quartet by Perron's superior officer, Captain Purvis, a political economist who endorses the Socialist determination to write India off 'as a wasted asset, a place irrevocably ruined by the interaction of a conservative and tradition-bound population and an indolent bone-headed and utterly uneducated administration, an elitist bureaucracy so out of touch with the social and economic thinking of even just the past hundred years that you honestly wonder where they've come from . . . The most sensible thing for us to do is get rid of it fast to the first bidder before it becomes an intolerable burden.'[99]

Paul and Jim Corben had much to put up with in Bihar in 1946, after

Major Kimber had left, from their own boneheaded colonel. They prided themselves not only on superior efficiency, man-management and political judgement, but on fighting a tireless battle against harassment from above, against blinkered and incompetent authorities, especially against RAMO ('the real winners of any competition at being the bottom'),[100] and above all RAMO's commanding officer Colonel Ingles. He seemed to them to embody fossilised and patently false Edwardian attitudes with his perpetual grumbling, his resentment of Emergency Commissioned Officers and his embattled imperialism: so far as the firm of Scott & Corben was concerned, the Colonel was a menace. But it is not hard to imagine the rage and bewilderment of a regular soldier, sensing betrayal in Whitehall, facing a precarious future, shunted to the back of beyond to be mocked and baited by a couple of cocksure young captains whose theories made his blood boil. 'He's trying the old game,' Jim wrote to Paul, describing an evening's drinking which ended with the Colonel rounding furiously on his tormentor:

He started the old ECO game and the die-hard conservative policy. I wasn't having any and produced all the arguments you taught me (incidentally, thanks to you, I used them quite sincerely) and we both got very worked up with each other, he closing the conversation with the words, 'It's time you knew better than to discuss politics in the Army. You're just over-civilised and one of many who will break down the British Empire which the Army through blood has built up.'
   'Di-da, di-da. . . !' That's God's truth Paul![101]

What troubled Paul later, and perhaps at the time, was his own and his contemporaries' ignorance. He had tried to remedy it by contacting young Indian intellectuals at the university in Calcutta, where there was universal astonishment at rumours of a young English officer wanting a meeting. Such a notion would have been unheard of in peacetime when even the most civilised, Sandhurst-trained Indian officer could not conceivably have set foot in a British brother officer's home, and it was still practically impossible in 1945 for an officer to mix with civilians on equal terms. Paul's summing up – 'one did not, as an English soldier, easily meet many of the indigenous population'[102] – was an understatement. Like most ECOs, he got on admirably with sepoys, servants and bearers, and he was friendly if never intimate with the young Indians he met in the mess. His relations with his own men were warmly, even passionately cordial. When he left Bihar, he received cards and letters from Nimu Purkayastha, Nag and Sunshine, fondly recalling their off-duty chats over a beer under the mango tree, and he kept up a stately correspondence for years with the trusty Dass.

Soldiers in 10/10 Section dreamed of him at night, and some slept with his photograph under their pillows.[103] One, called Ahmed Sayeed Khan (Paul paid him the compliment of naming two brothers after him in the Raj Quartet), sent him a tremulous, tender seven-page love letter, which ended: 'Till memory fades and life departs, your love will ever remain in my heart.'[104] The tone of their correspondence suggests that one of the elements of Paul's happiness in Bihar was the freedom to indulge feelings long and ferociously suppressed at home. Whether or not it stopped short of physical expression, the simple, uncomplicated affection of boys like Ahmed carried none of the connotations of shame and secrecy that still surrounded attraction to one's own sex in England.

But Paul's attempts to make political or intellectual contact with his contemporaries in India came to nothing. Dulal Nag Chaudhuri, eventually one of the subcontinent's most distinguished nuclear physicists, personal scientific adviser to Nehru and Vice-Chancellor of Jawaharlal Nehru University, would become also in the 1960s a friend of Paul's: he had been a student in Calcutta in the war, and well remembered his own and his friends' bafflement when word reached them that an unknown Englishman in uniform wanted to talk.[105] The meeting was not a success. The gap between ruler and ruled proved unbridgeable. It did not take long for both parties to realise how little they could communicate from either side of a barrier not so much of hostility as of mutual suspicion and mistrust. In a sense the Raj Quartet embodied Paul's answer twenty years later to the young nationalist intellectuals with whom he had got nowhere in Calcutta in wartime. It was also his answer to the boneheaded colonels, the diehard conservatives, the truculent memsahibs whom he came in the end to regard with understanding and sympathy. He felt they had a right to be heard, and that no members of the human race – neither British memsahibs nor Indian sepoys – should have to contend, metaphorically speaking, with spit in their drinking water.

Much if not most of the next three decades would be spent thinking about India. At first Paul tried to write about it using conventional literary formulae, but he was never entirely convinced by his own attempts at oriental romance or jungle adventure; he said he always felt something of a sham when he wrote about the fighting in Burma ('The rest of us are nothing,' as a young British officer says of a hero closely resembling John Masters in one of Paul's early novels: 'The rest of us are dressed for the part').[106] Paul would eventually bring off his own most ambitious effects by altogether different means, deploying unheroic characters pursuing prosaic occupations in mundane settings with a panache and a panoramic sweep that required unremitting imaginative effort ('So much else had to be imagined too, like what it felt like to be a deputy commissioner, or a political agent').[107] His readers tended to assume that he had been born in India, brought up in a princely State, possessed firsthand experience of the political service or the Indian Civil Service. He disabused them gently with self-deprecation and jokes. He had been schooling himself in the distinction between art and life ever since as a small child he had learned to cultivate the sense of being an outsider, a displaced person, an observer never fully at home in his own environment. 'When I'm in India nowadays I usually manage to feel embarrassed, as an impostor would feel embarrassed, when people say "Which state was your father resident in?" ', he wrote in 1975, the year in which he published the fourth and final volume of the Raj Quartet. 'But writing fiction is of course the act of an impostor . . .'[108]

CHAPTER SEVEN

Down the drains of destiny

England, for soldiers returning home in 1946, was barely recognisable as the country they had left behind before the war. Trains travelling inland from the coast passed derelict blackened building shells, gaping sites, wildflowers invading craterous exposed basements in half-ruined cities. Churches had been gutted, town centres flattened, industrial and manufacturing bases effectively destroyed. People everywhere looked grey, pinched, exhausted, underfed and badly dressed. Luxuries were unobtainable on the open market. Essentials – meat, eggs, cheese, milk, sugar, tea, fuel, furniture, clothing, blankets – were all severely rationed. The new Labour government, struggling with wholesale social reconstruction, found itself hard pressed to feed and clothe, let alone find jobs and homes for the unemployed millions discharged in wave after wave by the armed forces. 'It was a shabby, disgruntled, impoverished society, alive with deserters, small-time criminals and black marketeers, which moved among the bombed houses and burnt-out buildings of London in which I settled that spring of 1946,' wrote Rupert Croft-Cooke[1] who, like Paul, had been to some extent prepared for what he found by the overcrowding, the shortage of basic necessities like food and drink, the squalor, discomfort and disorganisation of the long voyage home from India by troopship.

Almost the last thing slipped into Paul's hand, as he awaited embarkation orders in the transit camp after infuriating delays in May, had been a package from Jim (himself stranded for another six months with the company in Bihar), itemising a forty-point plan for action on their return.[2] Their homecoming was to be a glorious rampage across the southern counties, taking in pubs, bars, cricket and football matches, race meetings for Jim, theatre and opera for Paul, joint sallies to the Chelsea Arts and Southdown Hunt Balls, together with more long-term investments: point number 18 was 'Wedding – whose? (Jim's)', points number 30 and 31 envisaged an unbroken string of annual christenings stretching from 1947 to 1954 (with an optimistic 'Note, 51 onwards is Jimmy's share'). Jim, lonely and depressed after the collapse of his South African affair, envied Paul his prospect of domestic happiness, choosing presents for Penny with respectful enthusiasm in Calcutta, memorising the date of the Scotts' wedding anniversary on 23 October, and wistfully contemplating their reunion. He and Paul had planned their futures and their families in considerable detail over the past three and a half years, and Jim missed their evenings together ('I could have gone on for hours tonight had I been in the right drinking company,' he wrote on 20 May, the day after Paul finally sailed for home). But, if Jim in far-away Bihar could still set store by the old consolations, it must have been clear to Paul long before his ship docked in June that none of these dreams, except the drinking sessions and with luck the offspring, were likely to materialise in post-war reality.

The Scotts, unlike most wartime couples, had at least a place of their own in which to set up home. Penny's father had died in 1943, and she had used her small inheritance to put down the first payment for a tiny house on the far side of the Bourne in Southgate. By the spring of 1946, she had moved into 8 Hampden Way, within easy reach of Paul's parents on Bourne Hill but far enough away to minimise interference from Mrs Scott, who had initially envisaged the young couple moving into Paul's old room over the garage or, failing that, taking a house round the corner in Fox Lane. Penny scrubbed, cleaned and painted their new home herself, furnishing it with pieces collected from junk shops or contributed by friends. She saved ration coupons, sewed curtains and covers, hoarded dried fruit and egg powder for a celebration cake, dug and planted the garden ready for Paul's return. The last weeks of waiting were a time of euphoric happiness when the sun never seemed to stop shining.[3] She had meticulous instructions from his mother about Paul's special needs, how to feed him, how to protect his creative peace and privacy. His books and typewriter were laid out in an upstairs bedroom set aside to be his study.

Frances Scott had, as she said with some complacency, spoiled Paul in more senses than one. Penny, who made no literary or artistic claims herself, did not question Mrs Scott's estimate of her son's genius. At the start of their marriage Paul had introduced her to modern poetry, chanting it aloud in their rented room at Paignton in a strange, solemn, Sansomian incantation that left Penny none the wiser. Keeping her end up in these poetic sessions had been a strain ('The very look of him terrified me before we started'), but far worse was the humiliation of finding herself unable to make head or tail of *I, Gerontius* ('It's clear as daylight,' Frances Scott said scornfully, 'it's the eucharist'). If this episode undermined Penny's confidence, it can have been scarcely less shattering to Paul's. She and he both knew the depths of nervous trepidation behind his habitual bravado: like many people damaged and denied in childhood, Penny responded passionately and unconditionally to other people's inarticulate cries for help. Paul said he married her because being with her was so restful after his mother's critical abrasions. Penny, determined never again to repeat the *Gerontius* mistake, set herself from the start of their relationship to strengthen and mount guard over Paul's precarious self-confidence. One thing that always disconcerted visitors to their house was her habit of submission to his judgement. It was a pattern already established in the enchanted period leading up to their Piccadilly honeymoon, when Penny automatically fell in with Paul's plan to have two children: 'I would have approved of our leaping into the Thames that moment had he suggested it.'[4]

Penny, who had spent so much of her free time as a nurse faithfully typing and retyping manuscripts sent back from India, was well primed in 1946 to assist at the launch of Paul's post-war career as a playwright. He had come back eager to start at once on 'the play we've been waiting for me to write'.[5] For the first time in his life, he had not only a room of his own but three whole clear months, paid for by the army, to devote to writing: 'We never discussed my getting a job,' he wrote happily. 'I dashed around seeing or trying to see the people I imagined must know who I was. I studied the market. I wrote articles and stories.'[6] He, too, was buoyed up with elation at the start of this second honeymoon. The young Scotts struck everyone as a model couple, radiating faith, hope and energy. They called one another Honey Girl and Honey Boy: he was her dreamboat: she uncannily resembled a drawing he had made before he ever met her of his ideal girl. Soon their happiness was complete: 'Before the three months was quite up my wife said she hoped I didn't mind but it seemed that she was slightly pregnant. There were only two answers to that. The first was that I didn't mind at all, the second was to present myself at a place called the London Appointments Board, which was a kind of labour exchange for people who had emergency commissions.'[7]

But underneath their pattern of content lay an unresolved emotional conflict sedulously damped down by Paul and vigorously stirred up by Frances Scott. Paul's mother had rallied and regrouped her forces in the three years of his absence. Defeated in a frontal attack over the new house, she redoubled her assault where her daughter-in-law's defence was weakest. Penny's childhood had made her acutely sensitive to undercurrents of disappointment or dissatisfaction in others, for which she was apt to blame herself. Whenever they met, on visits to Bourne Hill and later at Hampden Way, Frances continually marvelled aloud at Penny's inexperience as a wife, her unfamiliarity with artists, the six-year age gap between herself and Paul, the toughness of the nursing profession as opposed to the sensitivity of writers, the unworthiness of women in general and Penny in particular to be helpmeets for Paul, not forgetting the change in Penny's appearance caused by a wartime eye operation which had left her with an attractive, asymmetrical fleck in one eye. Nothing escaped Frances' relentless disparagement. 'She was terrible,' said Penny. 'And terrifying. The energy of the woman – she *never* gave in. She had incredible strength.'

Frances's displeasure cast a cloud in the background to Paul's homecoming. He had toyed in India with the notion of tea-planting in Assam: long afterwards he told the writer and traveller Freya Stark that he would probably have stayed on in the Indian Army if he had not had a wife at home.[8] Marriage had removed his need for physical escape. Released from the threat of maternal domination, he could afford to view his mother more tolerantly than Penny, who had replaced him in the firing line. Sometimes she felt almost crushed between Frances's outspoken contempt and Paul's silent reservations, which dulled the gloss of her own happiness. He took a keen critical interest in her make-up, her dress sense, her décor and furnishings, so much so that he seemed to her to pull to pieces the little house with which she had tried so hard to please him. Years later, in preliminary autobiographical doodlings for what subsequently became *A Male Child*, Paul recognised his own feelings (including dismay at the pokiness of the new home) in the hero who 'has returned from the war overbearing, intolerant, "managing", determined to make good by leaving the country & going abroad, sentimental about his mother whom [his wife] hates.'[9]

Occasional peremptoriness was not the only sign Paul gave of keying himself up to face a homecoming he both longed for and dreaded. He had written to Penny beforehand asking her not to meet his train, so that he could slip home quietly rather than risk a scene. Each of them feared falling short of the other's expectations. He had come back to an uncertain future: 'I also returned to two other things I had left behind when leaving for India. A typewriter and a wife.'[10] Both mutely required him to perform. Paul, who from now on kept his ordeals strictly to himself, seemed to several people on his return from

India to have clamped down and be holding himself in. He gave his brother Peter a record of Max Bruch's violin concerto, the piece he had heard an airman play at Addison's Café in Torquay in 1940, when he himself was still a youthful poet dreaming of glory with the sound of imaginary applause ringing in his ears. He told Peter that it was to be their coming-home music just as Tchaikovsky's 'Pathétique' had supplied music for their going away. But Peter found his brother permanently changed after the war: 'Paul was a quite different person when he came back. *Quite different.* All the fervour had gone.' He had let the army choke it out of him. But his rigid, hard-won self-control and apparent lack of feeling were hard for Penny to bear. Unquestioning compliance had been planted in her deep and early by the aunt whose upbringing made her feel she was tolerated only on a sufferance that might be withdrawn unless she earned her keep. It had given her the habit of rushing forward to forestall or disarm criticism which made Paul instinctively recoil, and Paul's withdrawals never failed to wound her: 'The cool reserve that was so much a part of him came again as a shock to me, and gave me the unreasonable impression as it always did that I had displeased him.'[11]

Whatever Paul may have felt in retrospect, Penny maintained that he had greeted news of her pregnancy with an element of blank dismay, which is perhaps not altogether surprising in the circumstances. Job hunting was bound to prove a thankless business for a twenty-six-year-old with no paper qualifications in time of cut-throat competition when military experience was virtually universal. Paul's few pre-war contacts proved discouraging. He got nowhere with Captain Peter Baker, who had his hands full turning the Resurgam Press into a full-scale publishing house. Clive, ill and out of work, was preoccupied with troubles of his own. Paul persuaded J. B. Priestley to read one of his plays at some point, but Priestley made no move. Coming fourth in an Anglo-Palestinian International Play Competition brought neither recognition nor any prospect of production. Paul called on the chairman of the judges, the solicitor Harold Rubinstein, who promised publication at some unspecified date, making Paul as the only non-Jewish finalist of the four feel ignominious and out of place: the winner, Emil Burano, was a rabbi who had survived Dachau and settled in Los Angeles, the runner-up was another central European persecuted by the Nazis. Third place had gone to a girl called Toni Block,[12] a Londoner as young and inexperienced as Paul himself, although her play did at least achieve an amateur performance by Anglo-Palestinian club members.

'Mark, you sound horribly browned off,' Jim wrote sympathetically from Bihar in August. 'I am sorry to hear people are as bloody at home as they are out here – it comes as rather a shock.'[13] The only compensation for this depressing interlude was an introduction from Rubinstein (a man of letters and part-time playwright himself) to a woman called Joyce Wiener, who was in the process of setting herself up as a literary and theatrical agent in St John's Wood. Miss Wiener, who needed clients, took on all four finalists but held out no great hope of placing *Pillars of Salt*. Nor was she impressed by the scripts Paul had brought back from India, *After Our Labours*, and a sub-Hemingway monologue dashed off in August 1945 on board ship between Bombay and Singapore (Clive had been uncharacteristically scathing about this effort too).[14] Miss Wiener urged him to write something fresh but by the end of his three months release leave Paul recognised that for him, temporarily at any rate, the game was up.

He knew too much about insolvency to take the prospect of it lightly. Familiar as a child with the spectacle of his father shuffling cheque stubs, at his wits' end to pacify landlord and bank manager, Paul had grown up under threat of the penury and ruin that had engulfed the Wrights' venture at Kingsbury (George Wright, his wife, Gilbert's, and their three surviving sisters had all died in the war, leaving Gilbert himself, forlorn and threadbare, as the only survivor in his generation of the family shipwreck). In the autumn of 1946, it looked as though Paul had landed back where he had started ten years earlier as an audit clerk, only this time he had a wife and child to support besides himself. The girl at the appointments board offered a clerking job at £6 a week with the merchant bankers, Brown, Shipley and, when Paul protested, fixed him up instead in the Far Eastern Accounts Department of the RAF's Malcolm Clubs, a network of social clubs for airforce personnel set up in memory of Wing Commander Malcolm, V C, with headquarters in Belgravia. Nearly thirty years later Paul liked to claim that the job he had rejected went eventually to a Lieutenant-Colonel Edward Heath, who had by then risen to become prime minister:

The joke about the RAF Malcolm Club was that everyone who turned up there to help with the accounts had been offered Brown, Shipley. Subsequently, in my professional life, I was always meeting men who had been invited to join that estimable firm, but it is only about three years ago that I discovered who had done so. And then I wondered whether I had been wise to decline the opportunity . . .[15]

At the time, Paul's predicament was no joke. The only solution to his dead-end job seemed to lie in studying for the accountancy examinations again. The RAF Malcolm HQ presumably lies behind the seedy, one-room Knightsbridge club in *A Male Child* with its ex-service personnel ('the mufti, the uniforms, the medal ribbons, the moustaches, the women who had hung on and the women who had let go'),[16] and a membership turnover so rapid that it seemed more like a rehabilitation centre ('Every month a batch of customers passed the test and went'). Memories of this period supplied the mixture of social flux and personal despondency which is the keynote of *A Male Child*, where the ex-Indian Army captain Ian Canning trails aimlessly round London, trying to come to terms with his failure as a writer, calling on his pre-war contacts and being tactfully turned down by a well-heeled publisher:

In the taxi he talked of paper quotas, printing costs and the lack of talent amongst new writers. His overcoat had a velvet collar, the sort of coat which would make him sad at the advent of warmer weather . . . His shoes were so highly polished, his nails so well manicured that I gave his person my whole attention, until I became conscious of my own feet thrust out in front of me on the bristly floor mat. My shoes were dull, with thick traceries of lines and cracks between the toe caps and the insteps. My pre-war trousers, with no knife-edge crease . . . were beginning to fray at the turn-ups, and there was an old caked stain of mud on one leg. I looked up at my reflection in the glass which the driver's broad back turned into a mirror, and saw a long thin face which was my own, with a lick of pale colourless hair hanging over the forehead.[17]

Rescue came that autumn in the shape of another sleek, polished, prosperous, velvet-collared publisher, Resurgam's Peter Baker, who telephoned to enquire if Paul's services would be available as book-keeper for his publishing operation. This was a joint venture between Baker's brand new Falcon Press (named after the armoured car in which he had served with distinction, being twice captured by the Germans and twice escaping, working for the Dutch resistance, returning eventually with a Military Cross),[18] and the Grey Walls Press founded by Charles Wrey Gardiner of *Poetry Quarterly*. A transient network of little publishing houses had sprung up like goosegrass after the war, but this one had a more impressive financial base than most (guaranteed by the chairman's proud father, Reginald Baker, who had made a cinematic fortune out of Ealing Studios), together with considerable practical experience, literary flair, an adventurous and discerning list of authors, all contributed by Gardiner. The outfit operated from premises in an old oil shop at 6 Crown Passage, a narrow alley running between King Street and Pall Mall just off Paul's familiar Piccadilly beat. The general impression of faintly dubious optimism was nicely caught by another of Baker's new recruits at Crown Passage, Roland Gant: 'A brave signboard, mounted on a wrought-iron frame and swinging in the wind like a pub's, identified a warren of small rooms with trampoline flooring and a snakepit of plumbing as a janus-headed publishing house – the Falcon Press and Grey Walls Press.'[19]

The place was almost entirely staffed by poets (a thoroughly practical arrangement according to at least one of Gardiner's authors, given the startling inefficiency of so many publishing concerns run by non-poets),[20] ranging from ex-Resurgam junior recruits like Paul and Gant to the typographer Sean Jennett, the Czech symbolist Fred Marnau, and Gardiner himself. Even Baker was a confident and by no means incompetent lyricist in all styles from Tennyson's to the Georgians' and Stephen Spender's. The appointment of a book-keeper filled the last vacancy in Captain Baker's crew, 'hopeful veterans', in Roland Gant's description, 'still young but rarely feeling so ... wearing demob suits *faute de mieux*, and hair a shade longer than regulation as the only luxury not requiring coupons'.[21] Paul, characteristically inconspicuous in this company, seemed tall and slenderly built: 'This was deceptive, the illusion being aided by his angular face, smoothly-brushed dark hair and longish nose – an impression of a man tall and slim whereas in fact he was not much above average height and he was both broad-shouldered and muscular, this too hidden by his dark suit. A cool, level gaze gave no hint of jumping to rapid conclusions; he had a quiet and level voice to match.'[22]

Paul was successively promoted over the next twelve months from book-keeper to accountant, chief accountant, financial manager and finally company secretary (regular upgrading was not matched by salary increases nor was there ever, by Paul's own account, more than one person in the accounts department, namely himself).[23] Gant, who had originally agreed to fill in as general dogsbody on £6 a week while waiting to sail for France or emigrate to Canada, ended up four years later as publicity manager. The pair were initially wary of one another, 'wary also of Peter Baker, who was intelligent, amusing, somewhat deranged and highly entertaining beneath a plausible manner'.[24] A year younger than Paul, educated at Eastbourne College and destined for Cambridge when hostilities had broken out in 1939, Baker had, as he said himself, come out of the war in a hurry determined to conquer the book world in record time. His plans for the combined presses were imperial and expansive. He had insufferable energy, indomitable courage, a schoolboy taste in horseplay and fast cars. He was a boisterous driver, who circled roundabouts the wrong way round for fun and impressed his senior partner by skidding back to the office after lunch grazing the pavements, 'at fifty miles an hour down Shaftesbury Avenue, on the wrong side of the road, twisting the wheel

among the traffic of Piccadilly Circus, making people in the road jump
for their lives'.[25] Easily the best of Baker's wartime poems is 'The
Motor Race', which sounds like the confessions of a modernistic Mr
Toad: 'The screaming of wheels, the rending/ of holocaust gears, the
whining discordance/ of pained superchargers/ as men duel to death
on oil-stained concrete . . .'[26]

Baker had other points in common with Mr Toad, not least his
melting charm. He touched Gardiner's heart with his exuberance, his
bumptiousness, his dogged devotion to the firm: 'He is very doglike
with his brown doggish eyes, vitality, playfulness. A cheerful dog after
the marrow bone of life, a large temperamental dog sometimes with a
beaten look of depression, then jumping up to you full of
enthusiasm.'[27] Baker's rampancy was inspiring but also exhausting
and demanding. There were heavy drinkers at Crown Passage even
before the chairman added a whisky distillery to his many acquisi-
tions, starting a brisk traffic in bottles slipped discreetly under the
counter with the books by the packer in the basement. Gardiner, still
only in his forties but in some ways antediluvian from birth, felt at
times as if he had got mixed up with the Crazy Gang or Tommy
Handley's lunatic radio comedy show, ITMA. His colleagues perpetually amazed him: 'They laugh, they shout, they pound up and
downstairs from nine to six . . . No comic film could move faster. How
any business gets done beats me.'[28]

In fact the press was expanding at its chairman's favourite dizzy
speed. Grey Walls had built up a small but choice backlist since
Gardiner started printing odd books in 1940 in a shed beside the
railway at Billericay, and it quadrupled its annual output after 1946. It
published English first editions of Scott Fitzgerald's *Tender is the
Night*, and Nathaniel West's *Miss Lonelyhearts*, with a solid core of
classics as well as works by Rainer Maria Rilke, Raymond Radiguet,
Kenneth Patchen, Michael Ayrton, Mervyn Peake, Kathleen Raine
and Ruthven Todd.[29] The Falcon Press list was a broader and more
commercial proposition. Everybody lent a hand on the editorial side,
including the accountant and the publicity manager. Paul afterwards
enjoyed recalling his part in one of Baker's more straightforward
schemes for making a quick killing by rushing through a reprint of
Swinburne's *Lesbia Brandon*: in the event Paul dropped in every six
months for years to discuss progress over tea and muffins with the
scholarly editor, who produced at last a scrupulously annotated
text with an introduction almost twice as long.[30]

Paul and Roland Gant, both first-class story-tellers, collected a
lifetime's repertoire of Crown Passage characters, running from
Gardiner in his upstairs office (where he had installed a couch for

entertaining lady poets in the afternoons) to Mr Heighington, the packer in the basement, who looked and talked like Tommy Handley, and Roland's assistant M— who drank like a Shakespearian porter. Almost a quarter of a century later Paul still revisited the place in dreams, remembering 'nearly every physical inch of it: the washstand at the head of the staircase, the shape of Peter's room, the perpetual need for artificial lighting: Graeme's monkish room [this was Graeme Hutchinson of the Unicorn and Richards Press], and the dark at the top of *those* stairs where young M— used to be sick and desperate with erotic explorations and disappointments.'[31]

Paul struck colleagues and clients at the time as invariably amiable, if somewhat aloof (anyone beginning to form an inkling of Baker's business methods would have had a lot to be aloof about). He dressed soberly, ate his lunch out of a paper bag prepared by Penny and kept his head down as he had at school. He was now indisputably part of the world he had dreamed of as a teenager wandering round Bloomsbury without realising it was a book production district, and getting an authentic literary thrill from a first sight of galley proofs in Clive's flat on Bourne Hill. He had come a long way since then, although not appreciably nearer to being accepted by a society in some ways as self-contained and stratified as the army, and as conscious of its uniforms. Literary London seethed with factions: picturesque poets of the New Apocalypse in broad-brimmed black hats; intellectuals in French berets who 'tapped their Gauloise on their Sartre', in Dylan Thomas's phrase, and abominated all things English; literati from the older universities with supercilious smiles and drawling voices expressly designed to repel boarders ('all about me, long thin accents with yellow waistcoats and carefully windswept hair, one lock over the eye, bleated and fluted,' wrote Thomas after a raid on Oxford. 'In a drawl of corduroy at the tea turn, vowels were plucked and trussed').[32] Paul could not feel comfortable, then or later, in this sort of company. He never cut himself off as conclusively as Clive, who had retreated from the poetic scene after a salutary experience in a pub when three hard-drinking visionaries rode over him roughshod. They were the dashing Captain Baker, the still more flamboyant Tambimuttu of *Poetry London*, and Thomas himself, so much the worse for wear that he could not even stagger upstairs for supper: 'I tried to remain companionable on two glasses of lemonade,' wrote Clive, resolving that one such adventure was enough to last a lifetime.[33] Paul never objected to serious drinking but, so far as any form of literary chic or for that matter literary establishment was cconcerned, he remained, by temperament, choice and circumstances, essentially an outsider all his life.

Crown Passage, which surrounded him with poets, also continually confronted him with the spectacle of his own poetic failure. He had a couple of pieces selected in 1947 and 1948 for *Poetry Quarterly*, more as a matter of form than a mark of any particular respect by the editor, who made no secret of his scorn for the business side of publishing, going out of his way several times in these years to single out accountants as 'dead souls' and the enemies of true creation.[34] While his colleagues pounded up and down selling books, Gardiner held himself ready on an upper floor 'to assume the cloak of stars, the fillet of the poet-priest'.[35] Paul, toiling below over chronically disordered accounts, found his task made no easier by his employers' respective attitudes to money. Baker ran towards it joyfully as if it were an ocean, vast, bottomless and inviting, in which to dip and gambol. Gardiner turned his back on it as if it wasn't there. Squandering it was a necessity, almost a physical lust for Baker. For his partner, it was a moral issue. Gardiner, who constantly proclaimed his own reckless allegiance to the muse as opposed to the 'careful plodding of little men with wives to keep',[36] was openly contemptuous of the fate that had overtaken Paul under the same roof. Gardiner himself might look and dress like an accountant – short-sighted, stoop-shouldered, City-suited, often equipped with an umbrella and an attaché case as well – but he never lost sight of his vocation as a poet-priest. In his professional capacity he took the view, not uncommon among publishers at all levels, that authors who wanted to be paid were despicable money-grubbers selling their souls for trash 'in the trivial dustbin of dead reality'.[37]

Much of this was defensive protest from someone who, except during his alliance with Baker, never earned a living, let alone kept a wife: Gardiner married four times, and sired at least eight children, making it absolutely plain that their welfare was in each case strictly a matter for their mothers. His own devoted mother looked after him as long as she lived, supplying all his needs – books, leisure, a roof over his head, regular meals, in that order – as well as comforts like the couch at Crown Passage, and the £5 with which he had founded *Poetry Quarterly* in the first place. Swept along on Baker's ambition, he felt his own poetic concerns in danger of being flushed 'down the drains of destiny'.[38] Gardiner was a strange advertisement for the creative life, in some ways more of a dire warning. The one issue on which he never compromised was the need to suit himself. Even Baker's chaotic habits could not seriously impinge on the routine he had evolved at an early age, and from which he scarcely ever wavered: writing every night far into the small hours, reserving the afternoons for sex, walling himself in more and more effectively as he grew older behind what he called his 'indestructible barrier against life, my books'.[39]

Paul learned the lessons Gardiner taught, both positive and negative. One was that the creative act did not spell romance for him. In the cold autumn and bitter winter of 1946, it was already beginning to be clear that the literary life would always be, for Paul, a matter of hard work and ruthless self-discipline, rather than starry cloaks and priestly fillets. Another lesson (which took longer to digest) was that writing takes precedence over all other activities. A third was that the prospect which would increasingly absorb his thoughts, dominate his imagination, blot out everyday affairs – provide him in short with his own barrier against life – was India:

My heart began to beat at the thought of it, and the greedy desire for sun and tropical vegetation, the happy, sweating discomfort of it; the bright days and the colours; the grey days of turbulent skies and frenzied, waving palm leaves moaning against swift clouds.[40]

This comes from an early, cancelled *Male Child* draft, but it bears out Paul's saying to Freya Stark at the end of his life that 'after a few months back home I started thinking and dreaming India'.[41] In that first drab winter of post-war austerity and increased rationing, when the best most people could hope to eat was spam fritters, tinned snoek or a Woolton pie with blackmarket cigarettes and a bottle of Algerian wine for treats, when keeping warm meant an unending battle with power cuts, fuel restrictions, icy winds, freezing rain and phenomenal snowfall, the sensuousness of India was a powerful lure. Paul received loving letters from the men he had left behind him. 'Sir, I am doing well here and I am still in your old platoon,' wrote the faithful Havildar Dass on 28 October: 'I am remembering you all the time for your gentleness and kindness upon me. Sir . . . I cannot forget you.'[42] Nimu Purkayastha, of whom Paul was especially fond, wrote at greater length and even more affectionately, painting an Arcadian picture of Captain and Mrs Scott at home in a dusty landscape touchingly familiar to Paul:

By today, you are a Civilian walking on the roadside of your own land, which is [more] beautiful, than that you ever see in India; with someone who is none but your better-half in the light of the tired sun, with fine hands in your plain funny pockets. Want you enjoying much, now, sir! . . . Sir, I shall never forget of the days I passed with you . . . Sir, I lost you; – a best friend of mine and an officer. Joy and miseries mixed together with your departure not only from me but from the land of India & probably for ever & ever to come.[43]

Paul was also receiving rather more disturbing letters that autumn from Jim in Bihar, and later in Bengal. It had become increasingly clear that the transition to Indian independence under a Labour government, which the two of them had anticipated so confidently in the final stages of the war, was unlikely to run smoothly. They had been dismayed, even before Paul left India, when the British Cabinet Mission in Delhi narrowly failed to secure agreement between Hindus and Muslims over the terms on which they would accept federation. Paul was well aware that, if his ship had been further delayed in May, he might not have got away at all. Jim's demobilisation had been indefinitely postponed on account of growing unrest in Bengal and fear of worse to come. He took his section down to Barrackpore to organise the dropping of emergency relief supplies in devastating monsoon floods that summer: 'I arrived here 11 days ago with 11 men and Sunshine [another of Paul's old friends, Havildar Rahman]. Since when we have done 695,000 lbs mostly of rice but including biscuits, mepachrine, Malaria tablets, milk, salt, tea, dhal, bleaching powder and pamphlets', he wrote cheerfully, bringing back old times to Paul. 'My only regret is that you are not here to help me add up two and two and tell me I am wrong when it makes five.'[44] The section found itself besieged by visitors, reporters, cameramen, a team from Pathé News, streams of army and civilian highups ('we 'ad the Gov 'imself in a week ago! God it was funny'), all arriving to inspect the damage. 'This is being used as a first class piece of propaganda by the govt to show to the world apparently what the British Govt is doing for India,' Jim wrote cynically: 'Where's that flag?'

But he sounded less sure of himself in his next letter, dated 7 July, which described the ugly mood of hatred and aggression on the streets of Calcutta ('Paul, you have no idea how absolutely browned off I am . . . Everywhere you go they shout "Jai Hind" and "Quit India" and you are forever having to dodge the odd missile that comes hurtling through the air'). Jim was stunned. He could not understand why an Indian crowd should round on its British protectors, especially on someone like himself who had always responded with delight to India, sympathised with its people, and unconditionally supported their claim to liberation. Paul wrote anxiously at the beginning of August in reply to this letter, but the next one was still more alarming. It was written from Barrackpore on 16 August, the date declared a Day of Action by the Muslim League, which urged its followers to rise against the Hindus: 'All hell's let loose! The Muslims are having a pitched battle with the Hindus in every open space in Calcutta.' Jim reported shots and dwellings set on fire, a Hindu girls' school broken into and its inmates raped: the police were doing nothing, the army was standing by to be called in, even as he wrote a mob was surging up Chowringhee where Paul had spent so many happy leaves in the Grand Hotel. News of the rioting was broadcast hourly on military channels. To Jim, listening throughout the day, it seemed like some nightmarish parody of a Test match commentary broadcast from The Oval.

Over the next three days, more than 20,000 people were killed or seriously injured in Calcutta. The rioting spread rapidly to Bihar and East Bengal. The only comfort Jim could offer on 27 August, in reply to Paul's horrified enquiry, was that the violence appeared to be strictly intercommunal. British soldiers were no longer stoned or sworn at as Muslims and Hindus turned on one another, and the whole country moved inexorably nearer to catastrophe. Prospects for a peaceful handover of power looked bleak that autumn. Politicians in both countries were bitterly divided. The Indian Army was demoralised. The Viceroy, Lord Wavell, privately admitted himself defeated. The British Cabinet, in disarray, discussed replacing Wavell with Mountbatten. No precise policy could be formulated in advance. Mountbatten eventually left with instructions to do the best he could. No one cared to contemplate the possibility of partition, or the slaughter that would inevitably follow. People in India, and bewildered spectators like Paul 'far away in Inglistan', looked on with the dreadful sense of helplessness that he would one day re-create so powerfully in the background to the final volume of the Raj Quartet.

That work, which starts with the rape of a white woman during the Quit India riots of 1942, ends on the eve of partition in 1947 with the murder of a Muslim, dragged by vengeful Hindus from a halted train, which then moves on, gathering speed, bearing its cargo of departing British civilians and government officials smoothly away from the scene of a violence and destruction that would shortly engulf the subcontinent. An interested observer – Guy Perron, Paul's stand-in within the Quartet – is struck by something 'greasy and evasive' about the gliding motion of that train. In the autumn of 1946, Paul had apparently as yet no inkling of making India his subject, but he certainly came to feel later that there was something greasy and evasive about the way the British had left India, their lack of foresight or preparation beforehand, their precipitate haste at the time, and their invincible reluctance to discuss it afterwards. He said long afterwards that it was round about this time, perhaps in the aftermath of the Calcutta riots or the appalling massacres in the Punjab at the time of Independence a year later, that he decided to set about remedying his ignorance of Indian history and politics.[45]

He got firsthand reports from Jim, who arrived back in England at last on 30 November 1946, docking in freezing temperatures at Liverpool. He took the train to London, and went straight to Paul, who took him home from Crown Passage for the weekend to Penny in

Hampden Way. They had planned this reunion for months, Paul posting off a sketch-map of Southgate to India, Jim begging not to be left alone to face Penny who, in the last lonely months, had come to represent in his mind a peak of feminine perfection. He had no real home of his own to come back to after the war: Jim's father (who had been chairman of Gieves, the military outfitters in Piccadilly) had died in 1945, his three brothers had been scattered by the war, his mother – who had lost her own four brothers in the First World War and expected to lose her sons in the Second – had been an invalid for years, ravaged by Parkinson's disease. The Corbens' house on Marine Parade in Brighton, headquarters to a large and energetic family before the war, had become a melancholy place, virtually a prison to Jim's mother. The family had been kept together over the past six years by her husband's secretary, Olive Gradon, who wrote regularly to the four boys serving abroad, and did what she could at home for Mrs Corben.[46]

For as far back as he could remember, Jim had been surrounded by male company whether at home, away at boarding school or in the army, and he longed for change. 'I'm twenty-four and I've never sat in an armchair,' he said to Olive, explaining his determination to make up for lost time. Paul and Penny, in their snug little house in Southgate, embodied for him a blissful vision of comfort, warmth and domesticity. He had endowed Penny in his mind's eye with all the womanly qualities – charm, tenderness, beauty, daintiness and delicacy – he had never known in fact. Her photograph had been a familiar fixture for the past two years on Paul's table beneath the blackboard in 10/10 Section tent, and the prospect of meeting her face-to-face filled him with mock awe ('I am absolutely terrified of Penny')[47] that was at least partly genuine. Their apprehension was mutual. Penny had heard so much for so long about Paul's best friend that she was if anything more nervous than he was himself. Neither need have worried. Jim was an enchanting guest: he told stories, made jokes (one of Paul's about porridge blew up for Jim into a weirdly elaborate running saga that went on for weeks), fetched and carried for Penny, slipping into the pattern of her days so spontaneously it was hard to believe they had not known one another for years.

Over the next few months, Jim was often on hand, staying with the Scotts, making himself useful in Paul's absence at the office, becoming an appreciative third party much as Paul had once done in the Sansoms' marriage. Jim for his part was enthralled. In the course of their friendship Paul had initiated him into the mysteries of books, art, politics and now married life. He looked up to Penny, and made her laugh. There was nothing he liked better than to sit with her, talk to her, escort her through the ice and snow to the shops to wait in endless queues for the meat ration or a bit of fish. He even came with her to the antenatal clinic – part of Penny's romantic spell for Jim was that, when they met, she was already three months' pregnant – and no doubt he eased the problem of hostilities with Paul's mother. Jim and Paul were both the younger, favourite sons of difficult, fierce, demanding mothers, which had given a peculiar intensity to their relationships with women: 'Jim's mother was a strict disciplinarian, but he could always get round her,' said Olive. 'Jim could get away with anything.'

Jim was in no hurry to find a job that winter: he divided his time between Southgate and Sussex, helping with a stables belonging to one of his brothers at Lewes, playing with Paul's idea of planting tea, or starting up some other scheme together, mainly interested in catching up on the delights he had been cheated out of by the war. He would dash up to town to visit Olive at Gieves and Paul round the corner in Crown Passage, disrupting their respective offices (one thing Jim could not stand was the thought of a desk job) before whisking them both off for an uproarious lunch. He was exuberant, expansive, irresistible in this mood. He wasted no time in putting the plan drawn up in India into execution by getting engaged to Olive, and embarking with her on a hectic round of dancing, drinking, parties, balls and race-going. When Penny gave birth to a girl in the upstairs back bedroom at 8 Hampden Way on 7 March 1947, Jim was as pleased as if the child had been his own. She was a perfect baby, contented, plump and pink with a curl on top: they called her Carol Vivien, or Tidger for short. Her proud parents took her down to show to Olive and Jim in Brighton. A snapshot of the family on the seafront with Olive shows Penny beaming behind the pram handle, the baby invisible within, and Paul looking pleased if self-conscious at their side (he insisted on pushing the pram himself at home although, as he said, it made him look a bloody fool in Southgate).

Paul sent other snapshots of himself with the baby to old friends in India, including Nimu Purkayastha, who slept with the photograph under his pillow at night and kept it in the pocket of his uniform by day ('Pay Book pocket is best place for it, as money always requires to come out when Mr Scott and Baby Scott peeps through with smiling faces').[48] When Nimu received Paul's letter, written in November 1947, he was still serving with the RIASC in the reconstituted army, which had been ripped apart for division between India and Pakistan at the time of partition the previous August. The old Indian Army, in which Paul had commanded an integrated company of Hindus, Muslims, Sikhs and Nepalese, had broken up with a bitter sense of betrayal, and its destruction exacerbated the sickening and wholly unexpected violence that immediately followed Independence. Earlier unrest was as nothing to the panic and bloodshed which caused something like a quarter of a million deaths that autumn in the mass migration of peoples between the two new countries. Millions more were left destitute, starving, bereaved, homeless and hopeless. It was an explosion on a scale inconceivable when Paul and Jim left India. By late November, Nimu's platoon was still heavily engaged in mopping-up operations, helping to sort and settle Hindu refugees from Pakistan, as well as expedite the last Muslims fleeing India. Nimu sent news of these activities in answer to Paul's letter, and asked in turn for news of Captain Corben.

In the late 1940s, the Scotts made several excursions down to Brighton to inspect the Corbens' house and supervise their plans for married life. The two men went riding from the stables, although even Jim admitted that Paul did not look right on horseback ('He's left it too late, Penny,' he said loyally). Paul was as impressed by the young Corbens' new home as Jim had been by the young Scotts'. 'That *was* something,' Penny said. 'I remember Paul was astounded by the beauty of the place – the opulence of the Corbens compared to our threadbare, stringent, terribly poverty-stricken life. That caught Paul on the raw.' It was his first inside glimpse of the kind of life people lived on the Broad Walk at home in Southgate. If it made him look with unfavourable eyes on 8 Hampden Way, it also changed his view of Jim. The two men began to drift apart with tacit encouragement from their wives: Penny and Olive Corben each felt outclassed by the other, Penny by Olive's plush furnishings and glamorous life style, Olive by Penny's radiance, her new baby, the pedestal she occupied in the eyes of Olive's husband. Without India to cement it, the friendship fell apart altogether when Jim abandoned a brief experiment with estate agency and moved down to Southampton to try his luck in the building trade.

Paul was in any case finding congenial company at the office, where he and Roland Gant were increasingly discovering tastes in common. 'Books we had read and authors we admired filled much of the conversation as did books we disliked and writers we detested,' wrote Roland. 'There was a lot of music too, listened to and talked about – Wagner, Mozart, Elgar, the Ink Spots, Fats Waller, Louis Armstrong, blues singers like Bessie Smith – and bits of old Hollywood dialogue were thrown back and forth, with arguments as to words and intonation, story line and date.' Paul relished Roland's mimicry and wry asides when the job pressed hard on him. Crown Passage book-keeping was anarchic, current accounting problematic. 'We all did a bit of everything,' wrote Roland, 'but Paul had the commando assignment of capturing cheques from Peter Baker whose approach to cash-flow problems was epitomised by romping into the trade counter to grab a handful of notes from the till and shout, between guffaws, "I'm taking Eric Hiscock [doyen of book-trade columnists] out to lunch, Paul".[49] A major audit in the spring of 1947 engulfed even the time set aside for Paul's own work in the evenings. 'I have never worked so hard in my life – I really mean that,' he wrote on 7 June, enclosing a royalty cheque for Clive (who had reversed their roles by becoming a Falcon Press author and Paul's official client). 'I have had to give up (thank goodness) the evening study lark – it was just too much for me.' He was finding it hard to sleep: all his adult life Paul's dreams were vivid, often unsettling, sometimes violently disturbing. He said he arrived home from work after a nine-hour day 'weary and dejected', and usually took to his bed on Sundays 'to recuperate from the week's troubles'.[50] Hard work, long hours, discouragement and defeat as a writer made him cruelly unhelpful to Clive, who asked for comments on a verse play, *The World Turned Upside Down*, and received in July from Paul six pages of swingeing criticism with a rider recommending that he scrap the manuscript.

Penny, absorbed in the new baby, found herself seven months later with another on the way. This second pregnancy, coming so soon after the first, marked a low point for her too, adding physical exhaustion to the strain of coping with Paul's moroseness and his mother's disapproval. This had intensified as Frances Scott confronted the full extent and finality of her loss. Tom Scott was by now stone deaf, her own eyesight was failing, Peter was out all day at work, and Paul had effectively cut himself off behind a barrage of demands from the office and his growing family. Alone at home with no one to talk to except her husband who could not hear a word she said, magnifying her grievances, musing on the past, she fell into the habit of telephoning Penny with rambling accounts of family funerals and long-dead relations, which generally led to biting comments on the present ('Mrs Scott seldom failed to end the conversation with verbal abuse, telling me I was useless and why Paul had married me she had no idea').[51] Penny grew to dread these telephone calls. She had no defence against them: her mother-in-law had learned to conduct her attacks in private so that Penny could not turn to Paul, who in any case did not welcome complaints about his mother. The withdrawal of Jim's support made things no easier: he had been such a friendly and uncritical audience to their marriage that both had felt encouraged by seeing themselves reflected through his eyes.

Paul stored the memory of this reflection. Ten years later he would take it out and use it in *A Male Child*, which explores among other things the triangular relationship between Alan Hurst, his wife and his best friend, who moves into their house in December 1946, and provides company for the wife, expecting her first child in March. Ian Canning also acts as what he calls 'a buffer state' between Alan's wife and his fiercely possessive mother, who spends much of her time alone, nursing her unhappiness and drinking in her room. The widowed Mrs Hurst has points in common with Jim Corben's mother, whose misery was eased by drink, and whose situation Paul had glimpsed or guessed in Brighton. But her appearance, her attitudes, her feelings, above all her pent-up jealousy of her daughter-in-law come from direct experience. Ian (who is based on Jim only in so far as he exerts a strong pacific influence on this troubled household) feels sympathy for both women. He is unfailingly attentive to the pregnant Stella, accompanying her over icy roads on regular visits to the clinic, calling the midwife and waiting patiently downstairs at the onset of childbirth. But it is Mrs Hurst who, for all her ferocity and cunning, strikes him as the more poignant of the two. Ian is dismayed not by her egotism but by her pathos, her courage, her 'gallant attempts to look smart and well turned-out', and her unspoken appeals for help:

She continued to look into the fire, and the attitude of her arms, the way she held her head, added up to a sort of distracted misery which put her beyond sympathy and excited compassion: compassion, because overwhelmingly I understood her utter loneliness. That it might be the result of her own shortcomings, her own simple inability to deal straightforwardly and honestly, I took into account; but that only made her isolation seem more insupportable.[52]

Mrs Hurst is the mother of two sons: her favourite – dreamy, delicate and precocious – was a poet who died young. Alan, the surviving married son who served in India in the war, is a steady, reliable father-to-be with no talent as a writer and no ambition beyond holding down his job as an accountant. Nothing can compensate his mother for the loss of her other son: the golden boy who had belonged exclusively to her ('I knew every thought of Edward's. Every hope. Every plan. Every ambition. He held nothing back'),[53] and whose glorious achievements as a poet were to have made up for his father's inadequacies. Mrs Hurst broods and grieves over the past, stoking her resentment in the present. Ian cannot bring himself to tell her that she is mourning not for a real son but for a fantasy ('she had twisted the truth into a pattern of her own choosing, and to unravel it face to face, heart to heart, would be more than she could bear'). Paul could never confront his mother with the truth either but, in Mrs Hurst, he painted a portrait of Frances Scott mourning her lost poet, and venting her disappointment in Paul on the wife who bore the blame for turning him into a prudent, predictable conformist.

Paul shot up the ranks as an accountant, becoming company secretary to the Falcon and Grey Walls Press together with Convoy Publications by November 1947. He was writing again, although with no intention of confiding hopes, plans or ambitions to his mother. By the end of the year he had submitted two new plays, *The River* and *The Wilderness*, to Joyce Wiener who responded with alacrity. An enthusiast by nature, she was also a shrewd judge of both books and people. Short, plain, vivacious, often extremely funny, not yet middle-aged herself, she held pronounced views on the development and promotion of young talent. Paul, at this tentative point in his career, was everything she liked best in a client. His inexperience appealed to her, and so did his eagerness to learn. She had read English at Oxford before the war, and worked briefly with one of the big literary agencies, before leaving to set up on her own with a handful of Oxford contemporaries (Veronica Wedgwood, Naomi Jacobs, Caryl Brahms) for clients, Compton Mackenzie to lend tone (her sister Margery had been his secretary), and Georgette Heyer for serious financial ballast.[54] She worked from home in a tiny office in her flat in St John's Wood with a secretary typing at a card table set up in the lounge. Brisk, businesslike, punctual, at her desk 'ready to pounce' first thing each morning, she permitted herself little social life outside the agency, often sitting up half the night reading or correcting manuscripts, and typing long letters of advice and practical criticism to her authors.

Paul kept a few of them, and must have received many more in these years when he and Joyce toiled together to impose clarity, coherence and structure on his characteristically shapeless scripts. Her faith in him, once committed, was unshakeable. 'Joyce was a mother hen,' said another of her clients, Toni Block, Paul's fellow prizewinner in the Anglo-Palestinian Competition. 'She was overwhelming. She took you over.' Joyce undoubtedly bullied her authors and made them feel guilty, like a mother. She was also fiercely devoted to them, demanding and generally getting their devotion in return. Paul and Toni each produced new plays in 1947, and Joyce adopted the pair of them, carrying them off to parties, introducing them to contacts, organising their lives, never doubting her ability to make their fortunes and her own. 'No one could set you up like she did,' said Toni Block. 'There *never* was another agent like Joyce.'

Many people found her hard to take. She could be formidably rude. Publishers might quail at the sight of her, but people who worked with her learned to be stouter-hearted. 'Every now and then she might get hold of the hair on the back of your neck,' one of them said. 'But you always went back. She was much, much more than an agent. She was editor, confidante, sergeant major, shoulder to weep on – you name it.'[55] Paul eventually made the most of Joyce in all these capacities, but what he needed more than anything at this stage was to be taken in hand, professionally speaking, by a first-class sergeant major: 'together we launched an attack on Shaftesbury Avenue and the little theatres,' he wrote,[56] looking back on that heady spring of 1948 when Joyce made him feel that anything was possible.

Little-theatre clubs and clublets had sprung up as thickly as post-war publishing houses, and Joyce's assault was vigorous. She sold Toni's play, *Flowers for the Living*, to the tiny New Lindsey Theatre where it was a spectacular success in January, transferring afterwards to the West End; and she very nearly pulled off a similar coup for Paul a few months later by placing *The River* with the Arts Theatre. A flurry of excitement, speculation, meetings, discussions with a producer and wholesale script revision eventually petered out when the Arts Theatre backed off in May.[57] Joyce attacked again by dispatching the script to the BBC's infant television drama department. Over the next few months she got nowhere with the Mercury Theatre, Oscar Quitak's Under-30 Theatre (a long shot for a playwright who would soon be pushing thirty), Velona Pilcher at the Gate, and Clive's old partner, Jonathan Field, who had turned up as a producer at the Torch. Paul enjoyed imagining Field's dismay when Miss Wiener's latest protegé, the prospective saviour of the English stage, turned out to be none other than the author of *Pillars of Salt* ('oh my God. Another play to read by *him*'). Field talked vaguely of a production for *The River*, and even more airily about doing *Brilliant City* behind gauze curtains: 'I said by all means,' Paul reported briskly to Clive, 'but do it behind velvet curtains.'[58]

Joyce's encouragement produced a surge of well-being and creative energy. When *Pillars of Salt* was finally published by Gollancz as the third of *Four Jewish Plays* on 21 May, Paul could afford to be offhand ('I *loathe* the play & blush whenever I catch sight of a line of its dialogue,' he wrote to Clive:[59] total sales of 221 copies on subscription to Anglo-Palestinian club members and the playwrights' relatives confirmed his gloom). With two new plays going the rounds and a third out in hardback, already working on an idea for the next, Paul by mid-May was also rapidly drafting what he thought might possibly turn out to be the first chapter of a novel.[60] The Scotts' second daughter, Sally Elisabeth, was born on 30 May 1948, at the height of this productive and creative period. In an optimistic moment, Paul proposed moving to a better address nearer central London, more

TOP LEFT *Paul and Penny pushing Carol in her pram with Olive Corben at Brighton in 1947.* TOP RIGHT *Frances Scott – Grandma on parade – with Carol and Sally.* CENTRE LEFT *Paul's drawing of a cat.* CENTRE RIGHT *Paul celebrating with Penny in Paris after escaping from the wreck of the Falcon Press in 1950.* LEFT *Scott family at Brooklands Rise in the early 1950s.*

Hampstead Heath than Palmers Green, at 61 Brooklands Rise, NW 11. This remained ever afterwards in family legend a time of hope and happiness with Paul perched on a stepladder painting walls and singing pop songs, Penny handing his lunch up to him, the two babies looking on: 'we're trying to Redecorate our Home,' Paul explained to Clive, ' – so there are pots and pails (no jetty) all over the place, screaming children and typewriters clacking.'[61] The move had been inspired by Joyce, whose notion of furthering her young clients' careers included social supervision on matters like where to live, who to cultivate and what to wear. Joyce took a dim view of any writer rash enough to saddle himself too soon with small children. She freely criticised Paul's domestic arrangements, frankly deplored his background and made no secret of her jealousy of Penny. 'Joyce pushed Paul,' said Toni: 'Joyce fell in love with people, and their wives got in the way.'

For Paul, in the full flush of Joyce's approval, this was more gratifying than it can have been for Penny. Writing would continue all his life to supply many of the joys and pangs of love: suspense, anticipation, absorption, exultation, deflation and despair. Joyce's excitement raised the temperature for both of them as effectively as if they had in fact embarked on a love affair. Looking back long afterwards, Paul used the language of love to describe himself in the third person as a young man wrought up to fever pitch by Joyce: 'Basking in her praise, sharing her hopes, setting out after office hours trembling with expectation to meet an interested producer in St Martin's Lane, or travelling on a Sunday morning to meet the Television drama pundits at Alexandra Palace. Or, once, rushing to the phone because his wife had rushed upstairs, also trembling, and whispered – "It's Margaret Rawlings".'[62] The phone call led to nothing, like innumerable others. Paul got used in time to these theatrical fool's errands. The upshot of Joyce's little-theatre campaign was practically nil. The only person prepared to come anywhere near to staging a production was Velona Pilcher, who favoured continental authors, wore snuff-coloured corduroys, and had left the Gate to start her own 48 Theatre ('rather arty and precious and doesn't like anything English')[63] in a St John's Wood studio where, some time in early autumn, *The River* and *The Wilderness* opened a season of private playreadings organised by Toni and attended by as many little producers as Joyce could rustle up.

But Joyce had other plans in mind for Paul. The novel he thought he might or might not have begun in May never actually materialised. But the year after, at Joyce's prompting, he started another which he called *The Gradual Day*, and later *Dazzling Crystal* ('both titles from

Spender, the poet of my youth, the poet of my middle age, the poet, I expect, of all my days').[64] He worked on it throughout the winter of 1948–9 with Joyce, who edged him tactfully away from his characteristically amorphous expressionism towards a more analytical and structural approach. He read Kafka, and was overwhelmed as he had once been by Eliot, until Joyce put a stop to what he called his 'Kafka phase' by insisting he study logic ('I thought she was talking nonsense,' he said later: 'She wasn't').[65] If no one could set you up so brilliantly as Joyce, no one could take you down more thoroughly either. Paul was often reluctant to obey her instructions, sometimes downright mutinous, but he always capitulated in the end. 'Thank goodness you made me write novels instead of plays,' he wrote handsomely in retrospect.[66] At the time, *Dazzling Crystal* made the rounds with even less success, if possible, than his play scripts. It was rejected by seventeen publishers in the first ten months of 1950. Paul's own final verdict followed his standard pattern: 'I thought it was a work of genius. It was merely derivative and half-baked.'[67]

At some point he swapped manuscripts with Roland Gant. 'I read his first novel, which he said was unpublishable and was, and he read mine, which was also unpublishable,' Roland wrote. 'We said so to each other very nicely, each knowing that we were right.'[68] Wrey Gardiner (who had published Paul's 'Song for Kafka' in the 1947–8 winter number of *Poetry Quarterly*) was equally dismissive. All either of them could remember afterwards was a Kafkaesque flavour and a Soho setting, 'unlike anything else Paul ever wrote'.[69] Both had more pressing matters on their minds by 1950. Signs of impending disaster in Crown Passage could no longer be ignored. 'From where I sat it looked distinctly dodgy,' wrote Roland, 'but from where Paul sat, with the accounts in front of him and creditors on the telephone, the landscape was volcanic and about to become active.'[70] Gardiner, switching metaphors, reluctantly agreed: 'the rot had set in although gangrene was still far away'.

At the general election in February 1950, Peter Baker had been elected Conservative member for Norfolk South, defeating the Labour minister Christopher Mayhew, and claiming to be the youngest person in parliament as well as one of the most prominent. When the Deputy Speaker failed to recognise him, Baker was reassuring: 'Please don't apologise, I don't know who *you* are either. But *anybody* will tell you who I am.'[71] He hobnobbed with bishops, VCs and captains of industry. By his own account, he dazzled the Prime Minister (' "Peter Baker" remarked Winston Churchill, "that strange mixture of Jesus Christ and Senator McCarthy" '), and swept the Foreign Secretary (who had unwisely accepted a lift in Baker's car) off his feet: 'I completed five circuits of the roundabout on the Embankment before delivering Anthony Eden, green and apprehensive, at the House. He never forgave me for this.'[72]

Eden was not the only person feeling green and shaken. One of Paul's best stories in later life described Baker shuffling chequebooks as he shunted debts around the overdrafts of his assorted companies (which included in the end speculative property development as well as the Strathmore distillery, a printing works, a West End wine merchant and a factory making experimental inflatable aircraft hangars in Surrey). Like much that had happened in the past ten years, none of this was particularly amusing at the time. When Baker called a meeting in July to announce drastic salary cuts, Paul had already left Crown Passage: 'I had to stop thinking in the short term of my security, of my wife, my children and my mortgage, and take a long hard look at the organisation which employed me. Having done so, I resigned.'[73] He gave three months' notice but was immediately and acrimoniously thrown out. A general exodus followed. Both Falcon and Grey Walls ended up – 'three years and seven company secretaries later' as Paul put it – in liquidation. Baker, who stood trial at the Old Bailey in 1954 for fraud and forgery, was sent to prison for seven years.

Paul was thirty when he left Crown Passage. His first sustained attempt to reconcile his two divided selves had ended in catastrophe. He appeared to have failed comprehensively as poet, playwright, novelist. Now he was walking out on his job as an accountant with no prospect of another. His reaction, which would be much the same whenever a comparable crisis cut him loose in the future, was a mixture of elation and relief. He had extracted three months' severance pay from Baker ('I had not read the Laws of Contract for nothing'), and he celebrated by whisking Penny off for a week to Paris: a snapshot shows her looking charming in net gloves and a chic Parisian straw hat with Paul only slightly strained in the background. In later years he could be hilarious about the Crown Passage affair. But once, towards the end of his life, talking to an audience of fellow writers, he gave some inkling of the other side of what he felt that summer: 'Perhaps you *all* know it. The terrible cumulative weight of sustained failure.'

CHAPTER EIGHT

A prince among agents

'From 1950 things began to look up,' Paul wrote ten years later.[1] The
first thing he did with his new freedom was to sit down once again and
write a play, only this time, under Joyce's guidance, it was a ninety-
minute radio script closely based on his own initial experience with
No. 1 Air India Company in 1944. He called it *Lines of Communication*, and it took him three days flat. 'That's the best thing you have
ever done,' Penny said when he showed her the manuscript.[2] Joyce
thought the same, and so did the BBC's drama department. The
producer who summoned Paul to discuss plans for a production was
the young Donald McWhinnie,[3] tall, quiet, courteous, phenomenally
calm and intellectually surefooted. Paul, sufficiently cynical by this
time to take McWhinnie's uneffusive protestations with a pinch of
salt, put the matter out of his head until, one day when he was sitting
on the lavatory at Brooklands Rise, an envelope slid under the door,
pushed by Penny, containing a BBC contract offering ninety guineas
for *Lines of Communication*. It was, as Paul said wryly, 'a suitably
mystical experience', the one he characteristically picked for a mental
snapshot to mark his transition from an amateur to a professional
writer: 'I stared at this letter and contract for some time. After that the
image fades. You could say that an amateur went into the closet and
that a professional emerged. . . . I have often wondered in fact whether
the people who now live in that house have ever felt, in that closet, a
curious emanation for which there is no accounting, a sense of delight
so profound that it can only be called tranquillity, so that they find
themselves spending longer there than is either seemly or necessary,
simply to enjoy this rare, elusive aroma of peace from another world.'[4]
   Peace from another world sustained him on a second round of job

hunting that summer. At some stage during the past four years of failure as a writer, he had fallen back on the family facility for drawing, turning a sardonic eye on post-war London (as the political cartoonist Halki would do on post-war Bombay in *A Division of the Spoils*), and submitting a stream of astringent, unreassuring, decidedly un-Wright-like cartoons to *Punch*.[5] Paul's cousin and contemporary, Philip Wright's son David, had established a reputation as a graphic artist, painting fashionable beauties popular as pin-ups in wartime, designing a famous advertisement for Boleto stockings, going on after the war to draw the Carol Day strip in the *Daily Mail*.[6] Paul himself attended life-drawing classes at the local institute, bringing home rolls of vigorous male nudes, but he found no foothold as a cartoonist, and his application to follow in McWhinnie's footsteps as a trainee producer was turned down that summer by the BBC. He and other mutineers from Captain Baker's crew took to congregating at Josef's in Greek street, or L'Epicure round the corner in Frith Street, ever afterwards Paul's favourite place for celebrations, treats, reunions, the exchange of gossip and news. By the end of the year Roland Gant had found a job with Heinemann, Sean Jennett with Faber, and Graeme Hutchinson with the Phoenix Press (John Baker, who ran it, turned out also to be the employer of Paul's old friend Mr Fulbrook and his book bag).

Paul himself started work as a literary agent with Pearn, Pollinger and Higham in Covent Garden as soon as his three months' paid leave ran out at the beginning of October. Laurence Pollinger's son Gerald said that his father had found a place for Paul at the earnest request of Peter Baker's father, after a spot of bother with the signature on a royalty cheque from Falcon Press (Baker's eventual downfall came from letting his pen run away with him when it came to forging cheques in the names of creditworthier tycoons like Sir Bernard Docker, or the brewer Sir John Mann). But it seems more likely that, as both parties later maintained, Paul was taken on that autumn as his assistant by Pollinger's partner David Higham, who had no son prepared to succeed him in the business, on the understanding of a partnership in the offing.

Agency work suited Paul from the start. It exercised his talent for administration, kept him in some sort of contact with books and bookmen, even allowed time in the evenings for him to rework *Lines of Communication* as a novel. This was yet another strategy proposed by Joyce, who had fielded *Dazzling Crystal* back from sixteen different publishers by October 1950.[7] The seventeenth was Frank Morley of Eyre and Spottiswoode, who took Paul out to lunch on 28 November and somehow managed to turn rejection of the manuscript into a mark of confidence in its author. Paul came away from their lunch fired with a determination – already beginning that afternoon to formulate a plan – that would last him all his working life. 'I think it is the first time a publisher's really been honest about this ms. He said its sale would be about 1,000 copies, and they couldn't afford that . . . He accepted the fact that it was a legitimate piece of writing and I accept the fact that no one is going to publish it – yet. We'll shelve it,' Paul wrote cheerfully[8] the same day to Joyce, forwarding the first 17,000 words of his second novel for technical advice before submitting it to Eyre and Spottis-woode. The spur of Morley's honesty, coming at the end of Joyce's three-year training programme, set him off like a runner under starter's orders. He fell into a steady stride ('Mondays, Wednesdays and Fridays: two hours in the evening; Saturday mornings, 9.30 to lunchtime. Sundays: either morning or afternoon; or both if the mood's right'), and had the whole novel finished, typed out and delivered in just under four months.

He seems to have realised, almost as soon as Joyce suggested it, that *Lines of Communication* was no more than a rough sketch for something bigger: 'the play script is really the dialogue-synopsis of the novel, although, as you'll see, the tangents and undercurrents will be the novel's strength.' The idea of a tangential rather than a straightforward chronological or sequential structure was something Paul had been struggling to articulate perhaps as far back as *Gerontius* ('If we consider the ends/ the ends leading to the greatest end/ and the greatest end ending forever . . .'). He gave up writing plays partly because he could never come to grips with the notion, which he had already tried explaining rather clumsily to Clive, of a drama thrown off at a tangent to ordinary life ('The drama. . . ends when the tangent returns to the circle of life – the old circumference – but – if any message or lesson has been pointed – the life – or the circumference has suffered a change. The drama has enriched – or killed a lie – or straightened the path')[9]. The scheme for a novel whose strength lay in its tangents and undercurrents would find its final shape nearly a quarter of a century later in the Raj Quartet.

Johnnie Sahib, the novel based on his radio play, does not in fact come anywhere near achieving its author's original prescription: the format is too conventional, the content still too factual, for anything more than a bare statement of themes which would return as variations in nearly all his later novels. The book starts with the arrival of a stranger who will serve as a stand-in for the author (Jim Taylor as the newcomer, Johnnie himself and the Major were taken directly from Paul, Colegate and Kimber). The story is set in India, against a background of everyday working routine, and it deploys for the first time the twin themes of male rivalry between two types – one thrusting and aggressive, the other more reflective, sensitive and shrinking – and the obsessive need of a domineering senior officer to establish a hold over his charge or charges. Perhaps Frank Morley recognised *Johnnie Sahib* not so much for what it was as for what it represented: a preliminary marker, a staking-out of ground to be covered and boundaries explored. 'My second novel, which was published as my first, was dull, worthy and lousy,' Paul wrote in 1968, by which time he was halfway through the Raj Quartet. 'But it illustrated my limitations as they were then, and I have ever since worked within them, getting nearer and nearer to the ideas that belong . . . to my youthful attitudes.'[10]

Paul could hardly have found an editor more experienced in the promotion of youthful talent, or prepared to expend more energy on it, than Morley, who had begun his career as a publisher by recruiting T. S. Eliot for Faber & Faber. He was already in his fifties when Paul met him, the youngest of three brilliant Oxford-educated American brothers: Christopher Morley was a bestselling novelist in the States, Felix a Pulitzer-prize-winning columnist, Frank himself a founding director of Geoffrey Faber's firm in 1925, which he said would have been called Faber and Morley if only he could have raised £20 capital at the operative moment.[11] He had also been a founder member of Eliot's *Criterion* group, and the two remained close friends (*Old Possum's Book of Practical Cats*, subsequently relaunched as the musical *Cats*, was originally written for the Morley and Faber children). Frank was a huge man, hugely entertaining, hugely well-read, hugely discerning and disarming, with a disinterested passion for good writing and a knack of getting his authors to accept criticism which they might have found hard to take from anyone constructed morally or physically on a meaner scale. When he invited Paul to lunch, he had only recently returned from spending the war years in America to join Eyre and Spottiswoode, which would shortly pull off two major publishing coups with Patrick White's *The Tree of Man* and H. M. Prescott's sixteenth-century saga, *The Man on a Donkey*. Both were Frank's discoveries, both launched triumphantly on literary London by the sheer weight and impact of an enthusiasm which, at the end of 1950, he brought to bear on Paul.[12]

One of Morley's first moves on joining his new firm had been to revive the Eyre and Spottiswoode Literary Fellowship, an award of £500 for a first or second novel originally set up under Graham Greene and first awarded in 1948 to Rebecca West's son, Anthony. Paul left the lunch table in November fully intending to meet the closing date for entries, which was 31 March 1951. As a conscientious agent, he also rounded up more than half a dozen eligible candidates among the clients of Pearn, Pollinger and Higham, distributing application forms, forwarding manuscripts, and in due course returning them, with discreet lack of comment, when he collected the award himself in May for *Johnnie Sahib*.[13] Clive's long poem, 'The Witnesses', also won a prize that month in the Festival of Britain Poetry Competition, and Paul modestly resigned the Jetty Pail for the last time: 'I think this means that the famous old insignia we used to pass between us finds its permanent home with you,' he wrote, 'and also a brand new laurel wreath.'[14] The wreath marked the end of their friendship, for the Sansoms had decided by this time to settle with Ruth's family in Tasmania, where Clive hoped to rebuild his ruined health.

Lines of Communication, broadcast on 12 February, had proved so popular that the BBC was already making plans for a television adaptation. Morley, demanding only minor revisions to the novel, promised publication the following spring. Paul was caught up in a pleasurable flurry of preparation, obtaining official clearance from the War Office and unofficial clearance from Tony Colegate ('Give him this, he didn't turn a hair'),[15] recruiting the founder of his old air supply company, Colonel Newman, to check facts and film footage for the television version, contacting old RIASC cronies, arranging for presentation copies of the novel to be forwarded to Nimu (still with the Indian Army in Delhi), and Havildar Dass (back home among the paddy fields, bullock carts and mud huts of Andhra Pradesh). *Johnnie Sahib* was published to encouraging reviews on 25 April 1952, and *Lines of Communication* (adapted by Paul himself and the producer, Ian Atkins) was televised to a slightly cooler reception a month later. Paul was by this time deep in his next novel, *The Return of the Dove* (eventually renamed *The Alien Sky*), for Eyre and Spottiswoode.

If Joyce Wiener felt justifiably complacent – 'You are indeed a novelist rather than a playwright, and I am thankful we diagnosed it in time'[16] – the hopeful novelists among Paul's own clients must have been more surprised than pleased. Few writers welcome competition from their agents and, after a showy start, Paul rapidly retreated behind the protective cover which in later life would disconcert his readers by making him look more like an accountant or an agent than an author. Many of his clients at Pearn, Pollinger and Higham had no suspicion that he wrote at all. Some, when they found out, minded more than others. There would always be those who felt that any reasonably good review Paul might get had somehow been wangled at their expense, or alternatively that the time and energy required by his own books would have been better spent looking after theirs. Paul represented authors ranging from Arthur C. Clarke, the future Homer of space fiction, and his bestselling Australian compatriot Morris West, each of whom enthusiastically regarded any completed manuscript as a property ripe for development, to the poet D. J. Enright, who dreaded the thought of being hustled by commercial developers ('I liked Paul from the start. He was gentle, reassuring, rueful, pleasantly ironic').[17] Paul acted at one point or another in his years with Higham for Herbert Read, Mervyn Peake, Ronald Searle, Keith Waterhouse, John Fowles and Elizabeth David.

One of his earliest clients, recruited on the strength of an article in the *New Statesman*, was a young unknown Yorkshireman, an ex-librarian from Bingley, who turned up at the office on 5 September 1951 with an unpublished verse play, four articles and an idea for a novel to be called *Born Favourite*, or *Joe for King*. His name was John Braine,[18] and Paul sustained him over the next five years of setbacks and disappointments with patient, practical advice, reading his chapters as they were written, and eventually selling the completed manuscript in 1956 to Eyre and Spottiswoode, who published it as *Room at the Top*. 'One should ride one's authors with a light rein, but if possible sit the saddle alone,' said David Higham,[19] who liked his employees each to build up his or her own stable. As well as scouring the book pages and little magazines for outsiders like Braine and Enright, Paul roped in a sizeable contingent from Crown Passage, including Roland Gant, Charles Wrey Gardiner and Gardiner's new assistant, Muriel Spark, in those days still primarily an editor and poet (echoes of the Falcon and Grey Walls débâcle, together with recognisable portraits of Peter Baker and Gardiner himself, would turn up nearly forty years later in her novel *A Far Cry from Kensington*). He placed Gant's novels, but failed to find publishers for either Gardiner's latest manuscript, *Frail Screen*, or Mrs Spark's selection of Mary Shelley's poems.[20]

He did better with old Indian contacts, handling first and second novels respectively for Peter Green and Jimmy Leasor. The early 1950s marked the almost simultaneous launch of their three long-delayed careers, and Paul fell into the habit of comparing notes, lunching regularly with Jimmy at Ley On's Chinese restaurant in Shaftesbury Avenue, and drinking with Peter at the Dog and Duck between Frith Street and Dean Street (Paul's clients in those years of post-war austerity came in for a good deal of what he called Dog-and-Ducking). Both were immediately struck by Paul's seriousness and strength of purpose, although they could hardly have reacted more differently. Jimmy, who had come down from Oxford to work for Beaverbrook on the *Daily Express*, remained true to his vision of the writer's life as he had originally pictured it to Paul at Belgaum: a vista of glittering prizes – wealth, fame, fast cars, a historic manor house in the country – following on a rich harvest of bestsellers. Paul's ambition seemed dismally narrow by comparison, his outlook as an agent doleful and disheartening. Jimmy, never one to pass up a hot property, was happy to ghost stories at speed on spec for all comers – war heroes, big game hunters, the Vanderbilt sisters – making his first fortune in the mid-1950s from the true adventures of an escaped German POW, all of which struck Paul as essentially a waste of time: 'Old Scott was always against these things, always downbeat.'[21] Paul's lack of speculative enterprise, his indifference to short-term results, his determination to write regardless of market trends, appeared to Jimmy as bleak and self-denying as when the two had first glimpsed one another's dream castles in Belgaum.

It had seemed then to Jimmy that Paul felt himself marked down for failure almost before he began. Peter, on the other hand, charac-teristically sanguine, was amused by Paul's dry wit and increasingly impressed by the singlemindedness which was almost the only gift missing from his own literary and intellectual repertoire. He had abandoned an academic career after scaling the first heights (a double first at Cambridge, the Craven scholarship, a well-regarded doctorate on Roman magic, and the post of director of classical studies at Trinity) in order to mount a diversionary attack on Fleet Street, contributing regular columns of fiction reviews to the *Daily Telegraph*, non-fiction to the *Yorkshire Post*, and film criticism to *John O'London's Weekly*, while working on preliminary strategy for a major writing campaign. He approached Paul somewhat tentatively in January 1954[22] for advice about whether to strike first as an author with historical novels, travel books, translations, thrillers, biography or poetry (he concentrated in the end on the first and last, making occasional highly successful raids in all the other fields, with side swipes at drama and *belles-lettres*).

From the start each had unqualified faith in the other's ability to write. Each admired in the other qualities he had no wish to emulate himself, Paul delighting especially in Peter's prodigal inventiveness, his intellectual agility and daring, the nippiness and control he demon-strated on the tennis court or behind the wheel of a sports car as effectively as on the printed page. Time and energy were the prime factors in Paul's eventual analysis of Peter's prodigious output: 'The nature of real talent is always imponderable, although one's suspicion that it is mostly in direct proportion to energy is pretty well confirmed'.[23] Over the next decade the two would egg one another on, consulting and commiserating, exchanging manuscripts, diagnosing faults, pinpointing strengths, saluting one another's successes in private and in print, generally constructing the sort of support system one author can supply for another in whose work he genuinely believes.

Jimmy was the first, Peter probably the closest, of the fellow novelists whose friendship in these years far outgrew the original business association. But of all his clients the two who would between them do most to shape Paul's own career were older and more experienced India hands. One was Mollie Hamilton, born and bred in India of distinguished Anglo-Indian forebears, married to an officer of the Queen's Own Corps of Guides, whose post-war career took them, as she said, to 'all sorts of entertaining bits of Britain's fast-vanishing Empire'.[24] Mrs Hamilton was a children's author and illustrator in process of switching to romantic detective stories set in exotic locations, and published under her maiden name of M. M. Kaye. She represented everything that fascinated Paul and made him uneasy about British India, a milieu socially and intellectually at loggerheads with his own. This was the first time he had dealt personally at any length with a member of what had always seemed to him an insufferable élite, long overdue for exposure by right-thinking liberals as emotionally insensitive, racially intolerant, politically obsolete. She for her part had picked an agency at random for her third novel in June 1951, but it was not until five books and five years later that it occurred to her to ask the cool, correct, efficient but aloof young Mr Scott of PPH whether he was by any chance the Paul Scott who had written *The Alien Sky*. If he was staggered by her enthusiastic request to shake his hand, she was scarcely less taken aback by his astonishment ('Oh dear, did I really come across as some sort of Poona-Poona Memsahib?').[25] Mutual confusion erupted into laughter, 'and we were friends from that moment on'.

The other client who would one day take a shaping hand in Paul's affairs was Gerald Hanley, who wrote romantic, elegantly elegiac adventure stories exploring the use and abuse of power, sexual, social and political, against a background of Imperial dissolution. One of Paul's first jobs as an agent, in November 1950, had been to negotiate an American sale for Hanley's *The Consul at Sunset*, a first novel by a new client which would shortly prove a runaway success in Britain. Hanley himself turned out to be a picturesque, footloose and singularly elusive Irishman, a few years older than Paul, with a head-start both as novelist and army officer (seven years' service in Africa, India and Burma), as well as a far more rackety history of knocking about the East in different capacities, farming, filming or working as a BBC reporter. He took Paul under his wing, drinking with him on unexpected surfacings in London from Kenya, Kashmir or County Cork, swapping stories, capping army reminiscences, encouraging him to conduct business correspondence in Roman Urdu ('Dear Gerald, *Abhi Kya Kerenge, Sahib? Inglistan ya Kashmir wapas ane*

Paul as an agent with PPH, the only time in his life when he settled for prosperity and a safe job.

the young Executive 1954/5

BELOW LEFT *Gerald Hanley, already a best-selling novelist, when Paul first listened to the yarns he spun and left his desk to go Dog-and-Ducking in Soho.*

BELOW RIGHT *Roland Gant, who played Fats Waller and the Ink Spots, swapped first novels with Paul at the Falcon Press, and capped his quotations from old Hollywood films.*

wallah hai?' Paul wrote: 'Don't for goodness sake reply in Higher Standard!').[26] If his example seemed to Paul steadily more attractive, unsettling and subversive, Hanley in turn needed the steadiness Paul supplied. He treated Paul as part disciple, part confidant, part personal retainer, coming to rely on him not simply to unravel an increasingly complicated tangle of contractual arrangements, film deals, paperback rights and book club nominations, but for a variety of errands ranging from drumming up an emergency advance by return of post to locating the silversmiths in Villiers Street where Hanley had once dropped off a pair of pistols as the pair of them passed by on a roundabout route to or from the Dog and Duck.

Paul's great quality, from his authors' point of view, was prompt and unfailing sympathy. His readiness to enter into their affairs, his grasp of literary as much as financial problems, his fellow feeling as a writer were invaluable. Publishers welcomed above all his calm, competent, scrupulous reliability. 'As an agent he was always the voice of sanity,' said Maurice Temple Smith of Eyre and Spottiswoode, whose dealings with agents had left him with no great expectations. 'He was good-tempered, smiling, efficient. He replied the following morning. He wrote sense. He read your letters before he answered them.'[27] Paul negotiated terms patiently but firmly, without exaggeration, bluster or emotional blackmail. His judgement was sound, both on quality and on what would sell. He generated enthusiasm from publishers, and induced confidence in authors. The amount of time he was prepared to spend on each individual client was unheard of ('I am pretty sure Paul read every script he dealt with,' said one incredulous colleague).[28] He was, when necessary, master of the majestic put-down: 'I wish I could be so politely rude to people, instead of just plain rude,' wrote an admiring author,[29] comforted as much by the fact that Paul understood the enormity of her wrong as by the prospect of his righting it. He could be scathing with publishers who slashed his authors' manuscripts to ribbons, shot them in the back with inaccurate publicity, buried them under ignorance or indifference, delayed publication dates, defaulted on payment, dishonoured contracts or failed to read their own small print ('Many thanks for the two letters,' Peter Green wrote after Paul had steered him round a tricky contractual corner, 'which seem to me models of statesmanship – not to mention what might be called loopholemanship').[30]

He made the ideal foil for David Higham, who tended to deal in broad and sweeping panoramas with a comparatively impressionistic approach to detail. David was burly, mustachioed, patriarchal, conveying, as one of his clients[31] pointed out, an unmistakeably commanding air of Davy Crockett. Like Paul, he had adapted easily to wartime service in the army and retained a military frame of reference, casting his new assistant as a subaltern or second-in-command, someone to be shown the ropes, to take orders, deal with red tape, soothe ruffled feelings and straighten out administrative snarl-ups. It was a relationship that both understood and found congenial, and it expanded with time to take in an element of father and son as it became clear that none of David's four boys was likely to succeed him in the business. David felt that his youth had been swallowed by the First World War just as Paul's had been by the Second: emerging from the army in his late twenties in 1924, with a wife to support and a child on the way, he had shelved his ambition to write and found an opening with the literary agent Curtis Brown, leaving to set up on his own with Nancy Pearn (who died in 1948) and Laurence Pollinger in the 1930s. Paul's determination to write was one of his most appealing points for David, who had turned out a couple of stylised, symbolic dramas himself after the war before settling down to become a Sunday novelist. Paul in 1950 – recently discharged from the army, author of quasi-symbolic plays, obliged to set aside his writing in order to keep a family – reproduced David's own position twenty-five years earlier in the wake of the first war. In May 1954, Paul became a junior director of the firm (on £884 a year, or more than double his starting salary) along with Pollinger's son Gerald, Pearn's assistant Jean Leroy, and the company secretary, Monica Preston. From now on Paul, tacitly accepted as heir apparent, fell easily into the role of fond and dutiful son following in the footsteps of David's sympathetic and supportive father: 'I think that was the whole thing,' said David's second wife, Nell Higham. 'He was doing through Paul what he hadn't done himself. He had a burning desire to see Paul succeed.'[32]

Paul had successively aroused the same desire in all his mentors – his mother, Clive and Joyce Wiener – from each of whom he had by now learned all he could, so much so that by June 1952, six weeks after the publication of *Johnnie Sahib*, he told Joyce the time had come to part.[33] He explained that he meant to put his affairs in the hands of David Higham. If David was beginning to supply the warmth and understanding Paul felt he had never had from his own father, Joyce was behaving altogether uncomfortably like his mother. The two had started bickering over contractual obligations, each increasingly exasperated by the other's wilfulness and truculence. Paul resented especially Joyce's proprietary attitude to his scripts. By the summer of 1952, he had come to a full stop halfway through his current novel, *The Return of the Dove*,[34] first roughed out the year before as a radio play on Joyce's instructions ('I believe the writing of the synopsis will be invaluable to you').[35] Her initial reaction to the play in outline had been encouraging, but he felt he had outgrown being ticked off and told what to do in such exhaustive and peremptory detail: 'the edges need to be a bit sharper . . . it is more novel than play as it stands. I don't think it will be difficult to turn this material into a powerful play. . . . Only thing is that I think it worth while taking a blue pencil to it now so that it emerges as a dramatic enough piece. . . . You know now that you can do these things – even when they seem miracle-difficult. So go ahead and do it this time.'[36]

Each blamed the other when Joyce eventually failed to bring off a BBC sale for Paul's synopsis. At the end of May, in the aftermath of *Johnnie*'s publication, Paul lapsed into 'a general feeling of depression' sufficiently debilitating for him to consult a doctor, who tentatively (and incorrectly) diagnosed paratyphoid.[37] Joyce was in trouble herself that summer, grieving over her own mother's death, and making both her adopted protégés, Paul and Toni Block, feel not only insubordinate but ungrateful and unworthy. The two agreed in some bewilderment that Joyce seemed anxious to be rid of them.[38] For Paul, her emotional demands on top of her criticism of his work were too much to bear, and on 15 June he wrote sombrely outlining their difficulties, leaving her in no doubt as to his changed feelings, and breaking off the relationship:

I believe we are too similar in temperament. In my private life I am always torn in two by the parallel demands of earning a living and creative writing and I am consequently inconsistent, optimistic and pessimistic; at once full and devoid of understanding. For no good reason I can thrive on criticism and in another instance break under its weight. We are all entitled to our own temperaments but I am convinced that I must now put my agency arrangements on a less personal, indeed [an] impersonal basis.

I can well see that a charge of ingratitude can too easily find its home. One is helped over a hill and it is one of the perplexities of life that having been helped one grows suspicious of the need for help in the future. You know my work well enough, I think, to see that this problem is a very real one to me. . . . It is useless to end on a 'no hard feelings' note. There are, I am sure. And I hope you will not ring me at least until we have both re-adjusted.[39]

Joyce accepted Paul's ultimatum with dignity and perhaps relief ('I trust . . . that your chivalry – as well as your common sense – may prompt you to say as little as need be about this in outside circles').[40] Paul returned to the manuscript of the *Dove*, starting all over again, finishing a first draft by mid-October, and delivering the final, revised typescript by the end of November to Frank Morley, who was enthusiastic. So was his chairman at Eyre and Spottiswoode, Douglas Jerrold.[41] David Higham, rightly anticipating a Book Club Recommendation, sold the novel to Doubleday in New York in March, subsequently selling Paul's proposal for a radio adaptation via Donald McWhinnie to the BBC.[42] The title was changed at the last minute, after much agonising over alternatives, to a phrase from one of Kipling's poems,[43] and *The Alien Sky* came out on 18 September 1953 to reviews that made Paul's name.

The first edition of 5,000 copies sold out within a month. The radio play, directed by McWhinnie and broadcast the following July, would be followed by an even more successful television version in January 1956. *The Alien Sky* was a triumph, if not an out-and-out bestseller in Jimmy Leasor's terms, or for that matter John Masters'. *Nightrunners of Bengal* had proved one of PPH's most popular and profitable properties, handled personally by Laurence Pollinger: David Higham made no secret of his hope that with luck and good management Paul might one day sell as well as Masters. Only American readers, obstinately uninterested in British Imperial affairs, turned thumbs down on Paul's novel as they had done two years earlier on Hanley's *Consul at Sunset*. Doubleday reported 'a pretty dismal flop',[44] in spite of their best efforts at marketing the book as *Six Days in Marapore* with a dusky Hollywood beauty on the jacket, all crimson beestung lips and black beetling brows, under the slogan 'A Story of Romance and Dramatic Action'.

The Alien Sky takes place in the little town of Marapore on the eve of Indian independence in 1947. The story starts, like so many of Paul's novels, with the arrival of a more or less colourless stranger, the American Joe MacKendrick, and unfolds against a background of political unrest, erupting finally in mayhem and murder orchestrated by the student leader Vidyasagar in the name of Hindu nationalism and Indian liberation (S. V. Vidyasagar was the name Paul gave twelve years later in *The Jewel in the Crown* to another young Indian nationalist, wrongfully arrested in the Bibigar Gardens, in another little town with almost the same name, Mayapore). It paints an unsympathetic portrait of the British community, viewed mainly through MacKendrick's eyes – 'He . . . saw them with their heads in the sands, their rears ripe and ready for the boot. They were stubborn, these Britishers on the point of departure' – with the exception of the liberal English newspaperman, Tom Gower, who blames his country-men not so much for their past actions as for their present failure of comprehension. Gower comes close to Paul's eventual position in that, for all his apparent aloofness, what matters desperately to him, more even than the loss of his job or the collapse of his marriage, is the need to understand the forces driving the British out of India: 'One could never kill the wish to understand: only disguise it, so far as one could disguise the existence of a caged beast.'[46] One of the titles proposed and discarded for this novel was *Caged Beast*;[47] for Paul curiosity was always a ruinous passion, and one which he suspected would in the end devour him.

He did not push it too far in *The Alien Sky*, which falls back constantly on the standard patterns and shortcuts of conventional romance: Gower suspects his wife of having an affair with his assistant, who is shot dead at last by Vidyasagar (but not before it has turned out to be MacKendrick who all along intended seducing Dorothy Gower, so as to score a posthumous point in a long-standing rivalry with his dead brother, who had been in fact her lover). The style is pedestrian, the plot and personnel largely predictable but, if anything tugs at the edges and frays the formulae of Romance and Dramatic Action, it is the female characters rather than the male. Women, in so far as they figured in *Johnnie Sahib* at all, were regarded in the context of masculine adventure as hardly human, referred to in generic jargon terms – 'bints', 'biwi', 'chichi' – and treated as basic amenities essentially no different from drink, cigarettes or decent quarters ('The need of a woman was like the need of food or water, purely physical,' as someone says in Hanley's *Consul*, 'and when you had to have it, you bought it and ate it'). Women occupy the foreground of *The Alien Sky*, grouped round the enigmatic central figure of Gower's wife. 'Dorothy Gower is, in my own view, a failure,' Paul said,[48] meaning presumably that as a character she remains unrealised, a passive, muted presence, seen obliquely, glimpsed at a distance through a doorway or retreating to her room, breaking her silence only once to confide her shameful and corrosive secret to the stranger. She is the child of an English father and a native Indian mother: 'You'd think it couldn't matter less. That it was all a joke anyway. My father and mother taught me it wasn't a joke. I only had to watch them together . . . He hated her because being married to her made him an outcast too. It dragged him down to her level. And she hated him because he couldn't pull her up to what he'd once been.'[49]

When John Masters tackled the same theme in *Bhowani Junction* (which came out the year after *The Alien Sky*, and commanded sales beyond even David Higham's wildest dreams for Paul), the result was more assured, less muddled, far crisper, more emphatic and exciting, but in another sense much duller. Masters' half-caste heroine, Victoria Jones (Ava Gardner played her in the film), is a paragon of beauty, intelligence, political awareness and emotional maturity, beloved by representative specimens of the entire male population of Bhowani – British, Indian and coloured – thanks to whose outstanding chivalry she remains pure, ending up a respectable married woman happily reconciled to her racial origins. For all his vivid local colour and spanking narrative pace, Masters' solution to the problem of mixed marriage is worked out in permutations as schematic and impersonal as if he were negotiating a tricky hand at bridge. For Paul, the subject remained painful, dangerous, unresolved, morally and emotionally equivocal. *The Alien Sky* had started from a factual base: Paul had envisaged it in the first place as 'a short true story',[50] and the final draft retained at its core elements which, however transposed, blurred and bowdlerised, had come originally from Frances Scott. He said that his characters were haunted by ghosts, 'ghosts of their own past and of their own futures',[51] and it is the ghost of his own and his mother's past that stands behind Dorothy Gower, telling her sad story to the young MacKendrick, who listens not so much to what she says as to the sound of her voice crying.

This was the first and, until the Raj Quartet, the only one of Paul's novels to focus on the British community in India chiefly through its memsahibs: an elderly retired spinster, a homeless and increasingly desperate divorcée, Dorothy herself who has no refuge outside her wretched marriage, an old schoolfriend without even that: taut, strained, often unhappy women for whom time is running out, who hold the threads of hostility and tension between the races, whose lives reflect the themes of rootlessness, displacement and dispersal which Paul was already beginning to suspect would become his central preoccupation as a writer. The accounts he gave of his intentions at the time, in correspondence and dustjacket blurbs, come closer to describing subsequent achievements than anything he had brought off as yet:

The theme, or problem, underlying both *Johnnie Sahib* and *The Alien Sky* is my personal theme – personal as a writer, I mean . . . It is that men and women, in these years that concern us, are increasingly aware of the absence of roots . . . There is nothing artificial about this (I think and hope) for it isn't a question of moving people around & making them do this thing or that thing in order to prove a point: it so happens that – for me – whatever people do they automatically play a variation on this theme – for me – because of what is, I suppose, a state of mind in myself.[52]

If Paul was beginning to define his territory as a writer more clearly, it was partly perhaps because he felt for the first time settled in other ways, financially less precarious, confident enough to put down a few experimental roots himself in a place of his own. On the strength of *Alien Sky*'s success, coupled with his directorship in May at PPH, to mark Paul's status as a coming man, and also to please Penny, the Scotts moved for the last time in June 1954, round the corner from

Brooklands Rise to a larger, white-painted, semi-detached villa in Hampstead Garden Suburb, 78 Addison Way. Both girls caught chicken pox that month. Paul took a week off at Whitsun to help with the move. His study, upstairs at the back, looked out onto an oak wood at the bottom of the garden, where the local Play and Pageant Union was performing Christopher Fry's *Boy with a Cart* in its open air theatre. Dancers with bare feet and beads of amber dabbled in the dew on Midsummer Eve. 'If I look out of my study window these evenings, I see strange figures moving among the oaks . . . conversation in the home invariably begins "By my halidom!" or "Tell me, good wife . . ." '.[53] Penny liked the new house, which was roomier, almost rural, altogether more promising than Brooklands Rise. The two girls, aged six and seven, could play in the garden and attend a private girls' school run by nuns a mile or so away. They had been taught from earliest years to keep quiet, to avoid noisy games, never to disturb their father in his study. So far as they were concerned, he had always been out all day, shut away upstairs in the evenings, seldom available at weekends. Sally expressed her image of him in a drawing with the caption: 'Poppa going to work. Works and comes home.'

Paul's work schedule never let up, but he made up for it when he emerged from the study for family gatherings, outings or seaside holidays by the energy of his attention. 'You *really* knew when he was with you,' said Carol: 'He'd do wonderful things.' He threw himself into festivities like Guy Fawkes night or Christmas Day, which always began with the two girls opening their presents and bouncing all over their parents' bed as the whole family breakfasted off a huge tray, before separating to dress and meeting again downstairs for a ceremonial lunch. At times like New Year, when three generations of Scotts met to celebrate with streamers, whistles and paper hats, Paul and Peter would entertain the party with turns so lifelike that Carol and Sally, who had never so much as set eyes on a Wright, grew up on familiar terms with Gilbert who lisped, and Louie who brandished an ear trumpet. Afterwards Paul could switch off as abruptly as he had switched on: part of what made Christmas so memorable was that everyone knew that, by Boxing Day, Poppa would be back again at the desk.

The same thing happened with holidays when, for two weeks at the end of every summer, Paul gave himself up to his family. While the children were small, the Scotts took holidays at places like Jaywick or Clacton out of season, in early September, when boarding houses were cheaper, resorts less crowded and blackberries ripe enough to pick. Paul would sing as they walked down to the sea – 'Huge long walks,' said Carol: 'At a gallop. He was a dragon. Full of energy. And he loved the water. He had a very peculiar backstroke, like a drowning frog: he *shot* backwards: what a swimmer!' He built two-seater sand cars for the girls to ride in, but above all he drew for them. 'My chief memory of Poppa as an artist is on the beach,' said Carol, 'great flat beaches with the tide gone out. He would take a stick or a long stone, or sometimes use his fingers if he was doing a quick sketch, and draw on the sand.' Paul, not a descendant of the Wrights for nothing, produced his masterpiece in 1953, the summer of the young Queen's coronation, when he covered the beach with a full-scale coaching scene complete with outriders, postilions and a team of horses drawing the fairy-tale coronation coach. Paul in this mood could be uproarious, and the family revolved around him. He radiated light and heat. The children and their mother basked in his abundance. 'He was wonderful to be with,' said Sally: 'He was a different person.' Coming back to London meant shutting that other self away for another year, which gave a melancholy tinge to their homecomings.

The new house in Addison Way was near enough for regular Sunday visits to 63 Bourne Hill, where blue hydrangeas grew inside the gate (Penny disliked the flowers ever afterwards), and Grandma drilled her household with soldierly precision. The girls, too young to be allowed anywhere near the drawing-room, were packed off to play in the Victorian front parlour, where they pushed the chairs back and crawled under the long heavy Chenille cloth that covered the round dining table. 'Sometimes Grandpa Josser would honour us with a visit,' said Carol: 'I think he was sent out to smoke his pipe.' Already in his eighties, massive, white-haired, hugely tall and virtually silent, Tom Scott seemed stiff and unapproachable to his grandchildren, but his studio in the room over the garage, which had once been Paul's, was magically inviting, especially to Sally, with its spill jars, drawing boards, paints, pencils, even a game of bagatelle laid out beside the fire. Tom was remote but not intimidating, unlike his wife. Her housekeeping was as disciplined as the army's, her command of other ranks unchallenged, her turnout as immaculate as if for military inspection. If Grandma on the warpath struck terror to the heart, no one could hope to look so smart as Grandma on parade with curls dressed, hat cocked, shoes polished, creases knife sharp and back ramrod straight.

She regarded her grandchildren, much as she once had their mother, as raw recruits to be shaped up. They brought out all her old talent for organisation and imaginative training schemes, as well as providing admirable counters in power games with Penny. Grandma was endlessly taking them to unsuitable places, keeping them out too late, giving them impossible, impractical, extravagant presents. 'She was a

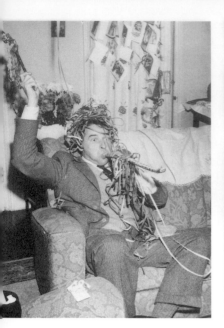

New Year celebrations. LEFT *Paul.* RIGHT *Paul, Arthur Pridmore, Eileen Scott, Carol and Sally standing at back with Penny, Frances and Tom Scott sitting in front.*

bit of a glamorous figure in her ancient manner,' said Carol. 'I loved Grandma. She spoiled us rotten.' Carol – blue-eyed and slender but square-jawed and stout-hearted even as a child – was her grand-mother's favourite, and could look startlingly like her. Sally, fair-haired and green-eyed, more Scott than Mark, said to be the image of her beautiful Great-Aunt Kate, got a cooler reception. She recognised granite in her grandmother, 'like a stone to stub your toe on'. Both girls realised as they grew older that the thrusting of a wedge between their father and their uncle Peter was being repeated in their own generation. It was as if, for one to enjoy the full sun of Frances's favour, the other always had to be in shadow.

A milder version of this split persisted at home. When Sally was small in 1952, she had fallen dangerously ill with pneumonia, monopolising Penny's attention and seeming ever afterwards, as any child that has been nearly lost always will do to its mother, perilously vulnerable, peculiarly at risk, in need of special care and protection. Carol, older and more robust, had been thrown back on her father so that subsequently the family tended to pair off: Poppa and Carol (or Kiki), Sally (or Sa) and her mother. But the main division was the one between the study, where Paul sat immured at his desk, and the kitchen, which was Penny's domain. It had yellow-painted walls and a coal-burning range with a cheerful fire to heat the water, a work table, a sink below the window overlooking the garden, and a big, solidly-built, wooden dresser with capacious, crowded shelves and

LEFT *Sally and Carol in the photo Paul kept on his desk.*
RIGHT *Family in the back garden at Addison Way underneath Paul's study window.*

cupboards. There were pots of geraniums on the windowsill, and cardboard boxes on the dresser for the cats. Two senior cats had moved with the family into Addison Way, where numbers quickly rose to eight: two black (Minty and Sooty who belonged to the girls), three tortoiseshell, a neutered ginger tom called Rota (after the antiquarian bookseller in Covent Garden, who had been a neighbour in Palmers Green), and a handsome pedigree Russian Blue brother and sister, called Baron and Beauty. The kitchen was always warm and welcoming with the radio playing and cats everywhere. 'Mama did everything in that kitchen,' said Carol. 'She did her baking, sewing, cooking. We did our homework. She wrote and read books.'

Penny made all the children's clothes: shorts, shirts, blouses, skirts and dresses. She knitted cardigans and jerseys. She stitched curtains with matching bedspreads and pillowslips embroidered with a pink C for Carol, a blue S for Sally. Home-making was her forte. Her nomadic history – a childhood spent on the move, years of shunting between nurses' homes and other people's houses on private nursing engagements – had taught her how to colonise any place where she might settle with a friendly, hospitable jumble of possessions. Everything she needed for survival and amusement could be laid out or packed away in her sewing box at a moment's notice. 'Mama could spend her whole day in one position: she could sew, do her nails, read a book, write a letter and stamp it,' said Carol. 'It was a kind of gypsy encampment.' Paul's self-imposed isolation was austere by comparison, and his study cramped: it contained a desk, two book cases (which gradually overflowed with books and box files), a single small window, and Bob Mason's jaunty portrait of the newly-made Lieutenant Scott. It was the room of someone who had dedicated his life to stripping away unnecessary clutter. People who came to the house marvelled at Paul's self-discipline. Other writers were enormously impressed: Toni Block, who liked and admired them both, could never understand how Paul could bring himself to leave the warmth and brightness of Penny's supper table to go upstairs and work. To Penny herself Paul's existence sometimes seemed, much as it did to Jimmy Leasor, lonely as a prison sentence: 'we three would paint and sculpt in clay, and cook our favourite cakes. Carol embroidered beautifully, and Sally knitted. We had interests galore, while Paul had only his work and his writing.'[54]

But Paul's perspective admitted no alternative. 'I had a wife, two children, a large mortgage, and a horror of ivory towers.'[55] His horror of affectation, any form of sham or make-believe, came from having spent his first twenty years with a prime fanatasist. His mother's ivory tower had by now become pretty well impregnable against reality: she told Penny that her father had been dean of a university ('caretaker more like', said Paul gloomily), and that her husband could command £300 a session for his fashion drawing ('why must she add a nought to everything?' said Paul). It made him determined that his own retreat should be a plain back bedroom, where he would work hard enough to pay all bills as they came in. The financial insecurity with which he had grown up had been alleviated, but not abolished, by his new prospect of prosperity. The move to Addison Way meant a substantial drain on an income admittedly assured but by no means princely and already heavily committed. Tom Scott's business had dwindled almost to nothing: a last crate of winter furs arrived from Noble's in the summer of 1953 or 1954, and this time it was Peter's wife Eileen – the two were married in 1952 with Paul as best man – who remembered seeing next season's fashions laid out in the studio. From now on Paul paid his parents' rent at Bourne Hill because, as he said, 'I was the only one in the family making any money'.[56] He was also about to take on school fees, the bane and bugbear of his childhood. The memory of his father going through the bank manager's returns fed nightmares of his own, in which he sorted feverishly through his cheque stubs, calculating the amount spent on the children's education and crying 'No! no!' so loudly that he woke himself as he reached the total.[57]

He discussed none of this at the time with Penny. Paul never directly confided his dreads and spectres, but his dreams grew worse at night as his withdrawal became more marked by day. Penny accepted his behaviour without comment, as she had done during the worrying months leading up to his resignation from Crown Passage when the girls were both still babies. Penny in those days would wheel them for miles in the big twins' pram, packing picnics for the three of them and staying out as long as possible so as to postpone returning home to face Paul's dejection, and what she always took to be his disapproval. She had learned to keep her distance for fear of repulse from the first week of their marriage when Paul, in the honeymoon hotel in London, had retreated into himself one evening, seeming not to see her and, when she touched and spoke to him, looking at her without recognition. It was the state Jim Corben had described as 'Paul thinking', and Mrs Scott as the sulks, but Penny had never encountered it before. Paul's curt 'No', when she asked if he was ill, was as unexpected as a slap in the face, and it felt like another slap when all she got, in answer to her anxious apology, was a brusque 'Stop nagging.'[58]

For her, it was an unforgettable shock, although for him it seems to have been no more than an unthinking, purely mechanical response. The lowering of an automatic mental shutter was a trick he had learned at his mother's knee: experiences like this one taught Penny what Mrs Scott had meant when she said Paul should not be interrupted in the arms of his muse. In her more prosaic moods, his mother admitted there was nothing to be done about Paul's sulking, any more than the cat's. It had been his method, evolved in boyhood, of asserting independence and at the same time exacting submission from his mother. Frances Scott, not above landing the odd blow below the belt herself, recognised her comeuppance, and respected him for it. But Paul never apparently allowed for the quite different effect on Penny, who had attracted him in the first place precisely because she had none of his mother's fighting instincts, and who reacted to his rebuffs by retreating in dismay herself.

Looking back long afterwards, Paul warned his elder daughter not to repeat his mistakes, in particular to guard against two of his best qualities which he had come to diagnose as failings. The first was his friendliness, the habit of being too accommodating to other people – 'probably a subconscious thing, to do with wanting to be liked by everyone' – and the second was his imperturbability: 'do try to throw your temperaments at work, rather than at home (another failing of mine!)'[59] As a young man, he had been over anxious to avoid anything like Joyce Wiener's extravagantly temperamental approach to agency. He became a byword at the office for tact, good humour and restraint. He was infinitely patient with moody, vain, overbearing, testy and importunate authors. 'Please don't apologise for the dramatics,' he wrote to Lal Green, Peter's wife, née Lalage Pulvertaft, whose novels he also represented: 'I once told a *very* dramatic author that we took on his temperament as well as his work: indeed you can hardly have one without the other.'[60] Nor, perhaps, would Paul have wanted to for, even as an agent, he retained the catholic sympathies of a novelist. On the one hand, he entered readily into the feelings of nervous publishers, who were apt to duck and shy away from some of his more notoriously tricky customers. On the other, he was himself too touchy, too raw, vulnerable and easily hurt not to respond instinctively to any author who felt, with or without reason, mishandled, let down, neglected, scorned or traduced by his or her publisher.

'My dear Paul, Truly you are a prince among agents!' wrote the Russian novelist, E. M. Almedingen,[61] when he finally found a home for the book over which she had come to blows with her former agent, A. P. Watt. She was a distinguished client with a history of misfortunes which were, as Paul said, by no means all of her own making.[62] Tall, dark and handsome, known on account of her stature and imposing presence as 'the grenadier', she had been born in St Petersburg in 1898, child of an aristocratic family with English connections on her mother's side (Tolstoy, dandling her on his knee, had predicted a future as a poet), and an academic background on her father's. She had survived the horrors of the Russian revolution, narrowly escaping starvation, shooting and imprisonment, to reach London in 1923, aged twenty-five, homeless and penniless, without family, friends or contacts. She built a literary career on irreducible obstinacy, will-power and gruelling hard work, producing a series of increasingly successful novels with Russian settings – *Froissia* and *Dasha* were the best known – just before the second war. A naturally autocratic turn of mind coupled with extreme self-reliance had never made for easy relations with her editors at Hutchinson. She could be imperious, critical and high-handed: she was exacting with herself, and saw no reason why her expectations of others should be less stringent. But she was also shrewd, sensitive and humane, a penetrating judge of books and people, unreservedly generous to those who passed her test. Repeated batterings had made her seem perhaps tougher than she felt. 'I do realise . . . that you need what I might perhaps call a literary arm to lean on from time to time,' wrote Peter Watt in a farewell letter full of respect, regret and perhaps a suspicion of relief, 'and that such an arm is not attached to the Hutchinson body.'[63]

She approved of Paul from their first meeting in July 1954, and cordially accepted his offer of an arm. He promptly sorted out her chaotic financial affairs, overhauled her contracts and repaired her relationship with Hutchinson (it gave her particular satisfaction when *Fair Haven*, the first book he handled for her, was exceptionally well received in 1956). Over the next decade or so, he consistently encouraged her to develop the scholarly, historical side of her writing, while she for her part read each new book of his as it came out, taking unaffected pride in his successes. They took one another out to lunch at the Epicure: both were chain smokers, both partial to the restaurant's special brand of Armagnac, both almost more inclined to squander funds they hadn't got on a treat in bad times than in good. Paul brought her home to dinner at Addison Way, and sometimes to spend the night. She became with time a kind of favourite aunt to the whole family, sending parcels of gladioli corms and tulip bulbs up from the country, and bringing presents for the children, who vividly remembered the sense of occasion generated by her visits ('A bulky woman with a great sense of style. She *swept* in,' said Carol: '*was* she royal?'). She was especially fond of Penny: Chris Almendingen (Edith Martha were her given names but she was Christine to close friends) was devoted to Paul, but she early suspected something up behind the scenes in his relationship with Penny, and redoubled her tokens of affection to them both.

Over the next few years, Paul developed the same kind of mutually supportive writers' relationship with Chris Almedingen as he had with Peter Green, only without the competitive element, or rather the bracing sense Peter always brought of everybody on their toes looking slippy and writing at the double with one eye on the ball. Like Chris, he was an occasional visitor at Addison Way on flying visits up from Cambridgeshire, dashing in with his book-bag on a rising tide of commitments and commissions, things to do, films to see, appointments to be kept and deadlines met. It seemed to the young Carol that he could polish off ten books sitting up in bed before breakfast, and have his review typed by lunchtime. Bob Mason also came to stay in the 1950s, and painted Penny. There were outings with clients to the Cock Inn at Cockfosters, and more formal gatherings for selected authors at home. Penny struck everyone as an exemplary wife and mother, a charming if somewhat self-effacing hostess, and Paul as an attentive host. They still seemed a model couple to the mild chagrin of some of Paul's women clients, who were not always best pleased to discover that he never looked at another woman. 'Paul was loyalty itself,' said Mary Patchett, who wrote enchanting, sometimes riproaring children's stories (*Ajax the Warrior*, *Tam the Untamed*) about animals in the Australian outback, dingoes and a wild horse called Brumby.

Mary Patchett was one of Paul's first and favourite clients: they had hilarious lunches together — 'I had more laughs with Paul than anyone'[64] — and summer expeditions to the zoo to pay their respects to the Indian otter, and the wild cats ('Paul loved lions, like I do'). Paul

delighted in Mary's candid, caustic wit, Mary in his answering
emollience. She was a gifted and exuberant grumbler, exaggerating
her own prickliness ('Disgruntled, porcupinally yours, Mary')[65]
purely for the pleasure of being professionally smoothed down by
Paul. Between them they perfected a kind of authorial double act,
Mary egging him on with more and more trenchant protests and
swingeing grievances against her publishers, Paul gracefully translat-
ing them into terms to which the offenders might respond. Mary's 'I
don't agree to *any* editorial alterations not sanctioned by me or you,
slummocky lot, never on time with anything,'[66] became Paul's 'Dear
Miss S., . . . She would be prepared to make any of the revisions you
suggest, provided she approves.'

Lunches with Mary became longer and more frequent. They
stopped going to restaurants and started meeting at her flat, swapping
gossip and stories sometimes half the afternoon. Mary was Australian,
divorced with a grown-up son, older than Paul and in some ways a
good deal more sophisticated. She had worked for Associated News in
Sydney, then gone into the beauty business, emigrated to England,
opened a salon and been Beauty Consultant to *Vogue* before the war.
'Paul was the most Regency man I ever met,' she said, 'elegant in
everything he did. His clothes weren't cut very well, or very well made,
but he wore them so elegantly. He had *such* taste.' Paul brought her
little gifts and paid her delicate attentions. She found him so charming,
so considerate, so boyishly sleek and slim ('I should have liked to pat
him') that she longed to look after him and make him happy. It was
Paul who suddenly drew back, putting a stop to the lunches,
explaining that they must no longer meet alone, and making it clear
that all invitations should from now on include Penny. Mary was too
practical, too experienced and far too attached to Paul to let it spoil
their friendship, but she never forgave Penny.[67]

Blaming his wife for Paul's abrupt withdrawals became something
of a habit among his friends, which was ironic, considering that Penny
suffered more from them than anyone. He himself had learned his
lesson from Joyce Wiener. It had made him adamant as to what
services he was prepared to perform for a client, and what not. One of
his specialities was soothing ruffled feelings. Another was the delivery
of home truths to publishers on behalf of authors whose reputations
for sunniness remained unclouded. Among Paul's unusual qualities as
an agent was the clarity with which he drew up limits, spelt out duties,
obligations and responsibilities. In heated disputes, it was partly his
grasp of tactics, partly the time and trouble he took to explain them,
that calmed all parties down. He could be unsparing in rebuke, and
magisterially firm. 'I think the cause of your dissatisfaction may be

that you entirely misunderstand the scope of an agent's work,' he wrote to an indignant client, who had threatened to leave PPH in 1954 after his first novel on grounds of general ineptitude, and in particular failure to secure reviews or advertising for him on the same scale as for *Alien Sky*:

We are not public relations officers. We are not publicists. We do not keep in tow a row of tame reviewers to write reviews of books by authors we represent. We control no papers or literary editors. We do not even control the publicity departments of publishing houses. Very well, you'll say, what the hell do we do? We act, in the first place, for the author, over matters of business. Money. We seek to make the best possible financial arrangements for the rights in works he writes and publishers publish. We try to ensure that the arrangements work, that the author gives away as little as possible and gets as much as we can persuade a publisher it is fair he should have. The agreements we draw up are the pointer to our success or otherwise. . . .

You cannot in all fairness blame us for your lack of reviews. If you do, you would, by the same token, have to pat us on the back for the reviews you got. What, for goodness sake, would our responsibility be for the one in this week's *TLS* [*Times Literary Supplement*]? Surely you see that there comes inevitably a time when the author, the agent and the publisher, having done their job, can only await the verdict: *of course*, you've 'spoken' to people. I have spoken to people too. *Of course* your friends tell you what a good book it is. . . .

What I refuse to take responsibility for is the reception in the press, and if you expect that of any first-rate agent who knows his business – where it begins and where it ends – you'll obviously want to look elsewhere. If you do it will be the greatest disappointment I've had as an agent, because I think we have done and can continue to do a job for you – and yours is the sort of work it gives me the greatest personal pleasure to be connected with.[68]

The recipient of this letter was Gabriel Fielding: brilliant, acerbic, assertive, dazzlingly ambitious, vehemently dramatic, violently sensitive, in short everything Paul liked best in a client. He was a descendant of the eighteenth-century Henry Fielding, writing under a pseudonym (under his other hat he was Dr Alan Barnsley, a general practitioner at Maidstone in Kent), and he had every intention of matching the achievements of his ancestor. His demands might be exhausting but the rewards were proportionately great, and Paul felt triumphant when Fielding's second novel, *In Time of Greenbloom*, caused a ripple of excitement in England in 1956, and something more like a wave in the US. It was the first of a trilogy that far outstripped Paul's own modest success in the late 1950s and early 1960s. So did John Braine as a novelist, and Muriel Spark, who published her first novel in 1956, taking Paul back as her agent, on Fielding's recommendation, in the summer of 1957 when she was working on *Memento Mori*. 'To say that Muriel regarded her gifts with expectant fondness would not be in any way an overstatement,' wrote her friend Derek Stanford of this period,[69] and Paul shared her expectations to the full. She sent him the first two chapters of *Memento Mori* on 26 September, describing her researches that autumn into geriatric hospitals, and picturing a ribald future for the pair of them – Granny Spark and Granpa Scott – in their respective senile wards. Paul negotiated terms with Macmillan, extricated her from the grasping clutches of a former publisher, and generally smoothed her path to fame and fortune over the next few years. Perhaps the most spectacular of all the literary launches he presided over in this decade with Higham were Spark's *Memento Mori* and Braine's *Room at the Top*, both manuscripts handled by him within a year of publishing his own *A Male Child*.

This third novel was begun in October 1953, finished on 27 February 1955 and published in March 1956. Peter Green considered it Paul's masterpiece[70] and so, privately, did Paul himself. *A Male Child* remained ever afterwards the dearest to his heart of all his early novels, and the only one he never disowned. Reviewers were impressed ('A distinguished, grave and original novel by a writer who gets better with each book he writes' said Pamela Hansford Johnson in *The Bookman*), although even the most respectful scarcely warmed to it. The book paints, with what one of his readers called Dostoievskian gloom,[71] a graphic picture of post-war rootlessness, the physical drabness and moral apathy of demobilised Londoners scrabbling about in search of jobs, homes, marriages and security. It revolves around the Hursts' haunted house called Aylward (a gaunt south London version of the Wrights' house at Richmond), as well as making occasional forays among out-of-work authors and dubious publishing ventures at the seedier, Crown Passage end of the book market. Frank Morley, nothing if not diplomatic, described it as a cross between *The Turn of the Screw* and Charles Addams's *New Yorker* cartoons with a dash of Eliot's *The Confidential Clerk* thrown in.[72]

A Male Child marks a turning point in Paul's relations with the past. He used Aylward (and seems to have been at least partly conscious of what he was doing at the time) for a kind of mental spring-cleaning, for turning out the cupboards and opening up the haunted attics of his childhood and early life. He dramatised the division in his own nature through the two brothers, Alan and the dead Edward Hurst. He drew a grim but not unforgiving portrait of his mother as Mrs Hurst, unable to come to terms with the loss of her dead favourite and savagely embattled with the wife of her surviving son. It is as though, having tendered romantic sympathy in *The Alien Sky* on one aspect of his mother's plight, he pushed it next to its ugliest extreme (early manuscript drafts leave no doubt that Mrs Hurst's maternal feelings are incestuous: 'what a man would call unnatural physical passion').[73] The author's sympathies lie with Alan who embodies the domestic virtues as husband, breadwinner and prospective father. The dead poet Edward – precocious, bookish, ineffectual, self-absorbed and self-admiring – is portrayed with the relish of a convert stamping out the last vestiges of a discarded self. 'But the other side of him would not lie down,' Ruth Sansom said, describing Paul himself in these years. For the rest of his life Paul would grow his hair long at intervals like a poet's, and experiment with unconventional clothes, but he always reverted in the end to the neat, inconspicuous, sober-suited character who struck chance acquaintances as resembling an accountant more than a freelance writer. Aylward, in *A Male Child*, remains riddled with memories of the dead Edward, whose ghost appears quite literally at one point peering through a windowpane.

Paul had originally envisaged it as a book about Alan Hurst, who would tell his story in the first person, but he found himself obliged quite soon to split the central character in two, introducing as narrator Alan's army friend from India, Ian Canning. Both incorporate traits borrowed from Jim Corben (Jim had lost touch by this time, but not before inviting Paul to stay with him in 1950 for the birth of the first baby – a male child – he had planned so long before in India). But essentially the two represent different sides of Paul himself, and it was their juxtaposition that excited him: 'At that point, I suppose, the thing caught fire.'[74] Ian's function in the text is to serve as interpreter for the inarticulate Alan who, as his wife says, must suffer 'the unhappiness without the kick of working it out for himself psychologically'. In preliminary notes for this novel Paul said he meant to explore 'the dark forces of nature' at work beneath 'the gloss of civilised society'.[75] If Ian was imported to provide psychological kicks, one of the main themes that finally emerged from the finished text was the image of marriage as a kind of prison house.

All the male characters supply variations on this theme. Rex Coles (a shrewd cartoon sketch of Gilbert Wright) explicitly compares marriage to a prison: Alan's friend David finds himself trapped into it: Ian escapes from it through divorce, and even Alan at one stage envies him his freedom ('I saw for the first time the marks of the prisoner on his brow. That they were self-inflicted through his own sense of duty made them no less moving to look upon').[76] But marriage is a prison Alan has entered voluntarily and, throughout the book, Alan stands for health and hope. He suppresses his own conflicts, relegating them to dreams so disturbed that he cries out in his sleep at night. By day he is vigorous, active, unreflective: 'himself the thrusting male, he deludes himself into thinking that he is needed by several people on several different levels to do their thrusting for them, to protect them, to fight their battles. This is the role he believes is allowed to men. He fights his own inner drive to break free, to "go out into the night & awaken his dreams of the hot spiced warmth of the East".'[77]

It is Alan's energy that rescues Ian from the slough of suicidal despond into which he has been plunged by failure as a writer ('I imagined much, started little, finished nothing and published not at all').[78] Ian is the archetype of all the passive observers – emotionally inert, intellectually alert, morally more or less depressed – in Paul's early novels. He contemplates gassing himself or throwing himself from a window, and is saved by Alan from swallowing an overdose of sleeping pills. He hates his own unprepossessing body, feeling ashamed of the contrast between his nakedness and Alan's handsome, muscular physique. Ian is ravaged by a mysterious illness picked up in India (he looks back wistfully to 'a time when the body harboured nothing malignant'), for which there is no treatment, and whose diagnosis leaves medical specialists baffled.

Many readers would in due course find the confusions and obscurity of *A Male Child* equally baffling. When Frank Morley had asked tactfully for clarification of the manuscript, Paul passionately defended it, refusing to make revisions, and saying he would sooner see it published as an abortion than decapitate it or cut out its deformities.[79] But he detected signs of Morley's mystification in even his most encouraging reviewers when the book came out, and by this time it echoed an uneasiness of his own. 'Pamela Hansford Johnson in *The Bookman* remarks on my allusiveness, my blurring of edges,' he wrote to another friendly reviewer in the month of publication, 'and these may be symptoms of the malady you are diagnosing. But what is it? Obviously I must become aware of it in some inner way before I can do anything about it. I'm not sure I should get rid of the illness – supposing it to be an illness – merely by telling myself that the book is to be about such and such.'[80] The note of urgency in this letter suggests that Paul was beginning to suspect that his problem as a writer went much deeper than any merely technical or structural difficulties.

Psychologically, he understood his predicament well enough, and confessed as much to Clive in Tasmania. Paul wrote to him somewhat awkwardly – 'I'm not sure what this letter can say since, in its way, it is some sort of apology' – on 18 December 1955, after reading an early copy of Clive's *The Witnesses and Other Poems*, in particular the one

'For Paul', and 'To One in Darkness', written at the time of Paul's homosexual ordeal in 1940. 'Perhaps it is because the darkness is over that I can write, or even see that it was darkness. It means something to me now because I see it from the right end. I've been a bad correspondent for many years, & no doubt shall continue to be, & as we all do, have gone through certain phases of one sort or another. I wish, possibly, that I had your particular brand of certainty . . . To read the poems again is like coming home. Thank you, Clive, for your continued goodwill which I have done little to deserve. I'm explaining it all very badly. But I *have* emerged into a certain lucidity, I think.' He ended by promising to send a copy of *A Male Child*, 'which may, I think, explain something of the past – not with regard to persons but with regard to one's understanding of them.'

Ruth and Clive knew enough to recognise the conflict between Paul's divided selves, and also his old fascination with the narcissistic Wildean imagery of mirrors which resurfaced in *A Male Child*. Ian sees his own face as a reflection of sickness, fails to recognise it in a mirror, sees Edward looking back at him from the glass instead of himself, until he is eventually persuaded by Alan to look beyond his own reflected image to other people:

Gently he was trying to teach me to ignore a condition that could not be diagnosed . . . I felt that what he offered me was life and sanity. He had taken me and shoved me unceremoniously in front of a mirror. But in it, mine was not the only reflection. There was his own and that of his mother, and all the other people who came and went, in and out of the rooms of Aylward: the human condition of which I was part and parcel.[81]

Ian's particular condition produces lassitude, apathy, stomach trouble, intermittent fever and depression. These are all symptoms of amoebiasis, a disease which Paul had also contracted in India, although it would not be diagnosed in him for nearly another decade. When he wrote *A Male Child* he was familiar with the form if not yet the name of his illness. But homosexuality was also a condition, untreatable and incurable, for all practical purposes impossible to recognise openly in those days. Paul had taught himself to ignore what could not be diagnosed. It remained submerged beneath the level of consciousness, buried too deep to be acknowledged to his family or friends or even to himself, but he was already obscurely aware that, if he could once find a way to confront his sexual nature in fiction without a blurring of the edges, it would immeasurably enrich him as a writer.

CHAPTER NINE

Something of Micawber

Paul felt himself heading in the late 1950s for some sort of crisis on the professional as well as personal fronts. He shelved his original plan to follow *A Male Child* with a long historical novel about Warren Hastings[1] in favour of a more practical proposition, a play called *The Colonel's Lady*, about a band of British cadets at an Officer Training School in wartime India galvanised by the arrival in the cantonment of a dashing divorcée at Smith's Hotel (a fictional version, first established in *The Alien Sky*, of Green Hotel, Belgaum). He dashed off a synopsis in January 1956, and discussed television possibilities over lunch at the Café Royal with a man from the BBC, who provisionally commissioned a script in April,[2] by which time Paul had a new novel in hand, also set in a military camp based on Belgaum. *A Male Child* had meanwhile got off to a slow start on publication in March after being turned down by eight different publishers in the US (Paul settled reluctantly as a last resort for disadvantageous terms from Dutton's Elliot MacRae). He blamed Frank Morley ever afterwards 'for giving that book the kiss of death at the top, right from the start, while all the time it was my best book'.[3]

Even Paul admitted that this was unreasonable, especially at a time when Eyre and Spottiswoode was struggling for survival, in low water financially, and facing a takeover by Associated Book Publishers in which Morley himself (confidently tipped to succeed Douglas Jerrold as chairman) would lose his job. Paul's position, already shaky, looked shakier still when his TV script was rejected that autumn on the grounds that its subject was out of date, and its heroine ('to all intents a historical person nowadays')[4] unlikely to interest a contemporary audience. Blanket dismissal of anything to do with Imperial India would become increasingly familiar to Paul as he himself grew steadily less interested in writing about anything else, but the problem this time was a matter of form rather than content. He had written the play for the actress Valerie White (who played Cynthia Mapleton in *The Alien Sky*) 'as a sort of up-to-date Edwardian comedy, very formal, non-existent in analysis',[5] and the effect is thoroughly contrived, neither quite witty nor paradoxical enough for its sub-Shavian sentimentality, too mechanical to work on any more demanding level. Donald McWhinnie eventually accepted it for radio under a new name, *Sahibs and Memsahibs* (the original title came from Maugham, along with the bland, knowing, ironic tone), casting Valerie White as the ex-Colonel's lady and Fabia Drake as her opposite number. Both actresses made the most of the characteristically sardonic humour which, as Peter Green pointed out, had never been allowed before to seep into Paul's writing. Peter also tentatively raised a longstanding and more fundamental complaint:

Here we are again, gnawing round the Far East military bone, time 1943: men in uniform, special conditions. What I'm beginning to wonder is, how necessary this very specialised field of operations is for you and, if it is, why? . . . Why you returned to the Far East again, I'm not sure. Because AMC [*A Male Child*] wasn't generally understood? Because the creation of it revealed things to you which were alarming, disturbing? All this is very impertinent . . . Believe me, Paul, I've given all this a great deal of thought and worry. If you think I'm up the pole, just tell me to go slide down a forty-foot razor-blade, and I'll do my best to oblige without damage.[6]

Sahibs and Memsahibs was not broadcast until the summer of 1958, by which time Peter's diagnosis must have seemed, if not impertinent, uncomfortably astute. Paul had in the interval produced two more novels, set respectively in Burma and Malaya in the later stages of the war, both dealing with men in uniform, both 'gnawing round' without ever actually closing in on a similar set of submerged conflicts. Both were mystical in tone and heavily symbolic, although what they symbolised remained far from clear even, as he frankly admitted, to their author. The first was *The Mark of the Warrior*, about the training of cadets in 1943 for the Burmese jungle war, with a hero haunted by the memory of his dead elder brother. Bob Ramsay's brother had been shot by the Japanese on the retreat to Imphal, leaving his CO, Major Craig, determined to bring out in young Bob the killer instinct – the true soldierly spirit, or mark of the warrior – he had recognised with approval in the dead John. Cadet Ramsay himself deliberately sets out to become his brother's double: 'He looked at his reflection in a mirror, and said, "Face yourself, Ramsay." The self which he faced was thinner. His cheekbones showed. His resemblance to John had strengthened. The mirror was like a window, through which John watched him and spoke to him.'[7]

Craig schools Ramsay to become invincible, eliminating weakness, pity, dependence, any vestige of fellow feeling for the men under his command, preparing him in stern and lofty solitude 'to be alone in the forest to kill'.[8] This tale of suspense, tension, danger and death is the closest Paul ever came to a masculine adventure yarn in the Masters manner ('It's simply saturated with nasty things like symbolism,' he wrote, adding smugly: 'I fell over backwards to tell a story that a fairly average reader could enjoy for its own sake').[9] Mollie Hamilton, who had known Jack Masters from his days as a cadet at Sandhurst right up to his triumph at Mandalay, recognised immediately what Paul was aiming at, and wrote to say she was sending her proof copy to Masters himself: 'I feel this is something he will really fall for. Ramsay is Jack to a large degree, and I shall be *most* interested to see what that type thinks of that type. Or if they don't recognise it at all!'[10] Masters made no response, perhaps because Paul's book caught him on the raw: *The Mark of the Warrior* begins with a flashback to the death of the elder Ramsay, an episode which fills Craig with guilt, first for exposing his men to Japanese ambush and, second, for prolonging their danger by not having the nerve to shoot and jettison his wounded second-in-command. Paul may have picked up in Burma rumours, which Mollie had certainly heard, of a similar incident involving Masters, who was said to have acted in fact with the ruthlessness the fictional Craig found sadly lacking in himself.

But perhaps he paid no attention because, as a piece of writing, the book posed no threat. Paul found the tightlipped conventions of the romantic thriller as unsatisfactory as post-Edwardian light comedy, and neither *Sahibs and Memsahibs* nor *The Mark of the Warrior* showed the slightest makings of a popular success. Bitterly disappointed by the rejection of his television script, further dismayed by sales of *A Male Child*, Paul was deeply discouraged to find the manuscript of his new novel turned down in America in 1957 even by Elliott MacRae.[11] His salary at PPH rose that year to £1248 (rather less, by his reckoning, than a publisher's editor might hope to earn) but his total earnings as an author came to £532.[12] Now that his attempt to combine writing with job security and a regular career structure seemed to be finally petering out, Paul's instinct was to advance rather than retrench. 'You've got to take risks if you want to get anywhere with writing. You've got to give up things,' he said twenty years later to the students in his American writing class, who understood him to be talking about his own life: 'Sacrifice was one of his themes. You felt that he'd taken risks, and he'd given up things.'[13]

In May 1957, the month in which MacRae refused *The Mark of the Warrior*, Paul travelled over to Ireland in his capacity as an agent to discuss PPH business with Gerald Hanley. They talked about their respective current and pending books, and exchanged commiserations over publishers. Hanley initiated his visitor into the delights of Dublin bar architecture in the course of an extended pub crawl which merged, in Paul's recollection, into a haze of Guinness fumes and Gothic.[14] They discussed the writer's life and its riskiness. Hanley was reassuring about what he called the jitters: the lack of security, the certainty of duns and debtors as against the unlikelihood of finding a crock of film rights at the end of the rainbow, or the more prosaic possibility of persuading a publisher to cough up some sort of long-term guarantee. They told one another that writing was what mattered, and one good thing to be said about money worries was that they made you write harder.

They cheerfully agreed that outsiders like themselves stood no chance of being accepted by the English literary establishment or, as Paul pointed out, of enjoying the pickings available on the old-boy network by way of 'advances for books never even begun let alone finished'. Theirs was a hard road, and they contemplated it with relish: 'people like you and me are plain bloody navvies without a trade union,' wrote Paul.[15] 'I have never been impressed by Oxbridge Eng. lit., but they know how to treat an advance. . . ,' replied Hanley: 'One must never forget, though, that these people look after each other, school by school.'[16] In the seven years since they had started doing business together, Hanley had lived in Kashmir with his Indian wife and children, filmed in Kenya, proposed moving to Italy, and eventually settled in County Cork in a house he regularly declared he would be forced to sell under threat of immediate destitution. He doubted if he would ever get over feeling jittery: there would always be moments when the fox terrier playing on his lawn looked more like a wolf at the door, 'but the freedom is worth the jitters'.[17]

Paul returned to London and his safe office job stirred, on the one hand, by Hanley's pathetic vision of himself reduced before winter to playing the violin on the pavement outside Hegarty's pub and, on the other, by the assurance that no matter what financial problems might loom, Hanley could always write his way out of them.[18] In fact, his current book was already selling comfortably, Paul was about to sell film rights in a previous novel, and Hanley's publisher, William Collins, would offer a financial guarantee before the end of the year. Paul's own position looked hopeless by comparison. But the weekend that was to have been spent discussing Hanley's future exerted both directly and indirectly a drastic impact on Paul's. On the boat going home, in the dining-car of the Emerald Isle Express, a picture floated apparently out of nowhere onto his mental screen: 'There was just an open space then and a man walking across it with blood on his cheek. Later I saw that he was walking away from a pavilion. All that remained then was to find out why he was walking away from the pavilion, and why the pavilion was there.'[19] The answers supplied his next novel, *The Chinese Love Pavilion*, which ends with the scene he had first imagined on the Irish boat train in May 1957.

But, before he could explore further, he had unfinished business with *The Mark of the Warrior*, for which he was about to receive an American offer of $1000 (or double MacRae's advance on *A Male Child*) from the solid, well-to-do, thoroughly respectable if not exactly go-ahead house of William Morrow Inc. The whole firm seemed to have fallen that summer under Paul's spell, starting with Thayer Hobson,[20] who acquired the manuscript in London in June and wrote in July, apologising in advance for inability to turn the book into a bestseller but making instead the kind of proposal most authors only dream of receiving from a publisher ('you'll just have to put this down as a case where your publishers are primarily interested in the quality and character of a book and not making a decision on the basis of whether or not they will have a big sale . . .').[21] Next came an exuberant note from Morrow's chief editor, John Willey, who had been indelibly impressed by Paul at their first meeting over a routine Higham lunch the previous summer ('I can't for the life of me remember the colour of his eyes, but I think of them as shining as we talked'),[22] and another from Hobson's partner, Frances Phillips ('looking to the future, as you know, dear Mr Scott of Pearn, Pollinger, Morrow is interested in authors rather than in single books').[23] All recognised something impressive and ungainly about *The Mark of the Warrior*: the sombre and authoritative note Chris Almedingen picked out on publication when she said it reminded her of a Dürer drawing or Leonardo's sketch of the Flood.[24] Gerry Hanley settled himself in his chair, 'a bottle of stout at the elbow and a cigarette going', to read the whole thing at a sitting: 'In your work this book takes you through that thin screen which hides things, and you are going to write some terrific stuff – that's what your book told me.'[25]

Paul's copy-editor for the *Warrior* at Morrow was Adèle Dogan, who set herself, even more energetically than any of his previous mentors, to coax Paul away from rhetorical cloudiness towards structural and analytical clarity ('You see, you know what you mean, and so your words convey more to you than they do to me. It isn't an easy book, and we'd like your signposts to be more lucid').[26] Adèle was young and determined, tactful, appreciative, endlessly patient: the long postal sessions spent working with her on this and the following novel proved invaluable to Paul, whose texts had, as he said, never before been subjected to such close, thorough and immensely intelligent scrutiny. It made him go back to his 'root-source', ponder, justify, explain ('now even I know what the damn book's about!'),[27] begin to work out what he was doing, and why, for himself as much as for her. He concluded that *The Mark of the Warrior* wasn't a book about soldiering at all: that its point was metaphysical ('You can still be metaphysical without losing the reader in mystery', Adèle wrote drily),[28] and that Ramsay's fatal jungle expedition (which ends with a restaging of his brother's death) was essentially a spiritual journey:

... a particular variation on what might be called the general theme of the Search, whatever that may be – for proof of identity, of existence, of God, what you will – and this is what Ramsay is looking for as unconsciously as Craig – only Craig looks for it in corporate existence, his fellow-men, Life, Esther, where Ramsay looks for it in himself, the Garden, destruction. For the subconscious Ramsay, the act of destruction is a creative act, a stripping away of one more onion skin.[29]

Paul's long letter to Adèle defining his intentions was written with hindsight in the light of his Dublin weekend, which no doubt explains why its imagery – the spiritual journey or quest for God in the Garden (by garden Paul said he meant the forest), ending in madness, destruction and death – corresponds in places less to the book he had actually written than to the book he was about to write, *The Chinese Love Pavilion*, which remained tucked away at the back of his mind while he wrestled with the *Warrior* that summer. He had experimented for the first time in that book with a split viewpoint, alternating between, on the one hand, the practical, responsible, guilt-ridden Craig, who is tended but also indefinably tainted by his devoted wife Esther, and, on the other, the solitary, celibate, sacrificial Ramsay who goes mad, according to Paul's note for Adèle, before willing his own death.[30] The two represent extreme versions of their creator's divided nature ('In the broadest sense, Craig and Ramsay are both looking for God,' Paul explained cryptically to Clive: 'The Ramsay image is the devil image almost; anyway, a potential sacrifice'),[31] but a narrative constantly shifting from one to the other proved thoroughly confusing to everyone, including Paul himself, as he finally admitted in another note to Adèle.

The Chinese Love Pavilion starts (after a brief prelude describing the pavilion itself) with Tom Brent, an ingenuous youth who has thrown up a career in accounting to sail for Bombay with romantic notions of exploring India, only to find himself after a year so discouraged as to be on the point of returning home to look for a professional opening in London after all. Brent's mind is changed for him by a masterful stranger, who makes a dramatic first entrance in a thunder storm, arriving out of the night, unannounced, hatless and streaming with rain. If Brent seems a fairly familiar figure, none of Paul's previous novels contains anyone quite like Brian Saxby (who retreats into the background after this opening encounter, exerting a powerful pull on the action thereafter while remaining largely unseen). Bronzed, bearded, big-boned, piratical, more (as his creator admitted) like a character out of Conan Doyle than Paul Scott,[32] Saxby turns out to have come from Sumatra by way of Ceylon, bringing with him a bag of smuggled sapphires and proposing shortly to set off on his travels again, heading this time via Assam for Malaya.

He carries young Brent off the night after their meeting to a quarter too shady for even the taxi driver to penetrate ('It seemed to me that all the cut-throats and beggars of Bombay were congregated there'), and plies him with illicit spirits in the upper room of a native dive, while recounting his adventures as traveller, explorer and shipwrecked mariner ('I'm never bored. I enjoy spectacular good health. I have been anywhere in the Far East you care to mention. I was born and bred west of Suez, and can only breathe east of it').[33] In the course of the evening the pair tell one another their respective histories, growing steadily wilder ('I had never drunk so much hard liquor in my life') and more confidential, exchanging aspirations and projecting visions, in an exotically transposed Bombay version of Paul's weekend in Dublin with Hanley. Brent and Saxby seem steadily less like outward-bound men of action, more like a couple of intoxicated novelists snugly holed up in a city pub, swapping tall stories and embroidering fantastic plots:

I was drunk enough to give rein to fancies inspired by his tales. We were in the warm close cabin of a schooner, a pearling lugger, two sailors afloat on the vast magic of the Pacific: we were in a ramshackle hut, two castaways bewitched by the pounding of the surf and the cries of parrots: we were at ease, old hands, half intent on the yarns we spun, but with knowledgeable ears on the drums which moaned and beat their breasts in the jungle from which our lamp-lit room protected us.[34]

This night marks the same sort of turning point for Brent as the Irish weekend did for Paul. Saxby urges him to follow his dream, aim for the peaks, risk all, read Conrad and trust his instincts – 'You and I speak the same language. . . . You are a romantic. You're probably capable of anything'[35] – above all to avoid being ensnared by tame dull domestic compromise in the name of financial security ('Turning tail and washing dishes is a mistake. Realistic maybe, but a mistake'). At times, the two of them might as well be discussing Paul's future prospects as an agent, growing increasingly prosperous with less and less time left for writing, rather than Brent's choice between being a businessman and a visionary or, as Saxby puts it, between the life of a respectable sahib and a coal-heaver.

This was the kind of vocabulary Paul habitually used in correspondence with Hanley, mocking what he called the Eng. lit. mandarins and picturing the pair of them by contrast as plain bloody navvies to the book trade. By the same token, there is more than an echo of Saxby, whether conscious or not, in a description Hanley sent Paul ten years later of what freelances like himself require from an agent: 'real female understanding of writers who come out of the night into Higham's with all their crap and problems (money!!) blazing smokily behind them.'[36] Brent comes to realise with time that Saxby is as much in need as himself of sympathetic understanding but, in the book's opening section, he is still too self-absorbed to be anything but overwhelmed by the older man's flattering attention ('He was senior in years and experience, possessor it seemed of a great fund of knowledge of the way of the world: the particular world, I told myself at that second, I surely aspired to').[37] He commits himself to the dream, which means India and the unknown ('Why India though? Why India?'), cancelling his passage home, abandoning his prudent plans for the future, setting off instead in Saxby's wake 'with all my luggage and very little money without knowing where I was going or how long it would take to get there.'

Paul began *The Chinese Love Pavilion* (which at one stage he called *Saxby*) with the New Year. 'I started a new book on January the first, and I think it is going to be IT,' he wrote on 3 February 1958, to his English publishers,[38] in a letter which also announced in strict confidence his intention of giving up his job as an agent to become a full-time writer. Hanley's example had forcibly driven home his feeling that he could no longer afford the price in time and energy of being an increasingly successful agent. 'Forgive me if I'm making you a shoulder to weep on!' he wrote: 'I don't think I've ever done it before, if only because I've never had time to take off from being a permanent wailing wall for other authors.' He drew an explicit parallel in this letter between himself and his hero, Tom Brent (called Tom Freshwater in the novel's first draft), whose story starts properly in 1945 – a decade after the decisive encounter with Saxby – when he is posted as an army observer to a Malaya full of men half demented after six years in uniform: 'Freshwater is typical of shagged-out Malaya. He (like me as an agent!) has come to believe he doesn't really exist spiritually, but is a sort of sympathetic receiving apparatus through which men who still believe they exist explore the mystery of their souls.'

Paul's decision to leave agency was taken in desperation on grounds of a necessity which overrode financial cost. 'I think I know in my bones that I'm going to make it as a writer, and I must have time to be one,' he wrote soberly. 'I can't at the moment afford to be one, as you will know ... But be one I must and be one I shall, full time, professional.' Paul addressed his letter to Eyre and Spottiswoode's new publicity manager, John Bright-Holmes, asking him to show it to Frank Morley's replacement on the editorial side, Maurice Temple Smith, and tentatively raising with both of them the possibility of a long-term guarantee. As an agent, he had already negotiated a deal of this kind with Morrow on behalf of Gabriel Fielding (*In the Time of Greenbloom* had been twentieth on the US bestseller list in 1957), and he would do his best in the summer to persuade John Murray to arrange something similar for Peter Green,[39] both of whom must have seemed better bets at that stage than Paul himself: an author rising forty with a single modest success to his credit followed by two semi-failures (sales of the *Warrior* on publication that March amounted, in Paul's gloomy view, to yet another 'financial disaster').[40]

Paul correctly anticipated that Eyre and Spottiswoode, financially pared to the bone and treated like poor relations after the takeover by ABP, would receive his suggestion without enthusiasm. He knew that, on any realistic view, he would have to postpone following his dream, but the humiliation still rankled three years later when he described with asperity to Hanley the material and imaginative poverty of English publishing houses: 'It always killed me when I saw ... a man bent with the need to *write* having to cap-in-hand it & getting a cold sniff and a hand-out like a soup kitchen.'[41] Maurice Temple Smith respected Paul both as an agent (it was Maurice who, as a very young editor, had seized the chance to publish *Room at the Top*), and as a novelist but, having been specifically recruited to run a tight ship, the best he could propose was a three-book contract on the same meagre terms as before. For Paul, with no alternative prospect of income save what he could drum up as a publisher's reader or book reviewer (he regarded literary journalism to the end of his life as a cross between prostitution and a circus act), it might as well have been a soup-kitchen handout, and his relationship with Maurice never entirely recovered from this initial impression of having been turned away with a cold sniff.[42]

It added a further crushing weight to the depression which for Paul had by this time become endemic. His complaint had been diagnosed as far back as 1952 as paratyphoid, and now, six years later, he underwent medical tests for diabetes, hoping against hope that whatever was wrong was 'just a general falling below par which will presently right itself'.[43] Lassitude, low fevers, dejection and paralysis of the will, all amoebic in origin, were becoming gradually harder to disregard. Specialists could neither propose a viable theory nor suggest a cure. In practice, Paul obtained respite through work. Long afterwards, when his condition had finally been diagnosed and treated, he liked to speculate in both general and particular instances about the effect on the British Raj of 'depressive and obsessive behaviour' caused by chronic amoebic infection in the bloodstream. A Muslim physician in the Raj Quartet develops Paul's own theory that the stubborn persistence which kept the empire itself intact owed much to the lethargy induced in the English by persistent tropical fever, 'the lethargy and its corollary, the concentration of mental and physical resources on a particular task'.[44] Paul's particular task at the beginning of 1958 was the first draft of *The Chinese Love Pavilion*, which he had completed by June.

His only other means of obtaining respite was drink, especially whisky, a palliative he had hit on with Jim in India at the same time as he contracted his disease. Paul approved of serious drinking: it was an immediately congenial trait in employers like Morley, McWhinnie and Morrow's John Willey ('a great gin man'),[45] and it launched him on fantastic spiralling flights of invention in sociable sessions with friends like Gerry Hanley, Peter Green and Roland Gant. 'Our wives had a lot to put up with in the course of these cabaret turns,' wrote Roland, 'which we ourselves found so hilarious at the time that tears of laughter fell into the drinks that were always to hand in large measure.'[46] Paul was never a public or disorderly drunk. He disliked pubs; some of his closest friends to the end of his life scarcely suspected that he drank at all, and very few caught more than a glimpse of the private, obsessive, quasi-medicinal spirit of his drinking alone in his room at home. He permitted himself only occasional lapses, times when he would come home at odd hours without saying or apparently even knowing where he had been, others when he passed out fully clothed on the floor. His behaviour could be unpredictable and his blackouts terrifying, but Paul never referred to these exploits next morning, and Penny learned to avoid any mention of her own alarm or bewilderment on pain of his severe displeasure.

The nearest Paul came to acknowledging how much he relied on her was in the person of Esther Craig, in *The Mark of the Warrior*, who selflessly supports and comforts her husband, supplying his needs, suppressing her own, unfailingly taking his part, calming his night-

mares, fetching him warm drinks in the small hours, or sitting by him
with the lamp turned low as if tending an invalid. Paul's somewhat
lopsided sketch of marital devotion is reflected from the other side in
Penny's own account of living with him in these years, worrying about
him, watching over him, waiting up for him, propping him on pillows
if he passed out, covering him with blankets, loosening his clothes,
leaving a lamp lit in case he woke, lying sleepless beside him sometimes
for hours to monitor his breathing. The silence between them on these
matters became unbreakable: each time it was as if, in the title of Paul's
early poem, 'It Never Happened'. But Paul understood quite well, at
any rate on paper, who had sat for Esther's portrait: 'In many ways
Esther is based on Penny – ', he wrote to Clive, 'and that is not to
suppose that Craig is based on myself – but the relationship between
them is, as you say, concerned with the less spectacular but continuing
aspects of marriage, and my understanding of these is gathered from
knowledge and appreciation of Penny. I'm not sure she's seen this yet,
probably not. I shan't tell her!'[47] If Paul never told his love in fact, he
paid her an equivocal compliment in fiction, for Esther's saintliness is
pallid and implausible by comparison with Craig's genuinely corrosive self-doubt or Ramsay's obsession. She has none of the vitality of
the worried and dissatisfied women in *Alien Sky*. Esther belongs to the
same reassuring world of conventional male fantasy as the docile,
compliant, musk-scented native girl laid on as a convenience, together
with food and a bed, to service Brent on safari in *The Chinese Love
Pavilion*.

Penny herself inevitably evolved her own strategems for survival.
Paul had finally resigned his old typewriter to her at the end of 1957,[48]
and in the evenings, when he came home from the office to shut himself
up night after night with the *Pavilion*, she began writing a novel of her
own downstairs on the kitchen table. *The Margaret Days* is decep-
tively simple, a fictional account of its author's experiences as a lonely
small girl farmed out to country people, written with a delicacy and
emotional directness at the opposite end of the stylistic scale from
Paul's intricate, oblique and increasingly ambitious constructions.
Penny did not consult him about it ('She's in the process, I believe, of
becoming an author herself,' Paul wrote to Chris Almedingen at the
end of the summer),[49] any more than he discussed his problems with
her. Both wrote steadily in spite of setbacks and illness. Penny's health,
never robust, had been showing signs of strain for some time. She had
been laid low in the spring of 1956 ('please give Penny my love, and I
hope she's better,' wrote Mary Patchett, adding unsympathetically,
' – sure it's not just that she's left you?'),[50] and again the following
summer with a suspected thyroid condition. After Paul's diabetic scare

Back jacket of Penny's first novel, published 1959. The Margaret Days is Elizabeth Avery's first novel and, like her heroine, she lived as a child with a foster-mother. 'But there,' she writes, 'the resemblance really ends. When I was ten I came down to relations in London determined to be a nurse. As soon as I was old enough I went as a probationer to a children's convalescent home, then to Queen's Hospital, London, and finally for general training to Derby Royal Infirmary.'

She later nursed at several hospitals, including Mount Vernon, and then took up private nursing and in this way satisfied her urge to travel and meet people in their own surroundings. At the end of one case in 1941 she stuck a pin in a map and as a result went to Devonshire. 'If the pin had slipped I should probably have married a naval officer. As it was I met and married a lance-corporal and we're about to celebrate our seventeenth wedding anniversary.'

Elizabeth Avery now lives with her husband (Paul Scott, the distinguished novelist and television playwright) and their two daughters, Carol and Sally, in Hampstead Garden Suburb,

in March 1958, she collapsed herself in May and was rushed to hospital ('struck down by what we thought was food poisoning!') for an emergency appendix operation, remaining in bed for at least a month.[51]

She was still convalescent at home in July when Paul's parents received out of the blue, after twenty years on Bourne Hill, a letter from their landlord giving a month's notice to quit. Paul and Penny prepared for upheaval at Addison Way, Paul evacuating his study, Carol giving up her bedroom, the whole family realigning itself to make way for the grandparents. But, if the prospect of sharing a house with her mother-in-law dismayed Penny, the move proved more than Tom Scott could bear. He was eighty-eight years old, and had been confidently ambling towards parity with his great-uncle, the celebrated nonagenarian Mark Scott of Selby, on the score of age if none other. He took to his bed at the news, and summoned his sons to sit by him. The flowers were falling from the lime trees as Tom Scott lay dying on Bourne Hill, and Paul said that for him lime blossom smelt ever afterwards of death and funerals:[52] perhaps he meant the funeral of the high hopes he had once had in that house as much as any actual burial. Tom Scott faded as inconspicuously as he had lived: 'he died in his bed, just finding it more and more difficult to breathe until in the end he gave up and in a couple of hours we had him down the stairs and out of the house and on his way to what they called a Chapel of Rest where he wouldn't be in the way or cause what the undertaker called unpleasantness. It was August.'[53]

Tom Scott died on Tuesday 5 August, the day after Bank Holiday Monday. Paul was away from the office all week, briefly cheered by Mollie Hamilton's letter proposing to forward the *Warrior* to John Masters, and pursued even at home by harassed and imploring authors who had failed to locate him in Dean Street (PPH had moved quarters the year before). One was Jimmy Leasor, who rang with condolences and apologies for intruding. Another was Kay Dick, an old friend and relatively new client, whose affairs were as she frankly admitted in more or less permanent need of urgent attention. A third was the best-selling novelist Mary McMinnies, married to a Foreign Office diplomat and stranded with her husband in Larnaca as the Cyprus crisis reached its violent climax that bank holiday weekend: '3 destroyers have dropped in. Aircraft zoom in . . . Jack & I are the last – literally the last . . . on this little frontier,' wrote Mrs McMinnies, armed with a gun in the drawer and poised for flight to Beirut, pausing only to post off a peremptory request for immediate funds. 'UNPARALLELLED CRISIS PULLING OUT SOONEST DEPENDING YOU PLEASE TELEGRAPH,' she cabled the day Tom Scott died.[54]

The funeral took place on Saturday. Paul said long afterwards that, as he and Peter sat at either side of the bed, each holding one of their father's hands, he had known with the writer's usual treacherous double vision that he would store what was happening for use in a book later.[55] His next novel, begun as soon as he had finished *The Chinese Love Pavilion*, would deal with a son's attempt to understand and forgive a cold, withdrawn father. More concrete memories surfaced later perhaps in Ada Lisle's deathbed in *The Bender*, and Barbie Batchelor's in *The Towers of Silence*. But at the time, or very soon after, he broke off his renewed struggles with the *Pavilion* in the autumn of 1958 to jot down a stray fragment on a separate sheet of his manuscript:

I begin with my father's death, because in everything else he was a failure. Failure is like a frame round the picture of our ambitions. The picture comes first, the frame last. So I begin with his dying which was successful. If he had no other talent, he had a talent for dying.[56]

Tom Scott's death brought Paul up sharp against his own past and his future. He was already uneasy about the new novel which had poured out of him in the spring so fast and furiously that he seemed almost to have lost control. He had shown the unfinished manuscript in June to Peter Green, who read it twice with mounting perplexity, astonishment and admiration. 'You're *writing* better than ever,' he wrote, saluting Paul's uprush of energy ('towards the end superb punch, speed and pungency'), but pointing out that the manuscript contained material sufficient for at least three separate novels: 'At the moment it's rather like eating curry, avocado pears, grilled trout and charlotte russe on the same plate – delicious individually, but they just don't mix.'[57] Paul's response was to make a fresh start, dated 26 July 1958, ten days after Peter's letter. 'I shivered when I read that you had torn up the first 40,000 words of the new book,' John Willey wrote from New York in August.[58] Paul returned to the script in September, writing as if his life depended on it, which in a sense it did. His father's death left him more than ever determined that there had been enough failure down three generations in the family, and that *The Chinese Love Pavilion* was the book that would make or break him.

It preoccupied him to the exclusion of everything else that autumn, when Frances Scott moved into Addison Way as a widow. She had spent her last days after the funeral at Bourne Hill in wholesale clearance, burning letters and documents, consigning the contents of the studio to a bonfire in the back garden, watching her old life go up in smoke in preparation for the new. She took over Carol's bedroom with the downstairs dining-room set aside for her private daytime use. Carol moved into her father's study, and Paul worked in his bedroom, or at a tilted folding table he had designed himself to attach to a bookshelf in the family drawing-room. The children, tiptoeing up and down more quietly than ever so as not to disturb him, found themselves commandeered by their grandmother. She had always demanded allegiance, rewarding Carol with an irresistible, wildly unsuitable, full-skirted, narrow-waisted New Look frock in plum-coloured taffeta, and appropriating Sally's stories as she had once done Paul's. Where she had been assertive, she now became over-whelming. 'She latched on to us children,' said Sally: 'It was a kind of taking over. There was no sense of her playing with us. There was a thwarting going on, a spoiling. It was a snatching of us from my mother.'

The family shifted and shook under Frances' impact. Even her favourite Carol was obscurely aware at the time of her grandmother changing from a figure of indomitable glamour, dash and vitality to something altogether more menacing, 'a driving knife or a wedge in our household'. When all five of them went on a seaside holiday to Dunoon in Scotland at the end of August, Carol twice walked in her sleep, a thing she had never done before – 'Something was up in the family' – shifting a wardrobe so heavy that even with Sally's help she could not heave it back into place next morning. Paul told Muriel Spark, who was visiting relations in Edinburgh and had proposed a joint outing, that things had not gone well in Dunoon. They went from bad to worse after the start of the school term, which left the two women for the first time alone together all day. The house rang in the mornings with thumping and banging as Frances turned out her room, relieving her feelings with such energy that she chipped the paint all round the skirting board, dented the vacuum cleaner and seriously damaged her bedstead. After she had dealt with the furniture, she would emerge dressed for parade to inspect her daughter-in-law, register complaints and draw up the day's charge sheet. Nothing ever gave satisfaction. Penny dreaded even her dismissals when Frances, 'her face screwed up with hate and fury',[59] would indicate the spot on her cheek where she required a kiss planted before either of them could set out for the shops.

'It was open war on Frances's part,' said Sally, 'and that my mother had to endure. She didn't complain to my father. The daily threats were never reported to him.' The root cause of the conflict was only too familiar to Paul, whose savage account of a similar relationship in *A Male Child* seems scarcely exaggerated in the light of what happened in fact two years later. He had clearly envisaged, if not evoked, the frustrated possessiveness of 'the woman . . . torn between love of the child of her womb and hate for the man he has become, the man who has escaped. A male child is born in love and hate – each being more ferociously expressed because they clash.'[60] Frances's fury seemed positively inflamed by Penny's passive resistance: the absolute refusal, or inability, of the one to answer back drove the other to ever more outrageous provocation. Acrimonious days were followed by broken nights and bad dreams. Interviews between Paul and his mother, when she handed over her £1 contribution to the housekeeping, became weekly ordeals. The household seemed locked into a nightmare re-enactment of the divisions at Wyphurst which had so painfully affected Paul as a boy. It was now Paul's children's turn to listen to his mother's voice and his own raised in the kind of altercation he described in *A Male Child*, 'angry, impassioned exchanges when we stripped the feelings from each other in he way dead stalks can be stripped of seeds.'[61]

The build-up of pressure became unendurable. Acceptance of Penny's novel that autumn was more than Frances could bear. Paul, coming home from the office one evening to find Penny silently weeping, delivered an ultimatum. There was a final, fearful scene between mother and son after which Mrs Scott left, pounding down the stairs, wrenching at the front door and slamming out into the night with a violence that shook the whole house. Sally, looking down from an upper window, watched her grandmother rush out in her black coat onto the street, brandishing a bag and glaring back at the house, taking her dismissal in a spirit that made it more like an act of aggression: 'She wasn't so much thrown out. She *swept* out.' It was in this sort of mood that, as a young married woman, Frances Scott used to descend, uninvited and unannounced 'with never a penny piece', on her sister Ruth in south London. This time she was seventy-two years old: she had lost home and husband, she had no means of her own, and she faced a second uprooting when she had barely begun to absorb the shock of the first. Feelings pent up for the better part of a lifetime had swirled out of control. To the family at Addison Way the battle seemed in retrospect to have raged for months on end, although in fact it can hardly have lasted more than eight weeks at the outside, for the Scottish holiday occupied the first two weeks of September, and Frances left the house in November. She took refuge with Arthur Pridmore, the father of her other son Peter's wife Eileen. He was a retired elderly widower, living alone just below Parliament Hill on the southernmost outskirts of Hampstead, where on 6 December, four months almost to the day after the death of her first husband, Frances Scott became the second Mrs Pridmore.

Paul did not see or speak to his mother again for years, nor would he write letters or answer hers. Frances's departure meant relief from pressure, an emotional respite and a return to working routine for the whole family. Paul made an immediate third start on the *Pavilion*, dated 11 a.m. on Sunday 7 December. He had already arranged with David Higham to take on an assistant, so that he might try a different regime in the New Year with two days off each week for writing. Penny was by this time at work on her second novel: the first, already in the preliminary stages of publication, showed every sign of being a modest but marked success. *The Margaret Days* is a charming evocation of the rural pattern still unbroken in her early childhood at the end of the First World War, with the miller grinding corn in his mill, people travelling by horse and trap, pies and cakes being baked on the kitchen range with a snowy white cloth laid on the solid wooden table, and sunshine outside the door. But the changes so soon to disrupt the external world are mirrored in the uncertainty of the central character, a small girl without parents or family of her own, passed from hand to hand like the parcel in a children's game which the players either don't want or can't keep. The setting is tranquillity itself – the book is suffused, as one of its reviewers said, 'by a calm country felicity'[62] – except that every so often the child, or the reader in the child's place, trips and stumbles over treacherous concealed gulfs of feeling. Physical security and emotional insecurity are woven together into the fabric of a text shot through with glints of unexpectedly quizzical wit.

The effect is both assured and disconcerting, and it came as something of a shock to Paul. Penny dedicated the book 'To H. B. with love' (Honey Boy and Honey Girl were the names they had given one another in the time of great happiness and mutual discovery at the start of their marriage). Years later, Paul marked the passage in Gordon Haight's life of George Eliot, where George Henry Lewes describes his initial scepticism over his own wife's first story: 'I confess that before reading the ms I had considerable doubts of my friend's power as a writer of fiction; but after reading it those doubts were changed into very high admiration.' Paul wrote 'H. G.' in the margin of his copy of Haight's book,[63] marked the page reference, and left it out for Penny to read. He had been initially taken aback by her accomplishment as a novelist ('Although I suppose it's disloyal of me to admit surprise!'),[64] and several of his friends remained dubious. Peter Green recognised Penny's gifts at once, and stoutly defended them against disparaging comments from Higham's reader, the formidable Doreen Marston (she was an old crony of Paul's: six years earlier he had given her the manuscript of his own second novel to report on without disclosing the author's identity, and perhaps it made her harsher with Penny's first than she otherwise might have been).[65] Roland Gant, by this time editorial director of Michael Joseph Ltd., was sufficiently impressed to offer publication the following spring. Paul handled Penny's professional début much as Lewes had acted for the exceedingly diffident George Eliot: correspondence with publishers was addressed to Paul as agent, not to his wife, who wrote under her maiden name of Elizabeth Avery (she had been christened Nancy Edith Avery: Penny was a nickname), and shrank from claiming a place in the literary world in her own right. She and Paul had always agreed that her role in their marriage should be supportive, and the success of this first novel – it was published on 4 May 1959 to warmly encouraging reviews – took them both by surprise.

Paul later underlined a phrase in Haight's biography from the letter the publisher had written accepting George Eliot's story without knowing who wrote it: 'If the author is a new writer I beg to

congratulate him on being *worthy of the honours* of print and pay.'
Time was running out meanwhile for Paul, who had produced nothing
as yet to justify, in terms of print or pay, his intention of becoming a
full-time writer. Part of the problem was to define precisely what sort
of book he was trying to write, and he had been wrestling with it for
almost a year when he made his third and last start in December. He
had originally envisaged a book set in Malaya at the end of the war and
divided along the usual lines between two central male characters:
Tom Brent (initially Freshwater), the shagged-out army observer, and
a newly commissioned, nineteen-year-old subaltern called Sutton,
who is so desperately anxious to prove himself a man that he ends up
mad, 'running amok in truly Malayan fashion'.[66] But Gerry Hanley
had been right in thinking that Paul had broken through some sort of
barrier in his last novel and, with the new one, the familiar scenario all
but disappeared in what Peter Green recognised as 'a tremendous
burst of creative ideas and plots and themes all struggling to get out at
once.'[67]

Peter disentangled three or four different strands in the first draft, all
working on different levels and belonging to different fictional genres.
There was 'a psychological military near-Ambler mystery' concerning
Saxby's disappearance in the jungle, combined with a more specifically political narrative about nationalist guerrilla activities, collaboration with and reprisals against the Japanese, the equivocal position of
the British occupying forces (elements from all these would eventually
be subsumed into the background). Next came 'a quite separate novel
about Sutton, Millie and the torments of growing into emotional
maturity', which was subsequently cut out altogether: Sutton's
relationship with the repressed homosexual Major Reid, and a few
surviving references to his earlier homosexual experiences at school,
suggest a strongly autobiographical slant. Paul finally settled for what
Peter called the 'theme of sex + personal exploration', centring on the
love pavilion itself. This is a gaudy little scarlet-and-gold pleasure
house, commandeered as an execution ground by the Japanese in the
war, requisitioned after it by the British Major Reid as a small private
brothel for the exclusive use of his young officers, including Brent,
who is temporarily attached to Reid's unit while conducting a semi-
official search for the missing Saxby (himself involved with Chinese
guerrillas as well as pursuing quasi-mystical errands of his own in the
jungle). *The Chinese Love Pavilion* would mark in the end Paul's
turning point as a novelist. It staked out a whole new political as well
as geographical territory. It confirmed his preoccupation with India
and the Far East. It attempted a long focus, ranging through time as
well as space, and experimenting for the first time with the complex,

many-layered plotting he would use in the Raj Quartet. It also began, more tentatively, to explore the powerful effect of physical images – the pavilion itself with its garden, Brent's murderous Malayan kris, Saxby's tropical plant house – which open up a whole new imaginative level in this novel.

But before he could tackle the final draft (which at this stage he called *Saxby*), before he could opt definitely for one sort of book over another, Paul had to be clearer about what sort of person he was. He said long afterwards, when asked how he created his characters, that all he had to do was imagine how he would have felt in their place. But, in order to look in his own heart and write, he had in some sense to understand and accept what he saw. Behind Paul's elaborate smoke-screens, his technical muddles ('I know I bit off more than I could chew, but . . . I don't get really *interested* until I've wound everything up into a *mess*!' he had written ruefully of *A Male Child*),[68] and his perennial problem with structure, lay a more fundamental evasion which he himself increasingly recognised as sexual. Several of his more perceptive friends suspected as much at the time, none more clearly than Peter Green, who urged Paul to strengthen his narrative by singling out a central theme:

I say this because it appears – correct me if I'm wrong – that the purpose of the whole novel at a deeper symbolic level (or so it strikes me both from the title, certain incidents in the book, and the ubiquitous and cleverly concealed sexual imagery and symbolism) is to explore the truth of man's sexual integration in all its aspects, simple and complicated alike. Especially the love–death equation: nothing could carry clearer implications than the pavilion being also the scene of execution – or, indeed, the Tereus-like fuck of the tongueless Hindi woman.[69]

This last episode (modified or missing in subsequent drafts) described 'in absolutely obsessive detail' Freshwater making love to a girl with no tongue. 'I keep coming back to it,' said Peter. 'It was a fantasy – a paradigm – a *reductio ad absurdum* – of what Paul thought a woman should be.'[70] In the final published text, Saxby thoughtfully provides an Indian girl ('She is an untouchable, and I am told, virgin')[71] along with bathwater and towels for the use of his guest, Freshwater/Brent: she remains silent throughout, although not technically dumb. But dumbness is no more than a logical extension of the kind of compliance expected from women like Esther Craig in the *Warrior*, where Paul first formulated his love-and-death equation. Ramsay in that book goes into the forest to kill (Muriel Spark had been fascinated by the way in which Ramsay seems to 'squeeze all the woman out of himself'),[72] while Craig makes it clear that what he himself fears in the jungle is impotence. Tormented by dreams of Ramsay, Craig wakes at night to lie sleepless beside his sleepless wife: 'He wanted . . . to hide himself against her and make his confession. His body was rigid with the effort it took both to do it and not to do it. How would he say it? How would he not say it? In the end, as always, he could only say it silently into his own darkness. I was no good, Esther. After years of playing at soldiers, when it came to it, in the jungle I was no bloody good.'[73]

The equation is worked out even more explicitly in *The Chinese Love Pavilion* with young Sutton, whose terror of impotence leads ultimately to madness and murder. The relationship between Sutton and his CO, Major Reid, spells out the premise underlying Ramsay's with Craig, or Taylor's with the Major in *Johnnie Sahib* ('In Reid's love for his officers there was undoubtedly the sexual element,' Paul wrote in preliminary notes, 'a homosexuality which never expressed itself physically but, unappeased physically, found its sphere in the mystique of hardship and bodily endurance').[74] Sutton, sufficiently experienced to recognise the Major's sexual sadism, is in some drafts reluctant, in others cynical and compliant. The character of Reid, altogether more complex, develops into an unflinching but not unsympathetic exploration of a brave, stubborn, profoundly repressed and puritanical temperament. The nature of the 'mark' Reid detects on himself – 'I had it on me as a punishment . . . it's there, like a mark on me'[75] – is made perfectly clear:

One day, I thought, he might wake up and know why and by whom he was being punished . . . the truth was he was punishing himself for sins only his subconscious mind had knowledge of. They were sins he had been brought to by other men who lived and died in the monosexual world of military splendour, where seduction was a matter of pace-sticks, coupling a business of bullets, and lying with women merely a reward for passing more important tests than those of natural love.[76]

Sutton, like Ramsay, passes the jungle test of bloodshed (Sutton is physically sick after the shooting of four suspected guerrillas, Brent morally sickened), and receives as his prize permission to take his turn, alongside Reid's other officers, with Teena Chang and her girls in the pavilion. But what should have been a reward turns into a hideous punishment: after his night with Teena, young Sutton is discovered next morning holed up with her dead body. Different characters offer different versions of what happened. Sutton claims that Teena killed herself with Brent's kris (in a cancelled draft, he says she attacked him first, whereupon Brent attacks Sutton). Brent in some moods believes Sutton, in others he holds Saxby ultimately responsible for Teena's death. On the whole he inclines to the view that Sutton killed her: 'However much he desired her . . . I think he found it finally impossible to prove himself what he would call a man. . . . He would have found the kris early on, in the pocket of the gown. I can see how it lay near them, unexplained, its handle and blade gleaming in the light of the oil lamp as he sat or lay with his heart thumping, unmanned and ashamed, and finding no outlet for his shame except in anger. There would have been a moment when Teena seemed to embody everything he found dirty and rotten.'[77]

Brent's tone of voice – calm, measured, enquiring, dispassionate, a voice never heard so clearly before in earlier novels – was perhaps Paul's greatest discovery in the *Pavilion*. It is as though he had somehow broken through to a side of himself which enabled him to contemplate, objectively and without distortion, his most primitive, punitive fantasies. On 31 May 1959, Paul brought his third draft to a violent conclusion with Teena dead and Sutton off his head, bleeding where she had sliced off his nipples with the kris, armed with a Sten gun, offering to shoot all comers, finally crawling away from the pavilion on hands and knees, howling for mercy, after being beaten up by Brent. It took Paul six weeks to type out and revise his 130,000-word manuscript, by which time he was filled with revulsion and self-doubt. He rang Maurice Temple Smith in despair, threatening ('silly hysterical me')[78] to scrap everything he had written so far: Maurice calmed him down, and David Higham restored his confidence after reading the whole script through at a sitting on 16 July.

Everyone who read *The Chinese Love Pavilion* that summer was struck by its unmistakable, uneven power. It would always remain something of a hybrid, retaining, even after extensive editorial attention and copious rewriting, traces of the conventional adventure story, the political thriller, the oriental romance. Teena and her girls remain standard male fantasy figures (Edith Sitwell protested on this score, and so did Storm Jameson, both supplying otherwise enthusiastic pre-publication publicity puffs).[79] There is a decided whiff of pretension about Saxby's quest for his soul ('Question I would ask,' wrote Morrow's gently ironic editor Adèle Dogan: '*How* do you look for a soul? In what kind of activity? Meditation? Murder? Prayer?').[80] But Saxby's mystical side represents the last gasp of an obscurantism going back at least to *I, Gerontius* which expired altogether in Paul's writing with Saxby's death. *The Chinese Love Pavilion* is full of dreamers, visionaries, sleepwalkers like Reid whose nightmares are balanced, and held in check, by the narrator's calm level scrutiny. Much of its imperfectly controlled, explosive force comes from images like the kris, destructive, desirable and (as Peter Green pointed out) a potent sexual symbol:

*Bob Mason's oil sketch
of 2nd Lt Scott posed,
like Dorian Gray,
against a crimson
background of hope in
Kashmir in March,
1944: the portrait with
its throat slit hung
afterwards in Paul's
study in London.*

The kris is the traditional Malayan dagger. Its blade is curved like a flattened
corkscrew. The kris in the drawer of my desk is perhaps an inch too short in
the blade but it is by no means a toy . . . Over the years the blade has grown
dull, sheathed itself in a kind of skin so that it no longer flashes in so lively, so
threatening a manner. But the memories it invokes grow sharper. Perversely
the kris has become a weapon of creation rather than of destruction.[81]

This is Brent speaking, but the kris in question was Paul's. He kept it
in his study together with the portrait by Bob Mason of himself as a
newly commissioned subaltern, a few years older than Sutton, about
to join his unit in the jungle which he, too, would reach just too late to
see action. Paul's portrait showed a side of himself he had done his best
to suppress. At one point, goaded beyond endurance (like Dorian
Gray) by the self he confronted in the picture, he slashed its throat,
hurling the painted face at his reflection in the mirror, and crawling
round the room on all fours (like Sutton) in a frenzy of self-disgust.[82]

He had been appalled to discover the damage next morning, having as usual no recollection of what had happened the night before. It was as though his daylight self, the humorous, unflappable, infinitely under-standing self beloved by his friends, could survive only by blocking off all knowledge of the frantic self-hatred released by drink or despair.

But in *The Chinese Love Pavilion* Paul tapped new and deeper levels of experience, which brought an immediately recognisable increase in authority as a writer. He was not particularly interested at this stage in factual or topographical accuracy: he firmly rejected the corrections proposed by his new assistant, David Bolt, who had served both with the army in Malaya and with the Malayan police.[83] What he was after was an atmosphere, a sense of people projecting individual obsessions in alien, occupied territory, 'a situation' as ambivalent and sharp-edged as the kris itself. Politically, sexually and psychologically, the book penetrates areas he had barely touched before. It was as if, in separating out the different threads of his novel, Paul had disentangled strands of his personality which he both liberated and brought under control. Endowing Brent with his own subtle and acute perceptions gave him access, through characters like Reid, to dangerous terrain: 'I was fairly sure that Reid wasn't aware of the nature of his own sexual impulses. In one way it was a relief. Actual awareness on Reid's part would have linked those deep-seated impulses with a permission,' Brent reflects in one of the cancelled passages which often sound as if Paul were impersonally discussing himself. 'But in another way his probable unconsciousness made me uneasy. A man going in ignorance of his obsessions could be as dangerous as a blind man directing traffic at a busy cross-roads.'[84]

Paul himself stood once again at a cross-roads in the summer of 1959. His manuscript reached New York in mid-July, together with a confidential letter to John Willey asking if Morrow could provide the sort of financial guarantee which would enable him to give up his job. The response was cautiously encouraging. By the end of August no less than seven people at Morrow's had read the *Pavilion*, John Willey ('I know it is an extraordinary book, and maybe a great one')[85] was exploring financial possibilities, and Adèle Dogan preparing an exhaustive schedule of textual notes, suggestions and queries. 'Paul had a marvellous mind,' said Peter Green, 'but it was an untrained mind. By the end, he'd trained it himself.' The later stages of this process are preserved in painstaking detail in correspondence with Paul's respective English and American editors over the next six months. Both urged him to simplify his effects and clarify his intentions: 'one needs a clear picture of confusion, not a confused picture,' Maurice Temple Smith said shrewdly.[86] 'Once we have brought to the surface that measure of excitement and drama which frequently now lies too quietly below the surface,' Adèle Dogan wrote, 'we'll have done all that is necessary.'[87] Major revision was completed in the New Year, followed by a last dizzy burst in which Paul restructured the ending, criss-crossing between three or more alternative versions, conflating Adèle's suggestions with Maurice's, justifying each to either, juggling, reworking, cross-cutting, until he felt close to collapse ('If I had to sit down and rewrite the scene I think I would end in a lunatic asylum').[88] On 12 January 1960 Eyre and Spottiswoode in London were reported 'absolutely wild' with excitement. 'Our immediate reaction is close to ecstatic,' Adèle wrote from New York on 20 January. David Higham concurred, and his American partner, Ivan von Auw of Harold Ober Associates, was already making contingency plans in case of major sales.[89] A publicity campaign was in hand, with publication set for the autumn.

But the price paid had been heavy. Paul said the *Pavilion* was 'written against a tide of fatigue which ebbed and flowed over three years'.[90] The family had celebrated completion and delivery of the manuscript with a Spanish holiday in September 1959 – 'Sun, sea, sand and champagne at 6s a bottle'[91] – at Tamariu on the Costa Brava. Paul said the place reminded him pleasantly of northern India, even of parts of Bihar:[92] the people were friendly, the village unspoilt, the weather perfect, Paul and the girls (now aged twelve and eleven) spent hours splashing about on pedal-boats in the bay. But the holiday had not turned out to be the liberation they had all hoped for, because Paul's book came too. He brought a carbon copy of his manuscript in a heavy suitcase, arranged for Adèle to post her report direct to the hotel at Tamariu and, although he never actually got down to corrections, he could not easily shake off the sombre and punitive atmosphere which had enveloped him for so long. The prospect of rewriting hung over him. He drank and brooded about it. This time it was Sally who noticed something up with the holiday: 'It was overshadowed by the sense of my father drinking too much – he would be sitting staring at the sands, not being with us – and by the sudden realisation that my mother was visibly suffering, visibly *not* having a good time.'

Penny herself gave some inkling of her predicament in these years to Peter Green, whose unyielding affection and admiration for Paul did not blind him to the growing strains in their marriage. 'I've tried to please him so hard for so long,' she said of Paul, 'and it's no good. I can't.'[93] As Paul wrestled with and closed in on his book, silent, wrapt, unreachable, sometimes scarcely speaking for days or even weeks at a time, Penny sank under an irrational sense of having failed him. From his point of view, the opposite was true. She had sustained and supported him through what had proved the most gruelling ordeal of his writing life. His love for her was like Craig's for his wife in *Warrior* – 'He had no need to touch her, no need of her touch'[94] – unswerving, unshakeable, essentially undemonstrative. At the end of his life, Paul acknowledged that the turmoil at home in his adolescence had prevented him ever expressing feeling face to face, or increasingly anywhere other than on paper. He could be very funny about his physical squeamishness: 'Don't bring any of these things to show me in the office,' he once warned Arthur C. Clarke, deep in shark, squids and octopi for a book on deep-sea diving, 'at least I don't mind just seeing pictures, or even a pickled one. But nothing in the flesh as it were.'[95] He had proposed to Penny on a dance floor, put the ring on her finger in a crowded railway carriage, and now he expressed his love, where he did most things that mattered, in his books. His two latest novels both began with a dedication, and ended with a muffled declaration, to Penny. Craig, on the last page of *Warrior*, is shaken by love for his wife – 'a kind of passion grew in him, an understanding of their mutual trust, of guilt he need not bear alone because she would ask to share it' – who presses his hand to her cheek 'as if to give him courage, take courage from him'. The last sentence of the *Pavilion* reaffirms the narrator's overriding faith 'in the love of one human being for another'.

This was as far as Paul was able to go, and it was not, of course, far enough. Penny had been unreservedly enthusiastic at the prospect of Paul's throwing up the daily grind at Higham's to make his fortune. For years she had watched him putting up barriers, feeling herself shouldered aside by each new book. In September 1959, when the longest and most demanding of them all was finally finished, Paul's drunkenness on holiday seemed to close the last chink through which he might have reached out to her. But he had staked everything, as boldly if not in quite the same romantic terms as Brent in his novel, and he was waiting that summer for the result of his last throw. The Scotts reached Tamariu on 5 September, and on the sixteenth John Willey cabled Morrow's offer of a guarantee for the next three years,[96] which Paul immediately accepted. His mood was reckless but not carefree. He had finally turned his back on financial or material security, but he would follow his dream in a spirit closer to young Ramsay's sacrificial sternness than young Brent's cheerful acquiescence. He was returning to London stripped for action, wound tighter and tenser than ever, ready to pare down his life so that nothing should stand any longer between him and his work. From his family's point of view, it was beginning to look less like a new freedom than a harsher form of the old enslavement. When they packed up to go home on 19 September,

Penny and the girls wept for the loveliness they were leaving behind, for the holiday that had not been an unqualified success, perhaps also for a phase of their life that had closed for good.

Paul's first move back at the office was to break the news of his resignation to David Higham, who had long expected something of the sort. 'I shouldn't like to go down to posterity as the man who stood in the great Scott's way,' he wrote in a cheerful, stoical valedictory letter to Paul.[97] There had been major upheavals at PPH the year before, culminating after much plotting and counter-plotting in final schism between David and Laurence Pollinger, who left to set up on his own, taking his son Gerald with him. A crucial factor in the Pollingers' departure had been Paul's decision to throw his weight behind David, and Paul's loss, at a moment when the disintegrating firm desperately needed holding together, looked like a catastrophe to his younger colleagues. It put their own futures at risk but, if they thought Paul was mad, they did not say so. What Morrow offered was £1800 a year for three years: Paul would produce a novel a year in return, putting all his earnings – freelance fees as a reader or reviewer, television and radio payments, all rights, royalties and advances – into a pool or kitty, to be administered by Higham's, who would advance him a fixed quarterly payment of £450, with Morrow making up any shortfall.

It was, as Paul said, no more than a secretary might hope to earn in America, although far more than any English publishing house would have offered without strings attached ('to them it seems big money,' he warned Gerry Hanley, 'and there is a bit of clanking, ball & chain').[98] Paul had turned down a job as senior editor at Collins which would have brought in roughly the same amount.[99] He reckoned he and Penny would be starting their new life with a joint capital of £300, and a mortgage ten times as big. He had earned £1000 from writing the year before, which was more than double his average annual figure (1958 was a freak year, on account of television and Pan paperback sales for the *Warrior*). Eyre & Spottiswoode's advance for the *Pavilion* was £400, increased on delivery to £650. Paul told Clive Sansom long afterwards that he had no regrets about leaving Higham's:

Although when I look back on what I actually retired on I think I must have been crazy. But sometimes I think writing demands a certain madness from those engaged on it, and sometimes withholds the best of its rewards until the right kind of gesture at it has been made. Of course one never counts on more than a year ahead (at least I don't). But something of Micawber is essential. I wonder whether that is really what was in Dickens's subconscious when he invented that gent?[100]

By the beginning of October 1959, Paul was writing to clients to announce his imminent departure. They were variously indignant, envious, appalled, filled with chagrin on their own behalf, and rueful satisfaction on his. Some were phlegmatic, others hysterical, one or two inclined to burst into tears at the prospect of a future without Paul to turn to in Dean Street. He had supplied every need from speedy and efficient financial first aid to the kind of slow, steady, knowledgeable tending publishers seldom go in for if they can settle instead for bumper cash crops. Paul was never too busy to read and discuss a manuscript: he sheltered nervous talents, supported frail ones, pruned back bogus growth, detected and cherished genuine achievement in the wildest and most undisciplined bolters. 'He literally identified with you as another writer,' said Kay Dick. 'Paul was an ego trip for an author. He would almost take over: become you.'[101] He had patiently shaped the careers of authors as different as John Braine ('you were the only one who recommended me to write a novel, and you were the one to place my first novel. I shall miss you very much'),[102] Morris West and M. M. Kaye (Paul had been the first person to read her *Shadow of the Moon* and the first to assure her, after sitting up with the manuscript into the small hours, that she had written a bestseller). He took as much trouble over unknown, unprofitable, often unpublished writers as over his most lucrative clients, and – almost unheard of in his profession – he urged them to ring him at home ('I don't stop being an agent & become an author as soon as I open my front door').[103] Chris Almedingen spoke for a great many authors when she wrote to reiterate, in characteristically generous terms, that they were losing a prince among agents.

Paul received wry congratulations from authors for whom he had successfully negotiated the kind of arrangement he now had himself. 'I still feel a little as if I've stepped off a high ledge into thin air,' the thriller writer Francis Clifford had written, escaping from a secure office job with Paul's help a year earlier.[104] On 1 October 1959, Paul officially gave notice to David Higham that he meant to step off his own ledge in six months' time. He celebrated the New Year by acquiring a little statue of Ganesh, the Indian elephant god, son of Shiva and Parvati, soul of wisdom and learning, giver of gifts and granter of boons. He told John Willey in New York on 16 January that he meant to 'burn joss sticks in order that we might have a bestseller on our hands', and sat back to see what Ganesh would do.

CHAPTER TEN

A long straight look in the mirror

Paul set up as a full-time writer, a week to the day after his fortieth birthday, on 1 April 1960 ('not – I hope – an appropriate day,' he wrote genially to Morris West).[1] Penny was delighted to have him at home for what both intended should be a fresh start, and charmed by Paul's plan of stopping work at midday so that they might break for a companionable drink together at the local pub before coming home to lunch at one o'clock. The only problem was reproachful or dissatisfied former clients who wrote and rang up in droves, asking Paul to clarify contracts, read manuscripts, intervene with publishers, overrule agency decisions, advise on financial strategy. Some threatened to leave Higham's, many more protested bitterly about supposed slights, slackness and inefficiency at the office in Dean Street. Paul responded diplomatically, smoothing out problems, explaining publishing schedules, suggesting tactics, putting in a word with one editor, dropping a note to another, urging patience and caution with a third. 'Why didn't someone tell me that *time* rushes by at the speed of an express train when you don't go to an office every day?' he wrote to Kay Dick in June.[2] 'I have never been so busy in my life,' he told Charles Wrey Gardiner two months later: 'The description "left agency to concentrate on his writing" now brings a wry smile to my lips.'[3]

Gardiner, who never entirely recovered from the catastrophe at Crown Passage, had just published his first book in ten years, called *The Answer to Life is No* (one of Paul's last jobs as an agent had been to sell the manuscript to Rupert Hart-Davis for an advance of £25). Drinking hard, quarrelling violently with the mother of his six small children, newly sacked from his job in a bookshop, with nothing

coming in but the rents from a shabby lodging house in Ladbroke
Grove which always ran out before the end of the week, Gardiner at
sixty was not an encouraging example for a newly fledged freelance.
'In circumstances like mine people are always curious to know what
you are going to do, what your solution is,' he explained helpfully:
'Their guess is as good as mine. I have no idea. I just want to be left
alone to write.'[4] So, increasingly, did Paul, who prudently proposed
that they meet for a beer at the Dog and Duck 'and then count our
pocket money before deciding what happens next'.[5] The days which
had seemed so invitingly empty were filling up at dizzy speed. Outings
to the pub with Penny first fell silent, then had to be stopped
altogether, and so did the unending procession of clients. The Scott
children learned young to field telephone calls: Poppa might be
thinking, working or out, but he must on no account be disturbed.

He could still find time in these early years for a spot of Dog-and-
Ducking, lunch with a colleague to keep up his courage at the Epicure,
long confidential sessions with one or two friends at somebody's house
in the evenings. 'Paul was a father confessor in people's lives,' said Kay
Dick, who welcomed him enthusiastically back that summer onto the
relaxed and rackety, colourful, convivial, thoroughly undomesticated
side of the book world which he had first glimpsed at Crown Passage.
Paul had known Kay as a tall, graceful, leggy young poet in a man's
shirt immediately after the war, a picturesque figure who embodied
what Gardiner called the thin, angular dream of Picasso's blue period
in London.[6] The intervening decade of living on her wits as a writer
had developed fortitude, stamina and a thick skin, without dulling
Kay's natural elegance or the eager habit Gardiner described of
bending forward 'as if she would dominate you with her blue eyes like
the small flowers you find on the very cold heights of mountains, but
which soften and deepen in certain eerie lights. Her beloved period is
the nineties, and she lives on her nerves and her books.'[7] Kay shared an
erratic and eventful existence with her friend, the novelist Kathleen
Farrell (Paul as agent had represented them both), in a shifting colony
of other authors, artists and intellectuals at 55 Flask Walk in
Hampstead. The pair invited Paul and Penny to their parties, and Paul
took to dropping round by himself to discuss their books and his own.
Kay's elegantly produced meditation on the *commedia dell'arte*, called
Pierrot, was due to come out with *Pavilion* at the end of 1960, and for
a while she sent him almost daily notes, bulletins and proposals in their
joint run-up to publication.

He would sit up talking and drinking, often well into the small
hours, long after the underground trains had stopped running, and
walk home alone the two or three miles over the heath in the pale

London nights, revolving ideas for his new novel, trying out six separate starts in all for what eventually became *The Birds of Paradise*.[8] It was Kay who found the description of the birds in Gardiner's *The Flowering Moment*, which Paul would reproduce on his title page: 'reading it gave me a tremendous knock,' he told Gardiner, '& illuminated all kinds of dark corners in the mind'.[9] By the middle of June, he had written 30,000 words of which only thirty pages seemed worth keeping. On 13 June, he sent Kay a note – 'Thank you for so kindly sheltering the Great White Bird of Paradise'[10] – with a sketch map showing his route home from Flask Walk the night before, looping over the heath, skirting the pond, winding northwards to 78 Addison Way. Characters and images from their respective books wove in and out of their lives that summer. Paul's review of *Pierrot* for *Books and Bookmen* suggests that he recognised more than a touch of Kay herself in her Harlequin: 'Handsome, gay, agile . . . A great intriguer. Lover of Columbine, but also fond of Pierrot. Possibly bi-sexual.'[11]

He saw Pierrot as an idealised *alter ego*: 'I should describe him as our conscience, the man one ought to be but isn't – patient, wise, humane, gentle, forgiving, charitable . . . he suffers at the hands of both masters and fellow servants, but preserves a moral detachment, is never embittered.' *Au clair de la lune*, Pierrot's theme tune, would wake echoes of this period in Paul to the end of his life. In the *commedia dell'arte* scenario acted out at Flask Walk, Paul played Pierrot to Kay's Harlequin, Pantaloon could be seen as a kind of composite publisher – 'He is money. He is power. He gives the orders. He dictates, he controls. He has found room at the top' – with the Doctor standing in for the equivocal critic who would hold Kay's and Paul's fates in his hand in the autumn: 'An Arts man, but Establishment Arts . . . He feels able to speak for every branch of knowledge, to make pronouncements. He knows absolutely nothing but has apt quotations from other men's work always to hand . . . A shrewd committee man, a limpet.' Paul despised himself for courting literary committee men. Kay had interceded unsuccessfully on his behalf with her friend Pam Snow (Sir Charles Snow and his wife, Pamela Hansford Johnson, represented in those days a peak – or in Paul's phrase a snow-line – of popular critical acclaim),[12] and he himself solicited quotable testimonials from established figures like Edith Sitwell, as well as distributing puffs to his friends in *Books and Bookmen*, but the uncomfortable role of self-publicist made him feel more than ever like a clown or pierrot.

Another of his contributions to *Books and Bookmen* that autumn was an article about Muriel Spark, who had followed up the triumph of *Memento Mori* the year before ('She has rather got to the stage of just glancing through to see how often the words brilliant, eccentric are mentioned', Paul reported fondly when the reviews came out)[13] by publishing *The Ballad of Peckham Rye* in the spring of 1960, with *The Bachelors* promised for October. Meanwhile she was writing *The Prime of Miss Jean Brodie*, planning her début as a playwright and considering film proposals for *Peckham Rye*. One of Paul's drily admiring Spark stories described her being wooed, as she was about to go on holiday, by the film director Ken Annakin: 'Apparently she said well what's in it for me, and Annakin said it would all have to be thrashed out, but that she could be thinking about it in Nice. "Thanks, I said. I was wondering what I was going to think about in Nice" '.[14] Paul escorted her to the Picasso exhibition at the Tate in April,[15] attended her parties in Camberwell, lunched or dined with her in town on their joint days off from the desk. She had changed perhaps more than anyone since Crown Passage days: if Paul was beginning to spread his wings, take short flights and make tentative landings in loose-living bohemian Hampstead, Muriel Spark stood poised for international take-off. His own major crossroads was also, as Paul said ten years later, the 'point when she was emerging from the rather homely Camberwell-based girl into the bird of paradise she now is, wearing couturier dresses in Rome and being photographed for *Vogue*.'[16]

He had always been fascinated by what women wore. Mollie Hamilton never forgot Paul's delight when, on the strength of his initial reaction to *The Shadow of the Moon*, she splashed a fabulous eighteen guineas on the hat of a lifetime. He thoroughly approved the same attitude in Muriel Spark, who baffled an interviewer round about this time by looking like Hermione Baddeley – 'jolly, motherly, buff-suited . . . not at all like a lady novelist'[17] – and declaring that she would throw up writing for at least a year, as soon as she made her fortune, and spend the money on clothes: 'I might even put up with Paris for the sake of them.' Paul felt similarly inclined himself in spurts of elation when it seemed as if success might almost be within his grasp at last. Macmillans headed their publicity pamphlet for *The Bachelors* with Paul's statement of faith in Muriel Spark ('I believe she has done more outstanding work in a short space than any other living writer'),[18] and she returned the compliment with a promotional piece for Eyre & Spottiswoode ('I love *The Chinese Love Pavilion*. It is enchantingly exotic, sensuous and colourful. Everyone should read it'). They jostled one another at the Book Society, his novel getting a recommendation in June, hers up for consideration the month after. the *Pavilion* was scheduled for publication on Thursday 29 September

1960 and *The Bachelors* on 13 October. 'We are coming out more or less together,' wrote Paul:

Ours will be the best books of the month. Ours will be the best books of the Autumn. We shall drip with mink, diamonds (you), Italian silk suits and sharkshin bathing trunks (me). I picture me somewhere in the sun which is why I choose silk suits and sharkskin trunks. I find after 20 years of not caring a damn about how I look or what I dress in (between 17 and 20 I was a bit of a peacock) I am looking with an upsurge of interest at the shops in Regent Street, Shaftesbury Avenue etc. I think I'm probably a teddy boy at heart. I lust after Italianate short jackets and tapering trousers.[19]

In the event, the nearest Paul came to basking in Mediterranean seas that summer was a two-minute dip in icy water off the north Norfolk coast on a family motoring holiday. He hired a baby Austin at the beginning of September, and drove for the first time since he left the army – 'my absolute lust for driving fell on me again'[20] – covering 1,400 miles in fourteen days with only three nights away from home, making a round tour of East Anglia, calling on Peter and Lal Green at their cottage outside Cambridge, taking day trips to places like Oxford, Stratford-on-Avon, and Marlow. At Whipsnade Zoo a peacock stood for twenty-five minutes admiring himself in the car's shiny bumper, which Paul, thinking of the white peacock in the completed first section of *The Birds of Paradise*, took to be a good omen.[21] He was back by the middle of the month – 'my mind is beginning to go (pre-pub nerves)', he told Mary Patchett – to face the kind of exposure which always made him feel like a performing monkey: his first television appearance when Peter Green interviewed him for ABC's *Book Man*, a handsome advertising campaign ('I can't wipe the silly grin off my face,' he had written to Maurice Temple Smith when he opened the *Bookseller* to find a four-page advance spread for *Pavilion*),[22] and the suspense of waiting for what turned out to be almost universal acclaim in the press. Preliminary sighting shots from Geoffrey Grigson in the *Spectator* the day after publication made Paul feel 'dirty and useless, close to that special form of contemplative suicide writers mock themselves in',[23] only to be dramatically rescued on Sunday by a generous, perceptive, wholly unexpected accolade from the *Observer's* leading fiction reviewer, John Davenport.

Mediocre sales in America were amply outweighed by a freak pre-emptive bid from a thrusting young executive at the New American Library,[24] who snapped up US paperback rights on a tip-off before publication for $17,500 of which Paul took half. He found himself selling translation rights, being wooed (inconclusively as it turned out) by his very own film producer,[25] putting down the first payment on a car, dreaming of selling the house, going abroad, perhaps even returning to India and taking the family with him.[26] Maurice, who reckoned to have sold nearly 10,000 copies in the first month, was still hoping four months later to make 20,000: in fact sales over two years reached just over 15,000, roughly three times as many as any previous Scott novel.[27] Paul arranged to have his portrait painted again (the original painting had reappeared with its scar mark on his wall) by Bob Mason, now a schoolmaster in Kent, who planned to hang the picture in the Royal Academy summer show on the strength of its illustrious subject's reputation (it was in fact exhibited at the Royal Society of Portrait Painters a year later).[28] Paul's letters show the provident, prudent, sober-suited sceptic grappling almost comically with the teddy boy in him that autumn. 'Arthur, I'm having the most fearful trouble,' he wrote to Arthur Thompson who, under his pen name of Francis Clifford, had stepped off a ledge into thin air twelve months before Paul: 'Every time I sign a cheque for money I haven't got I get a heart attack.'[29] He put on more of a swagger for Gerry Hanley, picturing himself retired with wife, children and typewriter to a hut by the sea in the sun,[30] and he was frankly ecstatic to Peter Green ('the new Anglia in a heavenly Ambassador blue is gleaming at the front gate').[31]

One thing that puzzled several people about Paul, even at the height of his euphoria, was that he seemed unconvinced, as if he were trying out a new role and could not feel comfortable with it. 'He was highly emotional,' said Maurice Temple Smith, 'you had to tread very, very carefully because he had a skin too few.' Paul himself complained bitterly to David Higham that Maurice had 'only two attitudes, the off-hand and the high hand, chiefly off-hand'.[32] In a less disillusioned moment he said with equal truth that Maurice's practical hardheaded approach made him feel, 'as authors often do when talking to their publishers – like something that's wriggled out from under a stone, naked and ashamed.'[33] People who knew Paul best often recognised this kind of shrinking in him, an elusiveness apparent even in moments of greatest intimacy, when his absorption in others made him seem to blot himself out. 'Fond as I am of Paul (he made you want to protect him), he wasn't memorable,' said Kay Dick: 'It was as if he cast no shadow, or looked in the mirror and left no image. I can only remember his moods.'

Kay, restless and unsettled herself in the early 1960s, sensed in Paul an underlying desperation which made her long to console him. They reinforced one another professionally, commiserated over their respective difficulties at home, agreed that they were both souls in torment. Paul talked about his father, and his overriding sense of having failed his parents. 'He had *no* happiness in his life,' said Kay. 'He was like a friendly dog that everyone wanted to pat.' Their relationship was tender, romantic, melancholy, tinged with regret on both sides. Paul showed Kay an unguarded side of himself that struck her as painfully vulnerable. They made love and, when it was over, Paul said gently: 'You'd have preferred it if I had been a woman.'[34] Kay found him infinitely considerate and unbearably sad: 'Afterwards his eyes filled with tears. I asked him why he cried, and he said, "Not about us". He went off with tears in his eyes, and I knew it was because of his life: and that we had made love because of his life.'

Paul withdrew immediately into his new book, and urged her to do the same: 'Please forgive my silence and disappearance but I'm not fit for human consumption.'[35] Visits stopped, telephone calls were blocked, letters produced apologies and excuses. Paul left messages to say he was working night and morning on his novel, reviewing in the afternoons (he had taken on a fiction column for the *New Statesman*), reading twelve books in a week, for all practical purposes unreachable. He had retreated behind barricades manned by his family as if to a lair where there was no need to keep up a front: nothing could have demonstrated more clearly the need for protection and support that underlay his urgent lifelong protestations about his marriage. 'Penny & I, believe it or not, are coming up to our nineteenth anniversary,' he had written to Adèle Dogan on her engagement earlier that year: 'perhaps I can't wish you more than we have had together.'[36] A gala outing on the day itself, 23 October, would be followed by a day or so off at Christmas and a further celebration to mark completion of the first draft of *The Birds of Paradise* in March 1961. 'Penny, by the way, has been wonderful as always in the last two months since Christmas (and before!)', Paul wrote to John Willey: 'she's been conducting a kind of Operation BOP, & we've hardly been out of the house together since Jan. 1.'[37]

Operation BOP, like all the other similar operations mounted before and after it, meant that, apart from occasional unpredictable excursions announced at short notice and as often as not countermanded without warning, Paul had spent five solid months in seclusion upstairs in his study, writing, brooding and drinking. The fresh start that was to have put the marriage on a more companionable basis had petered out almost at once: 'After a few weeks we were just two people estranged from one another, not speaking, sitting in silence, a silence that bordered on enmity.'[38] Holidays no longer brought the family together. Ever since the trip to Spain when the *Pavilion* came too, Paul had been reluctant to take any kind of break for fear the work in progress might give him the slip ('He was terrified,' said his daughter Sally, 'as if he were holding onto the string of a balloon'). After he gave up his job, outsiders gradually stopped coming to the house, and the few who still did found it a strain. Chris Almedingen was one of the people who worried most about the effect leaving agency was having on Paul. Always a grave and penetrating critic, she had grasped the significance of the submerged conflicts running through his work, especially *Pavilion* ('it confirmed my idea of you – formed after *Mark* – that in you we were going to have a great novelist'),[39] together with the risks entailed in exposing them. Visits to London confirmed her uneasiness. Her letters in the early 1960s are full of oblique concern for Penny – tributes, loving messages, enquiries about her health – and equally tactful support for Paul. 'Chris, dear, in the end one realises one's friends *are* one's friends because it is only with them that you can speak the language you're born with,' Paul wrote when the *Pavilion* came out: 'Finding you speak it you become friends. . . . Perhaps you did not know that, underneath that rather bland agency face, I was a mass of wretchedness, far more tender than perhaps I looked.'[40]

Paul and Chris Almedingen each recognised in the other an intrinsic wariness, reticence and self-reliance. Both had felt themselves from earliest childhood to be misfits, rejected by the societies they lived in, and excluded from the intellectual world to which they aspired. Chris, who had never known her distinguished academic father (he had severed all connection with his family in Petersburg when she was very small), had been brought up in isolation and penury by a proud, fierce, strong-willed, half-English mother who taught her, as Paul's mother had taught him, to expect no quarter, admit no defeat, to curb emotion and put her faith in books rather than people. She had come to trust and depend on Paul as an agent: he had rescued her so often from adversity, advised and attended her so faithfully through the whole gamut of writers' complaints – indifferent editors, mercenary publishers, importunate bank managers, inhuman reviewers – that she took particular pride in presiding over his first steps on the stony uphill path of the freelance. She urged him to have faith in himself, reminded him of Tolstoy's saying that 'every writing hour left some of his flesh and blood and bones in the inkstand',[41] assured him that despair was good for the soul: 'Believe me . . . every stone of that road has hurt my own feet – Yes, I did know about the "wretchedness" – not its "why" and "wherefore" – which – anyway – should never be pried into – but the general landscape – and that's where your integrity comes alive in your work. Don't dismiss it as a paradox, it isn't meant to be: your strength is in that "wretchedness".'[42]

It was a shrewd diagnosis, especially from someone who recognised all too clearly what it might mean for Paul and his family. Chris's own early childhood had made her more sensitive than many of his friends to the effect of Paul's wounding withdrawals, his efforts to anaesthetise emotion, the drink he used as a barrier, the fury that erupted when he felt thwarted or blocked and which he displaced on those closest to him. Harsh experience made her fear the consequences of Paul's behaviour and, for all her quick sympathy, judge him more sternly than she otherwise might have done. 'He refused to look at himself as he was. He didn't take the responsibility as a husband and father that he should have done. This was where he was weak – lamentably weak. He failed in moral courage. Some people don't know they're doing it, but he did. *He knew what he was doing.*'[43] The defection of her own father had left Chris peculiarly alert to the needs of vulnerable, sensitive, intelligent children approaching adolescence, as Paul's daughters were when he left Higham's. Sally at twelve was already beginning to register the humiliating gap between the charming and popular father envied by her schoolfriends, and the father who surfaced only at home, unseeing, unpredictable, abstracted or drunk, shaken by sudden frightening rages, in one of which she watched him swing the telephone on its cord and smash it, as he had earlier destroyed his portrait. Nothing would any longer distract Paul from his purpose: 'this is what I gave up the office to do – ', he wrote to Kay, 'unmask myself as myself, and not sometimes have to disguise my frustrations.'[44] He recognised clearly enough the ruthlessness behind a determination that left no feeling to spare, no energy to listen or respond on any but the most superficial mechanical level: 'at the moment I'm not a good listener, not a good doer. . . Please, please just accept that I'm in great trouble with the book & no use to anyone . . . I can't *talk* about anything at the moment except on the merest level of daily doings.'

This is the state of mind described by Bill Conway, narrator of *The Birds of Paradise*, on periodic retreats from the world when he, too, goes into a kind of emotional hibernation or limbo, cutting himself off from family and friends:

it was not really a question of disliking people from having been in too crowded contact with them for too long, but of putting first things first, of using unaccustomed freedom to observe the world into which I had, in a sense, been born all over again; to rest the body so it could heal itself and waste none of its rationed fire to set light to the emotion you always had to burn when you become involved with others . . .[45]

Conway at forty takes a year off from a business career in the City to retire to a Pacific island, take stock of the past, and write his memoirs (Paul eventually dedicated the *Birds* 'To Wil Morrow with gratitude and thanks for my own sabbatical year'). He feels himself a failure as husband, father and son: his marriage has just ended in divorce, his relationship with his eleven-year-old only child has become as frigid and inhibited as dealings had been with his own father, who was British Resident in the Indian princely state of Jundapur. Conway looks back to his childhood between the wars, to the panoply and pomp of the Raj, tiger hunts, shooting and garden parties, and to the ambivalent, competitive games he played in the palace garden with two other children: an English girl called Dora, and Krishi, the Maharajah's son, who would grow up disinherited in independent India just as Bill Conway, destined to follow his father into the ICS, would find the ground cut from under his feet in the booming consumer society of post-war Britain, with the liberal tradition at an end and no empire left to govern. Bill's adult experiences are soured by defeat and discontent, where the images of his Indian childhood remain warm, sunlit, remote and gilded like the great, domed, wrought-iron cage on the lake island at Jundapur, erected by one of Krishi's ancestors to house a collection of rare and fabulous birds of paradise.

Paul said, looking back, that these birds had served as his 'mining tool', a symbol like the kris that enabled him to get at, or dig out, the book he was struggling to write. He described his excitement and absorption as he watched them materialise, shaky and flickering at first, gradually steadying as his imagination took leaps and jumps, speeding up, slowing down, pursuing the images that swung towards and away from his mental screen in vivid, jerky, cinematic projection.[46] It was the process Kay had glimpsed from outside in the spring and summer of 1960, when Paul told her he was 'talking to birds of paradise, waking & sleeping & getting panicky about their not talking back to me'.[47] He had spent hours stalking and waiting for them, standing at his high study window or gazing at the blank wall behind his desk: 'I remember . . . when the cage first came. A wet June Sunday afternoon at about four o'clock, staring at a white wall.'[48] Like the home-made films of his childhood, laboriously drawn out with mapping pens, assembled on strips of clear paper and pasted together overlapping in sequence, the book entranced and engulfed him. He took it with him in his head on the top of a bus to the zoo in Regent's Park (where he found his first live bird of paradise, watched a tiger in the cat house, and talked to the green Paraguayan parrot that became Conway's Melba), and on trips to see glass cases full of stuffed birds at the Natural History Museum in South Kensington. In the end what he was looking for turned out to be dead birds with their feet cut off, stuffed specimens like the British in India, strutting in their glorious plumage, according to a private Indian joke, looking as if they owned the place, only to fall off their perch, 'dead from the neck up and the neck down', when they found they had no legs to stand on.[49]

The Birds of Paradise is an elegant and intricate construction, a series of interlocking images and themes – illusion and disillusionment, dream and reality, innocence and experience or compromise – shifting this way and that as the light changes, or as Conway's contemptuous dismissal of the British and their Imperial delusions gradually gives way to more complicated feelings about people like his father, and Krishi's, who inherited the earth and saw it turn to dust and ashes. Paul said the first inkling he had had of the book was an imaginary woman in a doorway with a companion, a conventionally glamorous couple in an escapist setting ('But how romantic – this idea of a man and a woman on an island surrounded by birds of paradise. How romantic, how unlikely, how false'),[50] whose situation became, as he looked at it, steadily more mundane and peculiar. Perhaps he half realised that his own career as a novelist was already moving in a parallel direction, away from bland fictional stereotypes towards something altogether less popular and predictable. The nameless heroine in the doorway developed, on closer inspection, into a much older woman called Dora, tough, stoical, observant, first in a long line of memsahibs who would with time provide their creator with some sort of key: 'all the things that happened in 1939–45 are my keys to what is happening now,' Paul had said as he started work on the *Pavilion*,[51] and it was partly through women like Dora that he would begin in the Raj Quartet to unlock and examine the traumatic experience of the British leaving India, an Imperial reality still largely submerged in his lifetime, inaccessible to historians, unmapped in the novel, unacknowledged for the most part even by those who were part of it.

The Birds of Paradise ends with Bill, Krishi and Dora meeting again at Jundapur after thirty years, a bleak reunion redeemed by their humorous, tolerant, sceptical acceptance of themselves and one another. The same note runs through the central relationship between the two Conways, which begins with the son's high hopes being crushed by what looks like his father's betrayal, settles into a neutral estrangement on Bill's return from fighting in Burma after the war years, and ends in belated reconciliation after his father's death. Readers of the *Birds* often assumed that its author had been born into the ICS and brought up in India: Paul himself said he knew, when he finished it, that he could never write another book about India without revisiting the subcontinent.[52] But the novel's last sentence, in which Conway finally makes peace as a son, is also in some sense an acknowledgement of unfinished business between Paul and his own father:

I no longer think of Father as old and foolish and out of touch. . . . I see . . . that within all his silence and coldness there burned the likeness of a noble aspiration . . . and bitterly regret that not once in my life did I sit with him and let him feel that I understood how vulnerable is the illusion a man has of his own importance, not of his importance to others, but of his importance to himself. . .

Paul finished the *Birds* at 4 a.m. on 1 March after a ten-hour stint at the desk, staggered into bed 'drunk with success, horny with fulfilment', and slept for twelve hours, only to find himself assailed on waking by his usual doubts: 'it was all wrong. I knew it was wrong when I typed it. I knew it was wrong again when I thought about it. . . ,' he wrote to Gerry Hanley just over a fortnight later: 'Yesterday Penny read the whole book for the first time, and agreed it went wrong just before the end.'[53] He said he did not know how he could have faced himself if she hadn't also said firmly: 'In this book, you are a writer.'[54] Ferocious disappointment – 'screams of rage and exhaustion in the study'[55] –attended Paul's failure to meet his publisher's delivery date of 1 April. He had planned a holiday to celebrate the end of his first full writing year in the place where he had originally received his 'free pardon from agency',[56] the Hotel Jano at Tamariu on the Costa Brava. But, when the family piled into the car on 4 April, once again Paul's manuscript came too, and overshadowed them all as they paddled in the chilly spring sea, basked in the hot spring sun, drove up into the mountains, drank champagne and ate seafood at their favourite Bar Royal run by two old friends, Miguel and Maria Burgos. 'The three girls of the party all cried as we drove out of the village waving to the Spaniards, & I wasn't far off it myself,' Paul wrote to Chris Almedingen on 29 April. 'The Pyrenees were snow-capped and shining in the sun, the grape vines were in leaf, and the sky was that special blue. Aie! How cold and grey England looks, how full of trivialities the newspapers. Back to work on Monday to finish the book.'

He meant to reduce it by about a fifth as well as rewrite the ending: he cut savagely, driven by a sneaking suspicion he had written the first part of a series ('I've always sneered at sequences á la Proust, Snow and Durrell'),[57] or worse still a family saga. One of the episodes he removed was Dora's account of her marriage to an impeccably correct Indian Army subaltern called Harry Poynter, who subjected his young bride to sexual indignities so unspeakable that she was sick on the sheets. Bill and Krishi, Dora's two middle-aged former playmates and chivalrous childhood blood brothers, are simultaneously fascinated and appalled by revelations of her husband's 'sexual bestiality' (which include bondage, beatings, voyeurism, experiments with leather goods and gum boots, as well as smuggling an Indian bearer into the bedroom to tickle his scrotum with a goose feather 'because, he said, he knew she wouldn't do it for him').[58] When Poynter arrives at Jundapur to collect his wife, Bill finds himself reluctantly involved in a fist fight: an absurd, comical, slow motion knockabout with the pair of them plastering one another all over the palace, lurching on and off the terrace, crashing about in the hall, tumbling out of the front door onto the gravel drive, and ending up puff-eyed, bloodstained, weak-kneed, barely able to stand upright in front of a silently appreciative Indian audience. The whole affair is a sort of Marx Brothers replay of the sexual depravity followed by punitive violence at the end of the *Pavilion*, and it worried Paul for the same reasons.

The revisions which he had reckoned would take a month at most lasted for nearly two, and it was this final section that held him up. 'Despair walked in last night,' he told Hanley on 27 May. 'It's all wrong . . . I can't get it. Three sections near perfect (in mind). Last section like an old chucked-away French letter on Hampstead Heath.'[59] A similar cry of anguish went off on the same day to that most tender-hearted and considerate of publishers, John Willey, who implored Paul by return of post to forget Morrow's deadline ('Dr Willey will now prescribe the obvious. . . . Throw away the calendar, Paul – relax, relax, relax').[60] Willey seemed so seriously alarmed that his patient felt obliged to explain his symptoms as part of the routine for each new novel: 'I think it has to be despaired over in order to come right. . . . I suppose it isn't really despair at all, just an acute attack of self-criticism which can sometimes lead to a feeling that if a book is *this* difficult to get right none of it is right.'[61] Always wary of the transatlantic agony-and-ecstacy approach to the artistic process, Paul insisted that for him it was more of a job like brick-laying, which did not stop him plunging back into despair as soon as the last brick had been laid and the manuscript delivered at the end of June. 'I . . . have been & still am in a black & distracted state of mind,' he wrote on 11 July to Kay: 'Even gin didn't help. I went on a fearful bender but it made no difference.'[62]

Gin was becoming an essential part of the struggle to unmask. 'To go on a bender,' Paul explained formally to his Swedish translator, 'has almost come to mean, in English, to go on the kind of drinking spree that will strip the drinker down to his inner nakedness.'[63] Paul's working pattern, laid down in the early 1960s, involved drinking in his study sometimes all day ('I'm pissed as a newt writing this on gin,' he wrote to Hanley), continuing in the evenings alone or at parties, moving on, if necessary alone again, to Soho clubs after the pubs closed. He was beginning to hate company, or hate the effect it had on him, falling back more and more on old friends like Kay, Gerry Hanley and Roland Gant who could be relied on never to remonstrate, take offence or ask questions. Once, in the course of a heroic night spent 'drinking to a Celtic pattern' with Roland, the pair drove into Oxford at dawn: 'there was nothing to do but kick a college wall or two because we were not a quarter of a century younger and were very much down rather than up,' Roland wrote long afterwards. 'A bunch of wilted bluebells gathered on the way back and proffered by a shaky hand did nothing to help our homecoming.'[64] Paul turned up several times at Flask Walk in need of a wash and a shave, too bleary after drinking all night to remember where he had been. Once, when he had mislaid his car, Kay set off to search for it in Soho, leaving Paul to sober up on black coffee. 'Sometimes fear I'll become an alcoholic,' he wrote uneasily to Hanley in August 1961, returning again to the same 'fearful bender' he had mentioned to Kay:

The awful thing is that at a certain stage my mind seems to go blank (I mean during one of these alcoholic sessions). I remember being in a dreary drinking club, which must have been about 5.30 p.m., and there are flashes of being refused admittance to the Gargoyle or thrown out of the Mandrake, but nothing is really clear until I nearly got arrested at 3 a.m. on Haverstock Hill on suspicion of trying to pinch a car. Actually I was walking home, moneyless, all the way from the West End, and was looking for a place to kip. The police patrol car ended up by giving me a lift to the Whitestone Pond, at which place I more or less came to.[65]

Paul was reading Stendhal's *Journals* that summer, also Robert Musil ('I take him like aspirin and sometimes like a drug'), and dickering with a new novel, or rather with the image which he hoped would help him get at it. All he had to go on at this stage was the picture of a man walking somewhere on an errand connected with his unsatisfactory brother. 'Where is it? When was it?' he wrote on 25 July to Adèle Dogan: 'Is the brother as bad as I think other people think he is? Fascinating, this dumb charade business.' He came back again and again to the night on Haverstock Hill, giving Peter Green a memorable account in the Dog and Duck,[66] and worrying away at it in a letter to John Willey about the hero of his new London novel, George Spruce, a character so riddled with self-contempt that he retreats from the world altogether ('And in time, because you saw no other human face, your own face would be revealed. It would come out of its lair like a naked animal, attracted by the sun and a feeling of repose, and no longer ashamed of having no fur').[67] Like his creator, George ends up in the hands of the police on Haverstock Hill, after drinking all night in a failed attempt 'to get up courage ... to go and cut his throat on Hampstead Heath'. Paul prudently never posted this letter of 27 September, waiting until he could write triumphantly to Adèle a month later to say he had re-established control by combining the real and imaginary episodes in his novel: 'I know where it is now that this one brother was going when he set out from what was once a kind of village street – but is now Haverstock Hill – the one that leads to Hampstead Heath. The journey of one brother towards another or because of another is now the climax and not the beginning of *The Bender*.'[68]

Paul freely admitted seeing himself in *The Bender*'s George Spruce, or rather the side of himself that had started out as his mother's golden boy, handsome, promising, gifted, a charmer who might have wound up – if he hadn't gone to India and been driven to write – a lonely, improvident drifter, wasting his energy on dreams and living out of tins, like George, in a rented bedsitter. George's climactic bender ends in a club on Old Compton Street ('It might be the Gorgon, or it might be the Apocalypse'),[69] after which he trudges northwards via the Charing Cross and Tottenham Court Roads only to be picked up by the police, trying car door handles on Haverstock Hill, hoping to steal an unlocked car and drive it into a tree trunk as an alternative to throwing himself under a bus, or in front of an underground train. Having failed to kill himself, George turns up in the small hours on the doorstep of his brother Tim. A respectable accountant, model citizen and father of two, Tim is the son their mother failed to cherish, a tame, dull, hardworking plodder, who lives in a trim north London garden suburb and bitterly resents being burdened at forty with the problems of the feckless, footloose George. This most schematic confrontation between Paul's split selves (the Spruce brothers' childhood, circumstances and family background are directly based on the Scotts', with Vi Spruce as a cartoon sketch, gingerly but accurately drawn, of Paul's mother) remains uneasily balanced between humour and pathos in what he defensively called 'my occidental style' or 'Greater London Contemporary'.[70] He was always indulgent towards *The Bender* ('its parentage is straightforward enough. Me, in London, as it were'),[71] but it confirmed his reluctance to tangle further with the small-scale, domestic and urban novel practised by more successful contemporaries like John Braine, Kingsley Amis, Angus Wilson and C. P. Snow.

Financially, Paul prospered as never before in the summer of 1961. The manuscript of the *Birds* was enthusiastically received by both

*Friends and fellow novelists whose careers
Paul helped to launch in the 1950s*

BELOW *Chris Almedingen for whom Paul
was 'a prince among agents', and an
'Archduke/King/Emperor among friends'.*

ABOVE RIGHT *Mollie Hamilton (M. M.
Kaye), who considered her first encounter
with young Mr Scott of PPH as 'one of the
greatest pieces of luck that has ever come my
way'.*

*John Braine, who 'convinced himself he
would never have written* Room at the Top *if
I hadn't prodded him over several years'.*

Muriel Spark, 'dear patient Mu',
who always brought out the
Teddy Boy in Paul.

BELOW *Morris West, who required*
and got from Paul a decade of
patient promotion and development.

Arthur C. Clarke, the Homer of
Space Fiction.

Kay Dick, who played Harlequin to
Paul's Pierrot in the summer of 1960.

Morrow and Maurice Temple Smith, who threatened at one point to lock it up in his office and publish surreptitiously, if Paul showed signs of major revision.[72] Eyre & Spottiswoode readily agreed to an advance of £1000 and, on the strength of the New American Library deal (the first and last US paperback sale of Paul's lifetime), the Morrow guarantee was temporarily suspended as an experiment in its second year.[73] The family celebrated with wholesale redecoration at Addison Way in August, when Paul redesigned the dining-room in blues and greens as a garden room, ordering modern bucket chairs, white paint and lime-green carpeting throughout. He and Penny both felt that things might be different if only he could pull off a bestseller, as he nearly had with the *Pavilion* and hoped he still might with the *Birds*.

The refurbishing was a peace offering, an earnest of things to come, partly also an alternative to acknowledging the need for more fundamental repairs. Paul's genuine enthusiasm for the scheme was tinged with the bitterness Bill Conway felt for his grasping, material-istic wife in the *Birds* ('She is a great consumer, wholly committed to it'), who never staggered blind drunk and out of control, 'only sucked and munched her way steadily through life in the company of other suckers and munchers'.[74] Paul undoubtedly gave the impression at times that his family's demands were insatiable just as, in gentler moods, he admitted the opposite. He toyed briefly that summer with a novel called *The Careerist*, or sometimes *Married with Two Children*, which was to be a reversal or mirror image of *The Bender*.[75] Its ambitious, thrusting, upwardly mobile hero insists on doing up the whole house with white paint, purple carpets and harsh lime-yellow curtains, which makes his apprehensive wife, uneasy with his modern-istic furniture and car-sick in his new Austin, feel like a stranger in rooms that no longer seem to belong to her. It is as if the innovations, ostensibly designed to please her, were shouldering her aside in her own home.

Several people felt something similar was happening in these years to Penny, who seemed self-effacing to the point of retirement: often when the Scotts entertained a friend or former client of Paul's – Mary Patchett, Doreen Marston, Muriel Spark – Penny would literally retire from the table with a migraine, or take a taxi home alone from the restaurant. People who knew them were divided. Many of his friends held Penny solely responsible for keeping Paul back, mounting watch over him, jealously guarding his privacy on the telephone, blocking their access to him at home. Others took Penny's side. Chris Almedingen was one of several old friends who tried over the years to remonstrate with Paul about the way he treated his wife. Penny for her part fell back on ingrained, protective habits of covering up and concealment. Paul's drunkenness, as he said himself, 'wasn't the sort you'd notice':[76] he never stumbled or slurred: Penny was the only person who witnessed his desperation in private, and in public she was also often the only one to realise how much he had drunk. Liquor brought out his intrinsically elegant wit, buoyancy and panache. She marvelled at his composure, his lucidity and level-headedness, the magnetic quality of his attention. His brilliance entranced her as it did other people – 'There was always a ring round him at parties' – but others seldom saw him in darkness, with the light switched off and the party over, after the guests had gone home. A favourite tune from this period, a theme that would haunt Paul to the end of his life, was Shirley Bassey singing 'The Party's Over'.

Paul's writing friends were frequently puzzled or critical of Penny for her reluctance to play any part on the literary scene, especially since it had looked at one point as if the two might join forces like the Snows as a husband-and-wife team. At the beginning of the 1960s, when Penny was producing a book a year, they were photographed together, interviewed in magazines and newspapers, featured on BBC radio's *Woman's Hour*, included as local authors in Helen Craig's book about literary Hampstead.[77] Penny had followed her first novel with an equally successful sequel, *The Marigold Summer* (1960), which takes the same heroine through an unhappy, loveless relationship with an exploitative aunt and ends with a major eye operation ('this one is even better than *The Margaret Days*,' wrote Peter Green, ' – the slow tightening of the screw up to the actual moment of the operation, that frightful childish terror of being the victim of a complicated conspiracy, the extraordinarily subtle exchanges with Fielding, the whole minuscule hospital claustrophobia – it's brilliant').[78] In 1961, she published *Nurse Has Four Cases*, a semi-autobiographical, semi-fictional collection of sketches which disconcerted her publishers by qualifying neither as nursing romance nor as a *Doctor in the House* type of comedy ('The Doctor books are funny,' Penny protested to Roland Gant: 'I never found nursing or hospitals funny'). While Paul was splitting his personality so as to twist it this way and that in *The Bender*, Penny was making a similar experiment in *Sister Bollard*, a drily ironic account of what might have happened to someone like herself who turned down marriage and children in order to carry on nursing.

But, if she had settled at this stage into a career of her own, it would inevitably have meant changing the balance of their relationship, something for which neither was apparently prepared. It was tacitly accepted between them, at any rate after *Sister Bollard* came out in 1963, that pushing Paul forward entailed Penny's pulling, or being pulled, back herself. He had taken over her career from the start, continuing to supervise and direct it even after he left Higham's, defining her intentions to David, justifying her aims and techniques to Roland, treating her writing (as they had both always treated her life) as an adjunct to his own. He was generous and discerning when she showed him the finished manuscript of her first nursing book, but once again taken aback: 'underneath it all she can't help being her writing self and there is something about that writing self that has its own special fascination. I am still surprised about it!'[80] If Paul felt apprehensive about the emergence of that unexpected, independent writing self, perhaps Penny did too: and, considering what was happening in the upstairs study – the hair-tearing days, the screams of rage and exhaustion, the black and distracted moods – perhaps they both felt that one writing self was more than enough in any one household.

They celebrated their twentieth wedding anniversary on 23 October, 1961, with a drive out to Epping Forest, lunch in the country, and tickets for *Madam Butterfly* at Covent Garden in the evening.[81] Paul, who had by his own account been drunk on and off all week, embarked on a serious, seven-day bender which came to a head when David Higham rang up at midday on 1 November to announce that John Braine's film rights had sold for £30,000. Paul, who had been drinking steadily since half past ten in the morning ('just breathing in gin, and it not having any obvious effect!'), poured several more gins, booked a table at the Epicure, took Penny out to lunch, and rounded off the afternoon by buying her a Hardy Amies coat at Marshall and Snelgrove. It was cut on the bias with swirling skirts and a peplum effect to go with that autumn's big hats: high fashion suited Penny, but Paul suspected almost before they were out of the shop that the gesture had been yet another mistake. 'I suppose it made us feel worse in the end, because the children wanted new bedjackets or slippers or satchels, I forget which!' he confided to Muriel Spark, conceding gloomily that Penny would never have the life to go with her new coat, 'which I don't think she likes now that she's got it, but is too kind to say'.[82]

Paul was seeing a good deal that autumn of Muriel Spark, who mounted an energetic campaign to persuade him to join her with his next novel on Macmillans' list.[83] He enjoyed flirting with other publishers, being wooed by Peter Green in his capacity as literary adviser to Hodder & Stoughton, receiving simultaneous advances from Fred Warburg of Secker & Warburg, holding Roland Gant in reserve. His sense of never having been sufficiently courted by the new regime at Eyre & Spottiswoode was reinforced by reports that Maurice

Temple Smith had been seen out with a woman – 'another E&S author
. . . supposed to be very pretty and sexy', Paul wrote plaintively to
Muriel Spark, who always brought out the teddy boy in him: 'I mean it
made me wish I was pretty and sexy too, I mean the way Maurice
would wish to take me out to the Caprice and sign a contract for
£300,000 on the spot.' Paul called round on Maurice after his fling at
the Epicure, dropping Penny off that evening with a friend in the local
pub, and going on to consume the better part of a bottle of burgundy at
the Temple Smiths' house on Christchurch Hill, Hampstead. The
various anxieties which had been troubling him for months had finally
reached the surface, and Paul outlined them – his professional
restlessness, his fear of failure, his drinking, the trouble with Penny
that couldn't be resolved by lunch in the West End or a couture coat –
in a long, confessional letter to Muriel Spark, ending with the violent
response provoked by Maurice's coolness:

So there I am back in the pub, and only Penny knows I'm as drunk as a coot,
and J. buys me a double gin on top of the burgundy, and then I think I buy her
one and we drive very fast to Liverpool Street, so fast that it is early for her
train and time for more double gins. And I drive home and leave Penny at the
door to go in and get the midnight tea and drive round to the garage and as I
open the garage doors and switch on the light there is this feeling of This is
What The End is like, rather sordid and cold and all damp brick. And so I
back the car in and close the doors and leave the engine running and wonder
how long it is before the carbon monoxide poison begins to work.

And then of course I begin to get plain bloody scared and the Puritan in me
says Get out of this bloody car, Scott, and go and write your novel, and then a
very curious thing happens. There's a wind on a still night and the garage
door swings wide open, so that I nearly jump out of my skin, and get away
from that awful place very quickly. And in the morning when I wake up the
trauma is over and I sit down and work, and work well . . .

And the next day Maurice rings and says we must meet and I say yes, and he
says he'll collect me on Monday evening and we'll go out to dinner. And when
it is six o'clock on the Monday evening and pouring with rain . . . he rings and
says he's ricked his back and would I mind going round to them for supper?
So I say no, I don't mind, and walk round to the garage (15 minutes) in the
rain and come back and have a hot shower in order not to have pneumonia,
and change and drive over and spend a long time there telling him why I'm
thinking of leaving him. . . . And I fight down my trauma, and aren't drunk,
and remember the swinging door in the garage, and say that I don't want him
to put anything up because I'm only telling him what it is I *might* want if I
stay.

And that, dear patient Mu (if you've read as far as this), is my private confession to *you*. I mean I haven't of course even told Penny about the swinging doors in the garage which swung open as if someone with a lot of wind and force had yanked it back and no nonsense to let the carbon monoxide out.[84]

Paul had reason to feel wry about this strange scene in the damp garage (it was a mile away from the house because family cars had not yet been thought of when Hampstead Garden Suburb was designed in the early years of the century), when the Puritan in him finally got the upper hand over the would-be suicide in the fume-filled car. It represented an appropriately unheroic last stand for the self-admiring, self-pitying 'lonely little poet' of twenty years earlier, who had surfaced again in the teddy boy lusting after silk suits, and longing to be wined and dined at the Caprice. But, if this was an inglorious victory, it was also a decisive one, and its effects would declare themselves slowly over the next ten years in both Paul's life and his work. It meant harnessing and controlling the 'kind of puritan panic'[85] that had impelled him to finish the *Birds* on time, and to start a new novel before he had even revised the last. Where the punitive puritanical streak came from, or why, remained part of what he called 'the mystery of human behaviour', a mystery that was not to be solved, only contemplated, recognised and, if you were a novelist, portrayed as clearly as possible.

The nearest Paul came to approaching the origins and workings of his own particular mystery was allusively through parables or pictures. He personified it in *The Corrida at San Feliu* (the novel he wrote after *The Bender*) as what Spaniards call the *duende*, meaning an imp or goblin, the fierce, implacable spirit – Lorca said it 'burned in the blood like powdered glass'[86] – that supplies the dark notes without which a piece of music or writing counts for nothing. The writer Edward Thornhill, who is the central character in *Corrida*, describes his own personal *duende* as a derisive little black hunchback, chained by his leg in a dungeon, drawing on the walls, shrieking and straining to get at the one part of the wall beyond his reach: 'The book I would write is the picture he would draw on that part of the wall.' Thornhill's *duende* is an image of Paul's desperation, the mounting fear which never left him in these years that he himself might never get at the book he had it in him to write. At the end of his life he told the students in his American writing class that the worth or permanence of anything they might write would depend on the strength and egotism of what he called their writing personalities:

But, however strong or egotistical your writing personality is, the *alter ego* – the reflection of you that looks at what you are writing and have written – must be a critic that is almost impossible to please, or get a good mark from.[87]

Paul's *alter ego* in the early 1960s took many forms. One was the no-nonsense wind that yanked open the garage doors and made him nearly jump out of his skin. Another was the sneering face he hated so much in the mirror that, in January 1962, he briefly grew a beard to hide it ('I can't stand it,' he said and, when Penny asked what he could not stand: '*My mouth*'). The stern puritan voice ordering him back to work at his desk was a form of what Thornhill called the *duende*, which had shadowed him from earliest days: 'when I was born . . . something monstrous attended the lying-in, cursed me with the inability to see only what is there physically to be seen and left me with one of its own dark offspring to follow me and keep me up to the mark.'[88] Thornhill, who holds the *duende* responsible for his failure both as a man and a writer, says he encountered it first as a hunchback capering in the garden of his grandfather's house at Richmond where he had played as a child. The mocking malformed hunchback that capered and grimaced in Paul's writing goes back long before he ever went to Spain, or read Lorca, to the gothic grotesques that invade Dorian's sleep in *The Picture of Dorian Gray* ('nights of horror and misshapen joy, when through the chambers of the brain sweep phantoms more terrible than reality itself. . . . In black fantastic shapes, dumb shadows crawl into the corners of the room and crouch there').[89] Something very like Dorian's nightmare troubled young Sutton at the end of *The Chinese Love Pavilion*: 'Perhaps when she lowered the lamp and he lay there, impotent and ashamed, the black violent shapes he was no stranger to burst in and filled the room . . . or he may have slept and, waking, turned her to him in a last attempt to defy the ugly monster of perversion that gibbered on his shoulder.'[90]

Whatever its literary origins, Paul realised in retrospect that the answer to the ugly monster was not to deny or fly from it, but to admit its existence, even to accommodate its nature. At the end of his life, when he had written the Raj Quartet and reached a measure of self-acceptance, when he knew himself in some innermost recess of his being to be secure at last as a novelist, and when he was no longer tormented as a man by gibbering destructive demons, he told his students that they would get nowhere as writers unless each could locate his or her own personal *duende*. He said it was not only the puritanical fear that chains a writer to his desk: it was also the part of him that steps back, the unsparing critical intelligence that checks the headlong desires and fantasies of the romantic imagination. He could talk by this time familiarly, ruefully, even gratefully to his students about 'the demon chained in a dungeon of his being, who was ugly and mean, and constantly hissed at him that he was no good'.[91]

This stern, implacable critic, the *duende* who mocked his best efforts, the *alter ego* from whom it was almost impossible to get a good mark, were all parts played from infancy in Paul's life by his mother. The other side of her pleasure and pride in him had always been her great expectations, imperative needs and demands Paul felt he had no hope of fulfilling. His career in its early stages had been a collaboration. 'His mother was his best audience,' said Paul's daughter Sally: 'As he succeeded, his success was better reflected in her than in anyone else. So he could not get away from her.' It had taken nearly forty years for Frances Scott's spell to be finally broken, in a struggle which was short but so sharp that at its height even those most closely involved had not been able to predict its outcome ('For all I knew,' Penny wrote, describing the nerve-racking weeks when her mother-in-law had moved in at Addison Way, 'I was the one to be turned out of the house, if it came to it').[92] Paul said he loved Penny for her gentleness: he could trust her never to remonstrate or pick a quarrel at a time when he desperately needed a soothing pacific influence to counteract his mother's abrasiveness. With Frances cut out of his life, the situation changed radically. To the family at home it seemed that an essential constraint had gone: it was as if Frances's departure had released in her son a harsh, exacting, destructive spirit that was beginning to run out of control. Family unity disintegrated. Paul's drinking intensified. The dislocation between his two selves became more sharply marked than before, and could no longer always be contained in public. Old friends were increasingly aware of signs of strain in both Paul and Penny: 'It lay like a jagged knife between them,' said Kay, whose own increasingly explosive domestic tensions, alternating with suicidal despair in the early 1960s, made her sharply aware of Paul's.

One ironic compensation for his mother's loss was Paul's reunion with his Aunt Ruth, Frances's youngest sister, banned from the family circle on account of an earlier altercation, and still living in Brixton. Ruth Mark had all her family's warmth, humour and generosity without her sister's rancour or manipulative energy. She was big-boned and square-faced with the distinctive Mark nose, a deep gravelly voice and a fund of family stories. Great-Aunt Ruth was a delight to Paul's children, and their pleasure in one another was mutual. The girls and their father paid visits, brought her flowers, took her for drives and excursions, plunged with her into a past about which they knew nothing. She had worked for most of her life as cook-general to a family in Croydon called Dawson, confidently relying on them to provide for her old age until the elder of the two surviving Miss Dawsons died in 1961, breaking up the household and leaving Ruth, as she said, high and dry at sixty-five, facing retirement after thirty-four years in their service on a legacy of £10.[93]

She confided her shock and incredulity to Paul, who listened with sympathy and close attention (Ruth's relationships with her employers, and with her sister, were made virtually straight over to George Spruce's Aunt Ada in *The Bender*, and something of her indomitable spirit would be handed down after her death to Barbie Batchelor in *The Towers of Silence*.) Paul drew out her anxieties: insecurity, want, ill health and – worse than any material hardship – her meagre emotional harvest, her fearful loneliness, her painful diffidence in company, her growing, even more grievous sense of the futility and waste of her life. Rediscovering each other from this new adult perspective gave them both a precious sense of what might have been. 'You seem to cover all my rough edged bricks with velvet,' Ruth wrote to Paul soon after they met, and, a month later: 'Usually I think people are laughing at my nervousness but, when I came to you, I felt more comfortable than alone in my own room.'[94] In the dozen or so years of their late friendship (she died, aged seventy-five, in 1971), Ruth, like many others before and afterwards, found herself soothed and consoled, her fears relieved and her troubles made more bearable by Paul's sympathetic understanding.

Ruth responded with uncomplicated affection. Living alone, going nowhere by her own account after Frances put a stop to her Southgate outings, and possessing no family life of her own, she entered enthusiastically into Paul's, sending greetings for Christmas and birthdays, picturing family holidays, and sharing his pleasure in the new car which she named 'Little Bentley' ('I consider her my very own godchild, as I moved the bidding for a name in the beginning').[95] The only cloud hanging over aunt and nephew was the possibility of Paul's mother's reappearance, which filled both with apprehension. Frances Scott, now almost totally blind, widowed for the second time in 1963, made tentative approaches to Paul, which he rejected on the grounds that he would never again allow a wedge to be driven through his household. 'I do not feel myself divisible from my wife and family in this way,' he wrote to a social worker who had reproached him for failing to respond to a Christmas card from his mother: '. . . its receipt can, I think, only aggravate the sense she has of this divisibility, & in the long run such an aggravation would be more harmful to her than otherwise. Since the death of her second husband she has, as I know from my brother, been completely on her own and it is only natural that her thoughts should bend more acutely to the idea of reconciliation. But reconciliation with whom? With me alone?'[96]

It was a firm and courageous statement of an allegiance from which, in his own mind, Paul never wavered. People who met him in the last two decades of his life were left in no doubt as to his pride and affection for his children, his absolute dependence on his wife: one of the first things that struck new friends was always his devotion as a family man. After he left agency, his favourite form of professional entertaining was to lay on an outing for four: himself and Penny, the guest and his wife – Roland and Nadia Gant, John and Fern Willey, the Sansoms on a visit from Tasmania, Paul's Swedish translator Magnus Lindberg and his wife Gunilla – often driving the party out for lunch to country pubs like the Cock at Cockfosters, the French Horn or the Compleat Angler on the river at Marlow. Paul's hospitality on these occasions was overwhelming ('One had to struggle to keep up,' said John Willey),[97] sometimes almost as much so to Penny as to their guests: 'I remember Penny gushing her appreciation to Paul,' wrote John Willey, 'as if he were Zeus giving ambrosia to the Olympian family.' The Scotts and Willeys shared the same wedding anniversary ('If that isn't an omen of togetherness, I don't know what is,' said Paul),[98] a bond on which the two men congratulated themselves and each other annually by cable on 23 October.

Throughout the twenty years that they worked together, John Willey remained everything an author might desire in a publisher. Considerate, obliging, ardently enthusiastic, he counted it a privilege to publish Paul, defending him stoutly in public and private ('I conceived of my job . . . as Paul's *amicus curiae* in the States, his champion and interpreter inside the house, particularly to the sales department'),[99] and apologising with charm and delicacy to Paul himself for the repeated failure of American reviewers to appreciate, American readers to buy or Morrow to sell his books. There was no trace in Willey of that faint bracing note of reproof, the severe and disinterested critical penetration that stimulated and alarmed Paul in Maurice Temple Smith. Their climactic confrontation in November 1961, which had sent Paul straight home to shut himself in the garage with his car engine running, had culminated in Paul's demanding and getting Maurice's honest opinion as to what was wrong with his work. 'He put it rather well,' Paul reported to Willey a month later, when he had recovered his composure. 'He said he always expected me to do something really terrific . . . but that there was a kind of membrane in the books, the final membrane I might never break through but he thought I would.'[100] Maurice predicted great things provided the blockage could be cleared, and Paul cordially agreed: 'I see my job now as wholly devoted to the business of trying to break through it.'

But Paul's resolution did not prevent him feeling uneasy about Maurice's discernment, and Maurice's feeling that, for all its brilliance, *Birds* was not the book in which he had pulled off his breakthrough. It was published on 9 April 1962, as a Book Society

Choice, to excellent reviews ('the best overall press I've ever had'), and confirmed Maurice's premonition by selling 10,000 copies in its first few months, then stopping dead at between a half and two thirds as many copies as the *Pavilion*. The manuscript of *The Bender*, finished, typed and delivered to Eyre & Spottiswoode the same month, produced yet more of Maurice's disconcerting frankness ('I did not conceal from him that I didn't think it as good as his previous work').[101] Paul, always especially touchy about *The Bender* as he had been with *A Male Child*, was unpleasantly conscious of how often Maurice had proved right before. His dissatisfaction came to a head in negotiations that summer for a new three-book contract, when Eyre & Spottiswoode declined to commit themselves to a joint guarantee arrangement designed to lighten the load on Morrow. By June 1962 Paul had moved with *The Bender* to Secker & Warburg in the Heinemann publishing group, where he was warmly welcomed by his oldest friend in the publishing world, Roland Gant ('If things did not come full circle, a parallelogram had been described,' wrote Roland,[102] for Paul at Higham's had placed novels for Roland's wife, Nadia Legrand, while acting simultaneously as agent for Roland, who had himself published Penny's books in his previous job at Michael Joseph). Secker agreed to pay £2000 (or double Paul's last advance) on each of his next three novels, to be delivered at eighteen-month intervals, and also to produce £400 for a return visit to India. The Morrow guarantee was reinstated. Paul faced the future without the equivalent of a publishing *duende*, whose critical intelligence had always been able to get under his skin: 'I was not rich enough to give him the money,' said Maurice Temple Smith, 'and yet I wasn't dishonest enough to tell him it was a wonderful book.'

The Bender appealed to fellow freelances, who knew what it meant to live from hand to mouth without salary, security or future prospects, hardened customers like Peter Green ('*howlingly* funny: I laughed till I cried') and Kay Dick (who took a connoisseur's pleasure in the masterly showdown between George Spruce and his bank manager).[103] But it got a different reception from Chris Almedingen to whom it was dedicated in recognition of her support when Paul left Higham's. The two had grown very close in these years: 'My dear Paul, You are Archduke/ King/ Emperor among friends!' she wrote[104] when he recommended her latest historical biography to Morrow. She read her proof copy of *The Bender* in mounting dismay, and wrote grimly to Paul on 22 September:

Now – what I have to tell you is rather difficult – and my only *point d'appui* is that I know I can trust your generosity and that you, as I flatter myself, can trust my honesty. I must refuse the great honour you have offered me. The refusal is not coloured by the least reflection on this book as such. . . . I admit that actuality, like Pico della Mirandola's image of truth, has myriads of aspects & that no author can honestly deal with any except those which answer his own inner truth – but – and I fear you will have to forgive me again – *do* George and all the others really belong to *your* truth?

What disturbed Chris Almedingen was the mixture of autobiographical truth and falsity in *The Bender*. She had talked to Paul sufficiently about his mother to understand that a rough sketch was probably as close as it was possible for him to come to that tricky subject, and she knew him well enough to identify the origins of George's suicidal depression, his treacherous retreats from reality, his inability to communicate with his family 'because in the end you could only talk to strangers and to the telephone'.[105] She also recognised the bleak account of his failed marriage, delivered in gin-sodden monologue to anyone prepared to listen in the bar of the club that might have been the Gargoyle ('The awful waste. Years of each other gone. Years you've spent not looking at the truth. Not talking to her any more because there's nothing to say'). She felt there was a fundamental dishonesty in *The Bender*'s portrait of George as, for all his self-castigation, a lovable drunken rogue, and that private weaknesses should not be exposed in public if they were to be so readily excused. 'Paul tried to see himself – to look in the mirror – but he didn't have the courage.'[106] She discussed the manuscript, and what to do about it, with a friend, Frances Pilkington, who argued that, once Paul had invoked Chris's critical judgement ('He must have known he shouldn't have done it'), he left her no alternative but to deliver a verdict. Behind her personal disapproval lay a dispassionate regret for the squandering of what had struck her from the first as highly unusual gifts. 'I'm not really an introspective novelist,' Paul wrote to John Willey,[107] tacitly conceding the point which both Chris Almedingen and Maurice Temple Smith had tried to put to him: that, so long as he permitted himself the emotional half truths and evasions that weaken *The Bender*, he would continue to find his access blocked as a writer to the fund of compassion and broad objective understanding both recognised in him as a man.

After painful deliberation, Chris Almedingen travelled up to town to tell Paul in person what she thought of him. 'She felt the whole book was a prostitution of his talent,' said Frances Pilkington: 'she told him he knew it: and she told him what it cost her to be saying this to him.' The meeting was not a success. Penny was appalled, indignant,

heart by what was in the circumstances a cruel rejection, even –
perhaps especially – if it confirmed his own misgivings. He had
admitted Chris too far into his confidence, relied too heavily on her
Russian warmth, to have realised the need to protect himself against
her obdurate Russian pride. She made what amends she could but, in
spite of increasingly urgent pleas, heartfelt tributes and a last
valedictory lunch at the Epicure, the friendship faltered and failed.
Paul could not forgive her ('and *she* did not recover for many years,'
said Frances Pilkington). He dedicated *The Bender* instead to David
Higham (who proved more than happy to accept it, having himself
dedicated his last novel to Paul), together with his wife and children,
particularly Ben, who was Paul's godson.

Chris Almedingen was not the only reader to detect in *The Bender*
an attempt to keep abreast of contemporary trends, a suspicion all the
more hurtful because it was not wholly unjustified. George Spruce's
much younger brother Guy is a rapidly rising young playwright of the
fashionable kitchen-sink school, singled out by Kenneth Tynan for his
success with *A Pram in the Hall*, and hoping to bring off another hit
with *The Geyser*. *The Bender* was greeted on publication by a message
from Laurence Olivier, always on the look-out for fresh conquests
after his Royal Court triumph in John Osborne's *The Entertainer*,
who sent to say he was 'mad about playing George'.[108] Paul himself
was uneasily aware of his reputation as a lightweight with no
individual voice of his own, still saddled in his forties with what he
called 'that "steadily improving" and "could do better next term"
attitude'.[109] His childhood and youth had left him acutely sensitive to
real or imagined slights on the score of his background: 'it amuses me
and also saddens me a bit to realise just how much the agency stigma
still sticks to me when it comes to the Literary Establishment,' he
wrote to Gerry Hanley: 'I shall never be accepted by them.'[110] The
problem was partly literary snobbery, partly the company he kept,
partly also an inveterate curiosity which made him reluctant, in time of
sharply opposed and vociferously warring aesthetic factions, to
commit himself to one camp or another. His stint as reviewer on the
New Statesman might have conferred a measure of intellectual
respectability if he had not immediately agreed to stand in for Howard
Spring, in place of the regular understudy Richard Church, on that
staidest of snugly conservative organs, *Country Life*. 'Apparently old
Dick always takes over from old Howard when the latter is taking time
off. So now old Paul steps in,' he wrote cheerfully to Peter Green in
April 1962: 'Makes me feel my age.'

He was still seeing Muriel Spark that spring: she promised him a
birds-of-paradise quilt for his bed if her own play proved a hit in the

West End, but turned down his invitation to speak at the Writers Summer School at Swanwick in Derbyshire.[111] This was the first creative writing course in the country, founded in 1948, held annually, and open to all-comers, which in practice meant amateurs. Paul's own first talk had been such a success in 1959 that he came back two years running, bringing his family with him, as host for the whole week: his official hostess in 1961 was the romantic novelist Jean Plaidy (in 1962 it was Penny), and the school's chairman was Vivien Stuart, one of Mills & Boon's most prolific and popular sellers. Paul liked Swanwick precisely because it represented the opposite end of the book world from the showing-off, snobbery and cut-throat competitiveness of literary London, but it was characteristic that, having been roped in by what Swanwick's chairman briskly called 'the poor old cardigan brigade',[112] he made a point of turning up in August 1962 dressed in a way calculated to upset them. 'I couldn't believe the change in him,' said Paul's old opponent, Gerald Pollinger, an ex-RAF officer who took his former colleague's casual clothes and relaxed approach ('no tie, long hair standing on his collar, hippie look') as a personal affront.

Paul danced the Twist, charmed the students and made them laugh, laid himself out to be an indefatigable and irresistible host. 'The women flocked to him,' said Penny: 'He was the cat's whiskers, he was the bee's knees, always the centre of a group.' He was drinking harder than ever – 'This may not have been especially noticeable because Penny kept things running smoothly for both of us '[113] – sparkling in public, collapsing in his room after each session, slumped down with glazed eyes, silent, insensible, untouchable. He was thinking that autumn of reviving *The Careerist* as a follow-up to *The Bender*, and feeling his way into the character of his heroine, Guy Spruce's sexy, scruffy, long-haired, half-Indian girlfriend, Anina. Paul was specially attached to Anina on account of her failed ambitions as a poet, her habit of hitting the gin bottle, and the eternal identity crisis caused by her mixed parentage. He had put her in, then cut her out of the *Birds*, only to find she reappeared in *The Bender*, pestering him thereafter so persistently that he half hoped at one point he might have found another mining-tool, like the kris or the birds of paradise.[114] One part of Paul identified with Anina ('Very few people have realised she was a poet manqué,' he wrote fondly to Clive), while another suspected she might easily become a bore. He had for some time been groping towards a large-scale, possibly sequential work ('if the London novels catch on, perhaps they will one day form a complex'),[115] but it was not until the end of the year that he finally gave up the idea of setting it in London. 'To breath fresh air east of Suez might unblock all kinds of barrels', he had written longingly a year earlier.[116] By December 1962 he had the makings of a Far Eastern story 'The Panther House', which he told John Willey might 'one day develop into the really big book I want to write about the British in India'.

When Peter Green announced his decision to break loose, leave England with his wife and three children and settle to serious writing on the Greek island of Lesbos, or Mitylene, Paul warmly approved. Each had simultaneously reached a crisis, in Paul's case the last of many: 'Came the end of 1962 . . . I had to give myself a long straight look in the mirror.'[117] It meant reining himself in more severely than ever ('a tight money-string, a tighter time-string'), once again stripping down commitments, reducing his load as a publisher's reader, resigning from *Country Life*, refusing Peter's column on the *Daily Telegraph* ('God knows I need the money'), producing a new novel in twelve months flat, and returning at last to India at the beginning of 1964, after which he would decide once and for all whether he could live by writing and, if not, abandon the attempt in favour of a regular job. 'I don't lack confidence in what I can do, only in what is going to happen to it. And being patient and not lacking confidence in myself seems to involve cutting my short-term throat about reviewing.' Cutting his throat, even metaphorically, as he looked at himself in the mirror was a return to the old, familiar, self-destructive urge which was now to be curbed and exploited. Violent impulses require violent discipline, or, as Paul wrote to Peter on 25 April 1963, wishing him well in his Greek exile: 'This – to put it crudely – is my shit-or-bust year.'

He spent it, as he had spent the year before, shut up in his study, 'lost to the land of the living (except agent, publisher & postman)',[118] wrestling with his current novel *The Corrida at San Feliu* which had grown from a visit to the local bullfight on the family's holiday the summer before at Tamariu. Paul was also struggling with a tide of ill health which had been creeping in for some time and now threatened to swamp him. His drinking had for the last two or three years alternated with crash diets in which he sporadically attempted to give up gin altogether, or substituted alternatives like vodka or whisky. Whatever was wrong with his insides – the Bengal trots, Belgaum tummy, Spanish tummy – got steadily worse. He was prostrated with back ache, which he hoped was lumbago or writer's spine, but feared might be 'something like cancer, which my doctor always says is indigestion'.[119] By the beginning of 1963, he reported himself barely able to eat. 'Not well (ulcers) & I am on a kind of starvation diet, eating only certain things & all of them terribly slowly,' he wrote to his Aunt Ruth in April, and to Gerry Hanley, proposing a reunion in August: 'Maybe not curry. My insides are tender. Cancer of the womb, I think!'[120] Sometimes it felt like malaria, at others more as though he were dying. Roland Gant, who had some experience of tropical diseases, having contracted one himself during the war, took to ringing up daily to monitor the state of Paul's bowels and his mind. His sufferings were part of the characteristic, accelerating cycle of amoebiasis: acute stomach pain, perpetual cold in the lumbar regions, uncontrollable irritability, lassitude, depression and chronic inability to finish anything (all but the first two symptoms would be faithfully reflected in the *Corrida*'s hero, Edward Thornhill). His only hope of easing the pain, or nerving himself to make further effort, came from liquor but it was a dangerous remedy, as he had forseen in the *Birds*:

The alcohol he drinks in such terrifying quantities has an effect of brightening and darkening his eyes instead of filming them over. However drunk he is, he never slurs his speech, never throws himself about or has that look of the drunk, that look of wires and cables collapsing under the weight of the body they're meant to hold upright ... His body transforms liquor into pure energy. Finally the energy becomes more than even his body can stand.[121]

Throughout the twelve months of 1963, it was as if Paul's book were running a race with his health. He cancelled his return visit that summer to Swanwick, emerging from the study for publication of *The Bender* in April (reviews were respectful but sales discouraging), and again in September for what he described as 'the most disastrous holiday we've ever had'[122] (a car accident even before they reached Tamariu was compounded by two weeks of driving rain, thunder, lightning and floods that made the roads virtually impassable). The Scotts never returned to Tamariu, or took another family holiday, and Paul swore he would not go back again by himself to the States after a trip to New York for Morrow's launch of *The Bender* on his wedding anniversary, 23 October. The date had been carefully chosen by Willey but Paul, already homesick on the voyage out, said he had never felt lonelier in his life, in spite of a characteristically hospitable New York round of lunches, dinners, cocktails, outings and parties ('Don't know that I can stand much more of all this being entertained. On the other hand, can't bear to be alone').[123] He lunched with Muriel Spark, who showed him Greenwich Village, and confided something of his despondency to his American agent, Ivan von Auw's partner, Dorothy Olding, who was especially fond of Paul and did what she could to console him. He spent a weekend in Connecticut with the Willeys, who marvelled at how much he missed his family, and the importance he attached to telephoning Penny on 23 October.

New York City itself struck him as unfriendly and claustrophobic ('Towards the end I had fearful fantasies of not being allowed to leave, and a series of awful nightmares').[124] His disorientation was exacerbated by hot weather, exhaustion, disappointment over the muted reception of *The Bender*, and anxiety about the unfinished book he had left behind him. He ticked off the days until his flight home like a prisoner serving a sentence. He longed to escape back into *Corrida* but work was impossible in New York, and even in London he found his route blocked by a letter from Kay, whose own desperation had reached a pitch that summer at which she, too, had attempted suicide. Paul, who had neither visited nor written to her in hospital, sent her on 3 November a long, difficult, painfully honest letter acknowledging his second, precipitate retreat into silence and evasion ('there are occasions in life when I feel incapable of contributing anything that will help the other person'). Kay's crisis had come when he himself was struggling to write about an author brought so low by inability to finish his book that he eventually kills himself, as one or more characters had tried to do in all but the first of Paul's novels (suicide was the fate he had originally intended for both Tom Gower in *The Alien Sky*, and Bill Conway in *The Birds of Paradise*).[125]

Paul had spent the better part of 1963 'thinking myself into being Thornhill'[126] in *Corrida*. Handsome, distinguished, bronzed and fit, Edward Thornhill in his late fiftics has won every glittering prize success can offer an author: fame, wealth, leisure, critical acclaim, a beautiful wife and a seaside villa in Spain ('Playa de Faro is really Tamariu,' Paul wrote to Roland Gant,[127] explaining that he had drawn the Thornhills' villa, the couple in the local bar and the bullfight itself directly from life). He has nothing to do except write in the mornings, and drink a bottle of champagne every day before lunch. But he turns out to be secretly riddled by jealousy and self-doubt, locked in the kind of 'agonising reappraisal' Paul was undergoing himself, brooding over his life, his work, his drinking, the paralysis of feeling and will that prevents him from finishing his book, or making any move to repair the burnt-out shell of his marriage. He pictures himself as a wounded bull, or alternatively as a matador ('to be judged not only on the sublime poetry of a series of tenderly confusing veronicas, nor merely on the skill and grace and fine male arrogance of a set of well and dangerously placed banderillas, but pre-eminently on the sad passion, the punishing absolution of his performance in the faena').[128] The book ends with a bullfight after which Thornhill dies, driving homeny move to repair the burnt-out shell of his marriage. He pictures himself as a wounded bull, or alternatively as a matador ('to be judged not only on the sublime poetry of a series of tenderly confusing veronicas, nor merely on the skill and grace andf the picadors fell off his horse, another left his pic in the bull, and none of the Spaniards in the crowd could apparently tell which of the matadors was Ernest Hemingway's protégé, the great Antonio Ordonez.[129] Paul, who had not the faintest idea what was happening, said he mugged up the technical terms from a handbook when he got home, although plainly his heart was not in it ('Is my heart anywhere but in India?' he had written on the first page of his first *Bender* notebook).[130] But something like his authentic note as a novelist emerges intermittently, superimposed on fake Hemingway, in Thornhill's Indian story 'The Arrival at Mahwar', or his unromantic glimpse of himself from outside as a hot, cross, perspiring tourist in crimson shirt and blue terylene trousers, unable to make head or tail of the bullfight.

Corrida, originally subtitled 'The Spanish Papers of Edward Thornhill', consists of four separate short stories and an autobiographical fragment, supposedly cobbled together after the author's death from a mass of manuscript scraps and abandoned jottings, with an explanatory preface. Its separate sections transpose and reflect long-standing themes (rejection, betrayal, suicide, disgrace, fraternal rivalry over a woman), but it also looks forward to something quite different. Thornhill's major work is a trilogy of colonial novels, written over a decade – *The District Officer*, *The Commissioners*, *The Administrators* – and he remains fascinated, as he watches the tourists in his Spanish resort, by the English abroad: 'These were my lost administrators . . . a dead race now; as dead as the last Romans in a no-longer savage Britain, lifting their patchwork togas to keep them clear of the mud of an amoral civilisation; keepers of the old conscience, puzzled now, beginning to be defensively acquisitive.'[131]

The *Corrida* was finished and typed by the end of December 1963. 'You will see all of me in this,' Paul said to Kay Dick.[132] He was forty-three years old and he had produced eight novels, none of which had hit any kind of commercial jackpot or done more than scratch the surface of the kind of book he still felt he had it in him to write. Even close friends, who knew or guessed the strength of his ambition, sometimes wondered if he had not overrated his powers. His loyallest supporters could not feel especially sanguine about the long-postponed trip to India, now scheduled for February 1964. 'I know that David feels I have scraped the bottom of my barrel on India,' Paul had written two years earlier when he was first beginning to envisage 'a big scale novel about the British force and influence'.[133] He could hardly have picked a less promising subject at a worse time. Imperial India, still the more or less exclusive preserve of romantic or adventure novelists, was tacitly agreed by serious critics to be a subject on which E. M. Forster had long ago said the last word. The response to any attempt to reopen

Paul's own dustjacket drawing for the
Corrida, *showing the heroine of one of
Edward Thornhill's stories playing out the
role of picador with her husband/lover
transformed into the bull: the design was
rejected by the publisher for being sexually
too explicit.*
ABOVE RIGHT *Jacket for* The Birds of
Paradise *in 1962: Paul knew, when this book
was finished, that he could not write about
India again without revisiting the
subcontinent.* RIGHT *Indian flag on the
jacket of* The Jewel in the Crown *(1966).*

it was nearly always instinctively hostile, dismissive or ribald. One of Paul's best stories described Hermione Gingold making an entrance on a London stage after the war as a lady lecturer, hitching up a shoulder strap and announcing her topic – *India* – whereupon the whole audience burst out laughing.[134]

He knew perfectly well that going back to India struck sensible people as pointless, at best faintly absurd, at worst an admission of failure as a serious novelist. But his mood was not so much frivolous as grim. For Paul the trip was a last desperate gamble, one he had put off as long as he could and risked now only because he could see no alternative for himself as a writer. He told a reviewer, when *Corrida* came out, that in retrospect he realised he had for years been 'acting out Edward Thornhill without quite knowing it'.[135] Friends, colleagues, readers who knew him even slightly must have recognised Paul himself, standing behind Thornhill, as he compares a picture of his younger self with the face he sees in the mirror:

Even with the face in repose, with the eyes shut, I can feel the depth of the lines from the outer flesh of each nostril to the corresponding corner of the mouth. They are lines of inquiry and rejection, and have deepened in the flesh as the flesh has thickened and coarsened. . . . Those poet's eyes are now the eyes of a writer of prose, and that youthfully pro-consular nose the nose of a man who remembers every smell there is. It is the face of a man ruined by his own curiosity.[136]

OPPOSITE   *Marine Drive, Bombay*

PART THREE

1964–1978
Defeat into victory

CHAPTER ELEVEN

Passage to India

Paul flew to Bombay on Monday 24 February 1964, landing soon after dawn next day and registering all the usual tourist reactions: the magic of the flight itself, a first sniff of the east in Beirut, a second in Bahrain, the shock of the shanty towns outside Bombay airport with labourers squatting in the fields, heat rising even at that early hour of the morning, kite hawks scavenging and screaming overhead.[1] But he had not come as a tourist. He had no hotel bookings, no holiday plans or fixed engagements (except for a long-standing promise to look up his old havildar, Narayan Dass, now headman of his village in Andhra Pradesh), nothing but the loosest possible itinerary. He planned to stay two months, visiting the south for the first time, taking in places he had never seen – Madras, Benares, Lucknow, Kanpur, Agra, Jaipur – as well as Calcutta and Delhi, flying home on 17 April via Moscow with a stop in Stockholm to call on his Swedish publisher.[2] He knew why he had come and roughly where he was going, if not precisely what he was looking for, or how to describe what he wanted to his Indian hosts, who had never met anyone like him.

He had no job, no regular prospects, none of the hippie's incuriosity in the present or the sahib's nostalgia for the past. He wasn't interested in seeing the sights or fraternising with the British (the few he came across were mostly commercial developers, businessmen, engineers, out on contract without any particular interest in or connection with India). His own contract, if he had one, was too vague for words. He told anyone who asked that he had come to recharge his batteries. The closest he got to defining his purpose was probably in retrospect through images like the subtropical garden with its cropped lawns, regimental beds of canna lilies and wild tangled undergrowth, which might serve equally well as a metaphor for India, the Raj and its historical roots, or for the writer himself and the works he hoped to produce:

The range of green is extraordinary, palest lime, bitter emerald, mid-tones, neutral tints. The textures of the leaves are many and varied, they communicate themselves through sight to imaginary touch, exciting the finger-tips: leaves coming into the tenderest flesh, superbly in their prime, crisping to old age; all this in the same season because here there is no autumn. In the shadows there are dark blue veils, the indigo dreams of plants fallen asleep, and odours of sweet and necessary decay, numerous places layered with the cast-off fruit of other years softened into compost, feeding the living roots that lie underneath the garden massively, in hungry immobility.[3]

This painterly passage comes from the novel which grew directly out of Paul's return to the subcontinent, *The Jewel in the Crown*. The garden of the MacGregor house in Mayapore is the first thing noticed by the book's narrator, the anonymous Stranger – more of a device than a character – who also visits India in 1964, representing the writer at his most impersonal, asking questions, effacing himself, groping patiently towards a story which only slowly and tentatively comes into full view. Paul, like the Stranger, was endlessly inquisitive in India, observant, attentive, absorbent. More than a decade of reading, reflecting and writing about the end of the Raj had produced fertile ground, carefully prepared, well watered, ready to receive impressions as they came at random out of the air – from other people, chance encounters, accidental connections – seeding themselves in his imagination, and sprouting almost as soon as he got home into rich, dense and prodigiously complicated growth.

Paul was welcomed on that first morning at Bombay airport by P. C. Manaktala, the managing director of Allied Publishers, Heinemann's Indian distributors, who had been asked to find people prepared to put him up in Bombay, Madras and Calcutta. A host in Bombay had proved hard to locate until one of Mr Manaktala's colleagues consulted an old friend who, on the strength of her admiration for *The Birds of Paradise*, immediately invited its author to stay. Her name was Dorothy Ganapathy, and she lived in a roomy flat overlooking the dusty grass of the Oval maidan, fringed by coconut palms, garlanded with crimson bougainvillea, not far from the sea in the old Fort district at the heart of the city. Paul reached 3 Queen's Court with Mr Manaktala just before breakfast on a day of brilliant heat, still carrying the overcoat he had brought with him from a cold grey London winter.[4] He was met at the door by the cat Beauty, a small and normally reserved Siamese who leapt into his arms to inspect him before being caught and shut up with apologies by her mistress. Paul begged and was granted a reprieve for the cat. 'At first we were reserved,' said Mrs Ganapathy. 'That first week we were stiff and diffident: he as to whether he should ask me questions, me whether I should tell the truth or not. We were fencing.'

These were the formal preliminaries to an exchange which would last a lifetime. The two fell warily but with steadily increasing confidence into a detailed, free-ranging, mutually absorbing conversation about India which they would break off and take up again, arguing, explaining, confirming and confounding one another on paper and in person in Bombay, Delhi and London. Paul said afterwards that he had felt at home from the start in Dorothy Ganapathy's flat. To her he seemed 'like someone who had lived in India all his life, been home for a holiday and come back. Nothing was strange to him.' Paul came to feel as if he had always known her, while she for her part treated him with the affectionate indulgence of an aunt for a favourite nephew. Perhaps she reminded Paul faintly of his own Aunt Florrie. Dorothy Ganapathy was far more sophisticated, better educated – she had gone on from her convent school (where the name Dorothy had stuck instead of her given name, Draupadi) to Durham University and the Sorbonne – more widely travelled and better read, but at bottom she had something of the same courage and forthrightness.

She was the daughter of a distinguished lawyer, Sir Hary Singh Gour, educated at Edinburgh and Cambridge, himself the founder of Saugor University. Her husband, who had been medical officer of health for Bombay, had died young soon after the war, leaving her to make her own way on the hard path of a childless Hindu widow. She had set about it by taking in a couple of young men as lodgers (the current pair doubled up in 1964 to make room for Paul), and teaching herself to work the stock exchange, manipulating a tiny capital with conspicuous financial acumen. 'Politics and figures are my life,' she said, recognising that Paul's interests were not essentially political, and that he listened to the speeches broadcast on Budget Day, 29 February, for her sake more than his own. Dorothy read voraciously but neither she nor her friends were bookish people: 'I only dabble in the stock market, read and bash about,' she wrote[5] with characteristically misleading self-deprecation. She combined the impetuosity and pride of her Rajput warrior ancestry with a sense of sexual equality, an intellectual confidence and integrity by no means common among European women of her generation. She was small, upright, alert, with vivid, finely-cut features and delicate incisive gestures to match her firm, clear, forceful opinions. She had a curiosity as devouring as Paul's, a fierce temper and a smile of melting sweetness and gaiety.

Her own passionate love of her country responded unconditionally to his. She liked his courtesy, modesty, receptiveness, the ease and spontaneity with which he accepted the immoderately generous Indian hospitality Europeans often find baffling, if not positively suspicious. Paul took as much or more than he gave gratefully and with fascination. Life in Dorothy's circle still followed the sedate and civilised etiquette of a more leisurely, formal, hierarchical world with its emphasis on correct dress, official visiting lists, calls at Government House, its regular round of dinner, mah-jong or card parties, and bridge at the club in the afternoons. There were rituals for meeting, making friends, dropping in for drinks, the last especially precious since this was a time of prohibition in India ('As soon as you arrive in Bombay, search out a reliable doctor and get yourself certified as an alcoholic,' Paul advised another prospective traveller: 'That's the only way to get the hard stuff').[6] In an environment some might have found stifling, Dorothy had preserved an energetic spirit, a social verve and a broad practical perspective on relations between their two countries which Paul found invaluable.

Even her setting was richly symbolic. Queen's Road where she lived was lined with handsome, solidly-built, white or cream-coloured residential blocks put up between the two world wars. Her flat on the first floor was cool, airy, spacious, simply but comfortably furnished with polished stone floors and a garden of flowering or trailing plants – bougainvillea, cacti, sweet basil, geraniums – in tubs and pots on the deep shady verandah looking out over a pillared balustrade on the maidan or Oval with boys playing cricket where, as Paul said, the Raj had once played flat golf. The balcony faced directly across to the Victorian High Court, flanked on one side by the Public Works building and the stately Telegraph Office, on the other by Gilbert Scott's university with its majestic clocktower: great gothic piles from the high noon of empire originally built to command a view of the Arabian Sea which was cut off, sixty or seventy years later, by a range of scarcely less imposing art deco blocks, reflecting in their names – Queen's Court, Empress Court, Windsor House – the unclouded confidence of Imperial afternoon. 'Paul loved the sea,' said Dorothy Ganapathy: 'How often we would go together to the Gateway of India, or to Marine Drive. Hundreds of times.' The Gateway of India, built for the King Emperor George V, is a short walk from Queen's Road which runs parallel to Marine Drive along the curve of the western shore. Paul strolled down to the sea with his hostess on his first evening before dinner, and sat up afterwards talking with her and one of her young lodgers ('he talks and thinks in English') before retiring at midnight to jot down first impressions in his notebook:

The more I think & read & talk about Indian political (& social?) problems the more astonished I am at the old British attitude. Etc. It is difficult to put it into words, this sense I have of the British responsibility for lack of education & social advancement. We grafted a layer of highly sophisticated political behaviour & thinking on to those other layers of poverty & want. The two are hopelessly antagonistic, I should think. That is why it would be so interesting to stay with Dass in his village.[7]

E. M. Forster had recorded the same amazement and indignation more than half a century earlier, when he came across an imperial committee in Madras debating whether or not Indians might be trusted with a share in running their own country as civil servants.[8] Paul had read *A Passage to India* for the first time on his return to England in 1947, and he would read it again when he got home after this second visit. He had been utterly unprepared to find attitudes Forster encountered before the First World War still flourishing nearly twenty years after Independence. He admired *A Passage to India*, although he also had reservations (and would suffer, often unfairly, from comparison with it for the rest of his life), coming in the end to value it not primarily as a realistic novel, or even a social comedy, but for its powerful prophetic element.[9] Forster had grasped at an early stage the implications of a process that ended in the precipitate and humiliating retreat Paul himself had inadvertently witnessed as a young man. The more he pondered Britain's connection with India, and its tragically divisive conclusion, the more he insisted that responsibility could not simply be shelved or ignored because it no longer suited the British to claim it. The reckoning so tentatively begun with that first entry scribbled in Paul's Indian notebook on 25 February 1964 in Dorothy Ganapathy's flat would be completed, ten years and four novels later, with *A Division of the Spoils*, which starts with a party on Marine Drive in Bombay. One of the guests is the historian, Guy Perron, who feels that the past cannot be detached from the present and the future, and who reflects views that come close to his creator's as he prepares for the party in a flat like Dorothy's on Queen's Road:

Perron waited on the balcony and gazed across the Oval to the dark bulk of the Law Courts. For a moment – perhaps under the influence of that symbol of the one thing the British could point to if asked in what way and by what means they had unified the country, the single rule of law – he felt a pressure, as soft and close to his cheek as a sigh: the combined sigh of countless

TOP *View from Dorothy's flat in Queen's Court, Bombay ('Perron waited on the balcony and gazed across the Oval to the dark bulk of the Law Courts . . .')* LEFT *Dorothy Ganapathy with her husband just before the Second World War and* ABOVE *with the cat Beauty, who made Paul feel at home in Queens Court, Bombay in 1964.*

unknown Indians and of past and present members of the glittering insufferable raj.[10]

Paul saw almost nothing of the British that first week in Bombay. On Wednesday Dorothy gave a dinner party to introduce him to some of her closest friends ('we . . . discussed what everyone discusses in India: politics, partition, prohibition and Mr Morarji Desai'),[11] who laid on a crowded programme of entertainments, outings and parties. On Thursday Dorothy took him to call on Homi Banker, a senior official at the State Bank – 'a Parsee called (like Happy Families) Mr Banker', Paul wrote to Penny – who with his wife Nurgiz drove them out that evening at sunset to the Hanging Gardens on Malabar Hill, and to the five Towers of Silence where the Parsees of Bombay lay their dead, invisible and unvisited save by the vultures circling overhead. On Friday, a brilliant clear morning marking the first day of the spring festival or Holi, they took a boat with Mrs Banker from the Gateway of India to visit the ancient cave temples carved out of the steep rocky hillside on Elephanta Island in the bay. Paul counted 120 steps to the caves, where he gazed in silence at the great, grey Trimurti, the three persons or images of god: Brahma, Vishnu and Shiva (Creator, Preserver and Destroyer). He noted 'remarkable peace' on the face of the Preserver,[12] monolithic, foursquare, high as a house, staring out at the sunlit sea from the dark shadowy depths of his cave. Perhaps he also noted the skull and the snake of the Destroyer who erupted, according to the temple guide, in a lingam or column of fire to show that destruction has no beginning or end and is the greatest of the three processes, since the other two would be impossible without it. Paul sketched the stone lingam in his notebook, and brooded so long over Shiva's split selves that Dorothy bought him a little bronze image of the god dancing in a ring of fire.

Paul felt he had swung from one imaginative pole to the other that night at a memorable open-air performance of Chekhov's *Uncle Vanya* ('I came away . . . half convinced that the Indians are really strayed Russians'),[13] which he attended with two more of Dorothy's hospitable friends, Nello and Coocoo Mukerjee. The Bankers invited him to a Hindu wedding (a thousand guests or more by Paul's reckoning, and at least three thousand lights in the trees), the Mukerjees to a Chinese meal, the Manaktalas to Sunday lunch at the fashionable Sun'n' Sand Hotel on Juhu beach. Afterwards the whole party paid a call at Dorothy's suggestion on an Englishman in whose flat on Marine Drive Paul had his first encounter with the new breed of memsahib, embodied by two supercilious British women who seemed to have been struck dumb and deaf by the new arrivals. 'The air was icy, with me, too, because I came with Indians,' Paul wrote incredulously that night to Penny. 'It made my blood boil. You have to see this kind of thing to believe that it is possible. The commercial English here (& that's all they are) are even *allowed* to have a club to which Indians are not admitted. It's just like the old days. . . . The air of boredom and superiority was ridiculous, unbelievable. Well, I must not get hot under the collar. They were the first English I've met. But I don't think they were isolated examples.'[14]

Paul saw evidence of unofficial apartheid on all sides after this sobering incident: in the hotel 'permit rooms' which served forbidden liquor to thirsty Europeans, and the 'shacks' or beach bungalows belonging to foreign firms at Juhu where the British slipped away to drink on the tacit understanding that no Indian would receive an invitation ('How many ways are there of preserving a colour bar?' Paul wrote in his notebook). The Breach Candy Swimming Club was being picketed at the time of Paul's visit for sticking to the old 'Whites Only' rule. The famous Bombay Yacht Club had been closed down for turning even Indian princes away from its doors but Paul was assured that, if he were a member of Breach Candy, he would still not be allowed to take as his guest H.H. the Maharajah of Bharatpur (an old friend of Mollie Hamilton's with whom he planned to stay near Agra). The day before his visit to Juhu some of Dorothy's friends had invited him to a flower show. Memories of both episodes resurfaced in *The Jewel in the Crown*, when the Stranger finds the post-imperial British still operating an unacknowledged colour bar at the Mayapore Club, cold-shouldering Indian members in the lounge-bar just as they boycott social functions organised by Indians on the maidan:

There would seem to be an unwritten law among them that the maidan is no longer any concern of theirs. . . . You might ask one of them . . . whether she went to the flower show last month and be met with a look of total incomprehension, have the question patted back like a grubby little ball that has lost its bounce, be asked, in return as if one had spoken in a foreign language she has been trained in but shown and felt no special aptitude for: 'Flower show?' and to explain, to say to them, 'Why, yes, the flower show on the maidan', will call nothing forth other than an upward twitch of the eyebrows and a downward twitch of the mouth, which, after all, is voluble enough as an indication that one has suggested something ridiculous.[15]

Shocked and shamed by his compatriots, Paul had been further taken aback by Dorothy and her friends who, in spite of his remonstrations in the car coming away from Marine Drive, politely pretended they had noticed nothing amiss. Later, Paul and Dorothy would discuss the subject by fits and starts as the Stranger does with his

Rajput hostess, the elderly widowed Lili Chatterjee in the *Jewel*. Lady
Chatterjee's detachment, candour and kindness all come from
Dorothy as do some of her turns of phrase – 'bash off', 'have the other
half' – and her philosophical attitude to the rudeness and arrogance of
European women both under and after the raj ('They're mostly lumps.
In *those* days they were nearly all harpies').[16] Paul would dedicate his
novel to Dorothy, who found herself on publication so often asked if
she had sat for Lady Chatterjee that eventually she put the question to
Paul. 'Well, Dorothy, every character has to start from some human
being,' he said, reminding her that when she first read the manuscript
she had felt as if she already knew the people in it. She took him to
mean yes and no.[17] What is certain is that, by the time Paul left
Bombay on 3 March 1964, Dorothy had given him his starting point, a
jumping-off ground and a base to which he would return in fact and
fiction over the next decade. 'I think it may be a successful trip,' Paul
wrote, sounding a confident note for the first time to Penny on his last
night in Dorothy's flat. Her parting present to him next morning was a
little silver Ganesh – Ganpat or Ganapathy – the elephant god, giver of
good luck, prosperity and wisdom, the granter of boons and remover
of obstacles whom Paul had first invoked when he left Highams four
years earlier, and who would preside with his namesake, Dorothy
Ganapathy, over *The Jewel in the Crown* and the three novels that
followed it.

Paul left for Madras, watching the country turn from lion colour to
green as the plane flew south, and stepping out into a solid wave of
heat that made even the simplest errands exhausting. 'I have to go
everywhere by taxi,' he wrote to Sally two days later, '& stagger from
one to the other like the soldier reporting to General Custer in the
American Civil War.' He was met at the airport by Mr Ullal of Allied
Publishers, and put up in Madras by a wealthy businessman, P. L.
Kumar, and his wife who was Mrs Manaktala's sister. The Kumars
lived in a comfortable, capacious, well-appointed bungalow in the
residential district of San Thomé: 'Norrice Lea with palm trees and
heat' Paul wrote home unkindly (the inhabitants of Norrice Lea in
Hampstead Garden Suburb were thought by less affluent neighbours
to have altogether more money than taste). His hosts were considerate
but hardly seemed to know who he was (Mrs Kumar had to ask his
name on the first day), and he felt uncomfortable in a provincial
atmosphere at once stiffer and sleepier than bustling, cosmopolitan
Bombay. The household itself seemed in some ways more English than
Indian, except for the bearers who called him Master, offered to clean
his shoes or button his braces ('Quite like old times!'),[18] and pursued
him with a stream of raj stories about ghostly colonels and captains

they were convinced any English sahib must know. Paul, tired and strung up after his week in Bombay, was beginning to feel slightly unnerved by what seemed to him, fresh from egalitarian England, thoroughly dubious nostalgia for an Imperial past he thought had long since been disowned.

But he liked the sparrows that flew in and out as if they owned the house, the bougainvillea that spilled all over the garden, and the enchanting lizards that came out at night with big black bobbles for eyes and suction pads on their delicate transparent feet. He also rapidly revised his first unfavourable opinion of the Kumars, swapping music-hall memories with his host who had fond memories of the old pre-war London Palladium, and acquiring considerable respect for his hostess, an austere and disciplined woman of strict religious principles and unexpectedly liberal views, who made it a rule to fast on Mondays, and gave much of her time to voluntary work for the poor. Part of the reason for Paul's initial oppression in India was his obscure sense of being implicated in the human squalor that had survived British rule: Bombay's sprawling slum encampments, the hovels of the derelict with their terrible smell of ordure, had filled him with bitterness and shame.[19] Mrs Kumar's sister, Mrs Manaktala, told Paul that when she first reached Bombay from her native Punjab she had wept from horror and disbelief to see people reduced to such wretchedness.

The Kumars' friends came from the upper levels of the Madras business community, commercial or industrial managers, shipping magnates, high-ranking officials, many of them former civil servants under the British, sober, prosperous, conventional people who made Dorothy's more relaxed and cultivated, theatre-going friends seem almost raffish by comparison. They welcomed Paul at a continuous round of hot, sticky, over-formal, non-alcoholic evening parties (Madras, like Bombay, was the capital of a dry state) among guests to whom it was barely conceivable that any serious person could choose to write for a living. He found it hard to get used to the sexual segregation of even thoroughly Westernised Indian society (once he looked up from an interesting conversation with a young married woman to find, to his embarrassment, that he was the only man in the room), or the inquisitorial scrutiny of the few remaining British ('Funny how the English even abroad keep up that awful skin of reserve. You can feel them judging your social background, probing for it, & being careful not to be too friendly in case they come to the wrong conclusion. And who knows, you *might* be an Anglo-Indian').[20] He dined one night in a splendid bungalow, with fountains playing and coloured lights in the trees, belonging to the Sikh manager of the Southern Railways, and another with the general commanding the area (who turned out to be an old friend of Mollie's husband, Goff Hamilton) in the old Madras Artillery mess, an elegant colonnaded eighteenth-century building once inhabited by Warren Hastings (about whom Paul had planned ten years earlier to write a novel).

He visited the Kapaleswara Temple in Mylapore, and was taken by Mr Ullal to see the celebrated ancient shrines at Mahabalipuram where he drank coconut milk through a straw from the fresh, green, turnip-shaped nuts, and contemplated the vast sleeping stone Vishnu filling his tiny dim cell lapped by the waves on the seashore. But almost as soon as he reached Bombay, Paul had proposed cutting out visits to historic sites like Benares, Lucknow and Jaipur, and he left Madras after a week without ever seeing the great British stronghold of Fort St George. What interested him was not physical memorials or monuments but the past as a living root, running underground, throwing up and nourishing unexplained growths in the present. Perhaps his most significant encounter in Madras was with a Brahmin engineer called Golshran, an executive at the local English Electric factory whom he met and immediately liked at a party on Saturday night.[21] They discussed the causes and origins of racial prejudice, and the reasons for its tenacity. 'This man, almost my age, had a very good English friend whom he knew in England. Now that friend has come out to India and they are no longer friends because the Englishman has been caught up in the European colony,' Paul wrote to Penny on 8 March: 'Sorry to keep harping on this subject but it really amazed me.' The conversation confirmed from inside impressions already formed from observation in Bombay, and sowed another of the seeds that would grow in *The Jewel in the Crown*. Paul said that Golshran had been discreetly noncommittal about the English at first, confiding a deeper distress and sense of rejection only when pressed:

They are all right when they first come out, he said, but in six months they are spoiled because the others have got at them.

I stared, because what he said came straight out of E. M. Forster. He thought my stare one of disbelief.[22]

Paul accepted an invitation to see for himself at the English Electric factory, where he was shown round by a young engineer newly out from home ('He seems like a good man but will he be spoiled?'). In the management canteen, the British sat together at the top of the table with their Indian colleagues at the bottom, eating roast beef and Yorkshire pudding in a temperature of 100° Fahrenheit and an atmosphere so humid that the wallet in Paul's hip pocket was beginning after six days to come apart at the seams. He felt constraint and disapproval emanating from his countrymen at the top of the table, 'beefy engineers waiting to resist being put upon or in any way taken for a ride by Indians', and he got the distinct impression they felt he would regret having 'gone over' to the native side.

Paul looked forward with relief to leaving the next day, 10 March, for leafy Timmapuram in Andhra Pradesh, where he planned to spend nearly three weeks in the rustic retreat pictured for him in enchanting detail over the past few months in letters from Narayan Dass:

You must stay for one month in my home . . . it will be cool in my village. There are very big trees in my village. We have table electric fans in my home. When you come to my home we will both go to the next village in a double bullock cart; when the bullock cart is going – garland of brass to necks of the bulls which will make sweet sound. My village will be quiet and peaceful. You will enjoy plenty of Palm Toddy [whisky], fat chickens, eggs and fresh water fish.[23]

Indian friends to whom Paul mentioned his plan were unenthusiastic. They said he would be treated like a maharajah, and promptly changed the subject. He wondered if they suspected him of hankering after the bad old days when all sahibs were treated like royalty. Mollie Hamilton had been crisply dismissive ('2–3 weeks with the ex-Havildar will be, at a guess, two weeks too long unless you can brush up on the language').[24] But Paul longed more than ever to escape from the strain of being on his best behaviour, to lower his guard with an old friend, to relax and sort out impressions in tranquillity among the bowers of scented rose jasmine, Indian bean flowers and night queen creepers Dass had promised in his country garden. This village trip had been planned from the start as the centrepiece of Paul's exploratory journey across the subcontinent ('the rest is sight-seeing'),[25] to be balanced, after a short stop in Calcutta, by a stay in the palace at Bharatpur on the strength of Mollie's introduction. The first fortnight had been no more than a civilised and carefully cushioned preparatory phase: 'Bombay of course is Bombay, and not India at all,' Paul had reminded himself on his first night. His real initiation would take place in Timmapuram. He and Dass would sit under the peepul tree gossiping about their youthful exploits, and filling in subsequent developments (Dass had a wife and five daughters, the eldest of whom – born two years after Sally Scott – was already in need of a dowry at the marriageable age of fourteen: her father had commiserated with Paul in the past about the crippling expense of daughters, and responded with special enthusiasm to the title, *A Male Child*). They would open their hearts to one another: after dabbling in the shallows of middle-class modern urban life, Paul would submerge himself in the immemorial traditions of rural India.

Dass's wife had joined in the invitation, and Penny had strongly urged Paul to accept. It seemed a unique chance for him to mix with the people, to live simply and modestly among villagers still virtually untouched by the pace of twentieth-century change. Electricity had only recently reached Dass's village: no houses were as yet connected to the supply except his uncle's and his own, which boasted eight electric lights and a German radio as well as a portable fan. He owned a well and a primitive rice mill, and had started a palm-fibre business with his uncle, pressing Paul into service a few years earlier to enquire about outlets from London brush manufacturers.[26] Dass was Timmapuram's link with the outside world, an innovator and entrepreneur, president of the village council, a traveller to the big cities, the only man in the village who had joined the army and learned to speak and write English (Paul's rusty Roman Urdu was useless, as Mollie had suspected, for anything beyond simple army commands, and in any case the local language was Telegu). Dass's hero was Charles Dickens, whose story had fired him at school and from whom he drew inspiration for both Paul and himself: 'he succeeded and earned much in book writing some countless £s. His father was a poor Clerk, and sent Charles Dickens to shoe polish factory, from there his fate turned, and he came to the world as a good author. . . . I learn from him "Try and you will succeed".'[27] Paul had been drawn to Dass in the first place by his air of resolution and calm, cheerful efficiency. Over the years Dass had sent parcels of tea and glass bangles, promising to look out for tanned python skin to make belts or bags for Paul's daughters, and to lay on a cock-fight in Timmapuram to entertain his old master: 'our civilian exchange of letters had achieved from the beginning an intimacy that our military relationship had precluded and yet, curiously, had been founded on.'[28]

Paul hoped to expand the relationship in the domestic context he sorely missed in Madras. He had been especially depressed by a visit to Spencers department store – 'the Harrods of the Carnatic'[29] – which had traditionally catered to the British memsahib, supplying everything from groceries, glassware and gadgets to textiles and toys, from liquor to ladies' and gentlemen's tailoring. Spencers' customers seemed to Paul the female counterparts of the men he had met at lunch with Golshran ('To the English, India is an enervating place: you have only to look at the young matrons in the air-conditioned coffee room of Spencers in Madras, wives of technicians from Stevenage and Luton who seem a bit lost without their prams and cardigans, to know that they wish their husbands' contracts would soon end').[30] The contagious lassitude and indifference made him even more anxious to get away. He splashed out £4 or £5 at Spencers on a wickedly extravagant

Parker pen for Dass, with sweets for the daughters and a bottle of duty-free Chanel Number 5 for their mother. For himself, he laid in emergency stocks of 500 cigarettes and a bottle of Carew's gin, the last of his liquor ration, which he meant to eke out with illegal and highly intoxicating home-made palm toddy.

Paul boarded the overnight Howrah mail train on the evening of 10 March in a mood of joyful anticipation, having bidden farewell to the Kumars and refused their invitation to a last party, because he did not trust their servant to make sure he caught the train ('He was a devotee of Shiva the Destroyer'). Mr and Mrs Ullal escorted him to the station – 'They thought I was mad to go'[31] – and installed him in an air-conditioned sleeper. Dass was to meet him next morning on Elluru railway station so that the two might complete the last twenty or thirty miles to Timmapuram together by bus through the parched flat brown landscape of paddy fields fringed by toddy palms ('sticking up like brushes that have just finished sweeping subterranean chimneys')[32] past gaunt, primeval, mud-coloured water buffalo and occasional straggling mud-hut settlements. When the train drew into Elluru Dass was waiting, positioned outside Paul's carriage with military precision for a reunion full of military portents:

Startlingly, we were both dressed alike, as if still in uniform: cream-coloured slacks and pale green bush shirts. I embraced him. He submitted, standing to attention. 'Sir!' he shouted (the loudness of his voice was surely something new?) 'your hair has gone grey!' We had both imagined this meeting – this classic situation – for years but God knows what different pictures we had conjured of it.[33]

The Dass Paul encountered on Elluru station seemed in some ways more like the soldier he remembered – stocky, dignified, undemonstrative, invincibly competent and correct – than the much more unbuttoned character who had emerged in letters from India. It was immediately clear that fraternal informality was out of the question, nor would there be any leaping over artificial barriers of rank, religion or skin colour. Dass was a proud man whose prestige was bound up with having, like his father and grandfather before him, served under a British officer. In promoting him from naik to havildar twenty years earlier, Paul had greatly increased his consequence, and his corresponding obligations at home in the village. The continued connection with his former captain had been a source of enduring satisfaction: the prospect of an actual visit had enhanced his standing and raised expectations to a degree Paul soon realised he could not fulfil. The first shock was to find himself enthroned on an upright chair at the bus stop; a chair, with or without a white man sitting on it, was in itself an outlandish import in an Indian village where people squat, talk, eat, work and sleep on the earthen floor. The second was being obliged to occupy the whole front row of seats in the bus, with Dass at his back and the rest of the passengers crammed in behind.

Dass's house and his uncle's were the only two stone buildings in a village of 600 families. It consisted of three small bare whitewashed rooms with barred unglazed windows, thatched palm-frond ceilings and a separate kitchen in the mud-walled compound. Auspicious designs had been drawn in chalk on the floor of the verandah. 'N took his sandals off,' Paul wrote (he called Dass affectionately 'Narayanji', but could never persuade him to drop the 'sir' in return). 'I followed suit, removing socks and shoes. His eldest daughter appeared with a brass jug. Eyes downcast, she poured water over his feet and ankles and then over mine. Biblical ritual over, bare-soled, refreshed from the shins down, still holding up my trouser-legs like a paddler at Clacton, I followed N up the steps into the house.'[34] It came as a third shock to discover that, apart from two broody hens hatching turkey eggs in the back room, the entire house had been turned over to Paul. There was no sign of Mrs Dass who, as a good Hindu wife, could not be seen by any man but her husband: Paul realised as soon as he produced it that scent had been the wrong present. Four small daughters lined up in the living room with joined hands in the gesture of greeting, *namaste*, and filed out in silence clutching their sweets.

When Paul asked after the fifth and youngest child, Dass appalled him by saying she had died ten days earlier. It would have been an unthinkable breach of hospitality to put off his visitor, as a European host might have done in the circumstances, but Paul was shaken and hurt. 'I had thought of him as a friend, but he was treating me like a Sahib.'[35] He sensed that Narayanji was similarly shaken ('He made me feel . . . that after all these years I was a disappointment to him with my free-and-easy civilian manner, my protests about being given a chair in the open street, a bench to myself in the bus'). Paul was further dismayed, though by this time scarcely surprised, to find he was to eat alone on the single chair at the only table in the living room. The fan on the windowsill was turned on while he ate. In spite of the freshly plucked scarlet flower by his plate, he felt intrusive, expensive, unclean. His fork and spoon seemed to have been specially bought ('When I left perhaps they would be thrown away, and the whole house subject to rituals of purification'). The meal was served from behind by Dass's eldest daughter and his wife's unmarried sister, who covered their faces and fled when Paul turned to look at them. He slept through the sweltering heat of the afternoon, waking for tea and a walk through the village with his host:

He pointed things out to me. People watched us. It was a tour of inspection. My approval was being sought. Ideally I should have been armed with a walking-stick and a stock of questions. . . . I should have led, not followed, flourished the stick, invaded these people's privacy, turned things over, patted a child's head, cracked a prepared joke in the vernacular, and said, every so often, 'Splendid! Splendid!' . . .

But to me poor people struggling to survive in hard conditions are not children. They always strike me as far older, infinitely wiser, than myself. It is I . . . not they who need the smile of approval, of understanding, of recognition. . . . The defence against poverty, under-privilege, is dumb acceptance. India is a land of absorbent silence. N, I think, felt this too; but he had his duties as a host.[36]

Paul could never be sure about the unspoken communion with Dass that might or might not lie beneath their protests and counter-protests, their mutual bewilderment and incomprehension, as each stubbornly resisted the image projected on to him by the other. There were flashes of contact and contentment for both host and guest. Paul, for whom dusk and sunset remained always magical in India, loved the familiar ritual of bathing in the cool early evening in the walled compound under a fading turquoise sky pricked with stars, rinsing away the sweat and dust of the day with water fetched from the well and heated over an open fire ('Gratefully, reminiscently, I dipped brass scoops into copper cauldrons of hot and cold water'). That first evening, after another solitary meal, he and Dass sat together on the verandah, watched by the neighbours crowding into the compound below coming and going 'like members of a restless cinema audience who find the film amusing but finally incomprehensible'. It was so stifling indoors that Paul slept in the open with Dass beside him on a string bed or charpoy at the roadside, nudged awake by the wet noses of munching cattle, listening to the tinkle and creak of bullock carts, glad to escape from the ring of villagers waiting for him to put on a performance.

His dislike of being on display came to a head next morning, soon after first light, when he realised that Dass expected him to take a pot of water and squat in the fields to open his bowels like the rest of the village (Dass indicated that the use of toilet paper – 'all these people would laugh' – would outrage Hindu notions of cleanliness). Faced with a choice between being revolting or revolted, reluctant to pull rank or claim special privilege, Paul hoped that deference to his host's wishes would at least put paid to the notion of him as a sahib ('A sahib would have resisted; flourished the stick, selected a site, and got the chaps moving, digging a hole and erecting an enclosure').[37] But what was in theory a gesture of civilised compliance with the custom of the country felt in practice more like submission to Dass, who had tactfully mounted guard at a distance:

Soiled, angry, robbed of my human right to conduct my most private affairs in the way that suited me, I rejoined him on the road. The thought struck me that it had pleased him to humiliate me. I cast back in my mind for anything bad I had ever done to him: shouted at him in front of the men, refused him compassionate leave, docked his pay. Surely not?[38]

Washing his hands when he got home turned out to be another ritual observance that had to be postponed, so as not to offend Hindu susceptibilities, until total immersion at the end of the toilet. The second performance of the morning involved being shaved on the verandah before a crowd of inquisitive spectators by the barber or *nai*, who rejected Paul's shaving soap. 'Perhaps they thought there was cowfat in it. I didn't care. And I didn't see why I should be a sahib for part of the day, and a caste-Hindu when shaving and going to the loo. N couldn't have it both ways.' Resentful, edgy, off-balance, Paul refused to capitulate. Anger ('insisting on soap, I realised I had shouted') gave way to the terror of being blinded when the *nai*, having made a wretched mess of lathering Paul's chin, dipped his cut-throat razor in water and scraped it over cheeks, forehead and eyelids. By 8.30 a.m. on 12 March, less than twenty-four hours after his arrival in the village, Paul had written asking Ullal to send a telegram requesting his immediate return to Madras. 'It is an act of which I have never stopped being ashamed,' he wrote later,[39] but at the time he counted the days, reckoning that with the delay required for a train booking the weekend after next was his earliest possible release date.

Meanwhile every day began badly with the lengthy public performance Paul had reason to dread. By the time it was over, the sun had dispersed the cool of the morning. He was tormented by flies, bitten on his bare feet by ants and oppressed by the screeching of crows, 'enormous blue-black creatures with gun metal beaks'. Everything he did was closely observed by a small swarm of children – 'They are very sweet but oh god how they stare'[40] – who behaved as if they had never seen a white man before. Paul realised they probably hadn't, and hated himself for wanting to choke off their curiosity. 'I'm just no good at this with rifle and hound to Darkest Africa lark', he wrote ruefully to Penny. Jumpiness had set in with the shock of finding something nasty on his first evening in his dressing-gown pocket, 'sensing and then touching a dry sinuous creature', which turned out to be a large convulsive lizard. Paul imagined snakes concealed in the thatch dropping down on him from above, or a cobra rearing up in the dark from the path outside. 'Do not walk there, sir,' Dass warned him one night: 'at such times, in such place, snakes creep!'[41]

Paul had ricked his back on his last day with the Kumars in Madras, when he insisted on packing his bags himself instead of leaving it to the devotee of Shiva the Destroyer. He arrived limping in Timmapuram, and the limp got worse. Breakfast on his first morning turned his bowels to water. His amoebic infection flared up. He felt sick, and painfully aware of his unseen hostess toiling to produce copious meals of rice, dhal, goat's meat curry, which he sent back untasted. Dass offered castor oil, and Mrs Dass tried to tempt his appetite with stomach-churning oniony delicacies fried in clarified butter or ghee. He felt his fixed smile become strained then disappear altogether on embarrassingly frequent trips through the village to the stinking, insanitary but mercifully enclosed latrine attached to his host's rice mill. 'One's internal miseries could not be concealed from an observant population. I made that journey many times a day, with increasing hate in my heart. The hatred sprang from fear. I was afraid of being desperately ill, of never getting away, of dying in that dreadful place where I was treated like an animal.'[42]

Wherever he went he was set up and stared at like a zoo exhibit: obliged to hold court from the verandah at Timmapuram on a hard kitchen chair, perched on another while waiting interminably for buses that were never on time, ushered towards a third at the cock-fight illegally organised by the deposed local maharajah (Paul doubted if he had ever been more than a small landowner, or zemindar), whose mouldering palace seemed an anti-romantic parody of Krishi's in *The Birds of Paradise*: rundown, almost ruined, with empty cages that had once held tigers dotted round the grounds, and dilapidated, disused elephants' stables. The cocks tore at one another wearing specially fitted razor-sharp spurs, the crowd was controlled with whips by the 'maharajah's' two dissolute sons, Paul was installed with his feet in the cockpit on the seat of honour, which was beginning to seem to him in some moods no more than his due. He felt himself growing peremptory, exacting and querulous. At the toddy-tappers' village in the jungle, where he walked one dark night with Dass to collect a bottle of illicit liquor ('It tastes like drains'), his hosts produced a string charpoy:

There I sat alone in the middle of the clearing, feeling like Sanders of the River, watched of course by a circle of wide-eyed children, wearing – I realised – my Sahib face. Odd how that defensive look comes back to you automatically![43]

Paul would return again and again in fact and fiction, in lectures,

essays and articles to what he called 'Sahib's Face'. He defined it as a
mask of superiority which was also an essential protective covering
and, even at his lowest point in Timmapuram, he diagnosed the reason
for it as fear. On a trip with Dass to Elluru, near the end of his first
week, he said he could feel it clamping his features into a harsh,
illiberal mask he loathed and could not do without.[44] After six days in
the village, cut off from all contact with Europeans, unable to summon
help if he needed it, dependent on people whose thoughts and feelings
he could not fathom, whose language he did not speak, and whose
customs he found impossible to follow, he had grown timid and
unsure of himself. He was unbearably agitated by the noise, stench and
squalor, the press of people, the fly-ridden carcasses in the meat
market, the leper holding up his stumps at the window of the bus. He
could hardly take in what was happening to him, or the changes that
had already happened: 'Timmapuram was like heaven by comparison,
when we got back'. Sometimes he blamed Dass unreasonably for
inflicting such ordeals on his superior officer, at others he imagined
himself Dass's prisoner. He brooded on fantasies of escape and
incarceration, of never again seeing his passport which he had
entrusted to Dass for safekeeping. His back hurt, his right leg had gone
lame, his dysentery weakened him so much that at one point he
wondered if he were being punished for having defied Dass in the
matter of the latrine. He had no means of knowing the whereabouts of
the nearest doctor. His fear of dying and being buried or burned in
Timmapuram, like the Dasses' baby, alternated with the suspicion
that he had been lured there 'for some awful purpose which would
only be revealed when I announced that it was time for me to go'.[45]

Looking back two years later, he recognised paranoid delusions, but
at the time he understood only intermittently that he was losing his
grip on reality. Little things made him hysterical: when Dass criticised
him for smoking too many cigarettes, he said he would scream if he
didn't smoke. Before he came, he had worried about running short of
drink or cigarettes, but what he dreaded most in the event was finding
himself without ink and air-letter forms. He wrote daily, sometimes
two or three times in one day, on a note of rising panic to Penny. At
intervals he would remind himself who he was by dropping a fresh
bulletin – 'This letter is my link with everything familiar and dear to
me' – into a box on a post beside the dusty road, which gradually filled
up with his letters, and was emptied irregularly two or three times a
week. He longed for her replies, reading them over and over again,
although he found it hard to grasp her news about her own and the
girls' doings. Chill, dark, rainy London, people who spoke English and
possessed private bathrooms, 78 Addison Way and the family in it, all

seemed a cruel illusion in sunny Timmapuram. He turned to Penny as he always had done in times of misery and trepidation, swearing this was the last time he would leave her ('Never, never shall I voluntarily go away alone again'), making no further entries in his Indian notebook, recognising letters home as his only safety valve: 'I look at my surroundings sometimes & I feel I was MAD! to come here.'

But even in the thick of distress, as one side of him plunged helplessly into labyrinths of doubt and confusion, another side knew quite well what he was driving at. 'One day I shall probably look back on this visit and be glad not to have missed it.' After he had written *The Jewel in the Crown*, Paul would look back, as he had foreseen, and itemise some of the specific Timmapuram incidents he had drawn on in the novel. One of his pleasanter memories was a visit with Dass to a Hindu temple two miles away, the Tirupati Temple, to pay observance, or *puja*, to the Lord Venkataswara in the name of Vishnu the Preserver: Paul was allowed into the inner sanctum, where the priest poured coconut milk into his cupped palms, offered him a garland of roses, and made the red *puja* mark on his forehead. He would pass on the experience more or less intact to Daphne Manners in *Jewel*:

Daphne's visit, of course, was really mine (as was her suspicion that she had drunk cow's urine): and Robin White seated on the wooden chair being shaved and anticipating the razor cut that would blind him . . . was me. Even Miss Crane, seated on a chair by the roadside, on the morning she left Dibrapur with Mr Chaudhuri, and feeling like 'something in a zoo', was me. . . . In a way, too, the children she taught were mine.[46]

Robin White is the civilised, reflective Mayapore Deputy Commissioner, reaching the end of his Indian career (as a young man beset by apprehension, loneliness, bouts of dysentery, he had reluctantly acknowledged a defensive need for the Englishman's mask of superiority) with undiminished love and respect for the subcontinent and its people. Edwina Crane in the novel is an elderly mission-school teacher, who gives English lessons by teaching her Indian pupils the names of people and things in a picture of Queen Victoria with her Imperial subjects, called 'The Jewel in Her Crown'. Paul said that he got the idea from Dass's small nephew, Balarama Krishna, who would come with his friends every evening to learn English by identifying first the contents of Paul's room, then the pen-and-ink pictures he drew for them on paper.[47]

But whatever it was that Paul had sensed and felt in Timmapuram would work itself out on a deeper and more disturbing level than accurate reproduction of topographical or sociological detail. He said that memories of the meat market in Elluru lay behind the Chillianwallah Bazaar in the native quarter of Mayapore, where Hari Kumar goes to live with an aunt on his arrival from England.[48] Some sort of seed had been sown when Paul wrote to Penny on 17 March, the day after the trip to Elluru, that the 'whole thing has given me an idea for a short novel'. The emotional dislocation he described in Timmapuram – his impotence, his stupefaction, his feelings of being menaced, hemmed in and trapped – would all be recreated in Kumar's devastating initial experience of India, and his painful acclimatisation. It is gradually borne in on Kumar that the everyday physical horrors – dirt, din, heat, insects, reptiles, screaming crows, stinking latrines, indigestible food – are only part of a moral and spiritual continuum from which he can expect no escape ('Waking in the middle of the night on the narrow string-bed . . . he beat at the mosquitoes, fisted his ears against the sawing of the frogs and the chopping squawk of the lizards. . . . He entered the mornings from tossing dreams of home and slipped at once into the waking nightmare, his repugnance for everything the alien country offered').[49] Paul had been sickened, like Kumar, by the Indian milkman's routine trick of starving a calf and strapping its corpse to a post for its mother to nuzzle so as to cheat her into letting down her milk. Like Kumar, he had been threatened by loss of identity, by exposure to syphilis and leprosy, by the sense of being deadened, depleted, drained of courage to face the outside world. 'This place is a kind of nightmare, basically, only one never wakes up from it,' Paul wrote to Penny on his last day in the village, speaking for the first time in Kumar's voice.

Paul planned to leave on the night train for Hyderabad on 19 March, giving Ullal's telegram as his excuse. The evening before his departure he found his bed strewn with jasmine petals. Mrs Dass paid him the honour of appearing at last for a farewell photograph, although she neither spoke nor looked at him, and he left loaded with flower garlands: 'I did not feel I had deserved them. I was leaving under false pretences of having some lectures to give in Madras. I was escaping from the kind of hospitality I did not understand, for all my previous experiences of India and Indians. I wanted to get back into my white skin. The bus was late. Would it ever arrive?'[50] He said he had reached screaming point by the time he and Dass finally gained Elluru, after an excruciating, unscheduled one-and-a-half hour wait for the bus, only to find the train was late too. His reservation had not been confirmed and there was no sleeper available. The station master urged Paul to beware of robbers, or dacoits, and the guard warned him not to answer if anyone knocked. 'Sir,' said Dass, 'lock the doors. Close the windows. Guard your property and your life.'[51] He got away in the end on the slow local passenger train, managing to transfer at the first halt to the night mail, sharing a compartment with three sleeping Indians in dhotis where he settled down thankfully, un-washed, in his 'filthy trousers and shirt', on a spare berth without sheets or pillows, to drain the last drops of Dass's crude jungle toddy. 'I arrived in Hyderabad next morning, still stunned and vicious. I knocked the hand of a beggar woman off my arm, gave the tonga wallah less than he asked for, ignored his protests and stalked into the Ritz Palace, called for beer and complained about the price.'[52]

A soothing shower, iced beer, clean linen, cooling fans, fresh laundry and the unspeakable privilege of a private bathroom restored some sense of proportion. There were telephone messages waiting for him, invitations to stay in Madras, an air-conditioned car to take him out to lunch with a friend of Ullal's called Mr Kulkar. Paul attended a British Council party, where he found admirers of *The Birds of Paradise*, and visited the museum, but was not impressed with Hyderabad ('The old Nizam only has 7 palaces left, poor chap').[53] Four days' rest and recuperation at the Ritz did much to diminish his anxiety, calm his stomach and lessen the pain in his leg. A Canadian fellow guest, employed by her country's information office in Delhi, explained that Europeans needed to stick together for fear of being exploited, and that friendship with Indians always had to be paid for (' "How often did you try?" I asked. "Well, for Chrissake, only the once," she said').[54] Kulkar told him a sobering story about some young Indians he knew in London who had been unable to eat for a week from dread of being obliged to make use of anything so disgusting as a china pedestal with water in it.[55] Paul began to get used to the luxury of waking in the morning without the sound of crows, to wearing shoes, shaving with soap, walking on carpets, drinking and talking with other people. He said his relief was indescribable: 'But already in that relief there was the shadow of something that appalled me – the growing shadow of my ingratitude, my ridiculous irrational fears, my utter dependence upon the amenities of my own kind of civilisation.'[56]

On 24 March, he flew to Madras to spend three pleasant, peaceful days staying with Balaraja Srinivasan, an understanding host himself still readjusting to India after working in Liverpool (the Kumars, solicitous and sympathetic as ever, were in the middle of moving to Delhi). Srinivasan was a friend of an old Higham's client, Monica Felton, a remarkable woman in her late fifties, author of perceptive, unorthodox books about unexplored people and places. She was a disabled but intrepid traveller, an outspoken observer, an experienced India hand who would supply Paul over the next ten years with useful

advice and otherwise inaccessible information. He had first got to
know and like her, and to admire her courage, in London in the heat of
a public scandal that blew up on her return from a visit to the Korean
war in 1951, when she openly condemned atrocities perpetrated by
British troops operating as part of the United Nations force. She had
been disowned by the British left-wing establishment, losing her job in
local government, resigning as governor of the London School of
Economics, being threatened with criminal proceedings (even, according to Paul, impeachment for treason), eventually leaving the country
to start a new life in India.[57] Paul had not seen her for more than ten
years, but her smile as she limped towards him (she had been out of
town on his first visit) was enough to bring back all her old
cheerfulness and fortitude under fire. Conversations with her and
Srinivasan steadied Paul and helped him regain a clearer perspective,
in reassuring contrast to the pessimistic Canadian at Hyderabad, or
the young women shopping in Spencers who seemed unable to meet
the eyes of the Indian bearers:

When I first saw them I laughed, thought them pretentious little girls trying to
act like memsahibs. When I saw them again two weeks later I didn't laugh. I
knew that by not looking at the servants they betrayed what else it was they
were trying not to see; the poverty outside, the squalor, the filth, the whole
shocking ambiance of India encountered for the first time by a woman who
not long ago was comfortably chatting to her friends in a new town
supermarket. It was an India for which they did not feel an ounce of
responsibility. The empire died almost before they were born.
    But in the fortnight's interval I had discovered the ease with which I could
get into a state of shock just as deep, perhaps deeper.[58]

    It was the Canadian woman at the Ritz who first gave Paul the term
'cultural shock' to describe what had happened to him in
Timmapuram. He could not believe how little it had taken to tip him
over into mistrust of his hosts, how quickly he had discounted their
humanity and concern. He remembered the trouble taken to please
him and forestall his needs: the tokens of respect and affection, the
fresh flower laid on his table each day, the electric fan and the German
radio placed exclusively at his disposal, the girl who knelt to wash his
feet when he entered the compound, the boy who carried heavy
buckets of water twice daily for his bath, even the *nai* who refreshed
him after shaving by a massage with coconut oil. He recalled with
shame how often he had repaid Dass's thoughtfulness with irritation
and barely concealed resentment. Paul said afterwards that he had
learned more in ten days in Timmapuram about racial hostility and
colour prejudice than in twenty years of liberal thinking at home.[59]

He celebrated his forty-fourth birthday, 25 March, by deciding to cancel his visits to Russia and Sweden, booking a flight home instead from Delhi on 18 April, and dining that night with Monica and Srinivasan, both of whom warmly endorsed his change of plan. He felt physically, emotionally and mentally exhausted ('my mind now seems to refuse to accept any more impressions').[60] He caught a feverish chill in Madras although the temperature was in the high nineties, his right leg had gone numb, a lump was beginning to form at the base of his spine, he suffered twinges of sciatic pain so sharp that sometimes he could scarcely move.[61] When he took up his journey where it had been broken off by boarding a plane for Calcutta on 27 March – Good Friday – he was still in a state of deep, delayed shock. Allied Publishers had found people to take him in once again, but first he was to spend a weekend with yet another stranger, an anglicised, public-school-educated Bengali called Neil Ghosh, to whom he had been recommended by Mollie Hamilton. When the plane landed at Dum Dum airport at midnight, two and a half hours late, Paul was relieved to find Ghosh still waiting with his Australian girlfriend, Caroline Davies. Mollie had met them on holiday in Kashmir the year before, and been immediately struck by Neil's singular charm, good looks and flawless Eton-and-Oxbridge manner. Paul, less susceptible to English upper-class urbanity, preferred the girlfriend who, he maintained ever afterwards, was by far the more interesting of the two.

Caroline Davies was a nurse: large, forthright, sturdily-built, what Paul called a 'skirt-and-blouse girl'.[62] She was calm, competent and dependable at a time when he badly needed someone on whom he could depend. It was one week and a day since his escape from Timmapuram. He had always had an abnormally high tolerance of pain but he was finding it hard to cope with his physical distress ('when I got up to Calcutta . . . I was pretty well dragging the leg behind me')[63] and the nervous anxiety that had come flooding back with the delay on the flight. Neil was expansive and entertaining but it was Caroline who took Paul in charge, persuading him in spite of an ingrained dislike of doctors to see her employer, an Austrian Dr Hahndel, who prescribed painkillers and arranged X-rays. In the course of the next week, she would take over Paul's hotel bookings, reschedule his flights, organise reservations unobtrusively and without fuss. She had the delicacy of feeling, the firmness and compassion that make a good nurse, qualities she shared with Penny: Caroline, too, responded intuitively to anyone in distress, let alone anyone as near collapse as Paul on that Good Friday night in Calcutta. 'I can't stand much more,' he wrote next morning to Penny, describing classic symptoms of amoebic infection on top of his lameness. 'The feeling of chill, and the aching leg take away all my concentration & I have a feeling that now I'm only wasting time. Can hardly bear to contemplate the constant moving about between now & Delhi ... am beginning to *hate* my suitcase!'

Paul's reactions to Neil Ghosh[64] were, by comparison, altogether more complicated. Neil was quite unlike other Westernised Indians in that he had been cut off from all Indian influence in earliest childhood and brought up in England, where he received the same training as any other public school boy being groomed for a responsible position under the raj. When he was shipped back in 1938 at the age of nineteen to an India he could barely remember, he sounded, behaved and thought of himself as if he were British. His position was unique in Calcutta, where he was known as 'the black Englishman'. He had shone at school – winning scholarships, making friends, performing effortlessly on the cricket field and as a popular all-round sportsman – and it had given him a polish and poise, an easy deferential charm, a generosity and attentiveness to other people that made him hard to resist. Caroline clearly adored him, and so in their day had a great many other women. Mollie Hamilton and her sister, running across him by chance on a tour of their own childhood haunts the year before, had found him an uncommonly agreeable companion, with a debonair wit and clipped delivery that made it hard to believe he was not English. Both agreed they had never met anyone like him and that, if the raj had not shut up shop without warning, he would undoubtedly have ended by holding high office, very likely governing a province. 'Instead of which, he is left stranded,' Mollie wrote later to Paul: 'black is your hat, speaking impeccable BBC English & *rotten* Urdu (& probably worse Bengali!); still with a foot in both countries and at home in neither.'[65]

Neil's history was curious and sad.[66] He came of a zemindar family in East Bengal, landowners and jute-growers. His mother had been ceremonially married at ten years old according to Hindu custom to a bridegroom she had never seen. In her world power and authority had no connection with literacy; she could not read or write or speak English, and she knew nothing of the far away country to which her husband decided to send their three eldest children – Neil at six with his younger brother and sister – alone halfway round the world in search of a British education. Neil's father was an army doctor in the Indian Medical Service, Lieutenant-Colonel A. M. Ghosh, who had hit on this scheme as the only way of ensuring that his children should not grow up second-class citizens in their own country. Neil and his brother were sent to Wolborough Hill preparatory school at Newton Abbott in Devon, moving on at fourteen to Blundells School, while their sister Uma went to Roedean. After four years their father brought over the rest of the family – his wife with her youngest son and the baby, Nilima, who was four months old – and installed them in a capacious house just outside Newton Abbott, staffed with servants and an English governess for the small children. 'The Colonel's family' were the only Indians in Devon, perhaps in the whole West country, certainly the only brown faces the local people had ever seen. Their father returned to India, having laid down instructions for a strict English regime which covered everything from their names ('Neil' was an anglicisation of Neel Baron Ghosh) to their table manners, their diet of plain unspiced English food, and a compulsory run, rain or shine, before breakfast. Their mother, stranded in a strange cold country without even an Indian ayah for company, unable to speak her own language or cook her native food, with no friend save the governess and no one to turn to but Neil (who adored her), pined, drooped and sickened. In 1934, both parents died.

Neil had always been their mother's standby, the one left in charge by their father, the handsome, dazzling, accomplished and admired elder brother: now he became at fifteen a father to his orphaned brothers and sisters. Four years later, with funds running low and war looming in Europe, the strange little dislocated, self-contained family was summarily ordered back to India by an uncle in Calcutta. None of them, except the youngest, ever fully recovered from this most extreme form of cultural shock. Uma at fourteen stubbornly refused to accomplish the transition from a schoolgirl in felt hat and gym slip, doing well at Roedean, to a prospective Hindu bride, veiled, mute, obedient, awaiting the same fate as her mother before her, in their native village of Bikrampur where buffalo were still slaughtered as a sacrifice to the gods. For Neil, the change was slower and at any rate at first much less drastic. An opening was found for him with one of Calcutta's great British mercantile houses, Bird & Co., where he was the first Indian ever to be offered equal terms with Europeans (including the coveted 'home contract', so-called because it came with a free passage to England every three years). The war, which creamed off his British contemporaries, ensured rapid promotion. When Paul met him, Neil was head of Bird's coal department, running one of the two or three biggest coal suppliers in the country, but his position was precarious. By 1964 Calcutta's British business community had been effectively disbanded, leaving Neil still living out a kind of princely post-Imperial make-believe, essentially fake but with vestiges of the panoply and privilege that had made a job under the raj for so long such a glittering prize.

He owned a share in a race horse, employed an excellent tailor,

Dipali Nag photographed by Paul in her garden: 'From the house there is the sound of a young girl singing . . . There are ragas for morning and evening. This one is for morning. The dew is not yet off the grass. The garden is still cool.'

belonged to the best clubs (arriving before the war to find himself barred from all but the Calcutta Club, on grounds of skin colour, was one of countless snubs that had strengthened an obstinate fighting spirit). He had a lavish entertainment allowance, an ample staff of bearers, and a splendid chauffeur-driven green Studebaker. His palatial, air-conditioned apartment in Lansdowne Court, one of Calcutta's most up-to-date blocks, could and frequently did comfortably hold up to 150 guests at a time. He was a brilliant raconteur, an extravagant thrower of parties and a reckless giver of gifts. He could sing risqué nostalgic songs, play the harmonica, stand on his head, and eat a whole raw green chili as a party piece. He was a long-standing prop and pillar of Firpo's Bar on Chowringhee, next door to the Grand Hotel which still stood with its elegant arcade of shops, its view of the broad leafy maidan, its terrace where clients might drink and dance under the stars as if nothing had altered. Paul was guest of honour that weekend in Lansdowne Court at the kind of informal gathering Neil liked best, with music turned up loud on the gramophone, company pouring in, whisky flowing like water (Paul was especially grateful, after five weeks in two dry states), and a selection from his unrivalled collection of records – Peter Sellers, a skit on the recent Profumo affair, the *Black and White Minstrel Show* and the BBC's *Scrapbook for 1940* – playing to remind all present, satirically or sentimentally, of change and decay. 'We were more English than the English!' Paul wrote to Penny next day. There was something about his good-natured, high-spirited host that for some reason flicked a raw nerve: 'Ghosh v hospitable but not quite my cup of tea.'

Paul was collected after lunch on Sunday by Dr Dulal Nag Chaudhuri, a nuclear physicist at the university, in whose house he

Kapaleswara Temple near the Kumars' house where Paul stayed in Madras.

Neil's girlfriend, Caroline Davies, in Calcutta.

Neil Ghosh, the year before he met Paul and implanted the seed that grew into the Raj Quartet, with Mollie Hamilton (M. M. Kaye) in the garden of HH of Kashmir's former palace.

was to spend the next week. The arrangement had been made by Allied Publishers' manager Krishan Churumani (to whom Paul had finally been introduced by Neil Ghosh over drinks at the Grand Hotel), an old friend of Dorothy Ganapathy in Bombay and of Dr Nag's wife Dipali, each of whom had offered a home to the stranger in the open-handed Indian tradition that would have construed any offer of payment as a poor return for hospitality. The Nags lived in Behala on the far outskirts of the city, remote from urban bustle and traffic in a country district of farms, wells and fields, still scarcely built over, where Paul found at last the tranquil Arcadian retreat he had originally envisaged in Timmapuram.

Their house stood in the middle of a large tangled garden ringed with neem trees, mango, mehendi, scented white jasmine, tall date and coconut palms, and strung with sprays of trailing pink, white and crimson bougainvillea. The house itself was an old stone building, three storeys high, with many little, light, airy rooms opening out of one another, washed in soft clear colours – lime green, lemon yellow, blue, lavender, dusty red ochre and two shades of pink – with grilles and shutters at the windows. It was furnished in the Indian manner with low tables, brass pots and ornaments, flowers everywhere and cushions for sitting on the floor. From his L-shaped room on the first floor, Paul could look out on two sides at the green garden – 'Paul sat here for hours watching out. He loved palm trees'[67] – and he would mount every day to the flat roof to survey the crowded prospect of village houses, tropical foliage, carts, cattle, goats and men coming and going under a broad blue sky. He was endlessly interested in these people, and would go into minute particulars about their jobs, homes, families, characters and customs with his hostess, who patiently answered his questions. 'In the evenings he would talk, but mostly he liked to listen,' said Dipali Nag. 'He was a very good listener. He and I would talk lazily about so many things: Bengali history: Bengali girls: from the beginning he would ask about my music.'

Dipali Nag was a classical singer well known throughout India – 'a kind of Bengali Maria Callas,' Paul wrote to Penny – with an international reputation dating back to the years immediately after the war, when she had sung as a girl with Ram Gopal's company on visits to Paris and London. She was small, slender, delicate, with a presence of exquisite authority and grace. She had been taught by a highly respected musician, Fayaz Khan of the Agra Gharana, and now took pupils herself, teaching, playing and practising in her music room at the top of the house. Paul listened attentively, sending a chit on the third day to ask if he might come in person to hear the morning music. The girls, flustered but proud to sing for the English sahib, soon forgot all about him as he sat in a corner watching, becoming in some sense a pupil himself, absorbing the form of the instruments, the techniques of the singers, the sound and feel of the music. Dipali demonstrated the polished, wooden, onion-shaped tamboura, the two small drums or tablas, the Indian harmonium which Paul watched her play so often that she invited him in the end to play it himself. He was fascinated especially by a morning raga Dipali sang for him about a girl leaving her father's house to go to her bridegroom: a throbbing plangent lament with undertones of rising excitement, at once elegaic and anticipatory. Dipali translated the song for him to incorporate in *The Jewel in the Crown* (he told her he had put her in the book, without naming her, as the guru who gives singing lessons to the girl Parvati),[68] where the Stranger first hears it in the garden of the MacGregor house in Mayapore:

From the house there is the sound of a young girl singing . . . There are ragas for morning and evening. This one is for morning. The dew is not yet off the ground. The garden is still cool. A blue-black crow with a red-yellow beak swoops from the roof of the house looking for its breakfast. Where the sunlight strikes the lawn the dew is a scattering of crystals.[69]

The days passed uneventfully. Paul sat thinking, resting, recuperating, making occasional excursions into Calcutta, and dining quietly with Dipali in the evenings. Her husband and son were both away that first week, neither her servants nor her pupils spoke English, nothing happened and nobody came to the house.[70] The two found they could say almost anything to one another as they were swept up in the kind of intense, platonic and romantic intimacy the Stranger daydreams about, in *The Jewel in the Crown*, between the Indian prince who built the old MacGregor House and the classical singer who lived in it ('It was said that he came to visit her morning and evening, and that she sang to him . . . and that he became enamoured finally only of her voice, and was content to listen').[71] Paul had looked drawn and thin when he arrived in Behala, but he became with each day more relaxed and receptive. 'I can't thank you enough,' he said to Dipali, explaining, when she asked why, that she had given him peace. 'I had never come across anyone quite like Paul,' she said. 'That was why I was drawn to him. He was a recluse. He had that extraordinary power: the power of someone sitting quiet in a room full of people.'

Paul said that, before it came to fruition, a book had to be sat with, tended and watched over.[72] Ever since he left Timmapuram, he had had some dim idea for a novel at the back of his mind. He thought he might call it 'The Mango Rain', after a rain Dorothy Ganapathy had told him about that falls out of season and waters the mangoes: 'It is a ripener of fruit and refresher of spirits.'[73] The title struck him as symbolic, perhaps of the necessity for love and understanding between different races, perhaps of the needs of his own dry, parched imagination, perhaps of the story that was already stirring and forming at the deepest level of consciousness, and that would ripen when he got home. Another idea he toyed with was based on Caroline Davies and called 'The Temporary Memsahib': he told Dipali about her, and said he planned to put her in a book one day.[74] There was still something about her and Neil Ghosh that intrigued and eluded him. He felt on the point of grasping it but was always distracted, on trips into town, by the difficulty of hobbling about, by the great heat – the temperature had by now risen above 103° – the fearful humidity, and by the city itself.

He loved Bombay, but for Calcutta, 'the filthiest city in the world', he had a special affection. He rejoiced in its spacious layout, its majestic buildings, its intellectual energy, above all in the sense of life pulsing on its streets: 'The miseries and vitality of the entire sub-continent are brought to the boil in this explosive city,' he wrote in an enthusiastic review of Geoffrey Moorhouse's *Calcutta*, seconding Moorhouse's view of the city as an infected running sore on the body of civilisation, 'but nevertheless to be celebrated by a last chapter entitled *Zindabad*, which means, literally, the place where life is – here humiliated almost beyond endurance but stubborn and defiant.'[75] By the time Paul wrote this review, he could look back on *The Jewel in the Crown* and see how many of its themes and images had finally come together in Calcutta. It was Neil Ghosh who told him about Mother Teresa, an Albanian woman who had left her nuns' order to set up a refuge for people dying on the streets. Neil kept her in coal ('We never got the same amount after he retired,' Mother Teresa told Neil's sister when he died), and had once to his fury found two of her bodies in the boot of his green Studebaker (the car had been loaned to ferry them to the morgue, without Neil's knowledge, by his English wife who subsequently left him, and by 1964 was suing for divorce). Paul investigated no further, but Neil's and Caroline's accounts of Mother Teresa would in due course help give birth to Mayapore's Sister Ludmilla,[76] just as the Nags' home in Behala grew into the MacGregor House with its luxuriant garden.

Paul took a fond, sorrowful leave of Dipali on 4 April, returning for a couple of nights to Lansdowne Court before flying to Agra to see the Taj Mahal, then on for a last week in Delhi. By this time he knew, however obscurely, that he had got what he came for, and he wrote cancelling his visit to the Maharajah of Bharatpur. He paid a cautious courtesy call on another old soldier from No. 1 Air India Company,

Havildar Nag, (who laid on a sumptuous if sticky state tea at which Nimu Purkayastha, away on a posting, was represented by his wife and children), and he enjoyed a boozy lunch with the not unsympathetic editor of the Calcutta *Statesman*.[77] Caroline's doctor proved encouraging but unhelpful, coming in the end to the same conclusion as all the others who had tried and failed to diagnose Paul's complaint ('Dr Hahndel told me I must stop thinking that there is something seriously wrong with me').[78] X-rays showed only a minor fault ('asymmetry of the lumbosacral diarthrodial joints') at the base of the backbone. There was apparently nothing to stop him completing his programme, except that Paul suddenly realised his business was essentially done. On Tuesday, 7 April, after a bad night and a horrible, hungover morning during which he missed the plane to Agra, lost his temper in the airline office, and had his right foot run over by a cyclist, he decided on impulse to take the next available seat on a plane back to London, which turned out to be in two days' time. 'And then everything became the right sort of shape and feeling,' he wrote jubilantly next day to Penny.

The episode that had apparently made up his mind was a late-night confrontation over the whisky bottle with Neil Ghosh, which lasted until four in the morning. Paul had organised a farewell dinner at a restaurant for Caroline, Neil and his sister Nilima Dutta (who already knew of the strange Englishman's plans for a book: 'I longed to ask him, are you really going to write about my brother? But I was too shy'). But, for all his genuine appreciation, Paul remained wary. Part of Neil's charm was his arrogance, an unruffled, unruffleable assurance immensely attractive to his admirers, that seemed indefinably condescending to people like Paul, whose instincts cried out against it and the system it represented. Even Neil's voice was provoking. Like Hari Kumar, he spoke with the unmistakable upper-class drawl, 'the sharp clipped-spoken accents of power and privilege' that grate so disastrously in *The Jewel in the Crown* on the English policeman, Ronald Merrick, and make him fatally conscious at their first meeting of his own voice, 'a tone regulated by care and ambition rather than upbringing'.[79] From their first encounter, Neil had brought out something of Merrick in Paul, who arrived in Calcutta still badly rattled by his recent breakdown. It would be a long time before he could rationalise the disturbing experience of switching roles, of feeling himself change in Timmapuram from a cowed and stupefied victim – Dass's prisoner –to an aggressive, racist bully:

I became reluctant to go out. I wrote letters. I read old letters over and over again. I became emotionally attached to my own luggage, as though it were a fetish. Everything that reminded me I was English became precious. And

gradually I felt a Sahib's face superimpose itself on my own – as I thought –
mild and liberal one. I did not merely accept the chairs of honour, I expected
them. When crossed in a desire I began to raise my voice, to give him [Dass] a
hard time.[80]

This passage, written four years after *The Jewel in the Crown*,
represents Paul's final, most carefully considered and detailed analysis
of the experience he had fled from in Timmapuram. What seams to
have happened in 1964 in Calcutta was that Paul was brought face to
face in Neil Ghosh with the defensive mask of superiority he had
instinctively rejected in himself.

Neil for his part had his own reasons for feeling equivocal towards
an English visitor. His position in Calcutta, always awkward, was by
the time Paul met him untenable.[81] When he had first arrived in 1938
to find himself with a foot in two countries, he had felt cut off from his
Indian contemporaries far more decisively than from the British who
patronised, petted and laughed at him, and shut him out of their clubs
('The East India Company ruled Bengal,' as they say in Calcutta, 'and
the Bengal Club ruled the East India Company'). After the war, when
Bird & Co. showed what it thought of its Indian intake by recruiting
forty or fifty new assistants from home, Neil made himself briefly the
life and soul of their bachelor parties. But, with Independence and the
government's policy of compulsory Indianisation for British firms, his
support drained away as his English friends left or were picked off one
by one. 'Neil had no Indian friends,' said the wife of an Indian
colleague who had watched him being steadily isolated: 'He didn't
speak the same language – and I don't mean English.'[82] The exodus
accelerated in the early 1960s. Neil, who had been the first Indian to
join the firm, saw the last Englishman leave in 1969. The education for
which the Ghosh family had paid so dearly – Neil's attitudes, his
achievements, his manner, even his voice – all now counted against
him. In 1964 Neil described himself accurately enough in response to
his wife's divorce petition as having been demoted 'from an "up-and-
coming young man" in my firm to an "also-ran" '. Juniors were being
promoted over him. Bird & Co. had entered the final stages of a power
struggle which would end in 1965 with the appointment of an Indian
contemporary as chairman, after which Neil was forced to resign.

Never abstemious, Neil now became a serious drinker. On the night
that the two sat up talking, Paul, too, had been drinking hard for a
week.[83] After a convivial evening with less friendly undertones of a
kind both men were expert at picking up, Neil poured out his
bitterness and sense of defeat to Paul whose exemplary talents as a
listener, coupled with his passionate curiosity about the British in
India, made him a receptive confidant. Paul himself later told several

people that this was the night on which *The Jewel in the Crown* slipped within his grasp.[84] Neil, when he eventually read the book, confirmed that he recognised himself, or at any rate his early years, in Hari Kumar. Hari's family history, his anglicised name of Harry Coomer and his English public school background, his charm, sensitivity and stubbornness, his total alienation from India, the shock of finding himself humiliated and excluded by people he had thought of as his own kind: all these come from Neil Ghosh. The match is striking in both overall pattern and incidental detail. Neil's recall to India had meant parting from an English girl called Daphne, who would bequeath her name to Daphne Manners in the *Jewel*. Even Kumar's final metamorphosis, after arrest and incarceration, into an unrecognisable, all-but-anonymous prisoner – shuffling, cowed, acquiescent, aged beyond his years and speaking toneless Hindi – came from things Neil let fall about his next brother, who had given up an Oxford classical scholarship, failed to get into the ICS, disowned his past, and suffered a series of crippling breakdowns.

But, although Neil and others supplied external details, the core of the novel lies elsewhere. The crucial encounter in Lansdowne Court was on one level not so much a confrontation with Neil as with Paul himself. It set in motion the mysterious process by which a novelist shuffles and reinvents his past, turning himself inside out, fragmenting, transposing and refracting himself in the mirror of his imagination. Paul would describe this process, or something very like it, in the final volume of the Raj Quartet when, under interrogation in English, the prisoner Kumar seems to turn back into a former self, the Englishman he had once been, Harry Coomer. It is, according to a horrified witness, as if one man were 'looking out of the eye-sockets of another', and the effect is electrifying:

It was as though there were two men in the chair, the one you could see and the one you could hear. The one you could hear was undoubtedly Coomer, and once you were aware that he was Coomer the unfavourable impression made by the shambling body and hollow-cheeked face began to fade. The English voice, released from its inner prison, seemed to have taken control of the face and limbs, to be infusing them with some of its own firmness and authority.[85]

Paul had known from the first that his Indian novel would be an attempt to explore on the fullest possible scale relations between Britain and India, an affair that had apparently ended abruptly in 1947, but whose repercussions seemed to him painfully evident in mounting racial tension in Britain itself in the 1960s and 1970s. He would start *The Jewel in the Crown* with a rape, looking back to historical precedent (the assault on Daphne Manners was based on a similar incident involving a white girl at Amritsar in 1919), mindful also of his literary descent from Forster and of the debt he owed him.[86] He said that the image in the book's opening sentence of a girl running in a flat landscape had come to him without his knowing why she was running or where. He realised only after the novel was finished that she had in a sense been running from the kind of ugly, senseless collision between black and white – a physical rather than a moral violation – that he, too, had fled from in India.[87]

But the ambivalent heart of his novel, the emotional axis on which eventually the whole Quartet would turn, is the central confrontation between Kumar and Merrick. Kumar goes back to Paul's own crushing sense of rejection and loss, when his whole world had collapsed without warning on his being taken away from school at fourteen. Merrick with his grinding sense of racial superiority, his repressions, his punitive intolerance, springs from the self who had fought almost throughout Paul's adult life to stamp out impulses he mistrusted in himself. Merrick is a man without self-knowledge, with no understanding of his own or other people's private compulsions, 'a man, moreover, who lacked entirely that liberal instinct which is so dear to historians that they lay it out like a guideline through the unmapped forests of prejudice and self-interest as though this line, and not the forest, is our history.'[88] Merrick would provide a means of opening up unmapped territory, of exploring the dark illiberal authoritarian instincts without which there could be no true understanding of the Imperial past. Paul said, when he had finished the Quartet, that Merrick, like all his other characters, came from himself: 'It's all a writer can do – expose himself each time he writes a chapter.'[89]

The upshot in fact of Paul's encounter with Neil was that they broke off relations. Neil may have sensed that his confessions had gone too far, more likely he resented Caroline's attentions to her patient, perhaps he felt that he and Paul had each glimpsed in the other a darkness better not exposed. 'I had seen the darkness in him, and the darkness in the white man, in Merrick,' Sister Ludmilla says, in the *The Jewel in the Crown*, of Kumar's first encounter with Merrick: 'Two such darknesses in opposition can create a blinding light.'[90] For Paul, the evening undoubtedly precipitated some sort of revelation. But Neil had no intention of allowing it to be repeated and, when Paul returned to the flat after cancelling his flight to Agra, his host threw him out ('making it pleasantly but quite plain it was inconvenient for me to stay on at Lansdowne Court').[91] Paul rang the Nags, and seemed still acutely disturbed when he arrived at their house. 'It was the only time I ever saw him agitated,' said Dipali: 'There was a look of anger – horror – on his face.' She had opened the door wearing a white sari, which upset Paul (who had always appreciatively noticed her saris) so much that she changed it immediately. When he was calmer, he explained that for him in India white was the colour of death.

Dr Nag, back at home on this second appearance, remembered only his surprise when Paul reminded him that they had already met, twenty years earlier, as young men in wartime on either side of an impassable Imperial divide.[92] In due course Paul would send a copy of *The Jewel in the Crown* inscribed 'To Dipali and Dulal with many grateful thanks for, and affectionate recollection of, your hospitality and kindness to the Stranger – '. The book's epilogue is a grateful and affectionate, indirect tribute to the two women who between them presided over its inception: Dipali Nag who translated the raga with which it ends, and Dorothy Ganapathy to whom it is dedicated, and whose voice can be heard unmistakably on the last page behind Lady Chatterjee's protests about being described as a repository of tradition: 'a repository sounds like a place for storing furniture when you bash off to some other station. I suppose an Englishman could say that the whole of India is that sort of place. You all went, but left so much behind that you couldn't carry with you wherever you were going, and these days those who come back can more often than not hardly bother to think about it, let alone ask for the key and go in and root about among all the old dust sheets.'

Paul flew home to London on 9 April, dragging his bad leg behind him. His Indian journey had pulled him down physically and drained him emotionally, but it had also shattered the barrier he had been unable to break through, the membrane he and others had felt muffling and blurring his writing. When he left Calcutta, Paul understood more clearly the mystery he had contemplated six weeks earlier in Bombay, staring at the stone Trimurti on Elephanta Island and pondering the great human dance of creation, preservation and destruction. 'It is a difficult concept,' as someone says in *The Jewel in the Crown*: 'One must respond to it in the heart, not the intellect.'[93] Timmapuram, and what followed, had taught Paul to look into the darkest recesses of his own heart, to acknowledge with uncomfortable honesty what he saw there, and to recognise the inadequacy of stereotyped views of the outside world, and the Raj in particular: 'I understood better . . . the physical and emotional impulses that had always prompted the British in India to sequester themselves in clubs and messes and forts, to preserve, sometimes to the point of absurdity, their own English middle-class way of life. It was a simple enough lesson. One could learn it from books. It is better for a writer to learn lessons from life.'[94]

CHAPTER TWELVE

The end of the party and the beginning of the washing up

Paul made a first note of the novel that would eventually be *The Jewel in the Crown* on a card at the Epicure, by which time he already had a heroine – Daphne Manners – whose prediicament might be used to explore 'the whole of the British-India affair'.[1] The image of a running girl whom he later identified as Daphne had appeared on his inner screen during a disturbed night in May, the month after he got back from India. He was clear from the start that he would need a historical perspective and, by early summer, he had decided to set his story at the time of the Quit India riots in 1942, 'the last great confrontation between East and West in India',[2] when the British government attempted to forestall a campaign of civil disobedience by ordering the arrest of Congress leaders. All this required firsthand research, which would mean enlisting friends to check details about wartime emergency regulations, the experiences of imprisoned Congress sympathisers, and Indian Army procedure in case of civil disturbance. Over the next few months Dorothy Ganapathy and her legal contacts in Bombay, Monica Felton and her political circle in Madras, Mollie's husband, Major-General G. J. Hamilton (formerly of the Queen's Own Corps of Guides and the 7/16 Punjabis in Burma) all collected information, consulted friends or answered queries.[3]

At the same time Paul insisted emphatically that he was not, and had no intention of becoming, a historical novelist. He had tried and failed to write about contemporary London: 'Publishing is full now of clever young men for whom literature began with *Lucky Jim*,' he warned Monica Felton[4] (whose most successful book, *A Child Widow's Story*, found a publisher through Paul soon after he got home). But in the summer of 1965, immediately after he had finished *The Jewel in the*

Crown, he would define the task facing the modern British novel – the novel written by his own and Kingsley Amis' post-war generation – in characteristically prosaic terms as 'the end of the party and the beginning of the washing up'.[5] He meant that, whatever their intentions, he and his contemporaries could not help but reflect in their writing the restless, dissatisfied, post-industrial, post-Imperial consumer society ushered in after the war by, on the one hand, the breaking up of the empire and, on the other, the foundation of the welfare state. Each of these achievements, each billed at the time as a glorious liberation, had produced disillusionment over the next twenty years in a culture that no longer acknowledged any common allegiance, 'the culture of an intensely narrow age, masquerading as latitudinarian. Free and broad of speech, mean of heart. Radical in protestation, reactionary in performance. Satirical in style, pedagogic in manner. Tolerant on the surface, violently disposed underneath. A culture and an age of disenchantment with established processes, or disenchantment with the notion that any process should ever be established again.'[6] Paul recognised clearly enough the acquisitive instincts, the sour and disruptive currents at work beneath the surface of the swinging sixties in England. But he responded as enthusiastically as the dizziest swinger to the optimism of the decade, and its overwhelming vitality:

The vitality of a people . . . seeking new definitions of almost every aspect of human exchange. Tempers are short. Vulgarity is intense. The dangers are great. The possibilities are enormous. This *is* our society. This *is* our literature.

At the General Election in the autumn of 1964, Paul welcomed the Labour victory (Harold Wilson lived a few streets away, with a policeman on his doorstep, in Hampstead Garden Suburb, which gave the whole neighbourhood 'a curious feeling of walking the corridors of power'),[7] although he himself campaigned for the local Liberal party in a safe Tory seat. Invited to explain his own preoccupation with the outdated concept of Empire, he would point to Britain's now largely abandoned nineteenth-century industrial base, to the derelict Lancashire cotton mills that seemed to him as much a monument to the raj as any statue of Queen Victoria, to the flood of poor immigrants reaching England from the subcontinent in the 1960s, and to growing racial tension in cities like Birmingham.[8] At the end of his life, attempting to define his achievement in the Raj Quartet for a class of American students, he drew a chart on the blackboard, beginning before the First World War when Britain ruled a quarter of the globe, and ending in 1945 when Attlee's socialist government was elected with such high hopes to abolish once and for all poverty, exploitation, social injustice at home and Imperial domination abroad. 'You write for an age,' he said, 'and this is my age.'[9] He could never see the past as disposable, or detachable from the present and the future. In May 1964 President Nehru died, and sixteen months later war broke out between India and Pakistan on the dividing line drawn up by Britain at the time of partition. Paul, who had just finished writing *The Jewel in the Crown*, was appalled. 'But what is so interesting (historically) is that although there is an obvious and increasing feeling of responsibility, no one has yet traced that responsibility back to the failure of the British government to consolidate and unify. No one has yet had the courage to say that Divide and Rule has come full circle,' he wrote from London in September 1965 to Dorothy Ganapathy, adding sadly: 'All this is in my book, you know.'[10]

As he entered middle age, Paul felt a growing identity with his father – 'we're not just of our time, we inherit our own memory, and the memories and attitudes of our parents'[11] – together with a corresponding wariness. He said the denial of memory could be destructive but so could the contrary tendency to romanticise the past, or to retreat into it, as his father had done. The Raj Quartet would be written from what one of its characters calls a vigorous sense of history, 'vigorous because it pruned ruthlessly that other weakening sense so often found with the first, the sense of nostalgia, the desire to *live* in the past.'[12] Inevitably the Quartet would be accused of glamorising the empire by critics who made no distinction between nostalgia and the attitude Paul defined as its opposite. He would find himself also under attack, simultaneously but from the other direction, by embattled old Raj hands who resented his lack of complacency, his insistence on raking over old bitterness and failure, his inability to write off the past, or walk away from it as casually as if it were a stack of dirty dishes. He gave the same stern answer to both parties: 'To forget strikes me as the quickest way of making the same mistake again,' he wrote when he had published three out of the four novels of the Quartet. 'I'm not sure that there is genuinely any such thing as forgetting, but there are tender conspiracies of silence – and these may engender ignorance, always a dangerous thing.'[13]

For Paul, one of the consolations of age was the attempt to come to some sort of terms with the past, which included on a smaller scale making posthumous peace with his father (he even wondered at one point if Tom Scott's having been too old to fight in the first war might explain 'the sense I have of being much older than I am . . .').[14] He welcomed the falling away of the conflicts of his youth, and cheerfully described himself long before time as an old man. His wife said that, on his return from India in 1964, he already looked like an old man, contorted, bent double, hobbling with a stick and insisting less vigorously than usual on his reluctance to seek medical help. She persuaded him within the week to see an osteopath who diagnosed fusion of the coccyx, and cracked his spine back into place with a report like a gunshot. After that Paul could walk upright, but nothing helped to dispel the mortal fatigue, the chill and crippling lethargy that had disabled him in India and made him feel, back in London, as if he were dying. This time it was Roland Gant who took him in hand, recognised his symptoms, contacted a Parisian specialist in tropical medicine, booked Paul into the clinic and accompanied him across the Channel to Paris at the end of May.

Roland himself had been in and out of hospitals since the war, baffling science until he came across a pioneering half-Catalan, half Indo-Chinese physician in Paris called Georges Farréras, who had devised a system for the detection and cure of amoebiasis, rife in France in the 1960s among soldiers returning from Algeria. It is a complaint exceedingly hard to diagnose, because the amoebic parasite expires almost at once outside the human body and so remains undetectable in laboratory specimens, and harder still to eradicate because the amoeba flourishes deep in the lining of the intestine, remaining impervious to even the strongest toxins used to flush out the stomach and bowels.[15] Paul proved on examination to be harbouring the parasite and began an agonising course of treatment on 29 May. Dr Farréras's treatment was swift, concentrated, convulsive and brutal. It involved penetration of the intestinal walls by massive doses of a preparation called emetine (an alternative drug, conessine, had to be abandoned because of the suicidal tendencies – '*des impulsions au suicide*' – observed in patients), introduced in hundreds of intravenal injections over a period of eight to ten days. Only those with strong hearts could stand this violent bombardment. 'They shut my system down' was the most Paul would say about it afterwards.[16]

He had exhibited in India many of the physical symptoms of amoebiasis: exhaustion, insomnia, sleep so broken that it exacerbated rather than relieved his tiredness, sickness, nausea, extreme suscepti- bility to cold, *douleurs intestinales* or what his American agent called 'bathroom trouble'. But the less tangible disorders that had shadowed him for twenty years correspond still more closely to Farréras's profile of a typical patient, whose condition is apt to declare itself in violent swings of mood and uncontrollable irritation with those around him, coupled with a horror of the slightest disruption to his established daily routine: even the simplest procedures – Farréras cites getting up in the morning, washing, dressing, shaving or being shaved – tax his endurance to the limit. He suffers torments from anxiety, restlessness, lack of concentration. He is constantly and cruelly oppressed by self-doubt, impaired sexual drive, a sense of universal impotence and discouragement ('In extreme cases, there may be a crisis of nervous depression in which thoughts of death and suicide are not unusual'). He finds it hard to bring his mind to bear, and increasingly difficult to finish any project once begun. He develops a trick of blocking out his surroundings: 'The patient fails to register what is said to him because he registers nothing.' He will frequently be forced to acknowledge himself incapable of meeting the demands of ordinary life: if he manages by heroic effort to function normally, he may 'take refuge in an occupation which demands such patience and minute attention to detail that it isolates him from other people, and even from himself'. Paul and Roland discussed with Farréras 'the stop-and-start methods and eroded will'[17] that make Edward Thornhill, in *The Corrida at San Feliu*, a textbook case of amoebiasis.

The effect of the cure, if successful, is immediate, sensational and lasting, provided the patient protects himself with drugs from any further contact with the amoeba.[18] Paul was discharged in June, with instructions to return three months later with his wife and daughters (the families of people with amoebiasis are commonly found to have been infected themselves). He felt transformed, rejuvenated, twenty years younger. On 28 June he wrote himself a sharp note – ' "Risk all." The Indian novel I ought by now to be able to write. A complex of narratives . . .'[19] – and next day he started writing what would prove to be the opening section of *The Jewel in the Crown*. He worked on it steadily that summer, evolving characters, exploring themes, building up his complex of narratives, breaking off at the end of August for another three weeks in Paris, when Penny and the girls all yielded positive results to Farréras' tests and underwent treatment. Paul was pronounced cured, which gave the trip in his memory a golden glow: he drew the Paris roofline from the hotel window, made up absurd little jingles for the family to sing as he used to do on seaside holidays, explored the city, introduced the girls to the Left Bank and the *Deux Magots*, and generally revelled in the sensation of feeling entirely well for the first time since the war.[20] He sunned himself in the Tuileries gardens, dabbling bare feet in the fountain and basking in reviews of the newly published *Corrida*: they were more respectful than effusive, except for the *Observer*, which published a dismissal by John Davenport so scathing that its literary editor privately apologised to Paul's publisher.[21] The whole family, returning for a check-up after six weeks, received a clean bill of health, which they celebrated in late autumn sunshine by eating roasted chestnuts in the Luxembourg Gardens, and chasing autumn leaves on the Champs-Elysées.[22]

Unaccustomed well-being carried Paul through a sticky patch when he got home to find *Corrida* turned down by Penguin (who had done badly with *The Birds of Paradise* and worse with *The Bender*), hardback sales falling behind Morrow's payments, and Heinemann about to lure Roland from Secker (Paul would follow him in the spring to the mutual relief of all parties). The new novel floundered momentarily, but righted itself and drove steadily forward, passing a halfway mark of 100,000 words in early March, and reaching completion in June 1965, exactly a year after starting out.[23] *The Jewel in the Crown* was received with 'wild enthusiasm' in the Heinemann office and jubilation at Higham's. John Willey read the manuscript straight through twice over, and responded with characteristic generosity ('It is a brilliant book . . . young Kumar is a genuinely tragic figure. . . . That a man can almost literally become invisible . . . because of the accident of skin colour is one of the devastating thoughts of the century').[24] Even now anyone reading Paul's novels in chronological order cannot help but be struck by a sudden change with the ninth. It is not simply that the *Jewel* for the first time contains no one suffering even implicitly from the lassitude and alienation typically induced by amoebiasis (in later volumes of the Quartet, Colonel Layton's father turns out to have died of the disease, Captain Purvis kills himself because of it, and Guy Perron speculates about its incalculable effect on the evolution of the British Raj).[25] There is an unmistakable change in the texture of the writing itself: what was weak, bland, pallid, derivative and defensively clenched becomes robust, lucid and open with a strongly individual flavour. It is as if a cloud, the indefinable debilitating self-indulgent invalid sensibility that had always hung over Paul's novels, had given way to clear sky.

The impact on his life was different but no less drastic. Paul spent the better part of a year after his cure 'under a stone' as usual with the new novel. He would normally be in his study by seven in the morning, emerging for lunch (which he ate in silence, often standing up as a change from sitting at his desk), dining off a tray, sometimes coming down again at night to watch a little television, punching the buttons at random and gazing with vacant eyes at the screen. He said nothing could match the excitement and absorption of the images that flickered and unrolled in his mind's eye. Years spent struggling in the grip of amoebiasis had developed phenomenal powers of will and concentration. He kept the *amibien*'s invaluable ability to blank out: 'the patient may retain what he hears but not what he has never taken in,' Farréras explained. 'His memory with its "holes" plays tricks on

Neil Ghosh in his last year at Blundell's School, 1938.

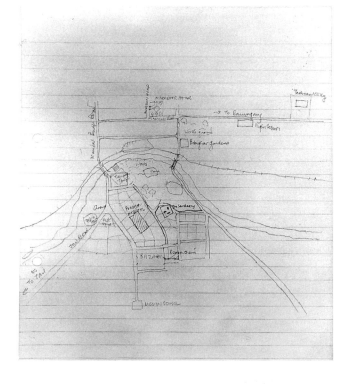

ABOVE LEFT *A page of* The Jewel in the Crown *manuscript.*

LEFT *Map of* Mayapore from Paul's *working notes.*

Ronald Merrick (Tim Pigott-Smith).

LEFT *Hari Kumar (Art Malik) and Daphne Manners (Susan Woolridge) from Granada TV's The Jewel in the Crown.*

'Nothing will come of it . . .' Paul had written to Dorothy Ganapathy when The Jewel in the Crown *was published in 1966, 'wouldn't it be marvellous, though, if some producer decided to make a film of the* Jewel *and sent me out to India for ages to help them with the script?'*

him.'[26] It was in one of these holes that Paul got soaked in a rainstorm without realising, until Penny met him in the hall when he got home, that he carried a furled umbrella. Long practice had perfected the art of excluding a real world that seemed flimsy and insubstantial compared to the inner reality at which he would gaze intently, and as far as possible without interruption, over the next decade. 'Almost every one of your waking hours is spent considering it, exploring it,' he wrote, explaining how the writer's preoccupation shuts out inessentials like a wife worrying over wet clothes: 'This is called absence of mind. But absent is exactly what the mind is not. At least it isn't absent from the place where its duty is to be – in the embryo book, wallowing through all the sticky, unmapped, unexplored regions of this extraordinary picture.'[27]

But to the explorer's family his voyage of discovery looked more than ever like a prison sentence. 'It was as if he had exiled himself to the one room where there was nothing but the typewriter and the blank page,' said his daughter Sally. 'It was the making of him as a writer, but the unmaking of him as a human being.' Penny had been Paul's lifeline in India, the safety valve without which he knew at the time that he could not have survived. He had poured out his doubts and fears to her on paper, lamenting the loneliness and misery of separation, the terror of hag-ridden nights, longing for her comforting presence, vowing repeatedly never again to travel without her. It was this crisis of desolation, and its crushing aftermath, that had finally forced him to seek help from Farréras. But treatment and cure meant that Paul, having ceased to be a patient with special needs, no longer required the protective care, the ceaseless and selfless solicitude Penny had faithfully supplied through all the years they had lived together. Paul was now in a sense off her hands. It meant a fundamental, permanent shift in her marriage, and it coincided with or perhaps contributed to the petering out of her own career. Her fourth book, *Sister Bollard*, which came out in 1963, is on one level a debate about women's opportunities which ends with the middle-aged Bollard – clear-eyed, unsentimental, stoically self-aware – turning down the triple chance of promotion, late marriage or early retirement because she prefers to plod on unchanged as a Ward Sister. But, although two more novels were going the rounds in 1964 and other manuscripts would surface at intervals over the next ten years, Penny never again found a publisher.

The two girls were fast approaching independence. Carol had already left school and, after a spell at a crammer's and strenuous arguments with her father (who urgently wanted for both his children the university education he had himself so bitterly missed), established her right to stop sitting examinations and go into the theatre. She had long been a pillar back-stage of the local Play and Pageant Union which had beguiled Paul in the family's very first week at Addison Way, and in May 1965, she enrolled at eighteen for a stage management course at the Royal Academy of Dramatic Art. She flourished from the start in the theatrical world. 'She's standing in for an ambition I once had for myself,' Paul wrote,[28] accepting defeat in the end with a good grace. Carol had always stood up to her father. She called him the Old Sod, the Old Grot or Grottso, Moany Bones, Four Eyes (after he acquired spectacles in 1966), and paid no attention to the rule of silence, the sick-room precautions, the habitual tip-toeing in and out of the study with cups of coffee, all of which had become second nature to her mother. Carol would cheerfully contra-dict Paul, Sally would argue with him about politics or history but, if the conversation grew heated, Penny was apt to leave the room. Carol remained affectionate, disrespectful and, if necessary, as obstinate as Paul himself. They had always paired off and, once her future had been settled in the first of a series of what Paul called 'crises on the daughter front',[29] their early alliance cemented itself into an adult friendship. Whenever Carol was at home, she and her father fell into the habit o taking long, companionable walks over the Heath on Sundays after lunch, when Paul would embroider fantastically convoluted stories about the Fairy Gazooka – a tarnished and thoroughly disreputable character with grubby wings and even grubbier habits who could always be relied on to cheer them both up – or sometimes a still more elaborate, contemporary Arabian Nights series, featuring Paul himself as the humble, woefully downtrodden and wistfully ingratiating sheikh Abu Ben Grottso.

Paul said Carol had inherited his sociability, determination and taste for hard work together with his theatrical and practical gifts whereas Sally, who drew and read as voraciously as he had done from childhood on, early showed signs of being a writer. Sally was seventeen in 1965. She had always shone at school, and Paul delighted as his own mother had once done for him in circulating news of her achievements, her twelve top-grade O levels, her four A and two S levels, and the further success confidently anticipated for her that autumn in the Oxbridge entrance examinations. In the spring of 1964, when Paul was in India (one thing that delighted him even in Timmapuram was a team of white bullocks 'with lovely black eyes made up like Sally's'),[30] he had dreamed that she had cut off her long yellow hair – only to find, when he got back, that his dream had come true.[31] Paul was a fond, proud, anxious, admiring but not at all lax or indulgent parent. He surprised an Indian friend, who held that children should be allowed to go their own ways, by the vehemence with which he insisted that on the contrary they had to be supervised, corrected, trained as strictly as you would stake, prune and tie a young tree.[32] At this stage, mid-way through the 1960s, Sally looked set to fulfil her father's most extravagant hopes of academic achievement just as Carol would shine in the theatre: 'their ambitions are a reflection of my twin interests, the theatre and literature,' he wrote guardedly to his mother,[33] with whom he had re-opened friendly but formal relations in the autumn of 1964, by which time Frances — wholly blind, partly deaf, increasingly frail, almost eighty years old and now safely installed back where she came from, south of the river, in an old people's home on Tulse Hill — no longer posed a serious threat.

Carol's course at RADA would finish in the summer of 1966 shortly before Sally set off for university, and the prospect of both daughters leaving home made the whole family restive. Paul, who still had periodic visions of taking off at some point with Penny, dreamed of a snug little retreat by the sea.[34] Both parents dreaded the girls going, which would leave them alone in the house with an invisible but insistent third presence, Paul's Indian novel, engrossing his waking hours and invading his dreams at night. 'It was always India, only India with him,' said Penny, who had hoped that going back might at last have got the place out of his system. She could never feel comfortable in the saris he brought her, or muster any enthusiasm for his Indian souvenirs: a plum-coloured sari from Havildar Nag, a brass tray from the Kumars in Madras, a silk scarf from Dipali Nag, and countless presents over the years from Dorothy Ganapathy, who urged Penny in vain to put on a sari to go with her dark eyes. Dorothy, who spent a month in London in the course of travelling in Europe in the summer of 1965, was invited to Addison Way for a dinner party which was not a success. Penny disliked the sensation of being looked over and found wanting that Paul's friends so often gave her, while Dorothy was startled by her hostess's declaration that she would never visit India because it had stolen her husband. Penny's view of the matter was, by Paul's own account, perfectly right. He freely admitted that India had stolen his heart as well as monopolising his thoughts and captivating his imagination. Again and again, ostensibly discussing professional necessities over the next decade, he would tacitly acknowledge the price that had to be paid in private. 'There are stresses and strains in the construction of a novel that we ignore at our peril,' he said to an audience of fellow writers, emphasising that defeat and despair were part of the creative process: 'Don't despair of despair.'[35]

The injunction was part of an account of the making of *The Jewel in the Crown* which Paul gave to the Writers Summer School at the Hayes in Swanwick. He had agreed to open the session in August 1965, in place of the Archbishop of York (who had declined along with all the other bishops approached),[36] and he returned to deliver a closing address two years later. Penny and the girls liked Swanwick: the amusements, the company, the folk-singing, the formal dance with an old-fashioned band, and the huge, rambling house with its spacious, high-ceilinged drawing room, its splendid conservatory, garden and grounds. Paul approved of a free family holiday without the inconvenience of being obliged to stop work, and all of them enjoyed the stir he made, the admirers who thronged round him whenever he appeared, hanging on his words, competing for his attention and packing the hall for his talks. He could be a brilliant lecturer on a good day, with a knack of raising, meeting and outpacing his audience's expectations without betraying by so much as a missed beat the often terrifying amount of neat spirits he still needed to nerve himself for a performance.

These were the years of the great Swanwick power struggle waged for control of the cardigan brigade by the dashing, imperious and hugely popular President, Vivien Stuart (who had her fifty-third book accepted in 1967 by Mills & Boon, and who took a special proprietary pride in Paul because of shared wartime experience in Burma, where she had driven lorries for the women's army corps). She kept Paul up to date with blow-by-blow, front-line reports on a mutinous campaign to break ranks and undermine her authority in the name of modernity, professionalism and literature's Angry Young Men, represented at Swanwick by the editor of *Books and Bookmen* and Paul's old sparring partner Gerald Pollinger. There were rows, rumbling rumours, muffled explosions, accusations and counter-accusations with Paul cast as referee or more often pig-in-the-middle. Dark talk of his having betrayed his old allies by becoming 'a "difficult" or "intellectual" writer' was countered by a stalwart Scottite, who announced 'she would gladly walk to Swanwick from Devon' to hear him.[37] Pollinger claimed that Paul lectured over the heads of his listeners. The President defiantly declared him 'the best darned speaker we HAVE EVER HAD AT SWANWICK'.[38] Paul emerged from their cross-fire in 1965 triumphant but shattered, drunk with elation and Carew's gin ('I spent the last day of it in bed under sedation! 300 authors under one roof is a horrible experience'),[39] retreating with Penny and Sally to recuperate in the course of a miserably wet week in a rented bungalow at Rottingdean on the south coast.

The two talks he gave at Swanwick were above all exercises in clearing his head. In them he stated problems, proposed and analysed solutions with exemplary directness and force. The first was written in July 1965, as soon as he had got the manuscript of *The Jewel in the Crown* safely out of the house, by which time he had long since acknowledged to himself and others that he had a sequel in mind. At Swanwick he permitted himself to contemplate big ideas – 'Movements in political and social history are, at an early stage, the dreams of writers' – while conceding their absurdity, and claiming for writers only the modest privilege of representing 'the collective discontent with established processes that leads to change and social development'.[40] The lecture, with the noncommittal title 'Aspects of Writing', surveyed the contemporary literary scene, noting its narrowly insular and domestic preoccupations, its preponderantly satirical tone, its often equivocal attitude to the emergent ethos of acquisitive aspirations and instant gratification, its energetic, aggrieved and angry young heroes ('What Joe Lambton wanted was power. . . . *Room at the Top* . . . forced us to recognise that *power* was what we had lost, and what we felt we couldn't live without, although for the life of us we couldn't see what kind of power it would be both pleasant to wield and humanly reasonable to exercise').[41] It touched on a theme that would become central for Paul – the warning that a generation which had watched the empire 'disappearing into the mists of territorial fragmentation and dangerous racial memory'[42] had not by any means disposed of its problems – and concluded that the British novel had sailed itself temporarily into a backwater from which it must somehow find a way to break out. What appealed to the audience at Swanwick, warming its cockles even where the argument passed over its head, was the note of subdued confidence, vigorous and invigorating, as if the speaker had himself already glimpsed the possibility of stretching and extending his reach.

His second Swanwick talk ('Method: The Mystery and The Mechanics', delivered two years later) was a practical and technical account of how he wrote *The Jewel in the Crown*, the kind of demonstration generally easier for a graphic artist than for a writer. Paul conducted his audience round the workshop of his imagination much as his father might have shown a party of interested visitors round the studio, starting from the physical base ('for a writer, going back home means back to the pen, pencil and typewriter – and the blank, implacable sheet of white paper'),[43] and giving a detailed, matter-of-fact account of the production process which for him invariably began with a visual image. In this case it was the running girl, tough, resilient, badly shaken, who mysteriously encapsulated for him 'the whole feeling of the British in India, and the feeling of India itself – a vast, flat territory, strangely forbidding, somehow incalcul-able, ugly, beautiful'.[44] He said that the right image would drill deep into the imagination ('Once I had got it, received it if you like, although naturally I gave it to myself, I could treat it as a mine whose veins could be explored and exploited'). He explained the mixture of experience, knowledge, hard thought and the prolonged effort of invention set in motion by that original emotional impulse ('Writing is not observation – it is feeling'). He described how he investigated the background and origins of the girl he saw running, decided on her location, felt his way into her character, tried to get close enough to see her face, connected her to her real-life counterpart, Neil Ghosh's Australian girlfriend in Calcutta: 'she was a big, husky . . . girl. My imagination fined her down, but at the point where the resilience of the girl in the image matched that of the girl in Calcutta, the fining-down process stopped – and Daphne Manners was born as tall, gangling – rather awkward.'[45]

He gave her a historical context at the time of the Quit India riots, which made it likely that she was fleeing from some kind of assault, and he remembered a similar episode during the same sort of turmoil just after the First World War at Amritsar in the Punjab, when an attack by Indian hooligans on an English mission schoolmistress had led to brutal and primitive British reprisals, which the Indians never forgot (the notorious General Dyer, determined to deal expeditiously with what looked like an incipient uprising had arrested six Indian boys at random and had them publicly flogged, subsequently ordering his soldiers to shoot on a peaceful, unarmed crowd of protesters walled in with no means of escape in Amritsar's Jallianwallah Barg). Having got so far with his first image, Paul balanced it by inventing another using a technique of reversal which he called 'going in through the back of the image',[46] a way of shaping and enlarging the narrative, which provided him with the mission school teacher Edwina Crane. Both women find themselves caught up by chance in the disturbances, and both eventually die in consequence. It was clear to Paul, looking back two years later, that their stories were part of a larger, long-term failure to bridge the racial divide. He was also perhaps beginning in retrospect to realise that behind Daphne Manners' relationship with her Indian lover, the affair that starts out with such high hopes and goes disastrously, irretrievably wrong with Hari Kumar's arrest, lay his own deep-seated sense of being displaced, dispossessed, a person never fully at home in the society in which he grew up.

Unacknowledged racial prejudice had caught him on the raw in India, pricking him all the more sharply because nobody wanted to talk about it. Dorothy Ganapathy had begged him not to write about it, when they discussed the kind of 'harpy' whose behaviour had dismayed him in Bombay.[47] He consulted Dorothy at the time about subsequent experiences, and she warned him about the extreme sensitivity of friends of her own with mixed blood. Dorothy's pride in her Indian nationality admitted no compromise, even producing a temporary rift with Paul in the summer of 1965 when she wrote, like Chris Almedingen before her, to refuse his dedication after reading the manuscript of the *Jewel*[48] (one of Dorothy's sisters was married to an English High Court Judge in Allahabad, and Paul had borrowed her daughters' names – Lakshmi and Indira – for two of the characters in the *Jewel*, whom he promptly renamed Shalini and Parvati).

By the time he finished the *Jewel*, Paul was already widening his focus, planning a trilogy which would go deeper and further into the affair between the races, proposing in his next novel to explore the opportunistic British attitude to conflict between Hindus and Muslims. 'History seems to have overtaken me,' he wrote sombrely to Dorothy on 30 September 1965, at the height of the fighting with Pakistan. He had already quoted to her the passage in his novel where Lady Manners identifies the creation of Pakistan as Britain's crowning failure in India.[49] He placed blame for the war ultimately on the British, detecting and deploring vestiges of old authoritarian Imperial attitudes in the Labour government's policy.[50] He said he had had it in mind from the beginning to end his Indian novel or novels with partition in 1947 and the massacres that followed, heralded by the episode of a Muslim being dragged from a railway carriage and murdered by Hindus. In the autumn of 1965, Paul still hoped that his next novel would lead him to this conclusion (in fact it would be nearly another eight years before he finally reached what he called 'the train scene' and used it to draw the whole Raj Quartet to a close), and that the trilogy could then be completed with a book about modern India.[51]

The autumn and winter were spent preparing, reading and thinking. Paul had evolved a basic structure for *The Day of the Scorpion* by April 1966, but was still dissatisfied with the beginning ('the material – the things I want to weave into it – is as intimidating as the north wall of the Eiger'),[52] and he was badly stuck again by July. Part of the trouble was the impending publication of the *Jewel*: 'If the first book doesn't make it the second inherits, automatically, a defeat,' he wrote to John Willey on 2 April. Advance reactions were encouraging. Heinemann had gone to the trouble of ordering an Indian flag, which had to be specially made and handstitched, for the jacket photograph. Paul typed out pre-publication extracts from the American trade press for Dorothy in Bombay, and got back a message for his publisher saying she meant to hold her little image of the god Ganesh in her hand until publication.[53] Dorothy's silver Ganesh had sat on a ledge over Paul's desk while he wrote *Jewel*, and in these weeks of waiting he poured out his nervousness over 'your book' to Dorothy more freely than to anyone else. She responded with loyal enthusiasm, circulating advance copies (devaluation of the rupee forced Allied Publishers to cancel orders), assessing reviews as they came in, demanding sales figures and enquiring anxiously after film rights. In the run up to publication she prayed every morning to Ganesh for Paul's success, and for rain (a late monsoon meant drought and fear of typhoid in Bombay), in the formula, 'Om Prakesh Om', which she had taught Paul, and which he had repeated to help his concentration whenever the writing went badly.[54]

He had reason to feel nervous. Disappointing sales of first *The Bender*, then the *Corrida* meant that the income guaranteed under renewed arrangements with Heinemann (£2,000 advance on each of two new novels in £500 quarterly payments) and Morrow (2,000 dollars a year) already exceeded his actual earnings. Neither of the last two novels had covered its advance, nor could he hope to produce a book a year. He had seriously considered, in the autumn of 1964, going back to some sort of office job, and he knew when he finished the *Jewel* that his future as a full-time writer depended on its success ('£2,000 a year into a £2,000 novel every eighteen months won't go,' he wrote flatly to David Higham).[55] Publication in America in June produced an accolade from Naomi Bliven in the *New Yorker* – 'With this review, I feel myself that at last justice reigns,' John Willey wrote solemnly on 2 July – followed by weighty approval from the oracle of the *New York Times*, Orville Prescott, after which the book sold out in ten days.[56] Dorothy described her guests standing to toast the *Jewel* at a party, in a letter which also triumphantly announced the coming of rain.[57] The book came out in England on 17 July to generally appreciative reviews. 'I think God Ganpati has heard our prayers,' Paul wrote to Dorothy three days later, reporting tentative approaches from a film producer which he urged her to discount: 'wouldn't it be marvellous, though, if some producer decided to make a film of the *Jewel* . . . ,' he added, briefly allowing himself to contemplate an impossible dream.[58] Friends at home were relieved and delighted. 'Goff and I snatched it from each other by turns and can almost be said to have read the same copy simultaneously,' wrote Mollie Hamilton,[59] who could remember the grown-ups endlessly discussing the Jallianwallah affair at the time, when she was a small girl in India. Heinemann planned to launch a library edition of Paul's novels with Ganesh as its emblem, and Dorothy discovered that, on top of all his other capacities and functions, Ganesh had been all along the Guardian of Writers.[60]

On 17 July 1966, Paul's publication day, Carol left home to take up her first job as assistant stage manager at the Summer Theatre in Frinton. 'It's also the anniversary (the 26th) of my joining the army, so there may be a significant conjunction of stars,' Paul wrote to Dorothy. 'The army led me to India, & before that to meeting Penny & to getting married.'[61] With the *Jewel* out of the way, Paul turned with relief to its sequel. He planned no holiday that summer, except for a short break at Seaford on the south coast where the horse painter, George Wright, had spent the last years of his life. The Scotts rented a charming house belonging to George's daughter Enid Huntley, the 'seaside aunt' who crops up occasionally in Paul's writings. Cousin Enid, now in her late seventies, was a favourite with the whole family: entering her front door was 'like stepping back into Victorian, or at least Edwardian times',[62] with potted plants on plant stands, brass and copper on the walls, a panelled dining room, chintz armchairs round an old-fashioned coal fire and a wooden verandah for sitting out on sunny days. But the weather was dreadful and Paul, who caught a heavy cold, stayed indoors with his manuscript.

Penny was still recuperating from a worrying series of accidents that had begun in the spring, when she cut her hand badly while opening a tin of catfood, infected the cut, and had to have a tetanus injection from which she took a long time to recover. In April, she dropped the telephone on her foot: 'She thinks she probably ought to go to bed & stay there (but then there's the danger of the roof falling in, isn't there?)' Paul wrote to his old friend Peter Green.[63] He kept his correspondents informed over the next few months as Penny repeatedly hit her hand ('She had better live in a plywood case as she keeps banging herself here, there and everywhere,' Dorothy suggested),[64] scalded it twice, and in July did the same to her foot. 'Poor Penny has been in the wars again,' Paul wrote to his Swedish translator, Magnus Lindberg, who had become a friend on visits to London, 'calmly stood pouring out a kettle of boiling water onto her foot instead of into a teapot. . . . I tell her we'd better start drinking cold tea.'[65] She broke a tooth in the autumn on the day they said goodbye to Sally who, having left school that summer with excellent A levels in English, Latin, Art and French, had decided to read English at York University instead of sitting the Oxford and Cambridge entrance examinations which would have meant another year at home. 'The sun went behind a cloud the day Carol left,' Penny wrote and, when Sally set off for York, 'the house was empty indeed.'[66]

Paul was immersed in his book that winter, shaping the whole and reorganising earlier sections ('I've relaxed by tearing the garden to pieces,' he wrote on 24 November to John Willey, 'getting rid of the weeds & hedging & ditching: which is rather like cutting and recasting, come to think of it'). He told Dorothy Ganapathy the following February that, apart from two days off at Christmas, he had been seated at the desk for the last three months, leaving the house only to dig and think: 'Gardening helps me clear away the fog of the morning and prepare for the evening stint.' By April 1967 he had finished the first half of *The Day of the Scorpion*, 100,000 words which by July had been typed out and lodged for safekeeping in David Higham's private cupboard.[67] He broke off briefly in August for a flying visit to Swanwick, with a fortnight beforehand working at Seaford, where Penny slammed her hand in the car door and had to embark on a depressing round of X-rays, hospital visits, hot wax baths and 'fearsome manipulative exercises'[68] to save the crushed hand. By October Paul's novel had reached the final downhill slopes, and in November it was almost finished ('only . . . one major and two minor scenes to do').[69] Penny was suffering from palpitations by this time, and seeing a heart specialist. Paul delivered the last 150 pages of his manuscript to the typist five days before Christmas, took to his bed with bronchitis, and summoned the doctor on Christmas Day for an injection to help him breathe.[70] Carol, at home between stage jobs, stayed on to nurse Penny, in bed downstairs with heart trouble, and Paul, who slowly recovered upstairs. When he said he thought he could fancy game pie and champagne, Carol bought a pheasant, cooked a pie and served it to him in bed with a half bottle of Moet and Chandon. It was Carol, the only member of the family still on her feet, who went up to town to deliver *The Day of the Scorpion* midway through January, departing herself the next month for a new job at the Forum Theatre, Billingham, near Durham, whereupon Paul took over as 'head cook and bottle washer!'[71]

Penny remained poorly, going into hospital for tests in March, being prescribed drugs without any conclusive diagnosis, and convalescing in April with Paul's seaside aunt at Seaford: 'I tell her she will rattle when she stands up if she goes on like this,' Paul wrote briskly to his mother at Easter.[72] Sally was also severely depressed in her second year at York, and struggling with problems of her own for which the university doctor prescribed sleeping pills, tranquillisers and anti-depressants in quantities which seriously worried both Paul and Penny. Carol celebrated her twenty-first birthday at Billingham with a crate of champagne from her parents. 'Daughters! Tell Goff I sympathise – I wish a couple of chaps would whisk my two off – I wouldn't be particular!' Paul wrote gaily to Mollie Hamilton, thanking her for a present of a stuffed bird of paradise and begging her not to send him a live scorpion.[73] Sally became formally engaged on his birthday, 25 March 1968, to the boy next door, Paul Cashmore.

Things looked up briefly that summer, although the house still seemed painfully empty. Even the cats were growing old. Paul said they looked lost and sad, wandering into the Cashmores' garden next door and crying, when the family was away.[74] Several of the original eight had died, or had to be put down, but the survivors still ran up trees and chased squirrels. Beauty, the female Russian blue, always a favourite and now twelve years old, had points in common with Paul's mother ('Energetic, agile, naughty, she cannot bear to see the others resting peacefully. Looks upon herself as someone to stir up some interest, get things moving').[75] Paul would stand for hours at his study window, pondering, reflecting, watching the cats and the owl that lived alone in a fir tree at the bottom of the garden. He put out saucers of milk for a hedgehog, and plates of scraps for the foxes that strayed from the oak wood. Penny was away on and off, down at Seaford, showing no definite sign of improvement. Paul went down too when he could, reporting a safari one hot day to Longleat, 'where the lions looked like so many publishers satiated on a diet of mutual agreement over terms.'[76] Penny's writing had been disrupted. She and Paul sometimes went whole days without speaking, and had long ceased to discuss one another's work: Paul told John Willey, when the *Jewel* came out, that they had decided Penny should not see the book before publication, which 'made it – in the household – an even more private affair than usual'.[77]

From Penny's point of view, Paul in these years was becoming steadily more forbidding, remote and inaccessible. Close friends who invited the Scotts to their parties got used to Paul coming alone, making excuses for his wife or, when they arrived together, to Penny's going home first and Paul's driving back on his own, unless he was so drunk he had to be put to bed on the spot. Penny seemed more retiring as Paul grew increasingly expansive. Once, in his own house, he went round distributing trophies (including the Malayan kris) to the guests, another time at the Gants he got so obstreperous he refused to leave and had to be knocked out by Roland (this was the famous occasion on which the pair set off in the small hours for Oxford). John Willey remembered another disconcerting dinner at the Gants when Penny disappeared upstairs on arrival to be followed shortly afterwards for the rest of the evening by Paul, and a night when the three of them wound up at a disco with Penny declining to dance: 'she and I sat on the sidelines, wallflowers that we were, while Paul danced up a storm with the many willing and able ladies present.'[78] Afterwards Paul drove them home in spite of Penny's remonstrances. 'Paul was up to the challenge,' Willey wrote admiringly, but Penny remained fearful, both of Paul's driving when drunk and of his knack of making these drives into a test of her faith in him. He would aim straight at a bollard, swerving at the last moment, which never failed to frighten her.

Less apprehensive passengers reported Paul a brilliant driver when drunk: at the wheel, as at the typewriter, drink steadied his nerve and sharpened his concentration, enabling him to take risks and carry them off as he never could have done when sober. Dancing became something of a hobby with him in these years whenever he could find a partner. He would dance the tango at the Rainbow Room in New York with his agent Dorothy Olding, who was devoted to him ('When I got to England, he was always the first person I would call') and, on his wedding anniversary, he asked Dorothy to dance with him in the drawing-room at Addison Way. Penny, who had again refused to dance, puzzled Dorothy and others by her invariable insistence on taking a back seat, literally on car outings, metaphorically on occasions when he and Paul entertained. Women like Dorothy Olding or Mary Patchett (who still saw as much as she could of Paul, meticulously including Penny in all invitations) could never understand what made Penny so edgy, so unappreciative of, even downright ungrateful for Paul's devotion. 'He was *so* gentle and *so* good,' Mary said wistfully: 'He would have been so easy to look after and make happy.'

But Paul himself understood very well what was happening to his wife at this time. He had written about a woman in precisely her position in his abandoned novel, *The Careerist* (or *The Marriage*) in 1963, and he would return to the subject again thirteen years later in the opening chapters of another unfinished novel, *Mango Rain* (or *The Careerists* or *Married with Two Children*).[79] The heroine in each case is a middle-aged wife immured at home, cut off from contact with the outside world, wholly dependent on a husband who narrowly controls her life while edging her firmly away from the centre of his own. Isobel Porter, in *The Careerist*, finds herself living a separate life under the same roof as her masterful, self-contained husband Nigel, doggedly pursuing her own routines ('she . . . prepared the living room for the evening session of silence that would be gravid with incompatibility, and not with companionable monosyllabic understanding'), meeting his needs and anticipating his demands in a spirit of stubborn, silent protest, 'as stringent as it was inarticulate'. Their relationship is epitomised by the kitchen, a kind of sore centre to the marriage, which has been modernised against her will to her husband's designs with all the hospitable clutter swept away to be replaced by clinical fittings, a vault-like cooking unit and implacable, blue-white, mortuary strip lights:

> For her, a kitchen had to prove itself by ordeals of fire and water: by gas rings that popped crossly at being turned on, stoves that sulked but could be raked and shaken until their teeth rattled, and made to grin with hot orange happiness behind crackling mica windows; by water that gushed and slopped and steamed and threatened to drown and scald and otherwise displayed its power to cleanse and make whole. But in this kitchen that Nigel had designed for her, fire and water (apart from the water that fell in shining rods from shining faucets) were powers that had been reduced to invisible forces you reckoned with in terms of calibration.

In *Mango Rain*, the wife finds her whole house turned into a kind of tomb, and herself growing wary even of the telephone ('a link with the world outside which she had begun to fear and no longer to cherish'). Her husband, David Chalmers, is a successful literary agent ('Books, books, books, she thought: I have had enough of books'). Nicknamed 'the Charmer', he is irresistibly attentive to others but less so to his wife, who increasingly resents being expected to entertain his favourite authors: to plan, shop for, prepare, cook, serve, clear away and wash up after meals at which she herself is apt to be treated at her own table as if she weren't there. One striking thing about both novels is how strongly the author's sympathies lie with the wife, who surrenders herself unconditionally only to end up used and discarded by a husband exclusively wedded to his career ('Marrying David she had found herself in a world of almost total obsession, what over the years she had come to think of as ingrownness'). It is was if, now that his own wife had been reduced more or less to a condition of dumbness like the mute, unprotesting, subservient women in his early fiction, the writer in Paul had begun to assess, truthfully and without self-deception, what that silent attentiveness cost.

'I . . . agree with your impression that the women are the best I have ever done,' Paul wrote to John Willey, discussing the manuscript of *The Day of the Scorpion*: 'In fact, I know I've not been all that good before. I was finally very pleased with the way Sarah and Susan came out.'[80] Sarah and Susan Layton belong to an old Anglo-Indian army family based on the hill station of Pankot, where the British retire to enjoy cheap servants, a mild climate, views that remind them of Surrey, and the pleasant consciousness 'of duty done without the depression of going home wondering what it had been done for'.[81] Sarah – quiet, efficient, dependable – joins the Women's Army Auxiliary Corps in wartime but finds herself increasingly needed at home to look after her family (her father, Colonel Layton, is interned in a German POW camp, and her mother – distracted, withdrawn, unable to function fully without his support – turns to drink for consolation). Sarah's pretty and popular younger sister Susan gets engaged to an officer called Teddie Bingham in 1943 and, when Teddie is posted away, plans a hurried wedding in the Muslim state of Mirat. Stones thrown and other disquieting eruptions at the wedding turn out to be connected with another officer, Ronald Merrick, Teddie's best man, said to have played a not altogether creditable role in a notorious affair that blew up over the rape of a white woman the year before at Mayapore. Teddie is killed in action, Susan bears his child but is unable to cope with his loss, becomes helplessly disorientated, loses all command or sense of herself, and ends up in a psychiatric hospital, while Sarah takes charge at home.

The Layton sisters started out with superficial resemblances to Paul's own daughters before taking on fictional identities for which, at a deeper level, he drew on himself. Susan's fragility and charm, her winning ways, her apparently effortless ability to captivate and disarm all comers mask an insecurity going back to earliest childhood, and a deep-seated dread of finding her own inadequacy exposed in public: 'Like when you lift a stone there's something underneath running in circles', she confides to her sister: 'I used to feel like a drawing that anyone who wanted to could come along and rub out.'[82] Sarah by comparison has never been tempted to surrender her sharply marked individuality for the sake of conformity with other people: she remains a sceptical observer, an outsider in Pankot society, without prejudices or preconceptions, startlingly so to more conventional characters like her Aunt Fenny (who softens on occasion to Sarah, 'but the softening only emphasised the lines that years of stiffening had left permanently on her, the private marks of public disapproval'). For large stretches of *The Day of the Scorpion*, it is Sarah who supplies a broader perspective on the narrow world of Pankot, and Sarah's tone of voice – level, reflective, humorous, enquiring – merges indistinguishably at points with the consciousness of the book's narrator. It was a voice Paul's friends immediately recognised: 'To read the *Scorpion* is to me . . . to listen to you personally,' Magnus Lindberg wrote from Sweden, 'to hear your voice and to see you before my eyes, to see your smile, the kindly sardonical glimpse in the corner of your eye . . .'[83]

The core of the novel, Paul's initial impulse, was already implicit before he began in his title. 'Scorpions are very sensitive to heat, which is why they live under stones. The rains drive them out into the open. There was an old belief that if you surrounded them with a ring of fire, they committed suicide. But actually they are shrivelled by the heat, and when they dart their tails they're not committing suicide but trying to attack,' he had written to Dorothy Ganapathy on 7 May 1967, explaining his metaphor for the British in India:

They were driven out of their places in the end, by a number of pressures – and were scorched by fires they had really set light to themselves . . . It's *The Day of the Scorpion* because the book is supposed to be taking us right up to the eve of independence – when we were all flushed out from under our stones.

When Paul wrote this letter, he had just reached the halfway mark of his novel at the end of Book One, 'The Prisoner in the Fort', which concerns unsuccessful British attempts to negotiate with the detained Muslim Congressman, Mohamed Ali Kasim, and the tensions between Hindus, Muslims and British simmering in the background to the Layton wedding. He was about to plunge into Book Two, 'Orders of Release', which would deal, in its first section, with the interrogation in 1943 of the prisoner, Hari Kumar, held without charge since his arrest by Merrick after the Manners affair (Daphne herself had died in childbirth nine months later, leaving a baby, Parvati), and, in its second, with Susan's collapse after her young husband's death, Sarah Layton's friendship with Kasim's son Ahmed, her brief, unsatisfactory affair with a British officer in Calcutta, and the conditional release of Ahmed's father.

A structure as complex as this second novel was in process of becoming could only be built on solid foundations after careful planning. At the same time, Paul insisted that the work must grow of itself, regulated 'by ear and sense of pace' rather than by any previously formulated blueprint. Five years earlier, when he had first contemplated the possibility of one day attempting a sequence, he had felt confident of shaping it according to the lessons so painfully learned from his earlier novels, 'relying on past experience . . . as you rely on what you've learned about breathing if you're a runner.'[84] Clearly this technique was beginning to work halfway through *Scorpion* where Sarah Layton and her family show signs of playing an integral part, not only as individuals in their own right, but in the overall structure of the sequence. As its scope widened, as themes and characters multiplied, as their orchestration became richer and more subtle, the quickening political and historical momentum of the Quartet – India on the verge of partition, moving simultaneously towards liberation and disintegration – would be mirrored on a domestic scale in the shaky equilibrium of the Layton family, whose affairs occupy a large part of the foreground.

The *Scorpion* was published on 3 September 1968. Paul celebrated by lunching with Roland Gant (he had lodged Penny at Seaford), and dining at the Connaught with Helen King of Morrow. He had dedicated the book to Fern and John Willey: she turned out to have been born under Scorpio, while he had long been Paul's most ardent and practical supporter, and was eagerly looking forward to the further instalments he predicted on the strength of this one.[85] It was well reviewed but sold worse than the *Jewel*, whose sales had turned out in the end to be respectable but no more. In the autumn of 1968 Paul's financial position, always precarious, was deteriorating again. His income had been bumped up over the past two years by a paperback deal with Mayflower that was about to run out. His application for an Arts Council bursary in 1967 had been rejected.[86] He had returned to reviewing for *The Times* and the *Times Literary Supplement*, which brought in an extra two or three hundred pounds a year, but his rate of production was slowing down, and his savings were more or less used up. 'In other words I hear the advance echo of the crunch', he wrote to David Higham: 'The problem can be fairly simply stated: how much am I worth, to whom and for what?'[87] The answer, in money terms, was not a lot. Paul could barely make ends meet on his publishers' guarantees, which brought in roughly £3,000 a year, and he worried constantly about whether, in view of static or falling sales, they would be maintained. An undertaking on the scale he envisaged, which appealed to neither popular taste nor intellectual fashion, required no ordinary commitment from publishers as well as author, and Paul could never count for certain on Willey and Gant holding Morrow and Heinemann respectively to the sticking point.

He himself needed no holding, but he was increasingly aware of the scope and mass of research involved on top of the immense effort of invention. 'Imagination is not enough,' he said: 'Knowledge is necessary.'[88] He had been making notes towards his next novel, *The Towers of Silence*, as far back as July, settling to solid work in September, and by early October was tentatively planning a return to India,[89] for which Heinemann had agreed to put up £500. On 30 November 1968, he wrote to Dorothy Ganapathy in Bombay announcing he had booked a flight for 4 January, which put him in such high spirits that he started his airmail form back to front ('well, this shows how mad I am, & excited!'). Penny had been back at home for some time, although still in pain from her hand, suffering from a bad back, and feeling generally shaky. Sally, who had switched from English to philosophy and was moving towards final examinations in her last year at university, was struggling with problems never entirely clear to Paul. She broke off her engagement that autumn, and at the beginning of December her parents were summoned to York to find Sally in hospital recovering from an overdose of sleeping tablets. She was evidently in no condition to explain what had happened, nor could Paul glean much reassurance from consultations with her tutor and supervisor. He was bewildered, his distress complicated by unacknowledged private hurt and resentment: he saw Sally's predicament as a kind of letting go, and contrasted it sharply with his own lifelong determination to pull himself up on the tightest of tight strings.

Of his daughters, Sally had always been in some ways the more like him, taking after the Scott family in looks, possessing intellectual and imaginative gifts in which he recognised his own. She had written long, ambitious, adolescent poems heavy with religious imagery (Paul's letters to her, analysing technical weakness and emotional imprecision, owed more to an old animus against *I, Gerontius* than to the comparatively innocuous verses Sally showed him), and he saw the makings of a dramatist in her first undergraduate plays. But Paul could not reconcile himself to her apparent rejection of the university education he had been cheated of through no fault of his own. He reverted to military methods, drawing up situation reports, listing options, establishing chains of command and communication ('It needs a clear line of instruction & information, in my opinion').[90] Old habits of authority reasserted themselves. He took the view that Sally could not expect privileged treatment in the form of an extended grant (financial strain was a minor but persistent worry), or extra time to complete her course. He pressed for a clear-cut decision ('She is either well & capable or ill & incapable') in a far from clear-cut situation. A fog of misunderstanding and cross purpose compounded the whole family's alarm and confusion. Mother and daughter drew together as they had done ever since Sally fell ill as a baby. The one bright spot Paul could discern in Sally's collapse was the way Penny rallied to look after her: 'Here we have one crisis after another (daughters) – but Penny, thank goodness, seems more or less operational again . . . ' he wrote to Mollie Hamilton on 13 December. 'Glad to hear that the work is moving along. Personally, I am deeply bogged down, not for lack of inspiration but in all these crises. What a year.'

Sally came home for Christmas, consulted a London psychiatrist who suggested a complete rest from brainwork, and was given permission by the university authorities to spend the first month of the spring term at home. Paul, who had wondered whether or not to postpone his Indian trip, was relieved that even a temporary plan had been formulated. However unsettled affairs might be behind the domestic lines, on the professional front he urgently needed to replenish resources depleted by more than four years' heavy slogging in a campaign that was beginning to look as if it might take another four. 'How I long for the softer airs and rhythm of India,' he wrote to Dorothy Ganapathy when it snowed at the New Year.[91]

CHAPTER THIRTEEN

The thick boot of envy and the leg-iron of contempt

Paul meant to go first to Dorothy's flat in Queen's Court, Bombay, then move on with her to Delhi, a city he had last seen as an officer in transit in wartime, when the Moghuls' Red Fort itself and the great plain on either side of the majestic Raj Path (then the Kingsway) in front of Lutyens' Viceregal palace were dotted and disfigured with tents, barracks, supply depots and makeshift hutments. He flew into Bombay on the morning of Sunday 5 January 1969, to spend a week resting, recuperating, revisiting old haunts, catching up on old friends, and repairing his relationship with Dorothy, which had suffered during a visit she paid to London the summer before at the height of Paul's family troubles when he had felt miserably unable to invite her to Addison Way, or to explain what was wrong. The two had lunched together at the Epicure, but it was only back in Bombay that they could talk freely again. Always a curiosity, now something of a celebrity with two Indian novels to show for his last visit, Paul was asked out and fêted all week. He and Dorothy took up where they had left off: they were fond enough of one another by this time, and familiar enough, to dispense with formal constraints. 'She stood up to him,' said the niece with whom Dorothy was to stay in Delhi, Mrs Kuldip Kaur Singh (known as Goodie). 'That was why he loved Auntie Dorothy. She lost her temper. She argued with him, and proved him wrong.'[1]

On 14 January they flew to Delhi where Paul had arranged to stay with the Nag Chaudhuris: Dulal had been made chairman of the government's Science Committee, and a member of Mrs Gandhi's Planning Commission (she would shortly appoint him Scientific Adviser to her Defence Ministry), which meant that Dipali had become one of New Delhi's most elegant and unconventional official hostesses. The job carried with it a large and beautiful bungalow on Tughluk Road – 'one of those sprawly old palaces' said Dipali[2] – approached by a semicircular drive curving past clipped lawns to a pillared portico, which opened onto a wide, cool entrance hall with polished stone floors stretching the length of the house to French windows at the far end of the drawing-room leading onto the garden. Instead of the peace and seclusion of rural Behala, there was a constant cosmopolitan bustle of people coming and going to meetings, concerts and parties, a mixed traffic of Dipali's old friends, mostly artists and musicians, and Dulal's government contacts, cabinet ministers and scientific delegates. Paul said the atmosphere of the house was like living in a Chekhov play.[3] He had his own rooms in the guest wing to the right of the hall, and found endless entertainment in his fellow guests: a lugubrious Dane called Eric, who was in love with Dipali, and a small, elderly gentleman looking like a brown acorn, dried up and exceedingly droll, an ex-Minister of Agriculture called Mr Sinhar. Paul drank his coffee and ate a fresh banana each morning in the garden, which was grander and more formal than Dipali's flowery green wilderness in Calcutta, with great crescent-shaped rosebeds, cornflowers almost as tall as himself, scarlet Indian honeysuckle climbing the cream-coloured walls, and small emerald-green parrots playing in the trees. There was a servants' compound with a buffalo or two, and a capacious kitchen garden (Mr Sinhar, who was said to be able to tell where any vegetable had been grown just by eating it, took Paul on a conducted tour diagnosing what was wrong with each plant).[4]

Paul would sit listening to Dipali's pupils taking their morning lessons in the yellow-painted music room which ran out into the garden. Dipali herself played and sang several times at evening gatherings: Paul was invited at one of them to accompany her on the tamboura, and once she sang simply for her husband and house guests. She noticed immediately, as Dorothy had done, how much more relaxed and happy Paul seemed than on his earlier visit, how often he laughed and how easy he was to please. She went shopping with him, showed him round the Red Fort and arranged a lunch with the novelist Ruth Prawer Jhabvala. On his last day but one, 29 January, she provided a ticket to watch the Republic Day parade along the Raj Path with buglers Beating the Retreat, a combination of Indian and Imperial theatricality which began with helicopters dropping thousands of crimson rose petals (Paul caught one of them) to carpet the route, and continued with flights of jets ('The last of them unrolls a striped aerial smoke-carpet of saffron, white and green. For a magical instant, before the thin vapours merge and blur and evaporate, the patriotic ribbon in the sky seems like a reflection of the long, straight road from President's House to India Gate').[5] Paul said he funked sitting in the VIP enclave, gave his ticket to Mr Sinhar, ducked the barrier and stationed himself in a service area under the ramparts of the Secretariat, which suited him better although he could not see so well. The march past made him uneasy ('I . . . was reminded how fundamentally disagreeable to me uniforms are, how vulnerable they make men look'),[6] and left a vivid sense of unreality: 'As Dulal said later, it was like a Cecil B. de Mille production. One expected Gary Cooper to turn up, dressed as a Bengal lancer.'[7]

But alongside the grandeur of official, republican New Delhi, Paul was getting to know a different and more prosaic scene. 'He explored the city in a very intimate way. He fell in love with Delhi,' said Goodie Singh who, with her Aunt Dorothy, acted as his guide on these explorations. Paul would join them after breakfast, and the three would set out together on a different expedition each day. They visited the Qutb Minar, the fluted pink sandstone victory tower built by the first Sultan of Delhi in the thirteenth century, and the mysterious, much more ancient iron pillar that stands near it, inscribed in Sanskrit and credited with the power to grant the wish – alternatively to ensure the return – of anyone able to put two arms round it and clasp hands behind his or her back (Paul managed this feat, according to Goodie). The three took coffee on the terrace of the old Imperial Hotel with its herbaceous borders, immaculate lawns and equally immaculate bearers in white pyjamas with matching sashes and turbans; they ate Sunday lunch amid the viceregal splendours of the Gymkhana Club where members sit out of doors under the neem trees in winter, and in dim lofty halls indoors in the heat of summer; and they visited the Golf Club standing on its course in the heart of Delhi, landscaped like an English park with peacocks and parrots sporting in the leafy glades as well as pheasants and hares.

But neither the private luxury nor the staggering public pomp of the raj interested Paul more than incidentally. What absorbed him was people. He was fascinated by a potters' colony beside a busy city road – families living as they must have done since medieval times in earthen huts on the red earth from which they make lamps and pots to sell for a living – or simply by sitting at home talking to the servants with Goodie and Dorothy as interpreters. Paul narrowly questioned the cook Mohammed, who came from the hills of north India, about his village, his family, where he worshipped, how much money he sent home, the ages of his children, when he meant to marry off the girls, what he would do for the boys. He went into the kitchen to watch

Mohammed prepare dhal and meat curry, and he talked at equal length to the orderly, Patel, from Maharashtra. 'Paul got to know Patel better than I did,' Goodie said.

Goodie was a soldier's wife (her husband, Colonel H. N. Singh, was away at the time of Paul's visit), descended herself from an old army family: her great-great-grandfather had been a sergeant at Lucknow, said to have smuggled the wife of his commanding officer out to safety dressed in his own wife's clothes, and her uncle had commanded the last Imperial victory parade at the end of the war down the Raj Path. Paul could hardly have found an abler or more enthusiastic guide. She was energetic, resourceful, a first-rate storyteller with a curiosity that matched his own and an inexhaustible fund of historical and practical knowledge. When the car would not start, Goodie made it go with a strip of tinfoil from her aunt's box of Turkish cigars. Paul was interested in everything she showed him, listening with the peculiar intentness that always encouraged people to talk. 'The thing about Paul was that he would never interrupt,' Goodie said. 'He had one hundred per cent concentration. He never glazed over. I never found, no matter how long I went on, that he had switched off and stopped listening.' He did not make notes but nothing escaped him. Once he watched Goodie doing business with a silversmith and recapitulated the entire dialogue for her afterwards, admitting, when she congratulated him on his Hindi, that he had not understood a word but followed every gesture and intonation.

After a week, she suggested driving Paul and Dorothy the hundred or more miles to Agra. They set off on 24 January, taking the great ancient trunk road used by the Moghuls, passing the same landmarks, the same bends, culverts and nullahs, stopping on the way to investigate anything of interest: 'A three or four hour journey always took six or seven with Paul,' Goodie said. They examined one of the pink, conical sandstone pillars erected at intervals along the route, with footholds for climbing, and niches in which lamps could be placed to light the tired, dusty Moghul armies into camp at night. They found a modern lamp, a little pink clay shell on the traditional pattern, about the size of a ginger biscuit, pinched together as such lamps always had been by women and children: Paul asked tentatively if he might have it, and Goodie left a chit in Hindi, weighted by a stone, to say it had been taken by an Englishman who loved India and asked forgiveness. She took him under a bridge or culvert to show how it was built, from the same small hand-made pink bricks and lime mortar as the Red Fort in Delhi: Goodie later presented one of the bricks to Paul, who took it back to use as a paperweight in his London study. They inspected the structure of the arch, she scraped a pinch of mortar with her pen knife and handed it to him to sniff. Paul said it gave him the feel of India, and hugged her: 'Goodie, would any tourist guide have gone under a culvert to show me this?' They passed a performing bear on the road, Paul's first elephant, and several working camels. Goodie spotted a wheelmaker's forge, braked, reversed, parked the car, and the three of them spent an hour watching the smith assemble a bullock-cart wheel, fitting the four wooden sections together with hub and spokes, then binding the whole with a red-hot iron rim.

At Agra, they stayed two nights at Clark's Shiraz Hotel ('lush in the modern sense,' Paul wrote to Penny: 'not quite my Indian cup of tea'). Paul rose early both mornings, and 'had imbibed half Agra' by the time his companions came down. They listened to a blind musician playing a one-stringed iktara (a dried pumpkin shell, bound in goat's hide with a single wire strung from a piece of wood to reverberate inside the drum-shaped instrument). Paul asked how much he should give, Goodie said four annas, her aunt disagreed, insisting he had enjoyed himself too much to be so mean, but Paul said the music had been worth more to him than he could pay: 'So I put what anyone else would in his begging bowl.' The musician was pleased by the compliment, and the two gravely shook hands. Paul asked to meet someone who had worked for the British and Goodie, whose husband had commanded the Parachute Brigade with headquarters in Agra, introduced him to Abdul, the English-speaking head bearer at the regimental mess. Paul talked for nearly an hour to Abdul, who had served and watched British officers all his life, having started as a boy washing dishes in the mess and worked his way up to mess steward. The trio explored the city, watching little boys of seven or eight carve exquisitely fine designs on wood as hard as rosewood in a shop whose owner explained to Paul that it was only at that age the fingers were nimble and the eyes sharp enough for the work: by forty a carver was ruined, his back bent by lumbago, his eyesight weak and his fingers too stiff to be any use.

In the evening, at twilight, they visited the Taj Mahal, and next morning Goodie drove them to Akbar's abandoned sixteenth-century city of Fatehpur-Sikri. Paul was impressed by what he described to Penny as an open air ludo board ('about ½ size of a football pitch') with a stone dais in the middle for the emperor to sit casting dice with slave girls as pieces. But he was more immediately intrigued by a dye works they passed on the road, with hundreds of strips and sheets of material laid out to dry on the grass. The coloured stuffs turned out to belong to a village of printers, who demonstrated every stage of the process, from the mixing of the vegetable dyes to the printing of the pieces in traditional patterns using carved wood blocks, explaining that they might expect to receive about one tenth of the sale price of their hand-printed cottons. On the way back, Dorothy bought a whole kilo of guavas which the three of them polished off at record speed, stopping for tea at a wooden shanty where Paul watched a villager spend four annas on a cup of tea and share it with a friend, who drank his half out of the saucer with noisy slurps. Paul said they enjoyed it so much he insisted on repeating the performance himself which, for Goodie, summed up his entire attitude to India. He wanted to try everything: he hugged Goodie, shook the beggar's hand, drank his tea from the saucer: she never saw him take precautions or swallow pills or seem in any way to hold back. 'He was so open,' she said. 'He touched everything. He always wanted to get the real feel: to get inside the skin of an Indian.'

She told him about her two daughters, and Paul talked lovingly of his own family, describing the girls, producing their photographs – 'his eyes grew bright with affection' – saying how much he missed his wife, and how dearly he wished he could share things with her. His letters to Penny in these weeks were full of the pain of separation and homesickness. It was not simply that he could not work without her ('you know how difficult work *always* seems to be, except when we're together, and the house is attuned to it'). It was her presence he missed, and his sense of being part of her. Paul was amazed when Eric the Dane grumbled in Delhi about having to go back home to his wife ('Personally, after a year without *you*, I'd be white-haired with longing').[8] His loneliness came to a head on the moonlit night he first saw the Taj Mahal. 'The thing about it is that it should be seen by 2 people who love each other. So for me there was a lack, and I kept thinking how much you would have liked being there, where you ought to be, hand in hand with Bear.' He told her the story of Shah Jehan, building the tomb for his wife Mumtaz out of white marble so pure that the light of a torch shines through it, and planning a black marble replica for himself with a river between spanned by a golden bridge: 'but he died before that was possible to arrange, & . . . they put his tomb next to hers. Since hers is in the centre, this produces a touching human effect of non-alignment.'

Paul went back to the Taj alone the next day, and was moved again by the non-aligned lovers. His letters to Penny return constantly to his worries about her and Sally, his longing to be home (he envisaged a glorious rampage for the two of them from one wild pub to the next – The Grapes of Wrath, The Four Horsemen of the Apocalypse, The Hand Over Fist), his sense of how horrified she would be by the dirt, smells and squalor of India, his wistful dream of winning a Premium Bond that would transform their lives so that they might travel out in luxury and stand hand-in-hand together by moonlight at the Taj Mahal. His letters were cruelly ironic, considering the terms on which they had lived before he left home, but they show what he meant when he talked sadly, at the end of his life, about the intensity of his emotions and his inability to express them except on paper. Goodie was in no doubt about the depth of Paul's feelings for his wife: he never explicitly suggested anything was amiss between them, but he talked a great deal about women in general. He said they were more observant than men, and their perceptions went deeper. 'A woman, especially an Indian woman, is like a basket. An open basket: it receives impressions, good or bad, it keeps on receiving and retaining.' He distinguished sharply between confident, self-reliant women, possessing the qualities he admired in Goodie and her aunt Dorothy, and the submissive ones who touched his heart: the kind of woman who, he said, would always be on the receiving end of kindness or abuse, always essentially dependent on a man.

At the end of a fortnight in Delhi, Goodie drove Paul and Dorothy to Jaipur in Rajasthan, where they were to stay with relatives of Dorothy's Bombay friends, the Mukerjees. Seeing a black-veiled Muslim woman in Jaipur, Paul asked if she ever lifted her veil or if anyone ever saw her face. Goodie said her husband might, but only in a tiny dark hut crowded with other people – parents-in-law, children, relations – where they could never make love except at dead of night, 'so he would probably *imagine* her face'. The woman herself would see it only in a spot of mirror glass mounted in a finger ring, the kind of tiny dolls' looking-glass sold in Rajasthan so that veiled women might look at their own faces. Paul tried to talk to the woman in black but she was too shy to answer the questions Goodie translated. 'Does she have a voice?' he asked and, to the woman, shaking his head so that she promptly shook hers in agreement: 'You have no voice?' The presence of these silent, veiled Rajasthani women, walking always four paces behind their husbands, had a sobering effect on all three friends. Perhaps it made Paul think about his own frustrated longing for a wife from whom he was separated by a great distance. 'In India, yes, one could travel great distances,' Sarah Layton would reflect in the last volume of the Raj Quartet. 'But the greatest distance was between people who were closely related. That distance was never easy to cover.'[9]

Paul flew back to Bombay with Dorothy on 2 February. He had little to show in the way of formal research: an insider's view of the current political situation from Dulal in Delhi, and some information 'on certain topics of value to me'[10] from his host in Jaipur, the Deputy Inspector General of Police, Lieutenant-Colonel Singha. 'My not very thrusting attempts in Delhi to be shown pertinent archives were not successful,' he wrote long afterwards, describing how he had found himself blocked on all sides when he tried to find out about the Indian National Army. 'I didn't persist because as a novelist rather than a journalist, the reluctance interested me almost as much, if not more, than the archives would have done.'[11] He traced his inconvenient interest in the INA back to a night in 1946 which he and a friend, waiting for repatriation in Bihar, had spent guarding an INA prisoner en route for questioning. Paul in those days had no idea what was involved, although he already sensed dimly that the issue of Indian nationalism, and the treachery of those who believed in it, was not as clear cut as the British authorities would have liked it to be.

Nearly a quarter of a century later hard facts were still extremely difficult to come by. The INA, recruited as an army of liberation by Subhas Chandra Bose from Indian troops in Japanese or German captivity, had been proscribed as traitors by the British, and tacitly disowned by the Indian government after 1947. It raised issues Indians seemed as reluctant to confront as the British themselves to come to terms with their own Imperial past. Paul could find no one prepared to discuss it until he flew down to Belgaum at the end of his stay to spend a night in the jungle at Jagalbet with a novelist he had met in Bombay, a Brahmin called Manohar Malgonkar, tall, rangy, aristocratic, a powerful and sometimes explosive personality: 'a very complex but interesting character,' Paul wrote after their first meeting, 'whom it was worth coming to India to meet (from the writing point of view)'.[12] Malgonkar, who had been commissioned in the war into the crack Mahratta Regiment, consulted a friend, Colonel A. Desai, president of Belgaum's Ex-Soldiers Association, who in turn lined up three former INA soldiers, or Jiffs, ready for Paul's arrival. Malgonkar met him at Belgaum airport on Tuesday 4 February, and drove him straight to Desai's farm where, with Malgonkar and Desai as interpreters, Paul questioned the three men exhaustively. It was clear to his fellow novelist that this brief encounter with Jiffs in the flesh had been all that was needed at this stage, a physical reality that 'had both filled up his mental image of them and given it definition'.[13] 'In one hour I learned *more* than in the whole month,' Paul wrote jubilantly that night to Penny.

Malgonkar was one of India's best-known novelists: his book, *The Princes*, had come out at the same time as *The Jewel in the Crown* and sold ('at least in America where it really matters')[14] infinitely better. He had known E. M. Forster and was a familiar figure on the British literary scene, stopping off frequently in London on his way to New York, and counting among his regular guests at Jagalbet his London publisher, Hamish Hamilton, and the travel writer and former controller of the BBC's Third Programme, John Morris, who had put Paul in touch with him in the first place. Malgonkar at this stage was far more successful than Paul, who was obliged to confess, when the two sorted out questions of literary precedence in the car on the forty-mile drive to Jagalbet, that he had never read a word his host had written. 'I was able to reassure him that I, too, had not read any of his books either,' Malgonkar wrote blandly: 'After the initial bit of sparring – if that was what it was – we seemed to take to each other.'[15]

Malgonkar read the copy of the *Jewel* which Paul gave him that night, and was immediately impressed by the authenticity of its military detail and atmosphere. Paul for his part relaxed in the Malgonkars' house at Jagalbet, designed to provide ideal writing conditions, peace, seclusion and breathtaking views of primeval forest tumbling away on all sides. Malgonkar, whose family had owned land in these parts as far as the eye could see before Independence, once lost a dog to a panther on a stroll after tea through the trees. Bitter green apaya trees and a brilliant red bougainvillea grew under Paul's window. There were little green bulbuls in the garden, scarlet-and-yellow minivets, and the ceaseless tapping of the coppersmith bird. Paul found Malgonkar's beautiful wife Coocoo soothing and sympathetic, hinting more to her than to anyone else on this trip about his anxiety over his wife and daughter in London. He liked even the dog round whom the life of the household revolved ('Delightful dog here who never *looks* at a human being, & buries his bones in places he forgets,' Paul wrote to Penny: 'He should go to a psychiatrist').

The Malgonkars gave a small lunch party for Paul next day, introducing him to an Englishman, Peter Goodbody, who had stayed on and now lived with his wife Maisie at Green Hotel in Belgaum, where Paul spent Wednesday night ready to catch an early plane back to Bombay next morning. Belgaum seemed almost unrecognisable and smaller than he remembered,[16] but Goodbody was excellent company, full of tall stories about the old days and, more to the point, the celebrated lawyer Bhulabhai Desai, who had been interned by the British and had led the defence at the INA show trials after the war in the Red Fort in Delhi. Goodbody claimed to have played golf at the Willingdon Club in Bombay with Bhulabhai's son, Dhiru Desai, and the Viceroy, Lord Willingdon himself (a massive sportsman who would turn out in huge boots, pyjama trousers tucked into red socks with a matching red silk handkerchief in the pocket of his tent-like, striped pyjama jacket, accompanied by an 'agi-wallah caddy who used to employ his especially prehensile toes to move the old chap's ball into the best possible position')[17]. Paul dined with the Goodbodys, promising to send a copy of *The Day of the Scorpion* – 'Scorpers as my publisher calls it'[18] – and flying back to find Bombay in uproar over the issue of whether Belgaum district should remain part of Maharashtra, or join Mysore State. There was burning, looting, rioting ('about fifty dead, I should think'), and a curfew lifted only in the early morning and for two hours every evening. Paul's meeting with another INA defence counsel, Sri Soli Batliwala, had to be cancelled (one of the first things he did when he got home was to send Batliwala a list of questions about timing, and the disposal of recaptured INA officers, NCOs and sepoys).[19] He made a dramatic exit on 11 February under armed escort at dead of night in an airport bus with wire mesh at the windows,[20] arriving home next morning to find that Sally, who had decided in spite of serious misgivings to go back to York, had left the same morning, missing him by a few hours.

He spent the rest of the month sorting himself out, catching up on correspondence, tying up loose ends and generally working towards a fresh start on the novel. In March, Sally collapsed again, and her parents were summoned to her bedside: even Paul, who never doubted her ability to bring off a first in philosophy, admitted it was unlikely she would be fit enough to sit her final exams in the summer. In April Paul's mother, approaching her eighty-third birthday, broke her hip. He described himself in these weeks as 'a sort of one-man disaster area all to myself. Domestic crises involving one daughter, and my ancient, near-blind mother who fell . . . and had to be visited in hospital in the wilds of Dulwich. The daughter business meant haring up to York for interviews with Registrar and Vice-Chancellor. That sort of thing. Depression, overdoses, that sort of thing. Settled now, I hope.'[21] This was written on 8 May, by which time Sally had fled back to take refuge at a psychiatric hospital in London where she again attempted suicide and remained under heavy sedation. Frances Scott, who had been slowly losing strength, died that month. Paul was distracted with grief, foreboding and agitation. Both parents, visiting Sally on her twenty-first birthday, 30 May 1969, were visibly distraught. She found her father in these months cold, condemnatory, harshly uncooperative with the psychiatric treatment that she saw as her only hope of support. To him, Sally's depression seemed a cruel reminder of the suicidal despair that had periodically engulfed him in the past. He felt threatened, and his instinctive response was to distance himself, stubbornly resisting what he saw as psychiatric interference, pressing hard for a physiological diagnosis of some identifiable disease or condition which might yield to medical treatment, if not to the assertion of parental authority.

It was impossible in these months of turmoil to settle to any kind of sustained work. At some point that spring, or perhaps in the almost equally disturbed winter before it, Paul wrote a stage play, *The Situation*,[22] a reworking in much greater detail of the section dealing with Hari Kumar's unofficial cross-examination in 1944 in *The Day of the Scorpion*. 'Kumar, always, exists like a dark shadow,' Paul had written, when he finished the *Scorpion*: 'The shadow gets longer and Kumar gets smaller. Or is it the other way round?'[23] His play, completed by May 1969,[24] was an attempt to confront more clearly the darkness at the heart of the work in hand. It is set in the windowless interrogation room where the British authorities, represented by the Governor's aide Nigel Rowan and an Indian colleague called Gopal, re-open the case against Kumar at the instigation of Daphne Manners' aunt, the former governor's widow, Lady Manners, herself an unseen witness of the proceedings. The play ends with a confrontation between her and Kumar, who begs to be left alone ('I like it here. I get on well. I give no trouble'), disclaiming all connection with Daphne or her baby on the grounds that he has become another person.

The young Kumar whom Rowan had known less than ten years earlier has grown unrecognisable to himself as well as to his interrogators: the cricketer wielding a graceful bat on the playing fields of his public school, Chillingborough, the aloof, elegant figure Daphne Manners had fallen in love with on the sunlit maidan in Mayapore, have both been replaced by a subterranean prisoner, immured in airless cells, blinking in the light of day, accustomed to solitary confinement without access to books, newspapers or writing materials. He describes how he has forgotten in prison everything he had been taught at Chillingborough, learning instead to eat dirt, to lick the floor, to live and work as a sweeper and cleaner of latrines ('They say the whole bloody country will be one vast shit-house when people like us have gone. Forgive me, Lady Manners. But that's what they say'). He also describes more fully than in the novel what happened on the night of his arrest, after Daphne's rape, when he was interrogated by Ronald Merrick, stripped, beaten, racially taunted, sexually humiliated, and driven close to killing himself − 'the one proof of cowardice, physical and moral inferiority' − resisting only because his death would have gratified Merrick. 'My suicide would have been a kind of sublimation for him. He could have *had* me then. Just by watching my dead body, carried out from the cell to the mortuary, which was the only way he *could* have me − and not feel himself contaminated.'

In the summer of 1968, the *Sunday Times* had published a series of sensational sexual revelations about Lawrence of Arabia. 'I remember the articles (who doesn't?)', Paul wrote eight years later,[25] tracing both Lawrence's extraordinary achievements and his corrosive self-contempt, his obsessive self-punishment, his need for regular secret beatings at the hands of young soldiers and airmen, back to depths of shame and guilt implanted in earliest childhood by his mother. 'Poor Lawrence. You could say that he was trauma-prone . . . his life blossomed in the desert only to be blighted by a growing sense of failure and (one must assume) bitter self-discoveries which made his hero-image pathologically and intellectually repugnant to him.' Paul would write in similar terms in retrospect of Merrick's bitter self-discovery in the course of his own 'long night of the soul' ('the night revealing several things to himself about himself in the underground room where he interrogated Kumar').[26] Details of Kumar's incarceration and torture by Merrick closely resemble the young Lawrence's ordeal in the prison at Dehra when he, too, was beaten, tortured and raped. 'The Turks . . . did it to me, by force,' Lawrence wrote long afterwards, discussing homosexuality with E. M. Forster, 'and since then I have gone about whimpering to myself Unclean, unclean.'[27]

Lawrence's reaction was to repudiate his public image ('I know the reverse of that medal, and hate its false face'), renouncing power and privilege, reverting to the anonymity of the ranks, rejoicing in his own degradation ('I came in here to eat dirt till its taste is normal to me'), and rejecting all attempts to appeal to his former self: 'The Lawrence that used to go about . . . is dead. He's worse than dead. He is a stranger I once knew.'[28] The new Lawrence chose celibacy, self-denial and close confinement, describing himself to Bernard Shaw as a sweeper and scrubber of floors ('a dustman and clerk and pig-stye-cleaner. . . . The officers fight shy of me; but I behave demurely and give no trouble'), and explaining his bondage to Shaw's wife, Charlotte, as a self-imposed life sentence: 'So long as there is breath in my body my strength will be exerted to keep my soul in prison, since nowhere else can it exist in safety. The terror of being run away with, in the liberty of power, lies at the back of these many renunciations of my later life. I am afraid of myself.' His only hope, he told Charlotte Shaw, was for the punitive and repressive side of himself to coerce the other: 'Normally, the very strong one, saying "No", the Puritan, is in firm charge, and the other poor little vicious fellow can't get a word in, for fear of him.'[29]

The cruel split, and the draconian suppressions, inherent in the kind of temperament Lawrence describes with such painful clarity had long been familiar to Paul. The initial revelations – subsequently published in book form as *The Secret Lives of Lawrence of Arabia*[30] – had appeared at the precise moment when Paul, having finished *The Day of the Scorpion*, was beginning to contemplate his next novel. The

Sunday Times article came out on 16 June 1968, and Paul made his first notes under the heading 'The Towers of Silence' in a new notebook dated 19 June.[31] Paul cannot have known, or needed to know, at this stage how uncannily close Lawrence's experiences at Dehra and afterwards had been to Kumar's. What he grasped was an essential and disturbing truth about the nature of brutality and repression. Lawrence's confessions come close in fact to the heart of Paul's fictional territory, 'the unmapped forest of prejudice and self-interest', an area of darkness (Paul had been indignant when V. S. Naipaul appropriated the title before he had even published his book in 1964),[32] where blind, irrational, vengeful and destructive impulses operate far from the historian's searchlight of conscious understanding.

He traced the root of fear, violence and suppression back as far as the massacre at Amritsar in 1919, and forward to growing tension in the late 1960s on the streets of Britain. Enoch Powell had made a notoriously inflammatory speech at Wolverhampton in 1968, comparing black immigrants to a spreading cancer, attributing their existence to treachery in high places and demanding drastic action, clinching his racist argument with talk of parcels of excrement and rivers foaming with blood. The speech led to Powell's immediate dismissal from the Conservative shadow cabinet and a wave of liberal revulsion across the nation accompanied by a parallel surge of popular support. It precipitated over the next few years a series of ugly and potentially explosive confrontations between black and white, and Paul examined the issues involved in a lecture, 'Enoch Sahib: A Slight Case of Cultural Shock', which he gave to the Commonwealth Countries League in London in November 1969. He identified a vein of narrow, defeatist insularity unscrupulously exploited for their own ends by politicians like Powell ('He has skilfully manipulated racial arguments so that they emerge as the semi-articulate protests of worried or terrified people he felt it his plain duty to stand up for, as spokesman, untainted himself by anything remotely like prejudice')[33]. He detected ignorance and fear behind Powell's appeal to floating voters like Paul's own aunt, 'the dear and ancient one who would vote for Mr Powell tomorrow, even though she lives in the quiet of a seaside town where a brown face on the promenade would be as rare a sight as a dodo among seagulls.' He drove home the point with a powerful, polemical account of his own experiences at Timmapuram, showing how readily the forces of reaction may override even the most impeccably liberal intentions.

Dangerous simplifications, and the authoritarian solutions they make respectable, are represented in the Raj Quartet by Ronald

Merrick, whose aggressive confidence, no-nonsense methods and 'unshakeable sense of his own authority' make him the kind of man always welcome in a tight spot, even though he may also come – as someone said of a similar character in *The Alien Sky* – to look more like the man who brought the tight spot with him.[34] Much the same might be said of Enoch Powell and, in a detailed historical analysis of the Raj Quartet, Professor R. J. Moore has traced unexpectedly close parallels with Merrick in Powell's background and Imperial outlook, his meteoric military career in wartime India, his romantic affair with the subcontinent and his firmly paternalistic attitude to its peoples.[35] Few if any of these detailed correspondences can have been familiar to Paul at the time: 'by Enoch Sahib, I do not necessarily mean Mr Powell. I mean any one of the people, like my aunt, in whom he has detected a readiness to withdraw from the problems of the modern world, and any one of the people in whom this spirit of withdrawal might yet be aroused.'[36]

Paul became depressingly familiar in the ten years he spent writing the Raj Quartet with the indifference and complacency behind what Gerald Hanley called the 'blockage about India': Hanley had warned him to expect mixed reactions in Britain, correctly recognising *Jewel* as 'the kind of writing which will help to dissolve that strange blockage'.[37] Paul grew used to disapproval from old hands who felt he blackened the raj as much as from young radicals who thought he glorified it: 'so much North-West Frontier flag-wagging for Moderns' was one smug dismissal of the *Scorpion* which Paul often quoted ('That young man obviously had a view – a received one – of British India. If he had to read a book about it, he wanted the view confirmed').[38] He was also regularly reproved by both parties for failure to write about the contemporary world. 'The neatest answer I can give is that, in my opinion, I have done and I do,' he said in another talk, 'After Marabar: Britain and India, a Post-Forsterian View'.[39] This was perhaps his most sustained attempt at self-justification as a novelist, delivered in India in 1972, but first sketched out in a lecture to the Royal Society of Literature in December 1969 (Paul's election as a fellow of the RSL was one of comparatively few signs of recognition he received from the British literary establishment in his lifetime: another was an Arts Council Grant of £1000, awarded at the second time of asking in 1969).

In his gloomier moments, Paul said that Forster loomed over literary India like a train terminus beyond which no other novelist could be permitted to travel by the critics.[40] More often he inclined to agree with Storm Jameson, who wrote after reading the *Scorpion* to say that as writers he and Forster belonged to two completely different orders ('at no single instant do your people tremble on the edges of caricature – they are all of them . . . complex human beings, passionately alive . . . again and again they cut down to almost frightening depths of human nature. The construction of the book, too, is superb. . . . It is a growing thing, living and moving on one level below another').[41] But, in 'After Marabar', he acknowledged that anyone writing about India did so in Forster's shadow, explained his own differences with *A Passage to India*, and explored its prophetic element: a vision that took in not only the prospect of Imperial decline and the failure of liberal intentions but also a fear that seemed to Paul increasingly to haunt the post-war consumer societies of the West, the message dinned home in the dull, thudding echo of the Marabar Caves: 'Everything exists. Nothing has value.'[42] Paul himself might be defined in this sense as a prophetic novelist, one who could never separate the present or the past from their consequences: 'One is not ruled by the past, one does not rule or re-order it, one simply *is* it, in the same way that one is as well the present and part of the future.'

This sense of continuity was much on Paul's mind when he turned back to his new novel in the second half of 1969. His play, *The Situation*, was still going the rounds. Although his theatrical agent Margery Vosper pronounced the script too static, and emotionally too anti-British (also perhaps sexually over-explicit, even for that permissive decade), it was briefly considered for West End production by Donald Albery.[43] Paul also gave it in July to Donald McWhinnie, who was directing at the Hampstead Theatre Club.[44] Carol, acting as his assistant stage manager, was impressed by his powers of concentration, his apparently limitless consumption of alcohol, and the memorable performances he elicited from actors in relatively short adjournments from the local pub for rehearsal. 'I never saw Donald drunk,' she reported, 'or perhaps I never saw him sober?' Paul laughed, admitting that nothing had changed in almost twenty years since the two first worked together in radio. McWhinnie recommended the play for television but it got nowhere,[45] perhaps because it had been written less for its own sake than as clarification or background notes to work in progress. Paul worked steadily on *The Towers of Silence* all through the winter of 1969 and the following spring and summer, announcing in August 1970, that he meant to break the novel at the end of what had become a thoroughly unwieldy first section, 'and make it the third in a quartet'[46]. He hoped to finish by the end of the year (in fact he dated the last notebook entry 19 January 1971), and complete the entire sequence for publication by 1972.

The Towers of Silence is the quietest, most domestic, most contemplative and elegaic of the four novels of the Raj Quartet. It serves as a bridge passage – Paul called it his slow movement[47] – between the excitements of *The Day of the Scorpion* and the gathering climax, violence and resolutions of *A Division of the Spoils*. It centres on the Layton family, exploring in greater detail events of 1943–5 set mostly in the hill station of Pankot – an isolated, predominantly female community of spinsters, widows, wives with sons or husbands at the front – against a background of distant European war, Japanese invasion of the subcontinent, defeat and dispersal on all sides. It charts the gradual, reluctant acceptance by one small insignificant section of the British civilian population in India that their time is up ('This sense of danger, of the sea-level rising, swamping the plains, threatening the hills, this sense of imminent inundation, was one to which people were now not unaccustomed').[48] The whole novel is focused through the eyes of an elderly retired mission-school teacher, Barbie Batchelor, who finds herself professionally redundant at the beginning of the book, and who spirals slowly downwards in the course of it through successive circles of isolation, rejection and rootlessness to madness and death. Barbie ends up a speechless outcast with no recollection of the past, forcibly parted from her possessions, physically restrained by cold water and winding sheets behind bars in the Samaritan Hospital at Ranpur. Her experience is mirrored at the opposite extreme by the radiant young bride, Susan Layton, who also finishes by succumbing (if only temporarily) to insanity and incarceration. One of the book's recurring images is the battered tin trunk of missionary relics from which Barbie cannot be parted, and which has to be endlessly sent for as she herself is shunted round Pankot, moving from house to house and from one family to the next, stowing her trunk away, bringing it out again, storing and sorting it, capsizing it in a thunderstorm at one point and spilling the contents piecemeal across the road. The trunk becomes an embarrassment, like its owner:

A comic but horrifying thought took hold: of old Miss Batchelor homeless, seated on her trunk in the midst of the bazaar, surrounded by her detritus . . . to the amusement of Hindu and Muslim shopkeepers who would interpret such a sight as proof that the entire raj would presently and similarly be on its uppers.[49]

Barbie, by Paul's own account, ran away with the book. Her story was to have formed an introduction, like Miss Crane's in the first of the four novels, 'but it separated itself & once I'd admitted that it had I was able to ponder it all out and adjust the rhythm'.[50] She embodied a side of her creator – 'There was a hell of a lot of Barbie in Paul. Nothing was too much trouble,' said Peter Green – that had always been drawn to the inarticulate and dispossessed. She was, like Shakespeare's Katherine of Aragon who had fascinated him as a small boy, 'a most poore Woman, and a stranger/ In your dominions'. Paul's aunt, Ruth Mark, Frances' sister, entered her last illness in the year he finished *Towers*, dying in her seventies alone among strangers in the tiny flat she called her rabbit hutch in a council block on Brixton Hill. She died on 5 September 1971, the last but one in her large family, followed by her sister Alice the year after, and Paul gave Barbie something of Ruth's brave spirit. But it was only after he had finished the book that he recognised, looking back, a part of himself in Barbie: 'I see now that her trunk of missionary relics . . . is really a symbol for the luggage I am conscious of carrying with me every day of my life – the luggage of my past, of my personal history and of the world's history – luggage crammed with relics of achievement, of failure, of continuing aspirations and optimistic expectations.'[51]

Paul dedicated *The Towers of Silence* 'To Penny with all my love', and, just as he reached the final stages, reviewed the second volume of Quentin Bell's biography of his aunt Virginia Woolf, in an appreciative article chiefly taken up with admiration and warm approval of her husband for 'devoting, one might say sacrificing, himself to the cause of looking after Virginia'. Paul concluded that their sexless marriage had been a thoroughly satisfactory arrangement on both sides, enabling Virginia to come to fruition as a novelist, affording Leonard Woolf the satisfaction of assisting her: 'sometimes subtly, sometimes directly, he ordered her life, put her as best he could in the way of coping with it, with what serenity she could muster, to do the work that mattered to her, to them both. . . . Professor Bell's portrait of his uncle is, I think, a very moving and human one. . . . The decision to marry Leonard was indeed a wise one. Through him she came into her own.'[52] Paul reviewed the book for *Country Life* in November 1970, agreeing to do it reluctantly, from financial necessity, in time he could ill spare, but finding in it an outlet for unexpressed and inexpressible feelings about his own wife, who provided the support without which he could not have coped with his life, or done the work that mattered.

But for Penny, once the girls had left home, prospects became bleaker and more sacrificial than ever. She played no part in the inner world which absorbed Paul for weeks and months on end, there were no more holidays or outings, visitors no longer came to the house, and she had no life outside it. Sally had returned to York in the autumn of 1969 to repeat her final year. Carol was also off again that autumn, stage-managing an extended tour of the prodigiously successful musical, *Hair*. Penny had spent the winter, with Paul immersed in *Towers*, writing a semi-autobiographical nursing book called *The*

Probationer and, by April, she had enrolled for a three-month, Back-to-Nursing refresher course at the Middlesex Hospital, continuing to nurse on the wards afterwards three days a week. Sally was rushed into hospital again in the spring term, spent the Easter vacation in York, proved too ill to sit her final examinations in the summer, and was given a degree without taking her papers, coming back at the end of June to be nursed at home. Paul decided not to tell Penny when Heinemann turned down her book that month.

Sally, who had developed an alarming tolerance to the sleeping pills and anti-depressants she had been prescribed ever since her first term at university, complained of blackouts, back pain, stiffness, dizziness, double vision, and Paul reported various, unsatisfactory diagnoses of what was wrong. He himself was suffering from his old trouble with the sciatic nerve, and being treated again by an osteopath: one afternoon in June, after a visit to his New York agent Ivan von Auw, he found himself suddenly crippled on the escalator at Marble Arch tube station, paralysed, bent double, in excruciating pain, '& being steered clear of by people who thought I'd had one over the eight at lunch'.[53] From August to October what Paul called crisis conditions prevailed at Addison Way. By November, *Towers* was drawing to a close, Penny was on sick leave from the Middlesex, and Sally had landed a secretarial job in publishing.

When Paul finally raised his eyes from the desk after delivering his manuscript early in 1971, he took a cautiously optimistic view. Sally had moved to a room of her own near Baker Street. Carol became engaged that spring to a bass-guitarist with the *Hair* company, an Irishman called Larry McLaughlin, whom she married on 19 April. Things were beginning at last to look domestically more settled. In May, Paul rented a large old, rambling house near Land's End in Cornwall – Churchtown House at Sennen Cove – and set off for a week with Penny, Sally and Sally's former fiancé, Paul Cashmore. It was the first time in more than ten years that Paul had gone on holiday without a manuscript, and the atmosphere was festive. They enjoyed the house itself and one another's company, the spectacular scenery, and a promising local pub called The Success Inn: 'it sucks us in and blows us out,' said Paul Cashmore (the two Pauls got on well, each encouraging and appreciating the joker in the other). They ate roast duck, drank lashings of red wine and took long sea walks. Paul brought his album with him and reverted to old Scott–Wright habits, making drawings and paintings in water colour of the harbour, the fishing boats and the cottages crowding the steep hilly slopes of Sennen. This radiant week in spring seemed like a fresh start, as well as a return to the old happy seaside holidays that had always recharged the family batteries, and restored their collective balance.

Two months later, Sally married Paul Cashmore. 'You ask what it feels like, marrying off two daughters in one summer,' Paul wrote warily to John Willey: 'Expensive – emotionally and financially. Also I think it proves (once again) that however onerous a responsibility may be, to be partly relieved of it is a kind of deprivation.'[54] The *Hair* tour had folded by this time without warning, Carol and Larry had moved in temporarily with his parents, Sally and her Paul (known as 'Pee' to distinguish him from 'the other Paul') were living in rooms not far from home in West Hampstead. Pee, who was a photographer, took a cheerful, relaxed picture of his father-in-law at home with a drink and cigarette, which Paul far preferred to more formal portraits for publicity and dustjackets. He hoped his worries as a father were over, although he still had misgivings: 'Murky depths of Victorian paternalism, lingering on in the bloodstream,' he wrote to Willey on 9 August 1971, noting the date as the centenary of his father's birth ('which is a pointer to how far back my racial memory goes').

The Towers of Silence was due to be published on 4 October by Heinemann, and *A Division of the Spoils* had already passed its first hundred pages in typescript. Paul had explained to both daughters and sons-in-law what he called his old-fashioned view that a marriage, once contracted, should be permanent, and that a wife's place was at her husband's side. Carol left at the end of September for Freeport in the Bahamas, where Larry had landed a job as guitarist with a hotel band at the Casino. Paul's letters developed into a wildly exuberant serial, complete with illustrations in the margin, relating the desert exploits of Abu Ben Grottso – 'May it please you, Oh Flower of an English Rose, Oh Gem of Freeport, Oh Lady with the ever open hand, to receive these Words and this Likeness in grateful thanks from the unworthiest and most disgusting of humble and insignificant eaters of filth'[55] – interspersed with much briefer and comparatively glum reports of what was happening at home that autumn.

Sally had felt, ever since she left home for university, that her father held her at arm's length. Her relationship with him had not recovered from what she took as a rejection two years earlier, when he had refused peremptorily to cooperate with her psychiatrist. She felt he had turned thumbs down on her, as Paul had once felt about his own father. It was as if she had become the skeleton in his cupboard – 'Almost as if I acted out the dark side of him' – and must bear the blame for a collapse over which she had no control: 'It was like a Victorian father's reaction. Blanket refusal. Such things cannot be in this family.' Paul for his part found himself confronted once again with a darkness he had never been able to face directly. It was only in retrospect, at the end of his life, that he could acknowledge that his daughter had been ill, unhappy, badly in need of a support he could not give. At the time, her predicament brought back painful memories of the years when he, too, had struggled with and succumbed to despair. The note of admonition in his letters to Sally as a student, urging her to accept her limitations and not fight the system, recalls his own younger self who had fought so hard at the same age to discipline and master unruly impulses.

Loss of control became once again a danger for Paul, who was drinking heavily, generally a bottle of spirits a day or more throughout this period. Furious eruptions, when he smashed or threw things, alternated with a mood of desolating self-hatred. Sally described him sitting on the stairs plucking at his face, as if he were trying to rip it away: 'The sense of dislike – that's what was left. The sense of a bad smell under your nose.' It was a gesture Paul had described in his books as far back as *The Chinese Love Pavilion*, where Saxby talks of wearing 'the face of a sahib', and tries perpetually to wipe it off ('He . . . slid his hand down his face as if removing the outer skin').[56] Penny in these years came to feel Paul's sneering face – the sneer he could not bear to see on his mouth in the mirror – directed more and more at her, and Sally, in whom Paul saw so much of himself, felt it too. His behaviour was sometimes so threatening that, although he never hit either of them, both were convinced that one day he would. Penny kept an emergency bag packed in case she had to leave the house at short notice. She had planned her re-training at the Middlesex in preparation for a time when she might need to earn her own living, and she secretly visited Erin Pizzey, who had recently opened the first refuge in London for battered wives, to ask advice. Penny had lived under strain in solitude for so long that simply to be able to talk freely, to share her anxieties and confess the fears that loomed sometimes uncontrollably (she told Mrs Pizzey that her husband had threatened to kill her with a pickaxe) was an inexpressible relief.

Just before Christmas Sally, who was five months pregnant, left Paul Cashmore and returned to her parents' house. She was locked so deeply into a pattern of depression, self-destruction and the drugs prescribed to combat both that even Paul, who vehemently disapproved of broken marriages, reluctantly admitted hers was over. It seemed to him one more failure in a long line of defeats. 'There was a kind of family breakdown going on,' Sally said. 'It was like a dance of death between the three of us.' Her return became a test of strength, or rather perhaps a test of vulnerability. Sally – sick, sedated, suicidally depressed, and in serious danger of losing her baby – claimed Penny's exclusive attention. Paul withdrew in dismay. By the first week of the New Year 1972 he had moved into Carol's old room, leaving the main

bedroom to the two women. The household was now formally divided
into two camps. Sally could not be left unattended which made Penny,
as Paul said grimly, 'something of a prisoner in her own home'. Paul,
living separately under the same roof, seemed to have manoeuvred
himself into the same position as his father before him: 'at the
moment, I'm mostly alone, in my study, or with my notebook, in the
pub.'[57]

He was preparing a set of lectures to be given for the British Council
in India. They had invited him in November ('the opportunity wasn't
to be missed,' Paul wrote to Gerry Hanley: 'Had reached a stage in the
last novel in the quartet when I realised how much I needed to go to
India again'),[58] and he had agreed to take part the following January
in a literary fortnight in Delhi to mark International Book Year. The
outbreak in December of the second war with Pakistan, which ended
after two weeks and the secession of Bangladesh in victory for India,
put paid to these celebrations, whereupon Paul's visit was rescheduled
as a lecture tour in February. 'It was a physical distancing,' said Sally,
'an abandonment.' But it was also a last-minute rescue from pressures,
both emotional and material, that had become too great to bear. Paul's
financial outlook at the beginning of 1972 was not encouraging:
Towers had sold 5,000 copies in England ('Heinemann seems to think
that good, so what bad is God knows'),[59] and appeared to be sinking
without trace in the US. Paul was living on advance payments for the
next novel which he had barely started, and on which he reckoned to
spend at least another year (in fact, it would take twice that). He had
no windfalls in prospect, no prizes, foreign rights, paperback or other
deals, nor could he hope to produce anything more lucrative until he
had completed the Quartet: 'my wretched slowness, and the failure of
the novels to make much of an impact on the market so far, leaves me
in no position to bargain,' he would write gloomily later that year to
Dorothy Olding. 'There is nothing to offer except a continuation of
the work.'[60]

He had already approached various publishers hoping without
success for a part-time job, and for nearly a decade he had been selling
his manuscripts for small but useful sums (never more than £1000 per
novel) to the University of Texas. But, after the final instalment due for
A Division of the Spoils in twelve months time, his income would dry
up altogether. On 22 January, a week before he left for India, he
braced himself to write to John Willey raising the question of the
future in general, and asking in particular for a loan, or an advance on
the $1,000 dollars due from Morrow in April, to keep the household
in Addison Way solvent in his absence. The British Council would pay
expenses but no fee. In December he had won a *Yorkshire Post* £100

award for the best novel of the year, but that had already gone on insurance and tropical clothing for the trip. Things seemed to be getting out of control in ways that had terrified him since childhood. 'The chaos of the past two weeks is indescribable,' he wrote to Mollie Hamilton on 28 January. Sally had miscarried the day before: 'a threatened event that has added to the complications, as you can imagine – with poor Penny coping at the hospital (visiting) & also trying to cope with an unidentified flying object (me).'

He flew off on Saturday night 29 January, landing in Bombay at 4.30 next morning, and plunging immediately into an official programme which left no time for the softer airs and rhythms that had refreshed him in the past. His opening lecture on Monday in the university's Convocation Hall – 'After Marabar', exploring in some detail his complicated relationship with Forster – was a disaster.[61] The text was far too intricate, too subtle and closely argued for delivery to an audience of barely a hundred people in Gilbert Scott's majestic building where Paul's words were swallowed up under the stained glass and gothic vaulting, fans whirred noisily, pigeons flew in and out, and traffic roared past outside the doors all standing open to catch the evening sea breezes. There was an official reception that night, followed on Tuesday by two more lectures and a dinner party at Dorothy's flat in Queen's Court. Next day Paul left to give another couple of lectures in Poona, putting up at the Turf Club, visiting Government House and the old garrison church of St George's, making a detour on the return drive to climb four hundred feet up a precipitous path under a broiling sun to see the rock temple of Karli. He arrived back in Bombay on 3 February in a state of near collapse. He was to stay with Sue and Partap Sharma:[62] she was the daughter of an old friend, Heinemann's managing director Charles Pick, and had just married a highly successful young playwright who arranged a gathering in Paul's honour of journalists and writers familiar with his work. He arrived late after the drive from Poona, looking pale, and turned paler still when the assembled guests raised their glasses in a toast.

He was exhausted, shivering and sweating, perhaps with fever or the panic commonly induced in visiting specialists by gruelling British Council schedules. He had lectured five times in four days, and was already wondering if he could keep up the pace in a dozen cities over three more weeks. His visit had been proposed by enthusiasts who had rightly recognised a serious British novelist writing about India as a rare opportunity, without also realising that it would be largely wasted if he lectured, without publicity or advance explanation, to audiences who had barely heard of him in places where his books were virtually unobtainable. It was a shock to find widespread ignorance in India about the work which had absorbed him for so long, and in which he was still immersed. Paul was depressed by his initial reception, constrained by the sense of being on display, uncomfortable under surveillance by his Council guides and minders ('*Very* discreetly, an eye is kept on one most of the time, you know').[63] They for their part were pleasantly surprised by his modest, straight-forward, unassuming manner, and the pains he took with each appearance. His path was smoothed in Bombay by Foy Nissan, a civilised and sympathetic escort who helped him turn his formal lectures into something more like impromptu talks. He had an immediate success on 4 February at the University of Baroda where one of the best English departments in the country, under Professor V. Y. Kantak, supplied knowledgeable and appreciative audiences; and another next day at Ahmedabad, where he made a dramatic, last-minute entry having covered three hundred miles in a taxi comman-deered by a courteous and princely fellow passenger, the Maharana of Jambughoda, after fog delayed their dawn flight from Baroda.

But he could not sleep, and was suffering by the end of his first week from an ominous loosening of the bowels, and equally ominous signs of having caught a chill. On 6 February he flew to Jaipur, with a four-hour stop at Udaipur, which he spent drinking recuperative brandies instead of visiting the famous floating palace, flying on next day for a crowded week of official engagements in Delhi, staying at the efficient but impersonal India International Centre, delivering four well-attended lectures, signing books, giving interviews, attending parties and dining one night in Tughluk Road with the Nag Chaudhuris. On Sunday 13 February, he reached Calcutta ('one feels one is at last in *India*'),[64] where he liked his roomy, old-fashioned hotel, the Kenilworth, and got on well with the Council's representative, a namesake called Tim Scott, who lived round the corner in an official bungalow near the maidan with an extraordinary, black-and-white marble art deco staircase, and a deep, cool, comfortable verandah with shady blinds and rattan chairs. Paul's letters home describe a hectic round of lectures, meetings, parties and press conferences, which he survived on copious draughts of Indian brandy and doctors' pills ('what is wrong with me is *fatigue* – almost total physical and nervous exhaustion from having to *perform*').[65] Dipali Nag, on a flying visit to Behala, attended one of his lectures. If he met Neil Ghosh again, he did not say so: Neil had touched his lowest point after his girlfriend Caroline left Calcutta in the years between Paul's two visits, resigning from Bird & Co., losing his company car and other privileges, mixing mostly with the dwindling few who had stayed on like himself:

seedy, aggrieved, disconsolate, hard-drinking refugees from a lost world. He had read and recognised himself in *The Jewel in the Crown*, but sceptical friends treated his claim to have been put in a book as just another of Neil's tall stories.

For Paul himself, the tour gathered speed like a dream – 'when I get home I suspect I shan't feel I have been in India at all this time'[66] – an impression heightened by reports from England of a miners' strike, a three-day week, power cuts, snowstorms, blackouts and emergency conditions. Penny described battling out each day through icy blizzards to visit Sally in hospital, returning at night to frozen pipes in an unheated house empty save for the decrepit, ancient Beauty, sole survivor at seventeen of the original tribe of cats. Paul and Penny each urged the other to seek courage and strength in spirits, raising their glasses to one another metaphorically by post. He left Calcutta by plane on 20 February, flying south to lecture on successive days in Madras ('am more or less out on my feet at the moment'), Bangalore, Calicut on the Malabar coast (where the rickety arrangements made for his reception collapsed altogether and so did Paul, exasperated after a 250 mile drive across the Deccan with another almost twice as long to face next day), and Dharwar, where he spoke for the last time:

> At the end of the lecture tour, exhausted and not yet recovered from the bad temper caused by a frustrating incident at the last port of call, I sat alone on the balcony of a guest house and watched the day die away across the rolling country of the Western Ghats. The land looked waste, arid, as if a fire that had burnt it all day was going out. Burning out too was my bad temper. I became tranquil and if someone had asked me then why I came to India again and again, I believe I could have described properly the way in which India always extends me by subtly undermining the structure of my Western responses and replacing them with attitudes that promise to lead to an ever fuller sense of identity with the place and its people.[67]

Paul spent two nights at Dharwar, fifty miles south of Belgaum, and was delivered by his driver on the morning of Sunday, 27 February, to Jagalbet where the Malgonkars had built a new house, like a dak bungalow, on the side of a wooded valley facing across to a hillside covered in dense jungle far from human habitation with no light to be seen at night. Paul, who had climbed four hundred feet up a rocky ridge to Karli Cave just over three weeks earlier, scarcely had strength to accompany his host on a gentle stroll into the forest in the cool of the evening after tea ('a short walk made him breathless, and his fingers shook as from a nervous tremor').[68] All he wanted to do was regroup, recover and unwind, and he could hardly have chosen a quieter place or more sympathetic company in which to do it. Mac Malgonkar had just finished a long article, 'Ootacamund Revisited', about the British in retreat after Independence ('here, on £10 a week, a man could hold his head high, and even join the Ooty Club').[69] Paul was fascinated by his findings, and vexed to learn that his own route up the coast from Calicut could easily have included Ootacamund in the Nilgiri Hills. He sat with Mac on his last night, on the back verandah under an almost full moon, both holding glasses, listening to the jungle sounds, talking of Ooty and its people:

I rather held forth about how it had become the last place of refuge for left-over sahibs, the koi-hais who throve best under the shadow of the raj but were hopelessly out of their element in any other environment. . . . Ooty somehow was more like the pre-war England they used to know than England itself. . . .

I told Paul how, like bees from a smoked-out hive clinging to a familiar perch, the sahibs and memsahibs had gravitated to Ooty. Originally, there had been about a hundred families but, at the time of Paul's visit, there could not have been more than twenty. They lived with their dogs and faithful servants, on their meagre pensions and nostalgia, in dank cottages which bore names such as 'Bramley Hurst', 'Llangollen' or 'Kenilworth'.[70]

The Malgonkars had once again arranged a lunch with Peter Goodbody from Green Hotel, Belgaum, with whom Paul had corresponded regularly in the three years since they first met. Goodbody had read *The Day of the Scorpion* in 1969 ('How accurately you have captured the atmosphere – muddle, depression and the dead hand of the absentee landlord, Whitehall . . . I take my hat off to you'), and, after this second visit, he would read *The Towers of Silence* ('What entirely flummoxes me is how you manage to convey the "milieu" with such accuracy – a species of seventh sense. Anyway, you've done it again').[71] In the interval, he had given advice, supplied background information, told stories and patiently answered Paul's questions about matters like Bombay's Willingdon Club, founded by the Viceroy with a mixed Indian and English membership ('The entire atmosphere was extremely tolerant. . . . What a different atmosphere to that you put over – so correctly – in your books'), and the legendary free brothel run for officers in wartime by a wealthy widow and her friends in the hill station of Kodaikanal: 'She was by all accounts the relict – (a lovely word which always puts me in mind of a busted paper bag blowing along the gutter) – of a tea planter.'[72] Paul would draw on Goodbody's account of this establishment for the dubious party at the house called 'Sea Breezes' on Marine Drive in his next novel. This second visit to Jagalbet proved as refreshing, and professionally as fruitful, as the first. Goodbody was a stimulating as well as a vastly entertaining character, and Mac Malgonkar was right in thinking that, when Paul left after two days to spend the rest of his last week catching up on the social whirl at Dorothy's flat in Bombay, 'the sahibs who had stayed on were very much on his mind'.

So was the far more pressing question of what he might find when he got back to England. Penny had sent little news of Sally, save to say she was still in hospital. Paul had returned brief, affectionate, apprehensive messages but, after a month away, he poured out his pent-up alarm and anxiety to Coocoo Malgonkar.[73] He confided his fears for his daughter, and his guilt at abandoning his wife to uncertainty and distress without support. He talked of the wretched life she led, her miserable daily journeys to and from the hospital, her difficulties when she got home to a cold house, and the fact that he should have been there to stoke the boiler for her. He said he should never have left her, that he had failed her over money and in other ways, that he ought all along to have done more for her. It was the kind of confession he could never make to Penny. His hostess, surprised and disturbed by this outburst from a virtual stranger, did her best to reassure him, but there was little she or anyone else could say. Five weeks' absence had postponed but not resolved the reckoning that awaited him in London.

When Paul flew back on Sunday 5 March, he found nobody at home. Sally, discharged that week from the Middlesex Hospital, had sought the support she could not get at home from her father in a community run by the psychiatrist, R.D. Laing. 'My wife is looking after her in the place she has gone to get better, so I am alone, here, and coping with chores!' Paul wrote on 8 March to the Malgonkars. He had both wife and child back within the week. Sally needed nursing in bed, and Paul went down with what he described as 'virus trouble'. As soon as she was strong enough, Sally left home again, withdrawing to a series of flat, retreats and refuges with friends where over the next few years she struggled for control of her life and health. She kept in close contact with her mother, who remained miserably divided by the conflicting and mutually exclusive demands made on her. There were threats and counterthreats of self-destruction. Once Paul swallowed a whole bottle of Sally's sleeping tablets, another time he locked himself in the study in a dangerous mood and emerged only after his wife had called the police. When Penny was laid low with flu, Paul told John Willey that he 'had what we call shadow flu (like the husband's shadow pregnancy) – which is virtually a way of claiming a bit of sympathy too, I suppose.'[74]

He could always see the funny side of their joint predicament, at any rate with outsiders. He took a firm line with the medical profession, blaming Sally's condition solely on the drugs prescribed by her doctors to relieve it, resisting psychiatric explanations, fearing perhaps rightly any attempt to implicate him in what had happened to her. Sally felt herself unconditionally rejected by her father. Paul, who had inherited a fortnightly column in *Country Life* after Richard Church's death the year before, gave a bleak account in a book review in January 1973 of relations between a father and his estranged, grown-up child: 'the terrible charade of human intercourse and family intimacy which takes place whenever the generations meet and the elder has to come away encouraged by pitifully marginal signs and criteria of well-being ... but deeply and bitterly oppressed by unacceptable but undeniable intimations of the inadequacy, the total irrelevance, of himself and his entire generation.'

As soon as some sort of equilibrium had been re-established at Addison Way, Penny resumed the 'secretarial duties' for which Paul had paid her £3 a week ever since he left Higham's ('her main job is to screen callers on the telephone, to go to the post office for me, and act as a tea- and coffee-girl, and generally run errands').[75] Her latest non-fiction book, *Back to Nursing*, was being offered to publishers in 1972 but her writing, like so much else between them, had 'become a delicate subject better not discussed'. Without Penny, he could neither live nor write, two functions he now found it hard to separate. She allowed him to turn into a virtual recluse ('It's the hermit in one, coming out', he wrote to Gerry Hanley)[76] for much of the ten years he gave to the Raj Quartet: 'nothing else matters except getting hold of enough money to keep the roof dry, the family fed & the book going'. He needed prison conditions but the person who provided them – screening callers, running errands, cutting him off from contact with the outside world – became perhaps inevitably the last person to whom he could turn for companionship or consolation.

He gave both without stint to his friends in these years. Paul kept up a steady stream of correspondence, becoming confidant and counsellor, enquiring tenderly after other authors' works in progress, calming stress, urging against overwork, lightening money worries, easing marital difficulties, mediating or making practical suggestions in every sort of domestic upset. He supplied disinterested and sensitive support in both short- and long-term troubles. Mollie Hamilton, struggling with her own most ambitious work over the same decade as Paul (like him, she had embarked in 1964 on an 'Indian historical', called variously *The Red Pavilions*, *The Far Horizons*, and eventually *The Far Pavilions*),[77] received regular encouragement in writing and on the telephone. They never discussed the contents of their respective novels: Mollie said that *The Jewel in the Crown* had disheartened her so much about her own writing that she refused to read any more of

Paul's books until she had finished her ten-year stint on the *Pavilions*.[78] But she consulted him, and implicitly followed his instructions, whenever she hit family snags, a writing block or a break in concentration.

Spurring her on became a way of sustaining himself ('however well-meaning other people's advice is,' Paul explained to Mollie, 'they're really only offering the advice they'd give themselves'),[79] but he found his own sensible prescriptions hard to take when he returned at last to his interrupted novel after the Indian tour of 1972. 'The India in my book seemed quite unreal, and its reality is only just coming back,' he wrote to Gerry Hanley on 28 March, nearly a month after he got back. He had asked his old friend Doreen Marston the same week, in the course of a long, comforting, gossipy lunch together, if she would accept the dedication of *A Division of the Spoils* ('I can't wait for the next novel,' she wrote: 'You know why, and I find it impossible to tell you how thrilled I was when I got into the taxi').[80] By the end of April, he was still 'gazing dazedly at the manuscript',[81] which was slowly beginning to come to life again, although a month later he warned John Willey not to expect quick results. 'The thing itself calls the tune and the pace.' He worked steadily and slowly that summer, uncomfortably aware that there was no possibility of finishing before the money ran out. He had no assets except the house he lived in, no savings, £800 a year from book reviews (*Country Life* had quadrupled his earnings as a reviewer), and an annual income of £2,000 from Heinemann plus $2,000 from Morrow, both scheduled to dry up when the current agreements ran out at the end of the year or soon after.

He faced his worst financial crisis since he had given up his job in 1960 at a time when he was unwilling or unable to call on his usual loyal supporters. Roland Gant had been ill, John Willey's wife Fern had died that spring, David Higham (whose firm had split apart again, leaving him once more with relatively inexperienced junior partners whom Paul scarcely knew) seemed at any rate temporarily to have lost interest in the progress of the Quartet, and Ivan von Auw (who with Dorothy Olding represented him in America) had just retired.[82] In mid October Paul reluctantly raised the problem through Dorothy with Willey, who responded at once with a wedding-anniversary cable, followed by a warmly reassuring letter. Paul reviewed strategy and tactics at length in his reply, which explained his fears, deplored his slowness – 'I was fascinated to read the other day that Cyril Connolly had defined literary sloth as the effect of the tug between genius and talent. . . . Personally I think literary sloth is an effect of creative fatigue . . . exaggerated in this case by weight of the last three books leaning on this one' – and frankly stated the strength and weakness of his position:

The situation would be relieved to some extent if only I could be certain when Division will be finished. The only certainty I have is that I shall just go on writing it until it is right because the whole sequence will depend on this last book . . .

As I think I said to Dorothy, I feel I have absolutely nothing to offer, nothing to stake, or put up, now, except this will and intention to write a good novel that will bring the sequence successfully to a close. Creatively time is not the essence – but time isn't free either, you have to buy it or invite investment in it . . . by and large I've bought time by spreading my total earnings as thinly as possible. . . . The habit of spreading thinly was connected with what I knew about my slowness. But in the last three years things have caught up on me. The Arts Council grant helped me to buy more time by reducing my drawings from Heinemann. I bought more time still by selling some manuscripts to Texas. But here we are, arrived at last at the point where there is nothing I can offer in exchange for time . . .

I have been wondering whether something could be worked out as between Heinemann and Morrow that would give me something like a sense of security. But, as I said to Dorothy, what this really means is that I am inviting a vote of confidence even greater than the one Morrow gave me in 1959, which enabled me to leave the Higham office.[83]

John Willey and his chief at Morrow, Larry Hughes, showed immediate confidence by increasing the advance already paid on *A Division* by half as much again, while Roland Grant and Charles Pick at Heinemann proposed to continue payment for another year on the same terms as before. It was, as Paul said, the best that could be hoped ('A finger in the dyke, if you will pardon the expression'),[84] and relieved immediate pressure. He returned to his novel, where he had broken off at the end of October, in the middle of what would eventually be the second section of Book One, 'Journeys Into Uneasy Distances'. The section starts with a premonition of catastrophe – a momentary, unexplained leap forward to what Paul called 'the train scene' with which he would close the whole sequence – when the Muslim, Ahmed Kasim, steps from his railway carriage into the arms of the waiting Hindu mob a week before the official hand-over of power, independence and partition, in August 1947. The train starts up again and moves off, after a brief bloody pause, carrying its load of British passengers, departing Imperialists, civil servants, police and army personnel:

It was the smooth gliding motion away from a violent situation which one

Chandni Chowk, Delhi.

Barbie Batchelor (Peggy
Ashcroft) with her
trunk: 'I see now that
her trunk . . . is really a
symbol for the luggage I
am conscious of
carrying with me every
day of my life – the
luggage of my past, of
my personal history and
of the world's
history . . .'

Red Fort, Delhi.

Guy Perron (Charles Dance) with Sarah Layton (Geraldine James) in Granada TV's Jewel.

Peter Green meeting himself when young as Guy Perron in the Raj Quartet.

witness never forgot. 'Suddenly you had the feeling that the train, the wheels, the lines, weren't made of metal but of something greasy and evasive.'[85]

The witness in this passage is a new character, Sergeant Guy Perron, who provides the novel's unifying commentary or consciousness: 'one had to find a way to come in from outside,' Paul explained later to Storm Jameson. 'One had to wrap it up, as it were, with a smile and a sense of openness. I needed and looked for a positive man. I suppose every book has to criticise itself, and Guy is the critic.'[86] Paul's lightning sketch of Guy Perron ('the sort of man it would be nice to have a drink and a laugh and a lunch with') is clearly based on Peter Green: each has an outstanding Cambridge record, an analytical intelligence and a powerful curiosity. But Perron is also a professional historian with the historian's impartial stance, methodical approach to evidence, broad perspective and emphasis on what Paul called 'lucidity and the calm rhythms of logical thought'.

Over the past twelve years, in the course of a systematic programme of reading, reflection and research, Paul had himself become a formidably knowledgeable Imperial historian. 'One day, it is to be hoped, someone – preferably an Englishman – will examine the whole situation in the light of our own failure to unify a country which we were always eager to describe, publicly anyway, as a sacred trust,' he had written as far back as 1961, discussing the partition of India in a review for the *Times Literary Supplement* of Penderel Moon's *Divide and Quit*.[87] He built up, before and during the years he wrote the Raj Quartet, an extensive, highly specialised library of books on British Indian history, social life and politics.[88] As a reviewer of books on Indian topics for *The Times* and *TLS* under Alan Pryce-Jones, he formulated, tested and developed over the same period the views which would supply the intellectual underpinning for *A Division of the Spoils*. 'The overall argument . . . is that the greatest contribution to the tragi-comedy of Anglo-India was the total indifference to and ignorance of Indian affairs of the people at home, who finally decided to hand India back in as many pieces as was necessary so long as it was got rid of. Which is what happened,' Paul wrote to Roland Gant on 9 May 1973. 'No one, that I know of, has yet said so.'

One theme that ran through his reviewing was mounting irritation with the unctuous half truths of nostalgia:

We want to know about the hour-by-hour *bandobast* [administration] in the political officer's *daftar*. . . . To hell with the peepul tree. That's just the romance. We want to know about the reality of the land records, about the cost of a canal or irrigation system, who paid for it and whether it worked. What did a forestry officer *do*? . . . How was a municipality funded? What was the cost of a primary education, and who bore it? Forget the duck, the tiger, the elephants, the servants, the loyal soldiers, the polo ponies, the topees, the ayahs, the *risaldars*. . . . Forget the dust, the sudden nightfall, the scent of jasmine and dung fires. Forget everything you have ever known and loved about India, and ask yourself, 'How did it *work*?' And there is hardly a book anywhere that tells you.[89]

This is the exasperation of a working historian, the prosaic grumbling of a Perron, who travels India with a notebook and schools his inquisitiveness with a discipline that is an object lesson in scholarly gathering techniques. Whereas, in *The Towers of Silence*, the reader was vaguely aware of waters rising, of anxious watchers in Pankot beginning to feel beleaguered and cut off, in *A Division of the Spoils* the sense of foreboding is sharply reinforced by rifts and fractures opening within the troubled Layton family. But the novel's sense of a historical tide turning in the background comes from Perron's awareness of the ground submerged beneath it. It is Perron who dissects the political cartoons in a Bombay paper of the popular satirist, Halki (a last salute to Paul's own ambitions as a cartoonist in London in 1947); Perron who notes the manoeuvrings of Indian politicians and British civil servants jockeying for a foothold on the steeply descending gradient of official policy laid down by the new socialist administration in Whitehall; Perron who examines the expedient compromises behind the British rhetoric of liberation; Perron who watches the violence simmering that summer as the secession crisis erupts onto the streets of Muslim Mirat; and Perron who speculates about the brutal realities underlying the collapse of nationalist aspirations so cogently advanced by the ex-INA Captain Sayed Kasim.

Perron makes vigorous use of what he himself describes as a practical, inquisitive, ruthlessly anti-nostalgic sense of history. He stands at the furthest extreme from his defeatist colleague, Major Tippit, brought out of retirement in *Scorpion* to take custody of the Congressman, M. A. Kasim, in the fort at Premanagar (on which Tippit is planning a monograph): 'I'm a historian really. The present does not interest me. The future even less.'[91] History is Tippit's excuse for turning his back on the convulsive upheavals tearing modern India apart. He blocks with 'mindless vegetable implacability' all complaints and queries from his prisoner, the stoical and clear-sighted Kasim, who finds himself physically immured by the British, politically estranged from his Muslim separatist compatriots, unable to endorse the cause of his nationalist son Sayed, 'out of rhythm with my country's temporary emotional feelings'.[92] This was very much Paul's own position during the writing of the Raj Quartet. He felt himself struggling against a kind of collective inertia; the dogged British determination to disclaim responsibility for the empire, its precipitate collapse and problematic aftermath; the greasy and evasive, perennial human instinct to glide smoothly away from violent disturbance. Paul confronted unpopular issues in the Quartet, and reached unpalatable conclusions. For him, history was an active force, a means of attacking sloth, complacency, misrepresentation and their fruits of hostility and fear. Understanding was for him a crucial weapon without which, as he wrote in a review of a book about racial prejudice in 1971, 'we must all limp on, wearing the thick boot of envy at the end of one leg, and the iron of contempt on the other'.[93]

Perron represents the historian at his most intrepid, charismatic and alluring, as well as personifying lucidity and the calm rhythms of logical thought. But, if Perron supplies a strong romantic interest in the Quartet (and in the television series based on it), its emotional heart lies in the opposite direction, with his superior Major (rapidly promoted to Lieutenant Colonel) Merrick, the least theoretical and most practical of men, an officer whom Perron initially mistrusts, subsequently despises and eventually comes to detest with whole-hearted and uncharacteristic venom. Merrick, moving steadily in the course of the four novels from one rung to the next up the official ladder of command and trust, reaches his high point (and his dreadful end) in *Division*. He believes in 'only two basic human emotions, contempt and envy'.[94] He is a man of the past. His insistence on the values of a world that no longer exists, perhaps never existed, makes him dangerously attractive in time of trouble – in Mayapore in 1942 or Mirat in 1947 – when his methods come as a relief even to people who deplore them. He has no reservations about Imperial power and privilege. He regards sceptics like Perron as traitors to their class and country:

He believes we've abandoned the principles we used to live by, what he would call the English upper-and-ruling class principle of knowing oneself superior to all other races, especially black, and having a duty to guide and correct them. He's been sucked in by all that Kiplingesque double talk that transformed India from a place where plain ordinary greedy Englishmen carved something out for themselves . . . into one where they appeared to go voluntarily into exile for the good of their souls and the uplift of the native . . . most of us are as bad as black to him. There aren't many real white men left.[95]

In so far as the Raj Quartet may be said to have a villain, it is Ronald Merrick. Racist, illiberal, manipulative, sadistic and sexually repres-sed, he represents the root of violence and unreason running underground. He acts on impulses seldom officially acknowledged ('One isn't supposed to talk about this kind of thing,' he says at one point to Sarah Layton. ' "I know," she said. "It's how we hide our prejudices and continue to live with them" ').[96] But one of the singular achievements of the Raj Quartet is that its portrait of Merrick, although scrupulously honest, is by no means unsympathetic. His actions, viewed through his own eyes, invariably look like sound, bold, courageous moves in pursuit of honourable ends. His worst enemies recognise his clarity, decisiveness and persuasive charm. Perron himself respects the energy of Merrick's 'powerful and inventive imagination'. His baleful influence is generally apparent only in the ruined lives of his captives: Kumar, the unlucky homosexual Corporal Pinker, Havildar Khan of the INA – 'the poor weary, shagged-out, shamed and insulted havildar'[97] – who hangs himself in *Division* after interrogation at Merrick's hands. Merrick's eventual marriage to Sarah Layton's unhappy and unstable sister Susan causes consternation in her family. But even Sarah admits kinship of a sort with Merrick and his narrow, blinkered kind: 'You are, yes, our dark side, the arcane side. You reveal something that is sad about us, as if out here we had built a mansion without doors and windows, with no way in and no way out.'[98] If Sarah Layton and Guy Perron between them forcefully present the attractions of the liberal spirit – a humane, informed, tolerant and open approach to relations between the races –Merrick's blind, compulsive, violence sounds a deeper note, the malign and sombre note of Lorca's *duende*, which is crucial to the emotional and imaginative orchestration of the Raj Quartet.

It completes a circle of creation, preservation and destruction that cost dear in human terms. Looking back long after he had finished the Quartet, describing his *duende*, Paul tacitly acknowledged that, in the interests of creation, he had invoked, if not cultivated, a destructive darkness in himself. 'It was as though he needed to keep some area of suffering,' said his daughter Sally: 'as if, having opened himself to that dark side, he required its presence.' 'The Philoctetes thing has interested me for years,' Paul wrote to a reviewer who had noted the use in *Division* of the Greek myth about the archer cast out by his companions because of his permanently open, stinking, suppurating, unhealed wound.[99] 'Philoctetes' is the pseudonym adopted by Hari Kumar, after his release from prison, when he earns a living by giving English lessons and contributing occasional journalism to the *Ranpur Gazette*. At the end of *Division*, on the night Perron learns the details of Merrick's murder in Mirat, a few days before he makes his one abortive attempt to find Kumar, he is haunted by, or perhaps dreams of a smell which he identifies as 'Merrick's smell . . . also the smell of the archer's wound'.[100]

Paul said, after the Quartet was finished, that he found echoes of himself in all his characters,[101] which accounts for the different identifications confidently made by different people according to the different sides he showed them. James Leasor recognised the Paul he knew in Merrick. Mollie Hamilton and others saw Paul as Perron. Peter Green was not the only one to find traces of Paul in Barbie Batchelor. A friend of Manohar Malgonkar's, one of Paul's earliest and most perceptive American critics, Professor D. W. Burjorjee (who had written to tell Paul, before they met, how clearly he recognised himself in Hari Kumar), said that the kindness, gentleness and generosity he knew in Paul were best reflected in that brave and disinterested statesman, M. A. Kasim.[102]

A Division, like its predecessor, took three years to write. Paul worked on it throughout 1973 with gathering momentum and few interruptions: celebrations for Carol's return from the Bahamas with Larry in February, a Swanwick lecture in the summer, a disastrous autumn holiday at Sennen (rain pouring down 'like a nineteenth-century painting of the Flood'[103] reflected Paul's resentment at time stolen from his manuscript), jury service in November, and a last-minute Christmas dinner laid on at Addison Way for John Willey and Dorothy Olding. Sometimes the book weighed like a ton of bricks, sometimes it free-wheeled downhill so fast it needed brakes. By winter it had entered its final stages, in the New Year it hung fire, and on 19 March 1974 Paul drew Carol's attention to his birthday in six days' time: 'I am not celebrating until I have finished my *@!&c+=% novel which means that I am not offering hospitality for a few weeks, but am open to receive congratulations and Loyal Greetings.'[104] In the event, he finished his *@!&c+=% novel on 25 March, his fifty-fourth birthday, almost exactly ten years after he started *The Jewel in the Crown*.[105] He felt relieved, depressed, deprived, elated, as if he had simultaneously given birth and been bereaved. Morrow reported customers so eager for the last book in the sequence they were said to be dying (one had already died) of frustration.[106] The manuscript, which took six weeks to type, was delivered to Heinemann on 29 April, and crossed the Atlantic in early May. THRILLED TO THE CORE, John Willey cabled, WHAT A NOVEL. WHAT A QUARTET. WHAT A MAN. WRITING SOON.

AND WHAT A CABLE, Paul telegraphed back: INARTICULATE THANKS.[107]

CHAPTER FOURTEEN

An elephant serenely pacing

Paul felt like a revenant from another world when he raised his eyes at last from the inner screen that had for so long monopolised his attention. 'Abandoning it is rather like throwing out one's colour TV set and reverting to black and white . . .' he wrote to John Willey on 2 August 1974. 'I look out of my window and see the buses and lorries going past and feel that I haven't seen things under my nose this past 20 years.' He talked almost as if his family were strangers to him. Carol had cut off her hair in the Bahamas ('She's a bit of a knockout to look at,' Paul wrote to Peter Green),[1] spent the year after she got back stage-managing the musical *Godspell*, and was about to join the BBC that summer. Sally had also reached a turning point, which would mean breaking her dependence on tranquillisers and sleeping pills after a final, fearful crisis in June ('usual thing, younger daughter, overdose, hospital,' Paul wrote to Mollie Hamilton: 'one never gets used to it').[2] Paul remained aloof and dubious, urging scepticism on Penny, viewing Sally's precarious victories with caution.

He himself felt washed up and worked out. The script of *A Division* was at the printers (editing – fined down by now to routine checking and collating in 'mammoth telephone sessions' with Roland – was completed by the first week in June, just over a month after delivery),[3] with proofs expected early in November. Paul drew up for Roland a Quartet cast list with notes on the subsequent fates of individuals (Kumar landed a teaching job, contacted Lady Chatterjee and kept an eye on the child Parvati's professional début as a singer; Sarah Layton married Guy Perron; Kasim became eventually governor of Ranpur),[4] but it was ghostly work. He could neither cut clean free from his characters' fictional claims nor feel himself still fully part of them.

Penny went alone that summer to the Swanwick Writers School, and brought back a virus infection which Paul caught. He meant to celebrate publication by taking her with him to New York: Morrow had signalled confidence in July in the shape of an advance of $1,000 on his next book.

He was trying to write again, 'tinkering with, prowling around, the idea for a new short novel, a sort of bridging thing, a farewell to India',[5] toying as an alternative with an account of his suburban 1920s childhood to be called *The Studio* or *Palmers Green*, along the lines of Ronald Blythe's *Akenfield*.[6] He wrote to his brother, asking for photographs and family albums, falling as he always did with Peter into a parody of Gilbert Wright – 'shall probably drive over to Fox Lane and park and look and think. And then get pissed (old man).'[7] He had in mind a Proustian memoir centring round his father, and hoped for the kind of success other writers had with 'reminiscences of childhoods not half as fascinating and bloody awful as ours'. Nothing came of these schemes. It would be at least another six months before Paul found he could so much as set one sentence after another, but he kept on trying 'because a writer only feels half alive when not writing'. He reviewed a life of H. M. Stanley that autumn, and quoted to John Willey the great explorer's account of how he felt when he got back from the Congo:

When a man returns home and finds for the moment nothing to struggle against, the vast resolve, which has sustained him through a long and difficult enterprise, dies away, burning as it sinks in the heart, and thus the greatest successes are often accompanied by a peculiar melancholy.[8]

Paul shared Stanley's pang. Sometimes he felt like a restive traveller impatient to take off again on another safari of the mind, at others like a prisoner released from a long sentence only to find he has lost touch with friends: 'Perhaps because I locked myself away too long to write this stuff, and lost contact. Emerging, I realise I don't know many people. It's a fault. One should,' he said a year later[9] in a letter to Storm Jameson, who had read *A Division of the Spoils* after rereading the three earlier novels, and wrote immediately, 'shaken and shaking' with excitement, to salute the scope of his undertaking, the splendour of his achievement, the risks he had taken and triumphantly pulled off as a writer: 'The book is marvellous, beyond praise by me, a good careful second-rate novelist.'[10] Paul was grateful but unconvinced. He said he could not be content with the Quartet or begin to think of it as a great work ('I sometimes think of it as a reconstruction of a ruined edifice, so exactly detailed that even the dry rot and the cracks in the walls show'), apologising for a depression which he knew must seem graceless and ill-timed. Other writers were only too familiar with its causes: 'These novels have come from the very marrow of your bones, the very stuff of your brain, the very life of your mind,' Storm Jameson wrote, urging him to recognise his need for a period of mental and emotional convalescence. 'I think that, just perhaps . . . rest may not be the only thing you need, and need deeply.'[11]

Division was published on 5 May 1975. Paul lunched that day at the Epicure with his dedicatee, Doreen Marston, noting that he had reached the same age as David Higham had been when Paul himself was taken on as a promising 'young-man-about-the-office' ('Now, when I go to see him, I feel older than he looks').[12] He sent a copy of the book to Dorothy Ganapathy in Bombay: 'I hope you will think it a fitting end to the enterprise which began at Queen's Court in 1964. You may even recognise the block of flats in one section as not dissimilar to the one I know so well and remember so very fondly, for itself, yes, but chiefly for its chatelaine.' He paid tribute to Dipali Nag: 'So much of the Quartet originated in Calcutta in 1964, when I stayed with you . . . I can still see almost every nook and cranny.' Publication, which had hung over him like an impending parturition, only strengthened a sense of anticlimax not to be dispelled by the most encouraging reviews. There was a handsome tribute to the whole Quartet from Philip Knightley in the *Sunday Times*, a faintly patronising thumbs-up from the reporter James Cameron in the *Spectator*, and a generous salute in the *TLS* from J. G. Farrell[13] (who had won the Booker Prize two years before with *The Siege of Krishnapur* about the Indian mutiny: *Division* was not among the novels shortlisted for the Booker in 1975). Paul's favourite notice ('the best and most perceptive I've ever had')[14] came from H. R. F. Keating in *Country Life*. Even Francis King, a staunch Forsterian, 'almost came near to – well, not tipping his hat at me but flicking his bow tie' in the *Sunday Telegraph*.[15]

Most critics acknowledged with more or less enthusiasm what Farrell saw as the Quartet's 'two great and time-resisting virtues', its extraordinary range of character and 'its powerful evocation of the British empire'.[16] But at a time when the tainted Imperial legacy was still too recent for objective viewing, and when fashionable youth favoured formal innovation rather than more sustained, long-term, large-scale experiments in the novel, it was hard to detect the peculiar originality of the Raj Quartet, which was perceived for the most part as a respectable piece of work, well and stoutly made, but not worth attention at any great length or from front-rank reviewers. This approach went furthest in the *Observer*, where *Division* rated second place in the weekly batch of novels reviewed by Anthony Thwaite who, after 'only a cursory reading' of the three earlier books, diagnosed something wrong with the whole Quartet: 'overall lack of essential spark, so that what I suppose aims to be . . . something with Tolstoyan impact gives off a Galsworthian smell of over-furnished blandness.'

Paul was disproportionately, perhaps unreasonably, upset by Thwaite's review, which summed up for him all the smug dismissals of the past decade. He consoled himself by posting off a cutting to Mollie Hamilton together with an elaborate exchange of memos, designed to cheer them both up, between Superintendent Thwaite and his superior Tonybenn Sahib, Chief Warder of Mudpore Jail, concerning the prisoner manacled in Cell 78, Addison Wing, an insignificant, elderly and eminently expendable imperialist caught trying to smuggle word out to a friend ('But what is Thwaite Sahib I am asking myself when honoured memsahib is remembering this writer's humble existence, hopefully also of wife and eight children pulling on as best possible circumstances allowing . . . The file will be sufficient, memsahib. Not to be bothered baking the cake . . .'). Mollie understood better than most Paul's low spirits and lack of resilience after ten years' hard labour. Her own novel, begun at the same time as the Quartet, was also at last nearing completion. She laughed so hard over the message from Mudpore Jail that she did herself an injury – 'Sadly report, your humble phrend is in consequence cracking three ribs besides dislocation of two jaws, & has ever since been in General Hospital . . .' – and she sent exuberant thanks for her copy of *Division*: 'salaams from heart's bottom of unworthy chela and from unworthy chela's husband's bottom too.'[18]

But when Mollie caught up at last with the Quartet, she read it with pride and pleasure tempered by dismay. She recognised immediately its power and durability but, as a potentially influential account of the empire she and her family had known so intimately and for so long, it aroused grave misgivings. 'Paul saw little or nothing of the Raj,' she said. 'He never met the real Raj. . . . I could have introduced him to so many people who would have helped put him straight on any number of points he missed, or got wrong. Or exaggerated. I didn't even think of it. I was charmed that he, like me, was mad about India, and that was that. I hadn't . . . realised that he, as a [captain] in the Rice Corps, would have seen a quite different India to the one I had seen, known and could talk to.'[19] Mollie was right, in the sense that she herself was one of very few representatives of British India in touch with Paul during the writing of the Raj Quartet – its strength and scope came precisely from its being the work of an outsider, who saw what those more closely involved could not have seen – and the only one he counted among his friends. She bitterly regretted the self-denying ordinance that had prevented her from reading the books as they came out, or from questioning Paul about what he was doing. She insisted it was inconceivable, to anyone who knew the British memsahib, that Sarah Layton could have embarked on a casual wartime affair in 1944, or permitted a bloodthirsty mob to molest Ahmed Kasim in 1947, and she said there was no question, given the integrity and efficiency of the Indian Police (Mollie's father had been Head of Central Intelligence), that malpractice such as Merrick's could have gone undetected.

These, and other disreputable aspects of British behaviour in the Raj Quartet, struck many readers at the time as doing damaging disservice to the Imperial past which they had known and loved. Dorothy Ganapathy reported embarrassed British Council representatives dissociating themselves in an interview on Bombay television from the Quartet's 'anti-British' stance.[20] Paul had been prepared for this kind of criticism, which he found understandable. What surprised him was the opposite reaction from old India hands, retired ICS wallahs, box wallahs who stayed on, the sort of people who might have had every right to object to an account that made no bones about the brutality, complacency, self-righteousness and rigidity of the British Raj. Perhaps the most unexpected of all those who wrote to Paul was Sir Herbert Thompson, British Resident in Jaipur, Hyderabad and Lahore, second-in-command of the Political Department at the time of Independence, successively right-hand man to the last two Viceroys, Wavell and Mountbatten (Paul said his was the sort of career Nigel Rowan had hoped for in *Scorpion* and *Division*). Thompson, having borrowed a proof copy of Paul's book from a neighbour, Nigel Viney of Heinemann, demanded to know who wrote it, insisting that its author, who clearly possessed inside knowledge, 'must therefore be . . . one of his former ICS colleagues under a pseudonym'.[21]

Once convinced of Paul's existence, Thompson sent him a letter dated 21 June 1975, full of amazement, admiration and gratitude for a reconstruction that tallied at every point with his recollection. 'There must, surely, be things I have got wrong?' Paul replied,[22] torn between delight and half-guilty denials ('I'm afraid I am not Perron. At least no more than any other character'), acknowledging himself a professional imposter as he always did when readers assumed he had been born or bred or worked in India. The upshot was a long, convivial, gossipy lunch with the Thompsons at Haddenham in Buckinghamshire, the first of many, which gave Paul the strange sensation of stepping through the looking-glass into a world he had so far projected only in his imagination. The situation became even more like something out of Lewis Carroll when he corresponded with Sir Conrad Corfield, Thompson's chief at the Political Department, who had left precipitately in 1947 after a head-on collision with Mountbatten. Corfield had played in fact the fictional role Paul had imagined for Sir Robert Conway in *The Birds of Paradise*, and had used his retirement to explain and justify his conduct in a book, *The Princely India I Knew*, which had been rejected by every British publisher he approached on the grounds that there was no interest in the subject. It was eventually published in Madras in 1975 by a historical society so specialised, academic and unworldly that Paul had some difficulty extracting the copy he subsequently reviewed in *The Times Literary Supplement*.[23]

Men like Corfield and Thompson, thrown out of India in 1947 together with a great many minor figures who wielded comparatively little or no power, had found themselves relegated in retirement at home to a kind of limbo, their voices for all practical purposes suppressed, their views ignored, if not publicly ridiculed, and their memoirs virtually unpublishable. For many of them the Raj Quartet signalled for the first time that history had not simply written them and the empire off: their messages and letters were not only appreciative but tinged with unmistakable relief at finding someone interested at last in comprehension rather than condescension, someone prepared to take them and their historical predicament seriously instead of dismissing them out of hand as intrinsically malevolent or absurd. 'It was, at least in part, the majestic figure of Paul Scott that made us news again, who pinned us down with a marvellous precision at a time when our whole strange edifice was about to collapse,' wrote Richard Rhodes James in a valedictory salute after Paul's death, speaking as the representative and descendant of real-life Laytons whose forebears had exploited India for generations. 'He got us right, in the big things and in the small, in the traumas as well as in the tea cups. Those of us who were part of the Raj are grateful for the trouble he took over us. . . . He has ensured that our past will never be lost.'[24]

'The denial of memory: it's a terrible thing. It weakens one,' Paul said,[25] and it was not only the British who felt this weakening denial. At the beginning of 1976 Paul received a worrying approach from General Mohan Singh, patriot and founder of the Indian National Army ('The INA was the bone of my bones, the flesh of my flesh, it was my most cherished child'),[26] who had apparently disappeared without trace after the abortive INA show trials in the Red Fort in Delhi in 1946. Singh had no cause to like the British – who had subjugated his country, denied his right to equality, and humiliated his most cherished child by treating INA officers as traitors – least of all a

British author rash enough to have included him ('Frankly, I thought he was dead,' Paul said)[27] in a far from flattering account of INA activities. If Paul was taken aback to receive a transatlantic phone call from Singh's son-in-law, he was still more so to learn that the son-in-law proposed posting him a parcel, which turned out on receipt to contain nothing more explosive than the General's memoirs, together with an official invitation to visit Delhi as a guest of the Punjab State. Like Corfield, Singh had found himself after the transfer of power defeated, derided and consigned by his countrymen 'to the limbo of oblivion';[28] like Corfield, he had written his memoirs in self-defence ('What pained us more than the personal injustice done to us was the unfolding of a diabolic plan for the deliberate falsification of the history of our Independence'); and, like Corfield, he felt that he had found in the author of the Raj Quartet the reader he was writing for, someone who understood at last the cause for which the INA had fought.

Morrow published *Division* on 11 August 1975. Paul's celebratory trip to the US had been postponed to the end of the month so that he could lecture in the fall semester at the universities of Texas, Maryland and Illinois. 'The academic interest there in the British Empire is much greater than it is at this end,' he reported to Herbert Thompson[29] (the only academic institution that had ever invited Paul to speak in England was Stamford School, where his wife's nephew taught). His original enthusiasm for taking Penny with him had dwindled with time. He seldom discussed his hopes or intentions with her and, as Sally steadily gained ground, Penny made plans of her own. She joined an art class, booked herself a place again at the Swanwick summer school, and arranged with a friend from nursing days to take her first holiday without Paul in Tuscany in June. On the day after she got home from Italy she fell in the garden and broke her wrist: although her arm was out of plaster long before his departure date, Paul decided to leave her behind on grounds of cost.[30] He flew to New York on Wednesday, 27 August (Air India gave him VIP treatment on the flight) to embark on the usual hectic round of parties, interviews and visits, travelling up to Connecticut with Dorothy Olding on Friday to spend a long, leisurely, boozy weekend catching up on gossip at John Willey's country house in Norwalk.

Among the most heartening of Paul's American reviews was a long and eloquent salute in the *Washington Post* from his old friend Peter Green,[31] who had returned from his Greek island to academic life as a professor in the large and expanding classics department of the University of Texas at Austin. Paul flew down to Austin at the beginning of September to spend two days with Peter and his second wife, and to lecture to Professor Roger Louis' newly founded British Studies group, which fielded a formidably knowledgeable array of practical experts, scholars and Imperial historians, the kind of audience guaranteed to put an unaccredited outsider off his stroke. The heat was sweltering – 'Texas was hotter than Bombay, for the time of year'[32] – when Paul arrived looking ill and unfit in his crumpled tropical suit. 'When I knew him in London, he was always lean and smart as a whippet,' said Peter, who suspected something fundamentally wrong. Paul's old horror of being obliged to perform ('you have to wear tie, collar & jacket, than stand under arclights in auditoriums, & give forth') was compounded by the dangerously high level of alcohol he had judged necessary to nerve himself for what proved a discouraging debut. He visited the library in the Humanities Research Centre to see his manuscripts preserved with Joseph Conrad's (*Almayer's Folly* and *Chance*), and sign the door alongside William Faulkner and Tennessee Williams.[33] But he flew back with a heavy heart to Washington, where talks at Rockville College and Montgomery College in the University of Maryland had been organised by Mac Malgonkar's friend, Professor D. M. Burjorjee, whom Paul had met and liked in London.

Bandy Burjorjee was a Parsee from Rangoon who had solved the problem of an anglicised background and education – he had written about what he called 'the Harry/Hari duality'[34] even before he first came across Paul's books – by settling in America and specialising in Anglo-Indian literature. He had recognised the Raj Quartet while work was still in progress as the most important development in his field since *Passage to India*: 'your tetralogy sets in motion again, and most powerfully, the Anglo-Indian stream in the genre of the Imperial novel,' he wrote to Paul in 1973.[35] The University of Maryland, where Paul was accepted as a major novelist, did much to repair his confidence after Texas, where he had felt exposed as an amateur historian. He stayed with Burjorjee and his American wife, enjoying the party they gave for him, and feeling touched when both John and Dorothy flew down specially from New York to attend. He liked Washington (especially a visit to the war graves at Arlington Cemetery which turned out, to Dorothy's disgust, to be the only sight Paul cared to see),[36] and he even liked getting back afterwards to Manhattan, where he stayed in a private apartment belonging to Morrow. He flirted pleasantly with Dorothy ('He was like a young boy,' she said indulgently), telling tall stories, inventing elaborate private jokes, arriving at her East Side apartment with red roses supposedly picked in Central Park (always an odd number to show he had gathered them himself), and dancing the tango with her at the Rainbow Room.

He was also flirting that summer with a new admirer, a graduate student at the University of Illinois at Urbana, who had written twelve months earlier to enlist his help with a dissertation on the Raj Quartet. Her name was Francine Weinbaum and she, too, had arranged through her supervisor, a Joycean specialist called Bernard Benstock, for Paul to lecture at Urbana. He had been flattered and disconcerted by her interest, and by how well-informed she proved to be about his work. She had cross-examined him with alarming thoroughness by post, starting with influences: he freely acknowledged Eliot, tipped his hat at Chekhov and Ibsen, but emphatically denied Forster – 'Frankly I don't think it would have occurred to anyone to compare me with Forster if he hadn't written *Passage to India*. . . . If I had written about Nottingham would I have been compared to Lawrence?'[37] She inquired boldly about factual models for characters like Merrick ('aim off for the sense of personal deprivation,' Paul replied, conceding Merrick's tangential relationship to his own nature),[38] and the actual locations of places like Mirat (Paul insisted that Mirat was politically his own invention, but admitted a vague geographical connection with Hyderabad).[39] She asked if he had ever been a poet ('Poetry. Oh dear. Yes, I intended to be a poet & because during the last war you could get almost any rubbish published I had some stuff appear').[40] Paul was taken aback by the acuteness of Mrs Weinbaum's perceptions, especially when she announced that the more she knew about his life, the better she would understand his work.[41]

She for her part was thrilled at the prospect of meeting her own real live author in the flesh, and correspondingly dismayed when Paul stepped off the plane. 'He was so beaten down by life. So tired, and so sad. You could see it in his eyes. And I *couldn't* understand how that had metamorphosed into the Raj Quartet.' Their initial sense of let-down was mutual ('he was rather disappointed that I was so young') but, although he seemed abnormally nervous each time he had to speak, his talks were an immediate success. He had got the hang of American college students by this time: 'Courteous, large-hearted, intelligent and amusing,' he reported to Dorothy Ganapathy: 'It was like being back in an Indian university.'[42] They loved his jokes, his patience, the trouble he took over explanations, his openness and obvious appreciation of them as an audience. Francine Weinbaum, as his guide and favourite disciple in the three hectic days he spent at Urbana, was swept up into the kind of intense, exhilarating intimacy at which Paul excelled. 'He had a tremendous sensitivity to the woman's point of view, and at times an uncomfortable ability to read my mind when I didn't want him to,' she said.[43] 'I don't know how to put this: he knew how to fulfil your needs, he really did. He could get inside you.' Paul stayed with the Benstocks, dined with the Weinbaums, sat in on two of Francine's classes (she was teaching *The Bender*, and Paul was unnerved by the personal questions it threw up), recorded interviews, gave a local radio talk, and generally expanded in the company of people who had not only read his novels but approached them without the prejudices and preconceptions that so often interposed in India and Britain. 'He was a tremendous hit,' said Francine. 'People he met in the US made it clear they thought a lot of him.'

He flew back to London on 19 September, having stayed up dancing into the small hours with Dorothy the night before, and was immediately laid low for the rest of the month with 'a monumental head and chest cold'.[44] His homecoming was cold in every sense. Sales of *Division* were not encouraging. Paul worried about mounting inflation, unheard-of prices – 'Everything leaps ahead except one's income'[45] – and an extra 8 per cent insurance added to income tax for the self-employed. Renewed efforts to find some sort of part-time editorial work got nowhere. He had been informally invited the previous winter to become chief editor for the Arts Council's New Fiction Society, but the offer was withdrawn without explanation to Paul's chagrin: he poured out the anxieties he could not confide to Penny in a long, unhappy letter to John Willey, including the correct suspicion that he had been turned down for a younger man.[46] He felt his house and himself in it becoming shabby, worn and threadbare. Friends noted that he no longer took holidays, or paid a typist to type his manuscripts for him. In October 1975, he was approached with an offer of help by the secretary of the Royal Literary Fund, acting on an anonymous tip-off.[47]

Paul must have been uncomfortably reminded of his own letters in the late 1960s to the RLF on behalf of Charles Wrey Gardiner, then on his uppers, pushing seventy, unpublished for years and about to be made homeless. 'I heard a story the other day of a man who lived in a cardboard house on a bomb site,' Gardiner reported blandly: 'When it got a bit soggy in wet weather he just built another. That seems what I should try for.'[48] Paul had written strongly in support of his application, acknowledging his own debt to Gardiner, declaring his admiration for Gardiner's disinterested promotion of other authors' work, and for his absolute integrity as a writer who had fulfilled his own prophecy, made a quarter of a century earlier before either he or Paul had left Crown Passage: 'To take up the pen in the middle of this life is a disaster, financial, cerebral, emotional, practical, and a kind of flying in the face of fortune.'[49]

In January 1976, Paul received another unexpected approach, this time from an American, Thomas Staley, a Joycean scholar and friend of Bernard Benstock at Urbana. Dr Staley, also an admirer (he described himself as one of the 'very respectful few' who recognised the Raj Quartet on publication as a major work),[50] was dean of the graduate school at the University of Tulsa in Oklahoma, where he offered Paul a visiting professorship that autumn. The two lunched together in Curzon Street on a bleak, chill Tuesday, 13 January: Staley was struck by Paul's reserve, his modesty, his reluctance to pull literary rank, the troubled undercurrents underlying his quiet manner and, when he agreed without demur to go to Tulsa, by something odd about his 'easy acceptance and simultaneous apprehension'.[51] Paul had in truth no choice but to accept any means of escape from an increasingly disastrous financial, emotional and practical situation. His net income that year amounted to £3,324: Staley offered him $12,000 for a term's comparatively light teaching. On 15 February, he submitted a formal application for assistance to the RLF ('Such a grant . . . this spring or summer would certainly help me to relax and concentrate: but these are luxuries, perhaps'),[52] in the event of the post at Tulsa falling through.

Paul's reputation in his own country was not so securely established that he could afford to sneeze at recognition, even from Oklahoma. He had always had admirers at home – 'I am very happy and proud, dear Paul, that you should like my work,' wrote Dame Freya Stark, whom he had met at a party in July 1975, 'because it is ant-like beside your Elephant so serenely pacing'[53] – but the first serious, sustained attempt to analyse and assess the achievement of the Raj Quartet came from an historian, Professor Sir Max Beloff, in an article in *Encounter* in May 1976.[54] Professor Beloff began by noting the marked indifference to India and its affairs prevalent at all levels in Britain since 1947, a profound reluctance to contemplate either the end of empire or its possible long-term consequences. He described the broad perspective and capacious range of the Quartet, the richness and complexity of its material – 'the subject is one to which the historian's technique, however refined, may not be able to do justice' – its imaginative and intellectual subtlety. He recognised at the heart of the whole enterprise its attempt to explore dealings on the subcontinent between the two peoples, and its success in conveying 'the full tragic significance' of their final reckoning. The essay was a generous and majestic tribute from one discipline to another (Anthony Thwaite, who was co-editor of *Encounter* at the time, could hardly have made handsomer amends for cursory treatment the year before), and it gracefully acknowledged that, at a time when detailed documentation was still almost impossible to come by, the novelist had penetrated areas not yet available for historical exploration:

Few historians have treated the fall of the British Empire as something that did not have to happen the way it did. . . . History is still being written by a generation that voted Attlee, Cripps and Bevan into power in 1945. Things will change as time reveals more of their handiwork. But the novelist need [not] wait.

Paul lunched with his publisher, Charles Pick, at the Garrick Club in May to meet Professor Beloff, who was taken aback, like Staley, by the incongruous impression Paul projected. Beloff said he looked more like some moderately successful provincial businessman, or perhaps an accountant, than a man of letters.[55] The two lunched again at the Epicure in July, six weeks before Paul left for Tulsa. Beloff had singled out two aspects of the Quartet by which Paul set particular store: its emphasis on work – the day-to-day practicalities of running the empire – and, rarer still, the importance it attached to women, the submerged other half, the wives and daughters of the empire whose existence tended in more conventional accounts to be either romanticised or ignored. Long sections of the Quartet are focused through women: not only perceptive and highly articulate observers, like Sarah Layton, Daphne Manners and Lili Chatterjee, but comparatively unimpressive, inconspicuous, virtually invisible women like Barbie Batchelor and Edwina Crane: passive witnesses who play no part in the decision-making process – who remain barely aware of its existence, let alone its ramifications behind the scenes – but who must gather themselves nonetheless to receive and absorb its impact.

They supply a slantwise, off-centre vantage point, one of the novelist's advantages over the historian, which Paul used for the last time in the book he had just finished when he read Beloff's essay in the spring of 1976. *Staying On*, intended as a kind of postscript or pendant to the Quartet, views India after Independence largely through the eyes of Lucy Smalley, who with her husband had figured briefly in *The Towers of Silence*[56] and subsequently hung on, making ends meet with increasing difficulty over the next twenty-five years at Smith's Hotel, Pankot. The seeds of the book go back to Paul's return to Belgaum in 1972, when he first heard Malgonkar's stories about Ootacamund and its left-over sahibs. Later he discussed their predicament with Mollie Hamilton, who showed him a letter smuggled out to her mother, Lady Kaye, from a widowed friend in Ootacamund: she had chosen to stay on, lonely, harassed and pitifully vulnerable, becoming in the end virtually a prisoner of the Eurasian couple with whom she lodged, who appropriated her meagre funds, intercepted her post and spied on her visitors. Paul agreed he had been startled by this letter, when Mollie asked afterwards if his book sprang from it.[57]

He had been perhaps still more shaken by a letter he received himself from Maisie Goodbody in Belgaum, writing to announce her husband's sudden death in 1974.[58] Peter Goodbody had suffered a heart attack in his late sixties while seated, like Lucy Smalley's husband Tusker, on his thunder-box (the Goodbody's cottage, untouched by modern sanitation, still had latrines with hinged flaps set into the outer wall and cleared by the sweeper from Green Hotel): 'When I found him, seated on a toilet round about midnight, one look at his face told me what must have happened.' It was a bald, grim letter and it anticipated a fearful future ('As far as I am concerned, it could not be worse'). Paul might have guessed something of the sort from Goodbody's richly comical accounts over the past few years of rising prices, falling income, heroic struggles to counter both by taking over the housekeeping – dusting, cooking, washing up, feats of elaborate domestic absurdity performed with improvised plumbing and no proper stove – and his tactical decision to eat in the hotel dining-room while gallantly holding his own in running fight with the hotel management. In his last letter, dated 11 December 1973, Goodbody described doing his own marketing like Tusker Smalley, haggling in the bazaar to the delight of ribald small boys and returning home festooned with bags and tins. He viewed his plight with much the same humorous detachment as Charles Wrey Gardiner: 'For how long shall we be able to continue? I just do not have the faintest idea.'

Paul had seen enough in Belgaum in 1969 and 1972, when he had been the Goodbody's guest at Green Hotel, to have formed a pretty accurate picture of how things stood. Their annexe in the grounds, with its beds of canna lilies, primitive kitchen and still more primitive bathroom, was precisely as he described in *Staying On*, and so was the hotel itself, lamentably decayed since its wartime heyday ('The place smelt of stagnant water and ancient damp: pervasive smells that attached to everything – the cane chairs, the faded cretonne covers of the ruptured sofas, the potted palms, the cloths on the tables in the dining room').[59] Green Hotel was owned by a Mrs Nanji (whose entrepreneurial dreams of sale or expansion had been thwarted by a newly-opened rival establishment draining off custom in the early 1970s), and run for her by a Parsee called Rutonji, cordially detested by Peter Goodbody.[60] Paul based the Bhoolabhoys – 'ownership' and 'management' in *Staying On* – on this couple, spiced with childhood memories of Charles Laughton's parents in their palmy days at the Scarborough Pavilion.

In circumstances, although not in character, the Smalleys too owe much to Paul's observation in Belgaum. L. J. C. ('Peter') Goodbody was an altogether more sophisticated and formidable personality than

Colonel Smalley, a man of singular wit and charm, a subtle joker ('so unlike Tusker Smalley,' said Mac Malgonkar, 'more Peter Sellers than Randolph Scott'),[61] with an inexhaustibly inquisitive, worldly, well-stocked mind. He had thought much about the British in India and read widely ('last evening I was reading Kalidasa's *Shakuntala*,' he wrote to Paul on 17 December 1972: 'When you & I were, if lucky, clad in woad, these people were producing unsurpassed literature'). Son of an Anglo-Irish Dublin family, educated at Wellington College and King's College, Cambridge, he had sailed for India as an exchange broker in the early 1920s, flourishing in the smart set of cosmopolitan Bombay and marrying a wealthy wife by whom he had two sons.[62] He emerged from the war having lost his money under some sort of cloud, arriving mysteriously alone in Belgaum (rumour said his wife had been murdered in America), where he was employed as a consultant engineer at the local sawmill and comfortably installed in Room No. One on the ground floor at Green Hotel, until he moved out into the annexe on his second marriage (rumour said it was never formalised) to the manager's secretary at the sawmill, a Eurasian Miss Clark at least twenty years younger than himself. They were accepted by neither British nor Indian society. 'In India there is no caste lower than an impoverished sahib,' wrote Malgonkar, who would also pay tribute to the Goodbodys by putting them in a novel, *Bandicoot Run*.[63] Goodbody set up a workshop for the manufacture of camera bellows, keeping his tiny work-force on even after the trade had become as anachronistic and outdated as himself. His fund of rich and racy pre-war anecdote contrasted starkly with the penury and encroaching squalor he endured so cheerfully in Belgaum.

   Goodbody himself had been popular in the town, unlike his wife, who was notoriously truculent, ill-disposed, raw, touchy and sarcastic. Her temper, always uncertain, became vicious after her husband's death. There was little future in India for people of mixed blood, and none outside it. In answer to her letter tentatively enquiring about the cost of living in Britain, Paul sent her three closely typed pages[64] laying out in detail the prices of everything from accommodation, medical care, clothing and cleaning materials to meat, drink, cigarettes, vegetables and bread. It was in the circumstances the kindest and most practical thing he could have done, but it must have come as a cruel shock to the recipient. Maisie Goodbody, once she had disposed of her few possessions and made enemies of all the people who might have been disposed to help her, depended for survival on the charity of local shopkeepers. Swami the baker sent her bread, and she received humiliating cash handouts from the local lawyer, son of a former carpenter at the bellows factory and sweeper at Green Hotel. She was taken in at some point, sick and starving, beginning to wander in her mind, by the sisters at the local mission hospial, and later she left Belgaum, rumour said to enter a home for the destitute in Bombay. Paul probably never learned the full details of her horrifying story – or how closely her end parallelled Barbie Batchelor's – but he knew enough to fear the worst, when he thanked her gently for her 'kindness to a stranger' on his two brief stays at Green Hotel. 'I think of them, really, far more often than I do of all the other places I visited,' he wrote on 5 January 1975.

He himself was still in the grip of 'the most impenetrable writer's block': he said he sat down most days at his desk, keeping his appointment with the muse, in Henry James's phrase, but for ten months after he finished *Division* the muse did not show up.[65] He had not got as far as the first paragraph of what he had envisaged as his bridging novel, *Mango Rain*, an instalment of the long-postponed *Careerists*, in which a London hero was to visit an Indian village based on Timmapuram.[66] He told John Willey on 17 January that he could have borne his money worries better if he had a book in hand, adding flatly: 'But I haven't. And I must tell you that I haven't. . . . I wish that as a boy I'd learned to build bridges or ships or centrifugal pumps because you can always go on doing that.' A month later, on 24 February, he had switched with relief to something simpler, a comedy ('*Staying On* goes better than *Mango Rain* ever did') which he described as his Indian *Bender*. It flowed, or trickled slowly, all through the summer. When Paul drove down to Buckinghamshire in July to lunch with Sir Herbert Thompson and his wife, they struck him as 'a couple of escaped characters from *Staying On* (escaped because they didn't stay)'.[67] By November, he was applying for help to Charles Pick's son, Martin ('What I'm basically after are anecdotes about all the marginally legal, or illegal things stayers-on got up to'),[68] who had worked in Bombay for the Oxford University Press. A month later, he suddenly realised that, even on their first appearance in the Raj Quartet, the Smalleys had been archetypal stayers-on, always getting themselves stranded after parties and 'having to cadge a lift home because the tonga had failed to come back'.[69]

The novel, which had reached two hundred typed pages by the end of January 1976, was finished, retyped and delivered by 13 April. Paul dedicated it to Roland Gant who, as he said, had been his friend longer than anyone else in publishing: 'it does, or rather is intended to celebrate 1946–76 (& beyond d.v.).'[70] It was Roland who first saw the book as a potential film with parts for Ralph Richardson and Celia Johnson (who would in fact play Lucy Smalley opposite Trevor Howard as Tusker in the television film made two years later). Paul

especially liked to picture the elegant Miss Johnson[71] delivering the
tirade in which Lucy finally makes her stand, a forlorn and faded
mouse at bay, turning on Tusker with a list of all the faults of people
born like him (and for that matter Paul himself) under Aries: egotism
and self-absorption, love of obfuscation, the need to dominate and
denigrate other people ('*I* have no friends because all our friends are
your friends, Tusker, not mine'). All she gets in answer to her
passionate appeal – which begins as pent-up accusation but tails off
into fear of loneliness and approaching death – is three terse words
from Tusker: 'You're pissed, Luce.'[72]

Everyone who read the book recognised something unbuttoned
about *Staying On*, a new ease and lightness, above all a pervasive
humour familiar enough to anyone who had ever talked to Paul but
kept until now on a tight string in his work. 'My impression of him
then was of someone unusualy grave, composed, almost introverted,'
wrote James Leasor, describing Paul when they first met in the army,
'but underneath was a much livelier character trying to escape and
finally did so with *Staying On*'.[73] With this access of confidence came
a general loosening-up, and a notably relaxed approach to the two
marriages at the centre of a novel: the Bhoolabhoys', which is
extravagantly and authentically if at times preposterously sensual
(people who asked if their couplings were based on personal
experience got no more than a noncommittal laugh from Paul), and
the Smalleys', which would be tragic if it were not at the same time so
absurdly funny ('I suppose that to laugh for people, to see the comic
side of their lives when they can't see it for themselves, is a way of
expressing affection for them, and even admiration,' Guy Perron had
said of the Raj in *A Division*).[74] The Smalleys' history – their courtship
and early years, their gradual estrangement, Tusker's stubbornness,
his wife's hysterical vexation ('She had protested. She had cried. She
had beaten him over the head with a newspaper. It had been like trying
to knock sense into something composed only of temper and vapours
and obstinacy and stupidity')[75] – goes back ultimately to Paul's
parents' relationship. At a time when his thoughts turned increasingly
towards the past, when he was planning his memoirs and including
more and more autobiographical material in his *Country Life* reviews,
Staying On was the nearest he came to carrying out his plan for putting
his father in a book.

But Tusker contains also a strong element of Paul himself. At the
heart of the book is Lucy's plaintive cry, the most poignant of all the
female voices lamenting loneliness, deprivation and neglect in his
books since *The Alien Sky*:

Tusker and I do not truly communicate with one another any more. . . . His silence is his silence and my loquacity is my loquacity but they amount to the same thing. I can't hear what he is thinking and he does not hear what I'm saying. So we are cut off from one another, living separate lives under the same roof. Perhaps this is how it has always been between us but only become apparent in our old age.[76]

Brusque, hurtful, umbrageous, full of unexplained anger and resentments, Tusker expresses other, gentler feelings only once, in a long, defensive, painfully constricted letter setting out Lucy's financial position in case of his death, and ending with a gruff declaration: 'Can't talk about these things face to face, you know. Difficult to write them. Brought up that way. No need ever to answer. Don't want you to. Prefer not. You've been a good woman to me, Luce.'[77] This letter, written the night before his final heart attack, is Tusker's last word to Lucy – 'the only love letter she had had in all the years she had lived' – just as *Staying On* itself was, more explicitly than any of his earlier books, Paul's own love letter to his wife.

The year in which he wrote it was probably the bleakest and most bitter of their marriage. Paul had ceased, or appeared to Penny to have ceased, to express anything but a hostility she could not understand or remedy. His face, when they were alone, seemed set in a perpetual sneer, the sneer of self-hatred that had come to include her too. 'He looked at her as if she were a bad smell under his nose,' said Sally. The harder she tried to meet or mollify him, the more evident it became that Penny was no longer the person who could please him. The two were shut up together for the greater part of that last year, and their desolation, at weekends when Sally joined them, was terrible to see. Paul was now permanently drunk or at least, like Donald McWhinnie, never sober. In the years spent writing the Raj Quartet he had used alcohol functionally, almost medicinally, as an essential fuel. 'It was his First Aid whenever he sat down to write,' said Roland Gant. He could not settle at the typewriter without a glass to hand: his first act on waking was always to finish the glass of whisky or vodka poured out the night before, then light up the first of the day's sixty or seventy cigarettes. By midday he had normally drunk the better part of a bottle of spirits, which would be polished off before bed time. What hurt his wife was not so much that he allowed himself to collapse with her as he seldom did outside the house, but that the dark and threatening side he showed her had blotted out the rest of him. The Paul for whom nothing was too much trouble, the tender, sympathetic, infinitely considerate friend, the masterful dancing partner who had swept Penny off her feet in the first place – the Paul she still loved, and whom other people still knew – had become a stranger in his own home.

She was desperate. He was scarcely less so. All lines of communication between them appeared irretrievably blocked. In February 1976 Paul travelled up alone to Shrewsbury to talk to readers of the Raj Quartet, an informal gathering of local enthusiasts organised by the novelist Joan Tate. He was to talk about fiction to a sixth-form group at Shrewsbury School on 26 February, and the next night to meet a group of about twenty people almost as familiar with his books as he was himself, an experience he found both touching and disconcerting. The invitation had included his wife, and, although Paul was adamant that she could not come, he must have thought of her when he summed up for the Shrewsbury boys his attitude to those who defined literature as a means of escape from everyday reality:

I believe exactly the opposite: I believe that all our many 'activities' only distract us, and are designed to distract us, from the actual business, rebarbative and mysterious, ironic and upsetting, of living with other people, and that this is the central concern of the novel, as it is the central problem of men and women who have to live with each other, making their moral decisions, and making the wrong ones, and having to cope with the anguish – and the joy.[78]

Apart from these three days in Shrewsbury, Paul's calendar was almost completely blank in the first half of 1976 while he finished *Staying On*. He rose at six and went straight to the study to drink, write and brood all day, dining off a tray, registering Penny's presence only with the look of disgust she had learned to dread. Completion of the book brought a brief respite. 'What a relief it is – for a few hours,' he wrote on 14 April, the day after delivering the manuscript to Heinemann: 'After that the reaction sets in: is it any good, you wonder.'[79] The manuscript of *Staying On*, corrected in a single editorial session with Roland Gant on 27 May, was already at the printers by the first week in June.[80] He plunged immediately into unfinished business, catching up on correspondence, making plans for the autumn semester starting at Tulsa on 30 August, looking forward to a week in New York first. 'Get out your dancing-shoes, please!' he had written jauntily to Dorothy Olding: 'Ball-room dancing, eh? Tangos, too. You'll leave me looking more than ever like Mr Palm Court of *1939*. . . . Still, I hope we'll cut a rug somewhere.'[81] It was a wonderful summer – 'hot, sunny, still' – and Paul dreamed of a return to Paris, where he had celebrated major turning points in his life in 1950 and 1964. 'I should like to be sitting on the rim of the pond in the Luxembourg Gardens, dabbling my feet in the water,' he wrote on 7 June to Francine Weinbaum, promising to meet her in just over a month's time in Manhattan, where he planned to spend his first few days staying with Dorothy in her East Side apartment.

This time he did not even dream of taking Penny with him: 'it's fine if there are two of you,' Francine had written, when he first consulted her in February about the Tulsa job, 'otherwise you sort of die quietly of loneliness.' 'Re Tulsa,' Paul replied: 'I guess I'll die slowly of loneliness then.'[82] Tension between himself and Penny was stretched taut. It seemed as if the side of Paul that had for years pushed his wife to the limit of her endurance was now determined to find her breaking point. She was convinced he found her hateful and, if she feared his violence, she feared even more his cold destructive loathing. She might have found a different message buried between the lines in *Staying On*, due in proof some time in late July, but she never read it. A week before the proofs arrived she finally reached breaking point. She had kept an emergency bag packed for the last twelve years but in the end she left with nothing but her handbag, walking out one day in mid July as if she were going shopping. She took refuge at Chiswick Women's Aid with Erin Pizzey, who rang Paul that night to say that his wife was safe and would not be returning.

Shock and blank incomprehension were followed by despair. He had to tell Roland what had happened because, when the proofs arrived, he was in no state to correct them. He also told Dorothy Olding, who learned with incredulity, outrage and consternation that Penny was starting proceedings for separation or divorce. 'All my fault, of course, at least, I can't blame her for anything,' Paul wrote: 'No third parties involved, on either side – just pressures . . . I'm not good at living alone, so I suppose the irony is that it turns out *I'm* impossible to live with, & am faced with the consequences, but also with a book that was oddly titled! Have begged her to come back, but she won't, I think.'[83] Paul was in a state of near collapse. After twelve years of austerity, self-denial and seclusion when he had stripped himself of all the usual props and comforts – parties, entertainments, holidays, normal social life, for long periods virtually all contact with the outside world – Penny was all he had left. Without her it was as if, in Sally's phrase, 'the scaffolding had gone from under him'. He had described his need for support in a cancelled passage from *The Corrida at San Feliu*, explaining the vocation of a writer's wife: 'She will hang on to him to the bitter end. This he suspects. In his way he is grateful to her. She is the only security he has. When he loses confidence in himself, in his future . . . in whatever it is, then he is grateful to [her] for still being there. Also of course he is in love with her.'[84]

Paul knew himself undone. The only people he could turn to were his daughters, who did what they could to comfort and sustain both parents. Carol, in trouble herself that summer with her own marriage, became an intermediary and a tower of practical strength: Paul said he did not know how he could have coped without her. Sally, summoned by telephone, spent a day at the height of the crisis at Addison Way where her father, distraught and weeping, poured out his bewilderment and hurt, protesting over and over again that things would have been different if only Penny had told him how she felt. He reiterated miserably to both daughters the fear of drama and eruptions that had bottled up his feelings in the divided household of his adolescence: 'I just want her to come back, or to hear that she *will* come back, if only temporarily, with no fuss or grand scene, which I simply can't cope with, but as if she's been out shopping or something.'[85] He could barely function, let alone work or think. One part of him acknowledged that he had lost his wife, and that it was too late to make amends. 'I do not want to be freed of you, as you put it,' he wrote to Penny on 1 August. 'The whole idea is utterly horrifying to *me*. If you mean really that *you* want to be free of me then I must try to accept that.' Another part, cut to the heart, remained mystified and disbelieving:

I can only go on asking you to return here, because my love although for so long not expressed remains as it always was, strong and deep, and necessary to me. In asking you to return I know I ask a great deal because the fact that you just walked out means you must have been deeply unhappy, or so I can only suppose, and for that I am contrite, but could not tell you to your face. I'm a mess. But I love you and there has never been and never will be anyone else. I must say that. But I must also say that I don't want to go on ruining your life, if that is what I've done. If your decision is irrevocable, you must tell me, please.[86]

It was irrevocable. She dared not see or speak to him or disclose her whereabouts. Everything was made worse by having to be done and decided in slow motion through third parties but with the utmost urgency. Paul was due to fly to New York on 22 August, and to hold his first class in Tulsa on 30 August. He could neither deal with proofs nor prepare lectures beforehand. He had to break off in turmoil and confusion from his distracted pleas and protests to make wretched arrangements about the heating engineer (a central heating system planned for Addison Way that autumn had been a final bid to please Penny), about filling in tax returns, paying bills and closing up the house. Carol was given power of attorney to take charge of incoming demands and pay out cheques in his absence. His last few weeks in England took on a nightmarish quality of grief and haste. He told Sally that he felt at times as if he were living in a Feydeau farce with doors opening, messengers entering, crises piling up ('The audience laughs like mad, because it's only serious from the characters' point of

Carol   *Sally*

view!').[87] At others, it seemed almost as if he were disposing of effects and winding up affairs after a death. Three weeks before he left he drew up a kind of testament, a letter of six handwritten pages dated 31 July 1976, addressed to Carol, as the elder daughter, 'and Sally, tho' Kiki is the first-born'.

It came with a package of mementoes, family snapshots, a bundle of Indian silver tea spoons and – 'my proudest possessions' – the many tiny, dulled bronze medals he had won at school more than forty years before for athletics. He wrote the letter in case of accident or mishap: 'There's nothing sinister in giving you this stuff: it's just that I regret knowing so little about my own father, & having almost nothing by which to remember him. My fault. But I have a feeling that if anything happened to me on the flights to or from USA, Mama would for emotional and very understandable reasons destroy stuff – & I'd rather that you & Sally saw it before chucking it out.' The letter accompanying these sentimental souvenirs was an unsentimental account of his early life. He looked back to his education, his early efforts and achievements, trying to work out what went wrong, describing the ethic of striving and attainment dinned into him from childhood by his mother (whom he never mentioned although her influence, far more than his father's, coloured his whole picture). He examined the legacy passed down in his genes for handing onward to his daughters ('As a boy I was also very bright, academically. . . . Sally has inherited that side of me, & you, Kiki, have probably inherited the other side, the one that says to you that you have to work that much harder than the next person, just to keep level'). He described the effect of leaving school early ('I ought really to have stayed longer at school, I suppose, to learn about unselfishness & working with others, & not always thinking just of myself & of trying to *make* it, alone'). What is missing is any reference to other people, and the feelings that come with them. Paul saw himself unsympathetically in a lopsided mirror, apportioning blame to no one but himself, mentioning his writing in passing only once, leaving his wife out of the reckoning altogether except for a single blurted exclamation on the last page:

I suppose the point I'm trying to get across is that whatever I am as a writer, forgettable or permanent, as a person I have been overly subjected to the ideas or idea of 'making something of yourself', & I repeat and apologize for anything in your own lives that suggests *my* conditioning has had an unhappy influence on you. I recall, for instance, how awful you, Kiki, thought it was that I should insist that you went to a crammer . . . but all it was is that I didn't want you to lose the important years, the years of full puberty, by having also to cope with the idea of survival by going out to work. The same thing applies to Sally. I *wanted* her to go to university – in a curious way you have both fulfilled *my* ambitions, one in the theatre & the other academically & artistically but good God at what cost, especially to Mama?

Sorry to sound off but, as I said earlier, I much miss knowing things about my father, another silent, stubborn, morose man, whom at times I hated because he seemed to give me nothing, but obviously gave me all that he had to give.

Chuck this letter out too. Or if you don't, please never mention it to me, unless it offends you & you want to give me a swipe. I love all of you very dearly. Papa.

The self-portrait in this letter is harsh, unforgiving and unfair. It would have been unrecognisable to the many friends who remained baffled by Paul's insistence, in the last years of his life, that he felt himself growing steadily more like his father. But it represents accurately enough the sense of waste and failure, personal and professional, that weighed on him as he flew off to America at the end of August 1976.

CHAPTER FIFTEEN

The tale is like a looking-glass

People who met Paul that autumn in Tulsa, Oklahoma, were struck by his charm and openness, his appreciative enthusiasm, his wit, inquisitiveness and inexhaustible fund of stories. Francine Weinbaum, who had seen him briefly in transit in New York to hand over her successful dissertation, said he told her in an aside that his wife had left him, pre-empting comment with a flow of jokes and anecdotes. The two graduate students, Bill Wheeler and Brian Murray, detailed to meet him at Tulsa airport on Sunday 29 August, found themselves captivated by their visitor before the day was out. Both faculty and students were amazed by Paul. Virtually no one on campus had heard of him before he got there, let alone read his books. He did not match their notions of a distinguished British visiting professor: they had expected someone supercilious, reserved and stiff, prepared to be disdainful about a city celebrated chiefly for its oil wells and as the buckle on America's bible belt. What they got was a pale, worn, unobtrusive and soft-spoken joker, clearly as adept as themselves at spotting and shooting down pretension. His two guides spent the whole of that first day and a great part of the next four months in his company. On the drive in from the airport they discussed the state of Britain – which seemed, from the vantage point of apparently boundless American prosperity and optimism in the late 1970s, to be sinking fast beneath a choppy sea of social, economic and industrial chaos – and looked out of the car windows at Tulsa's booming office blocks, brand-new shopping malls and spacious, one-storey, ranch-style suburbs stretching to the flat horizon as far as the eye could see. Paul noted the place names – Broken Arrow, Okmulgee, Muskogee – the men in Stetsons and snakeskin boots, the service offered at his nearest U-Tote-Um store: TWENTY-FOUR HOURS A DAY MILK and BREAD and SHOTGUN SHELLS.[1]

Tulsa and its people suited Paul. He liked their incongruities, and they liked his. He upset their stereotypes: after his first session in a formal classroom, he moved his creative writing class (known as Writing and Rhetoric, or Writ-and-Rhet for short) to his apartment, where he confounded his students by sitting on the floor, announcing that he did not take tea, and drinking gin instead like water, out of a red plastic cup. He had no academic qualifications but his unofficial credentials could hardly have been better chosen. The students loved his lack of ostentation, his elegant British accent, his no less elegant British irony and understatement. Even his clothes – safari jackets and bush shirts with, on special occasions in deference to the raj, a favourite blue, close-buttoned Nehru shirt – confirmed their hastly revised image of an eccentric English man of letters. Paul relaxed almost at once in Tulsa. He liked the huge blue skies, the brilliant clear air, the long hot days, the sudden spectacular prairie sunsets. He liked the slow dry native Oklahoman wit. He bought a polyester leisure (pronounced *leezha*) suit, the standard Tulsan uniform at the time: all he needed to complete the part, as one of his students pointed out, was a string tie and turquoise ring.

He liked his big, bare, student apartment with its matted, threadbare shag carpet and broken-bottomed sofa. It was equipped with nothing when he got it except an empty pink-painted fridge, a stove and a slightly cranky air-conditioner. Paul laughed, borrowed a pair of bedsheets, and set off with his minders to stock up on groceries, gadgets and plastic dinnerware at the discount store. He made no complaints. 'People relaxed around him,' said one of the graduate fellows, Maureen Modlish. 'He never showed off or made you feel inferior.' He liked the lack of pressure, and the fact that, because no one had more than the faintest notion who he was, nothing much was expected of him. He liked sitting on the floor, just as he got to like the narrow, inconvenient, shoulder-high strips of window looking out from his living-room over the road to the Bama Pie Factory, which released a different synthetic smell – pecan, cherry, chocolate – downwind each day. 'I am homesick for the Bama odours,' Paul told Donald Hayden, Tulsa's Dean of Liberal Arts, a year after he left.

Best of all he liked his students. The University of Tulsa, awash with oil money, relatively new, brash and rapidly expanding by 1976, had no indigenous tradition of learning and much to contend with in the way of condescension from older and more prestigious academic institutions. Junior status gave it, on the one hand, enviable freedom and willingness to experiment but, on the other, an exaggerated respect for academic orthodoxies. Paul had been dubious beforehand about the technological and highly competitive American approach to literature ('the whole system began to feel a little suspect to me,' Dean Staley wrote after being cross-questioned by Paul at their first encounter: 'The idea of assigning grades to creative work struck him as very strange').[2] He never mastered the grading system, simply awarding an A to every student in his writing class at the end of the semester. If he was staggered by the arcane and self-regarding labyrinths of critical theory, controversy, counter-controversy and revisionist heresy, he was frankly appalled by the pedantic jargon terms, the archetypal phenomenes and perceptual epistemology bartered as a substitute for solid reading. Besides Writ-and-Rhet, he was to teach a graduate course specially tailored for him, 'Imperial and Post-imperial British Fiction in the Twentieth Century', or Brit Fic for short. The opening session was not a success. The students correctly diagnosed that Paul, who had nerved himself beforehand with too many gins, was apprehensive, ill-prepared, uncertain of himself and them. He in turn was deeply discouraged when it emerged that no one had read the Raj Quartet, and further dismayed, when he quoted a passage from *The Cherry Orchard*, to find they barely knew of Chekhov either.

But after a shaky start the course gained confidence and momentum. The practitioner's ingrained disapproval of teaching literature as an academic discipline supplied a subversive undercurrent in Paul's classes to which his audience readily responded. For jaded graduate students, many of whom could expect to spend years in the grading treadmill, his democratic teaching methods were unexpected, his perceptions startlingly fresh and his mind prodigally inventive. He wasted little time on Kipling, skimmed Forster and was squaring up to Joseph Conrad by the end of his first month ('*Heart of Darkness*,' he reported to Sally: ' – rather like facing a giant'). He lingered long on Nabokov, who had always been his favourite novelist of the twentieth century as Thackeray was of the nineteenth.[3] He roped in congenial contemporaries like Anthony Burgess, John Braine (*Room at the Top* remained a source of fond, proprietorial pride: 'How it got on to a colonial syllabus, I don't know,' said Brian Murray), and Kingsley Amis. Responding as one imposter in academe to another, Paul took comfort and courage that autumn from Lucky Jim's example.

If the Brit Fic course was, by Paul's standards, relatively formal, it was the writing class that made his name legendary in Tulsa. He treated his dozen or so students, nearly all in their early twenties, as fellow writers. 'If you're going to be a writer, you know it now,' he said firmly, 'regardless of encouragement, or enormous discouragement.'[4]

He deflated their bids for attention but never undermined, or permitted anyone else to undermine, their confidence. He was a patient, constructive, conscientious and sometimes devastatingly funny teacher. He was also extraordinarily exciting. He convinced his students that they each had something individual to say, and he helped each find an individual voice in which to say it. 'Hear your own voice,' he said. 'In a difficult but subtle way, the dialogue of your characters has still to be in your tone of voice.' He set each week a simple, concrete, optional assignment. Once it was to write something beginning 'I remember' (a piece Paul singled out by a student called Patti Floyd became eventually the first story in her first published book).[5] At other times it was a play, a sonnet, a fairy tale (Paul himself chose Cinderella), a story starting from an image that had haunted him for years of a character or characters turning up somewhere in disgrace (another student, Sally Dennison, grew a whole first novel from this seed, setting it in the imaginary small town of Disgrace, Arkansas).[6]

Both in person and in precept Paul systematically overturned his students' more grandiose romantic notions of the creative writer. He made them write about what they knew, which often meant their unknown, unsung, prairie-farming Oklahoman grandparents ('Writing is a raid on the inarticulate,' he said, adapting Eliot's 'East Coker'). He shocked them by insisting that they entertain their readers, and that there was nothing glamorous about the writer's trade, which could be learned like any other only by unremitting application. He warned them in theory and in practice against intellectual snobs. At least two of his students, Sally Dennison and Steve Wood, were sufficiently impressed to write down every word Paul said. 'One needs a mentor,' he told them: 'Otherwise it's very lonely. You need someone to tell you to go on.'[7] He described his own apprenticeship and background. He told them his family history (Sally Dennison, who missed this class, heard its garbled and conflicting echoes passing round the campus afterwards like Chinese Whispers). He talked about giving up his job to become a full-time writer, and implied something of what it had cost him. He impressed on them the sacrificial risks involved. 'Find the key tone, the only tone of voice in which this thing would permit itself to be written,' he said. 'Before the key will reveal itself, it exacts a great sacrifice from the writer.'[8] He described the writer's need for a *duende* so vividly they never forgot his account of the ugly, gibbering, malevolent spirit that had taunted and pursued him. He said they must find their own limitations, as he thought he had finally reached his in *Staying On*: when someone tried to console him by saying he surely could do better than that, he threw his proof copy across the room so hard it burst its binding.

The classes also burst their bounds, expanding beyond official times and topics, spilling over into the students' lives and Paul's. 'We were discovering him,' said Sally Dennison, 'and he was discovering himself.' Students started dropping by in the late afternoon to talk and exchange gossip which, as always with Paul, shot away into wild fantastic spiralling inventions. Bill Wheeler and Brian Murray were both mimics, taking off campus figures and egging Paul on to do imitations of their imitations, culminating in a wicked take-off of himself being 'done' by Bill. Paul kept beer cans in his fridge for visitors who would sit up sometimes half the night listening to his stories. 'He talked *all the time*,' said Bill: 'he never turned us out.' They took him to Tulsa Philharmonic concerts, and to support the university football team with mascots, marching bands and twirling sequinned drum majorettes in the Skelley stadium. Once they improvised a picnic in a deserted garden at sunset by the great grey green Arkansas River. People would drop by to carry Paul off to parties or out to dinner. What he liked best was dancing to an old-fashioned band at the Shadow Mountain Inn which had a breathtaking view over night-time Tulsa. He would fetch up there with Bill and Brian or anyone else prepared to bring a girlfriend: afterwards he boasted that he had taught the boys at Tulsa not to be ashamed of dancing with the girls,[9] although in fact it was nearly always Paul who ended up 'dancing with the dates'.

The girls were charmed and flattered to be asked, for Paul remained as hard as ever to resist when he set out to please. 'I developed a need to impress this man,' wrote Sally Dennison: 'From that first class impressing him became a basic condition of my existence as a writer.'[10] Winning approval or encouragement from Paul was the metaphorical equivalent of being stroked for a cat. 'I wanted him to stroke me,' said Harriet Leake, who had returned to graduate school during a troubled patch in her marriage to a local millionaire and found, like many of his students, that she could not do enough for Paul. It became almost a competition to see who could impress him most, who would be asked to stay behind after class, whose turn it was to drive him to the liquor store (Harriet and Bill, possibly others as well, each did this particular run on a weekly basis: rumour said that Paul habitually picked up six quarts of gin or vodka at a time in his buckled briefcase). Harriet furnished his kitchen for him, so he could fix dinner on nights he wanted to stay in. When she and her husband took him out to dinner, Paul did justice to their French wines, and would often polish off a whole bottle of port gossiping with Jim Leake afterwards, but could seldom be persuaded to do more than push his Dover sole about his plate and eat at most two mouthfuls.

As word of the effect Paul was producing on his class got round the
campus, people vied more and more for his attention. Copies of his
books in Panther paperback (the Quartet was never published in the
US in paperback in Paul's lifetime) began appearing in quantity on the
bookstore's shelves. Numbers swelled in his Brit Fic course, and
faculty members started slipping him manuscripts of their own. He
dined regularly with the Staleys and he made an unexpected hit as a
dancing partner with the university president's wife. People who had
no connection with his classes began to lie in wait and hop out to
waylay him as he passed. By the second half of the semester he was
booked every night for cocktails and dinner: 'He was petted here,' said
Harriet Leake. Apart perhaps from his trips to India, this was the first
time in his adult life that he had given his full attention to other people
(he was writing nothing – again for the first time – in Tulsa), and they
adored it. Patti Floyd, who first saw him at a party given in his honour
where the guests surrounded him in an expectant ring, watched him
pass from one to the next, asking questions and listening to the
answers. 'He attended, he elicited, he was *utterly* self-effacing.' By the
end of the performance, which lasted well over two hours, the guests
were satisfied and Paul was drained.[11]

He poured himself out unreservedly for his writing class. 'I can still
see him smiling,' said Harriet, 'always looking down – he never looked
into your eyes – always into his lap. It was a private smile.' It was this
mischievous, elusive, beguiling, private smile that people remembered
about Paul all his life. His friends in India and at home all knew it well
and, in Tulsa, his Writ-and-Rhet group excelled one another to
provoke it. Paul became a kind of ideal father to them, individually
and collectively, perhaps especially to a slight, pale, Pre-Raphaelite
girl called Sharon Jesse, whose delicacy touched him ('she should eat
more,' he is said to have written in his report at the end of the
semester). Paul produced a cake for Sharon's birthday – 'We ate a lot
of cakes in that course,' said another student, Warren Brown – and
wrote a sonnet, which played on the falconry meaning of her
surname.[12] He read to the class, and taught them to play Consequences. He posed for group photographs, once with the stern look of
a Victorian paterfamilias, once on all fours at the bottom of a pyramid
of giggling and collapsing students. All of them realised that for those
four months cut out of his real life the Tulsa Writ-and-Rhet group had
become his family. They worried about his inability to eat or sleep or
look after himself, and they did their best to lessen his loneliness. 'He
hated to be alone,' said Brian Murray. 'He wanted someone always
there. He hated to be left.' Paul told Brian that often, after two or three
hours' sleep, he would get up and walk the streets, or stand for hours

on end in daylight staring through his high thin window. He welcomed interruption from these broodings. He never discussed his affairs at home but he talked a lot about his early struggles and his troubled relations with his father. To students who consulted him in crises – career decisions, love affairs, parental problems – he gave the kind of characteristically oblique help Bill Wheeler described himself and his friends getting not so much from anything Paul actually proposed as from the parables he told:

Paul seemed unable to begin a story without lighting a cigarette, and unable to light a cigarette without beginning a story. The two activities seemed to go hand-in-hand, the one fuelling the other. As he spoke, Paul lit cigarette after cigarette, pausing in his stories only long enough to light another cigarette before resuming his tale. During his stories, the grey ash of his cigarette lengthened in the air before the amazed eyes of his audience, in a long bending, unbroken arc, miraculously defying the laws of gravity.

Paul's stories also seemed to defy some less definable law. When someone asked Paul for advice concerning personal matters, Paul lit a cigarette and began a story. Paul's advice to young and old alike took the form of stories, long unbroken chains of events that unravelled before the ears of his listeners like the intricate plots of his elaborate novels, like the long grey ash of his cigarette. . . . Although Paul never actually gave advice to those who sought it, they left him at the end of an evening or in the deep blue-black of early morning surer of themselves, believing again in the impossible – no, the *possible* – in their lives – for in Paul's histories of all the men and women he had ever met, they had read the very circumstances of their lives.[13]

Paul insisted to his students that before you could start a story, you must know what you were aiming at: each beginning must have an ending – 'something to shoot for'[14] – and, in class and out of it, his mind turned constantly in Tulsa to his own beginnings, and his end. He quoted the famous lines with which Eliot (also reviewing the past at a turning point in his fifties) opened and closed 'East Coker'. Paul had brought his wartime first edition of the poem with him – the twenty-first birthday pamphlet given him as a young soldier by Geoffrey Ridehalgh – and his classes were overlaid and interleaved with Eliot's reflections on old age, failure and renewal, and his lapidary despair about writing. Paul fired his students, as Eliot had once fired him, with glimpses of truths they could not fully grasp in their twenties. He talked enigmatically in parables or riddles that seemed to apply equally to life and art. He described a fictional technique which he called reversal: 'One thing that takes the reader's breath away is *reversal* of characterisation, which transforms a sympathetic character into an unsympathetic one.'[15]

Some of Paul's students glimpsed or suspected in him a bitterness untapped in Tulsa. 'He never said a cruel thing about anyone,' said Brian Murray. 'But there was a seething resentment, and regret. The whole question of artistic disappointment was there. He struck me as someone with a lifelong depression.' Sally Dennison (whose novel was beginning to take shape under Paul's guidance) thought the same. 'When Paul turned up here, he was like someone in disgrace,' she said. 'He was shell-shocked. *It was him.*' The only one of his students who encountered Paul's other side as a teacher was Harriet Leake, who played the piano for him and who, in Paul's view, had the makings of a professional pianist. He was haunted by themes and tunes from the past that autumn: he could not hear *Au clair de la lune* played too often, but one night he asked for Chopin. Harriet, who would have given anything to please him, was crushed and shaken by the emergence of a Paul she had never seen before:[16] a strict, fierce, implacable martinet who rapped on the piano lid and made her play the piece three times before he could be satisfied, 'a critic who was,' in Paul's own words, 'almost impossible to please or get a good mark from'.

Time pressed as the semester wound towards its close. 'I've not got much more to say to you,' he told his writing class on 15 November.[17] The final session was a joint one at which he discussed the Raj Quartet, the only time he encouraged contact between his Writ-and-Rhet group and the Brit Fic people. This was the occasion when he drew a diagram of British Imperial history on the blackboard, starting with Kipling before the First World War and ending after the Second with the founding of the Welfare State and Indian Independence ('You write for an age,' he said, 'and this is my age').[18] He spent the week of Thanksgiving, 23–28 November, with John Willey and Dorothy Olding in San Francisco, which delighted him above all as a connoisseur of sunsets: 'I have seen some beautiful night-lit cities in my lifetime but none to compare with San Francisco.'[19] He celebrated Hallowe'en at a fancy-dress party with Bill Wheeler, who had felt so uncomfortable dressed up in a sheikh's outfit beforehand that Paul offered to put it on instead. 'So Paul went along and had the good time in the costume,' Bill said. Ever since he reached Tulsa, Paul had been in a sense having a good time in a costume, but soon he would have to lay aside his new persona and go home to resume the old. One of the girls at the party, noticing him sitting alone and dejected after midnight, asked him to dance: ' "I used to love to dance," he told her. "But now it's too late for me. I'll never dance again." '[20]

December was taken up with returning hospitality ('or as they used to say in India, "dining the station" '),[21] organising a students' wine-

and-cheese party and staging an elaborate, last, combined performance for both classes, which drew together the retrospective
threads Paul had gathered up over the past four months. 'Concluding a
fiction course is like writing a novel,' he said. 'You have to know the
point at which you want to arrive. Our time is limited, we feel a need to
do the best with it.'[22] For his 'Chekhovian Farewell' Paul produced a
tape recording made with help from selected students, giving strict
instructions to his audience about what to listen for, when to collect up
hats and coats, and how to make their exit. It began with the Jewel
Song from Gounod's *Faust* ('Listen for the counterpoint in the music,'
Paul wrote on the blackboard: 'It tells you "things are not going to
turn out lovely" ').[23] There were scraps of verse and prose, including a
rousing adaptation of Betjeman's 'Melstock Churchyard', with local
campus worthies substituted to weird effect for the chorus of Thomas
Hardy's Dorset tranters ('Tired hands will now grip pencils,/ Which
this morning held the plough,/ Thomas Staley, Donald Hayden/ Lie in
Tulsa's churchyard now . . .'). The centrepiece was Eliot's own stony,
sombre, fastidiously dry recording of 'East Coker'. Next came Paul
himself reading a passage from Conrad's *Youth*, and Shirley Bassey
singing in her throaty, richly seductive voice the song that took him
back to the early 1960s when he first left Higham's to set up as a full-
time writer:

> Now you must wake up, all dreams must end,
> Take off your make-up, the party's over –
> It's over, my friend.

A short pause for gathering up belongings was followed by the
twang of a guitar string breaking, the sound from the end of *The
Cherry Orchard* familiar by this time to Paul's students on both
courses. 'This "sound of a snapping string mournfully dying away"
was his illustration of honing to a sharp point, if only for a fleeting,
literary instant, the ambiguity and contrariness of life,' wrote Sharon
Jesse.[24] The students, filing out one by one in silence as they had been
told, took their leave of Paul standing at the door to say goodbye. He
had agreed to come back again the next year, but most of them
understood obscurely that this was his farewell to something
altogether more complicated and comprehensive than an unexpectedly successful teaching stint. The date was 15 December 1976. Two
days later Paul was booked to fly to New York, and then on to
London, arriving on 21 December to face his empty house. 'That
preyed on him,' said Jim Leake, Harriet's husband, who seems to have
been the only person in Tulsa with whom Paul discussed the
breakdown between himself and his wife. 'He certainly cared about

her. He said he came down one afternoon and she was gone. Smacked that ego pretty hard. *He sure was dreading going home.*' Paul wrote to Carol from Tulsa that Penny's leaving was always 'at the back or front of my mind', haunting every waking moment and encroaching on his sleep: 'I often wake up in the middle of the night & puzzle over what is going to happen to Mama, to the family, & to me.'[25]

He had agreed to give an interview in New York to Professor K. B. Rao, an Indian at Nevada University who was preparing a Scott handbook for Twayne's 'English Authors' series: they had talked for four hours at the end of August but this time the interview had to be broken off after thirty minutes because Paul was in no state to continue.[26] John and Dorothy provided what comfort they could, but there was little to be done except pour more drinks and reiterate their loyal indignation. Both took the view, shared in due course by a great many of Paul's friends, that his wife's defection was an incomprehensible betrayal. Carol and her husband Larry met his plane at Heathrow airport and took him home with them for a night before he returned to 78 Addison Way to pick up the threads of living alone for the first time in fifty-six years. He spent Christmas Day with his brother Peter, and Boxing Day at Carol's (Penny, who was now living on social security in a rented room in Swiss Cottage, had been there the day before). One thing that cheered him faintly during these macabre and melancholy family festivities was Eric Hiscock's column in the *Bookseller*, tipping *Staying On* to win the 1977 Booker Prize. 'Wouldn't that be nice,' he wrote to Dorothy Olding on 4 January 1977. 'Meanwhile, the new novel is taking a lot of shape & substance in my mind. I hope to start work on it next week.'

This was the last of many abortive attemps at *Mango Rain*, or *Married with Two Children*, in which Paul would explore the predicament of an oppressed, unhappy wife marooned at home, neglected and humiliated by a husband who reserves his charm for other people. David Chalmers is a version of Paul himself projected in a cold, unflattering light (Francine Weinbaum recognised herself in the eager, young secretary he acquires in the opening chapter), and the story takes place in London during the summer of 1976. Paul envisaged it at this stage as perhaps the first in the long-projected sequence now called *The Careerists*, 'mapping what has happened in England since 1945/7, the post-war, post-Imperial age'.[27] But the situation he started from was too close in fact, too painful and potentially explosive to have settled yet into a form that could be useful to him as a writer. He still hoped, although with no great conviction, for a reconciliation with Penny, something that could hardly come about while he professed himself to family and friends mystified as to why she had left him. He concentrated as so often before on practical arrangements to please her. 'He painted rooms, he put plants about, he made the drawing-room so elegant,' said Carol: 'He did *so* want her back, and he tried all sorts of ways of doing it.'

He planned to move his things into the dining-room while his study was redecorated in Stendhalian red-and-black, a scheme designed for him by Sally with scarlet painted walls and black chocolate carpet tiles. The old, cold, contemptuous father whose withering sneers Sally had dreaded for a decade and more seemed to have vanished as if he had never been. Paul entered enthusiastically into her plans that winter for applying to the Royal College of Art, taking unaffected pride and pleasure in having passed on the Scott-Wright gift. 'I *know* you are not deluding yourself about your graphic arts talent,' he wrote with a sympathy and generous understanding he had never shown her as a writer. 'Neither did you ever delude yourself about your dramatic talent. You were handicapped by illness & unhappiness, which led to lack of self-confidence, which I think is now coming back to you. Don't panic. Take it slowly.'[28] He inspected her portfolio, bought one drawing and commissioned another. Both accepted with gratitude and relief the final clearing of the atmosphere between them: it was as if Paul could at last spare time and energy to straighten out a relationship warped and deformed by the great weight of the Raj Quartet. 'He could claim me again as a daughter,' Sally said, 'and he claimed my talent.'

The two spent a great deal of time together that spring, seeing films, exchanging visits at Addison Way or in Sally's flat, exploring and enjoying one another's company. They re-established contact between the generations much as Paul had done with his Aunt Ruth nearly twenty years before across yet another of the rifts or chasms that opened so abruptly in their family. It was a time of peace, mutual confidence and goodwill. Paul pulled his depleted family together, drawing in Carol and Larry, gathering his children round him, 'getting to know us,' Sally said, 'in a way he hadn't when we were children and young people. He was picking up the pieces.' The past receded so far it became in some sense unimaginable. When Penny filed a petition for divorce in early March, Paul read her affidavit with horror and disbelief. 'But if this is true, I must have been a monster. You must have been afraid of me,' he said to Sally, looking up mildly over his reading glasses, quizzical, gentle, genuinely perplexed: '*Were* you frightened?'

Staying On was scheduled for publication in the second week of March. Paul noted philosophically that it was his thirteenth novel, due to be reviewed in the Sunday papers on the thirteenth of the month. 'Maybe we could arrange a meeting here that day,' he wrote to Sally, 'and I could ask Carol and Larry to join us, and I could cook some sort of Ibrahim-like hash.'[29] Ibrahim is the Smalleys' houseboy in *Staying On*, tactful, obliging and efficient, a shrewd observer in their household, one of Paul's modest and appealing *alter egos*. Paul himself cooked rarely but with style and confidence. Preparing a curry was for him an elaborate, leisurely, carefully co-ordinated solo performance with plenty of pauses to step back, light a cigarette, pour a drink and admire his handiwork: sudden flurries of masterly activity, spicings and tastings, sprinklings-in of cumin and coriander, wild tippings-on of turmeric, would be followed by slow meditative intervals ('Collapse. Recover. Start thinking about RICE').[30] The dhals, pulaos and curries that emerged from these long concentrated sessions were flanked by chutneys, pickles, relishes and evil, powerful sauces. 'The point about Chicken and/or Peas Pulao,' Paul explained to Sally, setting out the recipe for his *Staying On* celebration dinner in seven pages of meticulous step-by-step instruction, 'is not just that the rice should be coolish, initially fried, & yellow, but that the dish should be *mild*, & rely wholly on chutneys & pickles for excitement. After that, your mutton curry should be hot, very dark, red and yellow (the yellow being the butter) & served with either chappatis, nan, or (as I prefer) *plain* white Basmati rice.'

Publication week itself went well with a party at the Gants, assorted interviews and virtually unanimous acclaim from reviewers in the press, on radio and television. 'Well, *that* sounds like one to rush out and buy,' said Robert Robinson, the host on a thoroughly satisfactory BBC book programme,[31] warmly seconded by both C. P. Snow and Germaine Greer. Sales passed 4,000 in the first month, and the book spent what was for Paul an unprecedented seven consecutive weeks on the *Sunday Times* best-seller list. In May, Heinemann brought out all four novels of the Raj Quartet, using that name for the first time, in a single gargantuan hard back ('printed, appropriately enough, on India paper', Paul wrote to Dorothy Ganapathy),[32] which sold modestly but 'better than any of us had expected'.[33] The idea for the omnibus edition had come from Charles Pick's son Martin, whose active and infectious enthusiasm for the books gave Paul especial pleasure. 'Do you feel, as I do, that to be read and taken seriously by people far younger than oneself is one of the greatest joys a writer can experience?' he wrote solemnly to Freya Stark (who was a contemporary of his mother's rather than his own).[34]

He filled his empty house with company that spring and summer as he never had before. He held a family luncheon on his birthday and another for Sally's in May. He cooked a duck-and-orange Easter dinner for Peter and his wife Eileen, and threw a party to welcome

Dorothy Olding in June. Friends realised, as his students had done in Tulsa, that he could not bear to be alone. His marriage might be over, Sally's had ended in divorce, Carol's was finally disintegrating: his daughters, especially Sally, were aware of healing and reconciliation but also of the waste and wreckage implicit in the lines from his beloved 'East Coker' – 'What was to be the value of the long looked forward to,/ Long hoped for calm, the autumnal serenity,/ And the wisdom of age?' Sally read the Raj Quartet right through in the omnibus edition Paul gave her. When she had finished he took her out to dinner at the Epicure to ask if the book worked, and she knew from the tears in his eyes when she said yes that he was contemplating the price paid: a marriage too often strained beyond endurance, a life dominated and in the end destroyed by Eliot's 'intolerable wrestle/ With words and meanings'.

Paul's hospitality seemed to exhaust him. 'Felt frail afterwards' became a common postscript to his parties.[35] He hardly ate but he no longer left the house without a bottle of vodka in his briefcase, which he supped for breakfast, lunch and tea. He had for years suffered from winter asthma, prostrating colds and flu, cramps in his leg and an intermittent limp. Some time in March 1977 he contracted a throat infection which he could not shake off. 'It was a strange virus,' he wrote to Sally on 14 April, 'very debilitating, & even worrying at times, since it seemed to suggest other troubles, like cancer of the larynx! Which is something one can do without.' The sore throat had odd side effects ('weakness in the legs', 'colonic pains, appendix murmur etc.'), and was followed by a persistent rash. 'Look, what's all this about a skin cancer?' Paul protested sharply to Dorothy Olding on 13 May. 'At the present I have what we used to call in India a dhobie itch.'[36] Concentration was not easy. *Mango Rain* went into several drafts but none got much beyond the first fifty pages. Even writing a letter required an effort. 'Dorothy, please tell John I'm pleased with the new contract,' Paul wrote when Morrow agreed to a handsome $10,000 advance on the new novel, 'and that I'll write to him as soon as I can (as Tusker said of Lucy) get my arse off the chair'.

One project completed in these months was his version of Cinderella in which the heroine is a working girl who stays at home alone when the others go to the ball, seeing pictures and stories in the fire, dancing in her imagination through 'the castle of her history and her future . . .'[37] The story, first jotted down as a writing-class assignment in Tulsa, was now brought out and reworked. Paul had insisted to his Writ-and-Rhet students that, in anything they wrote, they should try to get at what he called 'the central emotional knock', 'the bit that knocks for you'.[38] He had been sitting on the floor reading

Sally's drawings of Paul's Cinderella from After the Funeral.
LEFT *'After the last funeral guest had gone she climbed the tower to her
room and took off the white dress . . .'* RIGHT *'She caught her own eye
in the glass and suddenly wept . . . she wept for herself; because oneself is
the person one always really weeps for in the end.'*

from Conrad at the time, and he knocked with his knuckles on the
ground to drive home the point. 'Cinderella knocked for him,' said
Sally Dennison: 'with Cinderella he was getting at the central knock.'
He explained that there were only so many basic plots, and that he had
long wanted to see what could be done with Grimms' tales. As soon as
he got home he turned to his daughter Sally, who did a drawing for
him that winter of Wilde's 'The Fisherman and his Soul', and who was
as excited as her father at the thought of collaborating on a book of
illustrated modern adult fairy tales. 'It resonated with his past, and
with my own past', said Sally, who had written and drawn fairy stories
as a small child almost as soon as she could hold a pencil.

The mutual confidence generated by this new project was precious
to them both. 'It was as if we were shuffling forward, coming nearer
and nearer, shyly, tentatively, each holding one side of the work. It was
like an offering,' she said. Paul discussed the scheme with Roland Gant
in April, insisting that he would have no other illustrator, and asking
for a contract before he returned to Tulsa. 'Hope you can manage the
weekend,' he wrote expansively to Sally on 3 May: 'It's *not* Country
Life, so we can have a leisurely, quiet and gravid time. Have had
further ideas about Snowhite and Sleeping Beauty . . .' Work had
always been a central, saving activity for Paul, who took immense
satisfaction in this new and equal relationship with his daughter. His

affection for her flowered alongside his belief in her professional capacities, released and reinforced by private jokes in long, peaceful and productive working sessions that spring and summer. He drafted and redrafted the text, she evolved delicate, clear, exquisitely detailed, pen-and-ink drawings. The Whittington Press agreed in May to produce a limited edition with Heinemann as distributors, *The Times* bought the story in June for Christmas publication, and Paul submitted the final version, which he called 'After the Funeral', just over a week before he flew to the US. 'Apart from working on *Mango Rain* in Tulsa,' he wrote on 22 July to Roland, 'I hope occasionally to work on Sally's and my next project (Snowhite: interesting things to be done about the mirror, & why dwarfs live in a forest).'[39]

Plans on the domestic front were more uncertain. 'There is, I think, to be a Division of the Spoils,' Paul wrote to Mollie Hamilton, 'but with only one of us Staying On, & in a house I may well have to sell.'[40] *The Far Pavilions* was finished at last in the spring of 1977 and Paul, who had been the first person to read *Shadow of the Moon* and certify it as a best seller twenty years before, offered to write the official reader's report for Allen Lane, warning Mollie that if he did not like the manuscript, he would say so ('Don't I know it,' she said stoutly). It was Mollie who had set the Raj Quartet in motion by introducing Paul to Neil Ghosh in 1964. She had started her own 'Indian historical' in the same year, and over the next decade and more the two had cheered one another on with an enthusiasm strengthened perhaps by the fact that, whether they knew it or not, they were developing different versions of what had started out as essentially the same plot. The hero of *The Far Pavilions* – an upperclass Englishman, orphaned in India as a small child and brought up to talk, think and behave as an Indian – is a mirror image of the hero of *The Jewel in the Crown*, and both reflect in the distorting glass of fiction something of Neil's predicament in fact.

Paul's report was extremely long and full of detailed advice ('most of which I took'). Once again he confidently predicted a best seller, lunching with Mollie to discuss his recommendations, chief among them his insistence that the inner logic of her story required the death of one or other of the two lovers, 'because the book darkens so towards the end'.[41] Mollie, who had always implicitly trusted Paul's judgement as a writer, agreed to try out his instructions. They touched lightly on his impending divorce – he offered no explanation save to say that he and Penny had stopped talking – and his return to America. She had been shocked to see how ill he looked, and she was appalled when he confided that he drank a tumbler of vodka first thing every morning. After lunch, as they parted on a corner near Piccadilly

Circus, he told her that he would never write about India again, and she asked him why. 'Because I've nothing left to say,' Paul said sombrely. 'And then he did a thing he'd never done before in his life. He kissed me.' He walked slowly away towards David Higham's office in Golden Square, and she watched with a forlorn feeling that she would never see him again. When he rang to say goodbye just before he left for Tulsa, his voice was unrecognisable, 'a croak: the voice of a stranger'. She told him she had been persuaded by her New York publisher not to change the happy ending of *The Far Pavilions*: 'Paul was disappointed with me. I said, "Honestly Paul, anyone would think you had a death wish." Odd that he should have said that – the book darkens so towards the end.'

Paul gave what he called his 'au revoir party' on 24 July, exactly a year after Penny left. He had sent her a message, through Sally, asking if she would be prepared to come to the party – 'As a guest. I can no longer hope for anything more' – in the wistful, chastened spirit his mother had so often used for appeals to him after the final break between them. She did not come, and on 31 July he flew to New York for the publication of *Staying On*. Uniformly appreciative reviews included a somewhat proprietary accolade from Malcolm Muggeridge ('He thinks he owns India'),[43] which filled the front page of the *New York Times Book Review*,[44] and was followed by an interview with Paul. Morrow celebrated by taking Paul out to dinner at an Indian restaurant to meet John Leonard of the *New York Times*, who had spent the summer reading the Raj Quartet ('I had lived for months in his mind. It was a very civilised place to be') in preparation for a thorough and thoughtful appraisal. 'As literary dinner parties go . . . this one was modest,' Leonard wrote afterwards. 'The Beautiful People didn't come. It was, instead of black tie, warm gin. And Scott was clearly a sick man, sad in body and soul, on his way to teach in Tulsa, Okla. Nevertheless he roused himself to several wicked anecdotes.'[45] Leonard was struck by what he called Paul's civility, the trouble he took to entertain the table, his generosity and composure in spite of evident distress: 'In pain, he was kind, not noisy. He advertised nothing of himself.'

Paul flew down to Detroit on 4 August, the day after publication, to take part in a four-day summer school, a sort of American Swanwick called the Cranbrook Conference, advising students on their work, reading and discussing his own. At the final public session on Sunday, he read Lucy's speech accusing Tusker of obfuscation and demanding some kind of financial assurance about her future if he should die: an outburst compounded in equal parts of indignation, contempt, grief, fury and appeal. The effort drained him, and he spent the better part of

Paul in the garden at Addison Way, alone in the summer of 1977, a year after Penny left him.

the next three weeks holed up alone at John Willey's house in Norwalk, where John joined him at weekends. He flew down to Tulsa, stopping for a weekend with the Burjorjees in Washington on the way, and arriving on 28 August to find a reception committee waiting. Half a dozen of his former students had prepared his apartment, stocked the fridge with drinks, painted banners, hired a van to drive out to the airport, and clapped him as he stepped off the plane. There was a party that night in Paul's apartment. The students, sensing his exhaustion, tried to slip away but he detained them, sitting on an uncomfortable upright kitchen chair, gathering them round him, lighting a cigarette, settling into the old, familiar, inviting ritual, preparing to summon up another surprise party given nearly twenty years before by Muriel Spark in Camberwell:

Clearly this would not be an early evening: Paul had wrapped up a story for us in brown paper and twine and had every intention of making delivery. Wordlessly, quickly, we found places on the floor, couch, chair, and waited for the writer to speak.

At first his words came slow as steps. Then, as his voice deepened with smoke and warmed with sips of gin, the story began to stretch, to shimmer to spin. It . . . was beautifully shaped in detail and suspense. We could see Muriel Spark's lively, overflowing flat, the meal she and a friend were still cooking, and waited for the 'big surprise' she had saved for Paul, and Paul had saved for us.[46]

The surprise turned out to be an unknown American, Mr Williams, whom Paul had done his best to draw out and set at ease, covering himself with confusion when he discovered later that the stranger's first name was Tennessee. The memory, with its characteristically offbeat climax, became a celebration of the storyteller's art, Paul's way of drawing his listeners hospitably into the rich, warm, lighted rooms of his imagination while shutting out failure, disappointment, and the dread they had all felt when they first caught sight of him at the airport.

To people who had not seen him for a year, the change in Paul was startling. He looked wan, shrunk and emaciated, his flesh was puffy and swollen, his eyes wept, and he moved with difficulty. If his students had been concerned, their elders were appalled. Paul himself maintained that he had flu, that the heat upset him, and once, to Tom Staley, that the ice cubes in his drinks were giving him stomach cramps. People close to him tried to believe that his slowness of speech and movement, his shuffling gait, his laboured breathing, drowsiness and depression were due to nothing worse than drink. Newcomers, enrolling for his classes on the strength of last year's legendary reputation (he was to supervise two writing groups), felt cheated and let down. His old students were sick at heart. Paul was senior, in both years and experience, to most of the faculty on that predominantly young and optimistic campus. It was not easy to determine who should take responsibility for someone so notoriously reluctant to seek medical treatment (before he left England Paul said he had refused to consult his general practitioner for fear of being forbidden to board the plane). After three weeks, Tom Staley made an appointment with his own doctor, Roger Atwood, who committed Paul to hospital the same day.

Paul enjoyed telling the story afterwards of how he had dropped into the clinic for a check-up and stayed six weeks. That first examination showed cirrhosis of the liver, which was colossally enlarged and had ceased to metabolise the phenomenal daily doses of alcohol it had so efficiently mopped up for years. Paul told Dr Atwood[47] that he normally drank a quart of vodka a day, and smoked sixty to eighty cigarettes. The liver failure had been triggered probably about five months earlier, some time in April, which was when Paul said he first began suffering from weakness in the legs, fatigue and emphysema. He had stopped eating, he was seriously anaemic, and he complained of rectal bleeding which made him fear a return of amoebiasis. He was too weak for an exploratory operation when he entered St Francis Hospital on 23 September: the doctors hoped to build up his strength with blood transfusions, to clear his lungs, drain the fluid from his swollen abdomen and restore his protein levels with careful feeding. He gave up drink immediately and cut down on smoking, but he refused utterly to stop teaching, continuing to conduct his writing workshop from his private room, setting assignments, reading manuscripts, making notes and receiving students at his bedside. They were alarmed and apprehensive: at least one was painfully reminded of the description, at the end of *The Towers of Silence*, of Barbie Batchelor in the Samaritan Hospital in Ranpur.[48] It was Paul who soothed distracted visitors so successfully that friends who came or called in consternation often found themselves laughing extravagantly from pleasure and relief by the time he had finished.

When preliminary explorations disclosed cancerous cells, Carol flew out on 1 October to be with her father, staying with the Staleys and doing much to restore the atmosphere he needed of calm, undismayed courage and serenity. Mollie Hamilton telephoned every day. *The Far Pavilions* was already showing signs of fulfilling Paul's predictions and he had urged her, before he left England, to spend a part of the proceeds on something like diamonds for herself. When he protested in Tulsa that so many gossipy transatlantic telephone calls must be costing a fortune, Mollie said in her best Babu accent: 'But, sir, you are telling me to do this.' 'What d'you mean?' Paul said with some asperity. 'Sir, you are telling me to buy diamonds. And every word that falls from lips of the master is a diamond to humble chela.' Even Paul, flattery-proof and instinctively resistant to compliments, was disarmed as always by her absurdity. He rang her on the morning scheduled for his operation, 20 October, announcing indignantly that instead of the condemned man's lavish breakfast to which he had been looking forward all he got was a glass of water. He said: 'Wish me luck, Moll.'[49]

The operation confirmed the initial diagnosis and showed that it was too late to prevent cancer of the colon spreading to the liver. Paul adapted well to a colostomy, seeming to pick up strength, regaining his appetite, finding no problem in managing without alcohol and rationing cigarettes. Dr Atwood discussed his findings with Paul in detail, explaining that the cirrhosis could probably be cured but that the cancer had gone too far to be eradicated, and that his best hope after radio- and chemotherapy would be a remission, possibly a long one, perhaps even lasting several years. The facts were explained to Carol, and to Tom Staley. Paul remained patient, practical, sanguine and composed. He appreciated the irony of the situation, setting himself once again to defuse the doom-laden currents of hysteria and despair that threatened to overcome his friends. He began with Dorothy Olding, who had borne the brunt of the past few weeks, acting as a clearing house for news and bulletins between Tulsa, New York and London. Paul resumed control of his affairs as soon as he left hospital on 4 November, making it clear at once how he proposed to handle them.

He signalled his intentions at dinner with Tom Staley and his wife by declaring that he meant to track down the culprit who had given Dorothy the false impression that he was terminally ill. There was a pause for the Staleys to digest this announcement and work out its implications in a silence charged with almost farcical drama and intensity. 'I was sitting there thinking, *wait a minute – ,*' said Tom Staley: 'You know, and I know – you know what I know – and I know what you know – and you *know* I know – what the doctors said. *And* Carol knows. She talked to the specialists. I thought, it's terminal: *he* knew I knew. He knew what he was doing. He wanted to make it clear how it was going to be. *No one was going to let on.*'[50] Astute, appreciative, deeply worried about Paul, Tom accepted with admiration and astonishment what amounted to a pact between them. It was a strategy that had always worked well for Paul, going back perhaps to childhood, certainly to the poem, 'It Never Happened', which he had written disowning an adolescent love affair in the last summer before the war. Paul knew that he was dying, and that he had written his own story in *After the Funeral*: 'But he did not want to believe his own prophecies,' said Sally Dennison.

Paul returned on 4 November to an apartment transformed by Carol, who had reorganised his shabby rooms, banished their air of neglect, cleaned the sticky kitchen floor, arranged flowers on the table and put up Bill Wheeler's pumpkin lantern for Hallowe'en. Paul was eating well and even beginning to gain a little weight, although his clothes still hung on him: Carol scoured Tulsa for a pair of braces and came home with red suspenders which became a great joke to his visitors. His gentleness and humour gleamed as they had always done for Carol, who had never known her father's violent dark side. The two resumed their old companionship with delight and greater confidence than ever. They talked easily, comparing notes, catching up on one another's news, discussing the past and what had gone wrong in their family, Carol asking questions about her parents' marriage and Paul answering with a freedom not often possible between parent and child. They talked about India and his love for it. 'In Tulsa, we were going there together next year,' Carol said long afterwards: 'we both knew we wouldn't.' The two drew close during these weeks which both remembered, in spite or perhaps because of the threat that hung over them, as a time of shining happiness: 'You turned it into a sort of holiday for me,' Paul wrote to Carol when she left to fly home on 15 November.

She was returning as his representative to accept the Booker Prize,

Paul had enjoyed imagining Celia Johnson playing Lucy Smalley in Staying On *('Oh what fun that would be!' he wrote to Carol in 1976) long before Anglia TV bought the rights for a film which was made, with Trevor Howard the year after he died.*

Britain's most prestigious literary award. *Staying On* had been shortlisted in October, plans were already in hand for Anglia Television to film the book, and encouraging rumours had for some weeks been crossing the Atlantic about the Booker judges' deliberations: 'we resembled a bunch of terriers looking for a rat,' said the chairman, Philip Larkin, 'we couldn't describe it, but we should know it when we found it.'[51] News of their supposedly still secret decision, following hard on what looked like Paul's recovery, was received in Tulsa with jubilation. Paul had corrected his proof copy of *Staying On* there the year before, and his students thought of it as 'their' book, much as *The Jewel in the Crown* was Dorothy Ganapathy's ('I wrote a book about her because she deserved it,' Paul had told them). They were elated and exultant. The university authorities, who had paid Paul's hospital bills in full, waived any further teaching requirement, and the Leakes put their private plane at his disposal, but Paul declined both offers, just as he had earlier refused to allow Donald Hayden to take over his writing class. He was very conscious of the debt he owed to Tulsa and to Tom Staley – who had recognised him at a time when he had received little or no other official recognition – and above all to his students, who would freely acknowledge their debt to him in return as they became increasingly aware with time how much Paul had taught them. 'Paul Scott is easy to remember,' Steve Wood wrote ten years after Paul left Tulsa, using the formula devised for one of his first writing assignments:

I remember his characters meeting in disgrace. I remember the *duende*. I remember sitting in various chairs or on the floor in his apartment after he moved the class off-campus. I remember him sitting on the floor, but even when he did we looked up to him. I remember him reading a student's story out loud with tears in his eyes. I remember rewriting fairy tales. I remember John Braine. I remember talking to him. I remember listening. I remember the Chekhovian Farewell. I remember being spellbound by the Raj Quartet for an entire summer of reading. . . . I remember seeing him standing at his shoulder-high windows, looking out into what I believed could only be India, his India, the India he shared with those of us who read his work. I remember him offering me a beer and cooking us omelets. I remember him drawing his lungs full of air through his nose and realising why his novels are filled with smells and scents.[52]

The Booker dinner was held at Claridges Hotel on 23 November. Carol stood in for her father, accepting his applause and a cheque for £5,000. Sally Dennison, who dropped in after lunch that day to see Paul, found him alone, looking at his watch. 'They will all be sitting down to dinner right now,' he said, and Sally suddenly understood that his version of Cinderella had been, like so many of the stories he told in Tulsa, a parable about the writer: the outsider who feels excluded or cold-shouldered by the rest of the world, the dreamer whose ball takes place in his or her head. 'It struck me then how like the story it was,' she said. Telephone calls came through all afternoon from London and New York with messages of congratulation and enquiries from the press. The *Tulsa World* sent a reporter with a bottle of sparkling catawba juice done up like champagne. Paul had turned down all invitations for Thanksgiving the next night, so Jim Leake smoked him a whole turkey of his own, delivering it with a pan of Harriet's famous sweet potato casserole, her cornbread dressing and cranberry sauce, half a home-baked cherry pie and half a pecan pie. 'He *was* pleased,' said Harriet, 'but I don't think he ate even a mouthful.'

Paul seemed in these last weeks in Tulsa curiously suspended between two worlds. Penny, who had not seen or spoken to him for nearly a year and a half, resumed her role as his wife that autumn, accepting his need of her as soon as she learned that he had cancer, slipping back into place just as he had once hoped she might with no fuss or explanations as if she had indeed come home from nothing more serious than a shopping trip. She had moved back to Addison Way and set about house-warming – cleaning, polishing, stocking the kitchen, tidying the garden – preparing a welcome for him, as she had done in the same 'euphoria of happiness' thirty years before when he first came home from India. They exchanged letters of solicitude and longing. When Paul left Tulsa in December, virtually his whole class came with him to the airport, covering his exit with a specially concocted Singing Telegram ('You danced and left us no traces,/ Not even red braces . . . It's time to pack up,/ All tales must end,/ The Party's over,/ It's over, my friend'). He knew that Penny would be waiting for him at home with the two girls: 'It was as if we had never been separated, as in the early days of our marriage,' she wrote afterwards. 'He had expressly instructed us not to meet him, as he had instructed me all those years ago.'[53] She felt that the slate was wiped clean between them. Paul drank fruit juice, and talked to her as he had not done for years. She said that the two were almost magically at one, as they had been when they first met, except that now his tawny yellow eyes had turned blue ('cancer had stolen the pigment').

The whole family spent a quiet peaceful, united, unexpectedly joyful Christmas, seeing no one, hardly leaving the house, enjoying their own and one another's company. Paul and Penny lived thankfully from day to day, taking each moment as it came. 'That last winter was exciting, not depressing,' Carol said. Heinemann gave a party in the New Year at the Gants for Paul, supported on Roland's arm, to receive tribute from old friends and new admirers. *Staying On*, in its third printing, was back again among the best sellers in the *Sunday Times*. The one-volume Quartet was also reprinting. 'So it has been an odd but in one sense very good and happy year for me.' Paul wrote on 2 January 1978 to Clive Sansom in Tasmania,[54] summing up his restored family fortunes, looking forward to the filming of *Staying On* in the summer, hoping 'that one day the TV people will do a 26 part serial of the Quartet, then I can go on doing what I've so far managed to do, write what I want & take my time over it.' At the end of a long period of retrospect and stocktaking, Paul seemed no longer troubled by the pressures that had driven him all his adult life. 'I am very content,' he wrote on 8 January, and perhaps for the first time he meant it.[55]

He prepared for his course of radiotherapy, dreading the prospect of long exhausting expensive journeys to and from the hospital. 'What's it like, Moll?' he asked Mollie Hamilton, who had successfully endured a course of radiation in the early 1960s with help from Paul, whose hospital visits always made her laugh so much it hurt. She told him the treatment would be dreadful but effective – 'Anything I can do, you can do better'[56] – and sent him the nearest thing she could to a 'taxi tied up with ribbons with a chauffeur inside', a cheque to cover a year's taxi fares on the strength of the *Far Pavilions'* American earnings, threatening that if he turned her down she would order him instead a stag's antler hatstand from Harrods. Paul capitulated gratefully: 'My mother used, when cross or crossed, to complain about "those stubborn Scotts" . . . I have been in my mind trying stubbornly to resist accepting so greatly undeserved a gift. But then I thought Scott stubbornness can be no match for that of a Kaye (& Hamilton to boot) and that, as you warn, things would only end up with the receipt by post of something like a sable belly-button brush with a solid gold handle.'[57]

He made a point of writing or ringing round as many as possible of his friends, cheerfully announcing his recovery, forestalling visits on the grounds that he still needed treatment, but explaining as he had once done to Carol that he was 'open to receive congratulations and Loyal Greetings'. Many who got no answer to their letters when *Staying On* won the Booker prize assumed, like Manohar Malgonkar, that Paul had been overwhelmed by success at last: 'ironically it was this somewhat lightweight offering that dislodged the stone that set the avalanche rolling. . . . The real heavyweights such as the Laytons and the Manners, Ronald Merrick . . . and the absurdly named Muzzy Guides had been hammering away at the door of the cave in vain, when that blaspheming army gadfly Tusker Smalley had come charging from behind and uttered the magic words: Open O Sesame.'[58]

All through January Paul grew slowly weaker. Joyce Wiener, his first agent, sent congratulations on the Booker,[59] and so did Jimmy Leasor, with whom Paul had laid plans for their respective first novels thirty-five years earlier on the troopship bound for India. On 12 February Paul entered the Middlesex Hospital for a second operation, which showed two days later that the cancer had spread rapidly, and that he had only a short time to live. His family and the few friends who realised what was happening gathered at his bedside. Mollie, who had seen an article of Paul's about Indian holidays in *The Times*, took it that he was well again and off on his travels in India. David Higham visited him, and almost immediately entered hospital himself: he had cancer, like Paul, and would outlive him by a few weeks. Roland Gant came regularly bringing news of publication plans for Paul's and Sally's Cinderella. Paul said he was pleased, 'and with a wolfish grin flickering across his bone-sharp features, he added: "I picked a good title in *After the Funeral*, didn't I?" '[60]

He died on 1 March 1978, just over three weeks short of his fifty-

eighth birthday. Dorothy Ganapathy, who had not even known that
he was ill, learned of his death in Bombay from a friend who saw it in
the paper. Neil Ghosh, who was born the year before Paul and would
die the year after, perhaps never heard the news, but he read *Staying
On* when it reached Calcutta, and said he recognised himself in Tusker
Smalley.[61] 'The tale is like a looking-glass in which you see yourself if
you gaze into it long enough,' Paul had written in *After the Funeral*. He
had himself looked long and hard in the mirror of his stories: he had
drawn with truthfulness and courage the destructive dark side of
human nature as well as its lighter frailties, humours and contradic-
tions: he had ranged far and wide in time as well as space: he had
explored above all the love affair between two nations, and its ending
in bitterness and division. The principle Philip Larkin discerned in
Staying On works as well for the Raj Quartet: 'although seemingly a
delineation of failure, the book resolves triumphantly into a study of
love – inarticulate and unfashionable love, perhaps – but a study in
which the end by death of a marriage is linked to the end by history of
an Empire, and the love that informs both . . . seems for this reason all
the stronger and more enduring.' Paul was fascinated by history and
its processes, the ways in which we acknowledge the past or try not to,
but he refused emphatically to be classified as a historical novelist. The
major problem for him in fact and fiction, past and present, was 'the
actual business, rebarbative and mysterious, ironic and upsetting, of
living with other people.'

Notes

Quotations not otherwise identified come from conversations with me, and letters not otherwise located remain in the possession of the recipients.

H.S.

Abbreviations used in these notes:

CL   *Country Life.*

DHA   Scott's office files, 1950–60, among the papers of David Higham Associates, Harry Ransom Humanities Research Center, University of Texas, Austin.

HRC   Scott papers, including most of his manuscripts and working drafts, at the Harry Ransom Humanities Research Center, University of Texas, Austin.

ML   Scott's private papers, including carbon copies of his correspondence, reviews, lectures, reader's reports, Sansom papers etc., at the McFarlin Library, University of Tulsa, Oklahoma.

MS   'My Story', unpublished manuscript by Penny Scott.

SR   'Scott's Raj', autobiographical draft outline for a TV book programme, May 1975, ML. Scott's books are referred to in shortened form, e.g. *Pavilion* for *The Chinese Love Pavilion*, *Jewel* for *The Jewel in the Crown*, *Towers* for *The Towers of Silence*, *Muse* for *My Appointment with the Muse* etc.

Chapter 1   Half close your eyes here – and you're in Mayapore

1 *After the Funeral*, p.2.
2 SR
3 Interview with PS by Caroline Moorehead, *Times*, 20 Oct. 1975.
4 Inf. from Peter Scott; Ada Grew was the daughter of Tom Scott's aunt, Ann Lindsey.
5 *Muse* p. 105.
6 Dustjacket blurb, *Six Days in Marapore*, Morrow, 1953.
7 SR
8 SR
9 SR
10 SR; *Paul Scott* by K. B. Rao, Twayne, 1980, p. 14.
11 MS + inf. from Penny Scott.
12 Inf. from Peter Scott.
13 *Muse* p. 45.
14 Peter Scott.
15 Edna Donagh, daughter of Frances Scott's brother Wilfred Mark.

16 Parish register, St John's church, Fenwick, & 1851 census.
17 See *Round About a Pound a Week* by Maud Pember Reeves, 1913 (Virago 1979); *Outcast London* by G. Stedman-Jones, Clarendon Press, 1971. Account based on birth, death and marriage certificates, 1881 census, rate books for St. Paul, Deptford (Lewisham Libraries).
18 MS
19 *Bender*, p. 45.
20 R. Mark to PS, 2 April 1967 & 8 May 1960, ML.
21 RM to PS, 17 May 1968, ML.
22 R. Mark to PS 11 Mar. 1968, ML.
23 R. Mark to PS 21 Aug. 1962, ML.
24 SR
25 SR
26 *Muse* p. 152.
27 SR ('real' crossed out in ms).
28 *Staying On* p. 85.
29 F. Scott to Ruth Sansom, 8 Feb. 1941, ML.
30 *Staying On* p. 142.

31 Ibid, p. 137.
32 Ibid, p. 147.
33 *Alien Sky* p. 150.
34 SR
35 *Muse*, p. 105.
36 Ibid, p. 140.
37 SR
38 PS to Peter Scott, 31 Aug. 1974, ML.
39 *Muse*, p. 152.
40 PS to Carol Scott, 8 May 72; my account of the Wrights based on inf. from Sheila Wright and Peter Scott, family papers & albums.
41 PS to Carol Scott, op. cit.
42 PS to S. Wright, 1 Jan. 1975, ML.
43 PS to Carol Scott, op. cit.
44 PS to Alan Jenkins, 4 Oct. 1974, ML.
45 Inf. from Sheila Wright.
46 *Staying On*, pp. 78–9.
47 PS, autobiographical note, 1960, ML.
48 Wrights' history based on 1851, 1861 & 1871 census returns, & Leeds directories.
49 PS's great-grandfather, Thomas Scott, m. 10 Nov., 1830, in St Andrew's church, Newcastle, Elizabeth Bewick, b.1806, d. Robert and Mary Bewick of Stamfordham: the three children of the engraver, Thomas Bewick of Ovingham, 1753 – 1828, all d. unmarried, and he had no niece Elizabeth.
50 Inf. from Pauline Hildesheim, grand-daughter of G. B. Scott's sister Mary.
51 'Conversation with Paul Scott' by Francine Ringold, *Nimrod: International Journal of Fiction and Poetry*, University of Tulsa, 1978, p. 31.
52 SR
53 SR
54 *Bender*, p. 14.
55 *Muse*, p. 44.
56 Ibid, p. 45.
57 SR
58 SR (phrase crossed out in manuscript).
59 SR; *Division* p. 103.

Chapter 2 Slow dreamy boats of recollection and swift thrusting boats of ambition

1 SR; *Muse* p. 152.
2 CL, 5 April, 1973.
3 *Muse* p 152.
4 *Three Weeks*, Duckworth, 1907, p. 13.
5 Ibid, p. 105; the next 5 quotes come from pp. 137, 47, 73, 205 & 137.
6 Ibid, p. 166.
7 Ibid, p. 246.
8 Draft entry for *Mid Century Authors*, 1966, ML.
9 Obituary, *Palmers Green & Southgate Gazette*, 10 Jan., 1930.
10 Ad. in the *P. Green, Winchmore Hill & Southgate Recorder*, 9 May 1912.
11 *Bender*, p. 24.
12 Inf. from F. G. Rudling, Ralph & Douglas Watkinson, school contemporaries of PS: WHCS prospectus in *Schools of the Edmonton Hundred* by G. W. Sturges, 1949, p. 118.
13 *Division* p. 209.
14 Autobiographical note, 1960, ML.
15 'I Find My Voice', unpub. autobiography by Clive Sansom.
16 SR
17 C. Sansom, unpub. autobiog.
18 F. G. Rudling.
19 Autobiographical note, 1969, ML.
20 SR
21 MS
22 SR
23 MS
24 SR
25 'The Father Figure', draft synopsis for TV play, ML.
26 *Bender*, p. 65.
27 SR
28 PS to Carol & Sally Scott, 31 July 1976.
29 *Division*, p. 272.
30 CL, 5 April, 1973.
31 PS to Carol Scott 19 April 1972.
32 *Muse* pp. 94–5 & p. 215.
33 Enid Huntley to PS, n.d. (1967), ML, Kate Scott d. 20 Jan, 1894, of metritis (inflammation of the womb), according to her death certificate.
34 PS to Diane Lloyd, 14 Jan. 1977, ML.
35 *Male Child*, p. 83.
36 Ibid.
37 *Mid Century Authors* draft entry, 1966, ML.
38 CL, 30 Nov. 1970; the film was based on a novel by Gene Stratton Porter.
39 CL, 18 Dec. 1975.
40 Inf. from Peter Scott.
41 PS to Carol Scott, 19 April, 1972.
42 *Muse*, pp. 153–4.
43 Ibid, p. 154.
44 CL, 4 July 1975.
45 CL 28 Feb. 1974.
46 Inf. from Geoffrey Ridehalgh.
47 Ibid, p. 15; previous quote from p. 79.
48 Ibid, p. 60.
49 Ibid, p. 60.
50 *Division*, p. 107.
51 *Muse*, p. 54.
52 F. G. Rudling.
53 PS to Carol and Sally Scott, 31 July, 1976.
54 PS to P. Goodbody, 8 May 1969, ML.
55 F. G. Rudling.
56 'Pleasure in Reading', draft article for *Times*, 1962, ML.

57 *Muse*, p. 154.
58 *Whatever Happened to Tom Mix?*, Cassell, 1970, p. 109.
59 Betty Jukes.
60 SR
61 Ruth Mark to PS, 25 Sept. 1963, ML.
62 Ruth Mark to PS, 1 July 1960, ML.
63 Ruth Mark to PS, 11 March 1968, ML.
64 SR
65 PS to Carol & Sally Scott, 31 July 1976.
66 *Muse*, p. 154.
67 *Birds*, p. 123.
68 Warren Brown, University of Tulsa, Oklahoma.
69 PS to Dr A. Dohm, 23 Jan. 1963, ML.
70 *Mid Century Authors* draft entry, 1966, ML.
71 MS
72 *Paul Scott* by K. B. Rao, op. cit., p. 15.
73 *Bender*, p. 93.
74 *Birds*, p. 108.
75 CL, 5 Oct., 1972.
76 Unpub. autobiog.
77 SR.

Chapter 3   Muse on the warpath
1 Cancelled draft, ts, HRC.
2 *I, Gerontius* (The Creation VI).
3 PS to Ruth Sansom, n.d. (Dec. 1940), ML; *Muse*, p. 156.
4 *I, Gerontius*.
5 PS to Carol & Sally Scott, 31 July 1976.
6 *My Life in Pictures*, Herbert Press, 1987, p. 28.
7 CL 13 Dec. 1973.
8 Autobiographical note, 1960, ML.
9 *The Bender;* PS to Leon Drucker, 28 May 1973, ML.
10 PS to Carol & Sally Scott, 31 July 1976.
11 Ibid.
12 Autobiographical note, 1960, ML.
13 Ibid.
14 PS to Richard Price, 11 Sept. 1971, ML.
15 PS to Storm Jameson, 25 Feb. 1975, ML.
16 SR
17 PS to C. & R. Sansom, 13 Mar. 1941, ML.
18 *The Silence of Dean Maitland* by Maxwell Gray (ps. Mary Leglee Tattiet), Kegan Paul, 1886, vol iii.
19 SR
20 Autobiographical note, 1960, ML; *Muse*, p. 154.
21 Inf. from Peter Scott; see also *Charles Laughton* by Simon Callow, Methuen, 1987, & *Pavilions by the Sea* by Tom Laughton, Chatto, 1977.
22 Autobiog. note, 1960, ML; *Muse*, p. 155.

23 *Muse*, p. 155.
24 Dec. 1938, Preliminary Exam., Association of Certified Accountants (C. T. Payne belonged to the Corporation of Accountants which required no formal qualification).
25 *Muse*, p. 155; *Bender*, p. 125.
26 Autobiog. note, 1960, ML.
27 PS to M. Spark, 13 July 1960, ML.
28 SR
29 Autobiog. note, 1960, ML.
30 PS to L. Drucker, 28 May 1973, ML; inf. from Peter Scott.
31 PS to Sally Scott, 30 April 1967, ML.
32 Review of Norman & Jeanne Mackenzie's life of H. G. Wells, CL 12 July 1973.
33 *Muse*, p. 155.
34 *Muse*, p. 156.
35 SR
36 *Palmers Green & Southgate Gazette*, 4 Aug. 1939.
37 *Muse*, p. 154.
38 *Bender*, pp. 64 & 69.
39 PS to Carol Scott, 26 Feb. 1969.
40 Steve Wood, Tulsa class notes, 1976.
41 SR
42 *Towers*, p. 337.
43 *The Picture of Dorian Gray* (1891), OUP, 1974, p. 36; next quote from p. 122.
44 SR
45 MS
46 PS to C. & R. Sansom, Torquay, n.d. (Feb/Mar 1941), ML.
47 Ibid, Dropmore, n.d. (29 Sept. 1940), ML.
48 Ibid, n.d. (Aug. 1941), ML.
49 PS to C. Sansom, n.d. (Aug. 42), ML.
50 Ibid, n.d. (Aug. 1940), ML.
51 'Paul's Early Poems', folder preserved by Clive Sansom, ML.
52 PS to C. Sansom, n.d. (Aug. 1941), ML.
53 PS to C. Sansom, n.d. (April 1940), ML.
54 Ibid.
55 'Paul's Early Poems', op. cit., ML.
56 Inf. from Ruth Sansom.
57 SR; inf. from Peter Scott.
58 PS to C. Sansom, 24 Sept. 1941, ML.
59 *Muse* p. 157.
60 *Muse* p. 44.
61 *Muse* p. 44.
62 PS to C. Sansom, 7 May 1944, ML.
63 *Muse*, p. 157; PS dates this meeting in June 1939, but both Ruth Sansom's memory and Clive's diary put in it Feb. 1940.
64 'Life of Clive Sansom', unpub. ms by Ruth Sansom: account based also on Clive's unpub. autobiography, & conversations with Ruth Sansom.

65 PS to C. Sansom, n.d. (early Aug. 1940), ML, & C. Sansom's diary, Feb. 1940, in the possession of Ruth Sansom.
66 *Jack. C. S. Lewis and His Times* by G. Sayer, Macmillan, 1988, p. 155.
67 C. Sansom's diary, op. cit., 22 Jan. 1940.
68 'Life of C. Sansom', op. cit.
69 *Gerontius*; *Muse*, p. 119.
70 'Life of Clive Sansom', op. cit.
71 R. Sansom to the author, Sept. 86.
72 PS to C. Sansom, 1 March 1941, ML.
73 R. Sansom to the author, Sept. 1986.
74 Ms preserved by C. Sansom, ML.
75 PS to C. Sansom, 24 April 1941, ML.
76 *Muse*, p. 157.
77 PS to C. & R. Sansom, 22 Mar. 1941, ML.
78 PS to CS, n.d. ML.
79 PS to Sally Scott, 26 Nov. 1966 ML.
80 PS to C. & R. Sansom, 22 Mar. 1941, ML.
81 PS to C. Sansom, n.d. (May 1940); Faber's archives record the arrival & departure of the ms on 18 & 26 June.
82 PS to C. Sansom, 24 May 1940, with enclosures, ML.
83 Ibid, n.d. (May 1940), ML.
84 PS to C. & S. Scott, 31 July 1976.
85 Unpub. autobiography, op. cit.
86 *Selected Poems. Clive Sansom 1910-1981*, privately printed, Hobart, Tasmania, p. 137.
87 MS
88 Synopsis, 31 Jan. 1956, ML.
89 Steve Wood, Tulsa class notes, 1976.
90 MS
91 Inf. from R. Sansom, Hobart, Tasmania, Mar 1988.
92 PS to C. Sansom, n.d. (June 1940), ML.
93 PS to C. & S. Scott, 31 July 1976.
94 *De Profundis*, Methuen, 14th ed. 1909, p. 89.
95 Inf. from R. Sansom.
96 CL, 28 Mar 1974.
97 N.d., ML.

Chapter 4   A twin who could be cruel as well as kind

1 This account based on inf. from PS's company clerk, E. J. Scilloe, on his unpublished ms, 'The Approach of War', Jan. 1989, & on the War Diary, 8th Bn Buffs, 1940–41, PRO.
2 PS to C. & R. Sansom, n.d. (17 July 1940), & 28 July 1940, ML.
3 Ibid.
4 PS to Carol Scott, 24 Oct. 1976.
5 *Male Child*, p. 11.
6 PS to R. Sansom, 3 April 1941 & Aug. 1940, ML.
7 Peter Scott to C. Sansom, n.d. (Aug. 1940), ML.
8 PS to C. Sansom, 28 Mar. 1945, ML.
9 PS to C. & R. Sansom, n.d. (June 1940, & 27 July 1940), ML.
10 PS to R. Sansom, n.d. (22 Dec. 1940), ML.
11 Ibid, n.d. (6 August, 1940), ML.
12 G. Armstrong to C. Sansom, Clive's ts copy, 20 Aug. 1940, ML.
13 PS to C. Sansom, n.d. (Aug. 1940), ML.
14 Narice Arlen: this account based on conversations with her and with Peter Lumley.
15 C. Sansom to PS, n.d., ML.
16 PS to R. Sansom, 26 Aug. 41, ML.
17 PS to C. & R. Sansom, n.d. (Sept. 1940), ML.
18 Ibid.
19 Ibid.
20 *The Dragon. A Paper for the Buffs & Men of Kent*, June & Aug. 1941.
21 PS to R. C. Hutchinson, 11 Dec. 1968, ML.
22 *Historical Records of the Buffs, 1919–48* by Col. C. R. B. Knight, London, 1951, p. 364.
23 PS to Carol Scott, 24 Oct. 1976.
24 'Southgate's Ordeal', *Palmers Green & Southgate Gazette*, 6 July 1945.
25 9 Nov. 1940, ML.
26 *Palmers Green & Southgate Gazette*, 15 Nov. 1940; Southgate Air Raid Wardens Reports, 8 Nov. 1940, Local Hist. Archive; inf. from Peter Scott.
27 PS to C. Sansom, dated 'Monday 25.11.40', probably a mistake for 28 Nov. ML.
28 Ibid.
29 PS to C. Sansom, n.d. (29 Oct. 1940) & 15 Nov. 1940, ML.
30 PS to C. Sansom, 15 Nov. 1940, ML.
31 Ibid.
32 PS to C. Sansom, 28 Nov. 1940, ML.
33 Ibid.
34 'Paul's Early Poems', Sansom papers, ML.
35 PS to C. Sansom, n.d. (early Dec. 1940), ML.
36 *Dorian Gray*, op. cit., p. 142.
37 Ivan Kapinski to Anna, Torquayovich, 25 Nov. 1940, ML.
38 PS to R. Sansom n.d. (22 Dec. 1940), ML.
39 Ivan to Anna, 25 Nov. 1940, ML.
40 Inf. from Narice Arlen (Stephen told her he had pulled strings to get the senior officer responsible removed or 'brass-hatted').
41 PS to R. C. Hutchinson, 11 Dec. 1968, ML.
42 PS to Diane Lloyd, 14 Jan. 1972, ML.

43 PS, army paybook, ML.
44 Peter Scott to C. & R. Sansom, 8 Feb. 1941, ML.
45 N.d. (Jan/Feb 41), ML.
46 PS to C. & R. Sansom, n.d. (early Feb. 1941), ML.
47 R. Sansom to the author, March 1988.
48 M. Hamilton to the author, 4 April, 1989.
49 *Dorian Gray*, op. cit. p. 107.
50 'Paul's Early Poems', Sansom papers, ML.
51 *Pavilion*, p. 230.
52 *Division*, p. 246.
53 Ibid, p. 248.
54 Ibid, p. 256.
55 Ibid, p. 259.
56 PS to C. & R.S., 13 Mar. 1941, ML.
57 Ibid, n.d. (Feb. 1941), ML.
58 Ibid, 13 Mar. 1941, ML.
59 Frances Scott to R. Sansom, 8 Feb. 1941, ML.
60 PS to C. & R.S. 13 Mar. 41, ML.
61 PS to Carol & Sally Scott, 31 July, 1976.
62 PS to Sally Scott, 18 Feb. 1968, ML.
63 *Dorian Gray*, op. cit. p. 119.
64 PS to R. Sansom, 26 Aug. 1941, ML.
65 *De Profundis*, Methuen, 1909, p. 42.
66 *Division*, p. 258.
67 PS to C. & R. Sansom, 13 Mar. 1941, ML.
68 Ibid, n.d. (Feb. 1941), ML.
69 Op. cit., p. 27.
70 PS to C. Sansom, 25 Nov. 1940, ML; P. Baker to C. Sansom, n.d. (Dec. 1942), ML; inf. from R. Sansom.
71 PS to C. Sansom, 4 April 1941, ML.
72 PS to C. & R. Sansom, n.d. (31 Mar. 1941), ML.
73 Ibid, 22 Mar. 1941, ML.
74 PS to C. Sansom, 24 Aug. 1941, ML.
75 Ibid, 28 Mar. 1945, ML.
76 Enclosed with letter, PS to C. Sansom, 24 April 1941, ML.

Chapter 5 The same mirror but a different reflection

1 PS to CS, 1 Mar. 1941 (Matelot spelt Maitalop: spelling standardised passim).
2 PS to C. Sansom, 3 Mar. & 22 Mar. 1941; his contributions, signed 'Quarter Guard', appeared in the *Dragon* from Mar. 1941.
3 PS to C. Sansom, n.d. (13 May 1944), ML; & see Chap. 6.
4 PS to R. Sansom, 3 Mar. 1941, ML.
5 MS
6 PS to Sansoms, n.d. (31 Mar.), & 3 Mar. 1941, ML; & inf. from P. Lumley.
7 PS to Sansoms 6 April 1941, ML; & inf. from Barbara Whelan (née Phillips), Leeds, Sept., 1988.
8 26 April 1941, ML.
9 PS to R. Sansom, 3 April 1941.
10 'Early Poems', Sansom papers, ML; PS to C. Sansom, 6 April 1941, ML.
11 PS to C. Sansom, 24/6 April, 1941, ML.
12 MS
13 PS to C. Sansom, n.d. (end June 1941), ML.
14 MS
15 'Local Poet's First Published Work', 6 June 1941.
16 *Dragon*, June 1941; PS to C. Sansom, May 1941, ML.
17 PS to C. Sansom, n.d. (June 1941), ML.
18 'The Third Sister', synopsis for TV play, ML.
19 PS to Eric Edwards, 19 Aug. 1951, ML.
20 Autobiog. note, 1960, ML.
21 *In the Meantime* by Howard Spring, London, 1942.
22 PS to C. Sansom, n.d. (June 1941), ML.
23 PS to C. Sansom, 24 Sept. 1941, ML.
24 PS to C. Sansom, n.d. (June 1941), ML.
25 *Poetry Quarterly*, London, April, 1942.
26 PS to C. Sansom, 15 June 1941, ML; inf. from Peter Scott.
27 PS to C. Sansom, n.d., Bourne Hill (end July 1941), ML.
28 MS
29 Sansom papers, ML.
30 MS; inf. from Peter Scott & Geoffrey Ridehalgh.
31 MS
32 PS to J. Willey, 23 Oct. 1960, Morrow papers, ML.
33 *Muse*, p. 159.
34 Percy Avery, obit., *Skegness Standard*, 24 Nov. 1943, & *Burton Chronicle*, 11 Nov. 1943.
35 PS to Sansoms, n.d. (June 1942), ML.
36 PS to C. Sansom, 13 March 1942, ML; poem in Sansom papers, ML.
37 PS to Sansoms, n.d. (1 April 1942), ML.
38 PS to C. Sansom, 'Monday 10 p.m.', n.d. (July 1942), ML.
39 PS to C. Sansom, 'Wed.', n.d. (Nov. 1942), ML.
40 Pub. in *Bugle Blast*, ed. J. Aistrop & R. Moore, Allen & Unwin, 1944.
41 PS to C. Sansom, 12 Feb. 1943, ML.
42 MS
43 Inf. from J. Leasor (who was the man next in line).

Chapter 6 Falling in love with India

1 SR (the definition came from the critic, Walter Allen).
2 Ibid.
3 *Jewel*, p. 240.
4 PS to Valerie Meidlinger, 28 Dec. 1964, & to S. Stander, 31 Dec. 1975, ML.

5 This & the next quote from *Male Child*, p. 10.
6 Inf. from Olive Corben, Nov. 1987.
7 *Male Child*, p. 9.
8 *The Gorgeous East* by Rupert Croft-Cooke, W. H. Allen, 1965, p. 4.
9 *Warrior*, p. 9.
10 SR; account of OTS, Belgaum based on inf. from J. Leasor & Geoffrey Bide; & on 'Memoir of Belgaum', unpub. ms by Capt. R. P. Williams of 12 Platoon, B Coy.
11 *Division*, p. 224.
12 SR
13 Tms. ML.
14 Robin White in *Jewel*, p. 323.
15 *Warrior*, p. 15.
16 SR
17 SR
18 *The Gorgeous East*, op. cit., p. 27.
19 SR
20 PS to C. Sansom, 2 Jan. 1944, ML.
21 Paddy Love to PS, 29 Dec. 1971, ML.
22 J. Corben to Olive Gradon (afterwards Corben), 2 Jan. 1944; inf. from Mrs Corben, Nov. 1987.
23 Inf. from Peter Scott.
24 SR
25 *Johnnie Sahib*, p. 39.
26 PS to C. Sansom, 7 May 1944, ML.
27 Portrait (reproduced on back of jacket) in possession of Carol Scott.
28 PS to C. Sansom, 23 June 1944, ML.
29 C. Sansom's diary; Unity Theatre minutes, Sept. & Dec. 1943.
30 PS to C. Sansom, 28 Nov. 1945, ML.
31 *Muse*, p. 158; a single speech from this lost ms survives among the Sansom papers, ML.
32 *Four Jewish Plays*, ed. H. F. Rubinstein, Gollancz, 1948, p. 142.
33 *Selected Poems* by C. Sansom, op. cit., p. 171 (dated on ms by Clive).
34 PS to C. Sansom, n.d. (13 May 1944), ML.
35 Inf. from R. Sansom; C. Sansom to PS, 21 Feb. 1944, ML.
36 PS to C. Sansom, 14 May 1944, ML.
37 *Dorian Gray*, op. cit., p. 122 (the previous quote on p. 77).
38 Ibid, p. 38.
39 PS to F. Weinbaum, 26 Oct, 1975, ML
40 Inf. from Olive Corben.
41 MS
42 PS (quoting the Hollywood screenwriter, Jeffrey Dell) to C. Sansom, 6 Aug. 1944, ML.
43 Inf. from J. Leasor, July, 1986.
44 'The Appointment', autobiog, fragment, ML.
45 MS.
46 R. Sansom to author, 8 June, 1988.
47 *Selected Poems*, op. cit., p. 168.
48 R. Sansom to author, 26 Nov. 1987.
49 PS to C. Sansom, 14 Sept. 1944.
50 My account of the development of air supply in Burma based primarily on unpub. first-hand ms accounts by PS's friend, the founder of No 1 Coy, Col. T. R. (Tom) Newman (a letter dated 10 Sept. 1940, from RAMO HQ, Rangoon, and an essay, 'Notes on the History of air Supply, RIASC', 16 April 1949), National Army Museum, London. Also on inf. from Allen Hill, 10/04 Section, No. 1 Air Supply Coy.; from Col. Kenneth Capel Cure, CO No. 2 Air Supply Coy.; 'Air Supply in Burma' by Lt.-Col. J. R. L. Ramsey, *The Army Quarterly*, vol. 55, no. 1, Oct. 1947; *History of the Army Service Corps*, vol. 4, 1939–46, by Brig. V. J. Moharir, New Delhi, 1980, pp. 45–9.
51 PS to R. King, 17 July 1975, ML.
52 Ibid; identification confirmed by Allen Hill of 10/04 Platoon.
53 Ibid.
54 *Defeat Into Victory* by Field Marshal Sir William Slim, Cassell, 1956, p. 373.
55 Ibid, p. 242.
56 PS to J. Mellors, 16 May 1975, ML.
57 *Johnnie Sahib*, p. 68.
58 J. Corben to PS., 5–7 June 1946, ML.
59 PS to R. King, 17 July 1975, ML.
60 J. Corben to PS, 27 Aug. 1946, ML.
61 *The Road Past Mandalay* by John Masters, M. Joseph, 1961, p. 165; see also *Imphal. A Flower on Lofty Heights* by Lt.-Gen. Sir G. Evans & A. Brett-James, Macmillan 1962, p. 10 and *The Forgotten Major* by David Atkins, Toat Press, 1989.
62 Dustjacket blurb for *Johnnie Sahib*, Heinemann, 1968.
63 PS to J. Mellors, 16 May 1975, ML.
64 PS to N. Purkayastha, 29 April 1951, ML.
65 PS to R. King, 17 July 1975, ML.
66 *Defeat Into Victory*, op. cit., p. 3.
67 Note on envelope containing PS's campaign medals, addressed to his daughters.
68 Inf. from O. Corben.
69 PS to Penny Scott, 17 Mar. 1964.
70 Ibid.
71 *Pavilion*, p. 221.
72 Note on campaign medal envelope addressed to PS's daughters.
73 *Defeat Into Victory*, op. cit. p. 438.
74 PS to Dipali Nag, 12 July 1966, ML.
75 J. Corben to PS, 2 June 1946, ML.
76 PS to C. Sansom, 23 June 1944, ML.
77 *Johnnie Sahib*, p. 19.
78 Peter Green to author, Sept. 1987.
79 P. Green to author, 12 Nov. 87;

conversations with him in New Orleans, London and Texas.

80 B. V. N. Dass to P. S., 9 April 1957, ML.
81 PS to Penny Scott, 17 Mar. 1964.
82 B. V. N. Dass to PS 15 Mar. 1958, ML.
83 Interview with F. Ringold, *Nimrod*, op. cit.
84 Ibid.
85 PS to Dorothy Eden, 4 Oct. 1960, ML.
86 B. V. N. Dass to PS, 9 April 1958, ML.
87 PS to A. Dogan, 1 Feb. 1960, Morrow papers, ML.
88 PS to D. Eden, 4 Oct. 1960, ML.
89 Ibid.
90 SR
91 *Nimrod*, op. cit.
92 N. K. D. Purkayastha to PS 10 Aug. 1946, ML.
93 *Nimrod*, op. cit.
94 CL 7 Nov. 74; PS to W. G. Archer, 28 Sept. 74, ML.
95 SR
96 PS to C. Sansom, 24 July 1945, ML.
97 *Division*, p. 13.
98 *Muse*, p. 120.
99 *Division*, p. 31.
100 J. Corben to PS, n.d. (May 1946), ML.
101 Ibid.
102 *Muse*, p. 120.
103 N. Purkayastha to PS, 23 Feb. 1948, ML.
104 A. S. Khan to PS, n.d. (May 1946), ML.
105 Dr Nag Chaudhuri to author, Calcutta, Feb. 1988.
106 *Warrior*, p. 59.
107 PS to J. Mellors, 16 May, 1975, ML.
108 Ibid.

Chapter 7 Down the drains of destiny
1 *The Dogs of Peace*, W. H. Allen, 1973, p. 25.
2 J. Corben to PS, 19 April 1946, ML.
3 MS
4 MS; inf. from Penny Scott.
5 PS to C. Sansom, 24 July 1945.
6 *Muse*, p. 159.
7 Ibid.
8 PS to F. Stark, 14 Feb. 1976, ML & HRC.
9 Ms notebook, HRC.
10 *Muse*, p. 159.
11 MS
12 London *Evening Standard*, 1 Dec. 1945; & inf. from Toni Block.
13 J. Corben to PS, 16 Aug. 1946, ML.
14 C. Sansom to PS, n.d. (May 1945), ML.
15 *Muse*, p. 160; & PS to R. King, 17 July 1975, ML.
16 *Male Child*, p. 117.
17 Ibid, p. 22–3.
18 *Times* obit., 15 Nov. 1966; *My*

Testament by P. Baker, Calder, 1955.
19 'Paul Scott', *Bookseller*, 11 Mar. 1978.
20 *Inside the Forties* by Derek Stanford, Sidgwick & Jackson, 1977, p. 87.
21 *Bookseller*, op. cit.
22 'Paul Scott remembered' by R. Gant, *The Making of The Jewel in the Crown*, Granada, 1983.
23 *Muse*, p. 160.
24 'PS remembered', op. cit.
25 *The Flowering Moment* by C. W. Gardiner, Grey Walls Press, 1949, p. 64.
26 'The Beggarman's Lute' by P. Baker, Resurgam Younger Poets, No. 1, Favil Press, 1940.
27 *Flowering Moment*, op. cit., p. 17.
28 Ibid. p. 42.
29 'Grey Walls Press' by Alan Smith, *Antiquarian Book Monthly Review*, London, Sept. 1986.
30 CL, 28 Mar. 1974; 'The Octopus of Love', unpub. autobiography by Wrey Gardiner in the possession of Alan Smith.
31 PS to R. Gant, 24 Oct. 1970, ML; & inf. from R. Gant.
32 *The Life of Dylan Thomas* by C. Fitzgibbon, Dent, 1965, p. 339.
33 C. Sansom's diary, 9 July 1943.
34 *Flowering Moment*, op. cit., p. 70.
35 Ibid, p. 78.
36 *The Dark Thorn* by C. W. Gardiner, Grey Walls Press, 1946, p. 196.
37 Ibid.
38 *Flowering Moment*, op. cit. p. 20.
39 'Octopus of Love', op. cit. p. 369.
40 *Male Child* ms notebook, HRC.
41 PS to F. Stark, 14 Feb. 1976, ML.
42 ML
43 N. Purkayastha to PS, 10 Aug. 1946, ML.
44 This & the next two quotes from J. Corben to PS, n.d. (June 1946), ML.
45 PS to F. Stark, 14 Feb. 1976, ML.
46 Inf. from Olive Corben.
47 J. Corben to PS, 27 Aug. 46, ML.
48 N. Purkayastha to PS, 23 Feb. 1948, ML.
49 'Paul Scott', *Bookseller*, 11 Mar. 1978.
50 PS to C. Sansom, 5 July 1947.
51 MS
52 *Male Child*, p. 126.
53 This & the next quote from *Male Child*, p. 131.
54 Inf. from J. Wiener's secretary, Barbara Woodgates, June 1987.
55 Inf. from Judi Dooling, May 1987.
56 Autobiog. note, 1960, ML.
57 PS to C. Sansom, 15 May, 1948, ML.
58 PS to C. Sansom, n.d. (June/July 1948), ML.
59 PS to C. Sansom, 15 May, 1948, ML.
60 Ibid.

61 PS to C. Sansom, n.d. (June/July 1948), ML.
62 *Muse*, p. 161.
63 PS to C. Sansom, n.d. (June/July 1948), ML.
64 Autobiog. note, 1960, ML.
65 PS to Sally Scott, 18 Feb. 1968, ML.
66 PS to J. Wiener, 13 July 1951, ML.
67 PS to Sally Scott, 18 Feb. 1968, ML.
68 'Paul Scott', *New Fiction*, April 1978.
69 Inf. from R. Gant; 'Octopus of Love' op. cit.
70 'Paul Scott', *New Fiction*, April 1978.
71 This & the next quote from *Time Out of Life* by P. Baker, Heinemann 1961, pp. 249 & 220.
72 *My Testament*, op. cit., p. 247; 'Primrose Path of an ex M.P.' by Peter Earle. *News of the World*, 20 Nov. 1966.
73 This & the next 3 quotes from *Muse*, pp. 161–2.

Chapter 8   A prince among agents
1 Autobiog. note 1960, ML.
2 *Muse*, p. 162.
3 PS to D. McWhinnie, 2 June 1960, ML.
4 *Muse*, p. 163.
5 Inf. from Sally Scott.
6 Inf. from Sheila Wright.
7 *Muse*, p. 162.
8 PS to J. Wiener, 28 Nov. 1959, ML.
9 PS to C. Sansom, 5 July 1947, ML.
10 PS to Sally Scott, 18 Feb. 1968, ML.
11 Inf. from Giles Gordon.
12 Account based on inf. from Maurice Temple Smith, May 1987; & from Christina & Donald Morley, July 1987.
13 DHA (it seems likely that the trip to Paris celebrated this triumph, rather than the previous year's disaster, the 2 events being telescoped in Paul's recollection).
14 PS to C. Sansom, 24 Mar. 1951, ML.
15 PS to R. King, 17 July 1975, ML; PS to H. F. Rubinstein, 12 Oct. 1951, ML.
16 J. Wiener to PS, 16 July 1951, ML.
17 D. J. Enright to author, 2 Sept. 1989; & DHA.
18 DHA
19 *Literary Gent* by D. Higham, Cape 1978, p. 212.
20 DHA
21 Inf. from J. Leasor.
22 DHA
23 P. Green interviewed by PS, *Books & Bookmen*, June 1962.
24 'Paul Scott remembered' by M. M. Kaye, *The Making of The Jewel in the Crown*, Granada 1983.
25 Ibid (M. M. Kaye dates this exchange to their first meeting, but according to DHA correspondence she did not realise PS's identity until 1956).
26 PS to G. Hanley, 19 Nov. 1953, ML.
27 Inf. from Maurice Temple Smith, May 1987.
28 Jacqueline Korn.
29 Mary Patchett to PS, 17 Dec. 1959, DHA.
30 P. Green to PS, 23 June 1956, DHA.
31 Diana Petre to author.
32 Helen Higham to author.
33 PS to J. Wiener, 15 June 1952, ML.
34 PS to Lee Bender of Doubleday, 20 Mar. 1953, ML.
35 J. Wiener to PS, 29 Nov. 1951, ML.
36 Ibid.
37 PS to Cyril Butcher, 9 June 1952, ML.
38 Inf. from Toni Block, July 1987.
39 ML
40 J. Wiener to PS 16 June 1952, ML.
41 D. Jerrold to PS, 16 Dec. 1952, ML; & PS to R. Miller, Eyre & Spottiswoode, 11 Nov. 1952 ML.
42 PS to F. Morley, 22 Mar. 1953, ML.
43 PS to F. Morley, 13 & 30 Jan. 1953, ML (the phrase comes from Kipling's verses about his birthplace, Bombay: 'Surely in toil or fray/ Under an alien sky/ Comfort it to say/ "Of no mean city am I" ').
44 Ivan von Auw of Harold Ober Associates to PS, 22 Aug. 1955, ML.
45 *Alien Sky* p. 50.
46 Ibid p. 142.
47 PS to F. Morley, 13 Jan. 1953, ML.
48 PS to Morchard Bishop (Oliver Stoner), 26 Sept. 1953, ML.
49 *Alien Sky*, p. 150.
50 PS to J. Wiener, 13 July 1951, ML.
51 *Johnnie Sahib*, draft dustjacket blurb, HRC.
52 PS to M. Bishop, 3 Oct. 1953, ML.
53 PS to Katherine Farrer, 25 June 1954, DHA; & to C. Sansom, 15 June 1954, HRC.
54 MS
55 Autobiog. piece, 1960, ML.
56 PS to C. & S. Scott, 31 July, 1976.
57 PS to Penny Scott, 29 Jan. 1969.
58 MS
59 PS to C. Scott, 24 Feb. 1969.
60 PS to Lalage Green, 6 Oct. 1954, DHA.
61 E. M. Almedingen to PS, 4 Oct. 1957, ML; the following account based on her 2 vols. of autobiography, *Tomorrow Will Come*, Bodley Head 1941, & *Within the Harbour*, Bodley Head 1950; & inf. from Frances Pilkington, Aug. 1987.
62 PS to Ivan von Auw, 22 July 1959, DHA.
63 P. Watt to E. M. Almedingen, 23 April 1954, DHA.

64 Conversation with M. Patchett, May 1986.
65 M. Patchett to PS, 30 July 1955, DHA.
66 M. Patchett to PS, 9 Feb. 1957, DHA.
67 Conversation with M. Patchett, May 1986.
68 PS to G. Fielding (Alan Barnsley), 8 Nov. 1954, HRC.
69 *Inside the Forties*, op. cit. p. 205. Correspondence with M. Spark in DHA & ML.
70 P. Green to PS, 16 July 1958, ML; & review in *Daily Telegraph* 9 Mar. 1956.
71 K. Farrer to PS, 14 April 1956, HRC.
72 F. Morley to PS, 14 April 1955, ML.
73 *Male Child* ms HRC.
74 PS to M. Bishop, 5 Mar. 1956, ML.
75 Ms notebook, HRC.
76 *Male Child*, p. 196.
77 Ms notebook, HRC.
78 *Male Child*, p. 78; the next quote from p. 18.
79 PS to F. Morley, 15 May 1955.
80 PS to M. Bishop, 5 Mar. 1956, ML.
81 *Male Child*, pp. 135–7.

Chapter 9   Something of Micawber
1 PS to F. Morley, 15 May 1955, ML.
2 PS to D. Wilson, BBC TV, 1 Feb. & 13 Mar. 1956, ML, D. Wilson to PS 4 April 1956, ML; 'Colonel's Lady' synopsis, dated 31 Jan. 1956, ML; BBC radio script of *Sahibs and Memsahibs* at HRC.
3 PS to John Bright-Holmes, Eyre & Spottiswoode, 3 Feb. 1958, ML.
4 D. Wilson to PS, 6 Sept. 1956, ML.
5 PS to D. Wilson, 19 Mar. 1956, ML.
6 P. Green to PS, 16 July 1958, ML.
7 *Warrior*, p. 67.
8 Ibid, p. 118.
9 PS to Adèle Dogan, Morrow, 21 July 1957, ML.
10 M. Hamilton to PS., 27 July 1958, DHA; inf. from M. Hamilton, & Masters' biographer John Clay.
11 D. Higham to Ivan von Auw, 29 May 1957, DHA.
12 Figure supplied by Bruce Hunter, David Higham Associates.
13 Inf. from Bill Wheeler, Tulsa, Oklahoma.
14 G. Hanley to PS 20 Oct. 1957 & PS to G. Hanley, n.d. (May 1957), HRC; this account of their friendship based on correspondence at HRC & ML.
15 PS to G. Hanley, 6 May 1961, ML.
16 G. Hanley to PS, 8 May 1961, ML.
17 G. Hanley to PS, 8 Feb. 1961, ML.
18 G. Hanley to PS, 29 Aug. & 18 Jan. 1957, HRC.
19 Draft of publicity material for J. Bright-

Holmes, Eyre & Spottiswoode, ML.
20 PS to T. Hobson, 29 Sept. 1966, ML.
21 T. Hobson to PS, 27 July 1957, ML.
22 'Memoir of Paul Scott', unpub. ms by J. Willey for author.
23 F. Phillips to PS, 9 July 1957, ML.
24 E. M. Almedingen to PS, 31 Mar. 1958.
25 G. Hanley to PS 29 Mar. 1958 & n.d. (April), HRC.
26 A. Dogan to PS, 25 July 1957, ML.
27 PS to A. Dogan, 21 July 1957, ML.
28 A. Dogan to PS, 25 July, 1957.
29 PS to A. Dogan, 21 July 1957, ML.
30 Ibid.
31 PS to C. Sansom, 22 June 1958. ML.
32 *Pavilion*, p. 21.
33 Ibid, p. 32.
34 Ibid, p. 33.
35 Ibid, p. 31; the next 2 quotes from pp. 31 & 33.
36 G. Hanley to PS, 25 Mar. 1972, ML.
37 *Pavilion*, p. 30; the next 2 quotes from pp. 37 & 38.
38 PS to John Bright-Holmes, ML (the *Pavilion* ms at HRC is dated '4 Jan. 1958. 1st start 10.10 a.m.').
39 G. Fielding file, DHA; PS to P. Green, 11 July 1958, ML.
40 PS to G. Hanley, 29 April 1961, ML.
41 PS to G. Hanley, 6 May 1961, ML.
42 PS to J. Willey, Morrow, 22 Oct. & 3 Oct. 1960; inf. from M. Temple Smith.
43 PS to M. Bishop, 30 March 1958, ML.
44 *Division* p. 156.
45 PS to G. Hanley, 29 April 1961, ML.
46 'Paul Scott remembered', *The Making of The Jewel in the Crown*, Granada, 1983.
47 PS to C. Sansom, 22 June 1958, ML.
48 PS to A. Warne, Maw, Ellis, Warne, 20 Nov. 1958, ML.
49 PS to E. M. Almedingen 26 Sept. 1958, HRC.
50 M. Patchett to PS, n.d. (April 1956), ML.
51 PS to P. Green, 13 May 1958, ML; E. M. Almedingen to PS, 8 June 1958, ML.
52 *Muse*, p. 250.
53 'The Appointment', ms fragment, ML.
54 DHA
55 Interview with F. Ringold, *Nimrod*, op. cit.
56 *Pavilion* ms. HRC.
57 P. Green to PS, 16 July 1958, ML.
58 J. Willey to PS, 29 Aug. 1958, ML.
59 MS
60 Preliminary notes for *Male Child*, ms notebook, HRC.
61 *Male Child*, p. 61.
62 Phyllis Young, *Yorkshire Post*.
63 *George Eliot* by Gordon S. Haight, OUP 1968, p. 213; PS also marked passages on pp. 214 & 215.

64 PS to P. Green, 19 Feb. 1959, DHA.
65 D. Marston to PS, 28 May 1974, ML.
66 PS to J. Bright-Holmes, 3 Feb. 1958, ML.
67 P. Green to PS, 16 July 1958, ML.
68 PS to M. Bishop, 5 Mar. 1956, ML.
69 P. Green to PS, 16 July 1958, ML.
70 P. Green to author.
71 *Pavilion*, p. 59.
72 M. Spark to PS, 5 Aug. 1958, ML.
73 *Warrior*, p. 34.
74 *Pavilion* ms ('3rd Start, 11 a.m. Sun 7 Dec. 1958'). HRC.
75 *Pavilion*, p. 183.
76 Ibid, p. 230.
77 *Pavilion* ms, dated 6 July 1959, HRC; PS confirmed this view to A. S. Khan, 30 Dec. 1974, ML.
78 PS to P. Green, 18 July 1959, ML; & M. Temple Smith to PS, 20 July 1959, ML.
79 Storm Jameson to PS 20 Aug. 1960, ML; & E. Sitwell to PS, 23 June 1960, ML.
80 A. Dogan to PS, 1 Sept. 1959, ML.
81 *Pavilion*, p. 12 (last 2 sentences, in ms at HRC, deleted from published text).
82 MS
83 Inf. from D. Bolt, Nov. 1989.
84 *Pavilion* ms, '3rd Start', HRC.
85 J. Willey to PS, 25 Aug. 1959, ML.
86 M. Temple Smith to PS 14 Oct. 1959, ML.
87 A. Dogan to PS, 1 Sept. 1959, ML.
88 PS to M. Temple Smith, 25 Jan. 1960.
89 I. von Auw to D. Higham, 15 Jan. 1960, ML.
90 PS to M. Temple Smith, 28 July, 1961.
91 PS to M. Temple Smith, 25 Sept. 1959.
92 PS to E. Cadell, 22 Oct. 1968, ML.
93 Inf. from P. Green.
94 *Warrior*, p. 57.
95 PS to Arthur C. Clarke, 21 Feb. 1955, DHA.
96 J. Willey to PS, 18 Sept. 1959, ML.
97 D. Higham to PS, 3 April 1960, ML.
98 PS to G. Hanley, 29 April 1961, ML.
99 PS to J. Willey, 28 Aug. 1959, ML.
100 PS to C. Sansom, 25 July 1966, ML.
101 Conversation with Kay Dick.
102 J. Braine to PS, 21 Oct. 1959, DHA.
103 PS to K. Dick, 13 Dec. 1958, HRC.
104 F. Clifford (Arthur Thompson) to PS, 29 Nov. 1958, HRC.

Chapter 10   A long straight look in the mirror

1 PS to M. West, 8 July 1960, ML.
2 PS to K. Dick, 14 June 1960, HRC.
3 PS to C. W. Gardiner, 20 Aug. 1960, ML.
4 'The Octopus of Love', op. cit.
5 PS to C. W. Gardiner, 27 Aug. 1960. ML
6 *The Flowering Moment*, 1949, p. 36.
7 Quoted by Derek Stanford, *Inside the Forties*, op. cit. p. 95.
8 PS to K. Dick, 5 May 1960, HRC, & to J. Willey, 9 May 1960, ML.
9 PS to C. W. Gardiner, 13 Sept. 1961, ML.
10 ML
11 Tms draft at ML.
12 PS to A. Dogan, 14 June 1960, ML.
13 PS to I. von Auw, 13 May 1959, DHA.
14 PS to L. Drucker, 24 May 1972, ML.
15 PS to J. Willey, 26 April 1960, ML.
16 PS to L. Drucker, 24 May 1972, ML.
17 Interview by Venetia Murray, *Books & Bookmen*, Mar. 1959.
18 *Books & Bookmen*, Oct. 1960.
19 PS to M. Spark, 13 July 1960, ML.
20 PS to F. Clifford (Arthur Thompson), 12 Sept. 1960, ML.
21 PS to R. Mark, 13 Sept. 1960, ML.
22 PS to M. Temple Smith, 11 June 1960.
23 PS to J. Davenport, Sept. 1960, ML.
24 Victor Weybright, J. Willey's memoir of PS.
25 DHA
26 PS to J. Willey, 30 Oct. 1960, ML.
27 PS to P. Green, 1 Mar. 1961, ML; actual figures from Bruce Hunter of D. Higham Associates.
28 Correspondence with R. Mason, autumn 1960, ML.
29 PS to F. Clifford, 24 Nov. 1960, ML.
30 PS to G. Hanley, n.d. (Aug. 1960), ML.
31 PS to P. Green, 18 Sept. 1960, ML.
32 PS to D. Higham, 24 Aug. 1961, ML.
33 PS to J. Willey, 22 Oct. 1960, ML.
34 Inf. from Kay Dick, who put this affair into her novel *The Shelf* Hamish Hamilton, 1984, p. 3.
35 PS to K. Dick, 29 Oct. 1960, HRC; further correspondence at ML.
36 PS to A. Dogan, 5 Mar. 1960.
37 PS to J. Willey, 1 Mar. 1961, ML
38 MS
39 E. M. Almedingen to PS, 6 Oct. ML.
40 PS to E. M. Almedingen, 7 Oct. 1960.
41 E. M. Almedingen to PS, 13 Dec. 1960, ML.
42 E. M. Almedingen to PS, n.d. (Oct. 1960), ML.
43 Inf. from Frances Pilkington, in whom E. M. Almedingen confided her anxieties about PS at the time.
44 PS to K. Dick, 13 Nov. 1960, HRC.
45 *Birds*, p. 147.
46 *Muse*, p. 18.
47 PS to K. Dick, 8 July, 1960, ML.
48 *Muse*, p. 18.
49 Ibid.

50 *Muse*, p. 17.
51 PS to C. Sansom, 22 June 1958, ML.
52 SR
53 PS to G. Hanley, 17 Mar. 1961, ML.
54 PS to J. Willey, 17 Mar. 1961, ML.
55 PS to K. Dick, 24 Mar. 1961, HRC.
56 PS to J. Willey, 26 Aug. 1960, ML.
57 PS to J. Willey, 27 Mar. 1961, ML.
58 Cancelled ms draft, HRC.
59 ML.
60 J. Willey to PS, 1 June 1961.
61 PS to J. Willey, 7 June 1961, ML.
62 PS to K. Dick, 11 July 1961, HRC.
63 PS to Magnus Lindberg, 25 Mar. 1963, ML.
64 Preface to *Funeral*.
65 This & the next quote from PS to G. Hanley, n.d. (Aug. 1961), ML.
66 P. Green to PS, 24 April 1963, ML.
67 PS to J. Willey, 27 Sept. 1961, HRC.
68 PS to A. Dogan, 27 Oct. 1961, ML.
69 *Bender*, p. 217.
70 PS to A. Dogan, 25 July 1961, ML.
71 PS to Rosaleen Whateley, 27 Oct. 1974, ML.
72 PS to D. Highham, 28 July 1961, ML; & M. Temple Smith to PS 24 Aug. 1961, ML.
73 PS to D. Higham, 2 & 21 Feb., ML.
74 *Birds*, p. 257.
75 PS to J. Willey, 27 Sept. 1961, HRC; 'Careerist' ms at ML; it was subtitled 'The Marriage' (PS to J. Willey, 3 Oct. 62, ML), subsequently shelved, & taken up again 12 Jan. 1977 as 'The Careerists, Mango Rain, or, Married with Two Children', ms at ML.
76 PS to Muriel Spark, 9 Nov. 1961, ML.
77 *Thirty Nine Writers of Hampstead*, London, 1962.
78 P. Green to PS, 27 Feb. 1960, ML.
79 Penny Scott to R. Gant, 21 Aug. 1960, DHA.
80 PS to D. Higham, 28 Sept. 1960, HRC; further correspondence in DHA.
81 PS to J. Willey, 26 Oct. 1961, ML.
82 PS to Muriel Spark, 9 Nov. 1961.
83 PS to M. Spark, 5, 17 & 21 Oct. 1961, ML.
84 PS to M. Spark, 9 Nov. 1961, ML.
85 PS to D. Higham, 2 Feb. 1961, ML.
86 *Corrida*, p. 79.
87 Steve Wood, Tulsa class notes.
88 *Corrida*, p. 94.
89 *Dorian Gray* op. cit., p. 131.
90 *Pavilion*, p. 90.
91 Inf. from Sally Dennison, Tulsa, Oklahoma.
92 MS
93 R. Mark to PS, Whit Sunday, 28 July & 29 Oct. 1961, ML.
94 R. Mark to PS, 21 Aug. & 16 Sept. 1960, ML.
95 R. Mark to PS, 28 Mar. 1961.
96 PS to Gladys Rocke, 5 Jan. 1964, ML.
97 Unpub. memoir.
98 PS to J. Willey, 11 Nov. 1961, ML.
99 Unpub. memoir.
100 PS to J. Willey, 11 Nov. 1961, ML.
101 Inf. from M. Temple Smith.
102 'Paul Scott', *New Fiction*, April 1978.
103 K. Dick to PS, 16 April 1963, ML; & P. Green to PS, 24 April 1963, ML.
104 E. M. Almedingen to PS, 18 May 1962.
105 This & the next quote from *Bender*, pp. 209 & 220.
106 Inf. from F. Pilkington.
107 PS to J. Willey, 4 Dec. 1962, ML.
108 PS to D. Higham, 21 April 1963, HRC.
109 PS to D. Higham, 14 June 1962, ML.
110 PS to G. Hanley, 29 April 1961, ML.
111 PS to M. Spark 18 Jan. & 25 Feb., M. Spark to PS 21 Feb. 1962, ML.
112 Vivien Stuart (pen name Alex Stuart) to PS, 3 Sept. 1964, ML.
113 PS to W. Smith, 13 Dec. 1962, ML.
114 See 'Careerist' ms, HRC; PS to J. Willey, 7 June & 3 Oct. 1962, ML.
115 PS to J. Willey, 4 Dec. 1962, ML.
116 PS to D. Bolt, 5 Dec. 1961, ML.
117 PS to P. Green, 25 April 1963, ML.
118 PS to M. Patchett, n.d. (1962), ML.
119 PS to M. Preston 28 July 1963, DHA.
120 PS to R. Mark, 25 April 1963 & to G. Hanley, 25 Aug. 1962, ML.
121 *Birds*, p. 187.
122 PS to Marjorie Harris, Swanwick Writers School, 26 Sept. 1963, ML.
123 PS to Penny Scott, 22 Oct. 1963.
124 PS to E. M. Almedingen, 9 Nov. 1963, ML.
125 See Ruby Miller of Eyre & Spottiswoode to PS, 13 Jan. 1953, ML; & *Birds* ms notebook, HRC.
126 PS to Nicholas G. Browning, 12 May 1965, ML.
127 PS to R. Gant, 4 Jan. 1964, ML.
128 *Corrida*, p. 82.
129 PS to J. Willey, 19 Sept. 1962, & to C. Sansom, 2 Dec. 1962, ML.
130 PS to R. Gant, 4 June 1964, ML; *Bender* notebook at HRC.
131 *Corrida*, p. 109.
132 Inf. from K. Dick.
133 PS to D. Bolt, 5 Dec. 1961, ML.
134 *Muse*, p. 91–2.
135 PS to Chas. A. Hout, 1 Dec. 1964, ML.
136 *Corrida*, p. 82.

Chapter 11 Passage to India

1 Indian spiral notebook, begun 25 Feb. 1964, ML.
2 PS to M. Hamilton, 15 Jan. 1964, ML.
3 *Jewel*, p. 63.
4 PS to D. Ganapathy 10 Feb. 1975, ML; this account bsed on inf. from Mrs Ganapathy, Bombay, Feb. 1988.
5 D. Ganapathy to PS, 10 Mar. 1965, ML.
6 'Paul Scott & India', unpublished memoir by Martin Pick.
7 Spiral notebook, ML.
8 *E. M. Forster* by P. N. Furbank, vol. i, Secker & Warburg 1977, p. 230.
9 See 'After Marabar. A Post-Forsterian View', *Muse*.
10 *Division*, p. 33; identification confirmed by PS to D. Ganapathy, 17 June 1975, ML.
11 'India', tms by PS, ML.
12 Spiral notebook, ML.
13 Draft review of *The Sweet Vendor* by R. K. Narayan, 1967, ML.
14 PS to Penny Scott, 1 Mar. 1964; further accounts of this incident in notebook & 'India' tms, ML; & in *Muse*, p. 98 ff.
15 *Jewel*, pp. 157–8.
16 Ibid, p. 65.
17 Inf. from D. Ganapathy.
18 PS to Penny Scott, 3 Mar. 1964; this account based on Mrs Scott's letters.
19 'India' tms, ML.
20 Spiral notebook, ML.
21 Account of this encounter based on PS's letters to Penny Scott; notebook & 'India' notes, ML; & 'Enoch Sahib' in *Muse*.
22 *Muse*, p. 99.
23 N. Dass to PS, 28 Jan. 1964, ML.
24 M. Hamilton to PS, 12 Jan. 1964, ML.
25 This & the next quote from spiral notebook, ML.
26 N. Dass to PS, 2 May 1958, ML.
27 N. Dass to PS, 1 Sept. 1948, ML.
28 Draft for abandoned article, 'Sahib's Face' (see PS to Jean Leroy of D. Higham Associates, 14 Sept. 1966), tms, ML.
29 'India' tms, ML.
30 *Muse*, p. 100.
31 'Sahib's Face', ML.
32 'India' tms, ML.
33 'Sahib's Face', ML.
34 Ibid.
35 Ibid.
36 Ibid.
37 Ibid.
38 Ibid.
39 Ibid.
40 PS to Penny Scott, 12 Mar. 1964.
41 PS to Penny Scott, 20 Mar. 1964

42 *Muse*, p. 102.
43 PS to Penny Scott, 15 Mar. 1964; further accounts in PS to D. Olding, 7 April, 1966, & to J. Willey, 18 April 1964, ML.
44 This & the next quote from PS to Penny Scott, 17 Mar. 1964.
45 PS to D. Olding, 7 April 1966, ML.
46 Ibid.
47 Ibid, & PS to Penny Scott, 13 Mar. 1964.
48 PS to D. Olding, 7 April 1966, ML.
49 *Jewel*, p. 220.
50 PS to D. Olding, 7 April 1966, ML.
51 Ibid.
52 *Muse*, p. 102.
53 PS to Penny Scott, 21 March, 1964.
54 PS to D. Olding, 7 April 1966, ML; & 'Enoch Sahib' in *Muse*.
55 PS to Penny Scott, 21 Mar. 1964.
56 *Muse*, p. 102.
57 PS to Penny Scott, 8 Mar. 1964; M. Felton obit. by PS, *Times*, 5 Mar. 1970.
58 *Muse*, p. 100.
59 PS to J. Leroy of D. Higham Associates, 9 April 1966, ML.
60 PS to Penny Scott, 26 Mar. 1964.
61 PS to Hugh Palmer, 21 Dec. 1975, ML.
62 *Jewel*, preliminary notes in blue foolscap notebook, HRC.
63 PS to Rosaleen Whateley, 3 Oct. 1964, ML.
64 Account based on conversations in Calcutta in 1988 with Neil Ghosh's sister, Nilima Dutta, & on his papers in her possession.
65 M. Hamilton to PS, 26 April 1964, ML.
66 Inf. from Ghosh papers, & from Nilima Dutta.
67 Inf. from Dipali Nag; account based on conversations with her in Calcutta, Mar. 1988.
68 PS to D. Nag, 6 Feb. & 12 May 1965, ML.
69 *Jewel*, p. 69.
70 PS's letters home suggest that Dr Nag was present but he and his wife confirm he was not.
71 *Jewel*, p. 64.
72 *Muse*, p. 58.
73 *Muse*, p. 59; PS to D. M. Burjorjee, 2 Aug. 1974, ML; PS to Penny Scott, 22 Mar. 1964.
74 D. Nag to PS, 1 Feb. 1965, ML.
75 Draft at ML.
76 PS to F. Weinbaum, 31 Dec. 1975, ML
77 PS to Penny Scott, 4 April 1964; & to J. Willey, 14 April 1964, ML.
78 This & the next quote from PS to Penny Scott, 5 & 7 April 1964.
79 *Jewel*, p. 131.

80 *Muse*, p. 80.
81 Account based on a private interview
    recorded in Calcutta in April 1988 by
    Pearson Surita with N. Ghosh's
    contemporary, Pram Prasad, who
    became chairman of Bird & Co. in
    1965.
82 Inf. from Armita Ghosh, Calcutta, Mar.
    1988.
83 Inf. from D. Nag.
84 PS to W. Olins, 1 Aug. 1975, ML; he
    said the same to M. Hamilton, & to his
    students in Tulsa in 1976.
85 *Division*, p. 291.
86 *Jewel*, preliminary notes in notebook,
    April 1964, HRC.
87 *Muse* pp. 60 & 62.
88 *Division*, p. 301.
89 PS interviewed by J. Tallmer, *New York
    Post*, 18 Oct. 1975.
90 *Jewel*, p. 132.
91 PS to Penny Scott, 8 April 1964.
92 Inf. from Dr Nag Chaudhuri.
93 *Jewel*, p. 137.
94 *Muse*, p. 59.

Chapter 12   The end of the party and the
beginning of the washing up
1   Attached to preliminary notes for *Jewel*,
    HRC.
2   *Muse*, p. 60.
3   See their respective correspondences
    with PS, ML.
4   PS to M. Felton, 27 Oct. 1964, ML.
5   *Muse*, p. 30.
6   This & the next quote, ibid. p. 37.
7   PS to D. Nag, 27 Oct. 1964, ML; & to
    M. Felton, 17 Mar. 1966, ML.
8   SR
9   Steve Wood, Tulsa class notes.
10 ML
11 'Conversation with PS' by F. Ringold,
    Nimrod, 1978, op. cit.
12 *Division*, p. 272.
13 *Muse*, p. 119.
14 PS to S. Jameson, 18 Feb. 1975, ML.
15 '*L'Amibiase. Quelques renseignements
    à l'usage de mes malades*', Paris, 1965,
    by Dr G. E. Farréras, & '*La Dysenterie
    amibienne*', Farréras' notes for patients,
    tms supplied by R. Gant.
16 Inf. from J. Leake, Tulsa, Oklahoma;
    also from R. Gant, who has PS's
    treatment notes (emetine derives from a
    S. American tree bark; conessine was
    sold in France in the 1960s under the
    brand names Roquessine or
    Néoroquessine).
17 'Remembering Paul Scott', *Making of
    The Jewel in the Crown*, op. cit.
18 See PS to the Sec., London School of

Hygiene & Tropical Medicine, 13 Dec.
    1968, ML.
19 *Jewel* notebook, HRC.
20 PS to R. Gant's mother-in-law, Irène
    Legrand, 20 June 1964, ML; & to N.
    Dass June & 23 Sept. 1964.
21 Terence Kilmartin to David Farrer of
    Secker & Warburg, 26 Nov. 1964, ML.
22 PS to D. Ganapathy, 26 Nov. 1964,
    ML.
23 PS to J. Leroy, D. Higham Associates,
    19 Mar. 1965, ML.
24 J. Willey to PS, 19 July, 1965, ML.
25 *Scorpion*, p. 60, *Towers*, p. 25,
    Division, pp. 25 & 156.
26 *L'Amibiase*, op. cit.
27 *Muse*, p. 27.
28 PS to Margery Vosper, 5 Mar. 1966,
    ML.
29 PS to M. Hamilton, 16 April, 1966,
    ML.
30 PS to Penny Scott, 14 Mar. & 12 Mar.
    1964.
31 PS to D. Nag, 19 May 1964, ML.
32 Inf. from Mrs H. N. Singh, Delhi, Mar.
    1988.
33 PS to F. Pridmore, 1 Sept. 1966, ML.
34 PS to G. Hanley, 10 Nov. 1965, ML.
35 *Muse*, p. 64.
36 Vivien Stuart (pen name Alex Stuart) to
    PS, 12 Mar. 1965, Swanwick Writers
    School, ML; further inf. on the school
    from its secretary, Marjorie Harris.
37 V. Stuart to PS, 21 Sept. 1964, & 8
    Mar. 1965, ML.
38 V. Stuart to PS, 21 Aug. 1965, ML.
39 PS to R. Mason, 1 Sept. 1965, ML.
40 *Muse*, p. 28.
41 Ibid, p. 34.
42 Ibid, p. 31.
43 *Muse*, p. 51.
44 This & the next 2 quotes from *Muse*,
    pp. 60–1.
45 Ibid, p. 62.
46 Ibid, p. 64.
47 D. Ganapathy to PS, 27 April, 19 Oct.,
    27 Nov. 1964, ML.
48 D. Ganapathy to PS, 11 Aug. 1965,
    ML.
49 PS to D. Ganapathy, 11 Sept. 1965,
    ML (passage beg. 'I have decided to
    leave Rawalpindi . . .', *Jewel*, p. 444).
50 PS to D. Ganapathy, 18 & 30 Sept., 11
    Oct. 1965, ML.
51 PS to Richard Sheed, 14 Mar. 1976,
    ML.
52 PS to J. Willey, 2 April 1966, ML, & PS
    to M. Felton, 15 April, 1966, ML.
53 PS to D. Ganapathy, 2 April, & D.
    Ganapathy to PS 7 April, 1966, ML.
54 PS, Heinemann publicity note, Oct.

1966, & PS to J. Willey, 6 July 1966, ML.
55 PS to D. Higham, 31 Oct. 1965, ML; also PS to D. Higham 29 Sept., & to P. Green. 26 Oct. 1965, ML.
56 PS to M. Lindberg, 23 Sept. 1966, ML.
57 D. Ganapathy to PS, 25 July 1966, ML.
58 PS to D. Ganapathy, 20 July, & to D. Nag, 27 July 1966, ML.
59 M. Hamilton to PS, 26 Sept. 1966, ML.
60 D. Ganapathy to PS, 2 Oct. 1966.
61 PS to D. Ganapathy, 6 July 1966.
62 Inf. from Sally Scott.
63 PS to P. Green, 15 April, 1963, ML.
64 D. Ganapathy to PS, 9 May 1966, ML.
65 PS to M. Lindberg, 26 July & 8 Oct. 1966, ML.
66 MS
67 PS to J. Willey, 18 Oct. 1967, ML.
68 PS to M. Harris, Swanwick, 1 Sept. 1967, ML.
69 PS to J. Willey, 17 Nov. 1967, ML.
70 PS to D. Nag, 9 Jan. 1968, ML.
71 PS to D. Olding, 14 Feb. 1968, ML.
72 PS to F. Pridmore, Good Friday, 1968, ML.
73 PS to M. Hamilton, 20 Dec. 1967, ML.
74 PS to E. M. Almedingen, 29 April 1961, ML.
75 PS's cat-sitting instructions to Cecilia Brown, 23 Aug. 1961, ML.
76 PS to Bruce Hunter, D. Higham Associates, 15 June 1968, ML.
77 PS to J. Willey, 9 May 1966, ML.
78 Unpub. memoir of PS.
79 Both mss at ML (an alternative draft of 'Mango Rain' in possession of B. Hunter, D. Higham Associates).
80 PS to J. Willey, 14 Feb. 1968, ML.
81 *Scorpion*, p. 54.
82 This & the next quote from *Scorpion*, pp. 341 & 150.
83 M. Lindberg to PS, 19 Jan. 1970, ML.
84 PS to J. Willey, 4 Dec. 1962, ML.
85 J. Willey to PS, 5 Feb. 1968, ML.
86 PS to P. Green, 14 Oct. 1967, ML.
87 PS to D. Higham, 14 Oct. 1968, ML; further inf. from B. Hunter, D. Higham Associates.
88 *Muse*, p. 19.
89 PS to J. Willey, 11 Oct., & to D. Higham, 6 July, 1968, ML.
90 This & the next quote, PS to Penny Scott, 24 & 25 Jan. 1969.
91 PS to D. Ganapathy, 28 Dec. 1968, ML.

Chapter 13   The thick boot of envy and the leg-iron of contempt
1 Inf. from Mrs Singh, Delhi, March 1988.
2 D. Nag to PS, 17 Dec. 1967, ML.
3 PS to Penny Scott, 28 Jan. 1969.
4 Account based on PS's letters to Penny Scott.
5 'India', 6 April 1969, tms fragment by PS at ML.
6 Ibid.
7 PS to Penny Scott, 30 Jan. 1969.
8 PS to Penny Scott, 24 Jan. 1969.
9 *Division*, p. 126.
10 PS to Penny Scott, 1 Feb. 1969.
11 PS to J. A. E. Heard, 8 Oct. 1975, ML.
12 PS to Penny Scott, 13 Jan. 1969.
13 Tms draft of 'Paul Scott's *Jewel* and After' by M. Malgonkar (pub. *Afternoon Dispatch & Courier*, 1987).
14 Ibid.
15 Ibid.
16 PS to Penny Scott, 4 Feb. 1969.
17 P. Goodbody to PS, 16 Mar. 1969, ML.
18 PS to P. Goodbody, 8 May 1969, ML.
19 PS to Sri Soli Batliwala, 17 Feb. & 8 Mar. 1969, ML.
20 PS to Leon Drucker, 17 Feb. 1969, ML.
21 PS to P. Goodbody, 8 May 1969, ML.
22 Notebook drafts and complete tms at ML.
23 PS to J. Willey, 14 Feb. 1968.
24 D. Marston to PS, 6 May 1969, ML.
25 Review of *A Prince of Our Disorder. The Life of T. E. Lawrence* by J. E. Mack, CL, June 1976.
26 PS to P. Goodbody, 14 May 1972, ML.
27 *The Letters of T. E. Lawrence*, ed. Malcolm Brown, Dent 1988, p. 360.
28 Ibid, p. 290; the 2 previous quotes from pp. 262 & 271.
29 Ibid, pp. 289–91; previous quote from p. 216.
30 By Philip Knightley & Colin Simpson, pub. Nelson 1969.
31 At HRC.
32 *Scorpion* notebook, entry dated 8 Sept. 1965, HRC; quote from *Division*, p. 301.
33 *Muse*, p. 95.
34 *Alien Sky*, p. 156 (Tom Gower's assistant, John Steele); quote from *Division*, p. 561.
35 *Paul Scott's Raj*, Heinemann 1990, Chap. 9.
36 *Muse*, p. 95.
37 G. Hanley to PS, n.d. (Aug. 1966), ML.
38 PS to M. Hamilton, 17 Sept. 1968; see also *Muse*, p. 115.
39 *Muse*, p. 115.
40 PS to M. Hamilton, 20 April 1962, ML; & PS to D. Nag, 9 June 1975, ML.
41 S. Jameson to PS, 23 Aug. 1968, ML.
42 *Muse*, p. 125; next quote from p. 119.
43 M. Vosper to PS, 5 Sept. 1969, ML.
44 PS to D. McWhinnie, 30 July 1969, ML.

45 PS to M. Vosper, 8 Sept. 1969, ML.
46 PS to R. Gant, 25 Aug. 1970, ML.
47 PS to J. Willey, 26 Mar. 1971, ML.
48 *Towers*, p. 48.
49 Ibid, p. 253.
50 PS to Richard Price, 11 Sept. 1971, ML.
51 *Muse*, p. 118.
52 CL, 30 Nov. 1970.
53 PS to M. Harris, Swanwick, 18 April 1973, ML; & PS to D. Higham, 21 June 1970, ML.
54 PS to J. Willey, 9 Aug. 1971, ML.
55 PS to C. Scott, 31 Oct. 1971.
56 *Pavilion*, p. 34; see also pp. 35, 65 & 236.
57 This & the previous quote from PS to C. Scott, 8 Jan. 1972.
58 PS to G. Hanley, 28 Mar. 1972, ML.
59 Ibid.
60 PS to D. Olding, 17 Oct. 1972, Princeton University Library.
61 Inf. from Foy Nissan (formerly Brit. Co. Asst. Rep., Specialist Tours Dept.), Bombay, Feb. 1988; & from his official report on the PS visit, dated 11 April 1972.
62 Inf. from Susan and Partap Sharma, Bombay Feb. 1988.
63 PS to Penny Scott, 11 Feb. 1972.
64 PS to Penny Scott, 13 Feb. 1972.
65 PS to Penny Scott, 17 Feb. 1972.
66 PS to Penny Scott, 16 Feb. 1972.
67 'Holidays in India', *Times*, 8 Feb. 1978.
68 'Paul's Scott's *Jewel* and After', op. cit.
69 Pub. in *Orientations*, Hongkong, Aug. 1973.
70 Ibid.
71 P. Goodbody to PS, 29 April 1972, ML; the previous quote P. G. to PS, 16 Mar. 1969, ML.
72 P. Goodbody to PS, 16 Mar. 1969, ML.
73 Inf. from C. Malgonkar, Jagalbet, Mar. 1988.
74 PS to J. Willey, 10 Jan. 1973, ML.
75 PS to A. N. Hunt of Maw, Ellis, Warne & Co., Accountants, 15 Jan. 1974, ML.
76 PS to G. Hanley, 28 Mar. 1972, ML.
77 M. Hamilton to P. S., 7 Sept. 1964, ML.
78 M. Hamilton to PS, Dec. 1968, ML.
79 PS to M. Hamilton, 30 Aug. 1974, ML.
80 D. Marston to PS, 26 Mar. 1972, ML.
81 PS to J. Willey, 29 April 1972, ML.
82 PS to D. Olding, 17 Oct. 1972, ML.
83 PS to J. Willey, 28 Oct. 1972, ML.
84 PS to J. Willey, 14 Nov. 1972, ML.
85 *Division*, p. 112.
86 PS to S. Jameson, 2 June 1975, ML.
87 *TLS*, 29 Dec. 1961.
88 PS's Indian library now at HRC; see also R. J. Moore, *Paul Scott's Raj*, op. cit.

89 Review of *Plain Tales from the Raj*, ed. C. Allan, *Times*, 24 Nov. 1975.
90 *Division*, p. 272.
91 This & the next quote from *Scorpion*, pp. 28 & 25.
92 *Division*, p. 443.
93 Review of *Rampal and His Family* by V. Sharma, *TLS*, 30 July 1971.
94 *Division*, p. 313.
95 Ibid, p. 209.
96 *Scorpion*, p. 217.
97 *Division*, p. 210; previous quote on p. 230.
98 *Scorpion*, p. 398.
99 PS to Benny Green, qu. *New Fiction*, 1978.
100 *Division* pp. 535, 550 & 597.
101 Interview by J. Tallmer, *N.Y. Post*, 18 Oct. 1975.
102 D. M. Burjorjee to PS, 2 Dec. 1986, & 2 June 1972, ML.
103 PS to J. Willey, 11 Nov. 1973, ML.
104 PS to C. Scott, 19 Mar. 1974, ML.
105 PS to D. M. Burjorjee, 2 Aug. 1974, ML.
106 J. Willey to PS, 30 May 1974, ML.
107 ML.

Chapter 14   An elephant serenely pacing
1 PS to P. Green, 31 Dec. 1974, ML.
2 PS to M. Hamilton, 18 June 1974, ML.
3 PS to J. Willey, 6 June 1974, ML.
4 21 Nov. 1974, ML.
5 PS to D. M. Burjorjee, 2 Aug. 1974, ML.
6 PS to R. Gant, 5 July 1976, ML; see also memo to D. Higham, 11 Mar. 1970, DHA.
7 PS to Peter Scott, 31 Aug. 1974, ML.
8 PS to J. Willey, 27 Oct. 1974, ML.
9 PS to S. Jameson, 2 June 1975, ML.
10 S. Jameson to PS, 30 May 1975, ML.
11 S. Jameson to PS, 3 June 1975, ML.
12 PS to D. J. Enright, 11 May 1975.
13 PS to L. Drucker, 21 April, & to R. Shead, 14 Mar. 1976, ML.
14 PS to H. R. F. Keating, 1 May 1975, ML.
15 PS to D. Olding, 11 May 1975, ML.
16 *TLS*, 23 May 1975.
17 *Observer*, 4 May 1975.
18 M. Hamilton to PS, n.d. (Aug./Sept. 1975) with Mudpore Jail papers, ML.
19 M. Hamilton to author, 9 Nov. 1989.
20 PS to D. Ganapathy, 4 April 1976, ML.
21 N. Viney to author, 3 Oct. 1987.
22 PS to H. Thompson, 26 June 1975, with Thompson's letters, ML.
23 *TLS*, 16 July 1976; *Princely India* pub. Indo-British Hist. Soc., Madras.
24 *Listener*, 8 March 1979.

25 'A Conversation with Paul Scott',
    Nimrod, op. cit.
26 *Soldiers' Contribution to Indian
    Independence. The Epic of the Indian
    National Army* by M. Singh, New
    Delhi, 1974, p. 199.
27 PS to F. Weinbaum, 4 April 1976, ML.
28 This & the next quote from *Soldiers'
    Contribution to Indian Independence*,
    op. cit., pp. 386 & 388.
29 PS to H. Thompson, 1 Aug. 1975, ML.
30 PS to D. Marston, 20 June, ML, & to
    D. Ganapathy, 14 July 1975, ML.
31 'Casting Off the White Man's Burden',
    Washington Post, 10 Aug. 1975.
32 This & the next quote from PS to H.
    Thompson, 26 Oct. 1975, ML.
33 PSA to Dr F. Warren Roberts of HRC,
    26 Sept. 1975, ML.
34 D. M. Burjorjee to PS, 2 June 1972,
    ML.
35 D. M. Burjorjee to PS, 30 June 1973,
    ML.
36 Inf. from D. Olding.
37 PS to F. Weinbaum, 19 Nov. 1974,
    ML.
38 PS to F. Weinbaum, 22 Nov. 1975,
    ML.
39 PS to F. Weinbaum, 31 Dec. 1975, ML.
40 PS to F. Weinbaum, 3 April 1975, ML.
41 F. Weinbaum to PS, 26 Sept. 1975; her
    successful thesis was 'Aspiration &
    Betrayal in Paul Scott's The Raj
    Quartet', 1976, Univ. of Illinois at
    Urbana-Champaign.
42 PS to D. Ganapathy, 7 Oct. 1975, ML.
43 F. Weinbaum to author, 10 Nov. 1986;
    & conversation with her, July 1988.
44 PS to D. M. Burjorjee, 23 Sept. 1975,
    ML.
45 PS to M. Goodbody, 5 Jan. 1975, ML.
46 PS to J. Willey, 17 Jan. & 24 Feb. 1975,
    ML; Martyn Goff to author, 3 July
    1989.
47 V. Bonham-Carter to PS, 8 Oct. 1975,
    ML.
48 C. W. Gardiner to PS, 4 Feb. 1968,
    ML; see also PS to V. Bonham-
    Carter, RLF, 12 June 1966, ML.
49 *The Flowering Moment*, Grey Walls
    Press, 1949, p. 97.
50 'The Meeting', Thos. F. Staley, *After
    Paul. Paul Scott's Tulsa Years*, booklet
    ed, Alice Lindsay Price, HCE/Riverrun
    Arts, Tulsa 1988.
51 Ibid.
52 PS to V. Bonham-Carter, 15 Feb. 1976,
    ML.
53 F. Stark to PS, 7 Jan. 1976, ML.
54 'The End of the Raj: Paul Scott's Novels
    as History'.

55 Inf. from Lord Beloff, Oxford, June
    1987.
56 *Towers*, p. 47–9, et passim.
57 Inf. from M. Hamilton.
58 M. Goodbody to PS, 27 Dec. 1974,
    ML.
59 *Staying On*, p. 221.
60 Inf. from M. Malgonkar, & from Guru
    Kulkani & other citizens of Belgaum,
    Feb. 1988.
61 M. Malgonkar to author, 27 Dec. 1987.
62 Inf. from Alison Fincham, archivist,
    Wellington College.
63 *Bandicoot Run*, Vision Bks., New Delhi
    1983, p. 333.
64 PS to M. Goodbody, 5 Jan. 1975, ML.
65 PS to J. Willey, 17 Jan. 11975, ML.
66 PS to F. Warburg, 26 Aug. 1975; ms of
    'Mango Rain' at ML, alternative
    version in possession of D. Higham
    Associates.
67 PS to J. Willey, 30 July 1975.
68 PS to M. Pick, 19 Nov. 1975, ML.
69 PS to Hugh Palmer, 21 Dec. 1975, ML.
70 PS to R. Gant, 28 June 1976, ML.
71 PS to C. Scott, 24 Oct. 1976.
72 *Staying On*, p. 84.
73 'Remembering Paul Scott' by R. Gant,
    Making of The Jewel in the Crown,
    Granada, 1983.
74 *Division*, p. 307.
75 *Staying On*, p. 182.
76 Ibid, p. 78.
77 This & the next quote, ibid, pp. 196 &
    197.
78 Tms of Shrewsbury talk, ML.
79 PS to Ronald Blythe, ML.
80 PS to J. Willey, 28 May 1976, ML.
81 PS to D. Olding, 13 Jan. & 22 Mar.
    1976, ML.
82 PS to F. Weinbaum, 14 Mar, & F.
    Weinbaum to PS 28 Feb. 1976, ML.
83 PS to D. Olding, 30 July 1976, ML.
84 *Corrida* tms, HRC.
85 PS to C. & S. Scott, 28 July 1976, ML.
86 PS to Penny Scott, 1 Aug. 1976, ML.
87 PS to S. Scott, 17 Aug. 1976.

Chapter 15   The tale is like a looking-glass
1   Unpub. memoir of PS by Brian Murray,
    & conversation with him, London, Nov.
    1987; conversations with William
    Wheeler in Tulsa, 1987 & 1989.
2   'The Meeting', *After Paul. Paul Scott's
    Tulsa Years*, ed. Alice Lindsay Price,
    HCE/Riverrun Arts, Tulsa, 1988.
3   For Thackeray, PS to S. Scott, 1976, &
    to F. Weinbaum, 15 Aug. 1974, ML;
    for Nabokov, PS to Oliver & Boyd, 26
    Feb. 1966, DHA; reviews of *Pale Fire*,
    Times, 15 Nov. 1962; *Nabokov* by
    Andrew Field, *TLS*, 8 Feb. 1968; *Ada*,

Daily Telegraph, 20 Oct. 1969; *Look at the Harlequins!*, CL, May 1975; & PS to Ben Travers, 10 Oct. 1968, ML.

4 This & the next quote from Steve Wood, Tulsa class notes.

5 *The Silver Desoto*, Council Oak Books/ Texas Monthly Press, 1988.

6 Tms synopsis of this unpub. novel with PS's notes & revisions at ML.

7 Steve Wood, class notes.

8 'Course notes' by S. Dennison, *After Paul*, op. cit.

9 PS to M. Hamilton, 31 Mar. 1977, ML.

10 'Course notes', op. cit.

11 Inf. from P. Floyd, Tulsa, 1987.

12 Quoted in 'The Writing Course' by Sharon Jesse, *After Paul*, op. cit. (jesses are the leather straps attached to the leg of a hunting hawk).

13 From 'The Storyteller', *After Paul*, op. cit.

14 Inf. from Sally Dennison, Tulsa.

15 'Course Notes'. *After Paul*, op. cit.

16 Inf. from H. Leake, Tulsa.

17 S. Wood, class notes.

18 Ibid.

19 PS to C. Scott, 1 Dec. 1976.

20 'Course Notes', *After Paul*, op. cit.

21 PS to C. Scott, 28 Oct. 1976.

22 'Course Notes', *After Paul*, op. cit.

23 Ibid.

24 'The Writing Course', *After Paul*, op. cit.

25 PS to C. Scott, 28 Oct. & 1 Dec. 1976.

26 *Paul Scott* by K. B. Rao, Twayne, 1980, p. 10.

27 Note with tms of 'Mango Rain' at ML.

28 PS to S. Scott, 7 Nov. 1976

29 PS to S. Scott, 8 Mar. 1977.

30 PS to S. Scott, 15 Mar. 1977

31 PS to S. Scott, 1 April 1977.

32 PS to D. Ganapathy, 4 April 1976, ML.

33 PS to S. Scott, 13 April 1977.

34 PS to F. Stark, 22 Nov. 1975, ML.

35 PS to D. Olding, 4 April 1977, Princeton Univ. Lib.

36 PS to D. Olding, 13 May 1977, Princeton Univ. Lib.

37 *After the Funeral*, p. 16.

38 Inf. from S. Dennison, Tulsa.

39 ML.

40 PS to M. Hamilton, 31 Mar. 1977, ML.

41 Inf. from M. Hamilton, plus her account in *The Making of The Jewel in the Crown*, Granada, 1983 op. cit.

42 PS to S. Scott, 21 July 1977.

43 PS to S. Scott, 11 Aug. 1977.

44 21 Aug. 1977.

45 *New York Times*, 8 Mar. 1978.

46 'Return of the Storyteller' by Faye Schuett, *After Paul*, op. cit.; PS had told the same story (with the ending given here) to his brother Peter.

47 Inf. from Dr Roger Atwood, Tulsa.

48 Bill Wheeler.

49 Inf. from M. Hamilton.

50 Inf. from Dr Staley, Tulsa.

51 Speech at Booker Dinner, pub. *New Fiction*, spring 1978.

52 'I remember', *After Paul*, op. cit.

53 MS; in the event, Paul changed his mind and asked Carol to meet him with a hired car.

54 ML

55 *Paul Scott* by K. B. Rao, Twayne, 1980, p. 150.

56 Inf. from Molly Hamilton.

57 PS to M. Hamilton, 8 Jan. 1978, ML.

58 Tms 'Paul Scott's *Jewel* and After' (pub. *Afternoon Dispatch & Courier*, 1987).

59 PS to D. Olding, 1 Jan. 1978, Princeton Univ. Lib.

60 Preface to *After the Funeral*.

61 Inf. from P. C. Manaktala.

62 Speech at Booker Prize dinner, *New Fiction*, Spring 1978.

63 PS to F. Weinbaum, 26 Oct. 1975. ML.

Paul Scott's works

Editions in brackets are those used for this biography

I. Gerontius. A Trilogy, Resurgam Younger Poets, No. 5, 1941 (Favil Press)
Johnnie Sahib, 1952 (Heinemann 1968)
The Alien Sky, 1953 (Panther 1974)
A Male Child, 1956 (Granada 1981)
The Mark of the Warrior, 1958 (Panther 1979)
The Chinese Love Pavilion, 1960 (Mayflower 1967)
The Birds of Paradise, 1962 (Penguin 1964)
The Bender, 1963 (Secker & Warburg)
The Corrida at San Feliu, 1964 (Panther 1974)

The Raj Quartet:
The Jewel in the Crown, 1966 (Heinemann)
The Day of the Scorpion, 1968 (Heinemann)
The Towers of Silence, 1971 (Heinemann)
A Division of the Spoils, 1975 (Heinemann)

Staying On, 1977 (Heinemann)
After the Funeral, 1979 (Whittington Press/ Heinemann)
My Appointment with the Muse. Essays, 1961–75, edited by Shelley C. Reece, 1986 (Heinemann)

Index

by Christine Shuttleworth

Illustration Acknowledgements

The author and publishers are grateful to the Scott family for permission to reproduce works in their possession, and also to the following (numbers refer to the pages on which photos appear):
Blundells School 312 (r); Camera Press 248 (top r), 249 (top and bottom r); O.Corben 140; Helen Craig i, 249 (bottom l); Douglas Dickins FRPS 117, 269, 297 (top), 360 (top), 361 (top); N.Dutta 297 (bottom r); D.Ganapathy 275; R.Gant 185, 267 (1); Mark Gerson FIIP 405; Granada TV 313 (top & bottom), 360 (bottom), 361 (centre); P.Green 140, 361; HRC, Univ. of Texas 312 (top & bottom); M.Hamilton 297; G.Hanley 185; W.Heinemann Ltd 267 (top & bottom r); M.Joseph Ltd 217; Kobal Collection 42 (bottom); McFarlin Library, Univ. of Tulsa 140 (bottom l), 173 (centre l); Merseyside County Art Galleries 39 (top); D.Nag 296; Palmers Green Library 1, 41 (top), 42 (top); F.M.Pilkington 248 (1); Popperfoto 248 (bottom r), 249 (top 1), 275 (top); *Radio Times* 141 (top l); R.Sansom 68. Whilst every attempt has been made to trace sources, this has not been possible in some cases. The publishers would like to apologise in advance for any inconvenience caused.

20611